Women's Periodicals and Print Culture in Britain, 1940s–2000s

The Edinburgh History of Women's Periodical Culture in Britain
Series Editor: Jackie Jones

Published Titles
Women's Periodicals and Print Culture in Britain, 1690–1820s: The Long Eighteenth Century
Edited by Jennie Batchelor and Manushag N. Powell

Women, Periodicals, and Print Culture in Britain, 1830s–1900s: The Victorian Period
Edited by Alexis Easley, Clare Gill and Beth Rogers

Women, Periodicals, and Print Culture in Britain, 1890s–1920s: The Modernist Period
Edited by Faith Binckes and Carey Snyder

Women's Periodicals and Print Culture in Britain, 1918–1939: The Interwar Period
Edited by Catherine Clay, Maria DiCenzo, Barbara Green and Fiona Hackney

Women's Periodicals and Print Culture in Britain, 1940s–2000s: The Postwar and Contemporary Period
Edited by Laurel Forster and Joanne Hollows

Visit The Edinburgh History of Women's Periodical Culture in Britain web page at www.edinburghuniversitypress.com/series/EHWPCB

THE EDINBURGH HISTORY OF WOMEN'S PERIODICAL CULTURE IN BRITAIN

WOMEN'S PERIODICALS AND PRINT CULTURE IN BRITAIN, 1940s–2000s

The Postwar and Contemporary Period

EDITED BY LAUREL FORSTER AND JOANNE HOLLOWS

EDINBURGH
University Press

Edinburgh University Press is one of the leading university presses in the UK. We publish academic books and journals in our selected subject areas across the humanities and social sciences, combining cutting-edge scholarship with high editorial and production values to produce academic works of lasting importance. For more information visit our website: edinburghuniversitypress.com

Edinburgh University Press Ltd
13 Infirmary Street, Edinburgh, EH1 1LT

First published in hardback by Edinburgh University Press 2020

Typeset in 10/12 Adobe Sabon by
IDSUK (DataConnection) Ltd, and
printed and bound by CPI Group (UK) Ltd, Croydon, CR0 4YY

A CIP record for this book is available from the British Library

ISBN 978 1 4744 6998 2 (hardback)
ISBN 978 1 3995 4679 9 (paperback)
ISBN 978 1 4744 6999 9 (webready PDF)
ISBN 978 1 4744 7000 1 (epub)

Contents

List of Illustrations

Figures

Plates

Acknowledgements

This volume spans eight decades of women's periodicals and print culture in Britain, from the Second World War to the present day. Organising a collection of essays to cover this period has been a complex task. We would like to thank all those at Edinburgh University Press who have worked hard through exceptional times to bring this volume to fruition, and especially our editors, Jackie Jones and Ersev Ersoy, for their vision, enthusiasm and guidance.

This collection would not exist without the hard work of all our contributors and we are very grateful for their collaboration, co-operation and collegiality throughout the process of putting the book together.

Laurel is grateful to Nick, Florine, Eden and Pierre, and her sister, Cheryl, for their love and support, and dedicates her work on this volume to her mother, Cevelia, who has lived through each of the decades represented in this book. Joanne would, as always, like to thank Mark.

Contributors to this volume gratefully acknowledge permission to use illustrations and thank the following organisations and individuals: Bauer Media Group; the Bill Douglas Cinema Museum Archive; the British Library Board; Feminist Archive North; Kate Charlesworth; Rhiannon Cosslett; Will Cotton; DIVA Media Group; The Fleece Press; the Glasgow Women's Library, Mike Goldwater; Hearst Magazines Ltd; Joy Hendry; Leeds University Library; Lesley Riddoch; Valerie Santiago; TI Media Limited; Ultra Violet Enterprises; the Women's Institute: NFWI Archives.

Every effort has been made to trace the copyright holders, but if any have been inadvertently overlooked, the publisher will be pleased to make the necessary arrangements at the first opportunity.

Introduction: Women's Periodicals and Print Culture in Britain, 1940s–2010s

Laurel Forster

The aim of this collection is to indicate the range and diversity of print media produced for women in Britain in the period from the Second World War to the early twenty-first century. This has been a long period of wide-ranging change for women in Britain in their personal, working and family lives, in their relationship to society and culture, and in what it means to be both 'British' and a 'woman'. The innumerable changes for women have included important aspects of increased ethnic diversity, disruption of the traditional British class system, and an acceptance of multiple female sexualities. This collection does not try to capture all these changes, but rather suggests ways in which print media primarily targeted at women have both reflected and directed the changing landscape and multiple ways of being a British woman.

Magazines and other print media have played their part in our understanding of the fragmentation of what it means to be woman in Britain in the late twentieth and early twenty-first centuries – anticipating and encouraging change, dispensing advice on how to live, suggesting new role models and raising current issues with their readers. Some print media forms, particularly commercial or consumerist magazines, have maintained a traditional approach to womanhood, presenting domesticity and femininity in various guises as the fundamental tenets or ideals of a woman's life. Within the period covered by this volume, however, the Women's Liberation Movement – with its demands, protests and consciousness-raising – used the form of the printed magazine to expose inequalities, report grassroots activism and bolster membership. Furthermore, other media forms – print and digital – influenced by an acceptance of British female diversity in the late twentieth and early twenty-first centuries, have come into being over this period, serving different groups of women, as well as a broad female audience. Of particular note is the explosion in feminist book publishing, the extensive use of pamphlets for women's political purposes, and the appropriation of online formats (e.g. magazines and blogs) for all matters of female concern, from craftivism to fourth-wave feminism. This represents a huge range of print media over this period, alongside which sit fundamental changes in the definition of 'womanhood'. This collection seeks to identify the work of some of these publications in reflecting these developments since the Second World War.

This introduction aims to provide a series of contexts for understanding and studying women's print media from 1945 to the present, when an extraordinary range of factors have affected women and media. First, the introduction draws attention to ways in which the very concept of 'womanhood' became much more fragmented after the Second World War. Plainly, it is not that single women, single mothers, working women, lesbian women and transgender women did not exist before the Second World War, it is that their visibility after the war has gradually increased to a common and legal acceptance of multiple categories of 'woman'. Following this, the second section of this introduction considers the important ways in which definitions of 'woman' have been shaped by changes in British society regarding age, class and ethnicity, and the role that women's print media have played in making those changes visible. One important political agent of change for women is feminism, and section three of this introduction considers how the occurrence of visible moments of feminism – in the so-called second, third and fourth 'waves' – has variously engaged with and impacted upon women's media. More conventional contents of domestic magazines representing traditional women's interests are considered in section four, with an introduction to ways in which these have become more specialised and produced burgeoning sub-genres of home, craft and food. Section five considers how important cultural phenomenon and crossover industries – some of them crucial to magazines' survival, such as celebrity and advertising – have increased their influence and commercial hold on women's magazines over this period. On the other hand, women's influence as publishing professionals is an important development over the time span of essays in this volume. Women had long worked in the publishing industry, but often at a low or subordinate level, and the late twentieth and early twenty-first century has been a period of women's determined entry into the previously male-dominated professions of publishing and printing, discussed in section six. It should also be noted that the critical study of women's print media has burgeoned over this period, and section seven outlines a range of methodologies which have developed to help us understand the complex field of women's print media. This leads on to section eight, an overview of the essays within this volume.

1. Becoming a Woman in the Postwar Period

At the end of the Second World War, a pocket-sized monthly 'service' magazine, *Housewife*, began to speculate about life for British women in the second half of the twentieth century. *Housewife* had only launched in February 1939 and had spent its war – like those other women's domestic magazines that had survived rising costs, paper shortages and general uncertainty – encouraging women to keep their spirits up, support those around them, and run their households along the lines of the 'Make Do and Mend' campaigns of the government ministries. The articles that determinedly looked forward to the end of wartime, however, did not always exude optimism about life after war. One such article, 'Father's Return', contemplated what might happen when, 'One of these days . . . a sunburnt figure in uniform is going to come walking up the garden path, through the front door, and into our lives again' (*Housewife* November 1944: 27–9). And with the return of the husband and father figure comes a warning not to 'delude ourselves into thinking we shall all carry straight on from where we left off. There is going to be a lot of adjustment to be done, and perhaps it might be as well to think over the difficulties now as well as the delights' (Ibid.: 27). Important changes were already being anticipated in this women's magazine. Alongside the prospective changes in the gender dynamics of personal relationships, there is also the sense of women's development: 'These war years must have given even the most frivolous of us a sense of real values. These five years have been packed with a life-time of experience from which it is impossible not to profit.' (Ibid.: 29). The clear message of this article is that things were not going to be the same after the war, not least because of the way that women themselves had developed in both their appreciation of the important matters of daily life and in their knowledge of their own newly discovered capabilities. *Housewife* magazine, easily dismissed as a domestic handbook for women, often pointed artfully towards areas of complexity in women's lives. The above article focuses mostly on the father-child relationship, and what we would now refer to as the psychological impact of this returning, or even new, presence in the family; but it also astutely points out that father's homecoming may not be the idealised familial and romantic reunion imagined. The process of adapting to new circumstances within the home and family is applied to the mother as well as the child. This magazine, which had been supporting women in their new roles and in facing the endless challenges of life on the Home Front, understood and tried to articulate how these experiences had also fundamentally changed the nature of women themselves. Besides becoming highly competent, thrifty and innovative housewives, women were members of the war services, deployed to work in factories, on farms and in myriad other ways to support the war. They were mothers, daughters, neighbours and members of society caring for their families and communities. Magazines used the multiplicity of women's roles to fill their pages with up-to-date editorial copy, as well as inspirational and encouraging articles.

At the same time, as the war ended, magazines started to produce more contemplative articles, expressing in broader terms a developing female consciousness both in the sense of the self and society. Sheila Rowbotham has argued that at the end of the war and in the early-1950s, there was a sense among women that it might be possible to 'escape from a fixed feminine destiny' (1999: 281). She points to how Simone de Beauvoir's now famous emphasis, in *The Second Sex*, on the process of becoming a woman 'resonated with a new generation ready to accept that one's womanhood was of one's own making' (Ibid.: 280). In posing her famous question, 'But first, what is a woman?', de Beauvoir (1949: 3) opened a radical debate about the category of 'woman', questioning gender relations and the stereotyping of women, and arguing against biological determinism.

In the pages of women's magazines, the end of the war (for magazine editors at least) was seen as a time of potentially deep and long-lasting change for women and, in their usual advice-giving role, magazines can be seen to take a 'psychological turn', an argument put forward by Tracey Loughran in Chapter 7. A focus on the increasing importance of women's psychology within women's magazines may be traced through what we now refer to as 'women's mental health issues', from so-called 'war nerves', to letters pages, agony aunts, early second-wave feminist articles about depression and the effects of medication, to more recent triumph-over-tragedy testimonials of sufferers (including readers and prominent women alike). It also forms the basis for the highly successful *Psychologies* (France 1970–ongoing; UK 2005–ongoing), a magazine devoted to all aspects of woman's inner life, and publications such as *Breathe* (2016–ongoing), with its specific focus on wellbeing and mindfulness.

However, the process of becoming a woman relates to relationships with family and society, as well as an interior journey. Magazines at the end of the war reflected on the prospect of rebuilding British homes, families and society and called for increased women's participation in this new era. *Housewife* speculated on the wider situation too, encouraging women to imagine that they would have a greater say in rebuilding society after the devastation of war. For instance, 'What I hope for in the post-war world' by Edith Pargeter, draws attention to social commentaries and writings such as the 'Beveridge Report', 'Health for the People' and 'Make Fruitful the Land' to suggest a Britain based on a caring society and co-operation in shared purpose (*Housewife* March 1943: 62–3; 102). The anticipation of improved circumstances for all was based on lessons learnt through wartime hardships. The magazine expected that women would lead the call for both an intelligent response to the madness of war and a sensible and fair distribution of wealth and resources.

In some ways women's magazines flattered their readers into believing that there would be a shift in gender power and a greater level of women's involvement in society in a postwar world. It was not claimed that women's abilities to participate in planning a postwar Britain necessarily increased over the duration of the war; although women were encouraged to have closer wartime contact with councils, agencies and governing bodies. It was more that magazines made plain the absolute necessity of women's contribution to society and brought their capabilities into a sharper focus. Pargeter's article anticipates changes in housing, international co-operation, economic structures, education and much more. Of her list of eighteen points articulating her hopes for postwar Britain, number six read: 'A more complete and confident partnership between the sexes, through the shared experiences of the war' (Ibid.: 63). Optimistic magazine articles targeted at housewives predicted a shift in consciousness in terms of a wider societal appreciation of women's abilities, as well as changes in gender relations within and beyond conventional marriage. At the very least, *Housewife* encouraged its readers to think of themselves, their status and their social participation in different terms. This is a weighty matter for a domestic magazine, and it asks women to reassess their own sense of worth, capability and self-reliance. For all such encouraging speculation, however, Jane Waller and Michael Vaughan-Rees have suggested that actually there were few opportunities for women to voice their questions and opinions about the building of postwar Britain, and that 'the women's magazines, in fact, provided practically the only outlet for such debate' (1987: 122). They suggest that 'the women of 1945 received nothing but the promises of a better life of brighter homes and consumer goods in the future' and that this was not enough, women wanted the wartime independence and comradeship to continue into peacetime (Ibid.: 127). Nonetheless, in the immediate postwar period, women's magazine editors enjoyed relative freedom from the pressures to please advertisers whose power, without goods to sell, was much diminished (White 1970: 125).

That said, and as demonstrated throughout this collection, the postwar women's magazine and periodical market in the UK does not necessarily treat women as a homogeneous group, but differentiates the reader not only by class and age but also by race and ethnicity, sexuality, work, lifestyle and interests, interest groups and politics. In what follows, there is mention of some of the key ways in which the landscape of postwar women's periodicals has been defined and delineated.

2. Age, Class, Ethnicity and Sexuality

Matters of age, class, sexuality and ethnicity shaped the British magazine market during the postwar period. This section brings to the fore the sometimes hidden, sometimes visible ways in which women's print media have approached the important issues of age, class sexuality and ethnicity.

Age was an important indicator of readership group at the end-of-war moment. White suggests that only after the war did society start to recognise adolescence as a crucial period in a young person's life, and the emergence of a new group of teenagers, 'whose modes of life, needs and interests were very different from those of young people of the pre-war period' (1970: 126). Age was also the differential between the home-service weeklies, such as *Woman's Weekly*, targeted at the older reader, and the modern competitors, such as *Woman* and *Woman's Own* (Ibid.: 126–7).

The women's magazine market became increasingly defined by readership age groups from the 1960s onwards. While some titles have explicitly targeted specific groups such as teenagers or (more recently) older women, many others work with a clear sense of a target age group that they can sell to advertisers. Given the potential power of teen magazines to shape young women's identities, much feminist research has unsurprisingly focused on these magazines. While there were already well-established comics for younger girls (Tinkler 1996), a new wave of pop and love-focused comics targeted at teenage girls was launched in the mid to late 1950s – including titles such as *Marilyn* (1955–65), *Valentine* (1957–65) and *Mirabelle* (1956–78) – soon followed by teen magazines – such as *Honey* (1960–86) – that began to explore independent lifestyles for young women (Ormrod 2018; Tinkler 2014; Carter 2016).

However, one of the most frequently discussed postwar teen magazines is *Jackie* (1964–93), partly because of its place in popular memory (e.g. it inspired *Jackie the Musical*, launched in 2016) and, in academic terms, because it was the focus of some of the foundational research in feminist cultural studies in the UK by Angela McRobbie. McRobbie argued that, while *Jackie* constructed a mode of youthful feminine identity that was different from the domestic femininities found in mass-market magazines aimed at adult women, it nonetheless positioned teenage girls in relation to domestic life. In particular, *Jackie* articulated an ideology of romance that made the 'world of the personal and the emotions', and the pursuit of romantic relationships with boys, the defining features of a young woman's life and helped to prepare them for future roles as wives (McRobbie 1991: 131; McRobbie 1981).[1] While *Jackie* was arguably more complex than McRobbie initially suggested, there is significant consensus that such titles as *Just Seventeen* transformed the teenage girls' magazine in the 1980s and 1990s, replacing the girl engaged in the anxious pursuit of romance with a figure with a greater sense of fun, confidence and independence – and an investment in pop and fashion – and offering advice on how to construct feminine identities through consumption (McRobbie 1991, 1994; Pleasance 1991). Furthermore, as Melanie Waters argues in Chapter 8, *Just Seventeen* constructed youthful femininities in a mass-market magazine that were, at least partly, informed by the second-wave feminism of the 1970s and 1980s. Never as radical as the feminist teen fanzine *Shocking Pink* (c. 1980–2; 1987–92),[2] many debates about *Just Seventeen* have suggested that '"feminist" independence was constructed around the idea that young women were "born to shop"' (Gill 2007: 187).[3] However, by the 1990s, sex had become the 'conceptual umbrella' underpinning new girls' magazines such as *More!* and *Sugar* which displayed 'boldness (even brashness) in the ways in which women's sexual identities are constructed' (McRobbie 1996: 177), representations that were also used to construct a wider 'moral panic' about young women's sexuality in the period (Tincknell et al.: 2003).

The market for teenage girls' and young women's magazines has declined in the twenty-first century. Many magazines aimed at younger women have become more celebrity, fashion and beauty focused. Magazines such as *Cosmopolitan* in the 2000s increasingly represented femininity as something needing 'constant vigilance, attention and self-surveillance', suggesting a woman's body, sexuality and self, required constant work (Gill 2007: 217). Meanwhile, traditional print formats have been challenged by online magazines and other digital platforms where, for example, vloggers offer beauty and fashion tips (Carter 2013). Many magazines have ceased their print editions and become online only. Yet, as Laura Favaro explains in Chapter 5, this has not meant the end of these publications – many have extended their reach as they expand across social and mobile media platforms, while some new digital magazines for young women make more explicit engagements with feminist ideas and activism.

Less attention has been paid socially or critically to magazines aimed at older women. However, Julia Twigg (2018) has demonstrated how magazines such as *Yours* and *Woman and Home*, and even more mainstream fashion magazines such as *Vogue*, target older women as consumers, negotiating what the magazines define as appropriate 'later-life' femininities. While these magazines offer 'a consumption-oriented version of empowerment through which older women can experience new opportunities, new freedoms', they also exert new forms of discipline as older women are required to 'shape their appearance to the cultural norms of acceptable femininity' (Twigg 2018: 346). In this way, despite significant differences between women's magazines targeted at different age groups, ideas about the construction of acceptable femininities through consumption practices occurs across age groups.

Consumption practices, often associated with the 'feminine', are always crucially important for commercial women's magazines. Joanne Hollows has drawn attention to the complexities of femininity and consumption practices, as labour and as identity formation (2000: 112–36). Magazines' and advertisers' knowledge of women's consumption practices form a clue to ways in which magazines target readers through social class. Cynthia White has suggested that education was the fundamental class distinction between groups of women just after the Second World War, and that domestic monthlies, such as *Good Housekeeping* and *Housewife*, were targeted at the middle and upper classes (1970: 132). Further, White has argued that changes in the composition of social classes after the war, 'pitchforked' many women 'into a style of life to which they were totally unaccustomed', and that this wider and heterogeneous population (in class terms) 'looked to the "glossies"' as arbiters of taste and fashion (Ibid.: 148). Magazines became handbooks for consumption practices and class allegiances. The role of the weeklies aimed at working-class as well as lower middle-class women, in consequence, can be seen to have intended to 'help women achieve the best possible results on a limited budget', with editors bearing in mind 'their readers' modest circumstances' (Ibid.). As well as matters of consumption and fashion, magazines also used the increased space given to letters and problem pages to deal with class-related questions of women and employment. White argues that, even in the face of increasing numbers of women taking up occupations outside the home in the early to mid-1950s, women's magazines still emphasised a domestic role for women in order to provide the 'right home-oriented selling climate' for advertisers. However, they also reproduced traditional images of marriage and home that represented white, middle-class women as the norm (Ibid.: 151–2).

Elizabeth Wilson has remarked on how the illusion of socialism after the war was 'achieved by contriving to make all classes appear "middle class"' (1980: 6). Wilson uses the example of the proliferation of domestic technology, or white goods, to replace servants: 'the woman wielding the hoover could become the symbol of the social revolution that had obliterated inequality; for women were above all *classless*' (Ibid.: 12, emphasis in original). Class equality, Wilson argues, became bound up with gender equality in the much-discussed position of the housewife, making it difficult to understand how 'an equalization of drudgery ever came to be misunderstood as emancipation' (Ibid.: 13). Women's war work had included new types of employment for working-class young women, such as factory or shop work, that many found preferable to domestic service. The postwar absence of servants was discussed in women's newspaper columns, and the government schemes for domestic organisation were largely rejected (Ibid.: 25). What did emerge was the rise of the consumer-housewife and, for Newsom, education was envisaged as 'guiding working-class girls towards middle-class taste' (cited in Ibid.: 36). Consumption, necessary for postwar economic recovery, led to commercial advertisers pressuring magazine editors to return to a 'narrow domestic formula' seen to benefit the middle-class and working-class housewife equally, with differences being not of class but of 'personality'(Mary Grieve, editor of *Woman*, cited in Ibid.: 37). Janice Winship has discussed how white goods intended for the middle classes were, by the 1950s, 'beginning to appear in working-class homes too' (1987: 42). She suggests that the job of women's magazines in the 1950s was to 'educate and reassure' women in their work of status-building through their homes (Ibid.: 43). Ballaster et al. suggest that the long history of women's magazines has played its role in shifting class determinations with regard to gender – in these magazines, the division between the masculine and the feminine has taken priority over divisions of social class with an emphasis on a 'common femininity' (1991: 127). The shift in reader address from 'lady' to 'woman' in earlier periods accompanied a shift in magazines from an emphasis on femininity as leisure to femininity as labour (Ibid.: 171). Further, Ballaster et al. argue that 'a discourse of "style" has replaced that of class in the women's magazine' of the 1970s and 1980s (Ibid.:125). If it suited the domestic economy and the women's periodicals market to ignore class differences, or at least to assume a ubiquitous aspiring middle class in magazine readership, then this questions whether class differences have in fact been overtaken, in women's magazines at least, by the focus on individualised concerns of femininity, style and taste. Social class may be understood in women's magazines to be refracted through available income and purchasing power: fashion and home decorating are two very visible examples of variable consumption practices. Women's magazines over the late twentieth century may have tried to give an impression of an individualised subjectivity in their editorial and features-led address; nonetheless, consumption practices have remained key. However, at the time of writing, there is a further moment of change with a newly invigorated turn to recycling, ethical consumption and an anti-consumption consciousness, brought about by concerns regarding environmental damage. It will be interesting to see how consumption-led women's magazines respond to this.

Important issues of age and class have been treated differently by women's magazines and their focus on consumption practices. Groups of women from varying age groups and class affiliations have come into and out of view as target markets. However, there is widespread evidence of a continued lack of visibility of black and ethnic minority women in British women's magazines. In 2017, 94 per cent of British journalists were white (Hirsch 2018), so the lack of diversity can be partly attributed to what white journalists think is interesting and sellable to audiences and advertisers. This is reflected in the relative invisibility of BAME women on the covers of UK magazines. In 2017, only 9.3 per cent of the covers of nineteen bestselling glossies featured people of colour. Some, including high-profile women's magazine *Marie Claire*, had none (Hirsch 2018). This is part of a wider picture in which glossy magazines tend to privilege a very narrow range of desirable selves: 'the situation is even worse regarding larger, older and transgender models' (Hirsch 2018). While, in Chapter 11, Estella Tincknell demonstrates how there has been some progress at *Vogue* magazine following the appointment of its first black editor Edward Enninful in 2017, she also shows how the apparent increase in diversity did little to challenge wider inequalities.

Meanwhile, women's magazines that target black and Asian British women are now well established in the UK. Such magazines are an important resource for women who do not find themselves or their experiences reflected in more mainstream titles in which whiteness is normalised. *Black Hair and Beauty*, currently the 'best-selling black magazine' in the UK (*Black Beauty and Hair* n.d.), is a part of a wider response to a long-standing association between whiteness and beauty and the marginalisation of black women's skin and hair in mass-market women's magazines. Launched in 1990, *Pride* was the UK's first monthly magazine for black women. It combines fashion and beauty and other staples of the contemporary women's magazines, such as news and entertainment, with stories of successful black women. Unlike its more mainstream competitors, *Pride* makes black women visible. However, despite *Pride*'s celebration of successful black role models, both magazines largely define black femininity in terms of consumption, partly reinforced through their dependence on advertising revenue for hair and beauty products (Helcké 2003).

In the 2000s, there were also a number of glossy South Asian women's magazines in the UK, including titles such as *Asiana* and *Asian Woman*, as well as more specialist women's magazines such as *Asiana Wedding*. As Linda McLoughlin's (2013; 2017) research demonstrates, magazines such as *Asian Woman* model themselves on mainstream glossies like *Cosmopolitan*, yet also evoke 'nostalgic notions of "untarnished" and "pure" Indian women' (McLoughlin 2017: 4). Foregrounding South Asian women who are marginalised in mass-market glossies, she argues that these magazines still privilege white Western standards of beauty, not least through frequent recommendations for skin-lightening products (Ibid.: 248). Like many mass-market glossies, these South Asian magazines frequently promote 'female empowerment' but rest on a 'neoliberal discourse of individualism' that privileges the choice to construct the self as a sexualised object through consumption (Ibid.: 248–9). Within these magazines, the pursuit of advertising revenue from hair and beauty industries impacts on the content (Ibid.: 152).

More recently, these more established magazines aimed at black and South Asian women have been joined by increasingly politicised and progressive entrants into the market. For example, *gal-dem*, in both online and print forms, is 'committed to telling the stories of women and non-binary women of colour' and more explicitly 'addressing inequality and misrepresentation' across a wide range of areas such as news, culture, politics, lifestyle and first-person pieces (*gal-dem* n.d.). While *Thiird* covers a similar range of issues, it is more explicit in its political mission, which is 'informed by decolonial and intersectional feminist thought' and a celebration of difference and diversity without 'tokenism' (*Thiird* n.d.) *Burnt Roti* is a crowdfunded South Asian lifestyle magazine that also prioritises the politics of racism, gender and sexuality, with a significant emphasis on mental health issues. These magazines not only challenge racial inequalities within both media texts and industries, but also attack some of the exclusions that underpin the implied subject of the 'women's' magazine (for more on non-binary identities in British periodicals, see Georgina Turner's discussion in Chapter 4). At the same time, while these magazines resist some of the pressures to produce content that creates an inviting space for advertisers and their budgets – and while they are free to access online – the pleasures of their print editions come at a price that renders them inaccessible to many readers (at the time of writing, retailing at £10 (*gal-dem*); £7 (*Burnt Roti*); and £8.95 (*Thiird*)). In this way, magazines like *Thiird* and *Burnt Roti* must also be understood within a recent wave of beautifully designed and highly-aestheticised niche lifestyle magazines for affluent middle-class audiences (Vercoe 2018).

Another notable exclusion from traditional magazines for women in Britain has been the range of female sexualities. Print media have proved very helpful in studying lesbian and other sexual identities. In 1992, Martha Vicinus considered that a lesbian history was in its initial stages, and she suggested that it was 'inhibited both by the suspect nature of the subject and the small number of individuals willing and able to pursue half-forgotten, half-destroyed, or half-neglected sources' (1992: 467). More recently, there have been histories of lesbian cultures in Britain, including those written by Rebecca Jennings (2007a; 2007b), Emily Hamer (1996) and Laura Doan (2001). Nonetheless, in 2009, Georgina Turner, commenting on a lack of knowledge about lesbian publishing in Britain, wrote an account of the British lesbian publishing tradition from the 1960s to 1990s, bringing to light a range of magazines including *Arena Three*, *Sappho*, *Rouge* and *DIVA*. Turner's writing in this volume – Chapter 4 – analyses the precarious publishing contexts for *DIVA* magazine.

Other lesbian publications, including the US magazine *The Ladder* (1956–70), have helped to illuminate lesbian histories and the historical ways in which lesbians sought legitimacy in the wider culture (Soares 1988). Marianne Cutler, for instance, has argued that publication of *The Ladder*, 'entered a public dialogue regarding the "problem" of homosexuality', asserting both the organisation's knowledge of female homosexuality and its right to participate in the discussion (2003: 235). Other articles have focused on lesbian subjectivities and Stefanie Snider (2010) has considered the representation of lesbian women's bodies in lesbian magazines.

Arena Three (1963–72) which was reinvented as *Sappho* (1972–81) was an early UK lesbian magazine, produced modestly at first and sent to subscribers who had gained their husband's approval, but which performed a significant social and psychological role for many isolated women (Forster 2015: 79–109). It did this through articles, commentary, face-to-face meetings and through recommended reading. In Chapter 10 of this volume Amy Tooth Murphy discusses how *Arena Three* encouraged a middlebrow and middle-class readership through an important part of the magazine: its literature and book reviews section.

The issues of age, class, ethnicity and sexuality remain pertinent and contested topics in women's print media, and all these issues were addressed in various ways in the magazines and print ephemera of the British Women's Liberation Movement of the 1970s.

3. Feminism

Earlier feminists of the suffrage movement had, of course, employed the printed form to mobilise their supporters by producing myriad feminist periodicals as official organs of their organisations (DiCenzo et al. 2011). However, in the 1970s, during the so-called 'second wave of feminism', the production of feminist magazines and newsletters was accompanied by a more pronounced sense of group participation, democratic accessibility and the expression of individual, as well as collective, subjectivity. Having said that, the British Women's Liberation Movement, and its magazines, has been criticised for its early dominance by white middle-class women, leading to assumptions about class and race. Nonetheless, feminist magazines offered new and enlightened perspectives, giving space to their readers' actual real-life experiences, and provided an alternative to regular publications for women. Some magazines suggest prioritising individual subjectivities, others aim to galvanise a group into political action or social awareness. Feminist print media of the Women's Liberation Movement argued for domestic, social and workplace equalities including legislation to establish women's rights to equal pay and equal opportunities – they highlighted women's history and offered a space for personal testimony and collective consciousness raising. For further detailed discussion on a range of feminist magazines see Delap and Strimpel, Bazin and Sedgwick in this volume, Chapters 2, 14 and 16 respectively. In particular, feminist magazines focused on hidden crimes against women, such as domestic violence and rape. They also sought to expose the plight of underpaid women, as well as the invisible work of women in the home and in their roles as child-rearers (see Sarah Crook's research in Chapter 21 for a discussion of the latter). For women, their Women's Liberation Movement group's newsletter or magazine was often a way of having a voice, of creating a safe space for women's opinions and of physically participating in feminist activity. Studying such rich material, however, encompasses the contradiction that, throughout this period, magazines were criticised as part of the oppressive regime, but were also employed as the medium through which women expressed their dissatisfaction with society, and used as vehicles for galvanising new members and organising into groups to oppose oppressive regimes.

Women's magazines have been both a focus of critical attention and a source of recovery of women's history since at least Betty Friedan's ground-breaking study in 1963. This dual position of magazines in relation to a feminist critical approach is far from new, but it is complex. One problem is that in the second-wave's burgeoning appreciation of magazines, its dependence on the printed form to develop the movement, and its understanding of the power of such communication for women, several blind spots were formed about women in Britain, largely to do with class and race. And while many feminist magazines such as *Women's Voice* and *Spare Rib* later did their best to rectify this, and while new magazines targeted at black, Asian and other British women were established, initial impressions of second-wave feminism had been established. This continues to shape wider representations of feminism – for example, Terese Jonsson (2014: 1,023) has shown how representations of British feminism in the left-liberal *Guardian* newspaper represent feminist activism as 'almost exclusively white'.

The story of second-wave feminist periodicals in the UK, like the story of the Women's Liberation Movement more generally, was fractured by difference and questions about the extent to which the feminist subject was white, middle-class and heterosexual. The key influence of socialist feminism on the British Women's Liberation Movement meant that questions about class became increasingly foregrounded, as Sue Bruley discusses in Chapter 15 in this volume. However, as Natalie Thomlinson's (2016: 433) research demonstrates, black feminist periodicals operated as a 'counterpublic' to the second-wave feminist counterpublic, 'carving out a space through which black feminists could contest racist hegemonic norms in general and criticize the (white) women's movement in particular'. In the 1970s, London-based campaigning periodicals *Speak Out* and *FOWAAD* reflected the concerns of the black women's movement, frequently using a 'Marxist framework' to critique the racism of the State (Thomlinson 2016: 437).[4] *We Are Here* started as a newsletter in 1984 and, after a hiatus, re-emerged as a magazine in the late 1980s. The publication paid far more attention to subjective analysis than to politicised personal life than the earlier black feminist magazines, taking on black men's role in reproducing patriarchal oppression and opening up more space for discussing issues about lesbianism (Ibid.: 438).

Another key black feminist magazine was *Mukti* (1983–7). Aimed at South Asian women (primarily in London), it combined practical help on the legal status of immigrant women, a forum for readers to share their experiences which had a consciousness-raising function, and a political education (Forster 2015: 111; Thomlinson 2016). Partly supported by public funding from the Greater London Council, *Mukti* was an ambitious project that was published in six languages, encouraged readers to shape the content and organised a range of community reader events. The magazine 'tried to help this marginalised group of women establish a positive sense of social identity on their own terms, supporting their fight against the racism of the time and the prevalent stereotypes of Asian women' (Forster 2015: 113).

Through the practices of consuming magazines like *Mukti*, Thomlinson (2016: 442) argues, 'the figure of the politically black woman was generated and circulated'. However, at the same time, the magazine also highlights the limits of a black feminist identity that did not always speak to the experience of Asian women. If *Mukti* demonstrates the difficulties of producing magazines that articulated a common black women's experience, it was also partly undermined by differences within the identity of South Asian women. As Forster (2015: 144) argues, 'In trying to provide a forum for women of a range of languages, ethnic origins, education, political engagement, caste and class it was a publication of diverse views and disagreement, trying to serve a fractured population.'

One way that women did express a sense of purpose was to create groups and meeting points for women, such as *Mukti*, who produced their magazine initially for women who could not attend the meetings. The creation of a feminist pamphlet, newsletter or magazine, and the creative connections between women writers and illustrators and the written text, were evident in some of the hand-drawn and handwritten magazine content. This aspect of many non-commercial feminist magazines is testament to this expression. A tradition of this kind of connection between print and the personal and homemade continued in the often hand-drawn zines of the 1980s and 1990s. Some zines were protesting as part of the Riot Grrrl movement and third-wave feminist ideas of individuality and self-identification. The expression of women's experiences and observations continued into the blogs, online zines and magazines of the twenty-first century, and even a fourth wave of feminism: some represent a return to activism, others are a reminder that sexism and gender inequality remain part of our society (see Kaitlynn Mendes's discussion of digital feminist cultures in Chapter 17 for more on these issues).

4. Homes, Craft and Food

While feminist magazines were interested in women's activism in the public sphere, as well as developing individual feminist consciousness, the magazine for women that prioritises and perpetuates the domestic arena is still very much in evidence. Reconceived ideas of femininity and domesticity may still be found in some of the longer-running magazines aimed at a mid-life, middle-class readership. Furthermore, there is a continuation of an agenda that speaks to women in the domestic setting, particularly in the areas of home decoration, craft and cookery, activities which have been variously revised and revived in the light of feminism. General interest women's magazines such as *Good Housekeeping*, *Woman and Home* and *Woman* – although now including front cover and feature content on celebrity, as well as self-help articles – still cover the women's domestic magazine staples of fashion advice, home styling, cookery and family. Further advisory articles on motoring, finances, gardening, travel and even a current trend for emotionally charged methodologies for tidying up all now form regular content for these magazines. Domestic matters have achieved fetishised heights in titles such as *Laundry* which uses ultra-high production values on uncoated paper and arty photography to glamorise aspects of domestic labour – picture the kitsch of historical appliances and elevate the drudgery of housework to a restorative and creative art. However, it is no longer necessary for magazines to assume that only housewives are interested in their homes or to assume that food preparation takes place only for families, or that craft is to be contained within a purely domestic setting. All three areas have seen growth and diversification in terms of magazine titles as they have become distinct interests in their own right.

The magazine that focuses on the home and interior decoration operates at the intersection of women's consumer magazines, professional art or architecture periodicals, and building or furniture trade journals (Aynsley and Berry 2005). The UK's first home magazine, *The House* (1897–1903) was short-lived due to its impassioned focus on design reform and endorsement of correct taste (Cohen 2005: 36). It was in the interwar period when other home magazines understood home decoration as an extension of personality, a pleasure and a creative pursuit that this periodical genre really expanded, and as Cohen argues, 'The periodical has become the pre-eminent forum for home decoration' (Ibid.: 41). *Housewife* itself, as mentioned above, morphed into *Ideal Home* in 1967, while other magazines dealing with interior design, gardening, holiday homes and home furnishings have proliferated and cater to a range of budgets and tastes from the high-end *Interiors* – an inspirational look-book for the wealthy – to the lower-budget *House Beautiful*, which frequently advertises supermarket homewares, with *Elle Decoration* (a spin-off of *Elle*) and *House and Garden*, amongst others, somewhere in between. The magazine creation of different moods, atmospheres and *mise-en-scènes* of the home implies a range of lifestyles, but also a process of education in taste.

Food is also ubiquitous content within women's domestic magazines, and has become a genre in its own right. Increased availability of ingredients and changes in the way we shop for food have played their part. *Family Circle* (1964–2006), a monthly magazine very much focused on feeding the family, achieved mass circulation and was sold only through supermarkets. Asda, Sainsbury's and Waitrose have all had their own food magazines, promoting their produce and corporate ethos. The BBC is also a huge producer of a wide range of magazines, including food magazines, with its flagship BBC *Good Food* magazine and other related media productions such as its webpages and cookbooks, the latter often authored by celebrity chefs of TV fame, sometimes relaying a culinary tourism from abroad. Alison James has argued that British food magazines 'are filled with recipes and detailed descriptions of food and wine which image the foreignness of foreign countries and lifestyles', offering a 'culinary expatriate cosmopolitanism' (1997: 77). Food within magazines has been seen as a source of anxiety, raising concerns about slimming for women, bodybuilding for men, and health for children. For men and women there are now specialist magazines addressing these concerns. Food magazines also address different levels of discernment regarding food, ranging from its role as a basic need through to meals for family fodder, and on to an aestheticised discernment of fine and exclusive ingredients. There has been much diversification in this field, with some magazines regarding food as a high cultural form, such as *Food & Wine* (Wilson 2003), and others, such as *Vegan Food and Living*, influenced by current food trends and increasing concerns about sustainability, the environment and ethical living.

Craft magazines have also seen a proliferation in titles over the period covered by this volume. Fiona Hackney reminds us that there were significant numbers of articles on home craft in home-based consumer or 'service' magazines of the earlier interwar period and has argued that they contributed to women's sense of modernity (Hackney 2006). However, home crafts, and associated magazines and websites, have become important in the late twentieth and early twenty-first centuries in different and distinctive ways: through a feminist intent, as well as through the increased focus on the home promulgated by the seemingly oppositional agendas of consumerism and an ecologically driven interest in the home-made. Home crafts have been seen as a form of feminist activism made visible at least since the US feminist magazine *Bust* (1993–ongoing), often undertaken by the younger activist who is technologically savvy (Hackney 2013; Bain 2016). In a drive to counter capitalist consumption and revalue female craft, women of all ages have turned to craft and its associated magazines. Groeneveld has discussed ways in which discourses of the 'new' knitting in third-wave feminist periodicals, and the rise of 'crafting as a feminist pastime', have led to other publications in book and online forms (2010: 262). She reflects on the political and feminist reclamations of this domestic craft, arguing that there is a complex relationship to accessibility and consumerism in these practices (Ibid.: 274).

Looking back to an earlier era, Hackney argues that 'Magazines such as *Make*, *Craft* and *Readymade* fuel the indie crafts movement' (2013: 176). Mainstream craft magazines may keep a feminist agenda or eco-commitment in the background, but, as Jo Turney (2004) discusses, they help explain ways that craft has an emotive impact. Turney has indicated that the current focus on crafts within the home, evident through specialist magazines such as *Cross Stitcher* and *Cross Stitch Crazy*, can be understood in terms of the way a craft artefact operates as an important 'transmitter of feeling' (Ibid.: 279).

The proliferation of subject-specific magazines, partly determined by the splitting off and subsuming of titles by publishing houses, and partly in response to the perceived formation of new readership groups, is particularly sensitive to trends. While such magazines are far from new in the period covered by this collection, publications in the areas of home decoration, food and craft can be seen to be competing for increasingly splintered and precisely defined readerships.

5. Celebrity, Advertising and Fashion

If magazines for women over this period have diversified to feed different audiences' requirements, in other ways some topics have become central and ubiquitous. The attention directed towards 'celebrity' since the turn of the century is not a phenomenon concerning women alone, but it certainly has had an impact on women's magazines, not least on the front covers which now tend to feature female celebrities more frequently than models. In Britain this obsession may have even started with a magazine. When the alien Spanish *Hello!* magazine hit British shores in 1988, it offered a new way of reporting the lives and loves of media 'stars' and royal icons. It provoked both approval and disapproval in its readers, who were fascinated with staged glimpses of the private lives of the upper echelons of 'Society'. Other magazines soon followed, some, such as *Best* and *OK!*, focusing on television personalities lower down the celebrity lists, and other publications that focused on unfortunate snapshots or gossip about their stars. While celebrity magazines are still a relatively recent phenomenon, they are a descendent of the film-star magazines of the interwar and postwar period, which Lisa Stead discusses in detail in Chapter 6. Celebrity is now an ever-present feature of women's consumer magazines, with high circulation titles such as *Cosmopolitan* on the one hand promoting young women's independence and social and sexual freedoms and, on the other, presenting their readership with images of photo-shopped world-famous beauties possessing unattainable glamour and body shapes.

Joke Hermes has questioned whether celebrity gossip magazines can be categorised as women's magazines and points to both similarities and differences in actual style and content (2006: 293). Hermes used interviews with readers to investigate how people derive meaning from celebrity gossip magazines and has summarised two categories of reading celebrity gossip magazines: 'serious and camp reading' (Ibid.: 294). The 'serious' reader may be conscious of the low status of this magazine genre but finds pleasure in 'vicariously enjoying the world of glitter and glamour', the focus on melodrama and family, as well as gaining inside knowledge and puzzling over the truth and lies about the stars in the way that fictionalised narratives work (Ibid.: 294–302). The 'unserious' reader employs irony and camp to mock and play with the magazine contents (Ibid.: 303). Whether the reader's engagement with these magazines is classified as serious or unserious, the celebrity magazine serves several social purposes. Rebecca Feasey (2008) has argued that they enable people to broach difficult conversations about contentious topics. Similarly, Andrea McDonnell (2014) has argued that popular celebrity magazines provide ways of making conversation with colleagues in the workplace.

Consuming images and gossip surrounding celebrities is often linked to the practice of consuming products endorsed by celebrities. Magazines have long been both enabled and restricted by the demands of advertisers; while advertising revenue has made magazine production possible in many cases, so too has the power of this vital income swayed editors and owners to create complementary content and create opportunities for product placement in content such as the short story, advice features and advertorials. The importance of advertising in women's magazines has been understood for some time. While critics such as Millum (1975) and Williamson (1978) have analysed the meanings of print advertising, more recent discussions of advertising in magazines have drilled down to the specific markets being targeted, for example through specific types of product, or women of different ages or diverse cultures. Both the different forms of advertising, such as the advertorial and online social media advertising, and the ways in which content stereotypes women according to role, class and cultural background have been discussed. Furthermore, recent work on advertising in nineteenth-century magazines has demonstrated that the connections between editorials and goods for sale is a long-established practice in the women's magazine. So pervasive is the need for advertising revenue, that some feminist and anti-capitalist magazines have also needed to make selective use of advertising (Hollows 2013).

6. Women's Postwar Print Culture Industries

The timespan of this volume covers a great expansion in women's print cultures. Simone Murray (2004) has described feminist publishing as 'Mixed Media' in her book of this title. She suggests that, 'Feminist presses must walk an impossible line between political authenticity and commercial viability; between financially risky first-book authors and low-risk, profit-generating "classics"; between ensuring sufficient turnover to remain solvent on the one hand, and, on the other, disguising any too flagrantly profitable operation for fear of intimidation' (Ibid.: 26). Women's publishing then, is fraught with tensions and competing identities. In Chapter 1 of this volume, Gail Chester's essay charts some of the technological changes that affected the whole of the printing and publishing industries and made it easier for women to access these worlds. The effects of technological developments were wide-ranging, from the normalisation of glossy paper and full-colour photography in domestic magazines, to the affordability of small-scale printing equipment, enabling the printing and production of magazines and leaflets featuring content rejected or ignored by larger publishers. Although often sexist, the underground or counter-cultural press of the 1960s, with its magazines like *Oz* and *Ink*, suggested a route for feminist publications that sought ideological change, in addition to legal, political, attitudinal and social change (Nelson 1989: 139–40). Lucy Delap and Zoe Strimpel in Chapter 2, and Catherine Riley in Chapter 3, discuss feminist publishing practices. Feminist publishing houses and presses were set up to publish work by female writers, past and present, and to open up opportunities for women to take more senior and influential roles in publishing. Publishing itself formed a strand within the Women's Liberation Movement, with Women in Publishing organisations in the US and then the UK. More women in publishing – and increased numbers of women involved in the creation, production, distribution and sales of printed media of all kinds – has had an impact on the content and contexts of women's magazines in the postwar period. They also had an impact on women-only publishing ventures discussed by Riley. In addition, networks of female booksellers formalised with their own trade journals. There were feminist bookshops, selling and lending works by women which were difficult to acquire, and performing social functions by providing spaces for women to meet and work (Hogan 2008; Delap 2016).

Female editors of newspapers and magazines have also been influential in women's print media over the period of this volume, and their role, influence and visibility, particularly in the new markets of the 1980s, has been noted. Anna Gough-Yates (2003) has discussed how, with interviews and features on magazine professionals becoming commonplace, the editor herself can be seen as representing the idealised reader of the magazine. In Chapter 7, Tracey Loughran emphasises the importance of early female editors and their expertise in shaping some women's magazines, and Charlotte Purkis describes in Chapter 13 how, in the specific field of performing arts journalism, some female writers rose to the roles of editors and critics for these specialist journals.

7. Studying Women's Print Media

The development of the study of women's periodicals and print media has led to new areas of interest, increased range of subject matter, and more detail and depth in critique and argument. Scholars have developed a range of approaches which demonstrate how print media, produced and consumed by women, both constructs women's consciousness and enables us to uncover women's histories. The postwar period has seen women's print media, in all its forms, become increasingly prominent as a subject of study. The critical field of book history, and its broadening out to the study of print culture, has provided a significant and foundational umbrella discipline for much of the study and recovery work represented in this volume. Discussing the field of print culture studies, Hammill and Hussey have captured the breadth of this burgeoning area of critical interest and indicated its reach. They suggest that:

> In this evolving area of print culture studies, the emphases are on the collaborative editing and production of printed materials, their material and visual aspects, their physical condition, their circulation in the marketplace, and the ideological dimensions of these processes. (2016: 5)

In this way, the field of print culture studies encompasses a wide range of aspects of print, from illustration and typography to the literary marketplace, editors and agents, to audiences and readerships. In addition, print culture extends to journals, newspapers, books, pamphlets, posters and more (Ibid.: 9,11). The form and individual qualities of such printed forms varies, as observed in this collection of essays, from hand-drawn and home-assembled pamphlets and zines to glossy, commercial, 'smart' magazines. Ritchie et al. (2016) note the particular usefulness of women's print media as historical resource, and even as valid historical evidence, in their collection produced after the 2012 *Women in Magazines* conference. This was an important inaugural conference, where, as Ritchie remembers, researchers presenting their papers felt that 'there was palpable relief at being able to talk about their findings without having to spend half of their allocated time explaining the validity of periodicals as historical evidence (Ritchie et al. 2016: 6, 1). Yet, despite this increased critical attention paid to women's print cultures, it is important to note that much of the current study in this vast field still discusses the 'tensions and paradoxes about the relationship between women and such publications' (Ibid.: 6).

This present collection contributes to this expanding field. It is interdisciplinary, drawing – as print culture studies do – on a range of critical fields and approaches. Contributors have approached print media from the disciplines of history, sociology, media studies, gender studies, oral history, politics and ethnography, using textual analysis, historical research, critical theory and interviews to provide context and critique. Because of varied content and quality – often incomplete information and irregular publication – print media is a complex field of study. It is understood, for instance, that the periodical form brings issues of temporality and redundancy and that there has been a tendency to 'cherry pick' content from magazines while ignoring the wider scope of their production contexts.

Important methodologies for studying print media have been suggested. Laurel Brake (1994) has identified many of the problems in dealing with runs of periodicals generally, and studying what seems like a never-ending form; she has suggested a holistic approach. In an important historical study, *Feminist Media History*, DiCenzo et al. (2011) argue for the importance of close analysis of primary material and the need to contextualise this material in relation both to historical contexts and current critical debates. They suggest a combined approach that encompasses both broader commentary and specific textual analysis through case studies.

Penny Tinkler has set out a helpful methodology specifically for writing about magazines (2016: 25–39). She makes a distinction between working *around* magazines – focusing on processes and contexts of production – and *with* magazines – focusing on the construction of meaning. Tinkler advocates an inclusive holistic research strategy that avoids a fragmented approach and takes account both of reader experiences, and 'what editors tried to achieve'. This includes contents that make up these composite texts (e.g. advertising), which are often lost in digitisation processes, and multisensory aspects of how people experience and make use of magazines. Furthermore, Tinkler emphasises the importance of contexts for magazines. Here, she introduces the idea of 'lateral mapping', a way of considering the 'range of magazines published for a particular constituency at a specific point in time' (Ibid.: 26), whereas 'longitudinal mapping' which looks backwards and forwards, 'considers the forerunners and successors of the magazines that are the focus of research' (Ibid.: 26–7).

Ground-breaking early works on women's magazines remain relevant for their revelations about the manifest and latent meanings of magazines and the complexities of ideological communication contained within this dominant form of women's print media. Early and important studies brought the field of women's magazines critical attention. Betty Friedan's (1963) *The Feminist Mystique* exposed the ways in which

American women's magazines portrayed women's lives as narrowly confined to domesticity, conforming to male editors' ideas of the 'new housewife'. While this work has since been criticised for Friedan's dual position both inside and outside the magazine industry, and for simplifications of femininity and culture, it remains an important touchstone in women's magazine studies (Johnson and Lloyd 2004; Hollows 2000). Marjorie Ferguson's (1983) *Forever Feminine* draws attention to the prevalence of images of femininity in magazines. In *Women's Worlds*, Ros Ballaster et al. (1991) argue that part of magazines' ongoing appeal to women readers is in the ways that they constantly address the never-ending problem of women's subjectivity (for an extensive critique of femininity and feminism see Joanne Hollows' *Feminism, Femininity and Popular Culture* (2000)). Janice Winship (1987), who wrote *Inside Women's Magazines*, uses a range of magazines aimed at different female readerships to emphasise the mixed messages of women's magazines and the mixed position of the reader. Winship observes that, although magazines may change over time, they still adhere to prevailing ideological patterns and this ensures the perpetuation of women's subordinate position in society.

In seeming opposition to some of this detailed work on femininity and subjectivity is the research into how readers actually make use of this mass media form. Joke Hermes (1995) in *Reading Women's Magazines* adopts an ethnographic approach to the periodical form, and findings from her interviewees reveal a level of ambivalence towards women's magazines. Ethnographic studies and the use of focus groups to discuss and report on the uses of women's magazines has become a significant approach. This methodology has been used in different contexts. For instance, Linda McLoughlin (2013; 2017) has sought to understand readers' cross-cultural views on femininity. Brita Ytre-Arne (2011) has discerned that magazines provide political or social information to their readers, while Feasey (2008) and McDonnell (2014) have both sought to understand the uses of celebrity magazines employing this approach. The focus group has been useful in providing direct evidence of readers' reading habits and opinions of magazines; they give a sense of how magazines really feature as material objects in everyday life. Such studies act as a check and balance to more theoretical deductions regarding the influence of mass media communication.

Historical studies of women's print media are now increasing in number and specificity. Cynthia White's (1970) *Women's Magazines 1693–1968* is a concise and wide-ranging critical history, and remains a valuable sourcebook because of its reach over time and the different types of women's magazine. Margaret Beetham's *A Magazine of Her Own* opened up the field of the nineteenth-century magazine for women, and while the examples in Beetham's volume, and in the academic journal *Victorian Periodicals Review*, are too early for the period covered in the present volume, both of these sources provide valuable methodologies for any scholar of women's magazines. Brian Braithwaite (1995) offers a history of the magazine industry workings in *Women's Magazines: The First 300 Years*. More specific and detailed studies of magazine histories or particular individual magazines (e.g. the recent volume on *Time and Tide* (Clay 2018)), or particular genres of magazine (e.g. fashion journalism) are also emerging (Best 2017). Histories that take a wider view of women's publishing and print media industry include Catherine Riley's (2018) study of the feminist publisher Virago and Lucy Delap's (2016) article on feminist bookshops (2016). The impact of women working in print media-related fields, as well as women professionals within print and digital publishing, is a history gathering increased attention as its relevance to contemporary feminisms and women's politics becomes increasingly evident.

Excitingly, more specific aspects of women's print media, such as those in this volume, are becoming more common. Work on important issues of age, race and class are inspiring studies of specific periodicals or groups of magazines. For example, the work of Angela McRobbie (1991) and Penny Tinkler (1996) reflects upon the girl or young woman and her liminal position as child/adult as represented in those magazines targeted at her age group. Nowile Rooks' (2004) *Ladies Pages* focuses on African-American women's magazines, and Erin A. Smith (2000) discusses working-class cultures in *Hard-Boiled: Working Class Readers and Pulp Magazines*.

There are also broader contexts for considering wider print cultures too. The magazine industry itself has been approached from a variety of angles, and Brian Braithwaite along with Joan Barrell (1979) have written helpful volumes such as *The Business of Women's Magazines*, which have aided scholars' understanding of the magazine industry. The commanding influence of advertising expenditure in women's magazines was brought to early attention by volumes such as *Images of Woman* by Trevor Millum (1975), and was given Marxist-feminist critique by Judith Williamson (1978) in *Decoding Advertisements*. Anna Gough-Yates (2003) has persuasively argued for the increased significance of the magazine editor and professional in the ways that magazines communicate with their female audiences.

This is an exciting time to be studying women's print media. Access to magazines, books and ephemera has been made easier through digitisation projects such as the *Spare Rib* digitisation project at the British Library.[5] Even though some images have subsequently been redacted due to copyright, it remains a wonderful resource. There have also been important digitisation projects of US *Vogue*, of modernist magazines (with accompanying publications, Brooker and Thacker 2013) and of British periodicals.[6] While some of these projects only just overlap with the time period addressed in this volume, they show the way for further, more recent periodical digitisations. Our understanding of women's relationship to culture, society and politics is being enhanced through critical work which views print media as socio-historical documentation, investigates meaning for readers and uncovers production history, adjunctive industries and professions.

8. This Collection

From paper shortages after the Second World War to the elimination of paper altogether in online magazines, changes to the woman's periodical over the postwar period have intensified. Mid-twentieth-century advancements in technology, printing techniques, publication processes, as well as the ubiquity of the Internet, have undoubtedly changed women's media for all time. Over the same period, women's lives in Britain have also changed in all manner of ways and magazines have reflected and constructed those numerous social changes for women over that seventy-year period. This collection of original and interdisciplinary essays – the fifth volume in this series by Edinburgh University Press – draws attention to the wide range of print cultures for women over seven decades. The range of essays included in this collection indicates both the history of publishing for women over the mid to late twentieth century and the early twenty-first century in Britain, and the diversity of audiences that use this material. Adopting an impressive range of approaches, the essays pay attention to the issues of race, class, age and sexuality, and discuss the diverse ways in which women were addressed and targeted as readers. While no single volume can represent all groups of women, these essays demonstrate the range of readerships for printed materials available to women over this long postwar period. By examining a range of printed matter, our contributors reflect in detail the important ways in which magazines contributed to, challenged or informed British women's culture. The collection spans domestic, cultural and feminist magazines and extends to ephemera, novels, pamphlets and other printed matter, as well as digital magazine formats. Over the second half of the twentieth century, women's relationships to their print media have survived huge changes in society, as well as changes in format. Throughout the essays, the range and significance of different printed forms for women are brought to the fore, from novels to newspapers, from pamphlets to periodicals and from hand-crafted zines to blogs and online productions. A range of approaches, including interview, textual analysis and industry commentary are employed in order to demonstrate the variety of ways in which the impact of postwar magazines may be understood.

Rather than attempting a history of print media, the collection highlights important issues including small circulation publications, as well as well-known and long-standing magazines. Taken together, the essays ask pertinent questions about the print cultures of the period. As print and the publishing industry became more accessible to women, so boundaries were increasingly blurred between magazine producer and magazine reader. Some essays present readers as producers, or produsers, and others discuss editors who were heavily invested in their printed output. The collection investigates the significance of print production processes, from the handmade and handwritten, to the Roneoed and photocopied, and on to the digital and online. Evidently, British women's print media since the Second World War must be approached from a variety of angles in order to understand it fully.

The collection begins with Part I, 'Publishing Industries and Practices', which seeks to explore the huge changes in publishing for women during the mid to late twentieth century and into the twenty-first century. This section pays attention to industry practices as they affected women, as well as feminist publishing enterprises and the range of texts produced specifically with female audiences in mind. The collection opens with Gail Chester's essay, which maps the publishing history of the feminist book over this long period since the 1940s, charting both the rejection and appropriation of the feminist book by feminist and mainstream publishers, including the heyday of the 1970s and the current resurgence in feminist publications. Following this, there is a discussion of the print culture surrounding the most famous British feminist magazine, *Spare Rib*. Lucy Delap and Zoe Strimpel discuss the motives and politics surrounding this important magazine, taking into account its strategies for financial survival, its approaches to its readership and its editorial tensions. Catherine Riley focuses on the feminist print culture and women-only publishing phenomenon of the 1970s and early 1980s. She argues that this phenomenon is feminist praxis that went on to influence all manner of genres, as well as the recovery of historical feminist books, some of which were bestsellers and enabled publishers to survive. Georgina Turner also draws attention to the practical challenges faced by an important and influential magazine for women-loving women:

DIVA. Here, Turner considers the ethics, production values and diverse approach to the magazine's target readership, against a backdrop of mainstream magazines and pressures to achieve advertising revenue. Looking to the future of magazine publication cultures, Laura Favaro discusses how young women's magazines, their relationship to their readers and the women's magazine industry have changed as they migrate or start up online.

Part II, 'Interacting with Readers', considers the ways in which magazines approached and addressed their target readership groups and audiences. This takes into account a range of age groups, including teenagers, and covers important aspects of postwar identity. Lisa Stead considers a specific group of magazine readers: fans of US and UK films of the 1940s. Fan magazines of this time, such as *Picturegoer*, had several avenues of communication with their readers, including discussions of wartime duties and domesticities. Mainstream women's magazines of the 1960s to 1980s, Tracey Loughran argues, attempted to rebuild the intimate space of women's magazines by including the reader. By accentuating letter-response formats – and by developing problem pages and the role of agony aunts – Loughran shows how some of the hierarchies involved in women's magazine were reduced. Drawing on Berlant's notion of 'intimate publics', Melanie Waters analyses the 'girl culture' of the younger reader and her magazines. Waters explores the extent to which *Just Seventeen* mobilised discourses of feminism to develop a feeling of intimacy among its young readership.

Part III, 'Tastemaking: Arts and Culture', considers different ways that advice and guidance is offered to women, and how this relates to wider social and cultural contexts, including women's reading practices. Stevie Marsden considers the history and impact of prizes for women's writing, and discusses the influence and publicity generated by the processes of judging cultural work. Amy Tooth Murphy explores Britain's first lesbian magazine, *Arena Three*, demonstrating how writers constructed a 'respectable' image through an association with middlebrow culture. From the perspective of elite cultural groups, the ruling class and celebrity, Estella Tincknell's analysis of the hugely influential fashion magazine, *Vogue*, reveals how the magazine is simultaneously cutting-edge and deeply conservative in its attitudes to fashion, celebrity, staffing and race. Eleanor Bell considers the increasing role of women writers in the Scottish literary scene, and maps this against a developing feminist consciousness. Pioneering work by women in magazines such as *Chapman* and *Cencrastus* have brought Scottish women's cultural work to the fore. Considering a participatory audience for the arts, Charlotte Purkis discusses those women of the 1950s and 1960s who were writing and editing music, drama and dance magazines such as *Theatre World* and *Ballet Today*. Purkis reflects on their writing and argues for a nascent feminism in these writing on performance culture.

What follows in Part IV, 'Feminisms and Activisms', demonstrates the important role of magazines in feminist activism. The political Left, and grassroots activism, has had a huge influence on the development of feminism and feminist activity. Victoria Bazin argues that magazines such as *Shrew*, *Scarlet Women* and *Red Rag* played their part in second-wave feminism's political positioning and offered space for discussion and debate, as well as a sense of collective agency for feminist activism. Sue Bruley continues the discussion about women's magazines on the Left in her analysis of *Women's Voice* and its troubled relationship to the masculinist political cultures of the Socialist Worker's Party. Bruley argues that an autonomous women's movement not only faced difficulties with existing political movements but also faced economic and social changes too. Claire Sedgwick takes a foundational second-wave feminist issue – women's reproductive rights – and compares the varying situations in the UK and the US, taking examples from *Spare Rib* and *Ms.*, two leading feminist magazines on different sides of the Atlantic. Kaitlynn Mendes considers the role of the digital in continuing the tradition of the feminist magazine. By examining the work of online feminist sites such as *The F-Word*, *The Vagenda* and *Feminist Times*, Mendes demonstrates that feminist DIY magazine culture is alive as a form of resistance and as a platform for a variety of feminist voices. In Rachel Alexander's discussion of *Harpies & Quines*, she demonstrates how the magazine attempted to create a distinctly Scottish feminist identity and how it positioned itself within broader print culture.

Part V, 'Negotiating Femininities', reflects on the ways in which magazines have shaped aspects of womanhood and notions of femininity. Cookery columns are a long-standing feature of women's magazines. Janet Floyd focuses on the representation of food in smart magazines to show how the magazine expressed relations between food and emotion which resonate in the anxiety of women's lives. Mary Irwin explores the production and content of the short-lived 1990s magazine, *Frank*, a woman's magazine shaped partly by the new wave of men's lifestyle magazines of the period. The magazine negotiated a complex response to a period often characterised in terms of post-feminism. Sarah Crook's essay tackles the subject of motherhood in second-wave feminist writings. Always a contested and contentious subject, Crook unravels some of the arguments put forward by women of differing views, in the pamphlets and magazines produced in the 1970s on the subject of motherhood, childcare and the Women's Liberation Movement. Fiona Hackney argues for a 'new consciousness' emerging in women's domestic magazines after the war, where women were encouraged by magazine editors, through the medium of fashion, to become involved in the wider society and community.

Our aim has been to open up a number of different contexts for understanding women's print media in the late twentieth and early twenty-first centuries and to showcase different critical approaches, as well as to illustrate the huge variety of subject matter in the field of British women's print media.

Notes

1. For a study of how teenage girls read and interpreted *Jackie*, see Frazer (1987).
2. For more on *Shocking Pink*, see Waters in this volume, as well as Gough-Yates (2012).
3. For more on 1980s and 1990s teenage girls' magazines, see Kehilly's (1999) research on how young people make sense of representations of sexuality in *More!* and *Sugar*.
4. For more on *FOWAAD* and its role in black British feminism, see Brixton Black Women's Group (1984); Bryan et al. (1997); and Samantrai (2002).
5. There are two parts to this – the full run of magazines: <https://journalarchives.jisc.ac.uk/britishlibrary/sparerib> and a curated website: <https://www.bl.uk/spare-rib>. The availability of the full run of magazines is threatened by a no-deal Brexit.
6. *Vogue* <https://www.proquest.com/products-services/vogue_archive.html>; Modernist Magazines (1880–1945) <http://www.modernistmagazines.com/index.php>; and British Periodicals (1681–1939) <https://journalarchives.jisc.ac.uk/britishperiodicals>.

Works Cited

Aynsley, J. and F. Berry. 2005. 'Introduction'. *Journal of Design History* 18.1: 1–5.

Bain, J. 2016. 'Darn Right I'm a Feminist . . . Sew What? the Politics of Contemporary Home Dressmaking: Sewing, Slow Fashion and Feminism'. *Women's Studies International Forum* 54: 57–66.

Ballaster, R., M. Beetham, E. Frazer and S. Hebron. 1991. *Women's Worlds: Ideology, Femininity and the Woman's Magazine*. Basingstoke: Macmillan.

Beetham, M. 1996. *A Magazine of Her Own?: Domesticity and Desire in the Woman's Magazine, 1800–1914*. London: Routledge.

Beetham, M. and K. Boardman, eds. 2001. *Victorian Women's Magazines: An Anthology*. Manchester: Manchester University Press.

Best, K. N. 2017. *The History of Fashion Journalism*. New York: Bloomsbury Academic.

Braithwaite, B. 1995. *Women's Magazines: The First 300 Years*. London: Peter Owen.

Braithwaite, B. and J. Barrell. 1979. *The Business of Women's Magazines: The Agonies and the Ecstasies*. London: Associated Business Press.

Brake, L. 1994. *Subjugated Knowledges: Journalism, Gender and Literature in the Nineteenth Century*. Basingstoke. Macmillan.

Brixton Black Women's Group. 1984. 'Black Women Organizing'. *Feminist Review* 17: 84–9.

Brooker, P. and A. Thacker, eds. 2009–13. *The Oxford Critical and Cultural History of Modernist Magazines*. Oxford: Oxford University Press.

Bryan, B., S. Dadzie and S. Scafe. 1997. 'The Heart of the Race: Black Women's Lives in Britain'. *Black British Feminism: A Reader*. Ed. H. S. Mirza. London: Routledge. 42–5.

Carter, F. 2016. 'A Taste of Honey: Get-ahead Femininity in 1960s Britain'. *Women in Magazines: Research, Representation, Production and Consumption*. Eds R. Ritchie, S. Hawkins, N. Phillips and S. Jay Kleinberg. New York: Routledge. 182–98.

Carter, M. 2013. 'Teen Mags: Still A Girl's Best Friend?' *Independent* 14 May 2013.
<www.independent.co.uk/life-style/health-and-families/features/teen-mags-still-a-girls-best-friend-8614418.html> (last accessed 7 November 2019).

Clay, C. 2018. *Time and Tide: The Feminist and Cultural Politics of a Modern Magazine*. Edinburgh: Edinburgh University Press.

Cohen, D. 2005. 'Why Did *The House* Fail? Demand and Supply Before the Modern Home Magazine, 1880s–1930'. *Journal of Design History* 18.1: 35–42.

Cutler, M. 2003. 'Educating the "Variant," Educating the Public: Gender and the Rhetoric of Legitimation in The Ladder Magazine for Lesbians'. *Qualitative Sociology* 26.2: 233–55.

De Beauvoir, S. 1949. (trans. by C. Borde and S. Malovany-Chevlaier, 2011) *The Second Sex*. London: Vintage.

Delap, L. 2016. 'Feminist Bookshops, Reading Cultures and the Women's Liberation Movement in Great Britain c. 1974–2000'. *History Workshop Journal* 81.1: 171–96.

DiCenzo, M., L. Delap and L. Ryan. 2011. *Feminist Media History: Suffrage, Periodicals and the Public Sphere*. Basingstoke: Palgrave.

Doan, L. 2001. *Fashioning Sapphism: The Origins of a Modern English Lesbian Culture*. New York: Columbia University Press.

Feasey, R. 2008. 'Reading *heat*: The Meanings and Pleasures of Star Fashions and Celebrity Gossip'. *Continuum: Journal of Media and Cultural Studies* 22.5: 687–99.

Ferguson, M. 1983. *Forever Feminine: Women's Magazines and the Cult of Femininity*. London: Heinemann.

Forster, L. 2015. *Magazine Movements: Women's Culture, Feminisms and Media Form*. London: Bloomsbury.

Frazer, E. 1987. 'Teenage Girls Reading Jackie'. *Media, Culture and Society* 9.4: 407–25.

Friedan, B. 1963. *The Feminine Mystique*. London: Victor Gollancz.

gal-dem. n.d. 'About'. *gal-dem*. <http://gal-dem.com/about/> (last accessed 5 November 2019).

Giddens, A. 1991. *Modernity and Self Identity: Self Identity in the Late Modern Age*. London: Polity Press.

Gill, R. 2007. *Gender and the Media*. Cambridge: Polity.

Gough-Yates, A. 2003. *Understanding Women's Magazines: Publishing, Markets and Readerships*. London: Routledge.

Gough-Yates, A. 2012. '"A Shock to the System": Feminist Interventions in Youth Subculture – The Adventures of Shocking Pink'. *Contemporary British History* 26.3: 375–403.

Groeneveld, E. 2010. '"Join the Knitting Revolution": Third-Wave Feminist Magazines and the Politics of Domesticity'. *Canadian Review of American Studies* 40.2: 259–77.

Hackney, F. 2006. 'Use Your Hands for Happiness: Home Craft and Make-Do-and-Mend in British Women's Magazines in the 1920s and 1930s'. *Journal of Design History* 19.1: 23–38.

Hackney, F. 2013. 'Quiet Activism and the New Amateur: The Power of Home and Hobby Crafts'. *Design and Culture: the Journal of the Design Studies Forum* 5.2: 169–93.

Hamer. E. 1996. *Britannia's Glory: A History of Twentieth-Century Lesbians*. London: Cassell.

Hammill, F. and M. Hussey. 2016. *Modernism's Print Cultures*. London, Bloomsbury.

Helcké, J. 2003. 'Magazines in Everyday Life: Negotiating Identity, Femininity and Belonging in Lifestyle Magazines for Minority Ethnic Women in France and the UK' <http://hestories.info/magazines-in-everyday-life-negotiating-identity-femininity-and.html> (last accessed 5 November 2019).

Hermes, J. 1995. *Reading Women's Magazines: An Analysis of Everyday Media Use*. Cambridge: Polity.

Hermes, J. 2006. 'Reading Gossip Magazines: The Imagined Communities of "Gossip" and "Camp"'. *The Celebrity Culture Reader*. Ed. P. David Marshall. Abingdon: Routledge. 291–310.

Hirsch, A. 2018. 'Glossies So White'. *The Guardian*, 10 April 2018. <www.theguardian.com/media/2018/apr/10/glossy-magazine-covers-too-white-models-black-ethnic-minority> (last accessed 5 November 2019).

Hogan, K. 2008. 'Women's Studies in Feminist Bookstores: "All the Women's Studies women would come in"'. *Signs* 33.3: 595–622.

Hollows, J. 2000. *Feminism, Femininity and Popular Culture*. Manchester: Manchester University Press.

James, A. 1997. 'How British is British Food?'. *Food, Health and Identity*. Ed. P. Caplan. London: Routledge. 71–86.

Jennings, R. 2007a. *Tomboys and Bachelor Girls: A Lesbian History of Post-war Britain 1945–71*. Manchester: Manchester University Press.

Jennings, R. 2007b. *A Lesbian History of Britain: Love and Sex between Women since 1500*. Oxford: Greenwood World Publishing.

Jonsson, T. 2014. 'White Feminist Stories'. *Feminist Media Studies*. 14.6: 1,012–27.

Johnson, L. and J. Lloyd. 2004. *Sentenced to Everyday Life: Feminism and the Housewife*. Oxford: Berg.

Kehilly, M. J. 1999. 'More Sugar? Teenage Magazines, Gender Displays and Sexual Learning'. *European Journal of Cultural Studies* 2.1: 65–89.

Latham, S. and R. Scholes. 2006. 'The Rise of Periodical Studies'. *PMLA* 121:2: 517–37.

McCracken, E. 1993. *Decoding Women's Magazines: From* Mademoiselle *to* Ms. New York: St Martin's Press.

McDonnell, A. 2014. *Reading Celebrity Gossip Magazines*. Cambridge: Polity Press.

McLoughlin, L. 2013. 'Crystal Clear: Paler Skin Equals Beauty – A Multimodal Analysis of Asiana Magazine'. *South Asian Popular Culture* 11.1: 15–29.

McLoughlin, L. 2017. *A Critical Discourse Analysis of South Asian Women's Magazines: Undercover Beauty*. London: Palgrave Macmillan.

McRobbie, A. 1981. 'Just Like a Jackie Story'. *Feminism For Girls: An Adventure Story*. Eds A. McRobbie and T. McCabe. London: Routledge and Kegan Paul.

McRobbie, A. 1991. *Feminism and Youth Culture: From Jackie to Just Seventeen*. Basingstoke: Macmillan.

McRobbie, A. 1994. *Postmodernism and Popular Culture*. London: Routledge.

McRobbie, A. 1996. 'More! New Sexualities in Girls and Women's Magazines'. *Cultural Studies and Communication*. Eds J. Curran, D. Morley and V. Walkerdine. London: Edward Arnold.

Millum, T. 1975. *Images of Woman: Advertising in Women's Magazines*. London: Chatto & Windus.

Murray, S. 2004. *Mixed Media: Feminist Presses and Publishing Politics*. London: Pluto Press.

Nelson, E. 1898. *The British Counter-Culture 1966–73: A Study of the Underground Press*. Basingstoke: Macmillan.

Ormrod, J. 2018. 'Reading Production and Culture: UK Teen Comics from 1955 to 1960'. *Girlhood Studies* 11.3: 18–33.

Pleasance, H. 1991. 'Open or Closed: Popular Magazines and Dominant Culture'. *Off-Centre: Feminism and Cultural Studies*. Eds S. Franklin, C. Lury and J. Stacey. London: HarperCollins.

Riley, C. E. 2018. *The Virago Story: Assessing the Impact of a Feminist Publishing Phenomenon*. New York: Berghahn Books.

Ritchie, R., S. Hawkins, N. Philips and S. J. Kleinberg, eds. 2016. *Women in Magazines: Research, Representation, Production and Consumption*. London: Routledge.

Rooks, N. M. 2004. *Ladies' Pages: African American Women's Magazines and the Culture That Made Them*. New Jersey: Rutgers University Press.

Rowbotham, S. 1999. *A Century of Women: The History of Women in Britain and the United States*. London: Penguin.

Samantrai, R. 2002. *AlterNatives: Black Feminism in the Postimperial Nation*. Stanford CA: Stanford University Press.

Smith, E. A. 2000. *Hard-Boiled: Working-Class Readers and Pulp Magazines*. Philadelphia: Temple University Press.

Snider, S. 2010. 'Revisioning Fat Lesbian Subjects in Contemporary Lesbian Periodicals'. *Journal of Lesbian Studies* 14.2–3: 174–84.

Soares, M. 1998. 'The Purloined Ladder'. *Journal of Homosexuality* 34.3–4: 27–49.

Thiird. n.d. 'Manifesto'. <http://www.thiiirdmagazine.co.uk/about-us/> (last accessed 5 November 2019).

Thomlinson, N. 2016. '"Second-wave" Black Feminist Periodicals In Britain'. *Women: A Cultural Review* 27.4: 432–55.

Tincknell, E., D. Chambers, J. Van Loon and N. Hudson. 2003. 'Begging For It: "New Femininities", Social Agency, and Moral Discourse in Contemporary Teenage and Men's Magazines'. *Feminist Media Studies* 3.1: 47–63.

Tinkler, P. 1996. *Constructing Girlhood: Popular Magazines for Girls Growing Up in England, 1920–1950*. London: Routledge.

Tinkler, P. 2014. '"Are You Really Living?" If Not, "Get With It!"'. *Cultural and Social History* 11.4: 597–619.

Tinkler, P. 2016 'Fragmentation and Inclusivity: Methods for Working with Girls' and Women's Magazines'. *Women in Magazines: Research, Representation, Production and Consumption*. Eds R. Ritchie, S. Hawkins, N. Phillips and S. J. Kleinberg. London: Routledge. 25–39.

Turner, G. 2008. '"The Road to the Lesbian Nation is not an Easy One": "Us" and "Them" in DIVA magazine'. *Social Semiotics* 18.3: 377–88.

Turner, G. 2009. 'Catching the Wave: Britain's Lesbian Publishing Goes Commercial'. *Journalism Studies* 10.6: 769–88.
Turney, J. 2003. 'Here's One I Made Earlier: Making and Living with Home Craft in Contemporary Britain'. *Journal of Design History* 17.3: 267–81.
Twigg, J. 2018. 'Fashion, the Media and Age: How Women's Magazines Use Fashion to Negotiate Age Identities'. *European Journal of Cultural Studies* 21.3: 334–48.
Vercoe, L. 2018. 'It's Journalism You Can Touch'. *British Journalism Review* 29.2: 38–44.
Vicinus, M. 1992. '"They Wonder to Which Sex I Belong": The Historical Roots of the Modern Lesbian Identity'. *Feminist Studies* 18.3: 467–97.
Waller, J. and M. Vaughan-Rees. 1987. *Women in Wartime: The Role of Women's Magazines 1930–1945*. London: Macdonald Optima.
White, C. 1970. *Women's Magazines 1693–1968*. London: Michael Joseph.
Williamson, J. 1978. *Decoding Advertisements: Ideology and Meaning in Advertising*. London: Boyars.
Wilson, E. 1980. *Only Halfway to Paradise: Women in Postwar Britain 1945–1968*. London: Tavistock.
Wilson, T. L. 2003. 'Tasty Selections: An Evaluation of Gourmet Food Magazines'. *Journal of Agricultural and Food Information* 5.2: 49–66.
Winship, J. 1987. *Inside Women's Magazines* London: Pandora.
Ytre-Arne, B. 2011. 'Women's Magazines and the Public Sphere'. *European Journal of Communication* 26.3: 247–61.

Part I

Publishing Industries and Practices

1

Culture Versus Commerce: The Publishing of Feminist Books Since the 1940s

Gail Chester

To many people, feminist publishing in the contemporary period has consisted of the books published by Virago and maybe The Women's Press, along with *Spare Rib* magazine. However, these publications, significant though they have been, are only a tiny fraction of the other material – pamphlets and zines, journals and magazines, posters, flyers, badges – that has poured off the presses, particularly during the 1970s and 1980s when the Women's Liberation Movement was most active (see Plate 1).

While the major explanation for the proliferation or paucity of feminist books at a particular time is the presence of a visible feminist movement, there are many other considerations. Since the 1960s there have been unprecedented developments in print and publishing technologies, which have impacted greatly on feminist and radical publishing, probably more so than on the more mainstream parts of the industry. From the 1960s, small offset-litho printing machines became affordable as letterpress was giving way to compugraphic typesetting. In the 1980s, desktop publishing (actually, not publishing, but the creation of documents using page layout software on a PC) allowed for more professional-looking design (for those who wanted and could afford it), while Gestetner duplicators were being replaced by photocopying machines and the risograph. These developments led to the setting up of many radical and community print shops and enabled the production of magazines, pamphlets and similar publications which would previously have been uneconomic – a trend which has continued into the 2000s with the development of digital printing – and have now made it affordable to produce quite small print runs of books. Social and economic conditions have also changed a great deal since the 1960s and 1970s, when the welfare state and cheap rent or squatting meant that people could afford to live on much less and throw themselves into political action, campaigning, writing and publishing. At any period, finding money has always been difficult for women, while the restructuring of the book industry since the 1990s has made life increasingly difficult for writers, which has only been exacerbated by increasing austerity since the late 2000s (Flood 2019a; Martin 2017).

But what is meant by a 'feminist book'? This is not a straightforward issue – first, one must consider political issues. Many mainstream feminists think it is unnecessary to challenge the whole structure of society and that explaining things politely will achieve equality, whereas more radical feminists believe a thoroughgoing overhaul of society is needed if women's oppression is to be changed. For example, should Sheryl Sandberg's book, *Lean In* (W. H. Allen 2013), be considered a feminist book, as opposed to Dawn Foster's book, *Lean Out* (Repeater 2015), which asks, 'If 1% are leaning in, what are the other 99% supposed to do?' It is clear that books at the liberal end of the spectrum are more likely to get published, at least by a commercial publisher. Even among women whose politics are definitely radical, there is some debate about the use of the word 'feminist'. For example, some black women refuse to espouse it, as they perceive 'feminism' to be a white woman's term. Women's writing, especially about women, has always been taken less seriously than men's, so in any genre, be it fiction, memoir or academic literature, questions will be asked about the quality of women's work – but just because a book is written by a woman and is about women, does that necessarily make it feminist?

Many topics that might have been considered feminist forty years ago would be considered mere common sense today – hopefully, that is one of the achievements of the Women's Liberation Movement. In the 1970s, books on women and judo and women and golf were welcomed into the Feminist Library,[1] something which might seem odd today. However, while pay parity in tennis and other major sports remains a live issue, and an increased interest in women's football is a recent phenomenon, there are clearly still feminist analyses of sport to be written. It is perhaps in fiction that the changes in society over recent decades demonstrate most clearly the dilemmas of deciding whether a contemporary novel is feminist.

During the period of the Women's Liberation Movement, around 2,000 identifiably feminist works of fiction and poetry were published by The Women's Press, Virago and other feminist publishers and self-publishing groups and individuals, as well as by a few mainstream publishers. However, it is common today for women to work outside the home, whether in relatively well-paid middle-class jobs or getting by on zero-hours contracts. Thus, women must still juggle their paid work with their caring and domestic responsibilities, while worrying about job security, promotion prospects, unequal pay or finding affordable childcare and housing. Such concerns are now part of everyday discourse, not the preserve of a few radical feminists. The novels of Sally Rooney, *Conversations With Friends* (2017) and *Normal People* (2018), both published by Faber and Faber – a long-established and renowned literary publisher – are an excellent example of the debate that has been prompted about women's writing, revealing that works may be considered feminist in that they take into account not just women's place in society, but also reveal antagonisms of class and generation. A number of older, privileged male authors have refused to acknowledge that literature such as Rooney's, which does not reflect their own preoccupations, could be deemed art (Foster 2019; Mullins 2019).[2]

If the definition of 'feminist' is problematic, then definitions of what makes a 'book' are no less so. The field of book history is littered with overlapping definitions to cover everything from the Rosetta Stone to the latest digital device. This chapter is concerned mainly with material where ink has been applied to paper, but in this era of e-books and social media, blogs and websites should also be included in the broad definition of 'books'.[3] Zines lie at the boundary between the print and digital worlds, often being distributed via both, having been produced on paper with scissors and glue. In many ways, zines are the natural daughters of the political pamphlet, something that is explored by Gillian Whiteley (forthcoming) in her history of the form.

The boundaries between pamphlets and books is often blurred, and the 'sexual politics' category in the British Library catalogue presents many such quandaries. One striking example is the self-published first edition of *The Politics of Sexuality in Capitalism* (1978), which was produced without a spine as a pamphlet, while the second edition, whose contents were the same, even though the format was different, was classified as a book. Thus the margins of what makes a feminist book remain fluid, and for the purposes of this chapter, it seems best to stick with the possibly simplistic definition that a feminist book is one that highlights, foregrounds or analyses the position of women in society, with the intention of improving it and, sometimes, even creating a little joy.

Publishing Feminism from the Mainstream

In her book, *Publishing the Postcolonial*, Gail Low (2010: xiv) suggests that the unprecedented interest of the literary establishment in books by black authors during the period of decolonisation 'can be rationalised as a complex of responses, including curiosity, concern, exoticism and opportunism'. When considering whether to publish a feminist book, a similar observation could be made. While 'opportunism' might seem a little harsh, the intention of mainstream publishers is to make a profit by watching social trends and then publishing books that they hope will appeal to interested readers, not necessarily because they are motivated by political concerns or indeed understand the market.

Jack Lindsay (1951) contributed an article on publishing to a special issue of *Arena* (a Communist Party journal) called 'The USA Threat to British Culture', which explained how British book publishing was being overwhelmed by the capitalist methods and cultural domination of the US. This article pre-dated the first major conglomeratisation of the British book trade by a generation, yet it accurately described what was to come, although it did not predict how the mainstream US publishing industry would be the first major source of countercultural and feminist books to reach Britain. This wholesale importing of texts from the US has posed a significant problem for the radical movements in Britain – at least since the Second World War – since such publishing can trick the unwary reader into believing that our cultural and political situations are more similar than they are. In the 1990s, Sally Munt (1997: 90) pointed out that: 'Many of the iconic texts [of Lesbian Studies] in the USA are imported for British use and appropriated there . . . It used to be that every vaguely sympathetic straight student had read Andrea Dworkin, now it is more likely to be Judith Butler. Both are separately identifiable as North American in their styles, both assume a North American reader.' Such American-centrism persists today, as, for example, with the controversy around Naomi Wolf's (2019) most recent book, *Outrages: Sex, Censorship, and the Criminalisation of Love*, which could be held as an example of an American author not sufficiently coming to grips with British history. But although we must maintain some vigilance about American cultural imperialism, we must also acknowledge that British feminist culture has been enriched by the works of Alison Bechdel, Audre Lorde and The Boston Women's Health Book collective, among many others.

Furthermore, our knowledge of political developments in Europe has too often been mediated by translations and authors being re-imported from the US, a famous case being Simone de Beauvoir's *The Second Sex*. Having been published in French in 1949, the first English language edition was issued in 1953 in Britain by Jonathan Cape and in the US by Knopf, who held the translation rights, in what was widely considered an inaccurate translation which omitted up to 15 per cent of the original text. Feminist scholars have argued convincingly that this was probably not primarily the fault of the translator (Bogic 2011; Simons 1983), but of Knopf being mainly interested in making as much profit as possible from sales. This US edition remained in print and was published as a cheap paperback by Bantam in 1961. Knopf consistently refused to have a new translation done, only relenting in 2009.

Between the 1940s and the late 1960s, while the women's movement was considered to be more or less dead, a trickle of feminist books was published in Britain by mainstream publishers with a somewhat radical sensibility – such as Penguin, Allen & Unwin, Gollancz, and Constable – as there were no feminist publishers at the time. In the period leading up to the Second World War, there were actually more feminist books being published, albeit by mainstream publishers, than in the period after it – this was most likely the long-tail legacy of the women's suffrage movement and political concerns connected with it, the effect of which had largely died out by the end of the war. Of the handful of obviously feminist books during this period, most harked back to earlier times, especially to the suffragettes and the history of women breaking into the professions,[4] as well as one or two classics such as *A Room of One's Own*, re-published by Penguin in 1945 and reprinted several times in subsequent decades. There were also a few titles which would later have come under the broad category of Women's Studies, such as Jeannette Foster's *Sex Variant Women in Literature: A Historical and Quantitative Survey* (London: Frederick Muller 1958);[5] Hannah Gavron's, *The Captive Wife: Conflicts of Housebound Mothers* (Routledge & Kegan Paul 1966);[6] Cynthia White's, *Women's Magazines, 1693–1968* (Michael Joseph 1970); and Eva Figes' *Patriarchal Attitudes* (Faber 1970; Panther 1972).[7] Interestingly, all of the early women's liberation classics which were originally published by mainstream publishers – for example, *Patriarchal Attitudes*; Betty Friedan's *The Feminist Mystique* (Victor Gollancz 1963); and Kate Millet's *Sexual Politics* (Rupert Hart Davis 1971) – were reprinted a number of times, fifteen times by 1981 in the case of Germaine Greer's *The Female Eunuch* (Cadman et al. 1981: 29), and several times subsequently. At the same time, Shulamith Firestone's more politically radical classic, *The Dialectic of Sex* (Cape 1971; Paladin 1972) – with its subtitle, 'The Case for Feminist Revolution' – languished for many years and was never reprinted by a mainstream publisher after its initial release, and then only by The Women's Press in 1979 and Verso in 2015 (Merck and Sandford 2010; Margree 2018).

There were a number of feminist or sympathetic editors based in the various academic publishers who thrived in the 1970s and 1980s, some of whom were able to establish women's studies lists, but this ecosystem was severely eroded as conglomeratisation of the publishing industry proceeded. Some of these editors found jobs in the conglomerates, while others joined the feminist publishing houses that were emerging. None of the feminist publishers distinguished between academic and trade books, which was a significant distinction in the mainstream trade. Thus, titles from feminist publishers occupied what was disparagingly called the 'mid-list' by profit-hungry mainstream publishers, but which meant they were read by both students and teachers at all levels, as well as by the interested general reader. As with so many aspects of feminist practice, this breaking down of accepted boundaries was not a carefully thought out plan resulting from expensive market research; it was a response to the demands of the publishers' politics and their connection with their readership. Most feminists, especially those outside academia, felt little or no sense of identification with the mainstream academic publishers, but, as the active Women's Liberation Movement waned, Women's Studies, which morphed later into Gender Studies, enabled the survival of a vigorous market in the publishing of highly priced theoretically orientated Women's Studies titles. These developments almost certainly contributed to the wedge that was driven between feminists within and outside academia, a development which was critiqued then, and has not been satisfactorily resolved since. An example of how this can be brought about is a book, *In Other Words: Writing as a Feminist*, which I co-edited with Sigrid Nielsen, and which was commissioned in 1985 by Hutchinson Education, the academic imprint of Hutchinson (Chester and Nielsen 1987) (see Plate 2).

Even in the mid-1970s, there was something of a division among women who worked in academia, based partly on the level of abstraction that they felt was admissible in the writing that they were producing. There was a lengthy and somewhat acrimonious meeting held at the Women's Research and Resources Centre (WRRC) in 1977 (see endnote 1), centring on what kind of publication the organisation should produce. The WRRC collective members who wanted to produce one-off pamphlets rather than an academic journal decided to form a subgroup for this purpose, and called their series 'Explorations in Feminism'. They began to disseminate important research that would not generally be considered significant by academic publishers, such as MA dissertations, and also work which was critical of the academic establishment, such as a pamphlet on sexual harassment in academia.

After the collective had produced about ten titles, they decided to find a sympathetic publisher to take on the series. This was not an easy decision, but going to a mainstream publisher seemed preferable to letting the Explorations in Feminism series die. Thus, in the early 1980s, the series was taken on by Hutchinson Education, and the WRRC publishing collective became its editorial collective. Hutchinson Education published about a dozen books in its Explorations in Feminism series, reprinting a few of the original WRRC publications and commissioning some new ones. *In Other Words* was one of the books that was freshly commissioned by Hutchinson Education, and was based on papers produced for a conference on feminism and writing in Edinburgh in 1985 – most of them needed editing for publication, and some new ones were commissioned. Not long after Hutchinson signed the contract to publish *In Other Words*, the company merged with a newer commercial publisher, Century, to become Century Hutchinson. This was the era of the great conglomeratisation of British publishing, so by the time that *In Other Words* had sold out of its print run of 3,000 copies in the mid-1990s (a startlingly large number by today's standards), the book had passed through the hands of five publishing houses – Hutchinson, Century Hutchinson, Bell and Hyman, Unwin Hyman, and Routledge Kegan Paul (most of which were themselves the product of previous amalgamations), before coming to rest with Routledge.

The contents of *In Other Words* show that it was a product of its time and not an academic book. In the mid-1980s, the Women's Liberation Movement was still vigorous and the book reflected its values – women taking control of their own lives and providing a support network in which such control became a possibility, while understanding that the personal is political. This approach is reflected in the table of contents, which is divided into four sections: What Women Write; Taking Control; Writing about Ourselves; and Support and Communication.

After *In Other Words* had sold out its first print run, its editors asked Routledge to consider issuing a second edition. They were told that its day had passed and it was not worth reissuing as interest in feminism was in decline, although the unstated reason for this was that *In Other Words* was aimed at a more general readership. However, in 2011, Routledge wanted to reissue *In Other Words* 'as a hardback facsimile edition and also an e-book . . . as part of a multi-volume set on Feminism, aimed mainly at the international library market' as part of a reissue programme, which is still in existence, called Routledge Library Editions.[8] The first WRRC pamphlets, published as a political act by a group of volunteers, cost under £2, *In Other Words* was published in 1987 at £7.95 for 250 pages, which was quite expensive for a feminist trade paperback then; while the Routledge Library Edition hardback, published in 2011, retails for £105.00 and the paperback sells for £35 – still beyond the means of most general readers – and you can rent the e-book by the month for a similar amount.[9]

Why Feminist Publishers?

In Britain, as elsewhere, feminists and other marginalised groups have consistently found themselves excluded from the mainstream publishing process. In 1972, Michelene Wandor – editor of *The Body Politic* (1972), the first anthology from the British Women's Liberation Movement – failed to raise interest in the volume among commercial publishers who judged women's liberation as 'not hot' and did not think that interest in women would last (Chester 2002: 198). It was eventually published by Stage 1, a very small radical publisher (also responsible for *The Little Red School Book* and works by Che Guevara and Fidel Castro) with a modest print run, using cheap typesetting, paper and binding. In contrast, *Sisterhood is Powerful*, the first women's liberation anthology in the US, edited by Robin Morgan, was published by Random House/Vintage Books in 1970, and although Morgan describes vividly in her introduction the many problems that she encountered with sexism and interference by male editors at Random House, it did publish a mass-market paperback of 600 pages with photographs, which also sold well in Britain (Chester 2019).

Lillian Faderman, the noted author of *Surpassing the Love of Men* (Junction Books 1981; The Women's Press 1985) explained how difficult it was for her to maintain her academic career and publish books about lesbianism in the US:

> I really would have liked to do a book on sexual minorities [instead of my first book, *Speaking for Ourselves*, the first anthology of multi-ethnic literature, published in 1969] — but that was impossible in the 1960s. Even if I could have found a publisher, I knew that my academic career would have ended before it began . . . Academic presses in the 1970s were open to feminist subjects, but I don't think they would have taken seriously books about lesbian literature or lesbian history . . . I didn't publish a book with an academic publisher until 1991, when Columbia University Press . . . offered to publish *Odd Girls and Twilight Lovers: A History of Lesbian Life in Twentieth Century America*. By then the subject was not only permissible, it was popular. After the hardcover came out and

did well in reviews and sales, Columbia held an auction for the paperback rights, and Viking-Penguin won. (Toor 2018)

Many feminist authors have had experiences similar to Wandor and Faderman, so it became clear that feminists needed their own publishing houses to produce the books that they wanted to write and that other women wanted to read. Virago – the first British feminist publisher – started in 1973, and is still in business today, unlike most of the other feminist publishers founded in the second wave (for more on Virago and feminist publishers in the UK, see Catherine Riley's discussion in Chapter 3). In the heyday of women's liberation, between the 1970s and the 1990s, feminist publishers produced books across the range of subjects of interest to concerned women – women who would not necessarily consider themselves to be activists, but wanted to understand their situation and what might be done to improve it. Many more works of non-fiction than fiction were produced, covering an expansive range of topics including employment, history, education, housing, the arts, motherhood, sexuality, politics, science, technology and, perhaps above all, health, a topic in which many women, whether feminist or not, often have had a deep interest. A popular sub-genre in feminist publishing was anthologies, where the short writings of different women were brought together around a particular topic. Such anthologies allow the same subject to be tackled from a number of viewpoints – they enable women who have many other calls on their time to be published; they enable groups of women from minority groups to have a platform (e.g. disabled mothers, black women or working-class artists (Chester 2002)).

When the first tranche of feminist publishers – Virago, Onlywomen, The Women's Press, and Stramullion – started in the 1970s, it was assumed that they would be able to cater for the interests of all feminists, as they shared much of their political outlook with their potential readers (even though there were obvious differences between the publishers from the outset).[10] Feminists were hungry for books that addressed their concerns, but during the 1980s some feminist publishers began to sense a rift with parts of the Women's Liberation Movement. Stephanie Dowrick, who ran The Women's Press then, 'perceived quite a lot of unease about [the Press] doing what they did, and seeming to do it well, [she] detected a kind of moralism . . . about what it means to some women to have a certain power, and other women not to have that power' (Cadman et al.: 41). Given the very different economic circumstances since the 1980s, it seems that, although feminists today are just as concerned with issues of morality and power, their focus would not generally be on judging women for running a successful business.

As time went on, it became clear that parts of the Women's Liberation Movement did not feel that their issues were being addressed by the existing feminist publishers. Thus, from the early 1980s, a number of new publishing initiatives began – Sheba (1980); Black Women Talk (1983); Scarlet Press (1984); Pandora (1983); and Honno (1986) – each with their own priorities, and each trying to move away from the London-centric, white, heterosexual bias that was felt to predominate. Unfortunately, apart from Virago, the only one of this group that survives is Honno, the Welsh feminist publishing house which publishes books in Welsh and English on Welsh women's experiences. But while those feminist publishers existed, they produced many ground-breaking titles that have undeservedly been allowed to languish out of print. In feminist publishing, as in the mainstream, very few books which dealt with class politics were published – the novel *Brainchild* by Eve Croft (Onlywomen 1982), and *Born to Struggle*, the autobiography of May Hobbs, the leader of the Night Cleaners' campaign (Quartet 1973) being among the rare exceptions, apart from the publications of the Federation of Worker Writers and Community Publishers, which, while occasionally hostile to women's groups, nevertheless gave access to being published to many working-class women (and men) (Chester 2019). Writing by black British women was hard to find (as opposed to importing books by black American women), and even trailblazers such as Beverley Bryan, Stella Dadzie and Suzanne Scafe's *The Heart of the Race: Black Women's Lives in Britain* (1985), one of the first non-fiction books that investigated the subject, and Heidi Safia Mirza's *Young, Female and Black* (1992) and *Black British Feminism* (1997) have been neglected by younger black British writers, so that this history is in danger of being lost. It is rarely taught at universities, nor does it appear in the timelines of what is effectively a whitewashed British feminist history (Evaristo 2019).

Various scholars have considered why Virago has outlasted almost all the other second-wave feminist publishers. There appears to be general agreement that a major reason for its longevity is that, along with its legendary marketing skills, throughout most of its history it has been incorporated within mainstream publishing companies. Virago started as an associate company of Quartet, but went independent in 1976. In 1981 Virago explained that 'It would be fair to say that many of the books that Quartet would not take on, because they thought they were not viable, became very successful. They did not see the audience' (Cadman et al. 1981: 40). Yet, only a year later, Virago became a wholly owned subsidiary of the Chatto, Virago, Bodley Head and Cape Group. In 1987 the Virago directors undertook a management buyout, only to become part of the British arm of the American multinational Little, Brown in 1995, which has since been absorbed into the Hachette Group (Chester 2019). In its latest incarnation, Virago seems to have mislaid its radical politics – although it has continued to publish good women's writing, it rarely takes risks to promote untested authors. Even though the feminist movement has become more visible again, Virago, ever the astute marketer, has chosen to focus, for example, on titles under the rubric of Virago Pride – although in 2018 it did publish 'our first anthology about intersectional feminism: *Can We All Be Feminists?* edited by June Eric-Udorie'.[11]

From its earliest days, Virago consciously presented itself as part of mainstream publishing (albeit a dissident part), as opposed to, for example, Onlywomen Press (set up around the same time), publishing only a few books a year that conformed to its ethos of radical lesbian feminism, and which remained resolutely independent until it closed around 2012 (Duncker 1999; Murray 1999) owing to its owner's ill health. In thinking about the reasons for Virago's survival, Catherine Riley (2014: 244–5) accurately describes the Butlerisation of feminism in the 1990s – not just the blurring of sexual identities (which many feminists have long advocated), but the adoption of personal consumption as an expression of, or as an alternative to, political identification (which many feminists have long been unhappy about). This was in keeping with the rise of neoliberalism – a development which Virago, with its more commercial orientation, was well placed to exploit. Interestingly, of the eight younger third and fourth-wave feminists who Riley cites as publishing feminist books against the virulent misogyny of much pop culture between 1999 and 2010, only one was published by Virago (Ibid.: 247). If the current feminist movement maintains its momentum, including more radical analyses, it will be interesting to see whether Virago will once again seize that marketing opportunity.

This apparent desire to appeal primarily to the mainstream market may help explain various decisions that Virago has taken in recent years towards notable feminist books and authors. For example, they refused to reissue *Heart of the Race*,[12] the first and widely respected anthology of black British women's writing, originally published by Virago in 1985, which has now been re-published by Verso – the earliest New Left publisher – in its feminist classics series. Verso has published ten titles in this series, as well as a number of writers across the spectrum of feminist politics, including four of Lynne Segal's more recent books and updated versions of five of Sheila Rowbotham's books. In 2013, Verso published *Out of Time: The Pleasures and Perils of Ageing* by Lynne Segal, with an introduction by Elaine Showalter. This would have seemed an obvious choice for the Virago list, as both Segal and Showalter are Virago authors, and indeed Segal was on Virago's advisory board (Showalter 2013: xv). From a marketing angle, second-wave feminists are getting older, as Elaine Showalter points out in her introduction.[13] This is borne out by the success of *This Chair Rocks: A Manifesto against Ageism* by Ashton Applewhite – self-published in 2016 and reissued in 2019 by Macmillan Publishers in the US and Melville House in the UK. A similar case, where Virago might have been expected to make a commercial as well as a political decision, is *New Daughters of Africa*, edited by Margaret Busby, which was published in 2019 by Myriad Editions, a feminist leaning publisher with a speciality in graphic books, among other things. Myriad was set up in 1993 by Candida Lacey, formerly of Pandora, and Anne Benewick, formerly of Pluto, and their strapline is 'Our mission is to make the personal political and the local international'. The original *Daughters of Africa*, also edited by Busby, was published by Jonathan Cape in 1992 and Vintage in 1993.

On the whole, it seems to have been left to long-established radical publishers to fill the gaps where one would hope to see feminist publishers taking a lead. Examples include Merlin Press's publication of a new edition of *Beyond the Fragments* (2013); Zed's long-term commitment to publishing feminist books with an internationalist perspective, including the books of Nawal el Saadawi; Lawrence and Wishart's two books on long-lasting and significant strikes led by women workers – *Trico: A Victory to Remember* (2018) by Sally Groves and Vernon Merritt and *Striking Women: Struggles and Strategies of South Asian Women Workers from Grunwick to Gate Gourmet* (2018) by Ruth Pearson. Meanwhile, after a few lean years in which Pluto published few books of contemporary feminist analysis, in late 2019 it published *Women and Work: Feminism, Labour, and Social Reproduction* by Susan Ferguson and *Furious: Technological Feminism and Digital Futures* by Caroline Bassett, Sarah Kember and Kate O'Riordan, and in 2020 it will publish *Feminism Interrupted* by Lola Olufemi.

The Renaissance of Feminist Publishing?

With the definite downturn in the Women's Liberation Movement from the early 1990s, and almost all the feminist publishers having disappeared, virtually the only feminist books from mainstream publishers were academic books, mostly with high-price tags and written in academic language off-putting to many women who consequently felt they were 'too stupid to be feminists'. One of the first books from the younger generation of feminist activists was *Reclaiming the F Word: The New Feminist Movement* by Kristin Aune and Catherine Redfern, published by Zed Books in 2010, followed by books by Kat Banyard, Laurie Penny and the more mainstream Caitlin Moran the following year. From the mid-2010s, mainstream publishers started to notice that a new feminist movement was happening, and so they cautiously started issuing a few books by feminists such as Laura Bates, Caroline Criado Perez, Finn Mackay and Reni Eddo-Lodge, most of whom were early activists in reviving the current feminist movement. However, the bulk of serious feminist analysis still seems to be coming from academic publishers such as Rowman and Littlefield, Palgrave Macmillan, Manchester University Press and especially Routledge. An example of a book that would previously have come from a feminist publisher is *Gender and Queer Perspectives on Brexit*, which contains many interesting feminist articles, published in 2019 by Palgrave Macmillan in its 'Gender and Politics' series, but costing £90.

The renewed feminist movement of today has gradually gained momentum since its revival around 2008, to the point where, by 2018, the publishing of feminist books could be seen as positively breaking through into the mainstream, although the variety of topics being covered has not yet reached anything like the range of those published in the 1970s and 1980s. There are a number of overlapping reasons for this: the contemporary feminist movement has been generally slow to focus on women's material situation, being surrounded by the grinding and unrelenting forces of neoliberalism,[14] and there has been a paucity of feminist publishers or feminist infrastructure to support them. During the period of the Women's Liberation Movement there was a variety of organisations such as Women in Libraries, Women in Publishing,[15] and Women in Booktrades, each of which organised their own meetings and conferences. There were three feminist bookshops – Sisterwrite and Silver Moon in London, and WomanZone in Edinburgh – as well as the network of around 100 shops (at its height) in the Federation of Radical Bookshops, most of which had a good feminist section, and there was the First International Feminist Bookfair, held in London in 1984. Running alongside the Bookfair in London, a Regional Book Week was held in twenty-seven towns and cities across Britain and Ireland, but the central organisers, mainly feminist publishers, alienated many within the radical book trade by striking a deal with WHSmith for their shops to carry promotional material and stock, even where there was a local radical bookshop organising events. Feminist Book Fortnight continued annually around Britain as a commercial promotion until the early 1990s, and subsequent International Feminist Bookfairs were held biennially in Norway, Canada, Spain, the Netherlands and Australia.

Happily, the shoots of a renewed infrastructure are springing up – in 2018 and 2019, New Suns: A Feminist Literary Festival with about fifteen stalls and a programme of talks, was held at the Barbican Arts Centre in London, while Jane Anger, now of Five Leaves Bookshop, Nottingham, one of the organisers of the First International Feminist Bookfair, relaunched Feminist Book Fortnight in 2018 with around 50 independent bookshops taking part. In 2019 a number of feminist bookshops opened in London: The Second Shelf, offering rare and antiquarian books, modern first editions, ephemera and manuscripts by women; Pages of Cheshire Street, which stocks books by women, trans and gender-diverse writers; and the Black Feminist Bookshop, a radical space of resistance, sisterhood and community, which began as a pop-up shop (Crockett 2019), along with The Feminist Bookshop in Brighton. Following in the footsteps of the Federation of Radical Bookshops, the Alliance of Radical Booksellers formed in 2011 with half a dozen members and today has expanded to over thirty, most of which have an active feminist section. More spectacularly, Emma Watson's feminist book club, Our Shared Shelf, on Goodreads, has nearly 230,000 members who are encouraged to read and discuss a chosen book every two months. How many of them do so is an interesting question, but even if it is only a very small proportion, this would be a lucrative income stream for the chosen publisher. Meanwhile, the highly commercial Foyles Books of the Year 2017 were all feminist titles: Naomi Alderman's *The Power* (Viking); Reni Eddo-Lodge's *Why I'm No Longer Talking to White People About Race* (Bloomsbury); and *Goodnight Stories for Rebel Girls* by Elena Favilli and Francesca Cavallo (Particular Books).

It seems likely that the 2018 centenary of (some) women gaining the vote prompted the mainstream industry to notice that not only was there a market for books commemorating this anniversary (of which about a hundred books were produced by publishers large and small), but also that there was a growing market for feminist books more generally. In the *Bookseller Buyers' Guide* for August 2018 to January 2019, there was a prominent feature about how sales of feminist non-fiction were keeping up momentum, especially in independent retailers, and there has been a slow build-up of new but very small feminist publishers, such as Linen Press, Aurora Metro, Silver Press, Victorina Press, Hammer On, Soundswrite Press (specialising in poetry by women in the East Midlands, and thus following in a long tradition of feminist writing groups self-publishing their own poetry), and Monstrous Regiment Publishing, mostly taking advantage of new digital print technologies which allow them to produce modest print runs economically, and which could also enable them to reissue important second-wave feminist books at a reasonable price, as well as increasing the variety of new ones. The new digital print technologies have also allowed the self-publishing of some serious feminist books, such as Jennifer Holmes' *A Working Woman: The Remarkable Life of Ray Strachey* (2019), which, in another era, would almost certainly have found their place with a feminist publisher.

Monstrous Regiment, a micropress based in Edinburgh and founded in 2017, is indicative of the newest wave of independent and intersectional feminist publishing. They say that 'their passion for publishing working class writers, as well as topics of intersectional feminism and sexuality, led them on a mission to curate bold and fresh content; the stuff they felt was often missing from bookshelves' (Monstrous Regiment n.d.). Even among feminists, it has taken many years to acknowledge the role that race and class play, as well as gender and sexuality, in determining who does and does not get published. I have written about my own experience of alienation as a working-class woman within the mainstream industry, and why the publishing industry needs to employ the widest spectrum of people to facilitate the production of the widest range of books, not only those that maintain the status quo (Chester 1996). The economic climate, lack of confidence and opportunity to meet the 'right' people makes it hard for working-class people, and especially women, to get to the writing stage, still less to imagine a career in publishing. When discussing exclusion from the book trade, as elsewhere in British society, issues of class remain highly contentious – but it is real (Hudson 2019). In a study exposing race, class, gender and pay inequalities, published in the journal *Cultural Trends*, researchers found that some 43 per cent of people working in publishing, 28 per cent in music and 26 per cent in design come from a privileged background, compared with 14 per cent of the population as a whole (de Waal 2016). Lack of diversity in the publishing industry is now coming to the fore, not for the first time, but hopefully this time real change may stick. Kit de Waal has been key in bringing the issue of working-class exclusion from writing and publishing to public attention:

> Three days after finding out I had a publishing deal, [I used my advance to set up] a scholarship for a writer from a disadvantaged background to do a Creative Writing MA at Birkbeck University, and asked people to spread the word deep into the communities that would least be able to afford two years of tuition fees for something they felt passionate about. The response was overwhelming, not only in that over 130 people applied for the scholarship, but professionals from the literary establishment, finding a mechanism for addressing their concerns, contacted me to get involved and their generosity has materialised: the staff at Waterstone's Birmingham are paying for the books from the reading list, a friend is paying for a laptop and stationery, Arvon are donating a week at a writer's retreat. And then Penguin Random House, Spread the Word, The Literacy Consultancy, The Word Factory and my agent, Jo Unwin, are all donating time, meetings, events, advice and support to another five runners up. And there's more, Birkbeck are running a Masterclass for a further fifteen applicants with many well-known writers lecturing for free. (Ibid.)

Nathan Connolly's edited anthology, *Know Your Place: Essays on the Working Class by the Working Class* (Dead Ink 2018) and de Waal's *Common People: An Anthology of Working-Class Writers* (Unbound 2019) both bring together established and emerging writers in a collection of essays, poems and memoirs which celebrate working-class life. Another person who has vigorously campaigned for diversity in the publishing industry is Nikesh Shukla, who compiled the essay collection, *The Good Immigrant* (Unbound 2017), where twenty-one British writers of colour discuss race and immigration in the UK today. It is striking that all these anthologies contain a high percentage of women authors, and they follow in the tradition of feminist anthologies which often allowed marginalised women to speak, and where diverse voices are encouraged to contribute to an overarching theme.

It is also striking that other major initiatives which have been prominent in encouraging more diverse people, especially women,[16] into publishing have also been mainly pursued by women and men outside a London-centric, white middle-class bubble. Kamila Shamsie, a British Pakistani writer whose novel *Home Fire* won the Women's Prize for Fiction in 2018, suggested that 2018 should be The Year of Publishing Women to mark the centenary of (some) women in Britain getting the vote. There was only one publisher which took up her challenge: And Other Stories, a small independent publisher of innovative contemporary writing from around the world, including many translated works, based in Sheffield. And Other Stories deemed the exercise to have been a success, in publishing terms as well as helping to raise consciousness across the industry, even though there were many detractors and mainstream publishers who were not prepared to take a financial risk (Yates-Badley 2018).

Conclusion

As Britain emerged from the Second World War, women were pushed back into the home, and the publishing of feminist books was at its lowest ebb in the twentieth century. It recovered and blossomed with the emergence of the Women's Liberation Movement in the 1970s and 1980s, and although feminist publishers had largely died out by the beginning of the twenty-first century, some feminist books continued to be published, not least because some of the gains instigated by the Women's Liberation Movement have been incorporated into an everyday understanding that woman's place in society has changed. However, not as much has changed in a positive direction as had been hoped. Many of the mechanisms which would facilitate women's (and other neglected groups') entry into the literary mainstream remain as elusive as ever. In 1987, Women in Publishing produced *Reviewing the Reviews: A Woman's Place is on the Bookpage*, which showed that it really wasn't – and thirty years later very little seems to have changed. In 2019 *The Emilia Report*, compiled by Danuta Kean and named after England's first published female poet, analysed the fortunes of writers of opposite sexes in the same market areas and found a 'marked bias' between male and female writers' media coverage (Flood 2019b). Similar research in other countries has revealed the same problems (Australian National University 2016).

The current landscape of feminist book publishing is inevitably mixed, as the apparently eternal conflict between culture and commerce continues undiminished. In 2018, Anna Leszkiewicz asked why publishing was suddenly obsessed with 'rebel' women and had produced so many titles using the same format. Her article lists twenty-eight books for children and at least eight books for adults published that year, following the success of 2017's *Good Night Stories for Rebel Girls* by Elena Favilli and Francesca Cavallo, which raised $1 million – the most funded original book in the history of crowd-funding. Katherine Cowdrey (2017) concludes that:

> [The books'] popularity shows the great progress mainstream feminism has made over the last few years. The idea that publishing would be revitalised by a series of gift books filled with the life stories of mostly dead, unconventional women would have been unthinkable a decade ago . . . But there's also an infantilising undertone at play, one that feels obvious when you consider the overlap between those aimed at adults and those aimed at children . . . These books are fundamentally more safe and marketable than, say, a compendium of contemporary cutting-edge activists, artists and leaders . . . An individualistic approach to feminism elides the fact that most of its successes, from suffrage to civil rights to legalising abortion, are thanks to grass-roots collective action.

The field of literary prizes is a major mechanism for boosting the profits of publishers, even though it is obviously also significant in boosting the visibility of writers, so unsurprisingly, it is another area of the publishing industry where women have been consistently neglected (Wynne-Davies 2015; see also Stevie Marsden's discussion of literary prizes in Chapter 9). The Women's Prize for Fiction was set up because of this very exclusion, and it has been mired in controversy since its inception – on top of the predictable and relentless misogyny, it has also been accused of elitism by small publishers, which can make the Women's Prize feel just as much part of the literary establishment as all the other prizes.[17] But whatever one's scepticism about various aspects of literary prizes, there can be no doubt that the awarding of the 2019 Booker Prize jointly to Margaret Atwood and Bernardine Evaristo felt like a significant moment in feminist publishing – and specifically in black women's publishing – and it was a moment of celebration to read in the joint profile of the two authors how much they value each other, older women, younger women, and women with curly hair (Armistead 2019). However, we would be well advised to heed the comments of Evaristo (2019) in an article published shortly after she won:

> Chidera Eggerue is a social media star, south-east London homegirl and feminist. She first came to prominence in 2017 when she created the hashtag #SaggyBoobsMatter on Twitter in order to promote the body-positive message that women's breasts and bodies are fine just as they are . . . A year later Eggerue published a self-help motivational book, *What a Time to Be Alone: The Slumflower's Guide to Why You Are Already Enough*, which entered the *Sunday Times* bestseller list the week it was published in 2018, when she was 23 . . . Eggerue, and other arts activists of her generation, are benefiting from the desire of the multinationals to be aligned with woke young people and to exploit their marketability. The revolution, or rather what we might think of as this countercultural moment, where those previously without a platform are having their say, has already been commodified. Those of us who are alert to the capriciousness of this *should* trumpet a note of caution to those who are swept up in the glamour of the moment. We need to ask ourselves how best we can effect change for our constituencies that is sustainable rather than fashionable. My answer is that the spirit of entrepreneurship, community and arts activism will sustain us long after it's no longer woke to be 'woke'.

Notes

1. The Feminist Library (previously the Women's Research and Resources Centre) is a London-based collection of materials from the Women's Liberation Movement founded in 1975.
2. Mullins' article also makes interesting points about the marketing of Rooney's books.
3. Not many feminist books started life as a blog, although Laura Bates' (2014) *Everyday Sexism* was an early example, and more recently Reni Eddo-Lodge's (2018) *Why I'm No Longer Talking to White People About Race* grew out of one. The long-term durability of blogs may turn out to be much shorter than publications produced by ink on paper. In December 2019, *Feministing*, one of the earliest feminist blogs, founded in 2004, announced that it would be closing within weeks, although during its lifetime it reached a peak of 1.2 million unique monthly visitors, far more than any feminist publication could achieve. Several other feminist blogs built on a model of paid staff and advertising have also shut in the past year, unable to sustain themselves in the current digital media world (see Goldberg 2019).
4. A search in the Girton College Cambridge library for feminist books published between 1945–65, while by no means a scientific approach, nevertheless produced the following interesting results: Vera Douie, *Daughters of Britain*, self-published, 1949; Roger Fulford, *Votes for Women: Story of a Struggle*, Faber, 1957: Judith Hubback, *Wives who Went to College*, William Heinemann, 1957; Virginia Crocheron Gildersleeve, *Many A Good*

Crusade, Macmillan and Co, New York, 1954; Josephine Kamm, *Rapiers and Battleaxes: The Women's Movement and its Aftermath*, Allen and Unwin, 1966; Monica Baldwin, *I Leap over the Wall: A Return to the World After 28 Years in a Convent*, Hamish Hamilton, 1950; Enid Moberly Bell, *Josephine Butler: Flame of Fire*, Constable, 1962; Nan Berger and Joan Maizels, *Woman – Fancy or Free?: Some Thoughts on Women's Status in Britain Today*, Mills and Boon, 1962; Vera Brittain, *Lady into Woman: A History of Women from Victoria to Elizabeth II*, Andrew Dakers, 1953; Pamela Brooks, *Women at Westminster: An Account of Women in the British Parliament, 1918–66*, Peter Daines, 1967; and Frederick Le Gros Clark, *Women, Work, and Age: To Study the Employment of Working Women Through Their Middle Lives*, 1962.

5. For more on Jeannette Foster and her difficulties finding a publisher, see Barbara Grier (1985) and Joanne Passet (2008), as well as the special issue of *Journal of Lesbian Studies* (Volume 18, no. 4) devoted to Barbara Grier and edited by Danielle M. DeMuth.
6. See the memoir of his mother by Jeremy Gavron (2015).
7. It was then republished by Virago in 1978 and by Macmillan in 1986 with a new introduction by the author.
8. Letter from Routledge commissioning editor.
9. See my forthcoming article on 'Purpose, Power and Profit in Feminist Publishing' in *Women: A Cultural Review*.
10. Cadman et al. (1981: 28–41) provide a thorough analysis of the interlocking practices and issues which preoccupied them – everything from raising the money to operate, to collective working, to rates of pay, to where they did their typesetting and printing.
11. Quote from Virago's online promotional newsletter.
12. Personal communication from Stella Dadzie, one of the editors of the volume.
13. Showalter (2013: xii–xiii) also provides a useful list of feminist topics and how they have changed over time.
14. Several books have been published analysing the relationship between the new feminist movement and neoliberal values – for example, Andi Zeisler (2016) and Catherine Rottenberg (2018), who also maintains a resource archive at <http://neoliberalfeminism.com/>.
15. In 2019 Women in Publishing completed the recording of its own history, conducting a series of oral history interviews with past members, which is lodged in the British Library.
16. Although it is true that there are more women than men working in publishing, although not in the most senior positions, they are overwhelmingly white and middle class, with a substantial representation of Oxbridge graduates.
17. Insofar as the intention of the Women's Prize has been to amplify women's voices, it could be defined as feminist, but defining its books as such is more questionable.

Works Cited

Armitstead, C. 2019. 'Booker Winners Bernardine Evaristo and Margaret Atwood on Breaking the Rules'. *The Guardian*, 15 October 2019 <www.theguardian.com/books/2019/oct/15/booker-winners-bernardine-evaristo-margaret-atwood-rule-breaking> (last accessed 14 December 2019).

Australian National University. 2016. 'Study Finds Gender Bias in Australian Literature'. Australian National University, 9 June 2016. <www.anu.edu.au/news/all-news/study-finds-gender-bias-in-australian-literature> (last accessed 12 December 2019).

Bates, L. 2014. *Everyday Sexism*. London: Simon and Schuster.

Bogic, A. 2011. 'Why Philosophy Went Missing: Understanding the English Version of Simone de Beauvoir's *Le Deuxieme Sexe*'. *Translating Women*. Ed. L. von Flotow. Ottawa: University of Ottawa Press. 151–66.

Cadman, E., G. Chester and A. Pivot. 1981. *Rolling Our Own: Women as Printers, Publishers and Distributors*. London: Comedia.

Chester, G. 1996. 'Book Publishing: The Gentleperson's Profession?' *Writing on the Line*. Eds S. Richardson, M. Cherry, S. Palfrey and G. Chester. London: Working Press. 141–8.

Chester, G. 2002. 'The Anthology as a Medium for Feminist Debate in the UK'. *Women's Studies International Forum* 25.2: 193–207.

Chester, G. 2019. 'Sex, Race and Class: The Radical, Alternative and Minority Book Trade in Britain'. *The Cambridge History of the Book, Volume 7: The Twentieth Century and Beyond*. Eds A. Nash, C. Squires and I. R. Wilson. Cambridge: Cambridge University Press. 616–45.

Chester, G. and S. Nielsen (eds). 1987. *In Other Words: Writing as a Feminist*. London: Hutchinson Education.

Crockett, M. 2019. 'The Triumphant Return of the Feminist Bookshop'. *Stylist*, March 2019 <www.stylist.co.uk/books/feminist-bookshops-uk-london-second-shelf-history/255823> (last accessed 12 December 2019).

Cowdrey, K. 2017. 'Small Publishers Protest "Elitist" Women's Prize Fees'. *The Bookseller*, September 12 2017 <www.thebookseller.com/news/micro-publishers-protest-elitist-womens-prize-fees-635471> (last accessed 12 December 2019).

De Waal, K. 2016. 'Whatever Happened to Working-class Writers?' *Herald*, 24 July 2016 <www.heraldscotland.com/opinion/14638710.whatever-happened-to-working-class-writers/> (last accessed 12 December 2019).

Duncker, P. 1992. 'A Note on the Politics of Publishing'. *Sisters and Strangers: An Introduction to Contemporary Feminist Fiction*. Ed. P. Duncker. Oxford: Blackwell.

Eddo-Lodge, R. 2018. *Why I'm No Longer Talking to White People About Race*. London: Bloomsbury.

Evaristo, B. 2019. 'These are Unprecedented Times for Black Female Writers'. *The Guardian*, 19 October 2019 <www.theguardian.com/books/2019/oct/19/bernadine-evaristo-what-a-time-to-be-a-black-british-womxn-writer> (last accessed 12 December 2019).

Flood, A. 2019a. '"There's No Safety Net": the Plight of the Midlist Author'. *The Guardian*, 19 June 2019 <www.theguardian.com/books/2019/jun/19/midlist-author-kerry-hudson-louise-candlish> (last accessed 10 December 2019).

Flood, A. 2019b. 'Male and Female Writers' Media Coverage Reveals 'Marked Bias''. *The Guardian*, 18 March 2019 <www.theguardian.com/books/2019/mar/18/male-and-female-writers-media-coverage-reveals-marked-bias> (last accessed 12 December 2019).

Foster, D. 2015. *Lean Out*. London: Repeater.

Foster, D. 2019. 'The Post-Recession Literature We Needed'. *Jacobin*, 28 May 2019 <www.jacobinmag.com/2019/05/sally-rooney-class-millennials-novels-normal-people> (last accessed 10 December 2019).

Gavron, J. 2015. *Woman on the Edge of Time: A Son's Search for his Mother*. Melbourne: Scribe.

Goldberg, E. 2019. 'A Farewell to Feministing and the Heyday of Feminist Blogging'. *New York Times*, 8 December 2019 <www.nytimes.com/2019/12/08/business/media/feminist-blogs-feministing.html> (last accessed 12 December 2019).

Grier, B. 1985. 'Afterword'. *Sex Variant Women in Literature*. J. Foster. Tallahassee: Naiad Press.

Hudson, K. 2018. 'Kerry Hudson Wrote About Working-class Novels. Then the Backlash Began'. *Observer*, 7 October 2018 <www.theguardian.com/books/2018/oct/07/working-class-writers-explosive-debate> (last accessed 12 December 2019).

Leszkiewicz, A. 2018. 'Why is Publishing Suddenly Obsessed with "Rebel" Women?' *New Statesman*, 6 July 2018 <www.newstatesman.com/rebel-girls-nasty-badass-women-history-feminist-books-publishing-trend-review> (last accessed 12 December 2019).

Lindsay, J. 1951. 'The USA Threat to British Culture'. *Arena* 2, new series 8, June/July 1951.

Low. G. 2010. *Publishing the Postcolonial: Anglophone West African and Caribbean Writing, 1948–1968*. New York: Routledge.

Margree, V. 2018. *Neglected or Misunderstood: The Radical Feminism of Shulamith Firestone*. Winchester: Zero Books.

Martin, M. (ed.). 2017. *Scratch: Writers, Money and the Art of Making a Living*. New York: Simon & Schuster.

Merck, M. and S. Sandford (eds). 2010. *Further Adventures of The Dialectic of Sex: Critical Essays on Shulamith Firestone*. New York, Basingstoke: Palgrave Macmillan.

Monstrous Regiment. n.d. 'About' <www.monstrous-regiment.com/about> (last accessed 16 December 2019).

Mullins, C. 2019. 'Why Can't We Make Up Our Minds About Sally Rooney?' *Electric Literature*, 4 June 2019 <https://electricliterature.com/why-cant-we-make-up-our-minds-about-sally-rooney/> (last accessed 10 December 2019).

Munt, S. 1997. '"I Teach therefore I am": Lesbian Studies in the Liberal Academy'. *Feminist Review* 56: 85–99.

Murray, S. 1999. 'Mixed Media: Feminist Presses and Publishing Politics in Twentieth-Century Britain'. PhD Thesis, University College London.

Passet, J. E. 2008. *Sex Variant Woman: The Life of Jeannette H Foster*. Boston MA: Da Capo Press.

Riley, C. 2014. '"The Message Is in the Book": What Virago's Sale in 1995 Means for Feminist Publishing'. *Women: A Cultural Review*, 25.3: 235–55.

Rottenberg, C. 2018. *The Rise of Neoliberal Feminism*. Oxford: Oxford University Press.

Sandberg, S. 2013. *Lean In*. London: W. H. Allen.

Showalter, E. 2013. 'Introduction'. *Out of Time: The Pleasures and Perils of Ageing*. L. Segal London: Verso.

Simons, M. A. 1983. 'The Silencing of Simone De Beauvoir: Guess What's Missing from *The Second Sex*'. *Women's Studies International Forum*, 6.5: 559–64.

Toor, R. 2018. 'Scholars Talk Writing: Lillian Faderman'. 19 February 2018 <www.chronicle.com/article/Scholars-Talk-Writing-Lillian/242551> (last accessed 12 December 2019).

Whiteley, G. Forthcoming. 'The Allure of *Pamphilos*: The Radical Art of Pamphleteering'. *Art, Politics and the Pamphleteer*. Eds G. Whiteley and J. Tormey. London: Bloomsbury.

Wolf, N. 2019. *Outrages: Sex, Censorship and the Criminalisation of Love*. London: Virago.

Wynne-Davies, M. 2015. 'Women Still Need to Fight for Publishing Deals and Book Prizes'. *The Conversation*, 5 June 2015 <https://theconversation.com/women-still-need-to-fight-for-publishing-deals-and-book-prizes-42836> (last accessed 12 December 2019).

Yates-Badley, E. 2018. 'What Became of the Year of Publishing Women?' *Northern Soul*, 1 September 2018 <www.northernsoul.me.uk/the-year-of-publishing-women-writers-and-other-stories/> (last accessed 12 December 2019).

Zeisler, A. 2016. *We Were Feminists Once: From Riot Grrrl to CoverGirl, the Buying and Selling of a Political Movement*. New York: Public Affairs.

2

Spare Rib and the Print Culture of Women's Liberation

Lucy Delap and Zoe Strimpel

This chapter will explore the motives and politics surrounding the formation and publication of *Spare Rib*, Britain's most high-profile feminist magazine in the period of the Women's Liberation Movement. The 1970s and 1980s were marked by extraordinary ferment, fluidity and experimentation in periodical publishing, allowing magazines to become 'the most significant arena for internal feminist debate' (Thomlinson 2017a: 43). As Agatha Beins (2016: 47) has argued, periodicals did not simply chronicle the Women's Liberation Movement, but helped constitute it. This function was all the more pronounced as large-scale feminist conferences waned after the fractious National Women's Liberation Conference in Birmingham in 1978 (Rees 2010). *Spare Rib* constantly experimented with new formats, ways of working and sense of its audience; it continued publishing until 1993, and thus spans the most active decades of women's liberation in Britain. *Spare Rib*'s visibility and ambition to reach women outside of the 'already converted' circles of mostly educated, urban women, has made it a dominant source for understanding the British Women's Liberation Movement. Nonetheless, its content did not reflect all strands of the movement and was greeted with both hostility and warm solidarity.

This chapter focuses on some key components of *Spare Rib*, highlighting the distinctive editorial practices and vibrant letters pages. It charts change over time, paying particular attention to distribution of the magazine and dilemmas faced around issues of profitability. Other British and international feminist periodicals are contrasted with *Spare Rib*, mapping out the influences and points of tension within feminist print culture. The chapter also considers the effects of the recent digitisation of *Spare Rib* by the British Library. The subsequent ease of access has begun to foster a role for *Spare Rib* as the 'paper of record' of the British women's movement, and we conclude with an assessment of the iconicity and representativeness of this magazine, as well as the challenges and opportunities of its digitisation.

With a budget of £2,000, *Spare Rib* was launched in July 1972 as a glossy magazine of a densely packed thirty-eight pages – a mixture of letters, features, news, quirky columns, history and a wild, vibrant visual offering of illustrations, photography, colour splashes and symbols, not dissimilar in appearance to magazines produced by the underground press. It was edited by Marsha Rowe and Rosie Boycott, who had been heavily involved in the underground press on titles such as *Oz* and *Ink*. However, like many women involved in the underground press, they had become increasingly frustrated and disillusioned by its undimmed machismo, sexism and exploitation of the 'sexual revolution' (Rowe 1982: 14–16). Aided by the increasing impetus behind the Women's Liberation Movement, Rowe and Boycott seized the moment and *Spare Rib* was born as 'a product of the counter-culture and a reaction against it' (Ibid.: 13).

Periodical Dynamics

For the first year and a half following its launch, *Spare Rib* more closely resembled a typical women's magazine than it ever would again, with editorial decisions taken by Rowe and Boycott prior to the development of a more full-blown collective approach. The magazine made its full commitment to the Women's Liberation Movement explicit from the start and promoted an extensive news offering. This was a period described by Rowe (1982: 20) as 'a jumble . . . carrying contradictory messages'. The magazine's 1972 manifesto set out an intriguing mixture of the individual and the collective, with a vow to '[cut] across material, economic and class barriers, to approach [women] as individuals in their own right' and also to 'aim at achieving collective . . . solutions to women's problems'.[1] In its first editorial, *Spare Rib* foregrounded its focus on the individual and subjective: it was to reflect 'our awareness of ourselves . . . not "as a bunch of women" but as individuals in our own right' (*Spare Rib* July 1972: 2).[2] In setting out to explore and advance the self-determination and experience of 'individuals', the latter phrase was revealing. It encapsulated the sensibilities of a period of women's liberation in which exploratory consciousness-raising practices were at the fore, before the more fixed identity positions that would shape the movement in the following decade locked into place. Also revealing was the emphasis on accessibility and multivocality – this was to be a 'magazine that is fluid enough to publish work by contributors who have not written before as well as by women and men who are successful journalists and writers' (Ibid.).

Before its launch, *Spare Rib*'s founding editors circulated a questionnaire to a nationwide sample of prospective readers asking the question: 'What is a liberated woman?' The answers formed the magazine's first letters page and emphasised the realities, challenges and confusions of daily life. Notably, respondents stressed ideas of the 'ordinary', in terms of selfhood and daily life. One potential reader suggested that a liberated woman was 'any ordinary sensible person who does not require "women's lib" or any other do-gooders to tell her how to react' (*SR* July 1972: 4). Another wrote in that 'in the context of marriage with no children and the wife working full time, I would say that a woman can be called liberated if her husband goes halves on the domestic chores, so they have the same amount of leisure time'; while a further reader thought a liberated woman was one who could reach 'the fullest potential in her career/family life' (Ibid.).

The tensions and contradictions of femininity (rather than the overtly politicised terrain of feminism) – motherhood, sexuality, conjugal relationships, distribution of household labour, clothes and beauty – shaped the early *Spare Rib* (Todd 1999). The first contents page announced (quirky) columns on cookery and beauty, features on the novels of Barbara Cartland and Georgette Heyer ('Carry on Romancing') and 'the aftermath of the bosom boom: attitudes to our breasts' (*SR* July 1972: 2). There were meditations on white weddings, such as Mary Stott's 'I promise to love, honour and obey' (*SR* August 1972: 6); the nuclear family, such as Micheline Wandor's 'Family Ever after: How Effective is the Family Structure today?' (*SR* November 1972: 10–13);

and a comic piece about going to the pub as a single woman by Fran Fogarty, 'The plight of the single girl in the pub' (*SR* August 1972: 18). It was feature-heavy, like *Cosmopolitan*, rather than news-led (although there were eight pages of news in addition to a news roundup at the start).

From the outset, *Spare Rib* foregrounded the work of women cartoonists, photographers and visual artists; the magazine sustained a close relationship with the See Red women's collective (1974–90), and showcased the immense creativity of the women's movement in challenging what theorists such as Laura Mulvey had termed the pervasive 'male gaze' of the visual arts (Mulvey 1975: 6–18).[3] The use of photography in *Spare Rib* was of interest to readers – they challenged editors when their photo captions only named the adults in photographs and ignored the children also present; they insisted on correct acknowledgements when *Spare Rib* occasionally misattributed a photograph, particularly where it had been taken by a woman. The early issues of the magazine regularly used male photographers, but later issues were much more dominated by women's photography. Overall the magazine aspired to high production values and professional editing, which lent itself to wider distribution. The *Spare Rib* collective was proud to have negotiated a distribution deal with the same company as the more conventional and heavily capitalised women's magazine *Cosmopolitan*.

Figure 2.1 *Spare Rib* cover, January 1974
(Image with kind permission of Valerie Santiago).

Periodical Communities

When *Spare Rib* was first published in July 1972, the British women's movement was already experimenting with different periodical formats and styles. The London Women's Liberation Workshop had launched *Shrew* (1969–78), produced in rotation by local London women's groups. As a deliberate nationalising move, the British women's movement also produced *Women's Struggle*, put together by the Women's Liberation National Coordinating Committee from 1970. Priced at a shilling, it listed the groups of the Women's Liberation Movement in the very early days. It was visually plain and lacked any journalistic writing, quite in contrast to the deliberately visual, professional-looking and news-oriented *Spare Rib*. There were also local news-sheets, such as the *Sheffield Women's Newsletter* (1971–80) and the Dublin-based *Fownes Street Journal* (from 1972). The women's movement had also inspired journals affiliated to political tendencies, such as *Socialist Woman* (produced in Nottingham from 1969) and *Red Rag* (1973–80). These periodicals took up varied styles – *Fownes Street Journal* adopted a bold and angry style, printed on cheap paper with the amateur hand-drawn graphics that characterised women's liberation and leftist magazines in this period. Its articles were direct, avoiding the exclusion caused by sophisticated language, with very short news items and articles. *Socialist Woman*, in contrast, was typed and very textually dense. It reprinted material from countercultural periodicals such as *Black Dwarf*, as well as national newspapers such as *The Times* and *Morning Star*.

Spare Rib's early issues looked dramatically different from other periodicals associated with the movement, and were priced significantly higher at 17½p. *Shrew* sold at 7p in 1971, while *Socialist Woman* was 6p; in 1972 *Spare Rib* was nearer in price to *Nova* magazine (1965–75) which retailed at 20p; both magazines shared ambitious use of colour printing, glossy paper, photographs and professional content (Cook 2015). Readers of *Spare Rib* made the direct connection to the *Nova* experiment with 'intelligent' women's journalism; a male reader, Ken Wilson, commented that an early *Spare Rib* feature on sex luckily avoided 'the Nova-esque (or would you prefer the Nova-lic?) style' (*SR* March 1973: 4). Unlike *Nova*, *Spare Rib* was always highly politically engaged and radical in its politics, with a firm commitment to women's liberation and engagement with New Left theorists such as Herbert Marcuse. When it did run recipes and dressmaking articles, these were oriented to saving money and liberating women's bodies from cumbersome clothes and deadening domestic labour.

Launched alongside women's titles including *Candida* (1972), *Cosmopolitan* (1972–) and *Viva* (1973–80),[4] *Spare Rib* was always critical of the women's magazine market; a reviewer in the first issue declared that '*Cosmopolitan* is to Women's Liberation what Little Black Sambo is to the Black Panthers' (*SR* July 1972: 33). Nonetheless, one reader complained that the first six issues of *Spare Rib* were too similar to the mass women's weekly, *Women's Realm*. Others feared that, like the women's weeklies, *Spare Rib* would attempt to attract readers by its coverage of sexual controversies (Wilson in *SR* March 1973: 4).[5] But others liked the combination of the 'traditional magazine format' that could appeal 'to the unconverted and even the non-extreme radical sections of the movement' (Eaton in *SR* September 1973: 6).

The *Spare Rib* editorial collective maintained a collaborative approach to other magazines of the women's movement and shared articles on occasion. *WIRES*, the fortnightly 20p magazine founded after the Manchester National Women's Liberation

Movement conference in 1975, for example, was sometimes invited to publish material that *Spare Rib*'s editors had deemed too controversial.[6] The listings pages of *Spare Rib* regularly advertised niche periodicals of the women's movement, such as *Sequel* (which termed itself a 'non-profit making bimonthly magazine for isolated lesbians'), another lesbian magazine *Artemis*, *Shocking Pink* ('A *real* alternative magazine for young women'), and *Mukti*, a quarterly Asian women's magazine founded in 1983. *Spare Rib* published birthday greetings notices each July, which provided advertising revenue and helped to chart the other periodicals with whom they exchanged or collaborated. In 1974 on *Spare Rib*'s 'second birthday', greetings and congratulations were advertised from *Gay News*, *Time Out*, *New Humanist* and *Movement* (the journal of the Student Christian Association), as well as from many publishers, bookshops and women-run businesses. By the fifth year of publication, *Spare Rib*'s 'birthday' issue listed greetings from a selection of trade unions, and the countercultural socialist paper, the *Islington Gutter Press*. *City Limits* (1981–93) also regularly advertised in *Spare Rib*, branding itself 'as forthright as feminism'. The flourishing of both feminist and countercultural magazines alongside *Spare Rib* encouraged cross-listing and supportive advertising between periodical titles, and even with national newspapers.[7] *The Guardian* women's page was an important interlocutor, and prominent *Guardian* journalists such as Jill Tweedie and Mary Stott offered their support to *Spare Rib*. But by 1984 *Spare Rib* had become critical of the lack of feminist content in *The Guardian* women's page, and its publishing model shifted closer to the radical global news focus of *New Internationalist* (a *Spare Rib* advertiser) and *New Society* (*SR* February 1984: 13).

Spare Rib's network, from the outset, extended beyond Britain. It featured coverage of feminist conferences and events globally throughout its life. The postbag contained letters, too many to publish, from women in countries including France, Germany, Sweden, the United States, Australia and New Zealand.[8] Many of these were requests for back issues, a number of which also stressed how unique and inspiring *Spare Rib* was; one German reader wrote, 'I don't know of any German magazine like *Spare Rib*', while a French correspondent asked for coverage of women's centres in Europe.[9] Even in early issues, the readership was clearly international; a member of the French *Mouvement de libération des femmes* was unimpressed in 1974 with what she perceived as *Spare Rib*'s bias and intolerance against men (J. G .G. in *SR* February 1975). Global coverage became more prominent from the mid-1980s. The February 1984 edition, for example, published Spanish-language poetry in its feature on the Chilean women's movement titled 'Vamos Mujer', as well as coverage of Indian, Danish, US and Palestinian women's news (*SR* February 1984: 49–51). July 1984 saw the translation of a feature from the German feminist magazine *Courage* (1976–84), as well as republished material from the Canadian feminist magazine *Kinesis* (1974–2001).

Spare Rib was available in the United States, and its cover price was quoted in US dollars from January 1979. One American reader noted how down to earth and realistic *Spare Rib* was compared to the feminist magazines of the American movement (Kustin in *SR* January 1975: 3; Farrell 1998). The US had seen the development of *Ms.* magazine at precisely the same historical moment as *Spare Rib*. Originally an insert in *New York* magazine, the preview issue in Spring 1972 featured well-known women's liberation writers such as Kate Millett and Anne Koedt, and promised to address 'women with deep, diverse ambitions, and those who have not yet had a chance to formulate ambition – women who are wives, mothers and

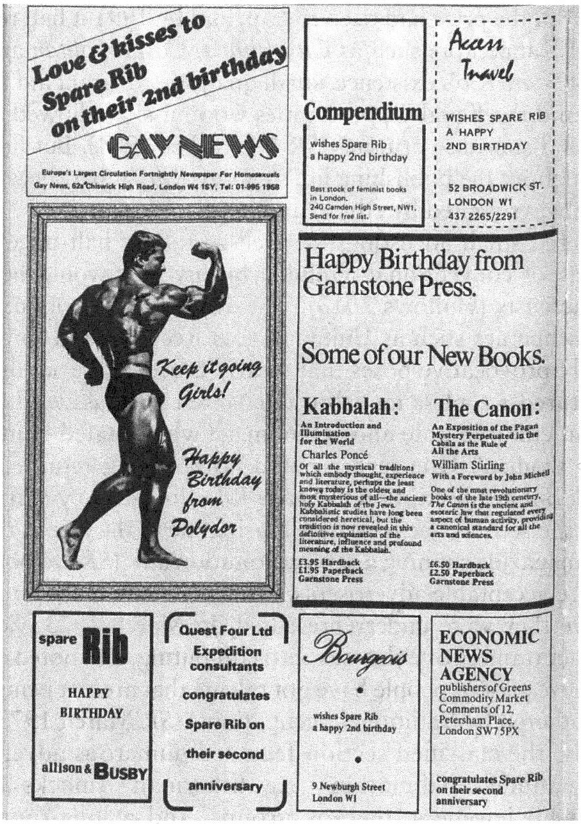

Figure 2.2 Happy birthday messages to *Spare Rib* on its second birthday, *Spare Rib* July 1974, inside cover.

grandmothers, or none of these' (*Ms.* Spring 1972: 113). Like *Spare Rib*, it included conventional adverts (for scotch and fur coats, noticeably more luxurious in tone than in *Spare Rib*) and became a successful mass-market monthly and high-profile face of the women's movement in the US. Like *Spare Rib*, *Ms.* was founded by women who were already experienced journalists and embraced professional production values. However, *Ms.* seemed less close to the turbulent movement dynamics that were to both energise and sometimes engulf *Spare Rib*. At 130 pages, *Ms.* was closer to the literary monthlies than the shorter, news-oriented format of *Spare Rib* (Thom 1997).

Breaking Even

The relatively high price of *Spare Rib* was always a bone of contention. In June 1974, a full-page accounts breakdown informed readers that, at 20p, less than half the income from sales went back to the magazine – the rest was absorbed by distributors, newsagents and wholesalers. It remained crucial to *Spare Rib*'s viability to obtain sufficient subscribers. By 1983, the price had risen to 65p, and by 1991 it had reached £1.50, in line with prices of competitors such as *City Limits*, *Cosmopolitan* and *New Society*. Over the course of *Spare Rib*'s existence, small quantities of grant aid from the Greater London Council and the Equal Opportunities Commission allowed the collective to extend publicity and subsidise printing (*SR* November 1984). But finances remained acutely tight throughout the publishing life of *Spare Rib*, in part because the advertising revenue was always limited by ethical and political sensitivities.

Spare Rib offered small ad listings, as well as full or half page colour adverts, including products of conventional feminine beauty that would be lampooned by critical feminist activists (Hollows 2013). The adverts were dominated in the early days by record companies such as United Artists Records, and sometimes featured women in sexually provocative poses that clearly caused editorial discontent. When Epic Records featured a topless model in the March 1973 issue, the *Spare Rib* collective included an editorial note above the image which stated bluntly, 'This advertisement exploits women'. One reader noted how, having returned home to New Zealand, she took out a subscription to *Spare Rib*: 'Imagine my extreme disappointment on opening the second one to arrive. Staring me in the face is the sell-out of all time – a feminist magazine running a sex-exploitation ad!' (*SR* October 1974: 3; Jolly 2008: 8, 12). More acceptable advertisers chose *Spare Rib* in order to attract women into careers where they were underrepresented. In March 1973, Control Data Ltd attempted to attract trainees of either sex into computing, and noted in their advertising copy: 'We believe a lot of people have got talents that are not being used, and a lot of people are smothered by traditional occupations' (*SR* March 1973: 40).

More typically, the classified section featured numerous adverts for comfortable or women-manufactured clothing (e.g. fisherman's smocks and dungarees), feminist and lesbian jewellery, therapy groups, and a long-running advert for Harmony Personal Vibrators that always apologised for the 'off-putting' phallic shape which wrongly suggested that it was an artificial penis. Clitoral stimulation, the manufacturers insisted, was the real function, and it promised to bring orgasms to 'women who have never before reached a climax' (*SR* May 1975: 40). Trade unions, development charities and local authorities began to advertise services and posts more widely from the late 1970s. But there was an air of unease at the presence of advertisements at all, and readers were sometimes troubled by the adverts for what one termed 'rubbish'; she asked for a statement refusing to endorse the items advertised which would 'explain the contradictions between the adverts and the articles to puzzled readers' (Duffy in *SR* November 1974: 3). By taking a critical stance towards advertising, the magazine struggled to remain financially viable, as early business correspondence makes clear.[10] Some readers were angered at the inclusion of any adverts. Another challenged this view, arguing: 'the women who have suceded [sic.] in building businesses, should they not be able to advertise their wares and services? . . . Should we not support our sisters? Or have I got the message and aim of feminism wrong?' (Tomrley in *SR* November 1990: 5).

As this exchange suggests, hanging over the magazine throughout its lifespan was the perpetual question of how it should secure financial viability without succumbing to what many readers and contributors saw as patriarchal capitalist politics. As Gail Chester et al. acerbically noted:

> There is a certain distaste on the part of the radicals in Britain to indulge in [selling]. There are two factors that contribute to this reluctance. One is the moral ambivalence towards and theoretical confusion about the role of money – should socialists or feminists sully their fingers with this most capitalist and patriarchal of objects? Secondly, there's a certain middle-class snobbery towards commerce of any sort. (1981: 76, 88)

In the early years, *Spare Rib* was the only women's liberation magazine that paid its writers (£1 per 100 words at the outset, although this amount would dwindle and then disappear entirely). The collective was 'torn' about payment since 'we all feel we don't want people working for *Spare Rib* . . . just because they're paid' (Ibid.) They recognised, however, that non-payment excluded many women from being able to work for the magazine. Nonetheless, finding suitable 'non-sexist' advertisers was a 'necessary but constant source of anguish' (Ibid.).

One way in which *Spare Rib* achieved a precarious financial balance was through its production of 'sidelines'. Its diary was a recurrent item, co-published with Sheba Press and offering useful features, such as a menstrual calendar in 1980, and information on how to lobby your MP in 1981. *Spare Rib Extras* advertised sloganeering tea towels ('You start by sinking into his arms, and end with your arms in his sink') and belts ('Women will belt up no longer'), as well as badges, stickers and Christmas cards. Readers sometimes volunteered their labour to pack and distribute such items.[11] Sidelines could also be used to solicit subscriptions, with readers in January 1975 being offered a free *Spare Rib* badge. The incentives were more generous in later years, with subscribers offered videos and price savings. Despite the innovative invitations to consume and subscribe, such strategies could only partially offset the fundamental weaknesses of distribution that *Spare Rib* faced.

The *Spare Rib* collective was always determined to achieve wide distribution beyond their subscriber base, and to place *Spare Rib* within mainstream newsagents such as WH Smith. One lesbian reader recalled that it was the only periodical with lesbian content which could be bought from the shelf; magazines such as *Arena Three* (1964–72) and *Sappho* (1972–81) required a subscription – although in reality, newsagent availability for *Spare Rib* was patchy (Koller 2008: 43; Marilyn Giddings in *SR* September 1973; for more on *Arena Three*, see Chapter 10).[12] The collective opted for both commercial and not-for-profit distributors, but still had trouble getting national coverage. In 1978 the collective advertised for 'someone to work at getting the magazine much more widely distributed in trade outlets around the country . . . It involves frequent trips all over Britain to local Women's Groups and to wholesalers and retailers' (*SR* July 1978: 33).[13] They also appealed to readers, 'Why not take copies with you to conferences? Pass them round at work? Show all your friends? Sell them in the streets?' (*SR* July 1978: 33). Drawing on similar tactics to the suffrage era feminist press, *Spare Rib* projected an active, committed readership, whose voices were always prioritised in extensive correspondence pages (Murray 2000). Overall, *Spare Rib*'s engagement with readers was intense and multi-faceted. As well as being relied on to help to distribute the magazine, and shape the magazine's agenda through letters, readers were also frequently implored to help finance it, not just through subscription renewal, but also by attending *Spare Rib* benefits and discos, buying its extras and finally through donations. Reader input was editorially central, fuelling sections such as 'Tooth and Nail' (1976–81), which printed egregiously sexist adverts that readers had spotted, and formed the basis of first-person viewpoint features that detailed the struggles of everyday female experience.[14] However, it was the letters pages that were the most sustained and dynamic manifestation of *Spare Rib*'s distinctive relationship to its readership.

Correspondence and the Relationship with Readers

The letters pages in *Spare Rib* were crucial for creating a community in which women were enabled and empowered to write, often as an extension of consciousness raising (Morris and Withers 2018).[15] As Lauren Berlant has posited, spaces like *Spare Rib*'s letters pages acted as an 'intimate public', which fostered 'emotional contact' between and among readers and the magazine. Such spaces were crucial in allowing women to link abstract concepts of the political and the personal, self and movement (Berlant 2008: viii; Waters 2016: 456). They were also vital for registering the 'tensions' in the magazine's community of readers and writers and provided a useful barometer of reader responses (Thomlinson 2017a: 433).

Spare Rib's correspondence captured the affective and intellectual challenges and rewards of feminist community and its periodicals as a whole; in Margaretta Jolly's thoughtful terms, feminist letters show 'poignantly . . . the struggle to realize ideals of sisterhood from within the puzzle of how to create genuine coalition and community across political gulfs of race of class or sheer differences of temperament' (2008: 4). Overall, however, it was 'the reciprocity between those who produced these periodicals and their readers' that was key to *Spare Rib*'s ambitious project of 'finding a new language' for women that reflected new and changing identities (Rowe 2015). Readers were constantly invited 'to join in the work, not simply as consumers . . . but as creators' (Thoms Flannery 2005: 1).

Letters began as a double page called 'In Our Own Write'. Over the next few years, the section expanded, and *Spare Rib* moved to further break down the barriers between reader and magazine. There were longer editorials, along with a more explicitly dialogic letters page; readers were in close conversation with each other and the collective. *Spare Rib* letters could even 'prompt shifts in editorial position' (Waters 2017: 460). But perhaps more important than this was their function in bearing witness to the magazine's attempts to work through internal dilemmas and dynamics. *Spare Rib* never hid from readers its own rifts and difficulties, from money to ideological differences. On the contrary, publishing and political problems could be shared with full honesty (or so it seemed). *Spare Rib*'s practice of rigorous self-scrutiny before the readers would be inconceivable at other magazines more committed to projecting a cogent, decorous editorial 'we' to readers. This honesty helped readers feel from the start that *Spare Rib* was a collective project for all women. It was repaid by letters that revealed strong feelings for and on behalf of the magazine. These could be loving or proprietorial, with letters frequently signed off 'Love' or 'In sisterhood' (a relatively standard *Spare Rib* sign-off). One early reader told how 'at last I've got this month's copy, hooray . . . I can't afford to subscribe so every month I walk a couple of miles in search of a copy'; another noted 'it is the only magazine that I can sit down and read from cover to cover without getting depressed' (*SR* September 1973: 3). Another thanked it 'for the encouragement and interest you have given me since you started up' (*SR* February 1974: 3).

With this sense of a collective and transformative project came sharp disappointments, with love and swingeing disapproval often mixed together. One London-based reader urged the magazine to 'please, please . . . hurry through your obvious period of infancy (too often reflected in the anger that comes through in your articles . . .). Not all of us are interested in the collective bargaining efforts of factory workers in the North' (*SR* 1974: 3). Another correspondent urged *Spare Rib* to reform; like other critical letters, its confident commitment to *Spare Rib*'s political purpose seemed to free the writer up to voice what could seem uncompromising critique. 'Although *SR* is a diamond in the slag heap of Sun/Mirror/Honey sexism and a sort of friend to a lonely feminist, it is sadly failing. God, it's all so middle class and TRENDY, really embarrassing . . . It's this sort of laughable world of dungaree-clad alternative bookshop types which must drive away the sort of women *SR* NEEDS to reach, the working class women' (*SR* 1980: 4). But throughout *Spare Rib*'s run, and in keeping with discursive modes forged within the Women's Liberation Movement, the fierce criticism of extreme honesty co-existed with, and did not preclude, extreme loyalty, attachment and care (Waters 2016).

Editorial Tensions

As the letters indicate, the magazine was continuously and robustly re-imagining itself. Any lingering similarity with mainstream women's magazines was reduced in December 1973, as *Spare Rib* announced that its editorial hierarchy would be replaced by an editorial collective. An in-depth explanation was offered in 'How and Why Does *Spare Rib* Run as a Collective?', a two-page editorial in February 1975 signed by Marsha Rowe (*SR* February 1975: 4–5).[16] Rowe offered readers a highly detailed account of how the collective was managing and experimenting with its daily working practices. She also elucidated the personal, political and intellectual imperatives to work collectively. *Spare Rib*'s collective was the fruition of 'the bridge between us' formed by discussion 'of our ideas together'. Collectivity was also a direct rebuttal of the masculinist structures that *Spare Rib*'s founding staffers had first assumed were integral to publishing. Ultimately, readers were told, the collective made manifest *Spare Rib*'s 'concern to identify *with* other women rather than against them' (Ibid.). It was not yet apparent how fragile this identification would prove in the face of the 'divisions and horrible things' that, in collective member Sue O'Sullivan's terms, would emerge in the early 1980s.[17]

The conversation about the structures and tone of the magazine continued with the April 1975 edition, which saw the first of a two-part series addressing the 'most frequently-asked questions about *Spare Rib*', under the headline: 'Why is your magazine so depressing?' This was an opportunity for a re-articulation of *Spare Rib*'s purpose, with the focus still firmly on 'ordinary' British women's daily lives – how 'women up and down the country are thinking, feeling, changing and organising at work, in trade unions, with kids, at school, at home, in bed'. What is perhaps the most interesting is the fact that the magazine still saw the need to be moderate, at least in some sense, in order to '[confront] the media image of women's liberation, of bra-burning and test-tube babies' (*SR* April 1975: 8).

The September 1980 issue, however, shared with readers a moment of far deeper internal ambivalence about the daily realities of publishing a magazine collectively. The collective noted:

> Recently [we have] come up against acute decision-making problems. We realised very abruptly that in fact we had never worked out a clear collective practice. A whole list of questions welled up:
>
> - Is consensus – everyone agreeing – what we aim for when we discuss what to publish?
> - Or is a majority decision good enough?
> - What about strongly felt minority opposition?
> - What criteria do we use for rejecting women's work?
> - Is it feminist practice to exert editorial control? When does editing become censorship? (*SR* September 1980: 3)

These questions would continue to shape the dialogue among and between *Spare Rib*'s editorial collective and readership; the tensions that resulted were persistent. In particular, with *Spare Rib*'s decision to suppress certain viewpoints came a great cost to the peace of the collective. The controversy in 1980 over the decision not to publish Ann Pettit's article, 'Feminism For Her Own Good', was shared in detail with readers.[18] Pettit was an anti-militarist and environmentalist who, in 1981, organised the Women for Life on Earth Walk, the women's peace march from Cardiff to Berkshire, which initiated the Greenham Common women's peace camp. In the article Pettit criticised what she saw as the growing gap in the movement between heterosexual and separatist lesbian women. The article was blocked by one collective member as being anti-lesbian. As a result, in September 1980, the collective turned, not for the first time, to the question of what it should publish, flagging its 'acute decision-making problems'. In this remarkable editorial, readers were informed how the decision to block the article came down to one collective member who 'felt so strongly that she'd withdraw her labour for the issue' if it went ahead. This had caused a serious emotional and operational fallout within the collective, and a group counsellor had been called in to help the collective move forward (*SR* September 1980: 3). Not only was this a candid account of the dispute, it acknowledged non-sisterly feeling, allowing readers to see and feel the thornily interlinked nature of politics and emotions.

Despite the ideal of 'an ethic of care', surging tensions between the collective and the individual could threaten the whole project (Jolly 2008: 9–12). In the December 1980 issue, Amanda Sebestyen wrote to explain her resignation from the collective. Sebestyen felt that *Spare Rib* was fearful of 'anything outside the tiny, admittedly beleaguered, world of the movement. Sexuality, religion, socialism – there's a Right Line.' She pointed to 'countercultural snobbery' and 'kneejerk' leftism, and the lack of consistency about editorial decision-making. As a feminist who leaned to the radical side of the movement, Sebestyen felt 'worn out' by the battles within the collective (*SR* December 1980: 19).

Diversity and Internationalism

From 1982, issues of race and anti-racism increasingly shaped the running and editorial content of the magazine (see Plate 3). A powerful source of tension and debate in this arena concerned coverage and attitudes towards Zionism and anti-Zionism following the Israeli invasion of Lebanon. A cluster of inflammatory articles and editorials in 1982 and 1983 kickstarted what became a heated, sometimes vicious and often hurtful dialogue that lasted until the magazine's closure (e.g. *SR* 126, January 1984: 4). In appearing to pit Jewish feminists (assumed to have strong ties and therefore implicit support for Israel) against feminists with the interests of Palestinian and 'third world women' at heart, editorial decisions on this topic became an incredibly divisive area for *Spare Rib*. Outbursts by the collective such as the one that saw a member claim that 'Jewish people should thank Hitler because without him the Jewish state would never have been created', rightly invited accusations of anti-Semitism. Painfully, the question of what Israel meant for feminism brought (white) Jewish feminists into conflict with black members of the collective (*SR* August 1982: 22–3; Thomlinson 2017b).

After a period of paralysis, *Spare Rib* eventually chose not to publish Jewish feminist letters that were identified as pro-'Zionist'. But feminist publishing was a collective project, and in choosing censorship over grave offence to some members of its collective, *Spare Rib* opened up a seam of unresolvable moral complexity. Over the next decade, this would erode the collective's ability to operate and lead the magazine (and some observers) to feel it had become 'unstuck'.[19] Melanie Waters (2016) and Sara Ahmed (2017) have written about the productive feminist potential of negative affect; the divisiveness of these issues in *Spare Rib*, however, charts a less positive process of highly personalised political disagreement.

These debates formed part of a general shift in editorial structure and stress. Having invited black women onto the collective a year before, there were more efforts to engage with black women as readers. A readers' meeting 'for women of colour only' was announced in 1983 (*SR* August 1983: 10). The announcement made clear that the arrival of black women onto the collective had not been smooth nor, from the point of view of the women of colour, handled well by the white collective members who had invited them.[20] The January 1984 editorial marked a divisive new era. 'Black women's job on the collective is at least ten times harder than that of our white colleagues', collective members wrote, 'and the fact that this has to be spelt out proves the importance of white readers' commitment to visible anti-racist struggle within the pages of *Spare Rib*' (*SR* January 1984: 3).[21]

There were also tensions over how Irish women were represented in the magazine and integrated into the collective. Roisin Boyd, the first Irish woman on the collective, left it in 1983 and contributed a stinging critique of how it had failed to recognise the specificity of Irish women's oppression: 'I was supposed to adapt and become part of *their* movement, culture and politics. I was never asked about what was happening in Ireland, whether things were different or the same' (*SR* August 1983: 58). The power between men and women was acknowledged, but not that between different groups of women, Boyd argued. *Spare Rib* did offer greater coverage of the Northern Irish troubles after Boyd's critique, but Irish women often felt that their complex struggle with state and paramilitary brutality, as well as patriarchy, was barely acknowledged.

In November 1985, *Spare Rib* decided to recalibrate and remodel the magazine based on the results of a reader survey printed in the April 1985 issue – the first such survey in ten years. The November 1985 issue presented the survey results as marking 'a departure from something old and the birth of something new' (*SR* November 1985: 4). Readers came from a wide variety of backgrounds; overall they were educated, yet with a surprising number not in paid work. They were voracious readers and politically active. Half defined themselves as heterosexual. The new *Spare Rib* tried to reflect this information, and the 'passionate responses' elicited by the survey were translated into a promise of more news coverage, and more coverage of Irish women, health, and events outside London (Ibid.: 35). Meanwhile, antidotes to the seriousness of the collective's preoccupation with race and identity struggles were provided in new regulars. There was 'Feminist Bedrooms', a 'light-hearted look at feminist lifestyles', plans for a column devoted to feminist astrology, and the arts section was revamped under the new jazzy heading 'Culture Shock'. Nonetheless, *Spare Rib* was sober about its task and position, and, gesturing to the global perspective that would eventually drive editorial direction, it noted that 'the worldwide position of women leaves much to be desired' (*SR* November 1985: 4). The magazine, despite an impressive thirteen years, still faced an uphill struggle.

Demise

From March 1990, the letters section prompted an intermittent new section called 'The Dialogue Continues' which featured point-by-point replies by the collective to readers' letters. This 'dialogue' concerned the proper meaning of feminism and the direction of *Spare Rib*, often prompted by an explosive set of debates about race, sexuality and class. The section was put in place after *Spare Rib*'s reply to an accusatory letter by a radical woman signed off as 'Manchester Feminist' in February 1990 which declared that *Spare Rib*'s 'brand of feminism I now recognise to be PSEUDOFEMINISM'. In aligning itself with the 'male leftie activism' concerned with 'third world struggles', *Spare Rib* had become 'A PERIODICAL FOR THE GIRLFRIENDS AND WIVES OF RADICAL MEN' (*SR* February 1990: 5). *Spare Rib* responded with a call for inclusive feminism: 'for us, there is no one enemy, or root cause from which all else spins' (*SR* February 1990: 7). Over the next two years, readers and *Spare Rib* locked horns over the direction of the magazine; key issues included the intended readership, as well as the limits of intersectionality particularly when, as some women insisted, in fighting for racial and class equality women were also fighting men's fights. Nikki M wrote in August 1990 that 'we must resist being co-opted into so-called wider struggles' (*SR* August 1990: 5). Yet other readers wrote to 'The Dialogue Continues' appreciatively, in full support of the magazine's intersectional approach. Thethani Sangoma declared that critiques such as Nikki's reflected a middle-class muddle about who the 'enemy' really was – it was not men but, as *Spare Rib* itself posited, capitalism which duped men as well as women into classism, sexism and racism (SR September 1990: 4). Dawn Collard asserted that *Spare Rib* was right to try to 'end all injustices/oppression' rather than being 'only concerned with women'; Victoria praised *Spare Rib* for its 'internationalism' that 'can be and must be the only approach by which the feminism movement worldwide may stride along in every country' (*SR* October 1990: 6; *SR* May 1992: 6).

The early 1990s saw a bitter and prolonged financial recession in Britain coupled with sharp public funding cuts (the Greater London Council, a key source of support for *Spare Rib*, was dissolved in 1986 by Thatcher's government). Long-standing distribution problems continued. In the February 1991 issue, one reader complained that WH Smith had hidden the magazine on its lowest shelf. Another was angry that her branch of the shop had put *Spare Rib* in the 'general interest' magazine section, grouped with the soft pornography magazines. She intervened, moving the magazines to the 'women's section', only to find that staff had moved them back several days later (*SR* February 1991: 4). But, at its core, the issue was financial non-viability. The price rose to a final level of £1.80. Benefits concerts, events, donations and publishing every two months rather than monthly issues helped – but were not enough. The dwindling of advertising revenue and falling subscriptions, themselves symptoms of an increasingly disparate feminist movement, spelt out the end.

Spare Rib's final issue was January 1993, six months after it went bimonthly to cut costs. The magazine stopped with an almost eerie suddenness. Although a date for the 'next issue out' was even given on the contents page (5 February 1993), it never arrived. Perhaps it wasn't obvious to the editorial staff either that this was the final issue. After all, the increased financial pressures of the open market combined with falling subscription rates meant that, since the late 1980s, each issue had been a struggle. Confidence in the magazine's futurity had long been impossible. By July 1992 'what was always a struggle' had been turned 'into a question of will we survive?' (*SR* July 1992: 7).

CONTENTS

ISSUE 235

FEATURES

6 Sheila Chandra - Weaving Our Ancestors Voices

10 L.A. - War Ina Babylon

32 Earth Summit - Green Imperialists Hit Rio

36 Palestine - 25 Years of Occupation: A Personal Testimony From Hanan Ashrawi

NEWS

41 BRITISH - Judith Ward - Freed at Last; Police Target Coventry Estate; Porn Ring Busted; Latin American Women on Hunger Strike in Styal Prison

44 AROUND THE WORLD Massacre in Bangkok; Communists Exit Afghanistan; The Moral of Coalisland

REGULARS

4 Letters

18 Music Disposable Heroes of Hiphoprisy; Najma; Diamanda Galas; Jody Watley; SR Pick of the Month

20 Film Basic Instinct; The Playboys; Movietalk

21 Television And Still I Rise; Teenage Diaries; The Body Beautiful

23 Performance Lóka Nátya; Asking For It; On the Boards

24 Books Toni Morrison's Jazz; Angela Carter's Wise Children; Catholics and Sex

27 Images To Po Me Te Ao; Revenge; Breaking Bounds

Ngozi Onwurah in The Body Beautiful - see page 21

Above: War Ina Babylon - see page 10

Left: The Palestinians of the Intifada - see page 36

29 Spare Time A Guide to What's On and Where; Lesbian and Gay Pride Listings; Something For Nothing

48 Pulse of the Movement Refugees Take Control; The Sistership; Free Kiranjit Ahluwalia

52 Job Ads

53 Classifieds

56 Parenting Could Your Child Have Glue Ear?; Choosing Childcare

57 Health Special Report: Ending the Culture of Silence - Women Speak Out On Reproductive Health And Power

SPARE RIB IS PRODUCED COLLECTIVELY BY Esther Bailey, Marcel Fakhry, Elorine Grant, Jennifer Mourin, Vuyiswa Ngqobongwana and Sarah Payton

DISTRIBUTION
Newstrade: COMAG
Tel: (0895) 444 055
Bookshops: Central
Tel: (081) 986 4854
Subscriptions: Spare Rib
Tel: (071) 253 9792

US Distributors: Ubiquity Distributors, 607 Degraw St, Brooklyn, New York, NY 11217 Tel: (718) 875 5491
Small Changes, 316 Terry Avenue North, Seattle, Washington 98109 Tel: (206) 382 1980
Armadillo & Co., 5795 West Washington Blvd, Culver City, California 90232 Tel: (213) 937 7674

PRINTING
BPCC Business Magazines
Tel: (0206) 851 665

THANKS THIS MONTH TO
Sharon, Annie Hole, Irene Shepstone, Renu Bhullar, Diane, Elisabete Cardoso, Patricia, Charity, Susan, Beauroo at the North American Guardian, John at BPCC and Roger at Lasertype

COVER PHOTOGRAPH
Courtesy of RealWorld

ADVERTISING
Spare Rib (071) 253 9958
June issue copy date: 20 June 1992

NEXT ISSUE OUT
27 June 1992

ENQUIRIES
Please send a stamped addressed envelope with all enquiries. SPARE RIB accepts unsolicited material but cannot be held responsible for the loss or damage of any correspondence. Due to the volume of material received we cannot return manuscripts.

SPARE RIB is available on tape for subscribers who are blind or partially sighted

SPARE RIB
27 CLERKENWELL CLOSE
LONDON EC1R OAT
TEL: (071) 253 9792
FAX: (071) 251 1773

Figure 2.3 The style and interests of the magazine changed significantly over the 1980s and into the early 1990s to a far more internationalist set of concerns. Contents page, *Spare Rib*, June 1992.

If *Spare Rib*'s end was sudden, it was not necessarily surprising; its internal disputes, particularly those around Zionism, had been a subject of public knowledge (*The Guardian* 1 November 1986: 26). Its closure attracted little comment in the national press, a fact that was seized upon gleefully in a lengthy article in *The Guardian* (the only major piece of coverage of the closure) by Eileen Fairweather, a former *Spare Rib* employee in 'Death by Suicide' (*The Guardian* 15 March 1992: A11). Fairweather's piece vented her bitterness over *Spare Rib*'s recent evolution. She described how the magazine that had been a 'unifier of the British women's liberation movement' had committed 'suicide', its 'lonely death . . . predictable [in July 1992] when, due to its perilous finances . . . it went bi-monthly and, a retailing source says, "almost no one bothered to complain".' Archival records of *Spare Rib*'s accounts in its final years are elusive, making it hard to corroborate or dispute Fairweather's assertion of *Spare Rib*'s 'rumoured . . . debts of £100,000'. According to the magazine itself, readership was an 'estimated 90,000' at this time (*SR* October 1991: 7). However, paired with the much lower peak circulation figure of 25,000 most commonly cited (taking into account that circulation, as copies sold, is always less than readership), this does not shed much light on revenue (Chester et al. 1981: 76; Dena and Shaila c. 1978). What is clear is a precipitous decline in the final two years; in August 1990, a familiar call for subscriptions ran '*Spare Rib* . . . Can you afford to be without it?' By August/September 1992, the line had a new add-on: 'It definitely can't afford to be without you' (*SR* August 1990: 7; *SR* August/September 1992: 5).

The scarcity of editorial resources was clear. By the final issue there were only six collective members (as opposed to roughly fifteen throughout the 1980s), which helps explain why many articles in the last few years were reprints. Loyal readers were well aware of 'financial problems' thanks to numerous appeals from 1991 onwards (Sudbury in *SR* August/September 1992: 4). If the collective had always looked to its readership for emotional and intellectual forms of engagement, it now looked to them for financial aid. '*Spare Rib* needs you' – 'It's midnight on the night before we send the 228th issue of *Spare Rib* to the printers. Things have got so tough here that we need to make an appeal for your help.' The aid solicited was donations – 'if everyone gives something, it will save *Spare Rib*' (*SR* October 1991: 7). Readers were also asked to try to get their workplaces to subscribe. As their letters (and appreciative editorials) made clear, readers responded to the call to arms, but it was not enough. The July 1992 editorial explained the decision to go bimonthly from the following month due to 'ever increasing costs' and general 'economic decline'. The new format would, it was hoped, free up 'more space to develop fundraising activities other than advertising, to bring in the necessary revenue' (*SR* July 1992: 7).

Spare Rib retained loyal and enthusiastic readers until the end and inspired the gratitude of black and working-class women for bringing them articles markedly different in focus from everything else on the newsstand. 'I think you're doing a wonderful and important job at a very difficult time in the Women's Movement,' wrote Ann Evans from Wales in the January 1990 issue – tellingly, the collective headlined this letter 'Not often we get a letter like this' (*SR* December/January 1990: 4). In a section headed 'Thanks!', the April 1992 issue showcased a cluster of appreciative letters from women responding to the magazine's appeal for financial help by stating that their renewal money was enclosed and thanking the magazine for being, as reader Alison Yap put it, so 'inclusive of difference' (*SR* April 1992: 5). Marienella, a working-class woman, wrote in October/November 1992 that she found *Spare Rib* 'unreplaceable' and 'unique' for its commitment to the 'cause of British and world feminism' (*SR* October/November 1992: 4).

But many readers expressed the frustration captured in Fairweather's disparaging piece. A letter by a reader called Chloe, in August 1992, hit such a nerve that it dominated the entire letters section of the next issue. Although not the first, Chloe took particularly forceful aim at the magazine's absorption in identity politics, particularly around race and class, saying that she had begun to feel 'the only one of your readers to be multiply-handicapped (sorry, differently abled) by being white, middle aged, middle class and heterosexual . . . you have largely abandoned the cause of British and world feminism and become too political'. Even more boldly, given the extreme tension between and among readers and the collective caused by debates surrounding Zionism over the preceding decade, Chloe wrote: 'Can I say something? *I am not in the least interested in the Intifada.*' At the end of her letter she reaffirmed that she wanted to see more light-hearted, relatable regulars like the erstwhile Feminist Bedrooms and, crucially, '*I do not want to read about the Intifada* – sorry!' *Spare Rib* responded by apologising 'to those readers who may find this letter as offensive as we did' but stating its commitment to debate (*SR* August 1992: 4).

The final issues of *Spare Rib* were pervaded with the collective's gloom about its own struggle for survival and the world beyond it. In its twentieth-anniversary edition, the collective observed that 'we find humanity in an ever-worsening crisis – political, economic, and spiritual' (*SR* July 1992: 7). This sentiment was echoed in the magazine's final editorial which linked the 'the current chaos and decay that surrounds us at the end of 1992' to deep personal fatigue: 'by this time of year it all seems too much and without further ado we are now signing off for our annual crawling-into-a-hole-to-sleep-for-two-weeks-solid' (*SR* December/January 1993: 5). A double-page feature in the middle of the issue entitled '*annus horribilis*' sealed the sense of gloom and entrapment – as a review of the 'state of the nation' that examined unemployment, health, education and poverty, it was clear that from *Spare Rib*'s viewpoint, things could hardly look worse (Ibid.: 46–7).

Conclusion

It may have exited the stage not with a bang but a whimper, but *Spare Rib*'s run of more than twenty years testified to a genuine tenaciousness in both business and cultural terms. And the story was far from over. More than twenty years later, as feminism in the UK began to galvanise large numbers of activists once more, a later generation attempted to revive *Spare Rib*. Charlotte Raven, a controversial journalist, was the main figure behind efforts to link a new version of *Spare Rib* to the thriving world of digital feminist content, as well as to revive the print version. But as Laurel Forster has documented, Raven's savvy commercialism estranged earlier *Spare Rib* readers and collective members. Despite Marsha Rowe's own ambitions for wide distribution and readership, she insisted that revival efforts respect the political motivations of the earlier magazine: '*Spare Rib* is not a brand' (cited in Forster 2015: 228). The magazine's legacy has been assured by the decision to digitise it by the British Library. Most of the magazine's content was made freely available online in 2015. This process was not without the moral and practical complexities that had always defined the movement – the project raised some sharp objections over its implications for intellectual property (British Library n.d.; Davies 2015). But with about 80 per cent of the content of *Spare Rib*'s 239 editions available, at least until Britain exits the European Union, on the British Library website, the magazine has entered its second major phase as the touchstone of modern feminist heritage in the UK, as well as paper of record for the movement.

Scholars of digitised print media have drawn attention to the mixed blessing they represent. D-M Withers (2015: 18) notes that the feminist archive 'does not automatically become richer as traditions are created, recorded or documented'. Instead, the process of digitisation requires attention to the technical systems, accessibility, commercialisation and selection that can filter and condition our thinking. Adrian Bingham (2010) has argued that digitisation can lead to cherry picking organised around thematic interests, without the deep contextualisation that is necessary to make historical sense of a media. For scholars using *Spare Rib*, it is tempting to allow this journal to speak for the entire British feminist movement. Writing about the challenges of creating the Sisterhood and After archive of oral histories at the British Library, Margaretta Jolly, Polly Russell and Rachel Cohen offer a salutary discussion of 'the primary ethical challenge' of aiming for representativeness of the Women's Liberation Movement (Jolly et al. 2012: 213). They remind us that appointing any one organisation, publication or set of activists as a proxy for the whole movement must be unsatisfactory, since women's liberation 'occurred as a result of a dialectical process between ideas, grassroots activism and campaigning'. Their question of how to '[honour] a movement that prided itself on its collectivity' applies to *Spare Rib* too (Ibid.: 213–5).

As this chapter has argued, representativity cannot be assumed and, if *Spare Rib* is characteristic of the movement, it is through its splenetic debate rather than any consensus over what a feminist platform might include. While other digitised feminist periodicals are slowly being made available, the current situation resembles the lone digitisation of *The Times* newspaper in 2003. *The Times* digital archive was relatively easy to access for scholars, and for a period, the absence of other easily available national newspaper titles made it the go-to resource for scholars eager to find newspaper sources to bolster their arguments. Despite having a relatively small readership, *The Times* became, for many historians, a proxy for educated public opinion, despite there being little evidence that it served this role historically (Hobbs 2013: 472–97). Those reading *Spare Rib* to access 'feminist opinion' must do so with caution, alert to the relative absences within this journal (e.g. the muted presence of revolutionary and radical feminism), as well as its biases to metropolitan content and to educated readers.

That *Spare Rib* is the first fully digitised British feminist magazine should not detract from the format's promise.[22] By allowing humanities scholars access to the fruits of complex digital programming – such as word searches across the entire run of the magazine – the *Spare Rib* online journal archive offers riches. Scholars of the women's movement, late twentieth-century periodicals and many more topics can deploy the insights of a vast possible array of metadata to probe this fragmentary history. Scholars based at the University of Sussex Humanities Lab have observed how digitisation offers the chance to 'track linguistic change . . . [plot] the placement of illustrations, and [map] locations mentioned within core texts' (Terras et al. 2006: 3). In the case of *Spare Rib*, such tools can enable the construction of an unprecedented topography of the women's movement, and help geographically plot the relationship between magazine and readers.[23] In making it faster and easier to track themes and changes in content, *Spare Rib*'s online archive also opens up new vistas in our understanding of the contours and daily contingencies the magazine faced.

Spare Rib's longevity, high profile and breadth of content is indicative of the extraordinary ambition of the British Women's Liberation Movement, from the heady days of 1972 to the plural and often painful debates of the early 1990s. It helped establish a feminist presence in the mainstream women's magazine market, as well as in bookshops, mainstream newsagents, libraries, women's centres, private homes and student unions. It circulated globally and provided an open and visible record of feminist collective decision-making, entrepreneurialism and print media expertise. Its pages record the activism that feminist Jan McKenley noted when looking back at her treasured *Spare Rib* diaries: 'It felt like we were absolutely in the world in the moment . . . life was just exploding.'[24]

Notes

1. *Spare Rib* Manifesto (1972), facsimile <www.bl.uk/collection-items/facsimile-of-spare-rib-manifesto> (last accessed 14 August 2019).
2. *Spare Rib* referred to henceforth as *SR*.
3. See Red produced posters for the women's movement and had been formed through an advert in the socialist feminist *Red Rag* magazine (See Red Women's Workshop 2016). On the visual culture of *Spare Rib*, see Chester et al. (1981).
4. *Viva*, a New York-based magazine, offered its target female audience heterosexual adult content. Its format was similar to *Playgirl* magazine, founded the year before. *Viva* was published by husband and wife team Bob Guccione and Kathy Keeton under the subtitle 'The International Magazine for Women'; Guccione also published the male equivalent, *Penthouse*. *Viva* included erotic fiction, reviews, interviews and fashion content, and launched the career of its fashion editor Anna Wintour, later editor of Vogue. Its first issue print run was reported to be one million, and the magazine was priced at $1 with a full-colour glossy cover. The price had reached $1.50 by the late 1970s, but the magazine was not profitable and was withdrawn in 1980.
5. Reader Ken Wilson was annoyed that 'articles on the still semi-taboo subject of sex make good copy, and you and your kind will continue to print them until a wearying public cries out for peace'.
6. The *WIRES* collective had a policy of publishing anything submitted by a woman that did not contravene the agreed demands of the Women's Liberation Movement, although the collective retained the right to reply. Despite their efforts to promote inclusion, few women came to their six-monthly readers' meetings, or responded to invitations to vote on editorial policy decisions (*SR* May 1978: 18).
7. *Spare Rib* cultivated its periodical and newspaper community but was also represented in other media. Anne Mortimer, a reader, wrote in 1973 that she had heard on Radio London that the July issue of *Spare Rib* might be held up (*SR* September 1973: 6). Radio stations advertised in *Spare Rib*, drawn by its strong emphasis on women's music production. The magazine had been critical of the sexism of the media in general and the radio specifically. This is evident in articles such as 'Local radio trivialises women's movement' (*SR* March 1975: 23) and 'Radio station sacks lesbian worker' (*SR* February 1987: 47). It reported on women-led pirate radio initiatives and reviewed both radio and television in its broadcast section. There was some collaboration between *Spare Rib* and the BBC, with Radio 4 broadcasting a live event from *Spare Rib*'s fifteenth birthday celebrations in 1987 (*SR* March 1988: 32).

8. A treasure trove of correspondence relating to all aspects of running *Spare Rib*, including particularly detailed accounts of the business side of the magazine in its first few years, is currently held at the Feminist Archive South (FAS), University of Bristol. For reader letters, see in particular DM2123/FA/Arch/56 *Spare Rib* correspondence, Special Collections, FAS, University of Bristol.
9. FAS, Box: DM2123/1.
10. FAS, Box: DM2123/FA/Arch/56.
11. When *Spare Rib* produced women's liberation greetings cards, the Wanstead and Woodford Women's Liberation Group packed and posted the items (*SR* February 1975: 31).
12. However, six issues later, a reader who had heard *Spare Rib* mentioned in *The Times* asked her newsagent who produced it and 'made it sound as ordinary as the "Radio Times"' (*SR* March 1974: 4).
13. On *Spare Rib* distribution, see Chester et al. (1981: 76–7) and *Spare Rib* March 1975: 4.
14. For example, 'Why I decided to have a baby' in 'New occasional series' (*SR* October 1977: 10–12).
15. Letters were not just key to the construction of the feminist movement; they 'have always been crucial to women's magazines' and a key site of identification and dialogue between reader and magazine (Forster 2015: 158; Waters 2016: 447).
16. *Spare Rib* was not alone in the feminist publishing milieu in choosing to operate as a collective. Feminist magazines edited collectively included *Scarlet Woman*, *Catcall*, *Outwrite*, *Red Rag* and *WIRES*, and *Off Our Backs* in the US.
17. O'Sullivan in *Sisterhood and After: The Women's Liberation Oral History Project, 2010–2013*. British Library Sound & Moving Image © The British Library and The University of Sussex. C1420/40, track 6.
18. See Margaretta Jolly (2003) for a discussion of Pettit's importance to the movement, as well as her falling out with *Spare Rib*.
19. Impassioned unpublished letters about *Spare Rib*'s handling of debates about Israel are held in the FAS collection – see, for example, DM2123/1/Box 53.
20. Reflecting on the arrival of black women onto the collective, Sue O'Sullivan pinpointed this as the moment that any assumptions about the *Spare Rib* collective's solidarity began to be dismantled. The collective decided that it 'needed more black women . . . we were rather unprepared, it was almost like "come and join us at our table, we will – we would love to welcome you to our table, would you like to sit down here with us at our table, oh excellent, you know." . . . I think that was really the one of the things that set the thing off kilter, in the very beginning.' (Interview for Sisterhood and After. C1420/40, track 6, transcript: 139).
21. On the tensions and also the productive attempts to realise multiracial collective working, see Natalie Thomlinson 2017b.
22. Other digitisation projects are likely to follow, including women's liberation magazines such as *Red Rag*. For a concise discussion of the significant advantages, as well as challenges inherent in the humanistic use of big data, see Martin Wynne (2015).
23. A mapping initiative is currently being undertaken by the project team of The Business of Women's Words: Purpose and Profit in Feminist Publishing, partnered with The British Library, <http://blogs.sussex.ac.uk/businessofwomenswords> (last accessed 21 August 2019).
24. McKenley in *Sisterhood and After*. C1420/15, track 3.

Works Cited

Ahmed, S. 2017. *Living A Feminist Life*. Durham: Duke University Press.

Bazin, V. 2017. '"A New Kind of Trade": Advertising Feminism in Spare Rib'. *Re-reading Spare Rib*. Ed. A. Smith. London: Palgrave. 197–212.

Beins, A. 2016. 'A Revolution in Ephemera: Feminist Newsletters and Newspapers of the 1970s'. *This Book is an Action: Feminist Print Culture and Activist Aesthetics*. Ed. J. Harker and C. Farr. Urbana: University of Illinois Press. 45–65.

Berlant, L. 2008. *The Female Complaint*. Durham: Duke University Press.

Bingham, A. 2010. 'The Digitization of Newspaper Archives: Opportunities and Challenges for Historians'. *Twentieth Century British History* 21.2: 225–31.

British Library. n.d. 'About the Spare Rib Digitisation project', British Library <www.bl.uk/spare-rib/about-the-project> (last accessed 15 August 2019).

Chester, G., E. Cadman and A. Pivot. 1981. *Rolling Our Own: Women as Printers, Publishers and Distributors*. London: Minority Press Group Series No. 4.

Cook, H. 2015. '*Nova* – Love, Masculinity and Feminism, but not as we know it'. *Love and Romance in Britain, 1918–1970*. Eds A. Harris and T. Willem Jones. London: Palgrave. 225–54.

Davies, C. 2015. 'Spare Rib Goes Digital', *The Guardian*, 28 May 2015 <www.theguardian.com/media/2015/may/28/british-library-spare-rib-feminist-magazine-online> (last accessed 15 August 2019).

Dena and Shaila. c. 1978. *Directory of Women's Liberation Newsletters, Magazines, Journals*. York, UK.

Erdman Farrell, A. 1998. *Yours in Sisterhood:* Ms. *Magazine and the Promise of Popular Feminism*. Chapel Hill: University of North Carolina Press.

Forster, L. 2015. *Magazine Movements: Women's Culture, Feminisms and Media Form*. London: Bloomsbury.

Hobbs, A. 2013. 'The Deleterious Dominance of *The Times* in Nineteenth-Century Scholarship'. *Journal of Victorian Culture* 18.4: 472–97.

Hollows, J. 2013. '*Spare Rib*, Second-Wave Feminism and the Politics of Consumption'. *Feminist Media Studies* 13.2: 268–87.

Jolly, M. 2003. 'Writing the Web: Letters from the Women's Peace Movement'. *The Feminist Seventies*. Eds H. Graham, A. Kaloski, A. Neilson and E. Robertson. York: Raw Nerve Books. 1–6.

Jolly, M. 2008. *In Love and Struggle: Letters in Contemporary Feminism*. New York: Columbia University Press.

Jolly, M., P. Russell and R. Cohen. 2012. 'Sisterhood and After: Individualism, Ethics and an Oral History of the Women's Liberation Movement'. *Social Movement Studies* 11.2: 211–26.

Koller, V. 2008. *Lesbian Discourses: Images of a Community*. Abingdon: Routledge.

Morris, B. and D-M Withers. 2018. *The Feminist Revolution: The Struggle for Women's Liberation*. London: Little, Brown.

Mulvey, L. 1975. 'Visual Pleasure and Narrative Cinema'. *Screen* 16.3: 6–18.

Murray, S. 2000. '"Deeds and Words": The Woman's Press and the Politics of Print'. *Women: A Cultural Review* 11.3: 197–222.

Rees, J. 2010. 'A Look Back at Anger: The Women's Liberation Movement in 1978'. *Women's History Review* 19.3: 337–56.

Rowe, M. 1982. *Spare Rib Reader*. Harmondsworth: Penguin.

Rowe, M. 2015. 'Background and Early *Spare Rib*', <www.bl.uk/spare-rib/articles/introduction-spare-rib-the-first-nine-years> (last accessed 16 August 2019).

See Red Women's Workshop. 2016. *Feminist Posters 1974–1990*. London: Four Corners.

Terras, M., J. Baker, J. Hetherington, D. Beavan, M. Zaltz Austwick, A. Welsh, H. O'Neill, W. Finley, O. Duke-Williams and A. Farquhar. 2017. 'Enabling Complex Analysis of Large-scale Digital Collections: Humanities Research, High Performance Computing, and Transforming Access to British Library Digital Collections'. *Digital Scholarship in the Humanities*. Sussex Research Online.

Thom, M. 1997. *Inside* Ms.*: 25 Years of the Magazine and the Feminist Movement.* New York: H. Holt.

Thomlinson, N. 2017a. '"Second-Wave" Black Feminist Periodicals in Britain'. *Women: A Cultural Review* 27.4: 432–45.

Thomlinson, N. 2017b. '"Sisterhood is Plain Sailing?" Multiracial Feminist Collectives in 1980s Britain'. *The Women's Liberation Movement: Impacts and Outcomes.* Ed. Kristina Schulz. New York: Berghahn. 198–213.

Thoms Flannery, K. 2005. *Feminist Literacies, 1968–75.* Urbana: University of Illinois Press.

Todd, S. 1999. 'Models and Menstruation: *Spare Rib* Magazine, Feminism, Femininity and Pleasure'. *Studies in Political Thought* 1: 60–78.

Waters, M. 2016. 'Yours in Struggle: Bad Feelings and Revolutionary Struggle in *Spare Rib*'. *Women: A Cultural Review* 27.4: 446–65.

Withers, D-M. 2015. *Feminism, Digital Culture and the Politics of Transmission, Theory, Practice and Cultural Heritage.* London: Rowman and Littlefield.

Wynne, M. 2015. 'Big Data and Digital Transformations in the Humanities – Are We There Yet?' University of Aberdeen, 21–22 September 2015 <www.slideshare.net/martinwynne/big-data-and-digital-transformations-in-the-humanities> (last accessed 8 March 2018).

3

The Impact of the Women-Only Publishing Phenomenon on Early Second-Wave Feminism, Literature and Culture

Catherine Riley

In the 1970s and early 1980s, a glut of feminist publishers emerged in the UK in the wake of the second-wave women's movement. White, middle-class feminist consciousness-raising was predicated on an exchange of ideas through women's writing and reading, making meaningful the refrain 'this book changed my life' as literature helped make the personal political. Feminist polemic and history by writers such as Sheila Rowbotham, Ann Oakley and Germaine Greer, as well as feminist fiction by Angela Carter, Jeanette Winterson and Alice Walker, for example, were all published (or republished) in the UK by the feminist publishing houses that sprang up in the UK during the 1970s and 1980s. These feminist publishers – including but not limited to Virago, The Women's Press, Pandora, Sheba, Onlywomen, Stramullion, Feminist Books, Honno, Black Woman Talk, Aurora Leigh, Urban Fox Press and Scarlet – were critical to early formulations of second-wave politics, producing not only new female-authored fiction, but also feminist criticism and theory. They also brought about a new understanding of women's cultural and literary past through their republishing and recovery of a raft of women's historical writing.

The second-wave feminist publishing phenomenon was important for two reasons. First, it enabled the production of literature by and about women, which helped to develop the feminist movement and gave space for the expansion of its ideas. Second, the act of publishing *was itself* a moment of feminist praxis – an enactment of feminist politics through an incursion into 'male' areas of economic and cultural authority. Women such as Carmen Callil at Virago, Philippa Brewster at Pandora, Lilian Mohin at Onlywomen and Stephanie Dowrick at The Women's Press put their politics into action through their work. These female trailblazers shifted the demographic of the publishing industry to make it one in which women could flourish, while also proving the market for women's writing – one that mainstream publishers would be quick to capitalise on. Second-wave feminist publishing thus brought together praxis and theory – deeds as well as words.

Examining and historicising the second-wave feminist publishing phenomenon also reveals the ways in which the literature it produced directed contemporary debates around sex, gender and culture. Second-wave publishers provided an outlet for exciting new writing by women that explored the debates around gender, the body and identity emerging from feminist politicking and theory. They also enabled new genres of female fiction writing to emerge, providing a space in which the romance novel, crime-writing and science fiction could be reimagined with different kinds of female protagonists and feminist thematics. Crucially, they also excavated a raft of historical writing by women that had gone out of print, reinvesting women's writing with value and republishing these texts for a new and eager audience.

The books that were made available by these new female publishers had a seismic impact on both the literary and cultural order of the time, questioning ingrained inequalities and challenging the status quo. Fiction writing from Alice Walker, Margaret Atwood, Angela Carter and Maya Angelou was published alongside key critical texts by Elaine Showalter, bell hooks, Dale Spender and Susan Griffin. This body of work, produced by women for women, put feminist publishing at the centre of the second-wave women's movement in the UK.

In this chapter, I will look first at the ways in which second-wave feminist publishers set themselves up, distinct from the mainstream industry: establishing a women-only space in which to produce and distribute books was no mean feat in the male-dominated book world of 1970s and early 1980s Britain. I will then turn to examine the kinds of books that were published in their early years, and the ways in which these intersected – and, to a large extent, actually directed – the arguments of second-wave feminism, in particular in regard to three stereotypes of female identity: the housewife, the mother, the sex object. The importance and impact of the feminist publishing phenomenon in these early years cannot be understated – they were a crucial tool in the construction and dissemination of feminist politics.

The Business of Feminist Publishing

In the early 1970s, ideas about women's roles in British culture – including literary culture – were constructed around three feminine 'ideals': the housewife, the mother and the sex object. These notions of 'appropriate' femininity meant that women were rarely considered capable of being good at 'business', and so the emergence of women publishers constituted a rare challenge: 'within major publishing houses, few women achieved anything other than minor positions . . . as late as November 1974 there were only six female executive heads of publishing' (Coser et al. 1982: 151). The new feminist publishers were encroaching into territory that had always been clearly demarcated as male. Diana Athill recalls the atmosphere of 1970s publishing in her memoir *Stet* (2000: 56):

> All publishing was run by many badly-paid women and a few much better-paid men: an imbalance that women were, of course, aware of, but which they seemed to take for granted. I have been asked by younger women how I brought myself to accept this situation so calmly, and I suppose that part of the answer must be conditioning: to a large extent I had been shaped by my background to please men.

The establishment of Virago in 1973, the first of the women-only publishing houses, was therefore a real venture into 'male' territory and a challenge to these notions of appropriate feminine behaviour. Evidence of the patriarchal attitudes towards women in business can be found in media coverage of Virago's launch – even by female commentators. Caroline Moorehead in *The Times* wrote the first article describing Virago's women as 'paper tigresses' (a term that was subsequently used to denigrate women in the industry) in which she is overly keen to describe Virago's launch as professional and competent – not something that would be a concern were she describing the unveiling of new male-run book business: 'the emphasis on professional is important: there is nothing amateur about either group. It shows in the jackets, the blurbs and the publicity' (*The Times* 11 February 1978: 14a).

This cultural antipathy towards working women was offset (to some extent) by the new feminist networks that were emerging, and on which Virago, and the other feminist publishers that followed their example, could draw for help. *Spare Rib* magazine had launched in 1972, and Virago's founder Carmen Callil was able to use the expertise and contacts of *Spare Rib*'s founders Marsha Rowe and Rosie Boycott in setting up her own venture. Initially, her publishing house was even to have shared its name with Rowe and Boycott's magazine: 'October 1972: this is it. "Spare Rib Books" it was going to be called. So it must have been within a few months of *Spare Rib* starting.'[1] In the end, Boycott chose the name Virago, and the new publisher's initial board meeting was between Callil, Rowe and Boycott, taking place on 21 June 1973 in Callil's dining room. There were new groups like Women in Media, the Arsenal women's group, and Virago's own Advisory Board which boasted a large number of literary, professional and academic women, as well as journalists, writers and publicists who supported one another and provided material as well as intellectual sustenance in the early days of these new publishing ventures. 'I don't think there were many other feminists in publishing,' says Ursula Owen, who had been introduced to Callil by a mutual friend and joined Virago as its first editor.

> There may have been but I don't think they were saying so. I was already part of a women's group, I was a member of a women's group that survived for seven years, that had lots of writers in it actually, and we did last for seven years with almost weekly meetings, amazing. It was called the Arsenal women's group.[2]

The emerging feminist community helped Virago's women find each other and helped them to work out ways of doing their business in the patriarchal world of publishing.

Virago launched its first list (of eleven books) as part of a co-publishing agreement with Quartet Books, whose (male) owners Callil knew well and liked. Virago took on Quartet's innovative 'Midway' concept for its first publications, a new smaller-sized format with paperback binding that was put out simultaneously to initial hardback editions that were essential for review purposes and libraries. This was figured as a practical move (Midways were cheaper to produce and so helped keep overheads low) as well as a political one in that it made the books more affordable, helping Virago to attract as wide an audience of readers as possible by offering cheaper editions. It shows that, from the start, Virago's women understood the need to innovate and were determined to make their business a success. Profit was as important as politics in their publishing venture, since making money through and for feminist writers was figured by Callil and her team as *in itself* a feminist act.

Following Virago, other feminist publishing ventures emerged. Onlywomen was the first, established just a year later in 1974 with the aim of publishing 'literature that challenged gender and sexual stereotypes' as well as to 'prioritise lesbian authors'.[3] Onlywomen was set up as a collective, where all members were trained to have a wide range of publishing skills so that they could be equally involved in the running of any aspect of the organisation, thus avoiding the formation of hierarchies. This collectivism was in contrast to the structure in place at Virago which had a clear chain of command – an issue that would be debated by feminists in the publishing industry as more women set up in the book business. There was discord between those who felt that the drive to produce books challenging the patriarchal construction of culture, economics, politics and literature as 'male' was fundamentally at odds with the capitalist principles that drove a profit-generating business, and those who felt that feminist publishing should be a profitable as well as a political exercise. In reality, there was collectivism at work in all these fledgling feminist presses, as none could afford *not* to have everyone chip in as and when required.

The tension between financial and editorial autonomy underpinned the efforts of all of the second-wave feminist publishers. Virago's solution was to reclaim the 'male' territory of commerce to maximise the reach it could achieve for its product: women's writing. Onlywomen's solution was to insist on a publishing process – from production to editorial to sales – that was outside of the male-dominated mainstream, necessarily curtailing its reach but maintaining the 'purity' of its mission to make books for and by women. It was a tension that remained unresolved, as some of the new feminist publishing ventures were established with male backing and others were grassroots driven from within the feminist community.

In 1977 The Women's Press was founded by the entrepreneur and publishing magnate Naim Attallah, who installed Stephanie Dowrick to run the business as managing director. Attallah recalls:

> It was set up with a hundred £1 shares, with me holding fifty-three per cent and Stephanie the balance of forty-seven per cent . . . to begin with, Stephanie was the only full-time employee and the whole operation was started in her living-room in her house in Bow. (Attallah 2007: 37)

Sibyl Grundberg doubled the staff number to two shortly after. In an interesting twist, Attallah's purchase of Quartet, with whom Virago had co-published its first eleven books, enabled him to set up his new women's press. As he explains, 'with the departure of Virago from the Quartet fold and the emergence of feminism as a serious movement, I felt that there was space for a new feminist list that would both reflect one of the most exciting political currents in society and make commercial sense' (Attallah 2007: 36).

Following The Women's Press, Sheba was founded in 1980 specifically to address the fact that 'if more women writers are published now than in 1965, it remains true that the majority are white, heterosexual, and middle-class'.[4] Sheba's dedication to black women writers meant that it was run as a not-for-profit workers' co-operative, situating itself outside of a system that it figured as historically racist and sexist. In its early years it published important black, Asian and minority ethnic women authors such as Audre Lorde, Barbara Burford and bell hooks, and its output during the 1980s included a broad range of first and third world black, Asian and minority ethnic (BAME) writers.

The inclusion of the different perspectives and experiences of black, Asian and minority ethnic women was a positive, albeit problematic, development as the feminist movement began to acknowledge and examine its failures to describe the different oppressions faced by women whose gender intersected with their ethnicity. Feminist publishers were not immune to these omissions – the publishing industry itself was (and remains) an overwhelmingly white, middle-class profession – but alongside Sheba, other women-only publishers began to prioritise a more diverse range of writing and writers. Under the direction of Ros de Lanerolle from 1981, The Women's Press became synonymous with a commitment to third world and black women's writing, and Virago also published fiction and poetry from Paule Marshall, Grace Paley, Grace Nichols, Audre Lorde and Bharati Mukherjee, as well as fiction from a large number of lesser-known BAME women writers. These feminist publishers took a risk in publishing such work, in a marketplace in which BAME writing was hugely under-represented in the mainstream.

The Women's Press and Virago benefitted, however, from smash-hit novels from BAME women – Alice Walker's *The Color Purple* (1983) for the former, Maya Angelou's *I Know Why The Caged Bird Sings* (1984) for the latter – which helped cement their association with the writing of BAME women from the UK and beyond, as well as secure the fortunes and viability of both publishers throughout the 1980s. Virago and The Women's Press were also involved with the establishment of Greater Access to Publishing in the late 1980s, an attempt to accelerate the inclusion of BAME women in the publishing industry itself.

Sheba was followed in 1981 by Pandora, established to capture the burgeoning feminist academic market. 'Pandora emerged out of Routledge and Kegan Paul's first tentative forays into women's studies publishing in the late 1970s with a feminist studies list overseen by former RKP publicity and editorial assistant, Philippa Brewster' (Murray 2004: 100). That Pandora was founded from within a reputable mainstream press gave it the advantages of financial stability, established distribution networks, and a strong presence in the UK (and US) academic marketplace. It boasted authors such as Jeanette Winterson, Jane Rule and Kathy Acker, as well as published important critical writing from Dale and Lynne Spender, Sheila Jeffreys and Jane Root.

Many other small-scale female-run feminist enterprises followed, and the establishment of a female foothold in the publishing industry was also confirmed with the creation, in 1979, of the 'Women in Publishing' (WiP) group. Its inaugural meeting, held in an upstairs room at the Globe pub opposite Baker Street tube station, was chaired by publisher Anne McDermid and led by Liz Calder of Cape (who was also the first woman on Cape's board) and Ursula Owen of Virago. WiP would go on to publish a number of important and influential papers on the state of the publishing industry for women, most notably *Reviewing the Reviews: A Woman's Place on the Book Page* (Women in Publishing 1987) and *Twice as Many, Half as Powerful?* (Tomlinson and Colgan 1989).

The emergence of all these feminist publishing ventures meant that women in numbers were, for the first time, in control of the book production process from start to finish. Holding the power to publish was figured early on as vital to feminism, an idea set out neatly by American second-wave feminist Charlotte Bunch in words evoking Virginia Woolf, whose own Hogarth Press had uniquely given her control of her writing, from start to finish: 'controlling our words corresponds to controlling our bodies, our selves, our work, our lives' (Bunch 1982: 140). The second-wave feminist publishers emerging in the UK in the 1970s and 1980s were an important moment of feminist praxis: the very act of setting up a women-only publishing house was fundamentally political, a challenge to the history, structures and practices of an industry which had for so long been dominated by men. In the act of setting up their own businesses, feminist publishers were challenging notions of 'appropriate' female behaviour. As Carmen Callil said of Virago: 'we had to make it a success so that it could take its place in the world. And that had to be *business* success.'[5] Turning a profit was just as important as publishing political ideas. In addition, they shifted the parameters of what was considered 'publishable' by proving that there was a (considerable and eager) market for literature written by women, and also changed perceptions of women in business, with women like Callil, Dowrick and de Lanerolle demonstrating formidable prowess as entrepreneurs while challenging the domination of the publishing industry by 'gentlemen in trousers', as Callil put it (Simons 1998: 190).

Installing women at the top of the industry challenged the 'great tradition' that had shaped a canon dominated by male writers. When women began to choose the books that were produced, they did not automatically reproduce the male bias that had for so long dictated what was published, reviewed and made 'canonical'. Publisher Liz Calder sums it up:

> I'm sure there is a correlation: men and women tend to favour their own gender. When I went to Jonathan Cape in the early Eighties there were very few female authors on their list. It was always very much a male province. (Quoted by Smith 2003)

The new feminist publishers challenged this male province and began the process of making the publishing industry an arena in which women as well as men could have cultural, economic and literary authority. Their success in business terms underpinned this change.

The Books

Because publishing was a male-dominated industry, female publishers and editors were rare – although women were found in numbers in the lower-status and lower-paid ranks of the profession. Literary value was still bound up with ideas of the canon, at that time an almost exclusively male preserve. Feminist publishers launched their ventures into a highly sexist literary as well as cultural domain which, in spite of the sexual revolution of the 1960s and its supposed assault on norms of all kinds, still saw women confined to limited and limiting gender roles. Writer Hilary Mantel recalls:

> Probably young women won't realise what it was like before. The star names among women – Murdoch, Spark – were treated like honorary men. Older, less-known women writers were only to be found in tatty library editions . . . I remember a man sneering at me at a dinner party circa 1975: 'Women have no tradition'. (Cooke 2008)

Challenging the hegemony of the literary canon was thus one of second-wave feminism's most urgent tasks. Kate Millett's (1969) book *Sexual Politics* was one of the first to undertake this task, followed a year later by Germaine Greer's *The Female Eunuch* (1970). Both set out an excoriating critique of the male bias in literature and the canon, using literary analysis to show the confinement of women in culture, economics, politics and elsewhere, and pointing out the hypocrisy and bias of the 'great tradition' set out by literary men such as Matthew Arnold and F. R. Leavis:

> Dr Leavis believed that he could identify a woman writer by her style, even though necessarily all that she wrote must have been a parody of some man's superior achievement. After all, there was not much wrong with Virginia Woolf except that she was a woman. (Greer 1970: 104)

These texts were a starting point for the new field of feminist literary criticism. Elaine Showalter, one of the second wave's most important feminist literary critics, wrote that 'the very term "feminine", applied to literature, has been a pejorative' and had led to the side-lining and devaluing of all women's writing, and consequently its canonical exclusion (Showalter 1971: 859). In order to prove this point, feminist critics – and, crucially, publishers – went about tracking down historical writing by women and introducing it to a contemporary audience.

Second-wave feminist publishers were central to this task. They were a crucial part of the community in which feminist literary criticism emerged, with connections already established between writers such as Greer and Showalter and feminist publishers such as Marsha Rowe, one of Virago's founding members. She recalls of Greer: 'I had gone to her launch party and also I was friends with musicians and the bass player lived in her house and was always saying, "well, she's up there typing away at this book" and no one quite knew what it was going to be.'[6] Virago and The Women's Press spearheaded the effort to (re)invest women's historical writing with value. Carmen Callil's experience as a PR executive within a mainstream publishing house – Penguin – had introduced her to the idea of reprint series, and she had noted the success of Penguin's classics both in terms of numbers of books sold and subsequent profit generated. She was keen to emulate this for her fledgling publishing venture. She was also aware of the work of feminist critic Sheila Rowbotham, a close friend of Virago's founding director Ursula Owen and a member of Virago's Advisory Group, who had published *Hidden from History* (1973) in which she concluded that the literary records of women's lives had been deliberately obscured in order to denigrate the legacy of women writers as well as perpetuate a patriarchal view of the world more generally. These two factors led Virago to establish its reprint library in 1977 – an idea that was quickly developed into the Virago Modern Classics series. Elaine Showalter's (1982) *A Literature of Their Own*, published by Virago in the same year that the Classics list was launched, acted as a critical guide to the texts that were included in the early years of the series.

The Virago Modern Classics set out to challenge the literary bias that had consigned so many women authors – even those who had been a critical and commercial success in their day – to obscurity. The first book in the series was *Frost in May* by Antonia White (1978), originally published in 1933 and reprinted by Virago on 15 July 1978. Callil chose the books in the series based on a desire to 'reveal, and indeed celebrate, the range of female achievement in fiction, and to bury, if possible forever, the notion that women novelists are confined to this ghetto of the imagination' (Callil 1980: 1001).

Virago went on to publish hundreds of 'lost' British women writers and the Classics list became, perhaps, its most famous hallmark. As well as having a huge impact in terms of re-shaping literary history, and expanding the canon to include many more women's voices, the series proved that 'there was rich value to be had from writing which stood outside the Great Tradition of English Literature,' and thus provided concrete evidence of the flimsiness of arguments that women had not written in the past, or not written well (*Sunday Times* 29 January 1984).

The Modern Classics were, then, a deliberate attempt to counter the historical pejoration and suppression of women's writing. The rapid expansion of the series during Virago's first decade was down to a combination of this political intent as well as financial necessity: 'the importance given to reprints is partly a reflection of their aim to establish the existence of women's culture more firmly in the public mind, and partly a financial consideration, since not only do reprints cost less than publishing a book for the first time, they also sell fairly well' (Cadman et al. 1981: 31). The Modern Classics made commercial as well as political sense.

The Women's Press similarly set out to republish historical women's writing. It launched with a reprint of Jane Austen's *Love and Friendship* (originally published in 1922, more than a century after the author's death), and this was followed by Kate Chopin's *The Awakening* (originally published in the US in 1899), Sylvia Townsend Warner's *Lolly Willowes* (originally published in 1926) and Elizabeth Barrett Browning's *Aurora Leigh* (originally published in 1857). As other second-wave feminist publishers began to emerge in the late 1970s and early 1980s – although none achieved the size and scale of Virago and The Women's Press – they too reissued out-of-print women's fiction alongside new writing that theorised the importance of such historical works. Taken together, these reprints helped to reinsert women writers into literary history.

The boundaries of the traditional canon thus came under fire during the second wave, with reprinted literature from feminist publishers being at the centre of these debates. Inclusion within the canon was important, since it denoted influence and authority, as literary critic John Sutherland explains: 'there are, in fact, few better preservatives of a novel and its author's fame than to be set for examination, to be judged as suitable research material by the committees which approve PhD topics, or to be approached by an American university offering the curatorship of manuscript material' (Sutherland 1981: 11). Feminist literary critics set about tackling the absence of women in the canon, with early texts such as *Rediscovery: 300 Years of Stories By and About Women*, published by The Women's Press (Dinesen 1981). The Women's Press also went on to publish a number of important texts by Dale Spender who made the theme of women's canonical exclusion central to her work. Her sister Lynne developed a theory of literary 'gatekeeping' to show that inclusion in the canon was policed by gatekeepers whose interests were served by the texts that they granted entry (Spender 1983). In other words, men kept women out in order to devalue their work and maintain the idea that only men could write excellent literature.

Redressing women's long history of exclusion from the canon, and therefore from literary value, is one of second-wave feminism's success stories (while the battle for so many of its other goals – equal pay, an end to male violence, shared caregiving, equality of opportunity – continues). Feminist publishers were vital to this effort because, crucially, they made women's writing from the past publicly known. They helped change the literary landscape for good, expanding the canon so that it included a fairer representation of the writing of great female authors alongside men. And debates about the formulation of the canon intersected with debates around gender, since what had been considered 'canonical' had often historically been overlain with ideas of what constituted 'acceptable' subjects and themes for male and female authors. Writer Margaret Atwood (1982: 199) puts it thus: 'when a man writes about things like doing the dishes, it's realism; when a woman does, it's an unfortunate feminine genetic limitation.' The interrogation of the concept of gender was therefore central to feminist explorations of the ways and means by which women were oppressed and contained, both in cultural and literary terms.

Defining gender was a crucial starting point for second-wave feminism. Feminist critics looked back to texts such as Simone de Beauvoir's *The Second Sex* (1949) and Robert Stoller's *Sex and Gender* (1968) to articulate gender as a set of cultural assumptions and psychological attributes, distinct from the anatomical differences between women and men. In the UK, texts such as Ann Oakley's *Sex, Gender and Society* (1972) further made clear this separation of sex from gender, providing a basis from which women could examine the ways in which specific roles and behaviours had been ascribed to them. In particular, the imposition of the roles of housewife, mother and passive sexual object as idealised forms of 'femininity' were identified and then critiqued. Second-wave feminist publishers played a key part in disseminating new theoretical material that deconstructed these three ideals and explored new formulations of female identity.

Women as Housewives

US writer Betty Friedan had problematised women's assignation to the role of housewife in her text *The Feminine Mystique*. She wrote: 'in 1960 the problem that has no name burst like a boil through the image of the happy American housewife . . . the actual unhappiness of the American housewife was suddenly being reported' (Freidan 1963: 19). Freidan's work sparked a raft of polemic – much of it published by the new feminist publishing houses – that similarly showed how the imposition of the housewife ideal was destructive and damaging to women.

Ann Oakley, whose text *Housewife* (1974) underpinned these early second-wave critiques, was a member of the advisory group that fed into the selection process for Virago's first published lists which, unsurprisingly, featured a number of texts that examined the housewife role. Indeed, in Virago's first title *Fenwomen*, author Mary Chamberlain (1975: 46–7) notes the difficulties faced by women in conforming to cultural expectations that they will not perform paid work, as well as the limited opportunities available to women who *do* seek work outside the home: 'I realised I couldn't get in anywhere. There didn't seem to be any firm round here that would take in girls. I gave the idea up then . . . I was ever so disappointed when I wrote round the firms and they said they didn't take girls.' Virago followed up this text with other explorations of the housewife figure, including Carol Adams and Rae Laurikietis's *The Gender Trap* (1976) and Joyce Nicholson's *What Society Does to Girls* (1977), while The Women's Press republished Cicely Hamilton's *Marriage As a Trade* (1981, originally published in 1909), a very early exploration of the confinements put on women by the cultural expectation that they will be wives and mothers.

Women-only publishers also played a crucial role in disseminating fiction that challenged the imposition of the housewife ideal. Margaret Atwood's (1980) first novel *The Edible Woman*, written in 1965 and published in 1969 in the US before its UK publication by Virago, is an example of this. Atwood explicitly acknowledges the influence of critical writing such as *The Feminine Mystique* in her introduction to the 1980 UK edition: 'like many at the time I'd read Betty Friedan and Simone de Beauvoir behind locked doors' (Atwood 1980: 8). *The Edible Woman* takes on gendered stereotypes to show how they strangle women's potential and suffocate their desires, using protagonist Marian to evoke Freidan's 'problem that has no name', and show how she loses her sense of self in the face of her impending nuptials and the assumption of the roles of housewife and mother. Her fiancé's pleasure in the prospect of marriage is presented in stark contrast to Marian's desperate gloom, reflecting the fate that befell the 'happily married woman': confinement to the domestic, private sphere of the home in contrast to her husband's public life.

Other writers followed Atwood's example, exploring in fictional terms the figure of the housewife and the problematic imposition of an idealised 'femininity' based on woman's confinement to private, domestic pursuits. In its early years, Virago published fiction writing from authors such as Zoe Fairbairns (1979) and Diane Harpwood (1981), who both wrote about the stultifying effect on women's lives of their containment within the home. The Women's Press also offered Joan Barfoot (1980) and Joyce Reiser Kornblatt's (1982) stories about women trapped within, or trying desperately to escape from, unhappy marriages that limit their sense of self. Onlywomen similarly published Eve Croft's (1981) story centred on a woman's failure to embody the housewife ideal. These books together created a new genre of writing that figured, and refigured, the housewife and began to chronicle the effect of its idealisation on women's psychological, emotional and physical well-being.

Women as Mothers

This critique of the housewife was interlinked with the problematisation of women's role as mothers. Germaine Greer argued early on that 'there is no reason, except the moral prejudice that women who do not have children are shirking a responsibility, why all women should consider themselves bound to breed. A woman who has a child is not then automatically committed to bringing it up' (Greer 1970: 262–3). Combating these dual assumptions – that women ought to bear children and then ought to be mainly responsible for raising them – became a central tenet of second-wave politics. It was of course therefore a central theme in much of the material printed by the feminist publishing houses throughout their early years.

In 1970 Shulamith Firestone published *The Dialectic of Sex: The Case for Feminist Revolution* in which she argued that reproduction itself was the basis of women's unequal status with men, and imagined a future in which conception and gestation occur artificially, free from the human body, as the end goal of feminism: 'not just the elimination of male *privilege* but of the sex *distinction* itself: genital differences between human beings would no longer matter culturally' (Firestone 1970: 11–12). Firestone's radical thesis was hugely important to the Women's Liberation Movement as it gained momentum in the 1970s, and was reprinted by The Women's Press in 1979 – Rosalind Delmar, a member of the Virago Advisory Group, wrote the introduction to the UK edition. The feminist publishers were an important outlet for other critical writing that examined the issue of motherhood. Adrienne Rich's *Of Woman Born*, published in 1977 by Virago, set up the idea that motherhood was a cultural imposition, and that cultural, psychological and medical discourses of motherhood had naturalised the link between the female sex and childcare: 'the patriarchal institution of motherhood is not the "human condition" any more than rape, prostitution, and slavery are' (Rich 1977: 34). Virago gave Rich the platform from which to explore ideas that would be hugely influential to second-wave feminism: such texts challenged the mainstream industry's 'gatekeeping' role in determining what was deemed publishable (or profitable), while also playing an active role in shaping the goals and challenges of second-wave feminism itself.

After Rich, Virago also printed (or reprinted) other texts that examined the impact and import of women's role as mother: for example, Margaret Llewellyn Davies' *Maternity* (1979), Tillie Olsen's *Silences* (1984), Catherine Itzin's *Splitting Up: Single Parent Liberation* (1984) and Denise Riley's *War in the Nursery: Theories of the Child and Mother* (1983). At The Women's Press, the feminist interrogation of the role of motherhood was evidenced most obviously by the publication of *Why Children?*, co-edited by Stephanie Dowrick and Sibyl Grundberg (1980: 10), who argued that '"Choice" is meaningless in a society which refuses to accept that responsibility for the care of children should be shared by all who benefit from their existence'. A great deal more material – both fiction and non-fiction – emerged from feminist publishers on this theme of motherhood, as the second wave situated women's oppression within the paradigm of (heteronormative) parenting models. (A Sheba reprint – *Rocking the Cradle* – explored the potential of gay parenting models to chip away at the edifice of patriarchy (Hanscombe and Forster 1982).) Stories of mothers and mothering were reimagined and retold as the second-wave publishers enabled the textual exploration and problematisation of the motherhood imperative, presenting troubling or challenging versions of the relationships between mothers and their children.

Women as Sex Objects

All this writing fed into the call for change that was articulated by the women's movement in the 1970s and 1980s, putting women-only publishing houses at the heart of feminist activism. The figuring of women as *objects* in sex, never *subjects*, was the third element in the gender category 'feminine' to come under feminist interrogation as the second wave evolved. The objectification of women's bodies was an important catalyst for the Women's Liberation Movement since, in spite of the so-called 'free love' era of the 1960s, women remained socially and psychologically constrained to one of two sexual categories – the active, desiring 'whore', or the passive, inhibited 'virgin'. Germaine Greer (1970) argued in her hugely popular text *The Female Eunuch* that one route to female empowerment was sexual promiscuity, a straightforward reclamation of the kinds of behaviours that men had historically owned (a position she subsequently recounted in her later writing). Other feminist writers similarly set out to address women's lack of sexual agency by putting them in charge of their own sexual choices, and troubling the corollary between sexual pleasure and a (hetero)sexist paradigm that always put men in charge.

Once again, the new feminist publishers were at the forefront of this exploration of female sexuality and sexual identity. They enabled literary examination of the ways in which the meaning of women's sexuality was forced onto them by patriarchal culture and then culturally policed. Virago's second published text was Nancy Friday's *My Secret Garden* (1975), a collection of women's sexual fantasies and one of the first of a new genre of feminist texts that looked closely at women's figuring of their own sexuality. Giving free expression to women's desires, as well as demystifying the female body, was figured as a crucial first step in creating a new, empowered female sexuality.

The Hite Report on Female Sexuality (Hite 1976), republished by Virago a year after Friday's text (it was originally published in the US in 1973), continued this trend, along with other 'self-help' sex texts such as Jane Mills' *Make It Happy* (1978) and Anne Hooper's *The Body Electric* (1980). Virago's Ursula Owen recalls: 'We did a sex education book called *Make It Happy* . . . sold a lot, caused a huge stir. People stood up in Parliament and said it should be removed from Dorset library, blah blah blah. You know there were masses of books doing that kind of thing. Dorset, you know! Lots of Tories.'[7] As Owen acknowledges, there was something of an outpouring of literature through which women – as writers and readers – were able to think about and better understand their sexual identities and be empowered by them. Unsurprisingly, in the sexist culture of the late 1970s and early 1980s, these books were figured (in the mainstream) as controversial and threatening, a challenge to the status quo that had long served to limit women's sexuality.

Publication of sex-positive texts was an important step in empowering women to feel free(r) to express their sexual desires and identities. Critical theory on female sexuality developed alongside these self-help texts, with one of the most urgent debates – around pornography – arising from two texts published by The Women's Press. Susan Griffin's *Pornography and Silence* (1981) and Andrea Dworkin's *Pornography: Men Possessing Women* (1981) sparked a debate around heterosexuality, representation and consent that would dominate feminist discussion for much of the 1980s and would to some extent serve to fracture the second-wave movement. Susan Brownmiller (1975: 15) had set the terms of this debate, arguing in *Against Our Will* that the threat of rape is the fundamental means by which male power is maintained: 'nothing more or less than a conscious process of intimidation by which *all men* keep *all women* in a state of fear.'

Following Brownmiller, Dworkin and Griffin posited pornography as intrinsically oppressive to women, arising within and from a heterosexual paradigm in which women *were always* subjugated by men. The Women's Press thus allied itself with a radical, separatist feminism that emerged in the latter part of the second wave as a response to women's legitimate anger at their long history of sexual oppression and subjugation. These radical ideologies which posited *all* heterosexual sex as inherently oppressive to women and advocated for a 'political lesbianism' that was not necessarily sexually defined were, however, hugely divisive for the second-wave movement.[8] Heterosexual women objected to the construction of their sexuality as innately oppressive, while lesbian women objected to the co-option of their sexual identity as a political one. Greater lesbian visibility – in both literature and culture – had been one of the second wave's positive outcomes, with lesbian lives and loves at the centre of much of the fiction and non-fiction published in its early years, again in large part by the new feminist publishing houses, in particular Onlywomen, which was dedicated to lesbian writing. Resistance to the perceived dilution of lesbian identity as a *sexual* identity – so long suppressed and denied within patriarchal culture – was therefore inevitable.

These conflicts arrested some of the momentum second-wave feminism had gathered during its early years. But they were also a (positive) consequence of a movement that had become more complex and multifaceted as it developed, moving beyond the simplistic unifying figure of 'woman' to consider and include the different perspectives of ethnicity, class, age, disability and sexuality. Black and minority ethnic women began to talk and write about the multiple oppressions of race, class and gender, as other marginalised groups of women started to describe the specificity of their oppression. These 'identity politics' debates, as they came to be known, marked the coming of age of second-wave feminism – its evolvement into what we would now call a more intersectional feminism, which included (although not without discord) more multiple and diverse representations of women's experiences.

The ubiquity of women's sexual objectification and representation as sexed bodies cut across all these different identity positions. Although, as BAME feminists such as bell hooks (1982) pointed out, black women's sexuality was more likely to be categorised as active or even bestial in contrast to white women's, the two binary categories of whore/virgin remained the only possibilities for understanding or describing female sexuality at the start of the second wave (and arguably to some extent still today). In response, female writers played a key role in imagining new constructions of female sexuality – and once again, feminist publishers were critical to the dissemination of this new literature.

Storytelling was a key element in the feminist exploration – and contestation – of women's figuring as sex objects, and so alongside the critical writing published by feminist presses, there also emerged bold new fiction that portrayed female sexuality in new ways. Novelists such as Angela Carter, Marilyn French and Marge Piercy, who began writing in the 1960s and 1970s, and Joan Riley and Jeannette Winterson in the 1980s, all created strong and subversive fictional characters who defied categorisation as sexual objects, and/or who allowed exploration of alternative constructions of sexual identity. All were published, at least initially, by feminist publishing houses.

These writers' depictions of women as sexually confident, curious or questing was in sharp contrast to the cultural ideal of submissive femininity – or its more pernicious corollary, the woman who was 'gagging for it'. In creating a space in which women could imagine and describe sexual relationships and perspectives that gave other women autonomy, feminist authors really did offer a radical challenge to the cultural as well as literary paradigms of mainstream culture. The role of the feminist publishers was thus a critical one as the second-wave feminist movement established itself in Britain: without them, women writers and the characters and concepts that they created and explained would have had no outlet or audience. They created a product and a momentum that feminism, arguably, could not have survived without.

Conclusion

Exploring the wealth of fiction and non-fiction writing that was the output of feminist publishers in the UK during the early years of the second wave is beyond the remit of this chapter. We can see, however, from the examination of some key texts and authors how central the women-only publishing phenomenon was to the women's movement in its early years. In providing an outlet for women's writing that challenged the sexist status quo, feminist publishing put itself at the heart of feminist political practice. The women at the helm of these businesses proved the market for fiction and non-fiction by female authors, helping women taking up greater space within the book business as writers as well as publishers.

Second-wave feminist publishing changed what was written, and what was read, by men as well as by women. The canon of literature was reshaped by its incorporation of women's writing from the past, excavated and republished for new audiences by the women's presses of the 1970s and 1980s – a phenomenon that continues to this day with publishers like Virago and Persephone Press. In contemporary literature, the types of stories that women wrote, who they wrote about, and how they were dealt with as writers, were all fundamentally altered by the interventions of the second-wave feminist publishing houses. We still have some way to go until women are given the same footing as men in the book business – as frequent analyses of review coverage and the gender split in publishing hierarchies show – but the route to parity was begun with the work that these women undertook through feminism's second wave. (For more on these issues, see Chapters 1 and 2.) The impact and importance of second-wave feminist publishing cannot be understated – its legacy remains in the books, and the changed book business, that it left behind.

Notes

1. Interview with Marsha Rowe, 15 July 2004.
2. Interview with Ursula Owen, 5 February 2009.
3. Anon., 'Collection: Records of The Onlywomen Press'. Genesis Project <www.londonmet.ac.uk/genesis/search/$-search-results.cfm?CCODE=1145> (last accessed on 14 January 2008).
4. Anon., 'About Sheba Feminist Press'. Maryland Institute for Technology in the Humanities <www.mith2.umd.edu/WomensStudies/ReferenceRoom/Publications/about-sheba-press.html> (last accessed on 14 July 2005) (para. 2 of 10).
5. Interview with Carmen Callil, 10 November 2004.
6. Interview with Marsha Rowe, 15 July 2004.
7. Interview with Ursula Owen, 5 February 2009.
8. The term 'political lesbianism' was coined by Adrienne Rich (1981) in her influential text *Compulsory Heterosexuality and Lesbian Existence*, in which she argued that heterosexuality was itself socially and psychologically imposed rather than a natural inclination. This essay was republished for a UK audience by Onlywomen.

Works Cited

Adams, C. and R. Laurikietis. 1976. *The Gender Trap*. London: Virago.
Angelou, M. 1984. *I Know Why the Caged Bird Sings*. London: Virago.
Athill, D. 2000. *Stet: An Editor's Life*. London: Granta.
Attallah, N. 2007. *Fulfilment and Betrayal: 1975–1995*. London: Quartet Books.
Atwood, M. 1980. *The Edible Woman*. London: Virago.
Atwood, M. ed. 1982. *Second Words: Selected Critical Prose*. Toronto: Anansi.
Barfoot, J. 1980. *Gaining Ground*. London: The Women's Press.

Brownmiller, S. 1975. *Against Our Will*. New York: Simon and Schuster.

Bunch, C. 1982. 'Feminist Journals: Writing for a Feminist Future'. In *Women in Print II: Opportunities for Women's Studies Publication in Language and Literature*. Eds J. Hartman and E. Messer-Davidow. New York: Modern Language Association of America.

Cadman, E., G. Chester and A. Pivot, eds. 1981. *Rolling Our Own: Women as Printers, Publishers and Distributors*. London: Minority Press Group.

Callil, C. 1980. 'Virago Reprints: Redressing the Balance'. *Times Literary Supplement* 12 September 1980: 1,001.

Chamberlain, M. 1975. *Fenwomen*. London: Virago.

Cooke, R. 2008. 'Taking Women Off the Shelf'. *The Guardian* 6 April 2008 <www.theguardian.com/books/2008/apr/06/fiction.features1> (last accessed 21 August 2019).

Coser, L. A., C. Kadushin and W. W. Powell. 1982. *Books: the Culture and Commerce of Publishing*. New York: Basic Books.

Croft, E. 1981. *Brainchild*. London: Onlywomen.

Davies, M. Llewellyn. 1978. *Maternity*. London: Virago.

De Beauvoir, S. 1949. *The Second Sex*. London: New English Library.

Dinesen, B., ed. 1981. *Rediscovery: 300 Years of Stories by and About Women*. London: The Women's Press.

Dowrick, S. and S. Grundberg. 1980. *Why Children?* London: The Women's Press.

Dworkin, A. 1981. *Pornography: Men Possessing Women*. London: The Women's Press.

Fairbairns, Z. 1979. *Benefits*. London: Virago.

Firestone, S. 1970. *The Dialectic of Sex: The Case for Feminist Revolution*. London: Jonathan Cape.

Friday, N. 1975. *My Secret Garden: Women's Sexual Fantasies*. London: Virago.

Friedan, B. 1963. *The Feminine Mystique*. London: Victor Gollancz.

Greer, G. 1970. *The Female Eunuch*. London: MacGibbon & Kee.

Griffin, S. 1981. *Pornography and Silence*. London: The Women's Press.

Hamilton C. 1981. *Marriage as a Trade*. London: The Women's Press.

Hanscombe, G. and J. Forster. 1982. *Rocking the Cradle*. London: Sheba.

Harpwood, D. 1981. *Tea and Tranquillisers*. London: Virago.

Hite, S. 1976. *The Hite Report on Female Sexuality*. London: Virago.

hooks, b. 1982. *Ain't I a Woman? Black Women and Feminism*. London: Pluto Press.

Hooper, A. 1980. *The Body Electric*. London: Virago.

Itzin, C. 1884. *Splitting Up: Single Parent Liberation*. London: Virago.

Millett, K. 1969. *Sexual Politics*. New York: Simon and Schuster.

Mills, J. 1978. *Make It Happy*. London: Virago.

Murray, S. 2004. *Mixed Media: Feminist Presses and Publishing Politics*. London: Pluto Press.

Nicholson, J. 1977. *What Society Does to Girls*. London: Virago.

Oakley, A. 1972. *Sex, Gender and Society*. London: Temple Smith.

Oakley, A. 1974. *Housewife*. London: Penguin.

Olsen, T. 1984. *Silences*. London: Virago.

Reiser Kornblatt, J. 1982. *Nothing to Do with Love*. London: The Women's Press.

Rich, A. 1977. *Of Woman Born*. London: Virago.

Rich, A. 1981. *Compulsory Heterosexuality and Lesbian Existence*. London: Onlywomen.

Riley, D. 1983. *War in the Nursery: Theories of the Child and Mother*. London: Virago.

Rowbotham, S. 1973. *Hidden from History: 300 Years of Women's Oppression and the Fight Against It*. London: Pluto.

Showalter, E. 1971. 'Women and the Literary Curriculum'. *College English* 32.8: 855–62.

Showalter, E. 1982. *A Literature of Their Own: British Women Novelists from Brontë to Lessing*. London: Virago.

Simons, J. 1998. 'Women, Publishing and Power'. *Writing: A Women's Business. Women, Writing and the Marketplace.* Eds J. Simons and K. Fullbrook. Manchester: Manchester University Press. 183–91.

Smith, D. 2003. 'Women Celebrate a Turn-up for the Books'. *Observer* 21 September 2003 <www.theguardian.com/uk/2003/sep/21/bookerprize2003.awardsandprizes> (last accessed 23 August 2019).

Spender, L. 1983. *Intruders on the Rights of Men: Women's Unpublished Heritage.* London: Pandora.

Stoller, R. 1968. *Sex and Gender: On the Development of Masculinity and Femininity.* London: Hogarth Press.

Sutherland, J. 1981. *Bestsellers: Popular Fiction of the 1970s.* London: Routledge and Kegan Paul.

Tomlinson, F. and F. Colgan. 1989. *Twice as Many, Half as Powerful? Report of a Survey into the Employment of Women in the United Kingdom Book Publishing Industry.* London: Polytechnic of North London/Women in Publishing.

Walker, A. 1983. *The Color Purple.* London: The Women's Press.

White, A. 1978. *Frost in May.* London: Virago.

Women in Publishing. 1987. *Reviewing the Reviews: A Woman's Place on the Book Page.* London: Journeyman Press.

4

Producing a Lesbian Magazine at the Turn of the Twenty-First Century

Georgina Turner

Introduction

Lesbian periodicals – those publications explicitly written by and addressed to women-loving women – are very much a twentieth-century phenomenon. With some notable exceptions, however, before the 1990s, lesbian periodicals around the world were typically relatively short-lived, made on a low budget and published irregularly, or sometimes a combination of all three. Their activities may have been curtailed by government diktat (such as at the collapse of the Weimar Republic, for instance, which brought about the demise of the German lesbian magazine *Die Freundin*, 1924–33), or hampered by the less overt hostility that discourages advertisers and makes reaching readers beyond local networks more difficult (as was the case for even some of the US's most successful lesbian newsletters between the 1940s and 1970s). Sometimes it was national politics that set or slowed the pace of development of a lesbian periodical press, as in Portugal and Japan; often, it was internal politics that saw lesbian publishing collectives implode.

In the UK, the call in Lord Wolfenden's report of 1957 for the decriminalisation of sex acts between consenting adult men was indicative of a shift in the discussion around homosexuality. The formation of the Homosexual Law Reform Society and the charitable Albany Trust in 1958 was symbolic of new-found empowerment as the debate moved beyond notions of *curing* homosexuality. It was an article about lesbianism in a 1963 issue of *Twentieth Century* magazine devoted to 'morals' that prompted the founding of Britain's first lesbian newsletter; having been outraged by the article's description of lesbians as 'ludicrous' and 'pitiable', Esmé Langley felt that 'it would do many people a power of good to be able to contribute to their own magazine' (*Arena Three* Spring 1964: 6).

Arena Three was dogged by financial difficulties – publicising the magazine was still fraught with difficulty and women often lacked financial autonomy – and it eventually ran out of money in 1970. In any case, the political landscape was changing, and prominent members of the UK's newly formed Gay Liberation Front were keen to take the magazine in a more explicitly activist direction, relaunching as *Sappho* in 1972. Under this title, the magazine lasted until 1981 when, once again, finances were exhausted (for a more detailed discussion of *Arena Three*, see Chapter 10).

Globally, the lesbian and gay press has shared a mutually constitutive relationship with broader gay and lesbian movements and, whatever the local contingencies, the

1990s is widely acknowledged as a – perhaps *the* – key period for both. Certainly, the changes at that time had an unprecedented commercial element, and even if the 'pink pound' was a distinctly male currency,[1] a handful of lesbian magazines appeared in the early 1990s in Britain. Among them was *DIVA*, in 1994. More than twenty-five years later, it is the only British news-stand lesbian title still in print – although, in common with so many commercial print magazines in the twenty-first century, that status is constantly under review.

The precarity of the contemporary magazine landscape is frequently discussed, yet the academic literature continues more often than not to focus on texts rather than production (Boston and Duffy 2016). There are several excellent studies of magazine culture (see Gough-Yates (2003), for instance), yet still much of what we read about magazine editing and editorship comes in the form of the generalised accounts designed for student textbooks; the biographies of renowned, typically American, editors (e.g. Lewis 2014); and insights shared by editors invited to speak to journalism students (e.g. Navasky and Cornog 2012). As Jolliffe (1995: 51) has noted, these often anecdotal, partial accounts tend to tell us more about individuals than editorial cultures. Jolliffe (1995: 60) further suggests that interviews are an imperfect approach compared to observational and ethnographic research; even an open and cooperative participant is unlikely to recount day-to-day practices without error or amnesia (Moeran 2006). Nonetheless, this chapter, which comes out of a long-running project looking at *DIVA* and its role in constructing a subcultural community (see Turner forthcoming), draws on interviews conducted between 2008 and 2018 with key members of *DIVA* staff, including its four editors. Carrie Lyell (editor), Louise Carolin (deputy editor) and Kim Watson (media and marketing director) were in post when they were interviewed in 2008 and 2009; Frances Williams (founding editor), Gillian Rodgerson (her successor) and Jane Czyzselska (third editor) were not.[2]

Like Freeman (2011), I argue that there is value in allowing these women to tell the story of producing *DIVA*, even as I acknowledge that this kind of oral history makes for a negotiated, co-created account. Staff experiences of magazine production are rare (Soronen 2018) and valuable (Greenberg 2015). The rate of change in digitised media industries demands that scholars pay greater attention to production cultures (Boston and Duffy 2016), even in those sectors about which we already know most; what we know about lesbian periodicals, and about Britain's lesbian press in particular, remains extremely limited. Thus, in this chapter I use these interview accounts to discuss the creation of *DIVA*, how its staff have steered the magazine through social and industrial change, and the challenges that they face moving into the future.

Launch

There is not the scope in this chapter to examine some of the precursors to, and the full extent of, the 1990s commodification of lesbian and gay culture (see Turner 2009 for more detail in the context of *DIVA*'s launch), but two media-specific developments must be noted. First, a number of magazines made by and for women-loving women appeared from 1989 onwards. Although geography inevitably played a part in the accessibility of these publications, women in London would have little trouble getting hold of *Quim* (an erotic magazine, 1989), *Lesbian London* (more akin to the older style newsletters, 1991), *Shebang* (freely distributed imprint from the publisher of *The Pink Paper*, 1992), and *Lip* (founded after a split in the group behind *Lesbian London*, 1993). Second, women-loving women were more visible in mainstream media than ever before, in the form of 'lesbian chic': the 'lipstick lesbian', a (hetero) sexualised, hyperfeminine image of Sapphic desire, was everywhere, from the cover of *Vanity Fair* to the soap-opera suburbia of Channel 4's *Brookside*.

The founder of *DIVA*, Frances Williams, was sceptical of both: when we spoke, she described lesbian chic as 'bollocks', and Kim Watson, *DIVA*'s media and marketing manager for more than twenty-two years, recalled that when the topic of *Shebang* came up in the office, Williams called it 'Shebollocks'. Both women recognised how crucial these things were to *DIVA*'s beginning, however. Williams was working as a news reporter on *Gay Times*, founded by Millivres Prowler Ltd in 1984. The proliferation of titles aimed at lesbians and bisexual women signalled the health of a market that had previously been disregarded as commercially unviable (if it had been considered at all). Even in the era of the 'pink pound', lesbians were stereotyped as having minimal disposable incomes and less interest in consumption than gay men, but Williams believed in the importance of economic power in the fight for equality.

'The company saw its primary audience as gay men,' she said, 'but since lesbians and gay men were now working and playing together more, there was more scope to argue the case. I wanted women to get a fair share of the capital and the resources; I wanted to start something'. Rival publication *Shebang* printed 5,000 copies of its first issue in December 1992, all of which disappeared – 'we under printed, for sure', said Watson, who was still working on *Shebang* at this point – and went up to 7,000 copies for its second issue in February 1993, after which it was published every two months. Williams used this to pitch for *DIVA* in purely commercial terms. Even then, Williams said, the Millivres chairman Chris Graham-Bell was sceptical about launching into this market.

The first issue was, essentially, a pilot: Williams had six months to put something together, alongside her work on *Gay Times*. She was determined that *DIVA*, like *Shebang*, would be a bimonthly publication before long, making the most of this cultural moment. 'There was so much happening, so much to write about', she said. 'It was a public duty to make it happen really. I was in this privileged position at Millivres where I could persuade them to have a go.' The taste for lesbian iconography in mainstream media meant that the launch issue attracted the attention of publications with far bigger and broader audiences. '*DIVA* wouldn't have succeeded, or had the awareness it had at the time it launched, had it not been for this obsession with lipstick lesbians all over the media', Watson said.

All 8,000 copies of *DIVA*'s first issue sold out. On the cover, a short-haired model looks straight down the camera at the reader from beneath a shimmering gold hat, complete with a peacock feather (see Plate 4). Wearing heavy Timberland boots, black lacy underwear and an oversized white shirt that she appears to be removing, her squatting position highlights a slim but muscular physique. Although some readers recalled being put off by the confident – verging on confrontational – stance (Turner forthcoming), Williams was pleased with the assertive cover image. Bright red coverlines promised features on the famous *Brookside* kiss, lesbians in comedy and literature, the Manchester scene, and lesbian fiction. 'I wanted it to be pleasurable, I wanted it to be attractive; I wanted it to be aspirational', Williams said, 'I was keen that it should have all the elements of a professional magazine'. The limited budget available to her at the time meant that this was never possible, although she fondly recalled an 'amateurish' fashion shoot in the first issue: 'There were never enough resources put into it, it was always just me trying to cobble it all together.' In its first two years in print, on average around sixty per cent of the pages in *DIVA* were printed in black and white to save money. 'It doesn't look very glossy now, but it was definitely thought of as glossy then', said Louise Carolin, who worked on the magazine from 1995, later becoming deputy editor; 'that in itself was quite controversial'. American lesbian magazines *Curve* (1990–) and *Girlfriends* (1993–2006) had been seen as incredibly slick compared to British efforts. Here, 'lesbians had never had a commercial magazine that they could go into the newsagent and buy before', Carolin told me. 'I remember people being quite suspicious of it', she recalled. 'Readers' expectations at the time would have been that a lesbian magazine would be pretty political, heavy going. Analytical. The idea of a glossy lesbian version of a conventional women's magazine was just off the edge of the planet.' There were of course women who were desperate to see lesbian culture with high production values and a sense of fun – they just were not used to seeing it. Something so overtly mainstream in its ambitions ran counter to the more artisanal, 'authentic' ideals of the 1970s lesbian feminist movement.

Williams, though, 'was very concerned that [*DIVA*] shouldn't be too wordy' – she was reluctant to compromise her idea of writing for readers who were as interested in gossip and popular culture as they were in politics and activism. Dubious about notions of 'community', Williams was uncomfortable with the burden of representation that such notions carried. '*DIVA* was a magazine you could buy if you wanted to and not buy if you didn't like it', she said of her original stance. But *DIVA* was soon the only lesbian magazine still running, and almost certainly the only one available to buy outside of London. 'You'd get letters from people who hadn't seen anything like it, and you thought, "Bloody hell, this is having an impact"', Williams remembered. 'For so long, lesbians had been treated as outsiders; the magazine was there to welcome them home to a warm, acceptable, public, visible place.' The use of spatial metaphor, as well as the notion of home, is something that recurs in the magazine; readers were not coming out, they were *coming in*.

DIVA's Role

In her editor's letter in the first issue, Frances Williams wrote that *DIVA* would 'put lesbians centre stage', celebrating lesbians in all their 'splendid diversity' (*DIVA* March 1994: 4). Throughout more than twenty-five years in print, a vocabulary of celebration and inclusivity has been shared by all of the magazine's editors. Asked to articulate *DIVA*'s purpose, each of Williams's successors echoed her words. According to Gillian Rodgerson, editor from 1997–2004, 'the most important role that *DIVA* could play was to make women feel happy and positive about their sexual choices' and 'to make people feel really terrific about being lesbians'. Jane Czyzselska, editor from 2004–17, listed *DIVA*'s jobs as 'connecting each other, making ourselves feel celebrated and seen, and that we matter'.

Carrie Lyell, editor since 2017, reflected on the consistency of *DIVA*'s message, even as so much else changed. '[*DIVA*] has changed massively: aesthetically, politically it's different, but at its core, it shouldn't ever make someone feel bad', she said. 'It should definitely be a voice that stands up in the sea of bullshit that women have to encounter on a daily basis. Even if it's no longer about protest, I think there's still a value in having a celebration of who we are and of our culture.' The question of who 'we' are presents its own difficulties (see below), but what has been consistent in *DIVA* is its unflinching representation and normalisation of sex and sexual attraction between women. This might, after all, be as much as its readers have in common.

'I did not ever want *DIVA* to ignore that', Rodgerson said, 'Sex is an important part of lesbian identity'. Throughout her tenure, there were readers who complained about adverts for companies selling sex toys, including ads featuring women modelling strap-ons; the images made *DIVA* a risky magazine to leave on the coffee table. Rodgerson felt that it was an essential part of their remit, especially before the Internet and mobile devices had put retailers (and pornography) into readers' back pockets. Readers in isolated, rural locations might need visual aids to know how to wear a harness.

Czyzselska took over in 2004 and found the debate ongoing but continued to promote sexual content. Among the magazine's themed issues was an annual 'sex issue', which always saw a significant spike in sales – so much so that there were two *DIVA* sex issues in some years. 'I was really proud of what we did there', Czyzselska said, 'because prior to the web really taking off, there were so few resources for lesbian sex that weren't porn made for heterosexual men. We needed to make sure that *DIVA* was a resource in that way.' Although the magazine was not always (or even, as time went on, often) overtly didactic, its staff recognised the role *DIVA* could play in the (sexual) subcultural capital of readers. In some ways, items such as 'The A–Z of Lesbian Sex' featuring women of all ages, races, and abilities, as well as reports from *DIVA*'s annual reader sex survey, epitomised the magazine: validating, informative and representative of the diversity of lesbian and bisexual experience. Set against the selectivity (and fictions) of lesbian chic, this was the kind of content that marked *DIVA* out as an authentic, insider voice: a magazine written by, for and about women-loving women. Set against the skinny, white, ableist consumerism of mainstream women's magazines, this kind of content allowed many, although not all, readers to see themselves as they really were.

DIVA was also where some women – again, particularly those living outside of major cities – saw *other* women-loving women for the first time, coming to realise that they were not alone or perverse in their same-sex attraction. Women who read *DIVA* in the mid-1990s recalled flipping first to the personal ads, often not intending to contact anyone, but simply to see whether there were other queer women nearby – seeing that there were was an affirmational thrill (Turner forthcoming). Its community-building function is probably what defines twentieth-century LGBTQ+ periodical publishing, especially so in the case of lesbian and bisexual populations, which were at times less visible, even in urban centres with dedicated gay spaces and organisations (Brandão and Machado 2016; Freeman 2011; Livia 2002; Koller 2008; Milillo 2008; Vigiletti 2015).

At the turn of the twenty-first century, Rodgerson was insistent that *DIVA* include a directory of small ads, at least in part because of its service to the community, connecting readers with gay-run or gay-friendly services whose advertising budgets often were not large enough to buy whole or half-page adverts. This strategy, which is akin to earlier lesbian feminist ethics of consumption (Murray 2007), meant that, in 2004, the directory made up around 20 per cent of the magazine. By 2019, it was only two pages (of 100), and although at least one of the advertisers remained the same (Shirley's Removals, established 1988), the ads were now full colour and occupied a quarter or half a page, rather than a black-and-white box at one-sixteenth of a page.

DIVA has undoubtedly become more commercial and less political – in Louise Carolin's own words, by 2007 it had gone 'from *New Statesman* to *New Woman*'.[3] Czyzselska, editor from 2004–17, was sometimes criticised for this, and remembered being asked about it when appearing on BBC Woman's Hour around the time of *DIVA*'s 200th issue. 'I said, "Well, I think it depends on what you mean by political: is it political with a capital P or a small p?" What is "political" changes?' As Czyzselska also pointed out, *DIVA*'s very existence is political, still the lone queer women's title, and its success in attracting bigger advertisers, has been crucial to its survival as such. In fact, it is being the lone queer title that now presents perhaps *DIVA*'s biggest 'political' issue: who is it for?

Defining the Audience

Whatever the criticisms of Jane Czyzselska's tenure (and it is worth noting that they tended to come from those of a more radical feminist persuasion), the magazine became noticeably and deliberately more inclusive of bisexual and trans women, as well as queer women of colour, both as subjects and as writers. It would be a mistake to infer from this that *DIVA* had in the past excluded such readers, because both Gillian Rodgerson and Frances Williams spoke of an imagined readership that included *any* women who were attracted to women. Yet how successfully, explicitly and consistently the magazine addressed them might be contested; certainly, readers argued about it (see Turner 2015).

In 2002, *DIVA*'s strapline changed from 'Lesbian life and style' to the less rigid 'For the lesbian in you'. In an ideal world, Rodgerson said, such identification of the audience would not be necessary, but politically, it was 'very important to have the word "lesbian" on the cover in great big letters for the non-gay world'. For Czyzselska, prejudice within LGBTQ+ community was a more pressing concern, and she made it her focus to challenge the enduring whiteness of much (mainstream) queer media and the stigma that was still attached to gender non-conformity, even among lesbians and bisexual women. For Czyzselska's successor, the fluidity of sex, gender and sexuality in the late 2010s means that any definition of *DIVA*'s readership feels provisional or contingent.

According to Carrie Lyell:

> It's actually quite difficult to market to a lesbian and bisexual audience when fewer and fewer people are inclined to identify themselves in that way . . . So how do you do it? You could say that you're a magazine for women-loving women, but because lots of readers don't identify as women anymore, that's a completely changing, shifting thing. It's something that we're trying to keep ahead of, but it's impossible. Sometimes I'm like, this is madness; who thought [a magazine for LGBTQ+ readers] was a good idea? But it's been almost 25 years, so I think we're getting something right, if we're still around.

Although we tend to speak of 'women's magazines' as if it were a single category, individual titles typically have a more specialised target readership, differentiated from others by age, professional or income status, and so on. Without alternative LGBTQ+ targeted rivals, however, such a deliberate narrowing of its readership might carry commercial and political risks for *DIVA* – even if the result is to chase the impossible: attempting to please everyone. It is a dilemma that other LGBTQ+ magazines have faced (Freeman 2011) and can feel like never quite satisfying anyone. 'It's hard when people say, "there's never anything in *DIVA* for me, I don't see myself"', Louise Carolin said. 'The problem is it's a 100-page magazine and we have to try and squish as many different kinds of lesbians into each issue as we possibly can.' To begin with, Williams had little idea who actually read *DIVA*, only her own sense of the kind of woman that she was writing for – someone like her. By the end of her own tenure, thanks to annual surveys, Rodgerson had a very precise idea of the average *DIVA* reader: a 36-year-old public sector worker in a long-term relationship. She and Carolin also recognised, however, that their readers might be in their teens or their eighties, and anywhere in between. That kind of range has remained the case, even as *DIVA* began to write more consciously for a younger market in the 2000s.

Age is one of the most obvious ways in which mainstream women's magazines differentiate their target readership, and the difficulty of doing so has often been at the root of reader complaints in *DIVA*'s case. Czyzselska said:

> We would get countless emails or letters from older readers who say there was too much about young people and it wasn't relevant to them, and then we would get countless emails from younger people saying there's too much about old people.

Like Rodgerson and Williams before her, she 'learnt pretty early on that you can't please all the lesbians all the time'.

As online publishing exploded, the editorial team discussed creating bespoke publications, utilising digital platforms to reach younger readers in particular. Branding content for 'young' and 'senior' audiences risked making assumptions about readers, however, and as Lyell pointed out, it is not always the case that older readers are the ones to prefer print products. Perhaps the most considerable obstacle to such targeted content was the cost involved. *DIVA* had always been put together by a very small team of staffers, without the kind of budget that would permit the necessary audience research for such radical editorial change.

Finances

The demise of *Lesbian London* came about one month after the first issue of *DIVA* launched in April 1994, but it had long been signposted in editorials about the group's financial struggles. Since unmarried women historically lacked financial autonomy, and stereotypes of lesbians as being either poor or politically opposed to consumption made them far less appealing to advertisers than gay men, it has often been the case that lesbian periodicals relied on volunteer labour or a single benefactor (Brandão and Machedo 2016; Freeman 2011). *DIVA*'s key commercial advantage was that it had the backing of Millivres and could share *Gay Times*'s distribution network (Turner 2009), but that meant that readers often assumed that *DIVA* had more money than it did. 'A wing and a prayer'; 'a shoestring'; 'magicking things out of nowhere'; 'a tiny budget': all of its editors have described *DIVA*'s finances in these sorts of terms, with Gillian Rodgerson remembering losing sleep if she made plans that went over budget. It may have looked a league apart from the likes of *Lesbian London*, but *DIVA* was for a long time also a labour of love.

Both Rodgerson and Frances Williams continued to write for *Gay Times* while editing *DIVA*; the two publications shared a layout designer, and Kim Watson worked on the business side. Williams recalled that day to day she was often the only person in the office working on *DIVA*. Rodgerson described a close working relationship with Watson and the designer Elizabeth Grant, as the three juggled various roles, including a books imprint (Rodgerson's responsibility) from the late 1990s. 'The three of us, we had a great time', Rodgerson said. Others in the office would contribute to conversations about, for instance, cover designs (with *DIVA* being nicknamed 'dykes in vests again'), but 'it was our baby'. Given her time over again, Rodgerson would have involved many more contributors than she did, but convincing writers to work for the low rates that DIVA offered was not always easy. Much of the content was produced in-house, and copyediting had to be light touch by necessity.

Under Jane Czyzselska the team remained small but planning for each issue, which was still largely month to month, was drawn out to a two-month cycle. With themed issues – the sex issue, LGBTQ+ history month, and so on – it could be longer, and since the change of ownership in 2016, every issue of *DIVA* has been planned around a theme. 'It makes commissioning much easier', according to Lyell, who relies on a range of contributors and heads up a team of three full-time members of editorial staff – the largest full-time equivalent staff that the magazine has ever had. In addition, 'we have someone who works on social media when she can, we've got a sub-editor who works remotely, we've got a designer, we've got two or three in our commercial team'. Soliciting advertising can also be made easier with a theme to work around (Moeran 2006).

When Williams launched *DIVA*, she was frustrated by the fact that women often assumed that the magazine was free and would baulk at paying a cover price. The stereotypical idea of lesbians having low incomes and minimal purchasing power was, she said, pervasive at that time, and for the same reason, Watson struggled to convince the companies advertising in *Gay Times* that they would see a return from spots in *DIVA*. According to Watson, speaking to mainstream (that is, non-LGBTQ+) advertisers on behalf of a lesbian publication was like 'banging our heads against a brick wall'. Unsurprisingly, the magazine concentrated on generating as much revenue as possible from subscriptions. Even to the end of the 2000s, 'you would get people saying, "oh, this is a family brand"', said Czyzselska. 'There was an assumption that somehow there was something sleazy about appearing in a lesbian publication.'

The size of its budget had an impact on what *DIVA* could do, and several members of staff spoke of the magazine being the poor relation in the Millivres stable, but editors also recall being given relative editorial freedom. Censorship, or the threat of it, was more likely to come as pressure from distributors, particularly over cover images, and some retailers continue to stock *DIVA* on the top shelf as if it were pornography – having to ask a member of staff to reach for a copy can be the difference between a reader buying that issue or not. *DIVA*'s availability in newsagents and supermarkets has been vital to its visibility and success, which has meant that negotiation with distributors or retailers made jittery by partial nudity or sexual references was sometimes necessary. It was usually a case of Watson speaking to distributors to point out that the front covers of many lifestyle magazines featured partial nudity, although Czyzselska did recall once having to rush back to the office to re-design a cover deemed too sexual by a supermarket section head.

Under the ownership of Twin Media Group Limited, which bought *DIVA* in 2016, the magazine's news-stand visibility appears to be changing – a number of readers suggest that it is becoming harder to get hold of in the sorts of city centre and transport hub locations in which they previously found it (Turner forthcoming). As an independent publication, income streams are different. Selling advertising space has become easier since unhitching from *Gay Times*; the commercial team has a tighter, more coherent brief. Extensions of the *DIVA* brand (see below) have also helped to make it more marketable to companies with large advertising and sponsorship budgets. Although some older readers have questioned *DIVA*'s relationship with corporate organisations such as Barclays, Lyell has remained firm on *DIVA*'s long-standing policy of avoiding advertisers selling self-doubt. 'The money that you might get from [an advert for weight loss] is not worth the readers that you will lose as a result.'

While Lyell suggested that tight control of *DIVA*'s spending might be partly explained by the need to preserve jobs at Millivres post-2008, the fact that Twin Media is a woman-owned and run company had made a difference. After years in search of the 'magic formula' for best-selling covers, the editor has said that she can now take more risks. 'We can put someone on the cover who is a bit older', she suggested. 'Before, we would have been told "no, you can't do that, this is not going to sell". Now, Linda [Riley, *DIVA*'s publisher] will say that representation is more important, so if we take a little bit of a hit that month, it's okay.' Lyell agreed that 'print is scary' these days (see below), but on the whole, she felt liberated by the move out of a larger publishing house.

Coping with Change

DIVA launched on the crest of a wave of popular cultural interest in lesbian lifestyles and iconography while, at the same time, LGBTQ+ people in 1990s Britain routinely experienced prejudice and violence, and were fighting for the removal of homophobic legislation such as Section 28.[4] In the 2000s, legislative change began to offer protections for LGBTQ+ people from hate crime and discrimination in the workplace, and to recognise same-sex unions,[5] while on television six seasons of *The L Word* (and others in its wake) put women-loving women in front of unprecedented audiences.[6] Neither media visibility nor social acceptance is unproblematic for LGBTQ+ people in Britain now, but clearly much has changed for *DIVA* and its (potential) readers.

For some, often younger people, sexuality and gender identity are no longer the issues that they once were. 'It's like are you left-handed or right-handed; it's just not relevant to them', Carrie Lyell said. 'And when you're living in that sort of environment, it's difficult to see why it's important to have a magazine like *DIVA*.' For those who have not encountered widespread social hostility in relation to their sexuality, its importance to their sense of self may be reduced. Over time *DIVA* has become more of a celebrity magazine, both by virtue of the fact that there are now more openly LGBTQ+ women in the public eye and because of demand from younger readers;

however, it continues to tackle issues around access and discrimination. Lyell has said that she and other members of staff have a very personal connection to the magazine, having found it as they came to terms with their sexuality. Nevertheless, to be 'post-gay' (Ghaziani 2011) is a privilege not enjoyed uniformly across the UK, let alone globally, and Lyell says that '*DIVA* might be the only place that you feel normal for a little while'.

Again, the question of what it means to be 'political' arises. *DIVA* in the 1990s was arguably more instantly recognisable as a subcultural text, even if it aspired to mainstream production values; today, it is recognisably a commercial consumer magazine, aspiring to stay relevant to the subcultural community it serves.[7] 'I jokingly said the other day, "if we rolled back a few rights then maybe *DIVA* would be more exciting, more political"', said Lyell, 'but, you know, I absolutely don't wish that. I think we've gotten to the point we are at in large part thanks to magazines like *DIVA*'.

According to Kim Watson, the two key challenges that *DIVA* has faced since the turn of the twenty-first century practically coincided: the first, the end of *The L Word*, is specific to a magazine such as *DIVA*, which between 2005 and 2009 put stars of the show on its cover no fewer than fourteen times – and many of these remain their biggest selling issues. With more potential cover stars than ever before, *DIVA* gave the March 2019 cover to the original *L Word* cast in anticipation of a series reboot. The two share a symbiotic relationship: the show marked a significant watershed in women-loving women representation on screen, and its stars made themselves available to magazines such as *DIVA* to a previously unprecedented degree. The second challenge is the same that every publisher has faced since the late 1990s: the impact of the Internet and digital technologies (Ellonen and Johansson 2015). Media consumption – habits, devices and so on – has altered radically, at the same time as producers of, and platforms for, content proliferated. Legacy publishers recognised that they needed to 'do digital', but often did not know how best to.

'It felt scary, I think', Czyzselska said, 'It took us a while to get our heads around how we could make it work for us'. Making digital a part of their existing business model risked self-cannibalisation (Bilton 2014). 'We had to make sure that we weren't giving too much away on different platforms or producing things that were detrimental to our newsstand sales. It was hard to figure out how to make that work.' *DIVA* launched a digital edition via Zinio in 2007, with tablet and mobile versions for new Apple devices following in 2008. By 2013, *DIVA*'s print sales were in decline, but the digital edition was growing by around 20 per cent year on year. The relaunched website was attracting 60,000 visitors per month, and the magazine's social media presence was growing. In 2019, Twin Media put *DIVA*'s monthly online audience at just over 130,000, with 26,000 subscribing to an e-newsletter; follower numbers on Twitter had grown from 30,000 to around 70,000. *DIVA*'s digital edition, available a week before the print magazine, was downloaded on average 30,000 times each month. Of 25,000 subscribers, 70 per cent took the print edition of *DIVA*.

'We've seen a bit of a resurgence in print', Lyell said, 'We've seen some of our subscribers move from digital back to print. It's not comparable to five or ten years ago, but it's enough to give us a bit of hope that print isn't dead.' Although it is difficult to establish why subscribers have returned to print, Lyell has suggested that younger readers like to be able to use pages from the magazine as posters, as well as having a copy 'to keep'. This is a rather marked contrast to those readers who smuggled copies home in the 1990s, and often had to find ways to get the magazine out of the house again in order to dispose of it.

Into the Future

Digitalisation has had a huge impact on print media, with magazines and newspapers predicted to continue suffering falls in print circulation and advertising revenue (print and online) globally. For *DIVA*, one particular consequence of an increasingly digital landscape was the level of competition for readers that it produced – the proliferating voices on websites such as *After Ellen* and *Autostraddle* brought competition, but also relieved some of the burden of representation that *DIVA* had been carrying. In 2018, that enabled the magazine to take an explicitly trans-inclusive stance, knowing that readers could go elsewhere if that upset them, but believing that competition generally helps to avoid complacency. 'People might not be buying other magazines', Lyell said, 'but they will be going somewhere else if they don't like what we're doing. It's good to keep up and see what they're doing and think, "okay, can we take a bit of that, can we learn from what they're doing?" It helps keep us fresh.' The inclusion of queer women in mainstream (typically heterosexual) women's magazines might also be seen to pose a threat to *DIVA* but, as Czyzselska said, usually 'they write about lesbians as "them", [rather than] "us"'.

Survival for magazines in the twenty-first century requires a different kind of business model – one that is 'digital first' when it comes to content (Bilton 2014), and in which the emphasis is on opportunities for publishers to reach consumers rather than the media through which that happens. Twin Media – *DIVA*'s publisher since 2016 – has prioritised *DIVA*'s brand profile, with events such as annual awards ceremonies, various UK Pride events, literary festivals and a music festival taking place under the *DIVA* banner, as well as a weekly *DIVA Radio* show. The additional income is, according to Lyell, what keeps the magazine in print. Like all of her predecessors, as well as current and former readers (Turner forthcoming), Lyell and her employers are passionate about *DIVA*'s continued existence: 'We will do everything that we can to keep it in print, but we have to also be aware that things are changing, and it's tough.'

Conclusion

Some of what has had an impact on *DIVA* since 1994 is the same as other, less niche, more mainstream print magazines have had to contend with: the swift and radical transformation brought about by the Internet and digital technologies. Magazines must satisfy two audiences – readers and advertisers (Marchand 1985) – and digitalisation has fundamentally altered both. For *DIVA*, so too has the socio-political climate, the culture and the notions of culture in and with which it and its readers exist. While empirical insights into magazine production are relatively few in the literature, the specificities of LGBTQ+ publishing over any significant period are rarely explored; both are gaps that I hope this chapter helps to address.

Notes

1. 'Pink pound' is a term used to refer to the purchasing power of the LGBTQ+ community, which was recognised in the mid-1980s and widely exploited throughout the 1990s. Gay men living in households with two good incomes and no children were particular targets.
2. Kim Watson was interviewed again in 2018, having left her role at *DIVA* in 2016.
3. *New Woman* was a UK women's magazine published by Bauer until its closure in 2008.
4. Section 28 of the Local Government Act 1988 prevented local authorities in England, Wales and Scotland from promoting (the acceptability of) homosexuality. It was not repealed until 2003.
5. These changes were put in place by the Criminal Justice Act 2003, the Equality Act 2010, the Civil Partnership Act 2004 and the Marriage (Same-Sex Couples) Act 2013.
6. *The L Word* (2004–9) was a US series from the Showtime network, focusing on the lives of a group of West Hollywood queer women.
7. Describing an LGBTQ+ community has long been problematic and insufficient, and its applicability seems only to become more contentious. I use it in this chapter largely as a shorthand reference, acknowledging its shortcomings but mindful that *DIVA* readers do constitute some kind of imagined community, insofar as they are a community of practice.

Works Cited

Bilton, J. 2014. 'Publishing in the Digital Age'. *Inside Magazine Publishing*. Eds D. Stam and A. Scott. Abingdon: Routledge. 226–47.

Boston, N. and B. E. Duffy. 2016. '"What actually matters": Identity, Individualisation, and Aspiration in the Work of Glossy Magazine Production'. *Production Studies, The Sequel! Cultural Studies of Global Media Industries*. Eds M. Banks, B. Conor and V. Mayer. London: Routledge. 213–26.

Brandão, A. M. and T. C. Machado. 2016. 'Organa: The First Portuguese Lesbian Magazine'. *Journal of Homosexuality* 63.4: 575–99.

Ellonen, H. K. and A. Johansson. 2015. 'Magazine Management: Publishing as a Business'. *The Routledge Handbook of Magazine Research*. Eds D. Abrahamson and M. R. Prior-Miller. Abingdon: Routledge, 197–208.

Freeman, B. 2011. '"A Public Sense of Ourselves": Communication and Community-Building in Canada's *LesbiaNews/LNews*, 1989–98'. *Westminster Papers in Communication and Culture* 8.3: 143–67.

Ghaziani, A. 2011. 'Post-Gay Collective Identity Construction'. *Social Problems* 58.1: 99–125.

Gough-Yates, A. 2003. *Understanding Women's Magazines. Publishing, Markets, and Readerships*. London: Routledge.

Greenberg, S. 2015. 'Editorial Roles and Practices. Exploring the Creative Enterprise'. *The Routledge Handbook of Magazine Research*. Eds D. Abrahamson and M. R. Prior-Miller. Abingdon: Routledge. 168–78.

Jolliffe, L. 1995. 'Research Review: Magazine Editors and Editing Practices'. *The American Magazine: Research Perspectives and Prospects*. Ed. D. Abrahamson. Ames: Iowa State University Press. 51–71.

Koller, V. 2008. 'CEOs and "working gals": The Textual Representation and Cognitive Conceptualisation of Businesswomen in Different Discourse Communities'. *Gender and Language Research Methodologies*. Eds K. Harrington, L. Litosseliti, H. Sauntson and J. Sutherland. Basingstoke: Palgrave Macmillan. 211–26.

Lewis, E. 2014. *The Man from Essence: Creating a Magazine for Black Women*. London: Atria Books.

Livia, A. 2002. '*Camionneuses s'abstenir*: Lesbian Community Creation Through the Personals'. *Language and Sexuality: Contesting Meaning in Theory and Practice*. Eds K. Campbell-Kibler, R. J. Podesva, S. J. Roberts and A. Wong. Stanford: CSLI Publications. 190–207.

Marchand, R. 1985. *Advertising the American Dream: Making Way for Modernity, 1920–1940*. Berkeley, CA: University of California Press.

Milillo, D. 2008. 'Sexuality Sells: A Content Analysis of Lesbian and Heterosexual Women's Bodies in Magazine Advertisements'. *Journal of Lesbian Studies* 12.4: 381–92.

Moeran, B. 2006. 'More Than Just a Fashion Magazine'. *Current Sociology* 54.5: 725–44.

Murray, H. 2007. 'Free for All Lesbians: Lesbian Cultural Production and Consumption in the United States during the 1970s'. *Journal of the History of Sexuality* 15.2: 251–75.

Navasky, V. S. and E. Cornog, eds. 2012. *The Art of Making Magazines: On Being an Editor and Other Views From the Industry*. New York: Columbia University Press.

Soronen, A. 2018. 'Emotional Labour in Magazine Work'. *Journalism Practice* 12.3: 290–307.

Turner, G. 2009. 'Catching the Wave: Britain's Lesbian Publishing Goes Commercial'. *Journalism Studies* 10.6: 769–88.

Turner, G. 2015. '"A Real Lesbian Wouldn't Touch a Bisexual with a Bargepole": Contesting Boundaries in the Construction of Collective Identity'. *Critical Discourse Studies* 12.2: 139–62.

Turner, G. Forthcoming. *Lesbian Magazine Discourse: Constructing a Subculture*. London: Bloomsbury.

Vigiletti, E. 2015. 'Normalizing the "Variant" in *The Ladder*, America's Second Lesbian Magazine, 1956–63'. *Frontiers: A Journal of Women Studies* 36.2: 47–71.

5

'Hey, here's the new way': Young Women's Magazines in Times of the Web 3.0

Laura Favaro

Introduction

If you wanted to find out about being a woman, you read a woman's magazine. There was nothing else, there wasn't the Internet.

(Founders of *The Vagenda* feminist blog, Baxter and Cosslett 2016)

Part of consumer publishing, women's magazines are an important locus of normative ideas about femininity. Since as far back as the late seventeenth century, they have been articulating a combination of continuity and change in response to wider shifts, cultures and sensibilities (Ballaster et al. 1991). Nowadays the industry offers a large array of publications, aiming to cover different stages of women's lives. For instance, there are titles for pre-teen girls (e.g. *Go Girl*), the '20-something girl' (e.g. *The Debrief*) and 'women aged 50 and over' (e.g. *Yours*). The range of magazines targeting the female population can also be categorised in terms of sub-genres. These can be broadly divided into: the weeklies, which span from fashion (e.g. *Look*) and celebrity gossip and news (e.g. *In Touch*) to 'real-life'-centred publications (e.g. *Chat*); and the monthlies, which include specific-interest titles (e.g. *Good Housekeeping*); and add the 'glossies'. These focus on lifestyle, beauty and fashion to differing degrees (e.g. *Cosmopolitan*, *Glamour* and *Elle*, respectively). From the mid-2000s the hybridised 'weekly glossies' such as *Grazia* have also been competing in the market. But since around that time, the industry has been facing a much more powerful contender for women's attention: the Internet, a great source of opportunities not just to access but to create and distribute media content, as well as to communicate and interact with others. Nonetheless, and against widespread prognostications, the huge popularity of the Internet has not entailed the demise of the women's magazine. While print circulation is declining, an online model is catapulting the reach of publications, especially those directed at younger generations.

This chapter aims to empirically document and critically analyse the changing and evolving form of young women's magazines in the Internet era, with a particular focus on the more recent period of a web that is social as well as mobile. While the label Web 2.0 (also 'social web') is still commonly used, innovations in the 2010s, many of which were set into motion by the release of the iPhone in 2007, have arguably brought about a generational transition into a Web 3.0 (Cabage and Zhang 2013). Using as case studies the UK web versions of the well-established titles *Cosmopolitan*, *Elle* and *Glamour*, as well as the successful online-only *SoFeminine* and *The Debrief*, this chapter maps key moments, challenges and developments pertaining to a range of issues with regard to text, production and readers. To that end, I draw on a heterogeneous body of data, generated by a larger research project on these media (Favaro 2017a): thirty-three interviews with producers,[1] as well as editorial texts, user-generated content, magazine public communications, trade press and news reports on the sector. In addition to the changes and challenges brought about by the Internet, the larger study was concerned with representations of gender, sexuality and intimate relationships, along with the ways in which women's magazines relate to – and reconfigure – feminism. These concerns are reflected in the present chapter, which is structured according to two key sets of distinct but interconnected challenges. The first pertains to the transition to the online environment in general, and adapting to the social-mobile web in particular. The second set of challenges, which have again prompted a number of transformations, involves the recent reinvigorated interest in feminist ideas that has been particularly notable among young women and in the media, especially online.

Adapting to New Technologies

> The media landscape has changed hugely in the last decade. The growth of digital has been huge and standing still isn't an option.
>
> Lauren Holleyoake, Publisher of Bauer Media UK's *The Debrief* (in Gavin 2015)

In the late 1990s what was then often referred to as 'cyberspace' began to be firmly configured as a place for commerce and audience commodification. The female user emerged as the new ideal consumer, a yet to be exploited goldmine for marketers, particularly appealing in light of the increasing number of women heading online and their recently achieved independent spending power (Sadowska 2002). By stressing communicative and community-building aspects, the market began to position the Internet as offering women novel opportunities to express their femininity (Gustafson 2002). Typically, however, the dot-com industries promoted segregated commercial online spaces for women. The quintessential model emerging out of this process was the 'affinity portal' or 'community site'. These niche-oriented products, such as US-based *iVillage.com*, offered message boards or discussion forums, shopping possibilities and editorial content resembling women's magazines.

The rising popularity of the Internet among women and the growing availability of similar free and updated content online threatened the already fiercely competitive women's magazine print market. In a survival effort, from the early 2000s publishers began to embrace the web (Duffy 2013a). After a number of different attempts, success was found in developing content specifically for online delivery, as well as in those strategies based around immediacy and reader interactivity, which often meant the incorporation of community spaces, notably discussion forums. As such, the web extensions of well-established print publications and the newer online-only titles became increasingly similar. In addition to their mutual influence, this similarity is due to media mergers and acquisitions. Further blurring boundaries, in the 2010s a number of magazines have shifted to an online-only model (e.g. *InStyle* in 2016) or to a digital-first strategy (e.g. *Glamour* in 2017). Moreover, large publishing houses are creating new digital-only titles. *The Debrief* by Bauer Media offers one notable example. Launched in 2014 and promising a 'modern take on traditional content pillars', this 'digital lifestyle brand aimed at constantly connected ABC1 female millennials', developed a model built on using native advertising[2] and real-time data to inform the content and social strategies, the delivery of content that moves seamlessly across platforms '24/7' and a 'tone & approach [which] offer a real representation of her life' (*The Debrief* 2017). Heralded as 'the cutting edge of publishing' (Cottrell 2014), *The Debrief* has won a number of industry awards, and has influenced transformations in the well-established larger publications like *Cosmopolitan*. Some of the central features or shifts that these newer models involve are briefly examined in the two subsections that follow.

From Months to Moments

> The shadow of the falling circulation is always over you . . . There are lots of experiments . . . Much of our conversations at work are about 'what should we do with the website' . . . It's sort of a slightly anxious time, waiting and seeing if this is going to work.
>
> But then it's heartening when things like *The Debrief* spring up because we could all go work there. So it's a real up and down. Something will fold and then something new will launch and figures are down in print and then they're back up on the website. So it's a really up and down, a real roller coaster. It's a precarious industry to work in. I know lots of people who've been made redundant, whose magazines have folded. (*Glamour* professional)

The 2008 global financial crisis and long subsequent recession prompted the closure of many women's magazines. On top of this, 'the Internet age' has entailed an 'unprecedented period of disruption' (Champion 2015: 24), with commentators even describing circulation figures as a 'bloodbath' and urging 'female readers to flick as well as click – or lose women's mags forever' (Fairley 2013). But the sector has once more demonstrated its remarkable resilience, positioning itself in recent years at the forefront of the emergent publishing paradigm, marked by an urge to 'find a sustainable solution to the digital challenge' (Champion 2015: 35). In a move characteristic of media convergence culture, publications – newly re-positioned as *brands* – are embracing cross-platform and trans-media strategies (Duffy 2013a). For instance: 'ELLE continues to be cutting-edge in its approach to modern publishing. It produces content across all platforms – print, digital, mobile and social media' (e.g. note the number of sites to 'follow' in Figure 5.1).[3] The expansion reaches far beyond the printed periodical to penetrate non-media realms, as the other Hearst publication in the sample boasts: 'Our highly successful events – from career masterclasses at Cosmopolitan Self Made to fashion catwalks at Cosmopolitan #Fashfest – take Cosmopolitan off the page or screen and into readers' lives'.[4] Further to 'magazine media 360', a new content strategy was central to the approach that Hearst calls 'months to moments', which steered the company's transition from print to 'compete in the mobile digital world' (Edwards 2015). While in the mid-2000s the digital strategy revolved around creating 'evergreen content that was perfectly optimized for search',[5] ten years later there is strong focus on 'high-frequency, newsy content optimized for social' (Edwards 2015).

Figure 5.1 *Cosmopolitan.co.uk* homepage, 2019 (partial screenshot).

Epitomising the 'months to moments' approach, *The New Glamour* is based on a mobile-first, social-first approach, with the website declaring on its announcement in 2017: 'wherever our readers are, we'll be there'. Similarly, the editor-in-chief of *Cosmopolitan US* enthusiastically explained in 2014:

> Brands need to be where the audience is and *Cosmo* readers live much of their life with their phone strapped to their hand. We are there with them as they wake up, as they go through their day and as they recharge at night. And when they need to unplug, they reach for the magazine. (Joanna Coles in Alderman 2014)

A third case in point is *Elle*'s current self-definition: 'a 24-hour fashion media brand'. One article titled 'Hearst's President of Digital on How to Win the New Media Wars' also emphasises as part of 'the mindset of a modern editor' the understanding that 'Today, media is participatory' (Troy Young in Kansara 2017) – that is, readers are now 'users' that are interactive and connected, who distribute and even produce content. This poses opportunities as well as challenges for media companies and their commercial partners, and in what follows I discuss one example of attempts by magazines to both control and benefit from young women's *produsage*.[6]

From Readers to Produsers

In the past few years social media analytics have become a crucial element of corporate communications, such as the media packs women's magazines prepare for advertisers, where figures for 'followers', 'likes', 'shares' and more can be seen regarding a growing number of platforms. Also standing out in this new discursive terrain is the absence of the term 'community', so central until recently, and usually linked to forums or discussion boards – a facility that also began to disappear in the early 2010s. One evident reason pertains to technological developments and the attendant changing patterns of use. In the context of a rapidly changing media(e)scape, forums are perceived as 'relics of web 1.0' (Davis Jones 2015). After all, glossies are built on the eternal quest for the new and upcoming, not to mention the most profitable – and social media referral has surfaced as the principal driver of traffic to the sites. This has been boosted by the rise in use of mobile devices, particularly smartphones. As the publisher of *The Debrief* put it: 'That girl is glued to her mobile phone . . . A clear opportunity emerged' (Holleyoake in Gavin 2015). Exemplifying recent shifts, the 2014 redesign of the *Cosmopolitan* website (see Figure 5.1) removed the forums which had been in operation for eight years and were very popular (see Figure 5.2), a move which, the magazine claimed, was 'developed

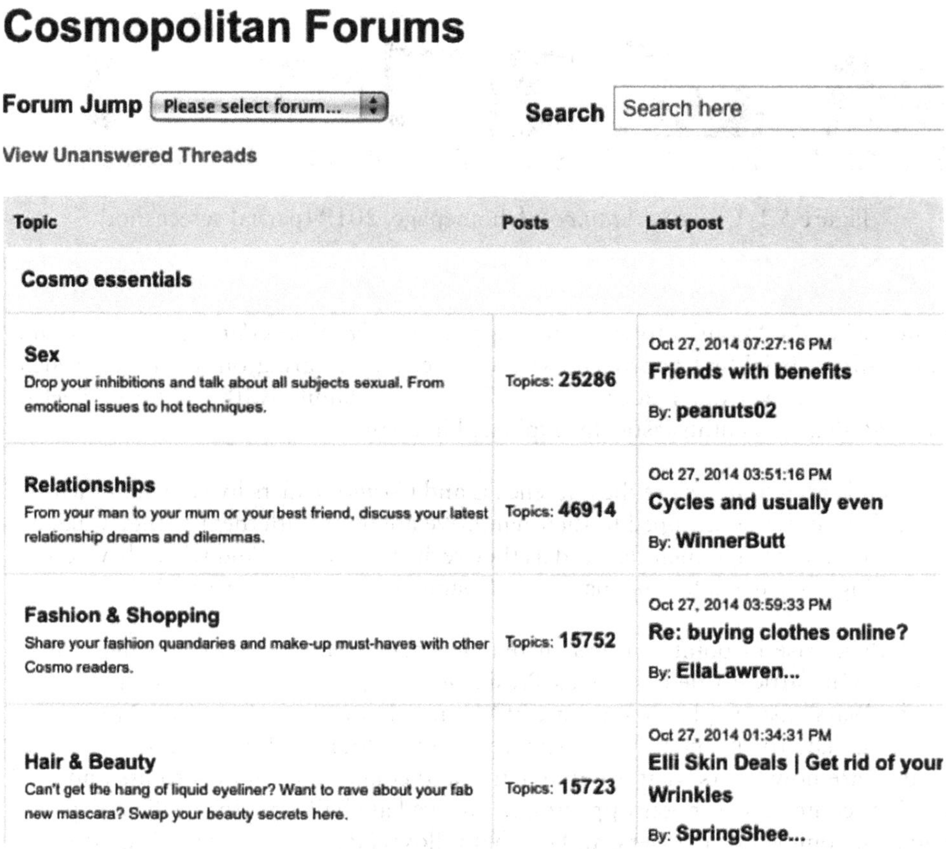

Figure 5.2 Forum homepage, *Cosmopolitan.co.uk*, 2014 (partial screenshot).

to prioritise mobile and social media'.[7] This contrasts with the seemingly celebratory observation a few years earlier by Louise Court, the then *Cosmopolitan UK* editor-in-chief: 'We have a really vibrant community on the website' (in Saner 2010). Indeed, the community was vibrant, and so the users lamented the forum closure as 'sad news' and an important loss, particularly because of the general consensus that 'these boards were a great source of advice and opinion' together with belonging and support. What is more: 'Our forum was a lifeline for so many of us'.[8]

Elsewhere I have examined in detail the decision by magazines to close the forums and instead promote social media platforms, tracing multiple determinants, and raising questions about power and exploitation (García-Favaro 2016). I have shown how, in part, this changing model of reader interaction responds to a corporate doctrine of control over young women's discourse. Notably, forum conversations about sex were deemed too explicit or even inappropriate by the editorial teams, in addition to causing conflict with advertisers. User-generated content intensifies what is already a complicated terrain for these publications: negotiating changing cultural sensibilities and practices concerning sex and sexuality with the boundaries of 'taste' and 'respectability' demanded by beauty and fashion brands. Closing the forums also responded to a desire to silence the critique expressed by users about the commodities and services of commercial partners, as well as editorial content. Respective examples from the *Cosmopolitan* forums are: 'Topshop is terrible quality' and '*Cosmopolitan* is a money-making franchise that exploits women for sales. Rather read something that will expand your mind, instead of poorly written drivel on celebs and bad sex tips'. As a features editor told me: 'we wanted the conversations to be in line with our content'. Magazine professionals explained that social media platforms facilitate the delimitation of user participation to commenting on individual editorial features, thus restricting 'conversations' to the topics selected by publications rather than those put forward by users themselves. Furthermore, under the new system, young women are 'put to work' for – more intense forms of – capital accumulation. In other words, the move away from anonymous discussion forums and towards social networking sites is part of a corporate effort to outsource new modalities of free consumer labour (Terranova 2000). For example, platforms such as Twitter and Facebook expand the 'work of being watched' (Andrejevic 2002) by enabling unprecedented levels of corporate surveillance, which smartphones further intensify in ever-increasing ways. Central too is outsourcing free, constantly targeted distribution work, in so far as publishers now rely on users 'sharing' across their networks the magazine content, which is now often doubly branded due to native advertising. It is for these reasons that, rather than communities, magazines are selling advertisers 'hyper-connected', 'addicted' and 'obsessed' social media followers who 'are plugged-in 24 hours a day, 7 days a week' (*The Debrief* 2014). Information packs also promise a reader who is an 'active social sharer', indeed 'sharing her life online is part of her daily ritual' (*The Debrief* 2016).

Despite their efforts, however, media companies are not in full control of young women's discourse online, nor can they fully ignore critique or the greater level of corporate accountability resulting from current internet technologies, cultures and uses. On the contrary, the ongoing collective and individual undertakings of female users are effectively forcing publications to modify at least some of their representational and discursive practices. In our interviews, industry insiders asserted that women's magazines are 'being . . . a lot more careful' in light of 'your younger audience', which is highly internet 'literate' and 'discerning'. This means that 'The moment you stop putting content that doesn't feel legitimate to them anymore they just won't visit you'. Moreover, as a digital health editor emphasised, social media 'has given people a platform to be able to say "this content doesn't work for me . . . so I'm gonna create my own or I'm going to yell at you about yours"'. Namely, dissatisfied users are potential content-producing competitors, as well as possible 'PR disasters' for companies, as described by another editor:

> Online is an interesting place because it's so youth-led and because the reader is so Internet literate, so the moment you start putting stuff that doesn't feel genuine online you'll be called out on Twitter, and there'll be some sort of PR disaster for you and probably the advertiser as well.

Particularly threatening for women's magazines are 'prominent feminist, female social media users', who can start a 'Twitter war' or 'social media trial'. Repeatedly mentioned in this sense was *The Vagenda*. Launched in 2012 by two young female journalists with experience in the industry, the blog (later developed as a book) defined itself as 'a big "we call bullshit" on the mainstream women's press'.[9] Holly Baxter and Rhiannon Cosslett (2016) additionally spoke of a platform for young women to 'tell their stories . . . without it being curated by some capitalist entity'. In the interviews with women's magazine producers the blog was repeatedly described as a 'rant' and 'mean', a 'violent attack' and 'quite scathing', as well as misguided, 'patronising towards' and even 'anti-women'. There were also, however, a number of expressions of sympathy towards the feminist intervention, and most interviewees conceded that *The Vagenda* had an impact on the sector, becoming 'a voice in the head' and leading producers to 'self-censor and check themselves'. Both these patterned responses were vividly captured in the words of a content director:

> The thing about *The Vagenda* is they've got a point. A lot of the content that they criticise is rubbish and should be criticised. I think overall they've been a force for good because you will – if you're in a features meeting and you're talking about a rubbish idea, there is a voice in your head going, 'well, what are *The Vagenda* going to say about this?' . . . It's the voice in your head going, 'this is not a good idea really'.

More generally, according to the producers of young women's magazines, this landscape where readers-turned-users, and (feminist) women in general, are speaking back is leading to 'more of an egalitarian approach to producing content', and is the reason why 'these magazines are starting at least online to approach subjects that their brand would not previously have touched'. It is to these editorial transformations, these adaptations to new ideas, that I now turn.

Adapting to New Ideas

> Everybody's talking about feminism at the moment. (Freelance writer, mid-20s)

Albeit with different levels of visibility and engagement, many countries in the West and beyond have in the past few years witnessed a resurgence of interest in feminism across spheres spanning from civil society to the corporate world. One notable constant in an otherwise heterogeneous terrain of voices, purposes and acts is the use of digital technologies and online platforms. As Ealasaid Munro (2013: 24, 23) observed, 'the internet works both as a forum for discussion and as a route for activism', and has been key to creating a 'call-out culture', especially present on social media, where sexism or misogyny are challenged 'insofar as they appear in everyday rhetoric, advertising, film, television and literature, the media, and so on'. Certainly, the newly invigorated feminism of the 2010s has been notable for focusing in particular on issues to do with the representation or treatment of women in the media and public space, as seen in *The Vagenda* initiative or in high-profile campaigns such as 'Lose the Lads' Mags' (García-Favaro and Gill 2016). Also key to making the 'return of the F-word' (Holmes 2013) take a transnational and youthful dimension has been celebrity and popular media cultures. Here, in sharp contrast to the notions of 'pastness' and 'redundancy', the othering, repudiation and at times hostility characteristic of the deeply ingrained postfeminist sensibility (Gill 2007), in the 2010s feminism surfaced as a 'trending topic', a 'cool', youthful, stylish, fashionable and decidedly desirable, even compulsory, self-identification. 'The New Do: Calling Yourself a Feminist', announced *Glamour US* in an emblematic iteration of this in 2013 (Holmes 2013). Also epitomising the break in young women's magazines from a long period of 'self-definition as decisively post-feminist' (McRobbie 2009: 5) is *Elle*'s proclamation to be a 'game changer with regard to bringing the new feminism to young women' (Candy 2013), following its 2013 Rebranding Feminism project, which aimed to 're-brand a term that many feel has become burdened with complications and negativity' (Swerling 2013).

With Rosalind Gill, elsewhere I have demonstrated how the 'new' or 'rebranded' feminism of women's magazines becomes coterminous with the ideological work many have argued was effected by postfeminism (Favaro and Gill 2018). We have problematised the emphasis on individualism, choice and consumerism, paired with a stripped-down notion of gender equality and a compulsorily 'positive' affective tone that avoids all the complex and difficult questions that feminism as a radical theory and social movement necessarily entails. Rather, it is re-configured as a floating signifier, with few, if any, implications for political action, marked by vague injunctions to 'empower', 'celebrate' or simply 'support' women. Through a language of empowered individual choice, magazines have continued to unabashedly promote everything from diet and exercise routines to cosmetic surgery – indeed, even to commercialise a feminist identity, as seen in articles such as 'Level Up: 10 Products Every Feminist Needs' (Zisman 2017) or in talk about 'Wearable Feminism' (*SoFeminine*). With regard to how these processes of depolitisation and commodification were explained or negotiated by the producers, a senior professional at *Elle* declared the following about engagements with feminism:

> Like anything else, it is constrained by the demands of the brand to trump. We are not a charity. It will always be done in the way that is appropriate for the brand and appropriate for the advertisers . . . If you asked the question, 'is it okay to be a feminist and wear makeup?', we're going to say, 'yes, of course it is and here's some that you can buy'.

Notwithstanding several references to 'commercial bandwagon-hopping', 'tokenism' and 'just lip service', in the interviews there was still a generalised enthusiasm about feminism 'finally coming to full force' and how, therefore, 'that's a massive consideration for everyone' in the industry. One research participant from *The Debrief* celebrated in an email:

> They [women's magazines] are pretty much all outwardly feminist, or dealing with conversations about feminism, which I think is really cool. Because if they're not, then they get called out on it thanks to social media – I remember last year a celeb mag did a '10 of the grossest bikini bodies of 2014' and it got such a backlash on Twitter it was really heartening.

Producers tended to express jubilation about the idea that 'it's a very very interesting time, and exciting' due to 'the new wave of women's journalism that's happening now' in response to feminism, the Internet and what was perceived as 'cultural a backlash against women's magazines', spearheaded by *The Vagenda* – as can be seen in this conversation with another professional at *The Debrief*:

> Participant: *Grazia*, the *Cosmos*, the glossies, they're aspirational, so everyone who reads them, the idea is that are reading something like, 'I want to be like that', whereas *The Debrief* is: 'I am that, and the people that work there are that'.
>
> Laura: Do you know what pushed this change?
>
> Participant: Yes, I do. It was publications like *The Vagenda* . . . They started this whole thing that 'hang on women's magazines are not ok'. Having a photoshopped picture of a 30-year-old woman on the front cover and then going in and being like, 'You need a £2000 coat. You need all of this make-up. You need to please your man'. That's all bullshit. *The Vagenda* basically started calling out all these magazines on these points that they were not – they were basically making women feel bad about themselves, and perpetuating this thing that women should be ashamed, women should try and be better. 'You're fat, that's not good enough. You need to be thin, and pretty and perfect in every single way, and be able to afford everything.' *The Vagenda* said: 'Hang on. This is not okay.' Then, suddenly, all the women's magazines, because they're in decline anyway, because print is in decline, it was the perfect opportunity to come out and be like: 'Hey, here's the new way.'

The following subsections outline two central, closely related features of such a new way or wave in women's magazines, as suggested in the interview extract above. First, in the words of industry insiders, publications are 'trying to be more relatable, more real'. The second theme pertains to their purported attempt to 'enforce positive messages', and in particular to encourage 'young women to feel good about themselves' and 'be confident'.

From Glossy to Genuine

Real life is the way forward (staff writer, mid-20s)

The idea of an intimate media-audience relationship lies at the core of women's magazines, which have a long-standing practice of presenting themselves to readers as a friend. However, a sense of producer-consumer proximity, together with associated notions about authenticity, has become particularly central for these publications in recent years (Favaro 2017b). For example, to explain the success of the website the publisher emphasised the following: 'tone and relatability is crucial and the fact that *The Debrief* is written for these girls by these girls (no one older than 26 is in the team!) has cut through' (Holleyoake in Gavin 2015). Professionals from different titles equally pointed out in the interviews that 'the team is made up of people that are in the bracket', claiming that magazines can subsequently give 'women millennials' 'what we need and what we want'. I was likewise assured by industry insiders that this approach is ensuring that the content offers increasingly faithful reflections of 'the(ir) real world'. One repeatedly highlighted content area was that of sex and relationships. Although there were a number of critiques, ranging from 'most women's magazines are still very heteronormative' to the use of sex as 'clickbait', in general interviewees expressed enthusiasm about the proclaimed idea that 'we're making a lot of strides'.

According to producers, 'magazines are listening', and in so doing have become 'pro-women' in their approach to sex and relationships. For instance, one freelancer stated that the 'focus on how to please your man' has 'turned into "how to have the best sex of your life", which is so much more positive and feminist and it acknowledges that women have sex for sex's sake'. It was additionally explained that while the previous breakthrough, headed by *Cosmopolitan*, revolved around the 'message that women enjoy sex, and that we should be allowed to discuss sex', then 'this new step involves talking about sex in a more realistic way'. I was told that this involves a growing move from expert (e.g. psychologists) and advice-based texts (e.g. by agony aunts) to first-person accounts of experience and opinion pieces by young women. These were respectively associated with the 'serious' and 'terribly boring' content and the 'smart, funny writing' – and with being prescriptive versus 'being real'.

Women's magazine producers explained that the approach to sex and relationships online is 'a lot more tongue-in-cheek, a lot more cheeky', 'bolder' and 'braver' than in print, as suggested by *SoFeminine*'s declaration to offer 'Sex tips from the subtle to the X rated. No topic too taboo . . . Keeping it real'. Diversity in sexual and gender practices and identities was also highlighted during the interviews to illustrate how 'there is a real movement towards a better, more real, discussion about sex'. 'The *Cosmo* website introduced lesbian sex tips which is so good', said a young professional from *The Debrief*. A senior member of staff at *Elle* pointed out: 'Certainly, 5 years ago people were not writing articles about transgender rights in women's magazines'. Interviewees explained that 'the younger generation' have a more 'fluid vision of sexuality', and therefore 'it would be strange to them if we weren't including stories about different types of relationships, or experimentation, or whatever. They would be like, "okay, this isn't real".'

The web was celebrated as responding significantly better than print media to millennial audiences, as well as to *women*. Once more vividly underscoring the producer-as-consumer identity of most research participants, a writer in her mid-20s described what young women today want: 'We want entertaining stuff, we want real life, we want honest things.' Other frequently mentioned descriptors are 'realistic', 'relevant', 'accessible' and 'relatable', with participants arguing that this is the type of content that is offered online in particular. One features editor summarised the print-online media distinction in this manner: 'Print media was giving you this kind of unrealistic blue print for living, online media is designed really to make you feel like it's your friend down at the pub talking to you.' In addition to non-commercial user-generated content such as personal blogs, the viral content model pioneered by digital media company *BuzzFeed* was highlighted as having been 'a wonderful eye opener for the women's magazine industry'. With the viral content, it was explained at *SoFeminine*, the aim is 'for our audience to see pieces that they can relate to and in the most personal way possible . . . because that's what they go to their friends for'. This 'friend factor' should then trigger a 'must-share' effect and, in this sense, I was told that online 'the more genuine the article . . . the better it does, automatically'.

In other words, content perceived as 'real' or 'genuine' by audiences is the shareable content that a business model based on virality requires. As the publisher of *The Debrief* put it: 'We have to make our content shareable but really that comes down to making it relatable' (Holleyoake in Gavin 2015).

The increasing centrality of content strategies based on ideas about authenticity was additionally framed by women's magazine producers as essential 'if you don't want to alienate your younger audience' who are 'very sophisticated consumers of digital media'. More generally, for one *Elle* senior professional, 'people have become even in the last 5 years much more sophisticated/cynical about particularly print media, glossy media in particular', highlighting that 'everyone understands how constructed those images are', and going on to note 'that's due to online'. She additionally spoke about the ways in which 'around the time the Internet became very mainstream, beauty standards had just become really unattainable'. Overall, in her view, 'all those things created and continue to create an appetite for more realism and more truth telling from media' – and this includes those working in the industry, both as consumers and as producers of content. For example, a number of research participants problematised the ways in which the models that women's magazine feature 'look nothing like me or any of my friends and don't even look like themselves'. With respect to the textual content, and illustrating the extraordinary investment in 'realness' that characterises the interview data, a freelance writer in her mid-20s declared: 'Everything that I write would be from my experience or my friends' experiences, so that way, in a way, I know it's reality. I know it's happening and it's real.'

The editorial approach perceived as more relatable, honest, real or genuine partly derives from the desire of women – both outside and inside the industry – for media that is close to their life experiences, and which breaks with past practices considered to be out-dated and variously injurious. At the same time, the emphasis on 'manufacturing authenticity' in commercial culture industries is, among other things, 'symptomatic of an era of destabilized communication hierarchies, participatory media, and reality television programming' (Duffy 2013b: 132). With regard to media (also, notably, to advertising campaigns) targeting young women in particular, the current 'rhetoric of real' (Duffy 2013b) not only responds to a marketing scheme designed to survive commercially – in a manner distinctive of 'cool capitalism' (McGuigan 2009) – it also operates to neutralise dissent, by co-opting disaffection, at a moment of significant levels of engagement with feminist ideas. An intimately connected manoeuvre is the prominence accorded to body positivity and self-confidence, which shall be examined next.

From Better Selves to Self-Love

In the interviews, producers repeatedly articulated a narrative of recent positive transformation in women's magazines: 'We have changed since the 90s and the noughties'. More specifically, it was explained that, 'when we're talking about the shift in women's magazines, at the core of everything we do is . . . always trying to enforce positive messages.' Others further detailed such a shift as an emphasis on 'how to feel great about what you've got rather than what you should be having'.

Body-positive content – epitomised by calls to 'love your body' – is now a stable feature of many women's magazines and beyond, particularly on social media such as image-based Instagram. In online publications it often takes the form of tip-based list-style articles, also known as 'listicles', a popular – and highly shareable – type of digital content. Increasingly prevalent too are first-person accounts, for instance: 'I hated my body, and this is how I learned to love it' (Smith 2017). More recently, there has also been an intensified preoccupation with female self-love in general, and particularly with instructing women on how to acquire or develop self-confidence, figured as the ultimate route to empowerment, success and greater efficacy in all areas of life. Once more, in addition to the special sections and even issues of print editions (e.g. *Elle*'s January 2015 Confidence Issue), featuring prominently in online women's magazines are listicles such as '8 Ways to Love Yourself' (Editors 2014) and '8 ways to feel more confident right NOW' (Elliott 2015).

Much like 'body positivity', also often referred to as #BoPo, the recent significance accorded to confidence is located within a broader cultural movement promoting female self-esteem, self-belief and positive self-regard, which is inspired by feminist ideas, as well as largely associated with social media. A case in point is *Elle*'s '8 Body Positive Heroes You Need to Follow on Instagram', women 'trying to put a stop' to the ways that it can promote self-doubt by 'making sure insta is more IRL (in real life)' (Brewster 2019). For one *Cosmopolitan* piece called '13 Inspiring Body-Positivity Moments From 2017', 'The past year was the *ultimate* celebration of self-love' (Selzer 2017).

As is the case with feminism, the recent emphasis on self-love in women's magazines was explained by industry insiders in terms of a business strategy 'to keep up with their competitors and with online'. It is intimately linked to the turn to 'authenticity' – as evinced by the focus on images of 'real women' (for a feminist critique, see Murphy and Jackson 2011) and on 'being more accessible and representative', as a writer celebrated. Participants additionally made connections to the fact that 'we are really held to account', particularly online. Others spoke of an industry-wide understanding that 'we've made mistakes in the past', with many stressing that 'we're all just women feeling the same things everybody else is feeling'. For example, one staffer discussed how these publications 'make you feel shit about yourself, especially when you just see loads of really skinny women everywhere and they are all really amazing looking'. That is, the interview data suggests that the shift in emphasis I have labelled 'from better selves to self-love' is at least in part a response to long-standing critiques of women's magazines – for example, for promoting unrealistic beauty standards, being stubbornly 'man-pleasy' (as interviewees put it), judgemental and, ultimately, harmful for women. It is often pushed by young female professionals who sympathise with these critiques, claim to feel 'passionate and strongly about women's confidence and their self-image' and identify as feminists.

There were also, however, a number of critical accounts in the interviews, such as the valuable point about 'the love of the body issue': 'it's better than the hate the body issue but it is still wasting a lot of time talking about bodies, dissecting and obsessing', in addition to involving 'still a lot of time and energy and money'. Indeed, in magazines (and many cultural sites beyond), current incitements to self-confidence often operate ideologically to obfuscate the continued surveillance, disciplining and judgement of women's bodies, with concomitant expectations to work on their 'improvement' (Favaro 2017c). One example is the article by *SoFeminine* '10 Hacks For Instant Body Confidence', which includes instructions familiarly rooted in patriarchal norms, as well as in consumer culture: 'put on some lipstick, go the extra mile and paint your nails, shave your legs' (Shoneye 2015). Also, the accompanying image – although at first glance

Figure 5.3 '10 Hacks For Instant Body Confidence', *SoFeminine.co.uk* (partial screenshot).

seemingly featured as a celebration of 'real women' – includes a link to a 'plus size clothing' shopping site, thus defining the models in those terms. What is more, the article itself is located next to a permanent website section on cosmetic surgery (see Figure 5.3).

Besides continuing to reproduce notions of lack and failure in relation to female bodies, what has been variously referred to by feminist scholars as a market-movement for self-esteem (Banet-Weiser 2013), a 'confidence cult(ure)' (Gill and Orgad 2015) or 'confidence chic' (Favaro 2017c), adds yet more levels of work – and consumption – to the project of normative femininity. Most notably, 'confidence' has emerged as an additional requisite of the (hetero)sexiness imperative – 'Sex appeal is all about self-confidence' states plastic surgery-promoting *SoFeminine* – as well as a key part of the 'mental makeover' (*Cosmopolitan*) newly demanded of women. Informed by positive psychology, and as seen in the closely related contemporary injunctions to 'Pump Up the Positivity' (*Cosmopolitan*), this form of labour requires constant self-vigilance and effort in the application of micro-techniques aimed at cognitive and affective (re)training with regard to their bodies, their sexual relationships, their parenting, the workplace and more (Favaro and Gill 2019). Ultimately, confidence is presented as a commodity, a choice, and fundamentally both the source and solution for the problems of women and girls – thereby privatising and *psychologising* the responsibility for (cultural, political and systemic) injuries and injustices, as well as the programme required to resolve them. Indeed, it is not coincidental that, just as an interest in feminism became evident across sites and with particular luminosity among young women (Gill 2016), these gendered neoliberal technologies of self-confidence and positivity have increasingly taken centre stage in women's magazines, in popular culture generally, and much beyond (Gill and Orgad 2015).

Final Remarks

Drawing on a rich body of data, this chapter has considered young women's magazines in reference to challenges of adapting to the rise of the social-mobile web, or Web 3.0, and to 'the new cultural life of feminism' (Diffractions 2016). Although organised into distinct sections for the purposes of discussion and clarity, these phenomena are different but interrelated, working together to trigger a number of transformations in all aspects or dimensions of these publications, not least in the assumptions made about readers and (hence) the type of content produced. In the words of an industry insider:

> It's all these different things, body confidence, feminism, the Internet . . . all these things have fed into a way that journalists, and all media, have had to think about what they're saying and writing, and what assumptions they're making about their readers. (Content director, late-30s)

The chapter has identified a number of themes or shifts which collectively contribute to what, for some producers, evidences a new wave of women's magazine journalism. I have highlighted the emphasis on being present across and beyond media platforms, producing content '24/7', and adopting a 'mobile-first', 'social-first' approach. Pointing to the closure of discussion forums and the growing importance of social networking sites, I have argued that the shifting models of reader online interaction in women's magazines problematise and complicate ongoing celebrations both in the industry and in some scholarly work about an increasingly democratic media(e)scape. The chapter moved on to examine a journalistic approach that is considered to offer a more authentic reflection of the lives and interests of female millennials, and the recent significance given to their self-confidence. Both emphases are in large part a response to (popular) feminism and digital cultures, such as the online practices of 'calling-out' and blogging, involving at the same time a series of old and new problematics. Notable among these is the continued centrality of consumption, as well as the inclination to call on women to turn away from analysing their pain or struggles in relation to the systemic injustices of patriarchal capitalist societies to instead place the emphasis on inculcating a self-regulating entrepreneurial spirit directed at undergoing personal rather than structural transformations. The 'turn to authenticity' and 'confidence chic' of women's magazines, and many sites beyond, are connected to the commodification and *neoliberalisation* of feminist values and aims, and ultimately exemplify the 'politics of ambivalence' that characterise contemporary 'brand cultures' (Banet-Weiser 2012).

The chapter has shown how the talk of women's magazine producers constitutes a heterogeneous, highly contradictory, discursive landscape in which long-standing passionate attachments to the genre and deep investments in its femininities tend to coexist with critical self-reflexivity, ambivalence and ideological dilemmas – often due to an awareness of, even agreement with, feminist perspectives about gender and sexual politics. Many professionals actively work to effect change, having to negotiate opposition from other members of staff, particularly those in more senior positions. More significantly perhaps, all those involved in the production of these media face an important number of restrictions that complicate incorporating new representational practices or approaches, ranging from the very real and serious threat of 'upsetting' advertisers, the publishing house or readers, to the fast pace of the work online, and other poor working conditions. In the latter sense, I was told that: 'We are hugely under pressure, massively underpaid. You feel like your job could be lost at any given moment. That is the culture of women's magazines.'

When confronted with long-critiqued practices, women's magazine producers repeatedly expressed: 'We are not a charity'. This means, for example, that there are powerful 'commercial pressures that are pushing you to focus your reader's minds on areas of their body that might need improving'. With regard to the incorporation of elements such as 'body-positive' content, one content director offered the following considered response:

> I would still defend women's magazines in doing this stuff because it's better that you do something than nothing, but you're not – They're not the perfect vehicle for it because there are all those contradictions, and there are all these questions. (Content director, late-30s)

In spite of all the contradictions and 'questions' inherent to these mainstream consumer publications, there was a strong investment by industry insiders in the idea that 'we'll never go backwards, the Internet's changed things completely', as someone at *Cosmopolitan* celebrated with reference to the more progressive features discussed in this chapter. Yet one *Elle* professional predicted that the focus on feminism 'will go away', indicating how these media are largely 'about the new and the next' (at the same time, as a *Glamour* member of staff pointed out, 'there's a cyclical nature to women's magazines'). Certainly, since the research documented here took place, *Elle* has stopped publishing its annual special Feminism Issue. But most vividly capturing the changing nature of the field, in particular the Internet but also women's magazines, notably in the digital era, is the closure of *The Debrief*: the very publication that was put forward in the data as key to influencing the transformations that have been the foci of the present chapter. 'After four years of championing feminist issues', as a trade press article reported, the publisher decided to 'focus resources' on glossy sister brand *Grazia* (Forsdick 2018). While some commentators spoke once more of 'a perilous time for magazines' (*Eulogy* 2018), others celebrated how 'a host of other publications remain committed to doing things differently', which was taken to evidence how 'the women's magazine has undergone a radical makeover' (Aroesti and Greenwood 2018). Offering a more nuanced understanding of recent developments, this chapter has shown how the 'new way' of young women's magazines in times of the Web 3.0 is multifactorial, contradictory and, ultimately, unlikely to bring about a significant rupture from the conventions of this still inescapable feature of the cultural landscape of femininity.

Notes

1. As part of larger fieldwork (Favaro 2017a), I conducted thirty-three interviews between December 2014 and December 2015 with producers, primarily writers and editors, who worked – or had recently worked – for at least one of the selected publications (see main text). Participants were predominantly female and within the mid-20s to early-30s range in age. Almost all had a first degree, many also had postgraduate qualifications, and most were based in London. The interviews were semi-structured, lasted just over one hour on average, and took place for the most part in cafés.
2. Native advertising was described by one magazine editor as a 'much more subtle' approach where 'customers pay the publication to hide the advertising'.

3. See <www.hearst.co.uk/brands/elle>.
4. See <www.hearst.co.uk/brands/cosmopolitan>.
5. 'Evergreen' content is considered to be always relevant to the target audience.
6. Now widely used, this portmanteau was coined in 2007 by Axel Bruns (2007).
7. See <www.inpublishing.co.uk/news/articles/cosmopolitan_site_goes_mobilefirst_7807.aspx>.
8. All comments by different users on the 2014 thread 'So the forum is closing . . .' (*Cosmopolitan.co.uk*).
9. See <http://vagendamagazine.com/about/> (last accessed 12 February 2016).

Works Cited

Alderman, A. 2014. 'Hearst Magazines Digital Media Introduces New Publishing Platform'. *Hearst Corporation*, 7 September 2014 <www.hearst.com/newsroom/hearst-magazines-digital-media-introduces-new-publishing-platform> (last accessed 12 November 2019).

Andrejevic, M. 2002. 'The Work of Being Watched: Interactive Media and the Exploitation of Self-disclosure'. *Critical Studies in Media Communication* 19.2: 230–48.

Aroesti, R. and P. Greenwood. 2018. 'From Glossies to gal-dem: The Websites Revolutionising Women's Media'. *The Guardian* 1 May 2018 <www.theguardian.com/lifeandstyle/2018/may/01/from-glossies-to-gal-dem-the-websites-revolutionising-womens-media> (last accessed 12 November 2019).

Ballaster, R., M. Beetham, E. Frazer and S. Hebron. 1991. *Women's Worlds: Ideology, Femininity and Women's Magazines*. London: Palgrave Macmillan.

Banet-Weiser, S. 2012. *Authentic™: The Politics of Ambivalence in a Brand Culture*. New York: NYU Press.

Banet-Weiser, S. 2013. 'Am I Pretty or Ugly? Girls and the Market for Self-esteem'. *Girlhood Studies* 7.1: 83–101.

Baxter, H. and R. L. Cosslett. 2016. *The Vagenda Two Years On: What Has Changed?* Event at Burley Fisher Books, 4 May 2016, London.

Brewster, A. 2019. '8 Body Positive Heroes You Need to Follow on Instagram'. *Elle* 14 May 2019 <www.elle.com/uk/life-and-culture/g27341302/8-body-positive-heroes-you-need-to-follow-on-instagram/> (last accessed 27 November 2019).

Bruns, A. 2007. 'Produsage: Towards a Broader Framework for User-Led Content Creation'. Proceedings of the Sixth Association for Computing Machinery's Special Interest Group on Computer Human Interaction's Conference on Creativity and Cognition, 99–106 <http://eprints.qut.edu.au/6623/1/6623.pdf> (last accessed 16 April 2016).

Cabage, N. and S. Zhang. 2013. 'Digital Citation Web 3.0 has Begun'. *Interactions*, September–October 2013 <http://interactions.acm.org/archive/view/september-october-2013/web-3.0-has-begun> (last accessed 12 November 2019).

Candy, L. 2013. Interview with *Elle* Editor-in-Chief Lorraine Candy. Link no longer active <http://empowering.hearst.co.uk/be-inspired/inspiring-interviews/editors-interview-lorraine-candy-elle/> (last accessed 10 August 2016).

Champion, K. M. 2015. 'Experimentation and Imitation: The Journey to Elle 360'. *The Journal of Media Innovations* 2.1: 23–40.

Cottrell, C. 2014. 'From Real-Time To Any Time: Lessons in 24/7 Marketing'. *The Guardian* 20 October 2014 <www.theguardian.com/media-network/media-network-blog/2014/oct/20/content-marketing-lessons-bauer-media-debrief> (last accessed 12 November 2019).

Davis Jones, K. 2015. 'Bodybuilding Forums Are One of the Last Relics of Web 1.0'. *Vice* 27 March 2015 <www.vice.com/en_uk/article/mvxveb/bodybuilding-forums-are-one-of-the-last-relics-of-web-10-456> (last accessed 12 November 2019).

Diffractions. 2016. Issue 6 'Feminist Ghosts: The New Cultural Life of Feminism'.

Duffy, B. E. 2013a. *Remake, Remodel: Women's Magazines in the Digital Age*. Urbana-Champaign IL: University of Illinois Press.

—. 2013b. 'Manufacturing Authenticity: The Rhetoric of "Real" in Women's Magazines'. *The Communication Review*, 16.3: 132–54.

Editors. 2014. '8 Ways to Love Yourself'. *Cosmopolitan* 4 January 2014 <www.cosmopolitan.com/health-fitness/advice/g3715/ways-to-love-yourself-celebrity/> (last accessed 27 November 2019).

Edwards, D. 2015. 'Months to Moments Strategy and Plans for Future Growth'. FIPP World Congress, Toronto, Canada.

Elliott, G. 2015. '8 Ways to Feel More Confident Right NOW'. *Cosmopolitan* 5 January 2018 <www.cosmopolitan.com/uk/body/news/a32330/confidence-tips-how-to-be-confident/> (last accessed 27 November 2019).

Eulogy. 2018. 'Spotlight on . . . Magazine Closures'. 1 June 2018 <www.eulogy.co.uk/view/spotlight-on-magazine-closures/> (last accessed 12 November 2019).

Fairley, J. 2013. 'Women's Glossies: Read 'em or Lose 'em'. 21 August 2013 <www.telegraph.co.uk/women/womens-life/10257082/Womens-glossies-Read-em-or-lose-em-the-case-for-womens-magazines.html> (last accessed 12 November 2019).

Favaro, L. 2017a. 'Transnational Technologies of Gender and Mediated Intimacy'. Unpublished doctoral dissertation. City: University of London.

Favaro, L. 2017b. 'Mediating Intimacy Online: Authenticity, Magazines and Chasing the Clicks'. *Journal of Gender Studies* 26.3: 321–34.

Favaro, L. 2017c. '"Just be Confident Girls!": Confidence Chic as Neoliberal Governmentality'. *Aesthetic Labour: Rethinking Beauty Politics in Neoliberalism*. Eds A. S. Elias, R. Gill and C. Scharff. London: Palgrave Macmillan. 283–300.

Favaro, L. and R. Gill. 2018. 'Feminism Rebranded: Women's Magazines Online and "the Return of the F-word"'. *Digitos* 4: 37–65.

Favaro, L. and R. Gill. 2019. '"Pump up the Positivity": Neoliberalism, Compulsory Positivity and the Victimhood/Agency Debate'. *Re-writing Women as Victims: From Theory to Practice*. Eds M. J. Gámez Fuentes, S. Núñez Puente and E. Gómez Nicolau. London: Routledge. 153–66.

Forsdick, S. 2018. 'Lifestyle Website *The Debrief* Announces Closure After Four Years of Championing Feminist Issues'. *Press Gazette* 24 April 2018 <www.pressgazette.co.uk/womens-lifestyle-website-the-debrief-aimed-at-millennial-women-announces-closure/> (last accessed 12 November 2019).

García-Favaro, L. 2016. 'From Produsers to Shareaholics: Changing Models of Reader Interaction in Women's Online Magazines'. *tripleC: Communication, Capitalism and Critique* 14.2: 346–79.

García-Favaro, L. and R. Gill. 2016. '"Emasculation Nation has Arrived": Sexism Rearticulated in Online Responses to Lose the Lads' Mags Campaign'. *Feminist Media Studies* 16.3: 379–97.

Gavin, J. 2015. 'Engaging Millennial Women: *The Debrief* Story'. *FIPP* 3 June 2015 <www.fipp.com/news/features/engaging-millennial-women-the-debrief-story> (last accessed 17 September 2016).

Gill, R. 2007. *Gender and the Media*. Cambridge: Polity Press.

—. 2016. 'Post-postfeminism?: New Feminist Visibilities in Postfeminist Times'. *Feminist Media Studies* 16.4: 610–30.

Gill, R. and S. Orgad. 2015. 'The Confidence Cult(ure)'. *Australian Feminist Studies* 30, 86: 324–44.

Gustafson, K. E. 2002. 'Join Now, Membership is Free: Women's Web Sites and the Coding of Community'. *Women and Everyday Uses of the Internet: Agency and Identity*. Eds M. Consalvo and S. Paasonen. New York: Peter Lang. 168–88.

Holmes, A. 2013. 'The New Do: Calling Yourself a Feminist'. *Glamour*, 16 September 2013 <www.glamour.com/story/the-new-do-calling-yourself-a-feminist> (last accessed 27 November 2019).

Kansara, V. A. 2017. 'Hearst's President of Digital on How to Win the New Media Wars'. *Business of Fashion*, 2 February 2017 <www.businessoffashion.com/articles/intelligence/troy-young-hearst-president-digital-new-media-wars-snapchat-facebook> (last accessed 12 November 2019).

McGuigan, J. 2009. *Cool Capitalism*. London: Pluto.

McRobbie, A. 2009. *The Aftermath of Feminism: Gender, Culture and Social Change*. London: Sage.

Munro, E. 2013. 'Feminism: a Fourth Wave?'. *Political Insight* 4.2: 22–5.

Murphy, R. and S. Jackson. 2011. 'Bodies-as-image? The Body Made Visible in Magazine Love Your Body Content'. *Women's Studies Journal* 25.1: 17–30.

Sadowska, N. 2002. 'Women's Internet Sites: A Search for Design Strategies to Engage the Female Viewer'. *Women and Everyday Uses of the Internet: Agency and Identity*. Eds M. Consalvo and S. Paasonen. New York: Peter Lang. 90–107.

Saner, E. 2010. 'Women's Magazine Sector is Bullish About the Future'. *The Guardian* 11 October 2010 <www.theguardian.com/media/2010/oct/11/womens-magazines-bullish-future> (last accessed 12 November 2019).

Selzer, J. 2017. 'Inspiring Body- Positivity Moments From 2017'. *Cosmopolitan* 21 November 2017 <www.cosmopolitan.com/health-fitness/g13352390/body-positivity-instagram-accounts/> (last accessed 27 November 2019).

Shoneye, T. 2015. '19 Hacks for Instant Body Confidence'. *SoFeminine* 19 October 2015 <www.sofeminine.co.uk/cosmetic-surgery/how-to-be-body-confident-s1596783.html> (last accessed 27 November 2019).

Smith, L. 2017. 'I Hated My Body and This is How I Learned to Love it'. *Cosmopolitan* 13 February 2017 <www.cosmopolitan.com/uk/body/health/longform/a49552/lauren-fitness-instagram-learn-love-body/> (last accessed 27 November 2019).

Swerling, H. 2013. 'ELLE Rebrands Feminism – What Does it Mean to You?'. *Elle* 1 October 2013 <www.elle.com/uk/fashion/celebrity-style/articles/a2322/elle-rebrands-feminism/> (last accessed 27 November 2019).

Terranova, T. 2000. 'Free Labour: Producing Culture for the Digital Economy'. *Social Text* 18.2: 33–58.

The Debrief. 2014. 'Media Pack.' Bauer Media <www.bauermedia.co.uk/uploads/Debrief%20.pdf> (last accessed 12 November 2019).

The Debrief. 2016. 'Media Pack'. Bauer Media <www.bauermedia.co.uk/uploads/The_Debrief_Media_Pack_2016_TEST.pdf> (last accessed 12 November 2019).

The Debrief. 2017. 'Media Pack'. Bauer Media <www.bauermedia.co.uk/uploads/Debrief_Media_Pack_2017.pdf> (last accessed 12 November 2019).

Zisman, H. 2017. 'Level Up: 10 Products Every Feminist Needs'. *Cosmopolitan* 17 November 2017 <www.cosmopolitan.com/lifestyle/g13509487/feminist-fashion-items/> (last accessed 27 November 2019).

Part II

Interacting with Readers

6

'There is a War on. Does She Know?': Transatlantic Female Stardom and Women's Wartime Labour in British Film Fan Magazines

Lisa Stead

The 1940s constituted 'something of a "golden age"' for British cinema, 'both in terms of popularity and creativity' (Taylor 1988: 6). While such assessment largely encompasses film production and stardom, this 'golden age' also extended to the extra-textual cultures of British cinema. The movies were consumed in a variety of media and modes beyond the nation's theatres through fan club activities, film-star endorsed marketing and, particularly, through film periodicals. While cinema culture was a staple part of mainstream newspaper and magazine content, it occupied its own distinct space in UK print culture in the form of the film fan magazine.

Movie periodicals became an important part of UK film culture from the early years of the twentieth century. They developed alongside a growing culture of cinemagoing to cater to the interests and tastes of both casual and dedicated spectators. A wide range of film papers developed within the domestic market, including such publications as *The Picture World* (1914–16), *Pictures and Pleasure* (1913–14), *Film Flashes* (1915–16), *The Picture Show* (1919–60), *Girls' Cinema* (1920–32) and *Photo Bits and Cinema Star* (1923–24). Such periodicals featured a range of contents including reviews, behind-the-scenes gossip, monochrome and colour star portraits, news about upcoming releases, and colourful, glamorous cover artwork. As I have explored elsewhere (Stead 2016, 2017a and 2017b), they also included a range of short fictions (both original and adapted), star interviews, advice columns aimed largely at female readers, articles offering a glimpse into the domestic lives of popular stars, screen star competitions for readers, and a range of advertising for products that were often promoted by prominent male and female stars.

Although British papers competed with American publications available for purchase on the UK market, British film fan magazines developed their own distinct identity. They were tailored to address national audiences along particular class and gender-inflected lines, and to process a national film culture, both in dialogue and competition with American cinema. Into the 1940s, British film periodicals were predominantly read by and marketed to women. As such, film magazines offer a distinctly gendered image of wartime British film culture, one which connects strongly to women's magazines of the period. Both genres of periodical showcased writings on fashion, dress styles and advice about domestic and romantic etiquette and, while film periodicals were for the most part not exclusively marketed to women, their address was markedly tailored towards a female readership through this kind of content.

Film magazines thus prove a valuable tool for interrogating changing models of femininity and their mediation through popular culture, most immediately through their construction of female star images. While recent research has begun to look in detail at the role that fan magazines have played in building participatory fan cultures,[1] historical film research more broadly has tended to use such periodicals as supporting sources, offering evidence for the popularity of certain performers or filmmaking trends, or the critical reception of specific films, particularly within classical Hollywood. In looking at British magazines in volume across the war years, this chapter instead considers the shape and structure of the periodicals on their own terms, illuminating how such extra-textual materials generated their own kinds of cinema culture and mediated film for a gendered British readership. Mark Glancy's research into the history of *Picturegoer* offers an invaluable foundation for understanding some of the ways film fan magazines processed and contributed to British culture in the Second World War,[2] suggesting that fan magazines 'should not be regarded as an open window to the world of film fandom, but . . . can be analysed as a representation of popular film culture in wartime, and one that was, itself, popular' (2011: 456). The specific representation of, and address to, women within this history merits deeper consideration, particularly in regard to contextualising the film magazine within a broader landscape of women's wartime print culture. This chapter offers a new interrogation of nationally specific print cultures of cinema by focusing on its wartime representation of female stardom, examining how British fan magazines responded to changes in the visibility and patriotic qualities of celebrity female labour in particular. In doing so, the chapter illuminates the distinctive role that the film fan periodical played in processing and disseminating wartime propaganda in relation to women's identities and images.

The chapter takes as its central case study the transatlantic star Vivien Leigh, whose treatment by British fan magazines across the wartime period illuminates a network of conflicted discourses on celebrity, patriotism and gendered labour, given her status as a star positioned uneasily between America and Britain. I examine Leigh's representation within the leading UK fan magazine of the time, *Picturegoer and Film Weekly*,[3] considering its complex attempts to both establish and discredit her stardom specifically in relation to war in a period during which 'stars figured much more prominently than individual films' (Glancy 2011: 474). Leigh's efforts at war work, both on screen in overtly patriotic roles and off-screen through practical labours such as knitting, visiting troops and tea making, sit against a wider backdrop of women's wartime labour. Women's work was essential to the national war effort, both on the public and domestic front. Robert Murphy (1992: 99) notes that by 1944, 'seven-and-a-half million women were working outside the home'. As a wartime woman whose labour and stardom was divided across the Atlantic, therefore, Leigh's relatively conflicted treatment within the magazine illustrates the broader complexity of its specific articulations of wartime femininity. Examining her treatment within *Picturegoer* offers a fresh understanding of how magazine discourses addressed UK audiences in the Second World War, charting the specific role that British fan papers played in creating and disseminating gendered representations of wartime femininity.

'Will the War Affect the Cinema?': Wartime British Fan Papers

British film magazines grew into a relatively standardised format across the 1920s and into the interwar period. Popular periodicals such as *Picturegoer* and *The Picture Show* focused on profiling and promoting film stars through interviews, editorial features and photographic material. They also blended film with a range of other pleasures and concerns, profiling fashions and cosmetics and including a plethora of short stories, domestic advice, etiquette tips, quizzes and competitions. Fan magazines profiled female stars in interviews and 'home life' articles, presenting them in and out of character in photographic and illustrated content. In tie-in short story adaptations (a popular aspect of many early British fan magazines), for example, stars could feature in character alongside representations of their off-screen image in photographs and advertising. As I have argued elsewhere (Stead 2016), a reader navigating the multimedia textures of the periodical (which combined prose with varied typography, illustrations, photographs and advertisements) could thus simultaneously navigate a range of articulations of modern womanhood through the figure of the female star.

Within a wartime context, magazines used such media-specific modes of address to negotiate contradictory discourses on national and international wartime female stardom and, by extension, models of wartime femininity. They related female star images to wider ideas surrounding female domesticity, independence and labour that were very much at the forefront of UK wartime culture. Sue Harper (1988: 168–9) suggests that 'women's images were appropriated to serve an extraordinarily wide variety of purposes' at this time. Describing them as 'endlessly polysemic', Harper cites the variety of modes of femininity employed in British cinema across the war years, signifying 'forbidden wilfulness . . . ratified monogamy . . . innocent sensuality . . . doomed feminism . . . proletarian doggedness . . . or aging support' (Ibid.). Fan magazines helped build these images by embedding characterisations within editorial commentary, review and feature writing. These formats contextualised fantasy with references to 'real' wartime life, but also encouraged readers to critique and participate.

When Britain declared war on Germany in late 1939, leading British film periodical *Picturegoer*'s most immediate response was to analyse the likely impact of the conflict on industry practices and everyday cinemagoing. In 'Will the War Affect the Cinema?', the article whose title heads this section, Hubert Cole outlined a range of concerns about the impact of war for cinemagoers in early 1940, considering the price of tickets and the problems of drearily propagandistic production (*Picturegoer and Film Weekly* 22 March 1940: 14–15). Such worries were not unfounded and reflected some of the problems that the UK industry and its cinemagoers were facing. The government ordered cinemas to close in September 1939 amidst fears of bombings, and though they swiftly rescinded the order, the industry faced further difficulty with the rise on the entertainment tax in 1940. For fan magazines specifically, wartime restrictions offered some even more immediate practical concerns regarding their sales and availability. *Picturegoer* informed its readers in August 1941, for example, that 'owing to further Government restrictions on the use of paper, it has become necessary, until such time as these restrictions can be relaxed, to issue "Picturegoer and Film Weekly" fortnightly instead of weekly' (*Picturegoer and Film Weekly* 23 August 1941: 3).

War did not, however, decrease the popularity of cinemagoing. By 1940, 'cinema admission figures reached 1 billion for the first time, rising to over 1.5 billion in 1943, 1944, and 1945' (Noakes 2015: 82). Cinemagoing was 'the country's prime leisure time activity', and 'an indispensable means of instructing and entertaining the nation in wartime' (Glancy 2010: 8), but cinemagoing was also 'a culture that encompassed both regular and selective cinema-goers, whose interests in entertainment and artistry did not sit easily together' (Glancy 2011: 474). Fan magazine sales kept a steady stream of entertaining content in the hands of their readers and attempted to make an address to both the more 'fannish' and casual viewer. While the country faced rationing, conscription, evacuation and austerity, British fan papers continued to offer a degree of glamour, escapism, excess and fantasy, not least in their all-colour covers and star portraits. They did, however, temper such presentation with a constant analysis of the value or meanings of entertainment amidst the conflict. A 1940 article reflected on the specific value of film in wartime:

> There are more urgent things to deal with than films. And those urgent things, so vital to our national existence, are being capably dealt with by millions of men and women . . . But human nature demands relaxation. Every hardworking man and woman demands escape from himself or herself for two of three hours a week so that they may thereafter carry on the important work with renewed energy and enthusiasm . . . Films are a necessity in wartime. (*Picturegoer and Film Weekly* 13 July 1940: 9)

Cinema in this understanding could simultaneously be a luxury indulgence *and* a site of patriotic affirmation. These themes play out consistently across *Picturegoer*, where war affected almost all of its regular features. Commentary about the charity work of particular stars featured in their interviews, for example, as did snippets about war work in gossip pages. Articles debated and discussed the impact of war on filmmaking and production on both sides of the Atlantic. Features profiled Ministry of Information films, taking viewers 'Behind the Guns' (*Picturegoer and Film Weekly* 13 July 1940: 10) and into munitions factories. Other articles promised titbits and anecdotes to 'amuse you in the long blackout evenings' (*Picturegoer and Film Weekly* 27 April 1940: 31).

Advertisements for women's cosmetics and domestic products also began to market their goods by relating them sympathetically to women's wartime experience. Beauty products offered relief from 'these days of stress and rush' (*Picturegoer and Film Weekly* 27 April 1940: 27). Contextualising the wartime adverts within the larger tapestry of each issue of the magazine gives a clearer view of the range of images of women and war that the paper offered its readers. In a 1940 issue, for example, Aspro painkillers pitched themselves to women 'On Active Service', featuring an illustration of a smiling young woman in a nurse's uniform in need of 'quick action in medicine' in 'these troublesome times' (*Picturegoer and Film Weekly* 23 March 1940: 30). The advertisement sits alongside interviews with, and images of, glamorous and fashionably dressed leading Hollywood stars, seemingly unaffected by such 'troubles'. Content could thus simultaneously exploit and obscure wartime realities, offering readers escapism, but also a variety of means to relate cinema to the war-inflected realities of their everyday lives.

Letters from readers published in *Picturegoer* attest to this, particularly when referencing the influence of war on cinemagoing habits, film preferences and the reception of particular stars. A letter from 'A. E. Cox, 60A Bolina Road, London' frames the writer's discontent with popular epics like *Gone with the Wind* (1939) by asserting that 'in wartime most of us go to the cinema for bright, snappy entertainment. We are not getting it because, in my opinion, films are too long and not light enough' (*Picturegoer and Film Weekly* 27 April 1940: 29). Other letters argue that newsreel content should not shy away from wartime realities. Letter writer Pauline Lindon suggests that:

> these vivid pictures of our battlefront are painful and harrowing, but they strike us, deep down inside, and we're not likely to forget them easily. And as propaganda, necessary propaganda, they will reach father than any words can ever do. (*Picturegoer and Film Weekly* 13 July 1940: 19)

In the same letters page, 'T. N.' alternatively expresses their frustration with war films, suggesting that 'it would be nice' if British producers 'stopped giving us films with stories that we have read about every day and what we have heard given over the air, about Nazi Germany' (Ibid.). Readers also comment much more directly on stars and their wartime responsibilities. A range of attitudes are displayed, from those feeling that stars should stay put in Hollywood and entertain audiences to those feeling that stars ought to 'make yourselves more useful by contributing handsomely to the Red Cross Fund, War Loans, or any other fund which takes your fancy' (*Picturegoer and Film Weekly* 23 March 1940: 28).

The image of the woman as labourer – both as stars seeking to 'make themselves useful' and as 'ordinary' women featured in magazine advertising and editorial content – was a central theme in magazine representations of wartime femininity. Women were increasingly mobile as workers in factories and armed services, yet such mobility gave rise to fears that 'working women would abandon, neglect or lose interest in femininity' (Giles 2004: 132). While British women were central to the construction of the home as a symbol of peace and the potential 'emergence of a new and better world' after the war (Ibid.: 137), they were simultaneously required to contribute as labourers beyond the home during the conflict. This gave rise to a complex dissemination of ideas of women's twin responsibilities, where 'policy decisions and . . . official schemes that attempted to organise the practical realities of carrying out a dual role . . . continued to address women's needs as either the needs of the worker or the housewife/mother' (Ibid.: 132).

As the war recruited ordinary women into spheres of work previously inaccessible to them, popular culture helped build an image of the labouring woman as retaining a grounding in domestic duties, making the worker/housewife a 'figure of national importance' (Ibid.: 133). Film fan magazines contributed to this in a range of different ways. Many adverts promised to help women to balance a worker/domestic identity through physical appearance, for example, enabling them to retain an essential femininity through cosmetics and dress, while indulging in traditionally more masculine labours. Hair-care advertisements called on women not to 'neglect your crowning glory just because there's a war on!' (*Picturegoer and Film Weekly* 27 April 1940: 33). Other advertisements focused on the more practical realities of women's war work, turning the factory in particular into a space for sharing beauty tips. A *Picturegoer and Film*

Weekly advertisement for Potter & Moore's Powder (see Figure 6.1) featured an image of a smiling female factory worker holding a wrench supported with the following text:

> Drone of machinery . . . clatter of metal . . . and overheard in one corner a snatch of feminine talk. 'What *do* you use that keeps your skin so young and lovely?' 'Potter & Moore's Power – Cream, nothing else. It's wonderful! So quick to use. So soothing. And it not only makes the skin look nice at once, but brings out the beauty of the underskin as well!' The noise of the machinery hasn't stopped. The munition workers carry on. (*Picturegoer and Film Weekly* 12 July 1940: 23)

The advertisement, accompanied by a further, tiny line illustration of a worker on the production line titled 'Munition Girl', creates a narrative in miniature. In doing so, it echoes the fiction-focused contents of the magazine where it included tie-in story adaptations and exploits the same discourses of gossip on which it relied in its letters pages, question and answer sections and interactive features, encouraging women readers to participate.

Figure 6.1 'Instant Beauty for Women in Wartime', *Picturegoer and Film Weekly*, 12 July 1940. 23.
(Courtesy of The Bill Douglas Cinema Museum, University of Exeter)

Picturegoer content offered working women readers escapism from labour through the glamour of star images and fantasy narratives, while also directly encouraging women's entry into the workforce. Advertisements positively profiled women as wartime labourers – in factories, as nurses, or as members of organisations such as the Women's Auxiliary Air Force – but also tapped more directly into the pressure women were under to balance domestic and public labour responsibilities. In readers' letters, the topic of women as war workers also surfaces. Cinema offers a reference point around which larger anxieties related to women and work coalesce, particularly because of its status as a public/private leisure activity and space (cinemagoing drew women into public space while offering a dark, enclosed, semi-private arena where women could temporarily escape domestic and public responsibilities and roles). Letter and poetry features created a kind of virtual community for readers beyond the cinema space itself, and during wartime this interactive network proved a useful platform for considering how war, work and leisure interconnected in women's daily experiences.

Readers' letters debated the place of cinema in women's working lives, which reflected the way many *Picturegoer* readers appeared to perceive the interactive aspects of the fan magazine as a space in which their voices mattered, and in which debate was encouraged. Several voices anxiously attempted to justify women's right to attend picture shows specifically because of their contribution to the war effort. For example, reader 'D. Whitlock' defends her status as a worker and her right to occupy cinema seats as respite from her labour: 'For two weeks now my sister and I have been working until 6.15 and lately 6.30 . . . we had to pay 2s for a seat and stand for over an hour.' (*Picturegoer* 12 June 1943: 9). 'Miss P. Gibbins' alternatively asserts that 'women shoppers' are just as much workers as any other labouring figure present at the cinema, suggesting that 'the women shoppers are having a very heavy burden to carry these days and hunting for food for hungry families is just as tiring, if not more so, than working in a factory' (Ibid.).

The wartime female star had a particular role to play within these discourses. She added a further layer of complication to questions of labour and gender, given that female star images had long occupied a seemingly contradictory position. Unlike the majority of their female admirers, female stars were able, both before and during the war, to remain in work beyond the marriage bar, and to generate their own independent income disconnected from marriage, inheritance or class background. In regard to a 'dual role', therefore, female stars had long navigated both domestic and public identities; their celebrity status implied a 'split between a private self and a public self' whereby the 'public presentation of self is always a staged activity' (Rojek 2001: 11), and fan magazines played a significant role in providing a platform for such staging along national lines.

Picturegoer primarily presented the interlocking themes of war, women and work by reporting on the tokenistic charity ventures of female stars. A double-page spread titled 'Personality Parade' from April 1940 is a typical example. A photograph of two stars is captioned: 'In addition to helping to keep British film production going and the troops entertained Margaretta Scott and Margaret Lockwood are doing their bit between scenes at Shepherd's Bush, knitting socks for soldiers.' The editorial further affirms their feminising domesticity with an assurance of their more traditional, home-centred qualities, informing the reader that 'Margaret Lockwood has all the domestic virtues. She probably "steps out" less frequently than any star in films, dislikes night clubs and swing music' (*Picturegoer and Film Weekly* 27 April 1940: 13). This kind of commentary, offsetting the dual image of labour on and off the screen with a reassurance of inherent domesticity, fits within the broader context of cultural representations of the Second World War in relation to women and the home front. Christine Gledhill and Gillian Swanson (1996: 1) suggest that 'stresses and strains appear in magazines, radio programmes, advertisements and films as traditional images attempt to accommodate new social demands made on women'.

The stresses of this kind of 'accommodation' are particularly apparent in the way that magazines used female stars to articulate specific attitudes towards patriotism and national identity with the threat and onset of war, especially in regard to the relationship between Britain and America. Mark Glancy (2014: 148) observes that papers like *Picturegoer* responded to war by ridiculing Hollywood 'for its neutrality and its isolation from world events', while praising British cinema for its 'stalwart patriotism', seeing it as 'a cause to be promoted and protected'. The war exacerbated pre-existing tensions between American and British star systems. These tensions are illustrated by the way fan magazines represented female star images. The pull between a more conservative, de-glamorised image of screen stardom embodied by many British actresses, and the extravagant, liberated and quintessentially modern femininity that American screen stars were seen to represent, was a long-standing tension in British fan magazines (Stead 2010). War magnified this tension, evolving a persistent attitude in British film culture towards film stardom 'and all its trappings of gossip, fandom and scandal' as 'somehow unseemly, *unBritish*' (Street 2002: 119). This was particularly the case where British fan papers criticised the opportunism of British stars who seem to use their contributions to the war effort as a thinly disguised play for extra publicity.

As a British actress who had just cemented her status as global icon through the thoroughly American image of Scarlett O'Hara, and who had secured her stardom through a contract with the American independent producer David O. Selznick, Vivien Leigh's star image was thus notably conflicted within these contexts. Because film stars 'remain at once inside and outside their mediatised roles as "characters"' (Leonard and Negra 2017: 29), Leigh's distinct transatlantic positioning caused particular tensions for her place within the propagandistic discourses of the fan magazine, and the extent to which her non-domestic characterisations did or did not take precedence over her off-screen, domestic star persona. She had the potential to be reclaimed as a national icon, yet was arguably not 'British' enough for wartime due to her divided loyalties across the Atlantic. While this offered ample material for criticism within the editorial content of British fan papers, her American qualities held alternative appeal for a female readership through the magazine's handling of her bodily image in photographs and illustrations. Leigh presented a glamorous image in her films and within fan magazine discourse, carrying connotations of the 'material comfort and security' of American culture through her associations with Hollywood (Stacey 1994: 105). As such, she appeared markedly removed from the everyday experiences and worker/housewife ideal of her British female audience and their contrasting contexts of 'material scarcity' (Stacey 1994: 105). In a time when, as Jackie Stacey (1994: 112) has argued, 'American glamour played a significant role in the changing constructions of British femininity', Leigh's hybrid status offers an engaging focal point for considering the work of British fan magazines in shaping these constructions.

'Californian Sun and American Applause': Negotiating Leigh for Wartime

When England announced its entry into the war in September 1939, Leigh was in America where she had been filming *Gone with the Wind* since January that year. Leigh had appeared in a handful of British films and plays prior to landing the role of Scarlett O'Hara, but this was the film that made her an A-list star and international celebrity. *Gone with the Wind* was still three months away from release, and Leigh had signed with Selznick to a seven-year contract, placing her at the heart of Hollywood stardom.

Following her Oscar-winning role in *Gone with the Wind*, Leigh went on to star in *Waterloo Bridge* (1940) and *Lady Hamilton* (1941), working on the latter with Alexander Korda. Leigh's roles in these two films, playing English characters in English settings, potentially signified a more overtly patriotic Englishness in counterpart to her embodiment of the quintessential Southern belle Scarlett. Yet both films were produced by American studios, the former by Metro-Goldwyn-Mayer and the latter through Korda's American company. It was not until December 1941 that Leigh was actually to return to British soil on a more permanent basis (according to Leigh biographer Kendra Bean (2019), Waterloo Bridge was 'contrary to popular belief . . . not filmed on location in London, but rather on the MGM backlot in California'). She starred in *The Doctor's Dilemma* at the Theatre Royal Haymarket the following March and travelled with the Old Vic Spring Party across North Africa performing for the troops in the summer of 1943. In June the following year, she starred in the Rank adaptation of George Bernard Shaw's *Caesar and Cleopatra* (1944), a grand-scale British production shot under the constant threat of 'air raids and gunfire' (Bean 2013: 92) at Denham Studios.

Bean has discussed Leigh's desire to contribute to the war effort in the early 1940s, including 'volunteering as an ambulance driver, an auxiliary policewoman, or doing fire watch duty on the roof of the [Haymarket] theatre' (2013: 89). In reality, Leigh's practical contributions came in the form of radio broadcasting, appearances at charity events, serving tea to the troops and participating in initiatives such a Natalie Wales Latham's 'Bundles for Britain' by knitting woollens for soldiers. An arresting cover for *Look* magazine from December 1940 shows Leigh with needles in hand, posed against a red, white and blue background. Her star image had the potential to function as a propagandistic national symbol through such off-screen labours.

Picturegoer covered Leigh's war work specifically in relation to her status as an international star. She had made infrequent appearances in the UK fan magazines since the mid-1930s after her early roles in films like *Look Up and Laugh* (1935), *Gentlemen's Agreement* (1935), her romantic pairing with Laurence Olivier in *Fire over England* (1937), *Dark Journey* (1937), *Storm in a Teacup* (1937) and her comic role in *A Yank at Oxford* (1938). *Picturegoer* reported on her during these early stages of career. *Picturegoer* writer Max Breen produced a handful of articles in 1937 and 1938 about the development of her star image in the wake of her highly publicised £50,000 contract with Korda. A double-page spread in April 1938 is scattered with head shots of the star, describing her as 'rather the garnishing than the nourishing element', but Breen held out high hopes for *A Yank at Oxford* having seen Leigh shooting the film, suggesting that 'Vivien has suddenly become Vivid' (*Picturegoer Weekly* 9 April 1938: 10–11).

Leigh appeared on the cover of the magazine several times across the war and immediate post-war period, testament to her increasing popularity. She further featured in editorial commentary, reviews and full-page photo inserts (a beautiful colour image of Leigh as Scarlett O'Hara on the 23 March 1940 issue is one such example). She again appeared on the cover in April 1940 in a full-colour, full-page head shot shared with Clarke Gable, promoting the UK release of *Gone with the Wind* (see Plate 5). Inside, Leigh appears in other guises. While the cover image shows her in her quintessentially American starring role, a double-page insert instead profiles *Waterloo Bridge* as a 'story of wartime (1914–1918) London . . . a vehicle for Vivien Leigh and Robert Taylor' (*Picturegoer and Film Weekly* 27 April 1940: 8). Further on in the paper, Leigh appeared in relation to yet another film – her British movie *Twenty-One Days* (1940) in the 'Shop for your Films' reviews section.

The magazine format multiplies Leigh's star image, and in doing so seemingly separates her American stardom from her English stardom. Her American glamour, petrified in the cover shot, is never followed up with any kind of feature or review and is instead offset against her more patriotic incarnation in *Waterloo Bridge*, where her image is presented as multiple and varied. A series of stills from the film show her involved in a range of activities and a range of costumes tied more explicitly to immediate wartime contexts, accompanying Taylor in full military uniform. The magazine also critiques Leigh for her acting ability in written editorial content: Lionel Collier, the reviewer for *Twenty-One Days*, suggests that like her co-star husband Olivier, Leigh 'seems to lack restraint' and is not 'wholly convincing' (*Picturegoer and Film Weekly* 27 April 1940: 23).

The notion that Leigh had more glamour than acting talent, getting by on her extraordinary physical beauty rather than her skill as a performer, was a criticism she endured throughout her career, particularly in regard to her ambitions to be recognised as a serious theatrical actress (George Cukor was to later describe her as a 'consummate actress, hampered by beauty') (cited in Lambert 2000: 115). A gossipy editorial feature from 22 March 1940 is symptomatic of this attitude. Reporting on Leigh's 'airy statement . . . that neither she nor Laurence Olivier cares to be known as a movie personality as they are both recognised in England as stage performers', Malcolm Phillips reminded the reader that: 'Miss Leigh . . . scored an overnight success in ONE play . . . If we were Miss Leigh, we would keep quiet' (*Picturegoer and Film Weekly* 22 March 1940: 4).

This emphasis on 'restraint' and the need to effectively silence Leigh's self-publicity connects her to a larger tension in British fan papers which showcased stylish, modern American stars while also seeking to represent less glamorous British actresses. American chic and screen charisma had been frequently offset in *Picturegoer* against the more conservative and de-glamorised qualities of English actresses across the interwar period – qualities both derided and praised by feature writers and letter-writing readers (Stead 2010). This tension was reflective of the wider emphasis on restraint, reserve, pictorialism and theatricality as markers of the national qualities of British cinema in the interwar period in particular. By late 1940, *Picturegoer*'s interpretations of Leigh's stardom were deeply enmeshed with her role as Scarlett O'Hara – a characterisation that placed her right at the heart of this tension – and the major success of *Gone with the Wind* on UK screens.

Mark Glancy (2014: 149) has discussed Leigh's treatment by UK fan magazines across 1940, singling out the recurrent attacks on her decision to stay on in Hollywood after the film was completed:

> In January 1940 . . . [*Picturegoer*] mocked-up a photograph of her in uniform as a WREN, and suggested that she should return to Britain to make films as part of her 'national service' and on officer's pay of £240 per year. In March 1940, an editorial asked, 'does she know there's a war on?', adding that 'perhaps it is easy to forget . . . when one is sitting safely 6000 miles away basking in the warmth of the Californian sun and American applause.'

The January issue to which Glancy refers signals the beginning of an increasingly uneasy portrayal of the star. Leigh is included here amidst a range of British actors and directors such as Alfred Hitchcock and Madeleine Carroll. A great deal of British talent had gone to Hollywood during the 1930s, and fan magazine editorial used the onset of war as an excuse to bemoan this exodus as a form of betrayal. Glancy notes that 'at a time when the USA remained defiantly neutral, working in Hollywood was portrayed as being one step short of aiding and abetting the enemy' (Ibid.). British stars who had made their name predominantly on American screens, therefore, were particularly vulnerable to criticism in an environment that 'forced the question of nationality into every crevice of public and private life' (Lant 1996: 13).

The inclusion of Leigh in this particular article offered an echo to editorial comments about the troubling lavishness and financial extravagance of *Gone with the Wind* included few pages earlier. Both features established an equation between Leigh, the 'problems' of Hollywood for British cinema, and the contrast between its exaggerated glamour and the more austere contexts of British filmmaking and British culture at this time. These early implications were more pronounced in the 2 March 1940 issue, where the initial editorial once again opened with a discussion of Leigh titled 'If this is true Vivien should be Spanked! There is a War On. Does She Know?' The article attacked Leigh for refusing to pose for portraits to promote the British film *St. Martin's Lane* (1938) (also known as *Sidewalks of London*) for American audiences. The writer Malcolm Phillips threatened her with 'spanking' and chastised her as 'naughty' for failing to appreciate the status of British films as 'essential to Britain's war chest', suggesting that her resistance spoke to 'the childish vanity that is the real name for most film star temperament' (*Picturegoer and Film Weekly* 2 March 1940: 3). In the process, the editorial created a division between pre-war Leigh as a *British* star and wartime Leigh as a brattish Hollywood product:

> It seems that while the Vivien Leigh of *Twenty-One Days* was glad enough to appear with Charles Laughton in *St. Martin's Lane,* the Vivien Leigh of *Gone with the Wind* is turning up her nose at the idea of spending a few hours of her precious time posing for portraits with the same Mr. Laughton. (Philips 1940a: 3)

The infantilising and eroticised language posits the unrestrained glamorous star body as a threatening entity that needed to be contained and chastised. A few pages later, the paper seemed to enact this punishment in an article featuring shots from the *Gone with the Wind* Hollywood premier that neglected to feature any pictures of Leigh. The omission of Leigh, given her status as the film's central character who features in almost every scene of the movie, seemed to purposely erase her from the paper in pictorial form as a way to reprimand her for her lack of patriotism, while leaving the seedy implications of a 'spanked' Leigh to linger in the imagination of a reader moving through the magazine in a linear order. The imagined image thus remains associated with her refusal to be photographed for more 'wholesomely' patriotic purposes.

The magazine's less favourable treatment of the star continued to the end of the year. A three-page feature by Hubert Cole dissected Leigh's star image, lamenting her typecasting as 'the tough girl' (*Picturegoer and Film Weekly* 7 December 1940: 8). The writer criticised her choice of unsympathetic screen roles with pointed reference to her American image as Scarlett, warning that 'unless Vivien Leigh breaks clean away from Scarlett O'Hara and all the other minor Scarletts, I fear she is going to find herself in the middle of a lot of grief' (Ibid.: 9). Three pages later, a more positive image of her *Gone with the Wind* co-star Clarke Gable was offered in an article titled 'Evolution of Gable', charting his career success. Leigh features in a small promotional shot of Scarlett and Rhett, but the image positions her wholly as support for Gable, rather than a leading star in her own right.

The hostility towards Leigh's 'Hollywood-made glamour' (*Picturegoer and Film Weekly* 22 March 1940: 4) is most acutely expressed through these kinds of uses of her image across the multimedia features of the paper. The mock WREN image, for example, was a composite of a promotional head shot and a superimposed illustration of the WREN cap (see Figure 6.2). This is a trick specifically available to the magazine as a mode of print media, able to rework bodily signification not only by omitting Leigh's image or printing unpleasant written commentary, but by literally remaking her image. The composite picture reflected the way that readers themselves often engaged with magazine representations, as evidenced in archival collections of fan scrapbooks and fan letters where readers cut out pictures and restructured them within their own journals and albums.[4] Unlike this kind of fan activity, however, which was often focused on acts of admiration for and memorialising of star images, the magazine uses collage and re-contextualisation to create negative associations. The WREN image informs the reader that Leigh is decidedly *not* like them. The uniformed star body, very clearly presented as a false construction, intervenes in the wider network of Leigh's on and off-screen image(s) in this way, structuring a critique of her Americanness through the specific tools of the magazine media.

Picturegoer's construction of Leigh's star image and its resonance for reading women is, however, open to other interpretations. Jackie Stacey (1994: 111) has suggested that 'American femininity . . . was associated with particular consumer products unavailable in wartime Britain', arguing that British women specifically found pleasure in the marked difference between their 'own experience of wartime Britain and Hollywood stars'. Such pleasure spoke to the difficulties that women faced in navigating the lived reality of conflicting cultural discourses attempting to maintain an imaginary of the wartime British working woman that did not disrupt 'the image of woman as homemaker' (Gledhill and Swanson 1996: 1). Fan magazines could magnify this conflict by routinely disparaging the American qualities of stars

January 27, 1940 PICTUREGOER and FILM WEEKLY

by MAURICE COWAN

We've made Vivien Leigh a Wren officer and her pay, for her National Service, would be £240 a year

Here's Alfred Hitchcock as he'd look as a major-general. Pay £4 10s. 6d. a day, plus allowances

Ronald Colman (London-Scottish 1914) is given the high rank of G.O.C. (2nd class) at £6 15s. 10d. a day

Madeleine Carroll gets the plum of the nursing service, matron-in-chief, £525 a year

Forbes. They will be given the rank of commander (with twelve years' service) and £2 8s. 6d. per day. Unless, of course, any of them insists on being a warrant officer marine gunner (after nine years' service) at 15s. 4d. a day, or an able seaman (after six years' service) at 4s. 6d. a day.

Now some recruits for the army. There are men like Sir Cedric Hardwicke, Basil Rathbone, Ronald Colman, Ian Hunter, Claude Rains, Miles Mander, Reginald Owen, Henry Daniell, Eric Blore, Arthur Treacher and Melville Cooper, who did their share in the last war. They deserve promotion. Colman (ex-London Scottish) would become a G.O.C. (2nd class) at £6 15s. 10d. a day, and the others colonels at £2 18s. 0d. Any one of them who would like to begin again as some of them did as a second lieutenant at 11s. 0d. a day or as a private at 2s. 0d. a day, and work his way up is welcome.

C. Aubrey Smith will be classed as a chaplain (1st class) at £2 5s. 4d. a day. And with him would go George Zucco (wounded, 1914-18).

That still leaves us a likely bunch of lads to enlist with R.A.F. rankings. Raymond Massey (captain with the Canadian Artillery, 1914-18) could top as air chief marshal at £6 6s. 8d. a day. Edmund Gwenn (also old campaigner, 1914-18) and Nigel Bruce (first member of H.A.C. to be wounded, 1914-18) air marshals at £5 6s. 8d. a day. The air vice-marshals at £4 10s. 6d. a day might include Lionel Atwill. That leaves us Cary Grant as air commodore at £3 1s. 0d. per day, John Loder (ex-serviceman) as group captain at £2 18s. 0d. per day and George Sanders, Reginald Gardiner, Peter Godfrey and Louis Hayward as squadron leaders at £1 14s. 2d. a day. Should any one desire the rank of flight sergeant the pay would be 15s. 6d. a day.

Now we come to the women. Here we have a nice variety of rankings, from a humble member in the A.T.S. at about 9s. 4d. per week (board and lodging provided) to matron-in-chief in the nursing service at £525 per year.

For the matron-in-chief I nominate Madeleine Carroll, and as other ordinary matrons at £160 a year we could have Anna Neagle (remember her Nurse Cavell), Merle Oberon (a charming Red Cross nurse in *The Lion has Wings*), Gladys Cooper and Edna Best. Should any of them care to rank as a sister at £85 a year or as a member of the Nursing Auxiliary Service at £2 per week (provide own uniform, and deductions if she lives in) the saving would be much appreciated.

For ambulance drivers at £2 per week I enrol Binnie Barnes, Ida Lupino, Heather Angel and Sophie Stewart.

The Wrens, too, must have their share. Flora Robson would be chief officer at £275 a year, and first officers at £240 a year could include Vivien Leigh, Greer Garson, Muriel Angelus, Anna Lee and Elsa Lanchester.

Here again any one of them can begin as an ordinary Wren at thirty shillings a week.

We must not forget to include a few writers. Dr. A. J. Cronin would receive the high rank of a major-general in the R.A.M.C. at £4 6s. 0d. per day, James Hilton might become a brigadier at £3 3s. 4d. a day, while Bill Lipscomb (captain and M.C., 1914-18) deserves to be a major-general at £4 10s. 6d. a day. Michael Hogan, another ex-serviceman, to be brigadier at £3 3s. 4d. a day and Roland Leigh and John Van Druten to be captains at £1 3s. 6d. a day.

It gives one quite a shock to see how many of our film folk are in Hollywood. Anyway, if they really want to do their bit, here is the solution to all the quota problems and to all our film problems.

After all, when David Niven left Hollywood to do his bit and gave up a £30,000 contract, he didn't expect even squadron leader's pay, £1 14s. 2d. a day.

7

Figure 6.2 'Personality Parade', *Picturegoer and Film Weekly*, 27 January 1940. 6–7. (Source: author's personal collection)

like Leigh, but her presence in their pages also offered women pleasurable access to a British appropriation of Hollywood glamour.

Her status as a fashion icon had specific resonance in this regard. Her relationship with dress and fashion in wartime was expressed most acutely in, yet again, her embodiment of Scarlett O'Hara. This may seem a strange observation, given that unlike *Waterloo Bridge* the film has no direct connection to the contemporary period. Yet Leigh's costuming offered an image of self-fashioning through dress that potentially held resonance for wartime British fans. As Mark Glancy (2014: 175) observes, *Gone with the Wind* features an extremely de-glamorised image of Leigh costumed in a single tattered pink dress for a huge portion of the film. Such sustained representation of the unspectacular star body 'was an abrupt break with Hollywood conventions'; yet such a break 'may have reassured some British women that their own, wartime shortages of cosmetics had not yet reached this crisis point'. As Robert Murphy (1992: 105) asserts, 'Britain's glamour-starved women were prepared to sacrifice a lot to feel exciting and seductive' at this time, particularly given the further potentially 'defeminising' influence of uniforms and working clothes that women were sporting for new wartime labours.

Scarlett's 'make do' attitude would seem to offer a specific connection to the way fan magazines encouraged readers to construct their own make-shift war fashions, echoing 'the principle of make do and mend' that had been instigated more widely in British culture at this time (Glancy 2014: 176). Fashion and beauty advice in *Picturegoer* responded to the restrictions imposed on women's dress and style options, suggesting ways they could make their own clothing. A full-page advertisement on the back cover of an early 1940 *Picturegoer*, for example, promises a 'Privilege Offer' to purchase a new dressmaking book featuring 'all kinds of smart and serviceable clothes', offering patterns that readers 'can make yourself' (*Picturegoer and Film Weekly* 2 March 1940: 36). A large illustration of an oversized book cover accompanied the prose, flanked by women in bathing suits, factory uniforms, trouser suits, evening dresses and everyday coats, gloves and headscarves.

The advert offers the reader an image of wartime femininity that is multiple, traversing the variety of duties, roles and identities that women could adopt. All of these images are filtered through the promise of self-making, cheaply compiling these looks from simple home patterns. The advertisement makes no direct mention of cinema, but its placement as the closing image of the periodical invites the reader to make connections and comparisons between themselves, these illustrations of 'everyday' working women and the star and character portraits contained within. In doing so, it in some ways superficially reconciles the contradictory demands of the dual role by presenting duality as in fact constituting a multiplicity of material options. When Scarlett transforms a set of green curtains into a lavish dress in the midst of the ruins of Tara, she offers a fictional echo to such budget dress patterns and make-do fashion advice. Although the prevalence of the image of Leigh as Scarlett across 1940s issues of *Picturegoer* most obviously speaks to the grand scale of the production and its publicity, it also suggests the wider resonances of that particular characterisation in its precise relation to the other magazine images of Leigh, contextualised within the interlocking coordinates of wartime labour, style and self-fashioning.

Conclusion

An examination of Leigh's wartime stardom offers new insight into the way that British fan magazines specifically mediated between films and their gendered audiences, and how distinctive contexts – war, work, the tensions between national film industries – were reflected by and processed through the print media of cinema. While papers like *Picturegoer* could frequently criticise a star for their lack of wartime patriotism, their magazine image remained composite and flexible, open to alternative articulations of female wartime experience. The screen glamour of stars like Leigh was therefore mediated in a range of ways in publications like *Picturegoer*, suggestive of the more media and gender-specific address of film magazines at this time, and their resonance for reading women.

By focusing on the distinct contribution of the film magazine to wartime propaganda, this chapter has aimed to illuminate the particular cultural role of film fan periodicals in shaping popular ideas about nationhood, patriotism and the war effort in relation to women's roles specifically. While it borrowed from, and adapted techniques from, its sister periodical the women's magazine in speaking to a female audience, the film fan magazine deserves particular attention for its own specific uses of particularly emotive and provocative star images circulating in film culture as a means to process wartime ideologies for its gendered audience. As this chapter has suggested, the film periodical adopted particular intermedial methods to interrogate wartime images of British femininity. An original exploration of the distinctive textual and visual strategies of periodicals like *Picturegoer* during this period thus highlights the significance of the film magazine as a prominent and influential component of women's wartime magazine culture.

Notes

1. Scholarly work into fan magazines and women's film history specifically has explored, for example, early American cinema fandom (Orgeron 2009); British fandom in the silent era (Stead 2010, 2013); the role the film periodicals played developing early star systems (Morey 2002); and the ways in which film magazines positioned women as 'viewers/readers/consumers' (Studlar 1996: 264) in the interwar period.
2. Glancy's (2010, 2014) research into wartime cinemagoing offers an essential overview of key contexts for cinema consumption and spectatorship during the war years.
3. *Picturegoer* went through many name changes during its existence. Full details can be found in the Appendix of this book. In the period covered by this chapter, the magazine was known as *Picturegoer Weekly* (1931–39), *Picturegoer and Film Weekly* (1939–41) and *Picturegoer* (1941–60). The references in this chapter reflect these name changes. However, for clarity, the title *Picturegoer* has been maintained throughout the discussion.
4. Examples can be found in archives such as The Bill Douglas Cinema Museum at the University of Exeter.

Works Cited

Bean, K. 2013. *Vivien Leigh: An Intimate Portrait*. London: Running Press.

Bean, K. 2019. 'Waterloo Bridge.' Vivandlarry.com <http://vivandlarry.com/vivien/waterloo-bridge/> (last accessed 19 August 2019).

Giles, J. 2004. *The Parlour and the Suburb: Domestic Identities, Class, Femininity and Modernity*. Oxford: Berg.

Glancy, M. 2010. 'Going to the Pictures: British Cinema and the Second World War'. *Past and Present* 8: 7–9.

Glancy, M. 2011. '*Picturegoer:* The Fan Magazine and Popular Film Culture in Britain During the Second World War'. *Historical Journal of Film, Radio and Television* 31.4: 453–78.

Glancy, M. 2014. *Hollywood and the Americanisation of Britain from the 1920s to the Present*. London: I. B. Tauris.

Gledhill, C. and G. Swanson. 1996. 'Introduction'. *Nationalising Femininity: Culture, Sexuality and British Cinema in the Second World War*. Eds C. Gledhill and G. Swanson. Manchester: Manchester University Press. 1–12.

Harper, S. 1988. 'The Representation of Women in British Feature Films, 1939–45'. *Britain and the Cinema in the Second World War*. Ed. P. M. Taylor. London: Macmillan Press. 1–14.

Lambert, G. 2000. *On Cukor*. New Tork: Rizzoli.

Lant, A. 1996. 'Prologue: Mobile Femininity'. *Nationalising Femininity: Culture, Sexuality and British Cinema in the Second World War*. Eds C. Gledhill and G. Swanson. Manchester: Manchester University Press. 13–32.

Leonard, S. and D. Negra. 2017. 'Celebrity'. *Keywords for Media Studies*. Eds L. Ouellette and J. Gray. New York: New York University Press. 28–31.

Morey, A. 2002. '"So Real as to Seem Like Life Itself": The Photoplay Fiction of Adela Rogers St. Johns'. *A Feminist Reader in Early Cinema*. Ed. J. M. Bean and D. Negra. Durham NC and London: Duke University Press. 333–48.

Murphy, R. 1992. *Realism and Tinsel: Cinema and Society in Britain 1939–1949*. London: Routledge.

Noakes, L. 2015. 'Gender, Grief, and Bereavement in Second World War Britain'. *Journal of War and Culture Studies* 8.1: 72–85.

Orgeron, M. 2009. '"You are Invited to Participate": Interactive Fandom in the Age of the Movie Magazine'. *Journal of Film and Video* 61.3. 3–23.

Rojek, C. 2001. *Celebrity*. London: Reaktion Books.

Stacey, J. 1994. *Star Gazing: Hollywood Cinema and Female Spectatorship*. London: Routledge.

Stead, L. 2010. '"So Oft to the Movies They've Been": British Fan Writing and Female Film Audiences in the Silent Era'. *Transformative Works and Cultures* 6 <https://doi.org/10.3983/twc.2011.0224> (last accessed 19 August 2019).

Stead, L. 2013. 'Letter Writing, Cinemagoing and Archive Ephemera'. *Reclamation and Representation: The Boundaries of the Literary Archive*. Ed. C. Smith and L. Stead. Farnham: Ashgate. 139–53.

Stead, L. 2016. *Off to the Pictures: Cinema-going, Women's Writing and Movie Culture in Interwar Britain*. Edinburgh: Edinburgh University Press.

Stead, L. 2017a. '"Dear Cinema Girls": Girlhood, Picturegoing and the Interwar Film Magazine'. *Women's Periodicals and Print Culture in Britain, 1918–1939: The Interwar Period*. Eds C. Clay, M. DiCenzo, B. Green and F. Hackney. Edinburgh: Edinburgh UP. 103–20.

Stead, L. 2017b. 'Silent Era Fan Magazines and British Cinema Culture: Mediating Women's Cinemagoing and Storytelling'. *Women Film Pioneers Project*. Eds J. Gaines, R. Vatsal and M. Dall'Asta. New York, NY: Columbia University Libraries <https://wfpp.cdrs.columbia.edu/essay/silent-era-fan-magazines-and-british-cinema-culture-mediating-womens-cinemagoing-and-storytelling/> (last accessed 19 August 2019).

Street, S. 2002. *British National Cinema*. London: Taylor and Francis.

Studlar, G. 1996. 'The Perils of Pleasure? Fan Magazine Discourse as Women's Commodified Culture in the 1920s'. *Silent Film*. Ed. R. Abel. London: Athlone Press. 263–97.

Taylor, P. M. 1988. 'Introduction: Film, the Historian and the Second World War'. *Britain and the Cinema in the Second World War*. Ed. P. M. Taylor. London: Macmillan.

7

'The most helpful friends in the world': Letters Pages, Expertise and Emotion in British Women's Magazines, c. 1960–80

Tracey Loughran

Introduction

The advertisement is simple: a line drawing of a door bearing the plate 'LETTERS', and text proclaiming, 'Behind this door, you'll find the most helpful friends in the world'. These 'friends' were the magazine's expert advisers on home-making, beauty, health, 'how it's done' and 'human problems'. 'IT'S A FACT', readers of *Woman* magazine were told:

> *WOMAN*'s Council of Editors, the experts that women trust, really *are* the most helpful friends in the world – they have the actual statistics to prove it! People all over the world, millions of them, seek their advice. And the letters keep coming in at an average of ONE THOUSAND A DAY. (*Woman* 4 March 1961: 27)

When this advertisement was published, seismic shifts in women's everyday lives were just over the horizon. Mass entry into the workforce, declining marriage and birth rates, rising divorce rates, the development of new contraceptive and reproductive technologies, and the effects of the Women's Liberation Movement meant that women's daily lives changed in all kinds of ways between the 1960s and 1980s. Mass-market women's magazines, traditionally conservative in outlook, struggled to respond to these dramatic changes.

As the magazine market shrank, publishers and editors experimented with many different techniques to recapture readers. One of the most influential and long-lasting of these changes was the increased space given to readers' voices within the magazine. However, despite this apparent 'democratisation', traditional forms of authority remained highly prized. Within magazines, authority and affective relations were constructed along gendered lines, mirroring power structures in the outside world. Only at the very end of this period, as a new generation of agony aunts started to make claims to experiential expertise, did letters pages really start to reflect changing social attitudes towards emotion, sexuality and gender roles.

In this chapter, I explore the deployment of letter-response formats in mass-market women's magazines' coverage of bodily, psychological and emotional health between 1960 and 1980, with a focus on *Woman* magazine.[1] I contrast male 'doctor' columns, which did not employ the letter-response format, with female 'nurse' columns

BEHIND THIS DOOR
YOU'LL FIND
the most
helpful
friends in
the world
LETTERS
Woman
189 HIGH HOLBORN, W.C.1
COUNCIL OF EDITORS
EDITH BLAIR Home-making
EVELYN HOME Human Problems
RUTH MORGAN Cookery
WYN MUNRO Knitting
VERONICA SCOTT Fashion
ANGELA TALBOT How It's Done
HELEN TEMPLE Beauty
JOAN WILLIAMS, S.R.N., S.C.M. Health
IT'S A FACT
WOMAN's Council of Editors, the experts that women trust, really *are* the most helpful friends in the world—they have actual statistics to prove it! People all over the world, millions of them, seek their advice. And the letters keep coming in at an average of ONE THOUSAND A DAY.
The greatest women's weekly magazine in the world also has the biggest, most varied library of FREE NEWSHEETS, continually being revised and enlarged. Ranging from Beauty Box's home perming hints to Health Department's layette lists, the newsheets cover almost everything in a woman's world: they'll be detailed during the coming weeks in case you've missed one you want.
Do remember: this wonderful personal service is for YOU. WOMAN's friendly experts are only a post-box away any time you may care to consult them.
Every recipe is tried and tested by experts in the Wooden Spoon Club
In Beauty Box you'll find newest salon treatments and wonderful cosmetics
Latest news of clothes and accessories comes to the fashion room
The health department's trained to help you with all problems of fitness
Woman
COUNCIL OF EDITORS BRING YOU
A GREAT FREE SERVICE
your PERSONAL SUCCESS BOOK
It's a unique personal plan for your success in every practical aspect of your home, appearance and health—you've never been offered anything like this before. The complete SUCCESS BOOK adds up to a handy reference volume on subjects you care about.
Backed by the expert knowledge that has made WOMAN's Council of Editors famous, each of the SUCCESS BOOK's sections is complete in itself as a pull-out booklet packed with up-to-date information and easy-to-follow illustrations.
Another wonderful WOMAN offer is waiting for you on page 29, a handsome portfolio to make your SUCCESS BOOK a permanent treasury of knowledge. Watch out, next week, for "How To Be An Expert Knitter." The later sections of your SUCCESS BOOK will deal with home decorating, cookery, health, flower arrangements and other important topics, all of them presented with your PERSONAL SUCCESS in mind.
THE FIRST SECTION OF YOUR SUCCESS BOOK
LOOKING WELL TURNED-OUT
IS AT THE BACK OF THIS ISSUE
27

Figure 7.1 'The most helpful friends in the world', *Woman*, 4 March 1961. (Image with kind permission of TI Media Limited)

that used it intermittently, and with female-led problem pages built entirely on this model. This comparison demonstrates the gendering of expertise and affective labour within magazines, as well as the complex construction of professional identities on and beyond their pages. Magazines depicted their female advisers' expertise as an extension of 'natural' feminine knowledge, and their advice to readers as part of an emotional relationship between women. The publication of letters aided the creation of this imagined bond between reader and adviser.

Within this affective relationship, authority was conveyed in different ways depending on the status and role of the adviser. By flagging nurses' status as health professionals, magazines helped these columnists to maintain a balance between authoritative distance and womanly support. Unlike the authors of 'nurse' columns, agony aunts had no formal qualification to bulwark their claims to expertise – indeed, publicly acknowledging their professional status as *journalists* might even undermine their status as the readers' trusted friend. Agony aunts' memoirs reveal tensions between their claims to professional authority and their reliance on emotional authenticity to justify their interventions in readers' lives. Looking at agony aunts' self-perception and public presentation of the role illuminates the extent to which claims to female expertise remained fraught, despite broader changes in women's social position in this period.

Magazine Markets and Changing Styles of Communication

Magazines have 'acted as private discursive spaces for women for centuries, offering an intimate zone of confidentiality and friendship' (Forster 2015: 158). From the inception of women's magazines, the publication of readers' letters has been crucial in forging this intimate space, 'a tradition . . . re-worked during 200 years of feminine journalism' (Beetham 1996: 2). Readers' letters, and the published or unpublished responses of advisers, helped to build a relationship between the magazine and its readers, and to establish the world within its pages as a 'supportive community' (Hackney 2016: 108). This had practical as well as emotional benefits for both parties. On opening a magazine, readers knew they were 'on "home ground"' and felt personally supported (White 1970: 299–300). For editors and journalists, readers' letters showed active engagement and therefore proved the success of strategies designed to foster 'loyalty, trust and identification with the magazine' (Tinkler 1995: 8). Of course, readers did not necessarily always agree with the magazine, or with each other. Correspondence in women's magazines offered a cacophony of voices, a potential 'space for dissension from the status quo', and witting or unwitting resistance to any 'desired image of womanhood' (Ritchie et al. 2016: 18). But, perhaps perversely, in enabling readers to feel on a more equal footing with the magazine, this capacity for opposition could actually strengthen their sense of a special bond.

Readers' letters continued to fulfil this crucial function of community-building within magazines throughout the twentieth century. However, the steady fall-off in magazine sales from the late 1950s, as well as changing forms of emotional communication, family life and gendered behaviour, prompted noticeable shifts in the deployment of readers' letters and letter-response formats. As the long 1960s took hold, existing mass-market magazines struggled to maintain their grip on audiences. Although in 1964 two-thirds of women in Britain aged sixteen and over still read a woman's weekly magazine – accounting for 12.1 million copies sold per week – the decline was noticeable and, in the long term, irreversible (White 1970: 216–18; Ballaster et al. 1991: 111). In response to fluctuations in the market, influential market research, and senior management beliefs that women's magazines had been 'wearing their skirts too long', publishers and editors experimented with ways to recapture old readers and appeal to new ones (White 1970: 222). The most drastic reaction was the launch of a new title, or the revamp of an old one, with more self-consciously 'liberated' or politicised content. Some, such as *Cosmopolitan* (1972–present), flourished; others, such as *Woman's Mirror* (1960–67) and *Nova* (1965–75), floundered after a brief period in the sun (Cook 2015; Froom, 2017). At the time, it was unclear what new formula might 'stick' and why.

Older mass-market magazines still held the lion's share of the market, but nevertheless felt themselves under threat (Ritchie 2014: 145). Such magazines were forced to make subtle changes in a more 'progressive' direction in the attempt to wrest readers back from these new competitors without alienating the core audience. This shift can be seen in the partial and uneven inclusion of (slightly) more daring content, but is even more evident in the widespread adoption of forms and styles intended to set up a more direct relationship between magazine and reader. These included the proliferation of interactive formats such as quizzes, the infiltration of readers' voices into conventionally 'top-down' formats such as features and advertisements, and changes in the prominence, presentation and pitch of pages incorporating readers' letters. The move towards less hierarchical relationships is most striking in letter-response formats, where there is clear dissonance between the openness of 1970s advice columns, and the formality or overtly moralistic stance of similar columns in earlier decades. Instituting this change in style and tone involved negotiating several competing demands, and it required considerable editorial and journalistic skill to strike the right balance.

This balance was particularly difficult to achieve in these decades for several interrelated reasons. The traditional function of the magazine adviser, to provide expert guidance, remained fundamentally the same – but times had changed, and styles of communication had to change with them. Mary Grieve, editor of *Woman* from the late 1930s to the early 1960s, believed that the growth of consumerism from the 1950s had resulted in a new 'climate of thought', in which it was no longer appropriate for the magazine to speak with 'such an authoritative, remote voice. The time of the monologue was ending; what was now needed was a place where a genuine dialogue could develop'. The magazine was now positioned as 'a partner in an exchange of ideas and experiences', primarily through the inclusion of readers' real-life experiences in different formats and features (Grieve 1964: 198). However, as the 'permissive society' gradually loosened traditional moral restraints, styles of communication and forms of personal relationship changed. Relatability, directness and openness came to be more highly valued as communicative styles. As the 1970s went on, rising rates of premarital sex, cohabitation, illegitimacy and divorce both reflected and spurred on greater discussion of sexual and emotional matters in public life (Cook 2004: 238–40). Magazine advisers had to adapt their tone and content accordingly.

At the same time, and partly because of this social flux, many women began to lose confidence in their own judgement and that of traditional and local sources of advice, such as family, friends and neighbours. In ever-greater numbers, they turned towards 'experts' such as nurses, psychologists and marriage guidance counsellors (Roberts 1995: 141–9; Davis 2012: 112–41). Grieve argued that in an age of 'enhanced communication', women craved 'trustworthy authority', yet had fewer sources of reliable guidance than ever before. Doctors were harassed, parsons had lost their traditional community role, and there was less personal service in supermarkets. In this context, magazines assumed a new importance as 'the only medium wholly devoted to communicating with women on their own terms' (Grieve 1964: 93–6, 210).

In the world outside the magazine, women simultaneously demonstrated unwillingness to be bound by traditional social norms or hierarchies, and an increased appetite for the authority offered by professional expertise. As professional expertise proliferated, magazines became important mediators of new 'psychological norms and languages' (Rose 1989: xii, 208). Within the magazine, advice columnists had to remain approachable by adopting more open and less judgemental styles of communication, but they also needed to speak with the authority that their readers craved. It was a difficult line to tread, and more difficult for some advisers than others according to expectations around gender roles and professional status. These complexities were usually smoothed over on the printed page but, as we will see, were revealed in agony aunts' expressed ambivalence in their memoirs about certain kinds of claim to expertise and authority.

Readers' Letters and Advice Columns in *Woman* Magazine

Woman magazine launched in 1937 as 'a trade paper for women at home', offering guidance on domestic matters such as choosing 'new curtains for the living-room, a husband or a frock' (Makins 1975: 170; Grieve 1964: 138, 177–8). Along with *Woman's Own*, launched five years earlier, it dominated the sector until the 1980s (Ballaster et al. 1991: 110). In 1957, *Woman*'s weekly sales peaked at nearly three and a half million – a postwar record not repeated by any other magazine. A decade later, *Woman* still sold an impressive two-and-a-half-million copies per week and held 22 per cent of the market share of women's weekly magazines – but no publication was immune to the wider decline in sales. From 1962, the magazine lost readers at an average rate of 3.6 per cent each year (Winship 1987: 40; White 1970: 217, 220, 232–5). The publishers responded with various experiments, including the launch of new magazines and concerted consumer campaigns, but none succeeded in recapturing readers in the longer term (White 1970: 194–7).

The fate of *Woman's Mirror* provided conclusive evidence of the risk attached to drastic reinvention. In 1965, this magazine had relaunched with a strikingly and self-consciously 'modern' design and much more radical and serious content (Froom 2017). Sales continued to decline, and in 1967 it merged with *Woman*. Attempts to retain something of the more serious edge of *Woman's Mirror* within the merged magazine had an adverse effect on *Woman*'s sales (White 1970: 224–9). The *Woman* editorial team therefore needed to boost the magazine's sales and retain the magazine's share of a shrinking market, but also had reason to be cautious about experiments that might push away the magazine's core readership. Readers' letters pages and advice columns were popular formats where limits could gently be tested; the form simultaneously allowed the editorial team to appear removed from risqué content, while actively soliciting further content from readers and providing the illusion of democratic conversation.

In these decades, *Woman* made determined efforts to develop a more reciprocal relationship with readers and to include a greater range of readers' voices. In the 1950s, it had introduced a regular readers' letters page, where women could communicate with both the magazine and each other (White 1970: 128). In retrospect, this innovation both marked and motored a new style of relationship between mass-market women's magazines and their readers. From the late 1960s readers' voices and stories were also increasingly included in *Woman*'s feature articles, including series on living with problems like mental illness (*Woman* 4 October 1971: 24), marriage guidance counselling (*Woman* 1 July 1972: 63–4) or experiences of pregnancy and childbirth (*Woman* 7 April 1973: 32–6). However, despite shifts in tone and content, and occasional changes in column titles and advisers, for the most part the type and template of pages that featured readers' letters remained remarkably stable over the period covered here. The superficial democratisation of the magazine masked the retention of traditional attitudes towards expertise and authority.

For parts of this period the magazine opened with a short communication from the editor (from 1975 named 'In a Woman's World'), followed by the dedicated readers' letters page, 'Woman to Woman'. The 'etiquette' column remained under the stewardship of Angela Talbot for most of the period, but changes of title to 'Socialsense' (1969) and then 'Actionwoman' (1975) reflected the increased emphasis on a range of practical, welfare and consumer issues. Evelyn Home's offer to 'Talk It Over' continued to head the problem page until Peggy Makins' retirement in 1974, when the column was rebranded under the names of her successors, Anna Raeburn (1974–8) and Virginia Ironside (1978 onwards). After *Woman* absorbed *Woman's Mirror*, Marje Proops joined the ranks as a second agony aunt. The format of her page went through several iterations, including the conventional 'Dear Marje', 'Counselling in the Round' (looking at the different perspectives of protagonists on their shared problem), in-depth analyses of 'The Human Dilemma' and 'Male Mail'. She departed in 1972 but continued to write occasional articles for the magazine. Readers' letters, the etiquette column and the problem page therefore formed a holy triumvirate for the expression of readers' voices throughout these decades.

There was one more advice column that often, but not consistently, featured readers' letters. Nurse Joan Williams' 'Talking about Health' (later 'Healthy Living') page sometimes included readers' letters, most often a single letter followed by a much longer explanation of the health or childcare problem that it had raised. In 1964, a new section ('From the Postbag') featured a series of shorter letters, but this was not included on the page every week. There were peaks and troughs in the level of readers' letters included on the page, with notable spikes in 1962 and 1966. The inconsistent use of letters on the 'Talking about Health' page illuminates the tangled relations of gender, expertise and caregiving within magazines, and the extent to which *professional* expertise was portrayed as inconsistent with the personal and affective relations established via the letter-response format. Even though *Woman* was staffed by an almost all-female cadre of professional journalists, ambivalence is the hallmark of (self-)representations of female expertise within the magazine's pages. The professional status of journalists was rarely acknowledged in the magazine; the presentation of magazine advisers as the reader's friend, who shared her domestic world, meant that female claims to professional expertise could surface only under specific, limited conditions. This is evident when we compare how expertise, authority and emotion were deployed in the columns of three different advisers: the male doctor, the female nurse and the female agony aunt.

Doctors and Nurses

The main women's magazines all featured a regular column by a female health professional. Unlike the etiquette column or the problem page, there was no settled format for the 'nurse' column across different magazines. *Woman's Weekly* ran two 'nurse' columns. Sister Helen Grove provided guidance on minor medical matters (e.g. what to put in a home first aid box, how to deal with backache, the causes and treatment of fungal infections) and sometimes answered readers' health queries; in 'Letters to Matron' an unnamed health professional replied to questions on pregnancy, reproductive and gynaecological problems and childcare. In *Woman's Own*, Ruth Martin's 'Woman-to-Woman Service' covered various female health problems, while her 'Mother-and-Child Service' dealt with practical healthcare for babies and children. These pages sometimes featured readers' letters, with the semi-regular inclusion of a 'Q&A' section from the early 1970s, but the emphasis was on factual and informative pieces about different aspects of health. Joan Williams' page in *Woman* contained similar elements to both the other columns. It dealt most often with pregnancy, childhood and parenting, and had a strongly practical emphasis: pregnancy diagnosis, healthcare and preparation for the expectant mother, and children's problems such as stammering or obesity. In the 1960s, the column most often took the form of a short informative piece, but also sometimes included responses to readers' letters on diverse topics like blood pressure, childhood illnesses or behavioural problems and vaccination. The column appeared less often from the mid-1970s and disappeared entirely later in the decade, perhaps because feature articles covered medical matters more frequently in this period.

The inclusion of letters on *Woman*'s health page constructed the reader as actively soliciting Nurse Williams' guidance, and as an important participant in the world of the magazine. However, even when readers' letters were not actually printed, the column constantly flagged Williams' helpfulness and availability. A piece might be framed as a response to readers' concerns: 'Unexplained medical terms can cause needless anxiety. Joan Williams, S.R.N., S.C.M., answers readers who want to know "What does it mean?"' Next to this piece, Williams' photograph was captioned, 'Our Health Editor is always glad to answer your letters' (*Woman* 5 October 1963: 33). The column constantly reminded readers that Williams would answer all letters by post. This message was reinforced elsewhere in the magazine. Evelyn Home often deflected medical enquiries to Williams, for example pointing out, 'This query concerning childbirth is not in my department, I'm afraid. Do write to Health Editor Joan Williams' (*Woman* 6 April 1963: 85). On occasion, Home explained that she had consulted Williams about the medical aspects of a problem, to ensure that she could comment accurately on the emotional side (*Woman* 1 July 1967: 60). Similar strategies were pursued in *Woman's Own* and *Woman's Weekly*, where readers were often directed to send in for leaflets, and reminded that advisers would respond to letters. *Woman's Weekly* readers were told that 'Matron has expert knowledge of child care and leaflets to guide you through pregnancy. You can always write to her at the address on page 5, and know she is eager to help' (*Woman's Weekly* 6 April 1963: 60). In such formulations, nurses were represented as emotionally engaged ('glad to answer', 'eager to help'), as well as experts on the health of women and children.

A comparison of 'nurse' pages with the 'doctor' columns in *Woman* and *Woman's Own* (there was no equivalent in *Woman's Weekly*) highlights the gendered construction of expertise and authority in magazines. In *Woman's Own*, Dr Roderick Wimpole (until 1974), and later Dr Michael Smith (from 1978),[2] wrote the 'Doctor's Diary', in which the doctor told of his recent encounter with a patient. In *Woman*, this brief was fulfilled by 'Dr Meridith', first in the 'Family Doctor' column, then in 'I went to the doctor' (from 1964), and then in 'Dr Meridith's Surgery' (from 1973; after 1978, the column appeared irregularly). In its first iteration, the column told the story of diagnosis and treatment of a specific ailment from the doctor's perspective, and in its revamped form simply switched to the patient's point of view, 'as told to' a *Woman* journalist. The change is indicative of the subtle shifts towards a more relational style of communication found elsewhere in magazines at this time – but, despite these superficial changes, the content, tone and overall 'message' of the column remained remarkably similar over this period.

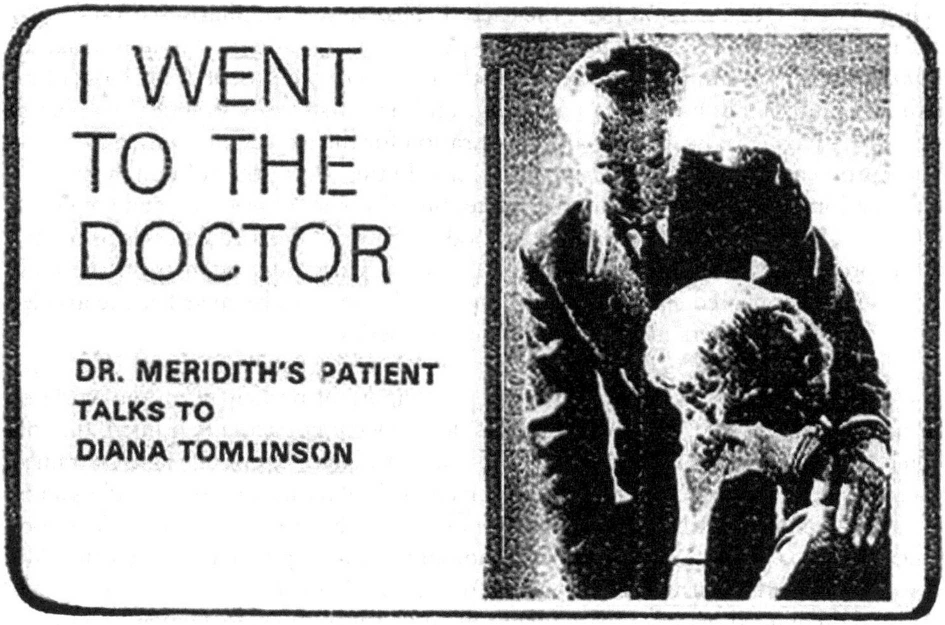

Figure 7.2 'I went to the doctor', *Woman*, 5 October 1968. (Image with kind permission of TI Media Limited)

These 'doctor' columns always followed exactly the same formula of describing symptoms and diagnosis, then listing methods of prevention and treatment. They dealt mostly with low-key complaints such as tennis elbow, sore throats, colds, cramp and headaches or, sometimes, minor emergencies such as burns. The columns emphasised preventive medicine, including the importance of regular health checks, and precautions such as breast examination or obtaining flu injections. Serious illnesses were either avoided or framed as the doctor's reassurance to a patient who had heard about the illness elsewhere, as in the case of a woman worried about taking any tablets at all during her pregnancy because of the Thalidomide tragedy (*Woman* 5 January 1963: 31). But while the conditions covered in the 'doctor' column might affect women or men of all ages, the doctor was typically consulted by an adult woman, either on her own behalf or that of her child or husband. The visual presentation of the columns further emphasised gendered differences in power. The 'Doctor's Diary' photograph showed the doctor's back, with the female patient facing the reader. The Dr Meridith column rarely pictured the doctor, but when it did, he was always presented as a shadowy presence behind the patient, or as looming over her seated or reclining figure. The combined effect of image and text underlined the disparity in knowledge and power between doctor and patient, and reinforced the authority of medical expertise.

The other notable feature of the 'doctor' column is the complete absence of readers' letters – particularly important if we accept that the 'form of the personalised letter and personalised response both enacts and addresses the idea of feminine responsibility' (Ballaster et al. 1991: 123). It was never suggested that readers might write to Dr Meridith, and the 'Doctor's Diary' column explicitly stated that Dr Wimpole was

✻ TALKING ABOUT HEALTH

hoping for a baby

Discussing delayed pregnancy, JOAN WILLIAMS S.R.N., S.C.M. emphasizes that, with rare exceptions, every young couple may become parents

IT is a known fact that within the framework of marriages where there is a complete and natural sex relationship, pregnancy will begin within a year for about eighty out of a hundred couples. And with only a further ten per cent will it occur during the second year.

Obviously then, a couple who have tried unsuccessfully for a whole year to have a baby are justified in thinking that something may be wrong. And they are equally justified in seeking medical advice. Indeed, they would be wise to do so; particularly if the wife is in her late twenties or older.

They may well find that the delay has a very simple explanation which is quickly revealed through a quiet talk with their doctor. For often the root of the trouble is their lack of true understanding in regard to marital relationship, and/or the fertile phase in the menstrual cycle.

adjustment

In this case, the putting into practice of necessary adjustments will probably lead to the desired pregnancy within a few months. Or maybe even sooner.

And if the doctor cannot find any obvious cause for the delay in conception? If he advises specialist investigation? There is still no cause for despondency or apprehension. For true sterility is rare, and there is every chance that the cause or causes of delay will be found through tests—none of which is in the least alarming.

(A brief description of what is likely to be involved is given in my free newsheet entitled "Routine Fertility Tests." This will be sent to any reader who would like to have it and encloses a large stamped addressed envelope with her request.)

causes

Among the causes of delayed pregnancy on the wife's side are spasm and blockage of the Fallopian tubes. Also an erosion (outgrowth of gland cells lining the canal of the cervix or neck of the womb).

Then there's a "dry" cervix or lack of normal cervical secretions. And the kind of discharge which kills the male sperm before they have time to enter first the womb and then the tubes for the purpose of fertilization.

Fibroids and tiny equally non malignant growths called polypi may also cause delayed pregnancy. As can inflammation of the womb, although, strange as it may seem, the condition of the body of the womb is not nearly so influential a factor in the picture of sub-fertility as is that of the cervix.

Anything else? Yes, much that is too intricate and too personal for discussion on this page. But there is one other cause of delayed conception, which can be touched on, and which is much more common than is sometimes supposed. This is a disturbance of the endocrinal glands: a disturbance which usually affects the pattern of menstruation and which is brought about by deep-seated emotional conflict.

That is why no woman should feel distressed or affronted if, at the conclusion of investigations, the specialist advises, not operation, nor cauterization, not hormone therapy, nor carefully regulated dieting, but psychiatric treatment.

In other words, a series of discussions in which a specially trained doctor helps his patient to bring up from the deeper layers of her mind, the shape and sources of her conflict. And then helps her to make a fresh evaluation of the situation, together with the necessary mental and emotional adjustments.

The resulting peace of mind and realistic thinking encourages a happier life, increased glandular harmony, normal menstrual cycle, and, eventually, conception.

This is a brief and necessarily incomplete picture of sub-fertility. Not all its causes can be recognized. Not all will yield to treatment, improved relationships and time. But many do.

And that is why—with rare exceptions—no married woman of childbearing years need give up hope of having a child of her own. For even if treatment fails, a seeming miracle can happen. Then one day her hopes will be fulfilled.

NEXT WEEK: New school ahead

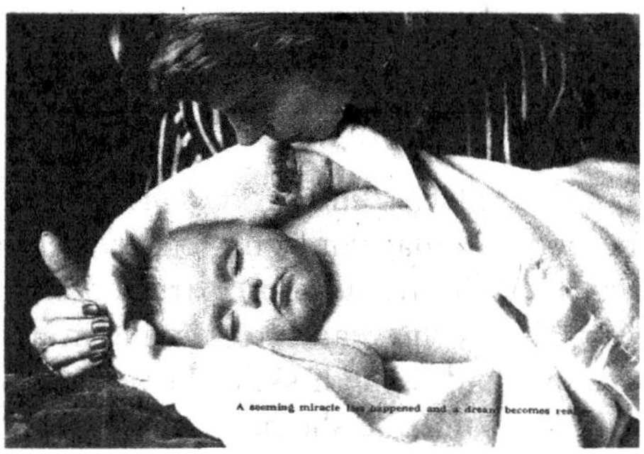

A seeming miracle [illegible] happened and a [illegible] becomes [illegible]

OUR FAMILY DOCTOR

CRAMP

She was a tall, slim, athletic looking nineteen-year-old.

"I'm going on holiday with friends next month," she said, "and want to swim a lot. I'm apt to get cramp and wondered how to prevent it?"

"When do you get cramp?"

"Mostly at night, but I'm worried about getting it while I'm swimming. Usually it starts just as I'm going to sleep," she added. "Always in my right leg. Here," touching her calf muscles. "But if I get up and stamp round the bedroom it soon goes."

"Does it happen any special night in the week?" I asked.

She said slowly: "Well, I've noticed it on Tuesdays and Thursdays."

"What do you do on those days that you don't on others?"

The answer was that she went to keep-fit sessions at a local gymnasium.

"Do you perspire a lot?"

"We all do, but we drink lots of lemonade and that sort of thing."

I explained to her that cramp is often caused by having lost salt through sweating.

"You get thirsty and drink a lot. "All the body fluids are salty, and the salt and water is carefully balanced. Lose water and salt by sweating profusely and they stay in balance. Replace only the water and the balance of salt gets upset and that shows up very commonly as a muscular cramp later on.

"You must try what people do in hot countries. Drop a salt tablet into the water or lemonade and you replace both salt and water. Then you won't get cramp."

On holiday, I told her, she was more likely to get cramp if she swam soon after a meal.

"Wait at least an hour after eating, and never swim when you are cold. Warm up your muscles by jumping about and doing a few exercises before you go into the water.

"If ever you do get cramp in the water, don't panic. Float on your back and use your hands and arms to scull yourself back to the beach. Then pull the cramped leg right up to your chest and massage the affected calf muscles. If you can get some heat into them—say from a handkerchief soaked in a thermos of hot tea—so much the better.

"And if you should get cramp again in bed at night pull your leg up to your chest. Then try to pull your toes up towards your chin. That lengthens and stretches the contracted muscles and the cramp will soon go."

I learnt later that she had a really wonderful holiday with never a hint of cramp. DR. MERIDITH

Figure 7.3 'A new life begins', *Woman*, 4 January 1964. (Image with kind permission of TI Media Limited)

unable to enter into correspondence. Essentially, both columns told the same story over and over again: the doctor never puzzled over a diagnosis for more than a few seconds, and the patient who followed his advice always responded with suitable gratitude. The formula of the column did not allow for any other outcome than the triumph of the doctor. In this way, the formal health content of women's magazines displayed deference to the figure of the male doctor, and boosted the prestige and authority of the general practitioner. The doctor column therefore constituted the doctor-patient relationship as a male-female association with an inbuilt imbalance in power – the doctor, the male authority figure, could always solve the problems of the woman, who was always in need of help.

The 'nurse' column, on the other hand, presented the nurse-patient relationship as an exchange between women, perhaps not as friends or equals, but as part of the same community (as *Woman's Own* had it, a 'Woman-to-Woman Service'). The content of the 'nurse' column reinforced traditional associations between women, caregiving and the female world of pregnancy, childbirth and childrearing. The nurse's tone was usually brisk but reassuring, adopting a caring language that the doctor's column avoided. Joan Williams told mothers not to worry too much about their children's problems in starting school: 'This is all very natural, so don't be upset about it' (*Woman* 4 December 1965: 22). Ruth Martin's column sought to reassure women that there was nothing to worry about, whether the problem was a retroverted cervix or the menopause (*Woman's Own* 6 January 1962: 51; *Woman's Own* 4 April 1964: 81).

Finally, the varied format of the nurse column (the practical guide, responses to letters, or discussions) meant that it did not hammer home the eventual triumph of medical expertise. The practical guide format simply stated what should happen if the patient followed a particular course of action, without recording her grateful response; and the letter and response format was necessarily open-ended. The nurse's expertise was carefully 'feminised' to replicate and extend the caring roles of 'ordinary' women, with only the persistent reference to her professional qualifications marking out her ultimate authority. This emphasis on formal qualifications served to separate nurses from doctors, whose qualifications were never listed (the title alone conferred sufficient prestige), and from agony aunts – who dealt in feminine and familial problems from a very different angle, and who *only* used the feminised letter-response format.

Agony Aunts and Problem Pages

More so than any other adviser, the agony aunt played a crucial role in setting up the perceived bond between magazine and reader. Her persona was 'an integral part of creating the fiction of the friendship or trusted relationship between the reader and the adviser that allows the reader to confide in a stranger' (Morris 2004: 12). Indeed, if the journalist had enough skill, the agony aunt would not be a stranger to the reader, but rather someone she had grown to know through familiarity with 'her views on intimate problems of marriage, on family relationships and on all the range of human emotion and experience' (Grieve 1964: 98). Because of her symbolic importance within the magazine, the agony aunt has had to bear unusually heavy ideological freight. Older traditions of feminist scholarship criticised the individualisation of female unhappiness on the problem page, and its failure to recognise that 'women's problems may have political origins, be politically structured, or politically transformable' (Ballaster et al. 1991: 146–7; Winship 1987: 77–8, 80). The problem page has also been viewed as reinforcing feminine stereotypes, both in terms of the all-suffering woman who seeks counsel, and the caring, nurturing, self-sacrificing adviser who provides it (Jackson 2005: 299).

While acknowledging the power of these critiques, recent historians have put forward more nuanced interpretations of the importance of the problem page. In these analyses, the emotional and practical exchange between adviser, correspondent and readers is crucial. The journalists who produced the page were well aware of its 'semi-public, semi-private' nature (Hackney 2016: 108). The adviser served up her one-to-one response for a mass audience, and so the problem page had to entertain as well as to guide and inform (Bingham 2012: 53). In working out how best to achieve this balance, advisers created a space 'where the boundaries between private and public, of what knowledges should and should not be spoken in public, [were] challenged' (Le Masurier 2016: 206). In pushing the boundaries of acceptable public discourse, problem pages made a significant contribution to the climate of reform in the 1950s and 1960s (Bingham 2012: 58). In turn, the relaxation of legal restraints against abortion and homosexuality in the late 1960s made it possible (eventually) for editors to print letters on topics that were once taboo, for advisers to respond more openly, and for readers to write more explicitly about what troubled them (Tebbutt 2017: 187, 192). These shifts coincided with the rise of the Women's Liberation Movement and, by the mid-1970s, mass-market magazines had started actively to encourage women's greater assertiveness in personal and sexual relationships – albeit without challenging the political status quo (Tebbutt 2017: 190–1; Cook 2015: 239–40).

As well as telling us about wider social shifts, problem pages provide insight into 'the day-to-day experience of ordinary people'; any genre that deals with real people's questions must also 'take account of real areas of difficulty and contradiction' (Morris 2004: 12; Ritchie 2014: 151). By reaffirming 'the social value of the mundane', problem pages can foster (temporary) confidence in readers' own identity and experience (McKay 2008: 99–101). In Bingham's view, ultimately problem pages 'encouraged readers 'to reflect on their lives, to claim sexual pleasure, and to reject unhappy relationships' (Bingham 2012: 60). For Claire Langhamer (2013: 39, 44), it is precisely because agony aunts mediated between 'the subjective and the prescriptive' that problem pages 'facilitate understanding of the dynamic relationship between everyday emotional experience and standards and norms'. Her study of mid-century problem pages focuses on the emotional exchange between readers and advisers, and shows how readers could push back against moral norms and specific guidance, while their letters 'showcased feelings and experiences which often defied prescribed solutions' (Ibid.: 52). Cumulatively, this newer scholarship highlights the importance of problem pages as windows into everyday life, social change, the authority of popular 'experts' and the agency of readers.

Expertise, Authority and Ambivalence

Woman is unique in that all three journalists who served as agony aunts in the 1960s and 1970s published extended reflections on their role. For nearly forty years, Peggy Makins wrote *Woman*'s problem page under the name 'Evelyn Home' (chosen by her psychoanalyst predecessor). When Makins retired in 1974, Anna Raeburn took over the page; and in 1978 she was succeeded by Virginia Ironside. Moving the focus to the agony aunt's own view of her role, rather than changes on the page itself, allows us to chart shifts in relationships with readers and perceptions of expertise and authority. This analysis suggests that problem pages undoubtedly reflected the broader social changes of the period, and that this can be perceived in the more direct and personal style of agony aunts. However, the nature of the work involved on the page, and primarily the relationship with readers that it entailed, in some ways prevented agony aunts from challenging either existing (gendered) forms of authority or the political status quo.

Unlike the doctors or nurses who served as advisers elsewhere in the magazine, none of *Woman*'s three agony aunts in this period had any formal qualifications for the role. They received no training and had no prior experience in psychology, counselling or the caring professions. They were all professional journalists who had learnt to counsel strangers only via prolonged exposure to their problems. As a result, they presented their claims to expertise as agony aunts with some ambivalence. In their memoirs, all insisted on their professional integrity as journalists. Makins referred those who might doubt her abilities to her years of experience on the page, her capacity to compare any problem with 'the histories of thousands of others, especially with those who have come through the same sort of unhappiness, and describe what has proved to be the best way of dealing with it' (Makins 1975: 191–2). Ironside categorically stated that 'no one employs me because I'm a nice person. I'm employed as a journalist to write a good, readable page. I'm employed for my writing and editorial skills rather than for my caring and compassion' (Ironside 1991: 131). A similar perspective led Raeburn to reject the title of agony aunt, and even the ultimate significance of this role in her career, stating that, 'I was trying to learn to be a writer and I began on a problem page. It was not the be-all and end-all of my life' (Raeburn 1985: 140).

In other ways, however, all three advisers downplayed the expertise needed to be a successful agony aunt. They maintained that no matter what advice they proffered, often the simple act of writing a letter that articulated their problems had the most beneficial effect on correspondents (Makins 1975: 184–5; Raeburn 1985: 139; Ironside 1991: 28, 105). When they highlighted the emotional aspects of the role, they de-emphasised the skill that it required and the power that they wielded, instead echoing the magazine's own presentation of the adviser's affective relationship with readers. Ironside believed that 'an agony aunt should be a friend – and a friend simply gives advice from the heart and the head, not from a book of theory' (Ironside 1991: 3, 113). Makins contended that 'I never wanted anyone to look on me as an authority, only as a friend in need' (Makins 1975: 162). But ambivalence is clear here too. The advisers did take pride in their work – and saw it as work. Raeburn described the problem page as primarily 'a vehicle for teaching', and the role of agony aunt as to mediate between 'the person with the problem' and 'all sorts of agencies and self-help groups and specialist disciplines'. To this end, she compiled a set of alphabetised files with links to reading and organisations on every relevant subject that she could conceive (Raeburn 1985: 134, 139, 141). Ironside (1991: 108, 20, 31) also saw her role as to provide information and produced or gathered nearly 150 leaflets on different problems. More than simply knowing where to find expertise if needed, she asserted her own importance as the last resort for people whom the experts had 'failed' (Ibid.: 111–12).

How can we explain these contradictory attitudes? The 'origin stories' put forward by all three offer a clue. All presented their eventual adoption of the agony aunt role as a lucky accident rather than professional manoeuvring. Makins initially took the post on a temporary basis (in 1937). As second sub-editor of *Woman*, she had believed that taking on the problem page would harm her journalistic prospects, but as a young woman with little life experience, she also felt unqualified to advise readers (Makins 1975: 39, 49, 129).[3] Anna Raeburn initially perceived the prospect of taking on the post as ludicrous: 'Here was I, 30 years old, marriage on the rocks, not respectable, not accomplished or even very experienced as a journalist, no white coat, no orthopaedic Oxfords, not a cardy or degree in sight. Why on earth should an established publication like *Woman* even look twice at me?' (Raeburn 1985: 126). Ironside (1991: 2) described herself as feeling 'totally inadequate' and 'overwhelmed at the idea of even being considered for such an exalted position' when she was offered the post.

Of course, these stories should not be taken at face value. They hint at ambivalence towards the agony aunt role, and the modesty with which experienced journalists had to present their achievements in order to maintain the caring persona on which their success was built. More than this, however, they convey a genuine conflict: between professional expertise as journalists and their largely experiential claims to be able to help with other people's problems. Unlike the authors of 'nurse' columns, agony aunts had no additional professional qualifications to bulwark their distinctly feminine form of authority, and so were subject to continual tension in justifying their claims to expertise to themselves and to others. However, when we look at the emotional labour agony aunts performed, it becomes clear that the nature of their experience, particularly in how the role forced them to engage with readers, was significantly different to the more standardised professional relations of nurse or doctor and patient.

Social Change on the Problem Page

Problem pages became more direct, explicit and supportive of female assertiveness in this period. This can be shown through agony aunts' responses to the problem of involuntary childlessness. Throughout the 1960s and 1970s, readers often wrote in for guidance on conception, adoption or convincing partners to start a family. As we might expect, towards the end of the 1970s, letters demonstrated greater openness about sexuality and bodily functions. Readers asked about ejaculation, orgasm, the long-term effects of the Pill or abortion, and the possibility of reversing sterilisation.[4] Advisers were more explicit too. When one woman confessed her fear that she could not conceive because 'after making love, the semen just runs out of me', Virginia Ironside wryly responded: 'Had Newton been a woman, this might have been the way he would have discovered gravity' (*Woman* 26 May 1979: 78). Moreover, the effects of the Women's Liberation Movement might be seen in Anna Raeburn's suggestion – radical for a mass-market weekly – that women could even try to see the benefits of the childless state (*Woman* 21 January 1978: 56).

Yet while the tone and style of the page shifted, advisers continued to dispense the same *kinds* of advice in these decades: emotional counselling rather than detailed medical information or technological solutions.[5] Readers were reassured that they did not 'have to go on feeling unhappy about this for ever', and pointed towards helpful agencies, services and books.[6] When women asked agony aunts about the causes of infertility, advisers could quash misconceptions, but not provide a diagnosis. They usually only told readers to consult their own doctors, or perhaps to contact the magazine's health editor for further information.[7] This approach reinforced the gendered division of labour in magazines' health coverage, where male doctors provided guidance on physical health and female advisers provided emotional counselling. At most, agony aunts reassured readers that doctors could offer specialist help (without specifying what this was), or urged them to be persistent if doctors did not take their fears seriously (implying less-than-perfect faith in medical counsel). Stylistic shifts that reflected important social changes also masked important continuities in both the focus of guidance and the relation of the agony aunt to other magazine experts.

In this regard, it is worth noting that agony aunts were reluctant to acknowledge the effects of social changes on the kinds of problem that they encountered. Makins traced broad shifts that had affected the problems seen on the page, including rising levels of female employment, the effects of birth control, and easier access to divorce. However, she also maintained that the problems received were 'changeless in essence, since they arise from the apparently invariable qualities which make up human nature' (Makins 1975: 75–7, 82–3, 150). Raeburn (1985: 138) did not comment on the issue at all. Instead, she stated that while anyone looking only at 'the outline of each case' might conclude that most problems were more or less the same, the important point is that they were experienced by different people, in different ways. While Ironside believed that there had been sweeping changes in the early 1960s and 1970s, she concluded that 'since then problems have been much the same, with only slight variations'. Like Makins and Raeburn, she insisted that ultimately the problems were not 'as important as the feelings behind them' (Ironside 1991: 166). All three advisers decoupled the problems that they had personally encountered from their social context, and instead stressed their timeless essence.

This deflection of social context could support feminist readings of the depoliticised problem page – but it can also be explained via the nature of the agony aunt's work, which involved more than producing a readable page. The problem page required intense and often emotionally draining labour. At the time of Makins' retirement, 'Evelyn Home' received between 400 and 500 letters a week. A team of behind-the-scenes respondents answered all letters, but the agony aunt held ultimate responsibility for letters that bore her name (Makins 1975: 54; Ironside 1991: 86–8). She had to sift letters to determine the urgency of a response, often encountering a range of distressing problems on the way, and to check the tone and accuracy of letters produced by the team. Agony aunts therefore dealt personally with a huge volume of problems, in a manner that involved direct engagement with the words of distressed people. In describing how they edited letters for publication, all three advisers emphasised the importance of searching for clues to the correspondent's personality, and tailoring her reply to the individual (Makins 1975: 160; Raeburn 1985: 138; Ironside 1991: 96, 102). Viewed in this way, the tendency to individualise was not – or not only – a symptom of depoliticisation; rather, it demonstrates the agony aunt's human response to a human problem.

In fact, Ironside was uncharacteristically prickly when discussing the question of whether problems had changed over the years: 'When you are on a battlefield tending the wounded, you don't look at the experience objectively, with a view to doing an anthropological survey of war in this day and age. You just get down to business' (Ironside, 1991: 44). Her tone hints at the emotional burden carried by agony aunts, who were continually exposed to the pain of others with no way of knowing whether they had helped or not. Advisers rarely, if ever, received feedback from correspondents. As a result, Makins (1975: 58) sometimes 'felt the job was meaningless and the trouble taken to find hope or comfort entirely lost'. In her book, Ironside (1991: 51) reproduced a long letter from a suicidal man and commented that, 'I will never know if my letter helped or if he got better of his own accord or whether he did indeed commit suicide'. She insisted that she did not find the work depressing, and that her own role differed enormously from that of a 'counsellor in the flesh': 'I do think about my readers, I do worry about them and I do take their problems home with me. But at the end of the day we never meet, and I never see their tear-stained faces, their bruises or their haunted eyes' (Ironside, 1991: 151–2). The imaginative force of this description underscores Ironside's deep sense of responsibility to her correspondents, and belies her claim that the emotional costs of the role were not high.

Conclusion

Looking at the role of letters pages within magazines is one way to understand the complicated relations of expertise, authority and emotion in these decades. The power structures within magazines mirrored those in the outside world. At the end of this period, expertise was still heavily gendered. Within the magazine, in order to deploy professional expertise, women still had to embark on affective relationships, while male experts were permitted to maintain their distance from readers. Emotional and sexual styles of communication underwent significant changes in these decades. However, the ambivalent placing of female expertise within the pages of the magazine suggests that, despite the resurgent feminist movement, at a fundamental level, gender relations remained unaltered.

But are the pages of the magazine the best place to look for such change? We can perhaps trace new attitudes towards gendered expertise and authority in agony aunts' implicit attitudes towards the role. Makins (1975: 125, 134–5), who came to maturity in the 1930s, still believed in the 1970s that 'women's basic impulses are maternal'. Consequently, she perceived her own role as 'Evelyn Home' in terms of acting as 'a mother-figure to millions'. This description implied a familial model of authority, one simultaneously absolute (who has more power than a mother over a child?) and firmly within the accepted model of female power. Her tone, including frequent use of 'my dear' and other such assumptions of seniority, bolstered this impression. On the page, she avoided reference to her personal life, instead maintaining as much distance from the reader as possible within the constraints of the form. Her successors, on the other hand, broke the carapace of the agony aunt open. In Virginia Ironside's view, Anna Raeburn's insistence on using her real name on the page 'said more about women's status than any replies which advocated women's liberation. It emphasised that this woman really was an individual in her own right and not just some fantasy dreamt up by a psychologist.' (Ironside 1991: 11, 20).

Raeburn carried this presentation of an authentic self throughout her work on the page, and in doing so modelled a new kind of female authority and expertise. She aimed to avoid talking down to correspondents, and instead to 'write from the point of view of identifying with the correspondent as much as possible', adopting 'a more direct approach, less diluted language', and breaking down the them-and-us-mentality of supplicants versus experts (Raeburn 1985: 133–4, 140). Her memoir is excruciatingly honest about her relationships with family and lovers, and her experiences of divorce, abortion, depression, grief, therapy, menstrual problems and domestic violence. She repeatedly quipped that her experience of agony was her main qualification to answer others' problems (Raeburn 1985: 70, 136). Ironside followed in her footsteps, asserting that readers had to know that 'agony aunts, too, can suffer just as many irrational, inane problems as they themselves'. She wanted 'someone who talks to me on equal terms, someone to reassure me by telling me that they, too, have felt as silly or mad as I do; and then telling me how they coped with it'. As a result, she aimed to convey herself in the column as 'a real person, someone, in my case, who's been divorced, been a single parent, got a child, spends half her time cooking and washing and worrying' (Ironside 1991:143–4).

This model of female expertise was based on an open admission of personal experience that aimed to connect the adviser with her millions of readers, and that could leave her intensely vulnerable. This approach may not have involved an overtly political reading of women's problems, but it did entail the sharing of lived experience with the practical aim of comforting and guiding readers. It perhaps only went halfway to making the personal political; but in demonstrating the messiness of women's lives, this approach set up a new kind of affective relationship with readers – one that might even have come closer to the kinds of emotional bond experienced by real rather than ideal friends, the kind who embrace each other's imperfections.

Notes

1. The research for this chapter was supported by a British Academy Small Grant. My thanks to Matthew Grant and Daisy Payling for their extremely helpful comments on argument.
2. An anonymous 'GP's Casebook' fulfilled a similar brief in the intervening years.
3. It is important to note that Makins was ambivalent about the role of agony aunt, as well as her own inexperience. This may reflect the narrow range of professional opportunities available to women in the 1930s, as well as the lower status of agony aunts at this time – by the time that Raeburn and later Ironside took on the role, agony aunts had achieved higher status within the industry.
4. *Woman*'s problem page: 11 February 1978; 18 March 1978; 17 June 1978; 1 July 1978; 14 October 1978; 6 January 1979; 7 July 1979; 14 July 1979; 26 January 1980; and 29 March 1980.
5. In part, this related to concerns about what could and could not be published. In the late 1970s, editors were still wary of potential moral objections to artificial insemination (Makins 1975: 142–4).
6. *Woman*'s problem page: 5 October 1963; 2 July 1966; and 21 January 1978.
7. *Woman*'s problem page: 4 March 1961 and 8 July 1961.

Works Cited

Ballaster, R., M. Beetham, E. Fraser and S. Hebron. 1991. *Women's Worlds: Ideology, Femininity and the Woman's Magazine.* Basingstoke: Macmillan.

Beetham, M. 1996. *A Magazine of Her Own? Domesticity and Desire in the Woman's Magazine, 1800–1914.* London and New York: Routledge.

Bingham, A. 2012. 'Newspaper Problem Pages and British Sexual Culture Since 1918'. *Media History* 18.1: 51–63.

Cook, H. 2004. *The Long Sexual Revolution: English Women, Sex, and Contraception, 1800–1975.* Oxford: Oxford University Press.

Cook, H. 2015. '*Nova* 1965–1970: Love, Masculinity and Feminism, but Not as We Know It'. *Love and Romance in Britain, 1918–1970.* Eds A. Harris and T. W. Jones. Basingstoke and New York: Palgrave Macmillan. 225–44.

Davis, A. 2012. *Modern Motherhood: Women and Family in England, 1945–2000.* Manchester and New York: Manchester University Press.

Forster, L. 2015. *Magazine Movements: Women's Culture, Feminisms and Media Form.* New York and London: Bloomsbury.

Froom, H. 2017. Woman's Mirror, *the 'New Woman', and Female Magazine Readers in the 1960s*. Unpublished MA dissertation. Cardiff University.
Grieve, M. 1964. *Millions Made My Story*. London: Victor Gollancz Ltd.
Hackney, F. 2016. 'Getting a Living, Getting a Life: Leonora Eyles, Employment and Agony, 1925–1930'. *Women in Magazines: Research, Representation, Production and Consumption*. Eds R. Ritchie, S. Hawkins, N. Phillips and S. Jay Kleinberg. New York and London: Routledge. 107–24.
Ironside, V. 1991. *Problems! Problems! Confessions of an Agony Aunt*. London: Robson Books.
Jackson, S. 2005. '"I'm 15 and Desperate for Sex": "Doing" and "Undoing" Desire in Letters to a Teenage Magazine'. *Feminism & Psychology* 15.3: 166–85.
Langhamer, C. 2013. 'Everyday Advice on Everyday Love: Romantic Expertise in Mid-Twentieth Century Britain'. *L'Homme Z. F .G.* 24.1: 35–52.
Le Masurier, M. 2016. 'Popular Feminism and the Second Wave: Women's Liberation, Sexual Liberation, and *Cleo* Magazine'. *Women in Magazines: Research, Representation, Production and Consumption*. Eds R. Ritchie, S. Hawkins, N. Phillips and S. J. Kleinberg. New York and London: Routledge. 201–13.
McKay, S. 2008. 'Advice Columns as Cultural Intermediaries'. *Australian Journal of Communication* 35.3: 93–103.
Makins, P. 1975. *The Evelyn Home Story*. Glasgow: Fontana/Collins.
Morris, P. 2004. 'From Private to Public: Alba de Céspedes' Agony Column in 1950s Italy'. *Modern Italy* 9.1: 11–20.
Raeburn, A. 1985. *Talking to Myself*. London: Sphere Books.
Ritchie, R. 2014. 'Young Women and *Woman*: Depictions of Youthful Femininity, 1954–1969'. *Women and the Media: Feminism and Femininity in Britain, 1900 to the Present*. Eds M. Andrews and S. McNamara. New York and London: Routledge. 143–55.
Ritchie, R., S. Hawkins, N. Phillips and S. J. Kleinberg. 2016. 'Introduction'. *Women in Magazines: Research, Representation, Production and Consumption*. Eds R. Ritchie, S. Hawkins, N. Phillips and S. J. Kleinberg. New York and London: Routledge. 1–22.
Roberts, E. 1995. *Women and Families: An Oral History, 1940–1970*. Oxford: Blackwell.
Rose, N. 1989. *Governing the Soul: The Shaping of the Private Self*. London and New York: Routledge.
Tebbutt, M. 2017. 'From "Marriage Bureau" to "Points of View": Changing Patterns of Advice in Teenage Magazines: *Mirabelle*, 1956–77'. *People, Places and Identities: Themes in British Social and Cultural History, 1700s–1980s*. Eds A. Kidd and M. Tebbutt. Manchester: Manchester University Press. 180–201.
Tinkler, P. 1995. *Constructing Girlhood: Popular Magazines for Girls Growing Up in England, 1920–1950*. London: Taylor & Francis.
White, C. 1970. *Women's Magazines, 1693–1968*. London: Michael Joseph.
Winship, J. 1987. *Inside Women's Magazines*. London and New York: Pandora Press.

8

'Everything a girl could ask for'? Fashioning Feminism in *Just Seventeen*

Melanie Waters

In October 1983 the first issue of EMAP's *Just Seventeen* landed on British newsstands in fighting form. Featuring a scarlet-lipped cover girl posing in a red headguard and boxing gloves, the new fortnightly magazine promised its young readers 'prizes, pop and plenty of punch' (*Just Seventeen* 20 October 1983: 1) (see Plate 6). While the sales of girls' magazines had dwindled in the 1980s (Sanders 1983: 42), EMAP's decision to task editor David Hepworth with producing a magazine that was 'more expensive . . . stylish [and] slightly racier' than other teen titles marked the publishing industry's renewed courtship of girls as consumers (Hepworth 2013: para. 11).

In light of twenty-first-century debates about the survival of print media in the digital age, and speculation about when the magazine industry is likely to heave its final death gasps, *Just Seventeen* has been nostalgically invoked as a cautionary tale about the volatility and precarity of the periodicals market. From its initial publication in 1983 until its usurpation by the monthly *Sugar* (1994–2011) in 1994, *Just Seventeen* led the market in magazines for teenage girls. Tim Holmes, working in the EMAP offices at the time, recalls that in its heyday *Just Seventeen* was selling 'half a million copies every two weeks and raked in advertising money like there was no tomorrow'. The magazine was so popular that EMAP 'devised its corporate strategies around [its] continued success', using its example to 'set new business models' and heralding its editors as 'magazine royalty' (Holmes 2008: xiii). By January 1985, EMAP had appointed a female managing editor, Bridget LeGood, to replace Hepworth and in February of the same year *Just Seventeen* moved from fortnightly to weekly publication because, it reminded its readers, 'YOU ASKED FOR IT!' (*Just Seventeen* 10 January 1985: 5). *Just Seventeen* continued to prosper during the boom in the magazine industry that took place in the 1980s and early 1990s, but its sales figures declined steadily from 1994. Holmes (2008: xiii) remembers that 'suddenly – almost between one issue and the next – teenage girls stopped buying it'. By 1997 the weekly that promised 'everything a girl could ask for' had lost two thirds of its readership and EMAP made the decision to rebrand it as a monthly magazine with the modishly abbreviated title of *J-17*.[1] Toppled from its throne by *Sugar* and *Bliss* (1995–2014) – which took many of their aesthetic cues from *Just Seventeen*, but offered edgier, sexier content – *J-17* limped on as a monthly for several years, before finally disappearing from shelves altogether in April 2004.

In order to understand *Just Seventeen*'s phenomenal popularity among British girls, and the means by which it engaged such an enormous readership throughout the 1980s, it is necessary to take account of the dynamic media landscape in which the magazine initially appeared. I draw on methodologies developed by Maria DiCenzo, Lucy Delap and Leila Ryan in their field-shaping work on suffrage periodicals to approach and analyse *Just Seventeen* in 'relational terms'. Unlike the suffrage periodical, of course, *Just Seventeen* was not an activist magazine; it was not affiliated to any social movement. A magazine for teenage girls, *Just Seventeen* nonetheless benefits from consideration 'in relation to publications that engaged with [it] directly', and against or through reference to which it sought to define its own position in a 'complex web' of 1980s' media (DiCenzo et al. 2011: 78, 200). For this reason, I analyse *Just Seventeen* alongside its early competitor *Jackie* (1964–93), the popular women's liberation periodical *Spare Rib* (1972–93) and the radical teen zine *Shocking Pink* (c. 1980–2; 1987–92) in order to explore how feminism informs the specific tuning of the magazine's content, politics and style. If the influence of mainstream magazines for girls is readily discernible in *Just Seventeen*'s regular items, I argue here that the progressive 'feel' of the magazine, and its ability to generate a sense of intimacy between readers that girls experienced as new and necessary, is indebted to discourses that were developed and put into circulation by the feminist periodical press of the 1970s and 1980s.

In this chapter I examine how, when and why the discourses of women's liberation are mobilised in *Just Seventeen*, with a view to understanding the ways in which feminism is used as an object of affective (dis)identification in the magazine. Informed by Barbara Green's path-breaking work on suffrage periodicals, in which she uses Lauren Berlant's theory of 'intimate publics' to illuminate the currents of feeling that animate the politics of activist publications, I ask whether this line of argument might be reoriented in consideration of magazines for teen girls. If the intimate public is a mediated zone in which constituencies of marginalised subjects experience the feeling of emotional contact and 'social belonging' through the shared consumption of certain 'narratives and things', then to what extent does *Just Seventeen* constitute an intimate public of girlhood (Berlant 2008: viii)? What role, moreover, is accorded to feminism in an intimate public that turns on the 'affective and emotional' attachments of its consumers (Ibid.: 170)? Using Sara Ahmed's work on 'stickiness', I investigate how feminism – though seldom named explicitly in *Just Seventeen* – magnetised *Just Seventeen*'s readership, developing the 'feel' of intimacy between its readers and producers by catalysing debates about modern girlhood.

I begin with an examination of the discourses of girlhood that *Just Seventeen* develops. In particular, I analyse the extent to which these discourses hinge on assumptions about readers' attachments to certain 'sticky' elements of traditional femininity, asking how the magazine measures the continuing lure of home and family against the promised rewards of education and professional work. I then go on to investigate how *Just Seventeen*'s coverage of 'progressive' topics intersects with, and diverges from, the coverage of these same topics in the feminist press. In doing so, I assess the ways in which *Just Seventeen* mobilises the feelings of its producers and consumers in order to facilitate discussions about politics without drawing hard political lines. Through special reference to the magazine's coverage of gender difference and discrimination, political events and campaigns, and sexuality, I argue that feminism circulates within the pages of *Just Seventeen* as a locus of fantasy and fear, offering readers a means of understanding the world as it is, and speculating about how it could be in the future.

Prior to *Just Seventeen*'s swaggering 1983 debut, *Jackie* had long held court as the steadfast and sensible companion to British girlhood. As one of the first magazines marketed at teen girls, and by far the most popular, *Jackie* has already attracted significant scholarly attention. Angela McRobbie (2000: 69), in her pioneering work on youth cultures, uses *Jackie* to outline the 'privileged position' that teen magazines occupy within the media, 'introduc[ing] the girl to adolescence, outlining its landmarks and characteristics in detail and stressing the problematic features as well as the fun'. Through its combination of picture stories, pop pin-ups, beauty pages, advertisements and readers' 'true experiences', *Jackie* assumes a 'common experience of womanhood or girlhood' in which 'all girls want to know how to catch a boy, lose weight, look their best and be able to cook' (Ibid.). The treatment of these core themes was scarcely affected by the political convulsions of the women's movement in the 1960s and 1970s. Even in the early 1980s, the 'Cathy and Claire' advice column continued to take a firm line on girls' obedience to authority figures (especially parents) and discouraged its correspondents from letting things 'get out of hand' with boys. A parade of wholesome-looking models smiled out from *Jackie*'s covers, positioned in close proximity to headlined content that gave the impression of being blithely incognisant of feminism's taking-to-task of sexist double standards and prescriptive accounts of compliant, domesticated femininity: 'Are you asking for trouble? How not to get yourself talked about' (*Jackie* 5 January 1980: 1); 'He ruined my reputation' (*Jackie* 24 May 1980: 1); 'Are you worth a second glance?' (*Jackie* 2 August 1980: 1). Unsurprisingly, given that the aspirational horizons of *Jackie*'s girl were so narrowly focused on snaring an appropriate mate, the moods that prevailed within the pages of the magazine were often at odds with the upbeat messaging and imagery of the covers. As McRobbie observes, 'the world of *Jackie* . . . is a cloyingly claustrophobic environment where the dominant emotions are fear, insecurity, competitiveness and even panic' (2000: 70).

If *Just Seventeen* defines itself in part through its rejection of *Jackie*'s myopic valorisation of heterosexual romance, then it is just as vitally shaped by the liberationist discourses of feminist periodical culture in the 1960s and 1970s. In her pioneering scholarship on girls, Catherine Driscoll observes that no 'girls' or women's magazines exist in a prefeminist state' because all are affected by 'the now inevitable questions of whether and how a woman is employed, feminist critiques of beauty culture, and other feminist propositions or practices' (2002: 280). *Just Seventeen* is no exception. The magazine's express commitment to providing girls with information about health, educational opportunities and careers, coupled with its coverage of 'taboo' sexual topics, registers the changes that feminism – as ideology, politics and mode of critique – had wrought upon the popular field of girl culture by the start of the 1980s.

With its signal abandonment of 'silly' romantic photo stories and its image repertoire of bright, bold, youthful femininity, *Just Seventeen* expanded the vista of girlish expectation, offering an appealingly empowered alternative to the 'neurotically dependent female subject' who was volunteered by *Jackie*, *Blue Jeans* (1977–90) and *My Guy* (1978–90) as the default model for girlhood. Instead, the new magazine set the stage for a fresh generation of 'sassy' girls' magazines, including *Mizz* (1985–2012) and *More!* (1988–2013), that responded directly to 'a new climate of confidence and self-esteem among their potential readers' (McRobbie 1994: 159). In contrast to both *Jackie*'s cloying sentimentalism and *Shocking Pink*'s darkly witty calls to feminist arms,

Just Seventeen conjured up a luminous world in which young women are primed to capitalise on the activist gains of the 1960s and 1970s without becoming mired in the discourses and politics of organised feminism. It was the first mass-produced magazine for teenage girls to imagine how recent legislative victories – including the 1967 Abortion Act, the 1970 Equal Pay Act and the 1975 Sex Discrimination Act – might influence the ambitions, experiences and perspectives of young women in Thatcher's Britain. At the same time, as a magazine that relied on advertising revenue from the manufacturers of beauty and clothing lines, it continued to celebrate 'fashionable' modes of femininity, emphasising the emergent triumph of the personal over the political in 1980s' discourses of girlhood.

In one of the only academic articles to reference the contributions of *Just Seventeen*, *Mizz* and *Etcetera* to the 1980s media landscape, Janice Winship draws attention to the shadowy presence of feminism in these magazines, arguing that the influence of the women's movement is insistently undermined by a commitment to individualism that precludes the possibility of political organisation and collective action. Noting the editors' studious avoidance of the 'label of feminism', Winship discerns in *Just Seventeen* and its competitors a feminism that dare not speak its name, presciently evoking, back in 1987, the ur-critique of postfeminist culture that would come to dominate the scholarly vista in the 1990s (1985: 37).

What it Feels Like for a Girl

In Berlant's characterisation, 'intimate publics' act as zones of contact for 'non-privileged subjects' who are 'marked by a commonly lived history' (2008: xi, viii). Drawing together individuals on the pretext that they are shaped by a shared 'emotional knowledge' that emanates from the 'experience of living as a certain kind of being in the world', intimate publics manufacture fantasies of social belonging that are circulated in and through the mass media (Ibid.). The periodical has, of course, long been conceptualised in similar terms. Manushag Powell (2011: 448) has argued that periodicals 'work as the connective tissue in studies of modern societies, pulling together seemingly disparate communities and interests', while for Heather A. Haveman (2015: 22, 5) they are a kind of 'social glue', providing spaces in which these individuals can 'receive and react to the same cultural messages at the same time'. In the intimate public and the periodical alike, the affective lure of a particular shared experience is sufficiently strong to diminish the perceived significance of other, more or less tangible, social differences. As emotion is the dominant currency in the intimate public, so the periodical's viability is contingent upon the success of the emotional appeal it extends to potential readers. According to Fionnuala Dillane (2016: 7, 5), after all, the periodical is an 'affective object', meaning that its 'capacity to communicate [and] the contours, scope, and effects of that capacity . . . are everywhere underscored by a relationality that is charged with affect and emotions'.

The charged relationality described by Dillane is discernible in *Just Seventeen*'s preview editorial, intimately entitled 'For Your Eyes Only'. In line with the fantasy realm of Berlant's intimate public, in which individuals who consume common texts and things can experience the 'feel' of intimacy and belonging, this editorial defines the girl, first and foremost, in terms of her position as a consumer of 'girl culture'. She is the target audience for *Just Seventeen*, a 'brand new magazine . . . put together with the girl readers of *Smash Hits* in mind' that all girls will want to consume: 'No matter how old you are, where you come from or how you pass your time, we think you'll agree that *Just Seventeen* is going to be everything a girl could ask for in a magazine' (*Just Seventeen* 13 October 1983: 2). While the girl is indeterminate in terms of her age, background and interests, 'girl culture' emerges from this editorial discourse as a magically unifying experience that cuts across racial, ethnic and economic divides.

If and how 'girl culture' might itself be classified is a question that has already been posed by scholars of feminine adolescence. Driscoll (2002: 267) argues that the term is 'difficult to strictly delimit because what is most obvious about it – girls – is what makes it hardest to define'. Claudia Mitchell and Jacqueline Reid-Walsh (2007: xxvi-xxviii) are equally speculative, suggesting that 'girl culture' might be best understood in relation to the broad categories through which it tends to be organised, which would include 'social practices', 'material culture', 'media' and 'bodies'. Invariably, the exact 'texts and things' that comprise 'girl culture' are forever changing, shaped by the historical, political and social imperatives of any given context, but the girl culture of *Just Seventeen* is as much significant for what it *does* as what it *is*. Girl culture, according to Driscoll, puts into circulation 'the things girls can do, be, have, and make, and in that process defin[es] what processes are particular to girls' (2002: 278). Because the scope of girl culture is so wide, and because its discourses are so diverse, the magazine – with its ability to 'capsize and contradict' – presents itself as an ideal venue for creating and debating experiences of girlhood (Powell 2011: 441). In brief, the 'girl culture' that *Just Seventeen* puts into circulation produces a sense of community by presenting readers with a selection of things by which they might be affected, and to which they might be moved to respond. The magazine's desire to generate a sense of shared experience, if not an identical set of responses, is enhanced by the intimate mode of address it adopts towards its readers: hailed insistently as 'you', the reader is co-opted into an imagined community of 'girls who want to know what's going on now, because next month is simply too late'. Readers are similarly bonded in their status as discerning consumers: 'Some people think they can tell you what to wear, who to like, how to behave, what's best for you. We reckon you can make your own mind up. What you need is information; you need to see what's around' (*Just Seventeen* 13 October 1983: 2). *Just Seventeen*'s appeal to the autonomy of the teenage girl is, of course, largely rhetorical; if she is free to choose what to wear, who to like and how to behave, then the magazine's carefully curated features, regulars, competitions and advertising determined the parameters of these choices, offering her a circumscribed selection of similar things (sanitary products, cosmetics, clothes, music) to 'choose' between.

What Berlant's 'intimate public' emphasises, and what I would like to explore further through more detailed reference to the content and style of *Just Seventeen*, is the extent to which the 'feel' of intimacy that comes from consuming 'common texts and things' is not consequent on consumers feeling the same way about these texts and things, but instead ensues from the shared experience of being affected – in one way or another – by these texts and things. In its presentation of the 'things girls can do, be, have, and make', *Just Seventeen* solicits censure as well as praise from its readers, and in doing so establishes the magazine as an intimate space in which – if not necessarily beyond which – girls' voices can be raised, heard and responded to.

(Not) Naming Feminism

If, as Winship contends, the nomenclature of feminism would operate as one of the few remaining taboos in a magazine that routinely discussed masturbation, abortion and underage sex, then it would be nonetheless instrumental in furnishing *Just Seventeen* with a narrative of progress that would situate the reader, alongside her peers, within a 'commonly lived history'. This history was established as a signal site of affective identification in the first of *Just Seventeen*'s main feature articles. Published in *Just Seventeen*'s preview edition, along with embryonic versions of regular items on street fashion ('Spy'), work ('It's a Living') and health ('Facts of Life'), as well as an interview with pop star Nick Heyward, a short story and Melanie McFadyean's advice column, Louise Chunn's 'The Opposite Sex' struck the keynote for the magazine's representation of young women's opportunities in the early 1980s. As the figure of the girl is habitually instrumentalised within feminist discourse as a pulsating, inchoate embodiment of past, present and future, so she initially appears in 'The Opposite Sex' as the offspring of past achievements, a 'sign of the times' and, simultaneously, the mercurial embodiment of feminist futurity:

> If you had been born 50 years ago, life as a girl would have been very different. Apart from having to wear a hat and gloves in public, your school and job opportunities would have been cut short. Your place in the world would have been neatly planned, from giggling girlhood to marriage and motherhood. Things have changed since then – but not as much as you might think. (*Just Seventeen* 13 October 1983: 22)

Written in the playfully intimate prose that would come to characterise *Just Seventeen*'s features journalism, 'The Opposite Sex' opens with a sobering reminder to its young readers that they are the fortunate beneficiaries of progress. Chunn's deployment of the direct address – *Just Seventeen*'s favoured vocative mode – co-opts the reader into a cross-generational sisterhood of girls. The mobile pronouns identifying the reader with her bridled ancestor generate a sense of emotional proximity that transcends time and space. Girlhood, it seems, is an affective experience; the feeling of being a girl – and being able to identify with other girls – is, in part, what makes one a girl. The strategies adopted here are strongly evocative of Berlant's account of 'women's culture', which she takes as her model for the 'intimate public' in *The Female Complaint*; namely, Chunn's article is conditioned on the presumption that subjects who are 'marked by femininity already have something in common' and are 'in need of a conversation that feels intimate, revelatory and a relief even when it is mediated by commodities and even when it is written by strangers' (Berlant 2008: ix). If *Just Seventeen* participates in a juvenile permutation of Berlant's 'women's culture', then the 'girl culture' it represents is, in 'The Opposite Sex', one that enables its consumers 'to feel that their emotional lives are already shared and have already been raised to a degree of general significance' (Ibid.). *Just Seventeen* trades heavily on this notion of 'general significance', producing a grammar of girlhood that structures itself around the everyday experiences that girls – past and present – are assumed to share in common:

> A lot of what makes you a girl is learnt when you are very young. You won't remember it, but you were always dressed in pink. Your brother wore blue. For

> Christmas you were given a doll. Your brother got a toy car. (*Just Seventeen* 13 October 1983: 22)

Here, particular experiences that may or may not resonate with individual girls are proffered as universal truths. To borrow Berlant's (2008: x) terminology, such experiences are 'understood' by other girls '. . . even when they "are not shared by many or any".' Presented in terms of their 'general significance', the validity of these experiences is supplemented by bullet-pointed comments from single-sex groups of boys and girls that detail the 'most annoying' things about the opposite sex, with the girls lamenting that boys are 'only after One Thing' and like 'music papers with long words in them', while the boys complain that girls 'take hours to make themselves look pretty – then won't let boys touch them' and read 'anything with kissing on the cover' (*Just Seventeen* 13 October 1983: 22–3).

As *Just Seventeen*'s first feature, 'The Opposite Sex' establishes an ideological and rhetorical grammar that subsequent articles would use as a pattern. As well as inaugurating the intimate mode of address that would come to characterise the magazine, Chunn's article also sets out *Just Seventeen*'s investment in heteronormative femininity as a default model for 'common' experiences of girlhood. Just as strikingly, however, it exemplifies in microcosm what Ros Ballaster et al. (1991: 155) describe as *Just Seventeen*'s 'surprisingly ambiguous' relationship to feminism, in which the magazine's 'progressive coverage of sexuality and employment', as well as 'inequality and discrimination', is 'undercut by content found elsewhere in the same issue'. As is the case with *Cosmopolitan* (1972–), at which similar accusations were levelled a

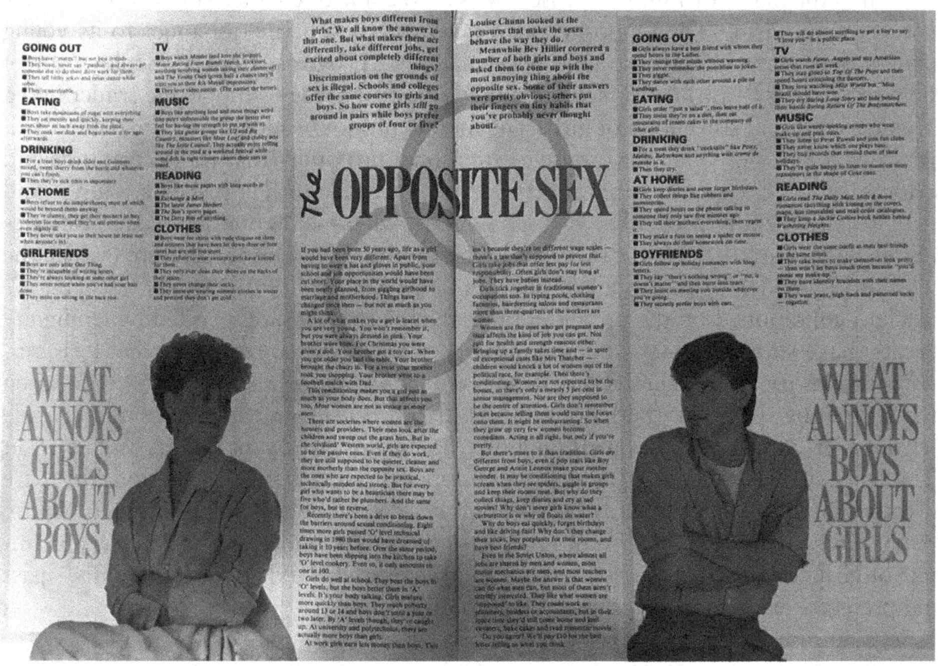

Figure 8.1 'The Opposite Sex', *Just Seventeen*, 13 October 1983. (Image with kind permission of Bauer Media Group)

decade earlier, *Just Seventeen* does give the impression of being 'progressive'. 'The Opposite Sex' is informed by sociological accounts of gender-role socialisation, of the kind set out in leading feminist studies including Ann Oakley's *Sex, Gender and Society* (1972) and Sue Sharpe's *Just Like a Girl* (1976), and Chunn uses landmark feminist legislative victories to plot her narrative of generational progress. The article reassures readers that the Sex Discrimination Act and the Equal Pay Act have all but eradicated structural inequalities, meaning that '[d]iscrimination on the grounds of sex is illegal', that 'schools and colleges offer the same courses to girls and boys', and that women and men are guaranteed the same wage for the same work (*Just Seventeen* 13 October 1983: 22–3). With such robust legislative protections in place, if things have not changed 'as much as you might think', it is because girls have *chosen* not to take up the opportunities that the activist campaigns of the previous decades helped to generate. Indicative verb formations abounding, Chunn instructs that girls 'earn less money than boys' not 'because they're on different wage scales', but because they 'take jobs that offer less pay for less responsibility'. Notwithstanding 'exceptional cases' like Margaret Thatcher, 'girls don't stay long at jobs. They have babies instead' (Ibid.). 'The Opposite Sex' is a masterclass in feminist ambivalence. In line with *Just Seventeen*'s determination to generate a sense of common experience that will stick with its nascent readership, the article presents girlhood as a prescriptive series of facts, predispositions and inevitabilities with which girls will be able to identify, but which are not readily reconcilable to feminism's ambitions for girls of the future. The overarching thesis of the article is that girls and boys are equally capable but constitutionally 'different'. As the daughters of the 1960s and 1970s came of age in the 1980s, the monumental gains made by second-wave feminism would enable them to fulfil their academic and vocational potential, but 'most' women would still 'like what women are "supposed" to like. They *could* work as plumbers, builders or accountants, but in their spare time they'd still come home and knit sweaters, bake cakes and read romantic novels.' *Just Seventeen*'s signal article thus twists into a now-familiar formation, offering an embryonic articulation of postfeminism's vexed neoliberal configuration of choice in which girls '*could*' if they wanted, but 'most' would choose not to.

If Berlant's 'intimate public' offers a framework for analysing periodicals as sites at which constituencies of 'non-privileged' subjects can experience a sense of belonging through the consumption of 'common texts and things', then Ahmed's concept of stickiness offers an insight into how this sense of belonging is achieved and augmented through the (re)mediation of particular 'sticky' signs. Feminism – in thought if not in name – is provocatively positioned here as an object of affective (dis)identification for the readers of *Just Seventeen*; as such, it is understood by both the producers and the consumers of the magazine in terms of its stickiness. As Ahmed (2004: 90–1) explains, a sign becomes sticky when it 'accumulates affective value' as a consequence of being 'used a certain way again and again'. Feminism does not have to be named explicitly in 'The Opposite Sex' for its familiar contours to be perceptible; it swirls menacingly as a potential source of 'bad feeling', a politics of troublemaking that seeks to destroy 'something that is thought of by others not only as being good but as the cause of happiness' (Ahmed 2010: 65). In the context of 'The Opposite Sex', feminism is liable to suppress 'natural' differences between boys and girls, deny girls the 'feminine' pleasures of baking and knitting, and force them to pursue activities in which they are 'not terribly interested'. While *Just Seventeen* uses elements of feminist discourse to frame its account of gender inequality, it also describes readers' affective attachments to those 'intractable and enduring' institutions – including heterosexuality and the family – that reproduce this inequality (Ahmed 2004: 12). For readers responding to *Just Seventeen*'s inducement at the end of 'The Opposite Sex' to 'pay £10 for the best letter telling us what you think', the article – which never refers to feminism directly – was nonetheless readable, simultaneously, as either a feminist critique of sexist double standards or as a rebuttal of feminism's militant attempts to erase the differences between men and women. Featuring in seven of the twenty letters published in the correspondence page of *Just Seventeen*'s second number, 'The Opposite Sex' established feminism's topical stickiness. It drew praise from some readers for acknowledging 'that there are more differences between girls and boys tha[n] the purely physical kind' when 'feminists persist in their claims for complete equality and consistently aim to be more like males', while others interpreted it as feminist call to arms. One 'Impressed Consumer' even proffered her own addendum to the article's perceived feminist logic: 'what about the fact that when girls sleep around or are seen with the opposite sex they're slags, etc. but boys are studs?! Forgot to mention it? Never mind. Thanks all the same' (*Just Seventeen* 3 November 1983: 36).

'The Opposite Sex' and the responses that it solicits offer a lucid demonstration of how the commonalities around which an intimate public forms might 'stick' with its particular constituencies: the stickiness of the content facilitates the sharing that takes place as part of the intimate public. In other words, readers adhere to one another through their engagement with sticky issues – of which feminism would be one. This is not to say that *Just Seventeen* adopts a consistent stance in relation to feminism, only that it is recognised as a site of consternation, or a 'sticking point', for young women; it refers to a set of ideas that are likely to rouse strong feelings – whether positive or negative – in the magazine's readership.

Feminine Pleasures and Feminist Killjoys

Just Seventeen's ambivalent approach to feminism is especially perceptible when the magazine's politics are regarded within the context of 1980s periodical networks. The currency of feminism in magazines for young women had been ably demonstrated at the start of the decade with the launch of the underground periodical *Shocking Pink*. As a self-funded, low-budget magazine 'written for and by young women', *Shocking Pink* warrants special attention in a discussion of *Just Seventeen*. While its small circulation figures render it distinct from any mainstream competitors, in its debut issue *Shocking Pink* pre-empted the editorial remit of *Just Seventeen* by two years: 'We feel that magazines like "Jackie", "Oh Boy" "Blue Jeans" etc don't give a realistic impression of our lives. We want a magazine that looks at fashion, music, books, makeup, relationships, and all the usual subjects, but from an interesting and realistic viewpoint' (*Shocking Pink* 1 1980: 3). With definitions of sexism, and items on racism, menstruation and the age of consent nestled alongside role-reversal fiction, a photo-story about coming out at school and advice about how to set up a support group for young women, the first issue of *Shocking Pink* identifies itself as a feminist concern. Its progressive politics and punk aesthetics were instantly welcomed by young readers, revealing the demand for magazines that departed from the 'stereotypes', 'pathetic love stories' and 'crap' promulgated by other teen offerings (*Shocking Pink* 2 1981: 2–3). With its confrontational politics, crude language and irreverent cartoons, *Shocking Pink* differed sharply from mainstream magazines for girls, but the content of its seven issues from the 1980s – which covered home-schooling, coping with sexist GPs, coming out, and the attempts by MP David Alton to impose restrictions on UK abortion law – suggests that *Just Seventeen* might owe a debt to its feminist forerunner.

The ideological intersections of the two magazines are especially palpable in their approach to matters of girls' health and wellbeing. *Just Seventeen*'s treatment of masturbation as part of its 'Facts of Life' series (17 November 1983: 19), for example, replicates the informed, reassuring tone of *Shocking Pink*'s article 'Masturbation' in its second number. As *Shocking Pink* (2 1981: 18–19) endorsed masturbation as a 'pleasurable and satisfying' activity, so *Just Seventeen* (17 November 1983: 19) lamented that this 'harmless and even necessary act is surrounded by so many cruel and silly myths'. Both items proceed to explore the biology of masturbation in strikingly similar terms, but if the prose is more or less interchangeable, then the 'feel' of the presentation is radically distinct. *Shocking Pink*'s article is illustrated by a provocative close-up photograph of a vagina, along with a series of scrawled doodles and celebratory marginalia: 'bath nights are fun again!', 'who needs a teddy bear[?]' (*Shocking Pink* 2 1981: 18–19). *Just Seventeen*, conversely, illustrates this instalment on 'Sexual Attraction' with a single, centralised line drawing of a girl and boy, turned away from one another and worrying in thought bubbles about crushes and infatuations. If *Shocking Pink*'s coverage of masturbation is consistently open, affirmative and joyous, then *Just Seventeen*'s is more equivocal: at a textual level, it recognises the 'pleasure' of masturbation, but the anxious imagery suggests that the feelings of shame that swirl around masturbation are not summarily dispelled by feminism's 'empowering' discourses about female sexuality. As Ahmed observes, the radical politics of feminism cannot divest us of our emotional attachments to certain 'sticky' norms, even when these attachments are not necessarily logical. Drawing on feminism's positive accounts of female masturbation, *Just Seventeen* offers its own 'progressive' approach to the topic, but it does so while acknowledging that the feelings of its readers might be regressively oriented towards guilt and shame.

Feminism's own sticky associations are established in 'Going Spare', a short report in *Just Seventeen* by Jenny Tucker about a forthcoming special edition of *Spare Rib*. In trying 'to attract a younger readership', explains a representative of *Spare Rib*, the edition will aim to place 'more emphasis on fashion and music, without losing the political tone of the magazine'. Tucker responds with exaggerated incredulity, proclaiming that *Spare Rib*'s special issue 'doesn't seem very likely' to attract young readers 'when there's a feature questioning the politics behind fashion; are girls pressured to wear the "right" type of clothes?' (*Just Seventeen* 4 October 1984: 59). Tucker's inventory of *Spare Rib*'s other youth-oriented features includes 'one woman's account of heroin addiction, getting the most out of your dole money, your first sexual experience and a variety of interviews with female singers'. Tucker queries the appeal of this 'pretty meaty' content to a target audience of young women, but *Just Seventeen* had, by its first anniversary, explored almost all of these topics in one form or another: money, drugs and homosexuality were covered in early instalments of the magazine's 'Facts of Life' series, and the very first issue had featured an interview with Annie Lennox in which the star discussed the sexual politics of clothes. Even Tucker's own column, in which the piece about *Spare Rib* appears, includes items – about Rape Crisis and new Family Planning Association initiatives targeting men – that would not be out of place in *Spare Rib* itself. *Spare Rib* appears here, however, in the guise of Ahmed's (2010: 66) 'feminist killjoy', threatening to displace the happy objects of *Just Seventeen*'s girl culture with the apparently grim topics and 'bad feelings' that Tucker gathers together under the sign of feminism.

There are, inevitably, moments when *Just Seventeen*'s coverage of 'live' news items overlaps with that of the feminist press. The occupation of Greenham Common Air Base by women opposed to its housing of nuclear arms is a case in point, with articles venerating and dismissing the actions of the protestors appearing across the mainstream and alternative periodical press throughout the 1980s. Offering a corrective to popular figurations of the women protestors as 'dykes' and 'dirty animals', Vicky Newell's warm account of her five days at Greenham for *Just Seventeen* turns on the feelings that she experiences during her time at the camp, where she is arrested repeatedly for her participation in the protests. With its photos of Greenham's wire fences and smiling protestors, Newell's personalised approach to the political controversy at Greenham echoes that of Roisin Boyd, Jan Parker and Manny, whose ambivalent responses to the camp, and the feminist politics of the protest, had been published in *Spare Rib* two years earlier (*Spare Rib* February 1983: 18–19). Stressing the normality of the Greenham women, Newell refers to them in terms of their 'families and responsibilities at home', but she also speculates sympathetically about the soldiers who guard the base, reflecting that they 'must feel silly facing women more like their grandmothers, mothers and sisters than the enemy' (*Just Seventeen* 3 April 1985: 22–4). This barometric sensitivity to feelings on both sides of a political dispute is broadly typical of *Just Seventeen*'s coverage of other current affairs in the 1980s, creating spaces in which the reader is confronted with competing ideas and left to 'make up [her] own mind'. From teachers' strikes to teenage pregnancy, the magazine used political crises to stimulate the mediation of feeling, and in the process withheld any final judgement about particular debates. *Just Seventeen* adopted a similarly 'personal' approach to the controversy generated by MP David Alton's Private Member's Bill, which in the mid-1980s threatened to amend and restrict the 1967 Abortion Act. As *Spare Rib* urged its readers to 'Dig out [their] "A Woman's Right to Choose" badges' and 'fight for their rights before it is too late' (*Spare Rib* October 1987: 8), *Just Seventeen* used the eventual failure of the Bill as a framing device for a 'Chatback' feature on abortion in which a group of readers shared their feelings about the current legislation (*Just Seventeen* 2 November 1988: 34–5). This – as with other features investigating 'feminist' issues – generated such a 'massive response' that it was followed up by another 'personalised' item, 'Answer Back', featuring letters from 'girls who have been through the experience [of abortion] themselves' (*Just Seventeen* 30 November 1988: 46).

Cannily drawing on aspects of feminist periodical culture, *Just Seventeen* is engineered in a such way as to *seem* progressive. The carefully curated selection of images, texts and things through which the magazine signifies its contemporariness highlight the autonomy of the 'new' freethinking girlish subject and her difference from the dewy-eyed girls who populate those unnamed publications that tell readers 'what to wear, who to like [and] how to behave'. At the same time, astute readers would identify inconsistencies between *Just Seventeen*'s rhetorical flourishes about independence, individuality and self-acceptance – in which readers were reassured that '*[e]veryone* is individual and has something unique and "special" about them' – and the particular models of youthful femininity that proliferated within its pages (*Just Seventeen* 21 December 1988: 37). In light of feminist critiques of Western beauty culture and simmering debates about intersectionality that were being addressed in other branches of the periodical press (not least by *Spare Rib* and *Shocking Pink*), the progressive gloss of *Just Seventeen* would look less than earnest to some readers. Tanya from Stirlingshire begins her letter by heralding *Just Seventeen* as 'the best magazine for [her] age group', but laments that it is 'let down' by its choice of models: 'I thought that an unconventional act like yours wouldn't sink to the capitalist idea of using "perfect" women who fit into the female stereotype to wear your clothes. Looking at these women can be bad for people's confidence and make them feel left out if they are plump or skinny' (*Just Seventeen* 17 November 1983: 44). The magazine's lack of racial diversity is also a source of debate. As 'two black teenagers who wish to see the media reflect more of everyday life as it actually is and not what you would like it to be', Donna McConnell and Sharon Sawyer wrote in to express their surprise at 'the lack of multi-racial articles for such a supposedly progressive magazine', wondering whether *Just Seventeen* is 'unwilling to touch upon potentially volatile subjects' (*Just Seventeen* 21 August 1985: 34). While similar queries about diversity in *Spare Rib* set the stage for an extended debate amongst editors and readers that would eventually lead to a radical reconfiguration of the magazine's scope, contents and personnel, the questions levelled at *Just Seventeen* remain unanswered. In contrast to *Spare Rib* and *Shocking Pink*, the magazine provided a space for criticism, but – it seems – little scope for change.

Who's that Girl?

Like her sisters of periodicals past, *Just Seventeen*'s girl is hitched to her time, a pivot point between tradition and progress, perfectly poised to capitalise on the feminist gains of previous generations. For this reason, she is invariably framed as a question: What will she do with her freedom? What will she achieve? What will she become? In *Just Seventeen*, the question of who or what the girl will be or become in the future is posed to her directly and repeatedly in the form of quizzes, surveys and questioning articles: 'How liberated are you?'; 'Are you the marrying kind?'; 'How good a shopper are you?'; 'A-levels: what are your options?'; 'Would you take your clothes off for £45 an hour?'. The question mark hovers hesitatingly as the concluding punctuation of many of *Just Seventeen*'s feature titles, a typographical cue to the reader to begin the (endless) process of subjective scrutiny that the magazine mandates as a route to self-knowledge and self-improvement.

The magazine's regular 'It's A Living' column suggested that it had high – and sometimes unconventional – expectations of its readership, showcasing interviews with women drag racers, helicopter engineers and record producers, while 'superwoman' Lindsay Shapero, author of the short-lived 'Dare' column, was pictured jumping out of planes, presenting television interviews and trying her hand as a gorilla telegram. If nothing else, feminism had expanded the precincts of girlhood; no longer confined to home and school, girls could go almost anywhere and do almost anything. At the same time, however, articles on sexual harassment, rape and unwanted pregnancies reminded girls of the dangers and responsibilities that would accompany their increased mobility.

While *Just Seventeen*'s articles and quizzes did not necessarily tell readers 'how to behave', they did identify certain types of behaviour as undesirable or risky, happily designating the tight parameters within which the modern girl should aim to operate. In the quiz 'A bitch or a doormat: what sort of friend are you?', for example, the reader's score determines whether she is a 'thoroughbred bitch', a 'wimp' or a 'perfect pal' – the latter of whom balances precariously on the friendship tightrope, refusing to 'be walked over' but ready with a 'shoulder pad to weep into' for any friend who offers 'the same attention in return' (*Just Seventeen* 10 September 1986: 21).

A more discursive account of female assertiveness was advanced in Rosalyn Chissick's article 'Do people walk all over you?' Some people, Chissick leads, 'ask to be walked over . . . Are you one of them?' In order to avoid their exploitation by 'friends, parents [and] work colleagues', readers were urged towards a regime of strict self-surveillance, excising any perceptible gestures of 'non-assertiveness' from their behavioural arsenal. Even when women have banished their bad habits, however, they must take additional care to ensure that their confidence is not misinterpreted. Dr Susan Jeffers, one of the experts that Chissick consulted in the article, cautioned that women '*need to know how to be tactfully assertive when dealing with men, as they have a tendency to interpret female assertion as aggression*'. Put simply: 'At work, a man who constantly gets his own way is "a shrewd business man"; a woman who does the same is "a bitch"' (*Just Seventeen* 20 October 1983: 34–5; emphasis in original).

This response to sexism in the workplace, in which the individual is tasked with managing the misbehaviour of wayward colleagues and exploitative bosses without being 'a bitch', is repeated in *Just Seventeen*'s more serious coverage of sexual harassment. In 'Harmless slap 'n' tickle . . . or sexual harassment?', Suzie Hayman traced the experiences of young women who have suffered sexual harassment at school or in the workplace. Ultimately, Hayman's article advises readers to be proactive: 'you can cope with it, or fight it. But you *shouldn't* put up with it'. The personal testimonies, however, act as sobering cautionary tales of what happens when young women do not 'put up with it': 'Chris' is fired when she reports being raped by her boss and 'Trish' is punished by her parents when she complains about a teacher who is later jailed for assaulting a thirteen-year-old girl. Jenny's informal course of action – which consists of banding together with female colleagues to undermine her workplace harasser – is presented as the most effective, but its success is contingent on the willingness of other women to 'rock the boat' at a time when unemployment was perilously high (*Just Seventeen* 9 August 1984: 52–3).

A later article from 1988 adopted a similar approach to the inevitability of sexism. Ranging over 'typical problems' that the reader is likely to encounter in the workplace, where 'most women will experience a form of sexual harassment', Penny Quinn's 'Sexual harassment: all in a day's work?' answers the question it poses in the affirmative. While Quinn identifies some potential sources of support, the article emphasises that there 'is no law against sexual harassment', so until such time as 'females feel free to voice complaints over harassment without fear of being laughed at', the 'solution' must lie with the individual: 'what can you do to help yourself?'. As well as keeping a 'diary of events' and contacting union representatives, Quinn encourages readers to '*tell* someone': 'if you *are* a victim of this type of behaviour, the way out of the situation is to share your problem with others, rather than becoming trapped into a frightened silence' (*Just Seventeen* 9 November 1988: 32–3). What is striking about these articles, and what they share in common with other items that focus on 'feminist' issues, is how closely *Just Seventeen*'s combined use of personal testimony, practical information and sympathetic intonation draws on patterns of presentation established in women's liberation periodicals. As a lifestyle magazine, *Just Seventeen* does not openly agitate for direct political action, but neither does it equivocate about the need for change. As Quinn proclaims, '[i]t is time that women who object to offensive behaviour from their male colleagues were taken seriously and not dismissed as being "up tight" or "over sensitive"' (*Just Seventeen* 9 November 1988: 33). However desirable changes to institutional structures and sexist attitudes might be, it is the individual's ability to negotiate the particular challenges of her own situation – albeit with the acknowledgement that she is 'not alone' – that takes precedence over collective action. Feminism, as both politics and critical methodology, is often implicit in *Just Seventeen*'s framing of sexist phenomena, but it is never named. Rather, feminism is obliquely associated with those women in Hayman's article whose complaints are dismissed as 'over sensitive', 'unnatural' or 'queer' (*Just Seventeen* 9 August 1984: 52), or with the aggressive, careerist 'bitch' that Chissick describes (*Just Seventeen* 20 October 1983: 35), not with the *Just Seventeen* reader, who might be forgiven for thinking that sexual harassment is 'a bit of a joke': 'Isn't it natural', asks Hayman, 'for men to whistle at girls and try to chat them up?' As *Just Seventeen* petitions for the legal safeguarding of women from sexual harassment in the workplace, it does so while seeking to distinguish between 'a whistle or a comment that makes you feel good, and one that makes you feel threatened' (*Just Seventeen* 9 August 1984: 52).

In contrast to activist periodicals, which have, since the 1960s, used the personal as a means of politicising women and spurring acts of collective dissent, *Just Seventeen* in the 1980s offers a more 'juxtapolitical' instrumentalisation of the personal, in which feeling is the basis for the reader's imaginative attachment to other subjects in the 'intimate public' of girlhood. Feminism is thus positioned as an object of affective (dis)identification within the magazine, one of the key means by which readers experience a sense of connection with – or disconnection from – other girls. In *Just Seventeen*'s coverage of reproductive rights or discrimination or violence or sexuality, feminism emerges as the lens through which producers and consumers of the magazine tend to assess particular political positions; it is always there, in features, quizzes, the advice pages and correspondence columns, shaping the feel of the magazine, and the feelings in it, even when it appears to be absent.

If no single magazine can deliver 'everything a girl could ask for', then *Just Seventeen* in the 1980s at least began the process of imagining how feminism might shape *what* girls ask for. Enabled and informed by feminism's language of intimacy, *Just Seventeen* created a space in which girls could 'feel' together, while also modelling modes through which the girl reader might articulate her desires, expectations and anxieties in that transitional adolescent moment when 'everything' appears to be within her grasp.

Note

1. An article in *Marketing Week*, '*Just Seventeen* Reduced to Monthly', records sales figures for January to June 1996 at 162,490.

Works Cited

Ahmed, S. 2004. *The Cultural Politics of Emotion*. Edinburgh: Edinburgh University Press.

Ahmed, S. 2010. *The Promise of Happiness*. Durham NC and London: Duke University Press.

Ballaster, R., M. Beetham, E. Frazer and S. Hebron. 1991. *Women's Worlds: Ideology, Femininity, and the Woman's Magazine*. New York: NYU Press.

Berlant, L. 2008. *The Female Complaint: The Unfinished Business of Sentimentality in American Culture*. Durham NC and London: Duke University Press.

DiCenzo, M., L. Delap and L. Ryan. 2011. *Feminist Media History: Suffrage Periodicals and the Public Sphere*. Basingstoke: Palgrave.

Dillane, F. 2016. 'Forms of Affect, Relationality, and Periodical Encounters, or "Pine-Apple for the Million"'. *Journal of European Periodical Studies* 1.1 (Summer): 5–24.

Driscoll, C. 2002. *Girls: Feminine Adolescence in Popular Culture and Cultural Theory*. New York: Columbia.

Green, B. 2016. 'The Feel of the Feminist Network: *Votes for Women* after *The Suffragette*'. *Feminist Periodical Culture: From Suffrage to Second Wave*. Eds V. Bazin and M. Waters. *Women: A Cultural Review* 26: 359–77.

Haveman, H. A. 2015. *Magazines and the Making of America: Modernization, Community, and Print Culture*. Princeton: Princeton University Press.

Hepworth, D. (Interview). 2013. 'The Magazine that Changed Our Lives', *Stylist* October 2013 <www.stylist.co.uk/life/the-magazine-that-changed-our-life/54772> (last accessed 20 July 2018).

Holmes, T. 2008. 'Mapping the Magazine: An Introduction'. *Mapping the Magazine: Comparative Studies in Magazine Journalism*. Ed. T. Holmes. Oxon and New York. viii–xviii.

'*Just Seventeen* Reduced to Monthly'. 1997. *Marketing Week*. 14 February 1997 <www.marketingweek.com/1997/02/14/just-seventeen-reduced-to-monthly/> (last accessed 20 July 2018).

McRobbie, A. 1994. *Postmodernism and Popular Culture*. London and New York: Routledge.

McRobbie, A. 2000. *Feminism and Youth Culture* 2nd edn. Basingstoke: Macmillan.

Mitchell, C. and J. Reid-Walsh. 2007. 'Introduction'. *Girl Culture: An Encyclopedia*. Eds C. Mitchell and J. Reid-Walsh. Westport CT and London: Greenwood Press. xxiii–xxxii.

Oakley, A. 1972. *Sex, Gender and Society*. London: Maurice Temple Smith Ltd.

Powell, M. N. 2011. 'Afterword: We Other Periodicalists, or Why Periodical Studies?'. *Tulsa Studies in Women's Literature* 30.2 (Autumn): 441–50.

Sanders, J. 1983. 'Teen Magazines: Reflection of the Frightening Eighties'. *Campaign* 25 February: 42.

Sharpe, S. 1976. *Just Like a Girl: How Girls Learn to be Women*. London: Penguin.

Winship, J. 1985. 'A Girl Needs to Get Street-Wise: Magazines for the 1980s'. *Feminist Review* 21 (Winter): 25–46.

Part III

Tastemaking: Arts and Culture

9

'When is a writer not a writer? When he's a man':[1] Women's Literary Award Culture in Britain 1940–2019

Stevie Marsden

Introduction

On Thursday 25 January 1996 a brand-new literary award was announced. Sponsored by the international telecommunications company Orange, the award was one of the richest literary awards in Britain, offering a £30,000 prize to the winner (at the time surpassing the £20,000 offered by the Booker Prize, and the £21,000 for the Costa Book Award, formerly known as the Whitbread Book of the Year Award).[2] The announcement of this new award – known as the 'Orange Prize for Fiction' until Orange ceased sponsorship of the award in 2013 – was met with disapproval and perplexity from some commentators. One columnist suggested that association with the award meant authors would 'arguably [be] tainted by the "lame-duck" brush' (MacDonald 1996: 2). Another accused the award organisers of holding a 'discriminatory gathering' (*Evening Standard* 26 January 1996: 9). The Orange Prize for Fiction, it transpired, was for women writers only.

The instantaneous, and to some extent ongoing, controversy of the Orange Prize for Fiction caused an immediate stir among culture and arts press, bringing to the fore important questions regarding gender discrimination in literature and publishing in the UK. Most importantly, the prize encouraged writers, publishers and readers to think about the various processes of adjudication for book awards, the gender-balance of judging panels and the significance of an awards' terms of eligibility. However, while the Orange Prize brought such debates into the realm of popular literary culture in the 1990s, the history of literary awards that are granted exclusively to women writers in Britain goes back to the late nineteenth century. As this chapter illustrates, trends in historic arguments concerning the technical and aesthetic quality of women's writing have consistently arisen in relation to literary awards that are reserved solely for women and, as a result, such awards tend to reflect broader systemic gender biases in literary culture. From the little-known Rose Mary Crawshay Prize, to the short-lived Fawcett Book Prize, and the unwavering Women's Prize for Fiction, this chapter highlights the history and impact of prizes for women's writing in Britain through the twentieth and twenty-first centuries. This chapter posits that lesser known awards, such as the Rose Mary Crawshay Prize, are antecedents for the likes of the Women's Prize for Fiction, the archetype in awards for writing by women. (N. B. In this chapter 'women' will refer to all women, including cis and trans women.)

Overlooking Women Writers: Literary Award Culture in Britain

Before moving into an overview and analysis of some of the longest running and most well-known awards for women writers that exist in Britain, it is worth positioning these awards within the wider historical context of awards for literature, and arts and culture more generally, in the UK and internationally. James F. English (2005: 1) contends that awards for the arts 'dat[e] back at least to the Greek drama and arts competitions in the sixth century B.C.' and John Street (2005: 821) suggests that one of the first arts awards was the *Prix de Rome*, established in 1663 in Paris. Such histories of arts awards indicate that they have been part of our cultural habitus for many hundreds, if not thousands, of years. This omnipresent history of awards makes them 'both an utterly familiar and unexceptional practice and a profoundly strange and alienating one' (English 2005: 1). Literary awards in particular have developed into a prominent subsection of cultural and arts awards. The proliferation of literary awards is often the starting point from which analyses of their impact and influence begin (see Best 2008: 5; English 2005: 17–18; Squires 2004: 38). Street (2005: 822) illustrated the growth of literary awards in the UK between 1901 and 1995, exposing how, since the mid-twentieth century, there was a near-consistent year-on-year increase in the number of literary awards established. It will perhaps be impossible to ever know the exact number of literary awards that are now in existence in the UK, as awards are established, dissolved, or put into indefinite hiatuses, on a regular basis.[3] The seeming precarity of literary awards has not, however, ever hindered their proliferation. There are believed to be up to 300 literary awards in the UK today (*Writers' and Artists' Yearbook* 2016). This is a startling amount if we are to take into account that Europe on the whole has more than 600 awards (Squires 2004: 38), even though France alone has 2,300 literary awards (Street 2005: 819) and there are 'at least 190 major literary prizes in the Anglophone field, and hundreds more minor, localized or specialized awards' (Driscoll 2014: 120). Such variety in the estimated number of literary awards throws into question the accuracy of such numbers, and reveals just how challenging it is to calculate how many awards there are.

A fraction of these literary awards are dedicated solely to women writers or writers of colour, and LGBTQ+, disabled and working-class writers, with many literary award shortlists and winners mirroring the white, male homogeneity of the literary field more broadly. While all awards are generally accepted as being open to women writers, with award eligibility criteria most commonly relating to an author's age, nationality, geographical location or type of writing (e.g. poetry, non-fiction, genre fiction), the winners' roll-calls of many major literary awards have reflected the overall neglect of women writers and their absence from the literary canon. Two of the oldest awards in Britain, the Hawthornden Prize (awarded to writers under the age of forty-one) and the James Tait Black Prizes (for fiction and biography) which were both established in 1919, are rarely awarded to women writers. Of the seventy-seven winners of the Hawthornden Prize[4] – which was established by the philanthropist Alice Warrender – just fifteen are women (between 1919 and 2017). Likewise, women make up around 30 per cent of winners of the James Tait Black Prizes: of the 103 winners of the fiction prize, thirty-one are women, and of the ninety-nine winners of the biography prize, just thirty were women (between 1919 and 2016). This is a trend reflected in other long-standing British awards. The Saltire Society Literary Awards, which are the longest-running series of awards for Scottish literature, include a Book of the Year

Award and First Book of the Year Award, established in 1982 and 1988 respectively. Of forty-one winners of the Book of the Year Award (established in 1982), only eight have been women. Women writers fare slightly better when it comes to the Saltire Society First Book of the Year, with sixteen of the thirty-six winners being women (between 1988 and 2017).[5] In further analysis of the Saltire Society Literary Awards I have argued that disparity between the number of women to men winners of awards is evidence of implicit stereotype bias which 'reflects the historical (non-)representation of Scottish women writers in literature more widely' (Marsden 2019: 62).

Other research has shown that not only are women less likely to win awards, but books *about* women are less likely to win. In 2015 the author Nicola Griffith examined the Pulitzer Prize, the Booker Prize, the National Book Award, the National Book Critics' Circle Awards, the Hugo Award and the Newberry Medal over a fifteen-year period (2000–15) to analyse the breakdown of women winners and the content of winning books. She found that 'when women win literary awards for fiction it's usually for writing from a male perspective and/or about men' and that '[t]he more prestigious the award, the more likely the subject of the narrative will be male' (Griffith, 2015). Gail Low (2015: 91–2) has also considered the gender imbalance of the Booker Prize, noting that:

> Since its establishment in 1969, the Man Booker, Britain's best-known prize for literary fiction, has been awarded to nearly twice as many men as women . . . the repeated marginalization of women writers is reflected in the somewhat sexist 'spinsterish' term 'Booker Bridesmaid', coined for Beryl Bainbridge, who was nominated five times but never won.

The Booker Prize (as it is now known following the cessation of Man Group's sponsorship of the prize in January 2019) has even worse figures when it comes to awarding writers of colour: of the fifty-two Man Booker Prizes awarded since 1969, only nine writers of colour have won the award and there have been a total of sixteen years when the prize's shortlist included no writers of colour (Temple 2018).

There are, however, areas of literary award culture where women writers have thrived for many years, but these tend to be genre fiction, particularly romance fiction and children's literature. For example, all but one of the winners of the Romantic Novelists' Association Awards (RoNAs) Novel of the Year Award, which has been awarded annually since 1966, are women writers. The one man to win the award was British author and creator of the comic strip *Modesty Blaise*, Peter O'Donnell, who won the award in 1978 under the pseudonym Madeline Brent. Women have dominated this award despite the fact that the award is open to 'the best in romantic fiction' (The Romantic Novel Awards n.d.) which is 'published by a traditional publisher' and 'written in the English language' ('Rules and Regulations' n.d.). In other words, there is no condition in the rules of the award that would omit male writers from being nominated. This pattern was finally broken in March 2018 when two male writers became the first in the RoNA's fifty-seven-year history to win 'under their own names' (Singh 2018). However, the fact that mainly women writers have won the RoNA Novel of the Year Award, and the one man who won was writing under a female pseudonym, may have something to do with the fact that romance fiction has habitually been viewed as a 'woman's genre', predominately written by, and for, women and therefore denigrated and marginalised as lowbrow culture, despite being one of the most 'popular of all genres of fiction' (Lee 2008). There is much scholarship discussing the complexities of romance fiction, women readers and writers, and the position of the genre within the literary canon (see Belsey 1994; Modleski 1984; and Radway 1984). In her influential study *Loving with a Vengeance*, Tania Modleski (1984: 14) notes how her examination of 'mass-produced fantasies for women' in the form of Harlequin Romance novels, gothic novels for women and television soap operas, was instigated by her 'concern that these narratives were not receiving the right kind of attention' (Ibid.) because they were predominantly enjoyed by women. Modleski continues stating how her study:

> [A]void[s] expressing either hostility or ridicule, to get beneath the embarrassment . . . to explore the reasons for the deep-rooted and centuries-old appeal of the [Romance, Gothic, Soap Opera] narratives. Their enormous and continuing popularity . . . suggests that they speak to very real problems and tensions in women's lives. (Ibid.)

The lack of acknowledgement of the dominance of women writers winning awards like the RoNAs further reflects this history of women's writing, and the romance genre specifically, being ridiculed or considered 'embarrassing' to both literary critics and popular culture more widely.

Women are also the leading winners of awards for children's literature.[6] The Eleanor Farjeon Award, founded in 1966, recognises 'outstanding contribution[s] to the world of children's books by an individual or organisation' (The Eleanor Farjeon Award n.d.). The award, created in honour of the children's author Eleanor Farjeon, was awarded to forty-eight individuals and six organisations between 1966 and 2016. Seventy-five per cent of the forty-eight individuals who won the award were women. Similarly, 65 per cent of the winners of the Kathleen Fidler award for novels for eight to twelve-year olds by previously unpublished authors (awarded 1983–2002) were women. Finally, more women writers have won the Carnegie Medal for new books for children and young adults (founded in 1935): of the seventy-eight winners, 54 per cent (forty-two) are women. Much like the romance genre, children's literature has historically been denigrated as inconsequential because of the great number of women writers contributing to the genre:

> It is perhaps not surprising that children's literature, the area of writing most dominated by women, is both the most culturally influential and most intellectually marginalized, nor that the standard histories of the subject have been written in terms of male 'landmark' writers judged by male-order literary standards. (Hunt 2008: 44)

Hunt also recognises the preponderance of women writers winning the Carnegie Medal around the mid-twentieth century and argues that, despite being award winners, women writers of children's literature seemed to 'exist in a shadowy parallel universe' (Ibid.).

Despite the acclaim and recognition that can come with winning awards, it seems that literary awards that have historically been won predominantly by women writers have gone largely unnoticed by the mainstream media and have in fact reinforced, as opposed to challenged, historic notions that there are areas of literature apposite for women writers, such as romance and children's literature. It could also be argued that the achievements of these women go largely ignored in comparison to their fellow writers in other areas of literature. Since many of the most influential and prestigious literary awards in Britain, such as the Man Booker and James Tait Black, are often awarded to literary fiction and, more rarely, genre fiction which is believed to have transcended the typical constraints of its genre, the fact that women writers appear to be less successful in these areas of literary award culture is viewed as being indicative of their non-success more broadly.

The systematic disregard of women writers in literary award culture, and the indifference towards the awards that women writers are more likely to win, has led to the establishment of literary awards for which only women writers are eligible. The aforementioned Orange Prize for Fiction (henceforth referred to as the Women's Prize for Fiction),[7] for example, is 'open to any full length novel, written in English by a woman of any nationality . . . published for the first time in print form [in] the United Kingdom' (Women's Prize For Fiction n.d.). Likewise, the Stella Prize, established in 2013, is open to 'female-identifying writers who are either Australian citizens or permanent residents of Australia at the time of entry' (The Stella Prize n.d.). Both of these prizes, according to their founders, were established in reaction to all-male literary award shortlists and the underrepresentation of women writers in book review pages. The complexities and controversies surrounding the founding of such awards in the British context will be discussed in more detail in the following sections of this chapter.

However, before considering contemporary examples of the exclusion of women writers in literary award culture in the UK and the awards founded to counteract this, it is worth considering the modern history of prizes for women writers in the UK and the ways in which earlier prizes led the way in the celebration of women writers. Accordingly, this chapter will present an overview of the Rose Mary Crawshay Prize, possibly the oldest literary award for women writers that still exists in the UK. Detailing the history of this prize, which was founded in 1882, is important to this discussion of literary awards for women writers in Britain from the latter half of the twentieth century to the beginning of the twenty-first century, since, from its founding, the Rose Mary Crawshay Prize was affected by problems that women writers, and the awards established to honour them, face to this day.

The Rose Mary Crawshay Prize: the Oldest Prize for Women Writers in Britain

Founded by the philanthropist and activist for women's suffrage Rose Mary Crawshay in 1882 and indentured to the British Academy in 1888, the Rose Mary Crawshay Prize is given to a 'historical or critical work on any subject connected with English Literature by a woman of any nationality provided that the nominated work is available in English'.[8] The award, which was originally called 'The Byron, Shelley, Keats in Memoriam Prize Fund' but is now known simply as the 'Rose Mary Crawshay Prize' (the 'Crawshay Prize' henceforth), was met with compliments from the poet Robert Browning who said, 'I have long been aware of your love for the poets and your munificence towards the women who study so as to intelligently honour them. Well done' (in Crawshay 1984: 30). In a similar vein, when writing to Crawshay about the quality of the submissions put forward for the award, the author Frederic Harrison said, 'The girls' essays are excellent . . . You must be gratified to feel that your effort has met with success' (in Crawshay 1984: 30). Significantly, Harrison's infantilising of the women writers who have been nominated for the award ('The girls') and surprise at the success of the prizes is not wholly dissimilar to the kind of reaction that the Women's Prize for Fiction would receive in the 1990s and 2010s, particularly when the sponsorship of the prize was taken over by Baileys (discussed in more detail later in this chapter).

Much like her philanthropic and advocacy work for social and political reform, Crawshay's approach to the award was meticulous and forward-thinking (John 2004). The indenture which saw the administration of the Crawshay Prize handed to the British Academy in 1888 detailed specific terms which suggest that Crawshay, and her fellow Trustees of the award Charles Hancock, William Michael Rosetti and Arthur Hewett Spokes, were keenly aware of the important components relevant to the management of a literary award. The 1888 indenture, for example, stated that information about the award recipients needed to be sent to particular periodicals, including *The Queen* magazine, *The Athenaeum* and *The Academy*.[9] It also specified that information about the award was to be 'published as paid advertisements in September of each year in the *Times* Newspaper or in whatsoever Newspaper shall in the course of years have succeeded to the position at this present time held by the *Times* Newspaper [*sic*]'.[10] The notice in the *Times* would not only list that year's Crawshay Prize winner, but also previous winners of the award. Such requirements indicate that Crawshay and her fellow award organisers were not only aware of the importance of acquiring newspaper coverage in order to promote the award, but that they were willing to invest in securing such coverage. The cost for the production of promotional materials ('circulars') and advertisements was included within the expenses of the award and amounted to £9.10.0 (just under £1,000 today).[11]

Another cost the award's expenses were cited to cover was the payment of 'examiners' (or judges) for the award. The adjudication process for the award, at least up until Crawshay's death in 1907, was as follows:

> Mrs. Crawshay employs a paid examiner to select for her twice the number of essays for which she has prizes to give; so that the final decision rests with herself . . . The rejected essays are not usually seen by Mrs. Crawshay . . . These essays are mostly returned to the authors corrected, with the excellent result that after several trials writers have succeeded in winning prizes. (Crawshay 1894: 31)

In other words, the examiner, or judge, read all submitted entries and then presented a shortlist to Crawshay who would select the winner. For their time adjudicating for the award, examiners were paid £10 (slightly less if there was a low number of submissions), which was £5 more than the secretary in charge of administration for the award was paid. This is a significant specification made by Crawshay and her fellow Trustees. The payment of judges for awards is something which is rarely discussed publicly, either by award administrators, the media or judges themselves. There is a general understanding that individuals who judge for well-known and wealthy awards such as the Booker Prize, Costa Book Awards and the Women's Prize for Fiction are paid, but the amount that they are paid is not publicly disclosed or discussed. Other awards, like the Saltire Society Literary Awards, which are the longest-running series of awards for Scottish literature, do not pay judges and are very open about this fact, maintaining that it is a positive attribute of the awards because, they have argued, it ostensibly assures the integrity of the judging panel.[12] However, including costings for the payment of a judge for the award suggests that Crawshay and the Trustees felt that award 'examiners' should be remunerated for their time and expertise, an act which effectively professionalised the role.

Arguably the most significant feature of the original terms of the Crawshay Prize was the requirement made for the composition of the awards' board of Trustees. The 1888 indenture stated that:

> The Trustees may be four men and one woman or three men and two women or two men and three women or four women and one man or they may be all women as the Trustees in their discretion shall consider best.[13]

Such terms meant that the board of Trustees, who oversaw the administration and management of the award, had to have at least one woman member at all times. Reflecting Crawshay's commitment to women's emancipation and equality in her political and philanthropic work, this condition reveals that Crawshay was aware of the importance of women being involved in the administration of an award for women writers. While the Trustees may not have been involved directly in the judging process, they were involved in the appointment of secretaries and examiners. Therefore, in at least guaranteeing the presence of women on the board of Trustees, Crawshay was promoting the inclusion of women at each stage of the awards' government. This is notable because the gender imbalance of literary award judging panels and advisory boards remains a problem today and has in fact been one of the factors that has instigated the formation of awards, such as the *Prix Femina* founded in France in 1904 in reaction to the all-male *Académie Goncourt* (English 2005: 61).[14]

In 1915 the Crawshay Prize was reformed and became 'The Rose Mary Crawshay Prize for English Literature', officially expanding the remit of the award to include a broader selection of critical works on English literature. The award would now be given to:

> [A] woman of any nationality who, in the judgement of the Council of the British Academy, has written or published within three years next preceding the date of the Award an historical or critical work of sufficient value on any subject connected with English Literature, preference being given to a work regarding one of the poets, Byron, Shelley, and Keats.[15]

This broadening of the terms of eligibility for the books that could be submitted for the award led to a rise in the number of submissions (although the British Academy would go through spells of having very few submissions and did not present the award in 1925, 1939, 1946, 1948 and 1971). One of the most recognisable names to have submitted a book for the Crawshay Prize was Muriel Spark who, in December 1951, submitted her biography on Mary Shelley, *Child of Light: A Reassessment of Mary Wollstonecraft Shelley* (1951). Spark's name was recognised by the awards' secretary, who, writing on the top of Spark's submission letter, noted that Spark had received the 'Observer Christmas Short Story Prize', worth £250, in December 1951. Unfortunately, Spark's work was not well received by one of the judges who wrote of *Child of Light*: 'I have read most of it (with difficulty) and find it well below the standard for a Brit. Acad. Prize. [*sic*] The lady splits her infinitives, speaks of reminiscing and motivating and altogether writes in an atrocious style.'[16] While Spark may have been unsuccessful in acquiring recognition for her Mary Shelley biography from the Crawshay Prize judges in 1952, the book has since been recognised as indicative of Spark's 'determination to rescue Mary Shelley from cultural amnesia and condescension' (Hughes 2013), a determination that Crawshay herself would likely have found an affinity for.

The Crawshay Prize continued to award women writers throughout the twentieth century but, by the late 1990s and early 2000s, concerns grew regarding the lack of recognition that the Crawshay Prize and its winners were receiving (a fact indicating that the stipulations noted in the award's original indenture relating to the targeted publicity of the award were no longer practised). A 2005 report reveals that the Crawshay Prize committee was keen to make the academic community and publishers more aware of the prize, and they started to place notices in the *Times Literary Supplement* with information about terms of eligibility and submission deadlines for the award. This promotion helped, particularly in eliciting books from different publishers, but was expensive and the committee eventually decided that they would ask publishers to make submissions and use the British Academy's literary editor contacts to find out about new, eligible publications (Shaffer and Barton 2005: 2).[17] Despite this, the Crawshay Prize still fails to garner much in the way of attention following winner announcements, likely because of its status as an award for academic and literary criticism as opposed to fiction, poetry or popular non-fiction, which is more likely to receive media coverage and increase the sales of shortlisted and winning books. Nevertheless, understanding the history of the Crawshay Prize is imperative when discussing the history of women's literary award culture in Britain because it is perhaps the oldest, and certainly the longest running, award for women writers that exists in Britain. Although the prize is for more academic, non-fiction writing, its history as a prize founded by a women philanthropist and advocate of women's suffrage, who was clearly aware of how the administration and judging of literature can affect how it is perceived – hence why Crawshay insisted on having at least one woman on the prize's board of Trustees, as well as ensuring media promotion of the prize (at least in the early years of the award) – makes the Crawshay Prize an obvious predecessor of other prizes for writing by women. It therefore deserves recognition for its role within the broader historical context of the emergence of awards for women writers in Britain.

'Celebrating excellence, originality and accessibility. . .':[18] Prizes for Women Writers in the Twentieth and Twenty-First Centuries

One prize established in the UK for women writers which followed in the footsteps of the Crawshay Prize was the Fawcett Society Book Prize, established by the Fawcett Society, a charity created in honour of one of Crawshay's contemporaries and friends, Millicent Fawcett (John 2004). Established in 1982 (and terminated in the mid-1990s), the Fawcett Society Book Prize was awarded to 'a work which has made a substantial contribution to the understanding of women's lives and experiences' (Book Trust 1995: 34). This 'women-only' award (Low 2015: 92) was presented alternately for fiction and non-fiction. Winners included Pat Barker (1983), Zoe Fairbairns (1985), Stevie Smith (1989) and Jung Chang (1993). Fairbairns would return to judge the prize in 1988 along with historian Lady Antonia Fraser and Equal Opportunities Consultant and Vice Chair of the Fawcett Society Jan Harding. An announcement of this all-women judging panel in *Spare Rib* magazine in 1988 reported that:

> All three judges feel strongly that the Prize, apart from being an individual winner, is a salute to all feminist writers, past, present and future and a recognition of women's and of feminist heritage. The judges are also keen to point out that the recognition of heritage makes it an appropriate prize to be associated with the Fawcett Society: campaigners for equality between the sexes since 1866. (*Spare Rib* April 1988: 31)

This quote indicates that the judges, and the Fawcett Society itself, positioned the award within the longer history of campaigns and challenges to the underrepresentation and disregard of women, not just in politics and society, but also in literature and culture.

The Women's Prize for Fiction, launched in 1996, is also part of this long history of awards that protest the neglect of women writers. According to the writer Kate Mosse, who was one of the award's founders and is now honorary director of the award, the Women's Prize for Fiction came about after 'a diverse group of journalists, reviewers, agents, publishers, librarians, booksellers – male and female – gathered together in a flat in London' to discuss the representation of women writers following an all-male Man Booker Prize shortlist in 1991 (Mosse n.d.). Describing this meeting, Mosse writes:

> There were long debates about the value or purposes of literary awards, of how they supported (or inhibited) reading, how publishing and reviewing might play a positive role in ensuring a wider range of authors . . . were celebrated. After some hours and several bottles of wine, the idea of setting up a new kind of literary prize – one which would celebrate women's creativity, one that would be truly international . . . – was born. A prize that would be fun! (Mosse n.d.)

When the prize was launched at the Institute of Contemporary Arts in London in January 1996, the organisers of the prize had secured an endowment for the £30,000 prize fund from a private donor, who was reported as being a 'mystery female benefactor known only as "Bessie"' (Burdon 1996). Some news articles used the Fawcett Prize as a point of comparison to highlight just how rich the Women's Prize was, with one noting that although the Fawcett Prize's 'list of past winners is impressive', readers 'hardly hear of it' since the prize was only worth £2,000 (*Sunday Times* 21 April 1996).

The Women's Prize was to be administered and judged by women only and the prize had secured sponsorship for administrative costs from the telecommunications company Orange after the Japanese pencil company Mitsubishi[19] pulled out following negative press surrounding critical comments from A. S. Byatt and Kingsley Amis.

On hearing about the award, the Man Booker Prize winning author A. S. Byatt said that she was 'against anything which ghettoises women' and that this was her 'deepest feminist emotion' (MacDonald 1996: 2). Byatt continued: 'My opinion is for the last 10 years or so it is observable that there have not been as many good women writers as men' (MacDonald 1996: 2). Kingsley Amis was also reported as saying, 'If I were a woman, I would not want to win this prize . . . One can hardly take the winner of this seriously' (Burdon 1996). The 'inevitable storm of controversy' (Burdon 1996) that followed the announcement of the Orange Prize is one which has followed the award throughout its twenty-five-year history. Most recently, the novelist Lionel Shriver, who won the Orange Prize in 2005 for her seventh novel *We Need to Talk About Kevin*, said:

> [I] feel perfectly comfortable saying it is not as meaningful to me to have won the Orange Prize as say it would have been to win the Booker. Most people who win that prize surely say the same thing: you have eliminated half the human race from applying . . . I took the money! But there is this problem of suggesting that we need help, that men have to leave the room and then we're prize worthy. (Cowdrey, 2016)

The founders of the Orange Prize, the most visible and quoted of whom being the novelist Kate Mosse, have always told the same origin story: they were inspired to start the award following an all-male Man Booker Prize shortlist in 1991. There was, they felt, a disparity in the representation of women writers in awards, despite the fact that according to Mosse '[w]omen write a huge number of novels' (*The Guardian* 2 January 1996: 5). The concerns of the Orange Prize founders were borne out by statistics: by 1992 only 10 per cent of writers shortlisted for the Man Booker Prize were women, and since the founding of the Man Booker Prize in 1969, twice as many men have won the award (thirty-one men as opposed to sixteen women).

This initial backlash to the prize – which came eighteen months prior to its actual launch – foreshadowed the kind of media response that the prize would go on to receive. Following the announcement of the prize, commentators argued that, in its exclusion of men, the prize was fundamentally sexist. There was a flurry of incensed headlines including: '£30,000 Prize for Women Only' (Holden 1996); 'Only Women Need Apply for the Richest Literary Prize' (*The Guardian* 2 January 1996: 5); 'Women-Only Book Prize Marred by Sexism Row' (*Independent* 26 January 1996); and 'When is a Writer not a Writer? When He's a Man' (*Evening Standard* 26 January 1996: 9). After commenting on the fact that women writers had that year won two of the biggest literary awards in the UK – Kate Atkinson received the Costa Book Award for her debut novel *Behind the Scenes at the Museum* and Pat Barker won the Man Booker for *The Ghost Road*, the third novel in her First World War trilogy – the author of this latter headline used Salman Rushdie as an example of the male talent that would be excluded from this new award for 'Miss World Novelist' (*Evening Standard* 26 January 1996: 9). The point being that, if Rushdie is considered the pinnacle of literary talent, how could an award that he is 'banned from entering' be of any value? (Ibid.). Mosse's response to these criticisms once again emphasised how women writers were generally neglected when it came to literary award culture:

> Ms Mosse, herself a novelist, said that while competitions like the Booker and the Whitbread were ostensibly open to both sexes they were perceived by many to be intrinsically male. She argued that despite both awards being won by women this year, it was a rare occurrence. 'Women write a huge number of novels, but for some reason they simply do not get on shortlists and when they do they rarely win. The idea is not to compete, but to put another prize on the map.' (*The Guardian* 26 January 1996: 5)

Such comments reflect the misunderstandings surrounding women writers and literary award culture more generally. When Mosse says that women write a lot of novels but do not get shortlisted and are unlikely to win if they are, what she is really referring to is the indifference towards *literary* fiction written by women and how this is ignored by award culture.

Unfortunately, debates surrounding the quality of literary fiction by women writers overshadowed the first year of the award, with two of the awards' judges – journalist and reviewer Val Hennessy and writer Susan Hill – commenting publicly on the 'abysmal' quality of the 146 entries submitted for the inaugural award (*Daily Telegraph* 15 April 1996). Hennessy reportedly stated:

> I have judged several prizes before and I have seldom come across so many books that were so bad . . . Some were just drivel. I am ashamed that some of the titles submitted were even published or that trees had to be cut down to provide paper for them, or that publishers saw fit to put them up for a major prize. (Ibid.)

Similarly, Hill apparently suggested that 'the quality of entries was abysmal, terrible' and that 'many of the books were by women with nothing to say . . . There is a paucity of imagination, major themes, big ideas and a paucity of wit . . . Instead there's lots of dirty words' (Dore 1996). In defence of these comments, Mosse admitted that some of the entries were 'bloody awful' but suggested the press focus on comments from the judges was misleading (*The Guardian* 16 April 1996). Such critique, which focuses on the technique and skill – or apparent lack thereof – of women writers, only acts to perpetuate historic and cultural perceptions of women as inadequate writers who are not on par with their male counterparts. Indeed, such criticism harks back to George Eliot's scathing 1856 essay 'Silly Novels by Lady Novelists' in which Eliot argues that novels by 'Lady Novelists are a genus with many species, determined by the particular quality of silliness that predominates them – the frothy, the prosy, the pious, or the pedantic.' (Eliot 1856: 442).

As well as the supposed sexism of excluding male writers and the lesser quality of writing by women, one of the main concerns of many commentators upon the announcement of the Women's Prize for Fiction was the relationship between the sponsor and the award, as indicated by the headline 'Orange a Controversial Colour for Literary Prize' (Burdon 1996). A commentator applauded Orange for supporting an award for literature, which was the 'most solitary and least promotable art', but did so whilst also bemoaning the 'discrimination' against male writers that the award upheld (*Evening Standard* 26 January 1996: 9). Yet, there are few literary awards that have so completely and committedly intertwined the identity of the award with a sponsor. It is possible that the founders of the Women's Prize for Fiction were keen to partner with a sponsor that would give the award credibility and would not obviously 'gender' the award. Orange, an international telecommunications and technology company, therefore, was a perfect partner. Even the branding of the award as 'The Orange Prize for Fiction' did not reveal the fact that the award was for women writers only, but, by the time Orange ended their sponsorship in May 2012, the 'Orange Prize' was internationally recognised as an award for literature by women.

The identity of the Women's Prize for Fiction was, however, complicated by the introduction of a new sponsor following the termination of the Orange sponsorship in May 2012. Realising that securing a sponsor for the 2013 award was unlikely in under twelve months, in October 2012 the award relaunched as the Women's Prize for Fiction, supported by donations from benefactors including Cherie Blair, and the writers Joanna Trollope and Elizabeth Buchan. Discussing this transitional period during an interview, Mosse considered the kind of sponsor that would take over from Orange:

> There remains the announcement of the heir to the Orange sponsorship. Four or five corporate suitors are in conversation with Mosse and her friends, who are coy about the state of play. 'It's unlikely to be an arms manufacturer or a cigarette company,' says Mosse. 'The orange label of Veuve Clicquot would suit our brand.' A champagne sponsor for women's writing? 'I wouldn't say no,' laughs Mosse. (McCrum 2012)

In 2013 the organisers of the Women's Prize for Fiction formally announced the new sponsor for the award: the Irish cream liqueur, Baileys. The introduction of this new sponsor brought with it what amounted to an entire image overhaul for the Women's Prize for Fiction, which was now to be referred to as the Baileys Women's Prize for Fiction. This change of sponsor also brought with it its own unique controversy and interrogations of gender dynamics, mirroring those that the award had received nearly twenty years earlier. However, this time around, commentators were concerned that the new sponsor relied on, and accentuated, gendered imagery to sell its products, a fact which appeared to undo a lot of the hard work the Women's Prize had done to be viewed as something other than the 'Miss World Novelist' award.

When news of the new sponsorship deal with Baileys broke in mid-2013, journalists were quick to suggest that the choice of sponsor was based on the 'needlessly gendered world of selling alcohol' (Magnanti 2013). Brooke Magnanti argued that '[Baileys] is the hen weekend of booze', continuing to question why another, different kind of sponsor had failed to take up this opportunity to support literature by women:

> Where is the forward-thinking tech sponsor, who realises their competitors are all but ignoring a vital half of the market, or else pandering to them with tiny crystal-encrusted pink phones? Where's the financial fund that has realised this is a competition about serious literature that attracts equally serious publicity? The spirits brand that does not taste like boozy cupcakes chewed up and spit back into a glass? Or even the fashion brand that recognises the opportunity for gorgeous, creative publicity around the announcement of the shortlist? (Magnanti 2013)

Significantly, Magnanti was not criticising the use of a drinks sponsor, but was concerned about the reputation of this particular drinks sponsor as a sickly-sweet drink for women. Magnanti juxtaposes seemingly opposing representations of femininity: one 'serious', 'gorgeous' and 'creative', the other 'pink' and 'boozy'. While she claims that 'the quality of writing and writers will not be changed', Magnanti also admits that 'the thought of women writers and Bailey's [*sic*] being paired rubs very much the wrong way' (Magnanti, 2013).

Well versed in responding to controversy surrounding the Women's Prize for Fiction, the administrators of the award appeared to pre-empt this criticism. On the announcement of the new sponsorship deal, Mosse was quoted as saying that the award organisers felt that Baileys was 'a great fit', suggesting that 'Everyone thinks of Baileys as a treat, as something which is about celebrating women and having a great time' (Flood 2013). The novelist Jenny Colgan also defended the new sponsor, saying that 'Baileys softens the image of the prize and brings together two great pleasures; reading a book whilst having a little glass of something or other. I think it's great for both sides' (Flood 2013).

The introduction of Baileys as a sponsor of the Women's Prize for Fiction remains an important development in the history of the prize and, as a result, is important in the broader history of literary awards for women writers in Britain. Baileys' sponsorship of the award brought to the fore, and accentuated, the gendered identity, and essentialist nature, of the award. Far from shying away from feminised imagery and discourse to promote the award, as the award founders had arguably done in the early 1990s when the award was sponsored by Orange, with the introduction of Baileys as sponsor the identity of the Women's Prize for Fiction was negotiated through what could be read as stereotypically 'feminine' imagery. For example, the all-women judging panels (which always include well-known or recognisable celebrities) were showcased more effectively than in previous years, with photos showing the women gathered together looking like a group of friends, or, perhaps, a book club. A short video spot, featuring writers, former judges and celebrities, such as Mary Beard, Caitlin Moran and Jennifer Saunders, talking about their favourite books by women writers was released in 2014. The women were invariably shown in cosy, domestic settings such as home libraries, living rooms and kitchens, reflecting an age-old image of the woman reader in domestic settings as discussed in Kate Flint's (1995) *The Woman Reader* (a title which, incidentally, won Flint the Rose Mary Crawshay Prize the year the first Women's Prize was conferred). The transition into the end card of this video draws attention to the Baileys logo, reaffirming the relationship between the sponsor and the award.

Another element of the marketing of the Baileys Women's Prize for Fiction that focused on the award's identity as an award for women writers in order to appeal to a female audience was the publication of the 'The Brilliant Woman's Guide to a Very Modern Book Club' as part of the #ThisBookClub social media campaign launched by the award in 2015. This twenty-nine-page guide included short essays from 2015 award judge Grace Dent and the 2012 chair of judges Joanna Trollope, as well as summaries of the award's 2015 shortlist and discussion points for book clubs. Alongside this award-specific content were supplementary materials which aimed to connect the prize to the sponsors' appeal to women, such as a tongue-in-cheek rundown of common book club members (including 'The High-Flyer', 'The Dreamer', 'The Hostess' and 'The Connector'), a list of high-street bars that are 'worthy of a modern book club' and an essay about the rise of the flat white martini which included a recipe for a Baileys flat white martini.

While there was nothing inherently wrong with these elements of the promotion of the Baileys Women's Prize for Fiction, they signalled a shift in the representation of the award from something which was focused solely on championing writing by women to all readers, towards a stylised and highly feminised campaign aimed specifically at selling the award to women readers. Furthermore, it seemed that the award's media-friendly partnerships with fashion brands and glossy magazines perpetuated clichéd ideas of what would most interest their target audience: cocktails, fashion and make-up. The approach taken by the Women's Prize for Fiction while it was sponsored by Baileys effectively essentialised understandings of women readers and femininity. Yet, such essentialising is an intrinsic element of literary award culture and, in the case of the Women's Prize for Fiction, the Baileys sponsorship and the related marketing was a manifestation of this fundamental characteristic of award culture. The Women's Prize for Fiction is arguably demonstrative of what Thomas Crisp identifies as the 'positivist essentialism' which may be temporarily deployed 'by a marginalized population for political purposes in order to displace a hegemonic majority' (Crisp 2011: 95). Crisp makes this argument in relation to the Lambda Literary Award for LGBTQ+, children's and young adult books, arguing that the decision taken by the Lambda Literary Foundation in 2009 to change the terms and conditions of the award so that only an author who self-identifies as a member of the LGBTQ+ community, as opposed to being a heterosexual or cis-gendered author writing about LGBTQ+ characters and situations, was an example of strategic essentialism.[20] Crisp's discussion of this change and the debate that surrounded it, reflects the kind of controversy that has surrounded the Women's Prize for Fiction and its exclusion of male writers:

> These debates often locate their nexus in awards for representations of traditionally marginalized people, with invested parties (i.e., authors, scholars, librarians, and publishers) disagreeing as to whether or not it's 'fair' for some of these awards to limit eligibility to those people who self-identify as members of the population being depicted. (Crisp 2011: 93)

One author in particular, Crisp notes, argued that further restriction to the prize's eligibility would mean that the Lambda Award would be further marginalised, effectively 'limiting its influence [and] causing it to be taken less seriously by those in the publishing and LGBT communities' (Crisp 2011: 94). Such comments could quite easily be applied to the reactions and controversies surrounding the Women's Prize for Fiction. However, as Crisp argues, far from being inherently complicated by their exclusionary nature, literary awards that are reserved for particular individuals (e.g. women, writers of colour, writers from certain geographical locations) use the 'temporary deployment of positivist essentialism by a marginalized population for political purposes in order to displace a hegemonic majority' (Crisp 2011: 95). In other words, awards for women writers are essentialist by their very nature and their accentuation of the literary production of women is a political statement that aims to highlight gender imbalances throughout the literary world. Indeed, it is no coincidence that many of the awards for women writers have emerged from the identification of a lack of recognition for women writers and the feeling that this deficiency needs to be rectified.

Conclusion

Preceding the introduction of *The History of British Women's Writing, 1970–Present* (2011), there is a chronological timeline of 'Recipients of major British literary prizes and honours' from 1970 to 2014 (Eagleton and Parker 2011: xvii). The list details the major award wins of women writers, such as Bernice Rubens' 1970 Man Booker Prize win for her novel *The Elected Member*, Carol Ann Duffy winning the Somerset Maugham Award for *Selling Manhattan* in 1988 and Andrea Levy's 2004 Women's Prize for Fiction and Costa Book of the Year Award win for *Small Island*. At first glance, this list seems comprehensive and indicates that women writers have in fact been consistently winning literary awards in Britain, at least since the 1970s. However, on closer inspection, gaps are evident. No 'major British Literary prize [or] honour', according to this list, was awarded to women writers in 1976, 1977, 1980 or 1982. In some years, there is only one notable win by a woman writer: Susan Hill won the Somerset Maugham Award in 1971 and Iris Murdoch won the James Tait Black Prize in 1973. As the list moves into the twenty-first century, more women are winning awards and accolades, but this acts to emphasise the apparent dearth of women award winners in the mid to late half of the twentieth century.

Yet, this history is incomplete. As evidenced in this chapter, women writers have found much in the way of award success in genres such as romance and children's, but since these are genres that are traditionally maligned because of their perceived lack of critical value, such accomplishments have been forgotten, falling out of contemporary literary award history. On the other hand, prizes like the Rose Mary Crawshay Prize elude mainstream attention, likely because of the specialist nature of the books that it honours. While it is imperative that such successes become part of the general discussion of women writers and their status within British publishing and literary culture, their existence by no means undermines the inequalities highlighted throughout this chapter. As discussed here, many awards for literary fiction by women writers have been established as a protestation or retaliation against the exclusion of women writers in award shortlists, judging panels and literary canons. Defying criticism and controversy, awards founded solely for women writers have been deliberate in their strategic essentialism by only celebrating the work of women writers who have traditionally been ignored by major awards and the literary canon. Consequently, they bring attention to these incidences of neglect, making such awards part of a broader history of political and social protest against the disregard of women writers.

Notes

1. *Evening Standard* 26 January 1996: 9.
2. The Booker Prize was known as such until 2002 when sponsorship of the prize was overtaken by the financial services company Man Group. Likewise, the Whitbread Award was so-called until 2006 when the awards were re-branded as the Costa Book Awards after Costa Coffee, a subsidiary of Whitbread PLC. However, for purposes of clarity, these two

prizes will be referred to as the 'Man Booker' and the 'Costa Book Awards' throughout this chapter, even if the names were different during the period in question.

3. In 2016 and 2017 alone several major awards were cancelled or compelled to pause presenting the award until sponsors could be secured. The seventeen-year-old *Guardian* First Book Prize (which awarded winners £10,000) and the Dundee International Book Prize (which promised a cash prize and publication of the winning manuscript) were cancelled in 2016 and 2017 respectively, and it was announced in 2016 that the £40,000 Folio Prize and £5,000 Fiction Uncovered award would not be awarded due to a lack of sponsorship.
4. The Hawthornden Prize was in a hiatus between 1944 and 1958 following Alice Warrender's illness and death in 1947. There have also been a number of years during which the prize was not awarded: 1959, 1966, 1971–3 and 1984–7.
5. See Marsden (2019) for a more detailed analysis of the gender imbalance of the Saltire Society Literary Awards.
6. This is a trend which has been identified in non-English language literary awards. In their analysis of gender and literary award culture in Flanders, Demoor et al. (2008: 39) illustrate how, while women writers are less likely to win major literary awards, 'Children's literature is the exception to the rule, thereby paradoxically reaffirming the traditional role patterns with women being associated with the upbringing of children'.
7. Following the cessation of Orange and Baileys as named sponsors of the Women's Prize for Fiction in 2012 and 2017 respectively, the prize is now referred to as the Women's Prize for Fiction and is sponsored by what it calls a 'family' of corporate sponsors, including Baileys, NatWest bank and the TV production company Fremantle (Campbell 2017).
8. Full terms of eligibility and nomination rules for the Rose Mary Crawshay Prize are available online on The British Academy's website <www.thebritishacademy.ac.uk/rose-mary-crawshay-prize>.
9. 'Indenture for Rose Mary Crawshay Prize'. 1888. BAA/EVS/12/3/2. Rose Mary Crawshay Prize Archives. British Academy, London.
10. Ibid.
11. Ibid.
12. In the press release announcing the winners of the 2016 Saltire Society Literary Awards, Saltire Society Executive Director Jim Tough said that 'Excellence is the common thread [of the awards], built on the integrity and freely given commitment of our expert panels' (Creative Scotland 2016).
13. 'Indenture for Rose Mary Crawshay Prize'. 1888. BAA/EVS/12/3/2. Rose Mary Crawshay Prize Archives. British Academy, London.
14. While both men and women are eligible for the *Prix Femina*, the judging panel has only ever included women.
15. 'Rose Mary Crawshay Prize for English Literature'. (n.d.) The British Academy. BAA/EVS/12/3/7. Rose Mary Crawshay Prize Archives. British Academy, London.
16. Helen Darbishire. Letter to unknown recipient. 29 March 1952. BAA/EVS/12/3/12 (File 1). Rose Mary Crawshay Prize Archives. British Academy, London.
17. Elinor Shaffer and Anne Barton. 'Rose Mary Crawshay Prize: Report of Committee'. 1 November 2005. BAA/EVS/12/3/17. Rose Mary Crawshay Prize Archives. British Academy, London.
18. 'About'. *Women's Prize for Fiction* <www.womensprizeforfiction.co.uk/about> (last accessed 17 September 2019).
19. There was some confusion in reports at the time about whether the company Mitsubishi that had originally agreed to support the award was actually the Mitsubishi car brand; however, the car brand is in fact unrelated to the stationers of the same name.

20. Crisp uses the work of Gayatri Chakravorty Spivak (1993) when explaining his understandings of strategic essentialism.

Works Cited

Belsey, C. 1994. *Desire: Love Stories in Western Culture*. Oxford: Wiley & Sons.

Best, J. 2008. 'Prize Proliferation'. *Sociological Forum*. 23.1: 1–27.

Book Trust. 1995. *Guide to Literary Prizes, Grants and Awards in Britain and Ireland*. London: Book Trust.

Burdon, J. 1996. 'Orange a Controversial Colour for Literary Prize'. *Press Association*, 21 January 1996.

Campbell, L. 2017. 'Women's Prize for Fiction Reveals New Sponsorship Model'. *The Bookseller*, 31 May 2017 <www.thebookseller.com/news/womens-prize-fiction-reveals-new-sponsorship-model-560886> (last accessed 11 April 2019).

Cowdrey, K. 2016. 'Women's Literary "Prizes are Problematic" Says Lionel Shriver'. *The Bookseller*, 9 March 2016 <www.thebookseller.com/news/womens-literary-prizes-are-problematic-says-lionel-shriver-324233> (last accessed on 22 December 2017).

Crawshay, R. M. 1894. *In Memoriam Endowed Yearly Prizes PRIZE ESSAYS by Competitors. 4th set*. Breconshire: Cathedine, Bwlch.

Creative Scotland. 2016. '"Visionary and Profound" Poetry Collection is 2016 Saltire Book of the Year' <www.creativescotland.com/what-we-do/latest-news/archive/2016/11/visionary-and-profound-poetry-collection-is-2016-saltire-book-of-the-year> (last accessed 27 September 2019).

Crisp, T. 2011. 'It's Not the Book, It's Not the Author, It's the Award: The Lambda Literary Award and the Case for Strategic Essentialism'. *Children's Literature in Education* 42: 91–104.

Demoor, M., F. Saeys and S. Lievens. 2008. '"And the Winner is?" Researching the Relationship Between Gender and Literary Awards in Flanders, 1981–2000'. *Journal of Gender Studies*, 17.1: 27–39.

Dore, R. 1996. 'Women Only Book Prize Entries Abysmal, Say Judges'. *The Daily Telegraph*, 15 April 1996.

Driscoll. B. 2014. *The New Literary Middlebrow Tastemakers and Reading in the Twenty-First Century*. London: Palgrave Macmillan.

Eagleton, M. and E. Parker, eds. 2011. *The History of British Women's Writing, 1970–Present*. London: Palgrave.

Eliot, G. 1856. 'Silly Novels by Lady Novelists'. *The Westminster Review*, October: 442–61.

English, J. F. 2005. *The Economy of Prestige: Prizes, Awards and the Circulation of Cultural Value*. London: Harvard University Press.

Flint, K. 1995. *The Woman Reader, 1837–1914*. Oxford: Clarendon Press.

Flood, A. 2013. 'Baileys all Round at Women's Prize for Fiction'. *The Guardian*, 4 June 2013 <www.theguardian.com/books/2013/jun/03/baileys-womens-prize-for-fiction> (last accessed 22 November 2017).

Griffith, N. 2015. 'Books About Women Don't Win Big Awards: Some Data' <https://nicolagriffith.com/2015/05/26/books-about-women-tend-not-to-win-awards/> (last accessed 22 December 2017).

Holden, S. 1996. '£30,000 Prize for Women Only'. *Press Association*, 25 January 1996.

Hughes, K. 2013. 'How Muriel Spark Rescued Mary Shelley'. *Times Literary Supplement*, 24 April 2013 <www.the-tls.co.uk/articles/public/how-muriel-spark-rescued-mary-shelley/> (last accessed 10 December 2017).

Hunt, P. 2006. 'Children's Literature'. *Encyclopaedia of British Women's Writing 1900–1950*. Eds F. Hammill, A. Sponenberg and E. Miskimmin. London: Palgrave.

Jeffreys, S. 1996. 'Women Caught in a War of Words'. *The Sunday Times*. 21 April 1996.

John, A. V. 2004. 'Crawshay, Rose Mary (1828–1907)'. *Oxford Dictionary of National Biography*. Oxford: Oxford University Press <www.oxforddnb.com/view/article/53008> (last accessed 22 November 2017).

Lee, L. J. 2008. 'Guilty Pleasures: Reading Romance Novels as Reworked Fairy Tales'. *Marvels and Tales*, 22.1: 52–66.

Low, G. 2015. 'Publishing and Prizes'. *The History of British Women's Writing, 1970 –Present*. Ed. M. Eagleton and E. Parker. London: Palgrave: 81–95.

McCrum, R. 2012. 'How Prize That Used to be Orange Was Saved – and Rebranded'. *The Observer* 13 October 2012 <www.theguardian.com/books/2012/oct/13/orange-prize-wfp-books> (last accessed on 22 December 2017).

MacDonald, Marianne. 1996. 'Women-Only Book Prize Marred by Sexism Row'. *The Independent*, 26 January 1996 <www.independent.co.uk/news/women-only-book-prize-marred-by-sexism-row-1325806.html> (last accessed 27 Sept 2019).

Magnanti, B. 2013. 'Why Baileys Sponsorship of Women's Prize for Fiction Leaves a Slightly Sour Taste'. *Telegraph*, 4 June 2013 <www.telegraph.co.uk/women/womens-life/10097826/Why-Baileys-sponsorship-of-Womens-Prize-for-Fiction-leaves-a-slightly-sour-taste.html> (last accessed on 22 December 2017).

Marsden, S. 'Why Women Don't Win Literary Awards: The Saltire Society Literary Awards and Implicit Stereotyping'. *Women: A Cultural Review*. 30.1: 43–65.

Modleski, T. 1984. *Loving with a Vengeance: Mass-Produced Fantasies for Women*. New York: Routledge.

Mosse, K. n.d. 'History.' *Women's Prize for Fiction* <www.womensprizeforfiction.co.uk/about/history> (last accessed 10 December 2017).

Mosse, K. 1996. 'Women when words fail'. *The Guardian*, 16 April 1996.

Radway, J. A. 1984. *Reading the Romance: Women, Patriarchy, and Popular Literature*. London: Verso.

Romantic Novelists' Association. n.d. 'Romantic Novel Awards' <https://romanticnovelistsassociation.org/awards/> (last accessed 17 September 2019).

Romantic Novelists' Association. n.d. 'Rules and Regulations: the Romantic Novel Awards 2020' <https://rnoty.secure-platform.com/a/page/Rules> (last accessed 17 September 2019).

Singh, A. 2018. 'New Romantics: After 57 Years, Men Break Through at the Romantic Novel Awards'. *Telegraph*, 13 March 2018 <www.telegraph.co.uk/news/2018/03/13/new-romantics-57-years-men-break-romantic-novel-awards/> (last accessed 11 April 2019).

Street, J. 2005. '"Showbusiness of a Serious Kind": a Cultural Politics of the Arts Prizes'. *Media, Culture and Society* 27.6: 819–40.

Spivak. G. C. 1993. *Outside the Teaching Machine*. New York: Routledge.

Squires, C. 2004. 'A Common Ground? Book Prize Culture in Europe'. *The Public* 11.4: 37–48.

Temple, E. 2018. 'The Man Booker Prize: By the Numbers' <https://lithub.com/the-man-booker-prize-by-the-numbers/> (last accessed 1 April 2019).

The Eleanor Farjeon Award. n.d. 'The Children's Book Circle' <www.childrensbookcircle.org.uk/pages/the-eleanor-farjeon-award> (last accessed 22 November 2017).

The Stella Prize. n.d. 'Guidelines and Submission' <https://thestellaprize.com.au/prize/guidelines-submission/> (last accessed 1 April 2019).

Women's Prize for Fiction. n.d. 'Rules' <www.womensprizeforfiction.co.uk/about/rules> (last accessed 10 December 2017).

10

Arena Three Magazine and the Construction of the Middlebrow Lesbian Reader

Amy Tooth Murphy

The 1950s and early 1960s in Britain saw increased professional and public interest in the topic of homosexuality, particularly from medical and sociological perspectives (Jennings 2007a: 149–50). Predominant professional discourse filtered down to the general public, facilitated by a willing media. The prevailing image of lesbianism that emerged was that of the pathologically 'masculine, immature and sexually aggressive' woman (Ibid.: 149). This stereotype, increasingly influential in the postwar period, posited the lesbian as dangerous, dominant and over-sexed. Her aim was to 'seduce weaker and more pliable women who were otherwise perfectly normal heterosexuals' (Albertine Winner, cited in Jennings 2007a: 149). These victims of predatory seduction were often cast as sexually naïve or fearful of heterosexual relationships, thus making them easy prey for the bullish and bullying 'congenital' lesbian. Lesbian tendencies were sometimes attributed, in psychoanalytic circles, to traumatic childhood experiences, or arrested development, and the cultural currency held by psychoanalysis in the postwar period did much to disseminate these ideas to the general public. Such imagery was not confined to Britain, and similar representations could be found in North America and Europe, where psychoanalytic approaches to non-normative sexuality were also in vogue. The dichotomy of the masculine and aggressive dyke and the passive and damaged younger woman (an age gap was often cast as a feature of these dysfunctional relationships) was profiled for a mainstream public in the 1968 British film *The Killing of Sister George*. In the tortured and torturous relationship between the main characters, 'George' and 'Childie', and the twisted milieu in which they reside, many of the popular and professional conceptions of lesbianism converged on the big screen.

Against this backdrop, in 1963 a small group of lesbian women, led by Esme Langley and Diana Chapman, came together to form the Minorities Research Group (MRG). Their aim was:

> [T]o conduct and to collaborate in research into the homosexual condition, especially as it concerns women; and to disseminate information and items of interest to universities, institutes, social and educational workers, writers, poets, editors, employers and, in short, all those genuinely in quest of enlightenment about what has been called the 'misty, unmapped world of feminine homosexuality'. (Cited in Hamer 1996: 166)

Aware of the need for a mouthpiece to communicate their mission, in Spring 1964 members of the MRG launched *Arena Three* (1964–72), the first British lesbian magazine. Written for lesbians and their supporters, its name 'signif[ied] its intentions of providing subscribers "with a special forum, platform, or 'arena' in which to meet a dozen times a year"' (Jennings 2007b: 136). Langley again held a central role, serving as lead editor for the majority of the magazine's lifespan. The editorial board set out to reach lesbian women but were also acutely aware of their role as spokeswomen for lesbianism to the wider public. Amidst a growing clamour the MRG and *Arena Three* sought to represent the voices of lesbians themselves. By directly engaging with public and professional discourses it was hoped that they could influence mainstream perceptions of lesbianism, and in doing so promote their own discourses as a counter to the notorious pathological figure of the lesbian so dominant in British culture. To that end, the magazine welcomed members of the medical and psychiatric communities, journalists and sympathetic male readers.

As the first lesbian magazine in Britain, and forerunner to *Sappho*, *Spare Rib* and even *DIVA* magazine, *Arena Three* has earned its place in the ancestral halls of lesbian culture. The vigorous debates ongoing through its 'Mailbag' pages paint a picture of 1960s lesbian ideological and political stances otherwise unobtainable. Until the emergence of *Arena Three*, there were no public platforms where lesbians could discuss their sexuality and surrounding issues. Indeed, Jennings (2007b) credits *Arena Three* with the key role in setting in motion the first stirrings of an ostensible collective lesbian identity. The magazine can also be seen as providing a space in which a nascent lesbian community could form. Many readers came from outside the urban centres of the South East and were therefore isolated from the majority of what little physical community spaces existed. These spaces were, in the 1960s, predominantly bars. Even those within reach of such venues were often isolated from them, by societal constraints as well as by choice. Therefore, the 'platform' created by *Arena Three* allowed for a new type of community to imagine itself and to form. From its very early days the magazine sought to facilitate this beyond its pages, through the creation of social groups around the country, and catering to a wide range of members' interests, from philosophy to board games.

However, far from catering to the lesbian population at large, *Arena Three* displayed a strong bias towards women from middle-class and professional backgrounds. This predilection can be seen throughout the magazine; in its stated aims, its features and articles, and through the ways in which its readership and its writers sought to construct within its pages a version of lesbianism that was acceptable and fitting for them and, indeed, for the mainstream public (Jennings 2007b). Although Langley claimed that the reader questionnaire of 1970 demonstrated a broad social demographic, there was an admitted slant towards professional women, with teachers and nurses being the most common occupations (*Arena Three* March 1971: 3). Some working-class women wrote to the magazine saying that they were being overlooked. One woman wrote that: 'nobody seems to want to know the ordinary working-class homosexual. As soon as I write to say I am employed as a car worker I have not heard from them again.' (*Arena Three* June 1967: 5). In spite of Langley's protestations to the contrary, backed by readers' letters refuting this reader's claims, the class bias of *Arena Three* cannot be ignored. From its articles on classical antiquity, to shopping for antiques, to its reviews of holidays in the South of France,

Arena Three reflected back to its readership a picture of themselves as educated, solvent and sophisticated.[1]

Research into twentieth-century lesbian history has frequently flagged up class status as both an inhibitor and facilitator of lesbian community formation. This is particularly true of North American scholarship. Notably Elizabeth Lapovsky Kennedy and Madeline D. Davis (1993) identified the central role of working-class identity in creating the lesbian bar community of 1930s–60s Buffalo, New York. In contrast, Esther Newton's history of the gay and lesbian community of Cherry Grove, New York depicts a community tied together through a shared professional and middle-class identity (Newton 1993). Throughout such discussions, it is consistently evidenced that class barriers play a critical role in defining 'appropriate' and sanctioned 'types' of lesbianism. More specifically, it has been shown that middle-class anxieties about respectability have resulted in conscious moves to distance middle-class lesbian identity from some of the commonly considered hallmarks of working-class lesbian identity; most notably the centrality of butch/femme roles and choice of social spaces, predominantly working-class bars in 'undesirable' locations. *Arena Three* can be taken as an exemplar of just these types of anxiety and their ultimate manifestation in the creation of a middle-class lesbian identity, formed as a direct rejection of perceived working-class lesbian culture.

Alison Oram (2007) has argued that *Arena Three*'s engagement with medico-scientific and psychiatric discourses was part of an attempt to demonstrate to the heterosexual world what they themselves already knew: that there was nothing distinct or unique about lesbians' biological or psychological make-up. By positioning themselves as spokeswomen, members of the editorial board were able to bolster the version of lesbianism that they sought to portray to the public via the media and socio-medical professions. And the defining characteristic of that image, I would argue, was normality. The MRG worked to promote a positive perception of lesbianism. For their purposes, positive was synonymous with normal. And 'normal', in this instance, often meant conventionally middle class in appearance, ideology and lifestyle. Keen to downplay lesbians' difference to the mainstream public, the MRG sought to portray lesbians as intelligent, responsible, solvent and appropriately feminine: in short, 'respectable'.

This propagandistic mission, I suggest, extended beyond direct engagement with medical discourses. *Arena Three*'s normalising agenda can also be seen in some of its responses to lesbian literature. In a thinly pseudonymous review for her own novel, *The Dark Side of Venus* (1960), Shirley Verel stated her authorial agenda as emphasising the 'normalness' of lesbians:

> No collars, ties, eton crops – there don't have to be. They're not really so very 'vicious' either . . . Who will class them, as homos with drunken fathers, murderous drivers, neglectful mums with v.d. – or even see them, through a strange irrational haze, as peculiarly 'evil'? (*Arena Three* May 1964: 7–8)

Verel's lesbian characters are, then, a foil to prevailing fictional depictions of lesbians, and her review an explicit rejection of a rogues' gallery of existing archetypes.

In this chapter I move the focus to *Arena Three*'s engagement with lesbian fiction, hitherto overlooked in historiography of the magazine, considering the literature chosen for review and the responses of both reviewers and readers. I will argue that *Arena Three*'s book review section can be taken as a window into the middle-class thrust of the magazine. Indeed, through the types of book reviewed, as well as the treatment that they received, the book review section played a central role in this middle-class positioning. Furthermore, I will suggest that this class bias is bound up with the political aims of *Arena Three* and the MRG as ultimately assimilationist.

In their study of Canadian magazines and middlebrow culture, Faye Hammill and Michelle Smith (2015) underscore the central role of middlebrow ethos and aesthetics in the creation of middle-class cultural parameters. They position the middlebrow as 'a mode of circulation, reception and consumption of cultural products' (Ibid.: 10), through which magazines contribute to a wider cultural milieu, including literature, music, shopping and leisure pursuits in general. Aspirational middle-class readers, they argue, came to mainstream magazines in order to combine pleasure with self-improvement, seeking the guidance and expertise of magazine editors and contributors in navigating the tricky space within which a cultivated and appropriate middle-class taste could be made and expressed. In this sense, magazines played a crucial role as tastemakers for a burgeoning middle class.

Although Hammill and Smith's study concerns mainstream magazines – a far cry from *Arena Three*'s limited and niche readership – their framework for understanding the intrinsic link between the middle class and the middlebrow is salient in considering the role of *Arena Three* and its book review section in setting parameters for a nascent middle-class lesbian identity. In particular, as will be seen, *Arena Three* evidences a conscious distancing from the 'contamination' (Ibid.: 12) of the lowbrow, as well as an ambivalent and suspicious attitude to highbrow cultural products. In the space between, the editors offered the safe yet satisfying ground of middlebrow novels, thus situating the middlebrow novel at the heart of a literary cultural circuit and lesbian cultural consumption. By devoting significant column inches to book reviews, the editors embedded the reading of fiction firmly into emerging middle-class lesbian identity, and *Arena Three* at the centre of lesbian print culture of the 1960s and early 1970s.

Defining Parameters: Respectability and the Rejection of the Lowbrow

Keen to engage with cultural representations of lesbianism, *Arena Three* ran a regular book review column. Literary editor, Claire Barringer, invited readers to submit reviews of lesbian-themed books and to send in suggestions for a running book list. The only guidelines for the list were that there should be no 'sludge' (i.e. pulp fiction), that it would exclude literature with only a passing or slight reference to lesbianism, and that preferably books should be written from the female angle (*Arena Three* April 1964: 2). In addition to Barringer's list, and regular reviews, the magazine also ran a subscribers' postal lending library.

In 1965 Gene Damon joined Barringer as a regular reviewer. Damon was in fact Barbara Grier, the American writer and publisher, and editor of the annotated bibliography *The Lesbian in Literature* (Grier 1967). Under the Damon pseudonym she edited and wrote for *The Ladder* (1956–72), the American lesbian magazine run by

The Daughters of Bilitis (DOB), the first lesbian rights organisation in the US. Damon brought a transatlantic angle to the column, reviewing American titles released by British publishing houses. She was also joined occasionally by Barbara Gittings, co-editor of *The Ladder* and a high-profile gay rights activist.

The appearance of Damon and Gittings gestures to the influence of American homophile politics on *Arena Three*. The DOB's tagline was 'A Woman's Organization for the purpose of Promoting the Integration of the Homosexual into Society'. The key word here is 'integration'. Historians have sought to delineate the assimilationist stance of the DOB (Gallo 2006: 2), and here I wish to extend that claim to its British counterpart. As the first lesbian magazine in Britain, *Arena Three* was undoubtedly a radical venture. The frequent advertisement rejections from mainstream newspapers demonstrate the major media taboo regarding promoting and condoning lesbianism. However, the magazine's preoccupation with respectability and public image was so great as to mute, to some extent, the radical impact of this new public discourse. I am not attempting to undermine *Arena Three*'s significance in lesbian representation and lesbian community formation. Rather, I am arguing that the greatly subversive move of promoting lesbianism was done in what can be seen as a conservative way of simultaneously arguing for lesbianism's own lack of subversiveness or deviance.

As will be seen, it was in its engagement with literature that *Arena Three*'s middle-class and assimilationist stances found their nexus. Through an explicit rejection of the majority of lowbrow pulp fiction and a pervasive suspicion of highbrow literature, the magazine's book reviews constructed a canon of lesbian literature that was decidedly middlebrow in its tastes. In doing so, the editors neatly formulated a stockpile of lesbian literature that managed to maintain in some ways a conservative angle on an obviously controversial topic. Although reviewers did sometimes turn their attentions to both high and lowbrow literature, the outsider status of these texts was always underscored. Ultimately, these reviews served to reinforce the overriding middlebrow slant of the magazine.

Having been traditionally overlooked in literary scholarship, middlebrow literature has in recent decades drawn the interest of scholars seeking to discern insights into the social and political world of readers of middlebrow fiction (Brown and Grover 2013). Such work has highlighted the socially and intellectually conservative slant of both the middlebrow novel and the middlebrow reader (Bracco 2003; Radway 1997). Rosa Maria Bracco (2003: 1–2) provides a succinct and useful overview of the middlebrow novel, identifying its central tenets and emphasising the middlebrow's investment and basis in respectability, morality and values over literary aesthetics and stylistics. In terms of middlebrow's own style, Bracco highlights the use of 'well rounded narratives, with clearly structured plots and definite endings'. The audience for middlebrow literature were assumed to be 'bound by a community of values' (Ibid.: 12). Those values, Bracco argues, were, once again, decidedly conservative:

> The term 'middlebrow' represented a symbol for the centre in more than one sense. It stood in the vast space between lowbrow fiction, designed merely to entertain, and highbrow works, increasingly alienated from a common reference of values. Its authors were from the middle classes and addressed a middle-class audience; they mediated between conflicts and extremes, and balance was their alleged trademark. (Ibid.: 12)

Furthermore, Bracco argues, middlebrow authors sought not to 'deviate from comfortably familiar presentations' (Ibid.: 10). These definitions of middlebrow literature can readily be applied to a range of lesbian-themed novels championed by *Arena Three*.

In keeping with Bracco's appraisal of middlebrow literature, *Arena Three* reviewers delineated a space for literature that was resolutely and consciously poised between low and highbrow publications. Lowbrow, in the context of postwar lesbian literature, can mean only one thing: lesbian pulp fiction. The 1950s and early 1960s saw the proliferation of lesbian pulp, following the phenomenal success of Tereska Torrès's *Women's Barracks* (1950) and Vin Packer's *Spring Fire* (1952). The 'golden age' of lesbian pulp that followed saw thousands of titles flood the newly emerging paperback market. Pulp, with its loose morals and distinct lack of 'respectability', was invoked by Claire Barringer in defining her Book List. Defining by exclusion, she stated baldly that there was to be no 'sludge' (*Arena Three* April 1964: 2).

In the September 1964 issue Barringer reported on a number of American titles with British publishers. With the vast majority of lesbian pulps coming out of America, it is no wonder that – despite Barringer's ban on 'sludge' – the novels featured in the magazine can all be considered part of the pulp canon. The titles themselves reliably signpost their pulp status: *The Odd Ones* (1960) by Edwina Mark, and *Stranger on Lesbos* (1960) and *Whisper Their Love* (1957) by Valerie Taylor. Barringer's short blurbs reveal a cross-section of 'melodrama', 'alcoholism', 'degradation' and plots of 'scarcely credible complications'. Her mildly disapproving tone is affirmed by a disclaimer at the end of her column. For any readers whose sensibilities were ruffled by the inclusion of trashy titles, Barringer reassures that: 'While endeavouring to cater to all requirements, the Book List does not intend to sink any lower than this. Compared to some American paperback horrors, the above section is reasonably well-written.' (*Arena Three* September 1964: 2). Despite the lesbian pulp genre providing, without doubt, the biggest overall source of lesbian-themed literature, in order for *Arena Three* to engage with such literature the specific titles had to distinguish themselves, being elevated above their counterparts to the status of what might be termed 'pulp plus'.

Valerie Taylor, one of the more prolific pulp novelists and author of what Yvonne Keller has termed 'pro-lesbian pulps' (Keller 1999) – that is, pulps with positive depictions of lesbianism – was also reviewed again in March 1965. This time, Gene Damon reviewed *Journey to Fulfilment* (1964), the third book in Taylor's four-part Erika Frohmann series (1960–88), following the lesbian protagonist Erika Frohmann through life's loves and losses. Damon's praise for Taylor was less qualified than Barringer's: 'All the paperback originals by Valerie Taylor are well above the usual run and can be recommended as good light reading with sympathetic casts and happy endings' (*Arena Three* March 1965: 6). Nevertheless, the reader is made aware that Taylor has distinguished herself enough from the unnamed hordes of pulp authors to merit her inclusion here.

Arena Three's casually dismissive treatment of pulp fiction is perhaps not particularly surprising. After all, the vast majority of lesbian pulp fiction titles were male-authored, derivative, sleazy and homophobic (Tooth Murphy 2017). In addition, it was not easy for uninformed readers to discern which novels were part of the small enclave of 'pro-lesbian pulps'. Therefore, it is logical that *Arena Three* reviewers would not wish to spend time wading through piles of formulaic trash titles resulting in endless negative reviews. Rather, a few cherry-picked titles would no doubt serve their discerning readership much better. However, that given, the number of pulps reviewed is still surprisingly low considering the popularity of the genre and the fact that for many women it was their only way to access explicit representations of lesbianism. Missing from *Arena Three* are numerous celebrated pulp authors such as Ann Bannon, Vin Packer, Sloane Britain and Paula Christian. These women, and others like them, wrote for a lesbian audience and, despite the formulaic constraints of the genre, wrote positive and often affirming accounts of lesbian love that survived against the odds (Tooth Murphy 2017). Nonetheless, *Arena Three* often featured middlebrow male novelists while overlooking lesbian authors of pulp fiction.

'Needlessly dark terrain': *Arena Three's* Rejection of Highbrow Literature

At the opposite end of the spectrum, *Arena Three* had a complicated relationship with highbrow literature. Rather than rejecting it outright – as with lowbrow literature – readers and reviewers often exhibited a suspicion towards what they considered to be highbrow. Perhaps surprisingly, a new edition of the much-revered lesbian tome, Radclyffe Hall's *The Well of Loneliness* (1928) was summarily dismissed by Barringer as 'got up in a flashy jacket by Perma Books, look[ing] more than ever like yesterday's mutton dressed as lamb' (*Arena Three* May 1964: 10). It should, however, be noted that not all classics received the same short shrift. In this same column Barringer recommended Djuna Barnes's *Nightwood* (1936), *Olivia* (1949) by Dorothy Strachey, Virginia Woolf's *Orlando* (1928), and even D. H. Lawrence's *The Rainbow* (1915). She also directed readers towards works by weighty authors such as Colette, Marcel Proust and Rosamond Lehmann. This backward glance at early twentieth-century classics is exceptional in Barringer's column. As she went on to explain, the purpose of the book review section was to keep members up to date with new publications. She particularly endeavoured to bring readers those works with 'a welcome sense of humour' (this perhaps explaining the unequivocal response to Radclyffe Hall). This distinction between classics and contemporary publications is important as, Hall aside, *Arena Three* conferred an inherent legitimacy to highbrow classics that was hard-won by newly published highbrow titles.

In general, contemporary novels pitched as 'literature' as opposed to 'fiction' had to go through something of an initiation process to ascertain their worth, the review format often being different from that of the standard novel. In the cases of Jane Rule's *Desert of the Heart* (1964) and Maureen Duffy's *The Microcosm* (1966), multiple reviews were given both for and against each work (*Arena Three* February 1964: 8–9; March 1964: 7; April 1964: 13; June 1966: 4–6). A recurring theme throughout is the way in which literariness is seen as not only off-putting but downright confusing; all in all, the kind of thing which can ruin a perfectly good book. In this rejection of literary aesthetics *Arena Three* signalled its affiliation with middlebrow tastes and mores, where realism and plot-driven narratives were the order of the day.

Desert of the Heart was first reviewed by two readers, Doreen Holley and Ann Bruce (a pseudonymous Esme Langley), in two separate reviews (*Arena Three* February 1964: 8–9). *Desert of the Heart* has since come to be regarded as a classic of lesbian literature and Rule has assumed a place as a doyenne of lesbian literary culture. However, as these reviews demonstrate, in 1964 in Britain she was as yet unknown to many lesbians. Indeed, both reviewers were less than complimentary. The main complaint given was that the book was 'confusing'. Holley bemoaned the convoluted nature of the plot, while Bruce stated, 'We end up more baffled and bewildered than we began'.

Bruce went on to more directly critique what she presumably saw as the over-literariness of the novel: 'The story is a weird and apparently pseudo-allegorical one, stiff with symbolic encrustations'. The implication here is that Rule's literary devices are an obstruction to the reader's engagement with the text. Bruce extended her own metaphorical conceit, depicting the novel as territory to be traversed: 'any beam of light on this needlessly dark terrain is warmly welcome', concluding that, 'Miss Rule's . . . explanatory mutterings would never get her a job as a professional guide'. Bruce's choice of metaphor is revealing with regard to the negative attitudes towards highbrow literature seen in *Arena Three*. Bruce suggested that in approaching a piece of lesbian fiction, a lesbian reader is seeking a guide or guidebook to lesbian sexuality. Overuse of literary strategies endangers the clarity of the plot, drawing the reader's attention from more important issues of lesbian life and identity. This definitively embeds *Arena Three*'s book reviews within the overarching ethos of the magazine where, through a wide variety of articles and reader's letters, the overriding focus for discussion is the issue of how to be a lesbian and live a (happy) lesbian life. The book review section suggested that literature could and did have a part to play in this process: by writing clearly and instructively about lesbianism fiction authors could be the 'professional guides' that readers sought. In this emphasis on realism and relatability over literary posturing, some of the reasons behind *Arena Three*'s draw to the middlebrow come into focus.

Tellingly, Bruce referred to Mary McCarthy as a foil to Rule, praising her 'cheerful precision'. McCarthy's *The Group*, published in 1963, follows the lives of a group of women, friends in college, as they embark on marriages, careers, parenthood, divorce, affairs and, in the case of the enigmatic Lakey, lesbianism. McCarthy's prose is clear and concise. There is no literary pretension about the novel. Rather, McCarthy employs a clear narrative structure to a wholly plot-driven story. In *The Group*, social, personal and cultural issues and concerns are foregrounded over and above literary devices and aesthetics. In comparison, Rule's deployment of mirror and desert metaphors and biblical allusions allows aesthetics to share centre stage with her characters. For Holley, *Desert of the Heart*'s happy ending, so often absent from lesbian literature of the time, was not enough: 'By that time I was past caring'.

Both Holley and Bruce also drew attention to what they saw as the rather unwelcome and uncomfortable sex scenes. Holley was put off by the casual way in which sex is treated by both bisexual and gay characters. Bruce squirmed over the 'purplish amorous encounters'. Here, highbrow and lowbrow fiction overlap, disconcerting reviewers squeamish about overt depictions of lesbian sexuality. A strange reaction, one might think, for a lesbian magazine, but not in fact out of place in *Arena Three*'s generally conservative stance. The magazine typically favoured a more measured and morally resonant depiction of sex, one which might fit more easily with their agenda of positive representation (Hamer 1996: 176–7).

However, not all readers looked unfavourably on Rule. In the following edition, an unidentified reader wrote that she was, 'still mildly seething' over the reviews (*Arena Three* March 1964: 7). The author of the letter praised Rule's 'brilliantly subtle and imaginative' work and accused Holley and Bruce of taking a 'superficial glance at a book of such depth of perception'. In the next edition Barringer wrote 'In

Defence of *Desert of the Heart*' (*Arena Three* April 1964: 13). Here she provided a glowing review of the novel, praising Rule's 'boldness' and 'vividly-drawn symbolic power'.

It is clear that *Desert of the Heart* proved to be something of a controversial text, arousing contention among *Arena Three*'s members in the wake of its publication. Positioning herself in the 'pro' camp, Claire Barringer might be seen as a potential advocate of highbrow literature, someone receptive to literary devices and nuance. And as has already been seen, she was certainly no proponent of pulp. However, two years later she was unequivocal in her criticism of Maureen Duffy's newly published *The Microcosm* (*Arena Three* June 1966: 4–5). Duffy's novel emerged from an original idea to publish a book of extracts from interviews she had carried out at the renowned London lesbian club, The Gateways. After a publisher advised her there was no market for such a book, she fictionalised the accounts and wove them together into a loose narrative centring on 'The House of Shades', a lesbian club recognisable as The Gateways (Duffy 2008). The novel is experimental in form, made up of various vignettes and pastiche set pieces, varying in style – largely stream of consciousness – from various interrelated characters. The novel is bound together by the recurring voice of Matt, a butch intellectual hiding in a job as a petrol-pump attendant. One of the more experimental features of the text is an extended flashback of nearly thirty pages to the story of Charlotte Clark, the eighteenth-century actress and cross-dresser, and also a lengthy flashback to the life of Boudica.

This time Barringer was put off by the prevalence of literary devices, affording the text none of the skill and dexterity that she found in Rule's novel. Rather than praise the book's experimental form, she appeared to see these features as indicative of sloppiness and bad writing. Imagining that the publisher must have rushed the novel out, she complained that it 'reads like a hastily-edited writer's notebook, with disjointed episodes, unfinished plots, experimental switches in time and style'. Furthermore, Duffy's postmodern approach to punctuation roused little interest in Barringer. Instead, it was merely something to overlook, to forgive the author for. The historical segments were irritating and 'inexplicable' to Barringer. As with *Desert of the Heart*, not even the book's optimistic ending was enough to rescue it: 'the fact that Matt finally renounces her petrol pump will be of small reassurance'. In addition to the technical faults that Barringer found with *The Microcosm*, she also apparently felt alienated and even disturbed by the central characters, and cautioned other readers that, 'To the uninitiated, the book's humourless butchiness will be a trifle alarming' (*Arena Three* June 1966: 4–5).

Here the highbrow again finds something in common with the lowbrow. Taking place largely in and around the bar scene, *The Microcosm* depicts working-class lesbian life; in particular, butch and femme models of lesbian identity. Suspicion risks tipping over into 'alarm' for the lesbian with more conservative sensibilities. In Duffy's novel, Matt is so butch that she refers to herself in the male pronoun. This gender ambiguity proved, alongside the style and form of the novel, to be a little too experimental. Regardless of the book's aesthetics, the focus itself was ultimately unseemly and disconcerting to Barringer.

However, in a similar manner to the *Desert of the Heart* reviews, Barringer's all-round negative review was countered by an enthusiastic review from Gene Damon, featured in the same column. Damon agreed that *The Microcosm* is not an easy read. But where Barringer found Duffy's literary devices mere distraction and poor writing, Damon found them stimulating, challenging and ultimately rewarding: 'the reader is required to think as well as enjoy, but it is not a novel to miss, for the reader comes away enriched' (Ibid.). Where Barringer condescended to the novel's unfinished appearance, Damon elevated and celebrated the novel as highbrow: '[N]o words do justice to this book, although I admit it lacks popular appeal, for it is truly an intellectual study, a novel of ideas, a thoughtful book. Hopefully one which will be discussed for years to come' (Ibid.). In making a claim for the book's durability, Damon, consciously or unconsciously, categorised the book as highbrow; a classic in the making. Furthermore, she cited various influences on the novel – Proust, Joyce and Fielding – explicitly installing *The Microcosm* within the highbrow literary tradition. Overall, this polemic approach to Duffy's novel, played out through both reviews, is even more pronounced than the contention prompted by *Desert of the Heart*. Significantly, both these novels have since achieved iconic status in lesbian literary culture, their literary merits certainly no longer considered a matter for debate.

In June 1964, *Arena Three* featured a review of Rosemary Manning's *The Chinese Garden* (*Arena Three* June 1964: 8). The novel is part of the sub-genre of lesbian-themed fiction set in girls' schools and follows the intelligent but naïve Rachel Curgenven through her school career at the austere and crumbling Bampfield boarding school, where both pupils and teachers engage in lesbian relationships against a backdrop of hypocrisy and moral outrage.[2] The *Arena Three* reviewer, A. Hughes, was impressed by the novel's descriptive, elegant and literate style. However, what hampers the novel for this reviewer is its plausibility, specifically its lack thereof. Overall Hughes finds the story 'difficult to swallow' in terms of the characters' reactions and interactions. In particular, she has difficulty with the adults' hypocrisies: 'While these ladies live in, contribute to, and presumably enjoy this decidedly camp atmosphere, they unaccountably throw up their hands in righteous wrath when [pupils] Margaret and Rena are caught in bed together.' (*Arena Three* June 1964: 8).

In a similar vein, the review takes issue with Rachel as unassuming narrator. Rachel is shown throughout the novel to be exceptionally well-read. Hughes cannot reconcile this with the character's startling naivety concerning lesbianism. She ultimately concludes that it is the 'want of perception, not intelligence on the part of the heroine, which accounts for the disparity between appearance and reality which is the major defect of this book'. The reviewer's main complaint is that the story is not realistic. Both *The Microcosm* and *Desert of the Heart* were criticised for obscuring a straightforward story with needless literary posturing. All in all, these reviewers demonstrate that what they really wanted from lesbian literature was unadorned realism; a coherent narrative that they could follow and buy into. The middlebrow novel, therefore, had much to offer and found much favour among reviewers.

Short Reviews for Good Reads: the Lesbian Middlebrow Reader

Accordingly – although they often inspired debate – highbrow novels were not the major focus of *Arena Three*'s book section. Instead, the magazine's stock-in-trade was the middlebrow novel. From issue to issue various middlebrow titles were recommended via short reviews with brief plot details and even briefer critical comment.

Ideologically, entertainment value was more important than any claims to 'authentic' lesbian literature written by lesbian women. The middlebrow novels featured by *Arena Three* are notable for their straightforward style, plot-driven narratives and lack of pretension to great literary merit. Very few of these titles have attained any lasting reputation, the majority being out of print and difficult to source. Indeed, middlebrow lesbian writing has not experienced the same critical surge of interest as pulp fiction has in recent years. Nor has it seen the same re-printing of more notable titles as part of the kitsch aesthetic revival.

So far, I have demonstrated that *Arena Three* writers and readers were happy to dismiss the vast majority of pulp titles as 'sludge', regardless of their treatment of lesbianism. I have further demonstrated their suspicion and ambivalence towards highbrow literature. As for that vast space in between, Janice Radway's (1997) landmark study of the middlebrow reader and the American subscription mail order 'Book-of-the-Month Club', is suggestive of the literary sensibility displayed by *Arena Three*. As with *Arena Three*, Radway argues that the Club's tastes and that of its readership were inherently conservative. In particular, Radway defines the middlebrow in terms of its conscious positioning against highbrow characteristics:

> Despite the traditional claims that middlebrow culture simply apes the values of high culture, it is in fact a kind of counterpractice to the high culture tastes and proclivities that have been most insistently legitimated and nurtured in academic English departments. (Radway 1997: 9)

Furthermore, the following, on how the Book-of-the-Month committee selected titles for their readership, is strongly reminiscent of the way in which the editorial board of *Arena Three* can be seen as consciously constructing a middlebrow corpus that suited the sensibilities of its readership:

> The judges were wary of the dispassionate, highly intellectualised aesthetic distance associated with experimental forms of literary modernism and the highly academic criticism that had appeared to legitimate it. As a consequence, their guiding philosophy of book selection was less an aesthetic, in the sense of a philosophy or theory of art, than an ethos, a practical disposition or orientation to books that evaluated them according to how well they harmonised with a reader's moral norms, ethical standards, and expectations about pleasure (Ibid.: 278).

The true test of a book, then, was that it should reflect 'the everyday perception of everyday existence' (Ibid.: 278). When applied to *Arena Three*'s reviews, this translates into readable, enjoyable books which depict lesbian characters that readers can relate to. This did not mean that works should be resolutely positive in their depictions of lesbian life. Rather, there were many featured titles with unhappy resolutions and unfulfilled loves. In practical terms, this is understandable, as happy endings were still very much in the minority for lesbian characters. However, it can also be argued that for many readers this echoed their own lives. Furthermore, as numerous readers' letters demonstrate, many women did not expect their own happy ending. In this sense, the novels reviewed in *Arena Three* did indeed reflect 'the everyday perception of everyday existence'.

The author's gender and sexuality were also not important for a book's inclusion. In many issues there were more male-authored texts reviewed than female-authored ones, and these were just as likely to elicit a positive appraisal.[3] A far cry from academia's drawn-out discussions over the question of lesbian authorship, this appears to support the idea that it was the story itself which was important, not the personal politics, or even the sexual orientation of the author. By accepting without question heterosexual male and female authors into its library, *Arena Three*, and by extension the MRG, was reconfirming its position as a mainstream and assimilationist entity, happy to engage in civil discourse with the heteronormative world.

Barringer and Damon's reviews were typically short and sweet, suggesting that lengthy critical dissections were not deemed necessary or desirable. Instead, they gave a very brief indication of the plot and tone of the novel, and perhaps some testament to or disavowal of the 'credibility' in terms of a lesbian plot. This had, of course, been one of the major downfalls of *The Chinese Garden*, in that the reviewer found it 'hard to swallow'. However, fanciful dealings were also encouraged and, in general, light reads curried favour. Brigid Brophy's *The Finishing Touch* (1963) was a 'Firbankian frolic' (Barringer in *Arena Three* May 1964: 10) and Louise W. King's *The Day We Were Mostly Butterflies* (1963) was billed as the 'delightfully lunatic adventures of the scatterbrained Miss Moppet and her lady truck-driver protector in and around Greenwich Village' (Barringer in *Arena Three* October 1964: 5). Genre fiction was also popular, with murder mysteries and thrillers featuring often. Ruth Rendell's first novel, *From Doon with Death* (1964) received a very positive review, being 'an excellent romantic mystery of the 30s school' (Damon in *Arena Three* September 1966: 6). Peter de Polnay's *In Raymond's Wake* (1965) involves a mysterious death at a Spanish resort with an 'odd collection of characters' and 'the most farcical pair of expatriate English lesbians imaginable' (Damon in *Arena Three* September 1966: 6). Laurence Meynell's *Double Fault* (1965) moves the murder to a country-house weekend, but the ensemble approach is familiar: '[the] large cast includes all types of homosexuals, none treated unfairly and none used as convenient scapegoats for the crime' (Damon *Arena Three*. September 1966: 6). As for Ian Fleming's *Goldfinger* (1959), Barringer's review offered no real praise or criticism, only passing comment on Pussy Galore as, 'the most delightfully outrageous name yet dreamed up for a Lesbian character' (*Arena Three* June 1964: 11).

Ghostly goings-on were also popular. Shirley Jackson's *The Haunting of Hill House* (1960) has the now familiar horror plot device of a group of strangers investigating paranormal occurrences in a deserted old house in the middle of nowhere. It has a fairly overt lesbian theme, one of the characters coming fresh from a big argument with her 'friend' and subsequently falling for one of the other women at the house. The woman in question is then seemingly driven mad by the mystical energies operating on the house and its visitors. Barringer has very little to say about the book, only passing brief comment on the lesbian storyline: 'the horrific effect on Eleanor's new-found love for Theodora' (*Arena Three* October 1964: 5). Robert Aickman's *The Late Breakfasters* (1964) is another case of uncanny happenings, with a strange and rambling plot and a procession of oddball gay characters. Once again, the supernatural occurrences are a backdrop to a female protagonist falling in love with another woman. Barringer's review of *The Late Breakfasters* is longer than usual and as well as outlining the plot she gives a more direct endorsement: 'there is much in this unusual book to amuse, to enjoy and to exercise the imagination. It will either cast a spell or leave you cold. I personally found it enchanting' (*Arena Three* July 1964: 6).

Away from the supernatural, the family saga also proved to be a popular formula where 'complicated' plots abound. Some examples include *Last Innocence* (1955) by Célia Bertin, made up of 'complex family relationships' in which a lesbian attempts to marry her brother-in-law (Barringer in *Arena Three* August 1964: 5); Marguerite Steen's *A Candle in the Sun* (1964), which revolves around a 'complicated family plot' (Damon in *Arena Three* September 1964: 5) (A man seeking to divorce his wife. It turns out that she is in a lesbian relationship with an old friend of his. He then meets someone else. Meanwhile, their daughter is in an undesirable relationship); and *The Round Mosaic* (1965), first of an intended trilogy, by Desmond Stewart: a 'lengthy' and 'complicated plot with an historical focus' (Damon in *Arena Three* September 1966: 5).

Although such plots may seem convoluted, the author was still expected to stick within acceptable boundaries of plausibility. Romulus Linney's *Slowly, by Thy Hand Unfurled* (1965), in which a latently lesbian wife and mother unwittingly destroys her family, including the death of her three children, was criticised by 'I.F' for being 'melodramatic and occasionally absurd' (*Arena Three* June 1966: 3). *The Compromisers* (1964) by Ernest Borneman, in which a woman sleeps with her female lover's husband in an attempt to secure her freedom, was given short shrift as, 'the most unconvincing story of any year' (Barringer in *Arena Three* August 1964: 5).

This glimpse into the stock-in-trade book reviews in *Arena Three* reveals that within what were generally cursory reviews, the magazine's writers were able to give their readership all the information that they felt was needed to ensure their reading pleasure. The picture of reading tastes that emerges is a simple one: plot-driven novels with lesbian themes that privilege reading pleasure above anything else. A fair degree of silliness was afforded for light-hearted novels. Conventional genre fiction with a queer twist in theme or characters was well-received. An acceptable amount of convolutedness helped to move family sagas along, but as soon as they veered too close to melodramatic or trashy they were out of favour. For the most part, aesthetics or literary worthiness did not come into the equation. The few contemporary novels with highbrow aspirations received reviews which were at best ambivalent or simply left reviewers unimpressed. Aside from the obvious fact that they dealt with lesbian themes, the books which did impress reviewers were generally conventional.

In literary terms they conformed to conservative style, form, genre, settings and scope. In this sense they conform to Tom Perrin's analysis of postwar middlebrow fiction:

> The attraction of such novels rests on their ambivalence: they at one and the same time allow readers an outlet for legitimate complaints about the hypocrisy of conventional values and also maintain the irresistible appeal of belonging to mainstream society. (Perrin 2011: 384)

Indeed, this concept of ambivalence is applicable to *Arena Three* at large. Despite a frequently embattled, and even antagonistic, tone with regards to both professional and public discourses about lesbianism, editors, writers and readers of *Arena Three* consistently demonstrated their longing for acceptance – for assimilation – into the very society whose castigations they so frequently derided.

Drawing on Bracco and Radway's descriptions of middlebrow fiction, *Arena Three*'s book review section can be seen as constructing a solidly middlebrow body of literature for its solidly middle-class cohort of readers. *Arena Three* and the MRG sought to perpetuate an image of lesbians as respectable members of society (Jennings 2007b: 155). The average reader concurred:

> The public image of the lesbian is so often a warped, unbalanced woman whose only interest, outside the minimal hours spent earning a living, is in gratifying an immoderate and irregular sexual lust. The thousands of other lesbians, who are probably no more highly sexed than their heterosexual counterparts, are just too normal and unremarkable in their habits and activities to be picked out by any chance acquaintances or colleagues, and are doing perfectly normal and useful jobs for the community, It is the image of these lesbians which needs to be put over. ('M.S.' in *Arena Three* October 1965: 13)

By reflecting a reliably 'normal' image of that readership back to itself *Arena Three*'s book review column played no small part in this assimilationist agenda. When *Arena Three* folded in 1972, after considerable struggles over distribution and financing, the lesbian community in Britain was poised on the edge of transition, as lesbian feminism and other branches of left-wing politics held increasing sway in both community and identity formation. The magazine's assimilationist stance was already looking out of touch. Late issues show an awareness of this step change, with articles on the Gay Liberation Front sitting somewhat uneasily among more familiar pieces, including perennial debates over butch identity and its desirability, and a nostalgic call for reminiscences about The Gateways, suggesting an awareness of an end of an era. Nonetheless, the next major lesbian publication, *Sappho* (1972–81), emerged as a phoenix from the flames, a direct descendant of *Arena Three*. This new magazine was spearheaded by news reporter, actress and gay rights campaigner, Jackie Forster, who had been a regular contributor for *Arena Three*. Although these two periodicals now appear to reflect very different forms of lesbian community, politics and identity, *Sappho* could not have existed without *Arena Three*. Moreover, the lesbian community which received this new magazine owed its existence in no small part to *Arena Three*. As the first lesbian periodical in Britain, *Arena Three* helped to set in motion new forms of lesbian expression that would play a major role in the coming queer movements of the later twentieth century.

Notes

1. Jennings argued for a broadening class base as the magazine expanded. However, as I argue here, the inherent class-based discourse remained in evidence, felt keenly by those working-class readers that it did acquire.
2. Examples include, Colette's *Claudine at School* (1900); Christa Winsloe's *The Child Manuela* (1933); Dorothy Strachey's *Olivia* (1949); and Brigid Brophy's *The Finishing Touch* (1963).
3. For example, in April 1965 only two books were reviewed, both with male authors. The same is true of January 1966 issue. In September 1966, out of seven books reviewed, four were written by men.

Works Cited

Bracco, R. M. 2003. *Merchants of Hope: British Middlebrow Writers and the First World War, 1919–1930*. Oxford: Berg.

Brown, E. and M. Grover. 2013. *Middlebrow Literary Cultures: The Battle of the Brows: 1920–1960*. London: Palgrave Macmillan.

Duffy, M. 2008. Oral history interview conducted by Sarah O'Reilly, *Authors' Lives*, British Library, C1276/03.

Gallo, M. M. 2006. *Different Daughters: A History of the Daughters of Bilitis and the Rise of the Lesbian Rights Movement*. New York NY: Carroll & Graf.

Hamer, E. 1996. *Britannia's Glory: A History of Twentieth-Century Lesbians*. London: Cassell.

Hammill, F. and M. Smith. 2015. *Magazines, Travel, and Middlebrow Culture: Canadian Periodicals in English and French, 1925–1960*. Liverpool: Liverpool University Press.

Jennings, R. 2007a. *A Lesbian History of Britain: Love and Sex between Women since 1500*. Oxford: Greenwood World Publishing.

Jennings, R. 2007b. *Tomboys and Bachelor Girls: A Lesbian History of Post-War Britain, 1945–71*. Manchester: Manchester University Press.

Keller, Y. 1999. 'Pulp Politics: Strategies of Vision in Pro-Lesbian Pulp Novels, 1955–1965'. *The Queer Sixties*. Ed. P. J. Smith. London: Routledge. 1–25.

Lapovsky Kennedy, E. and M. D. Davis. 1993. *Boots of Leather, Slippers of Gold: The History of a Lesbian Community*. London: Routledge.

Newton, E. 1993. *Cherry Grove, Fire Island: Sixty Years in America's First Gay and Lesbian Town*. Boston: Beacon Press.

Oram, A. 2007. 'Little by Little: *Arena Three* and Lesbian Politics in the 1960s'. *The Permissive Society and its Enemies: Sixties British Culture*. Ed. M. Collins. London: Rivers and Oram Press. 62–79.

Perrin, T. 2011. 'Rebuilding "Bildung": The Middlebrow Novel of Aesthetic Education in the Mid-Twentieth-Century United States'. *Novel: A Forum on Fiction*, 44.3: 382–401.

Radway, J. 1997. *A Feeling for Books: The Book of the Month Club, Literary Taste, and Middle-Class Desire*. Chapel Hill NC: University of North Caroline Press.

Tooth Murphy, A. 2017. 'The Kitchen: Lesbian Pulp Fiction's Radical Conventionalism'. *Queering the Interior*. Eds A. Gorman-Murray and M. Cook. London: Routledge. 51–63.

11

Always in with the In-Crowd: *Vogue* and the Cultural Politics of Gender, Race, Class and Taste

Estella Tincknell

The venerable fashion magazine *Vogue* has always associated itself with the interests of the ruling class, through the cultural and symbolic capital exhibited by the diffused aesthetic of its fashion spreads and through its unabashed attachment to the (white) scions of aristocracy as employees and the *haute monde* of celebrity culture as interviewees. *Vogue* is both cutting edge and deeply conservative in its articulation of fashion discourse, and the intersections of gender, class, race, taste, power and publicity are constantly reimagined and remediated to sustain its prestigious position as the world's leading fashion magazine with a strong pedigree. It is adept at responding to new inflections of power, at adapting to 'new times' and at transforming itself for new audiences while retaining its core loyalties. In this chapter I explore the relationship between *Vogue*, gender, race and class power in relation to the magazine's recent historic appointment of a black male editor and the scandal that this provoked around its track record of privileging whiteness. Drawing on Pierre Bourdieu's (1993a, 1993b) ideas, I consider the case in relation to the history of the magazine in the UK and to fashion as a site in which tensions around identity, culture and power are articulated and, ultimately, exposed.

'My *Vogue* is about being inclusive, it's about diversity'

In April 2017 British *Vogue* announced the appointment of its new editor, Edward Enninful, a black British fashion writer and stylist of Ghanaian heritage, who was at that point creative director of the US-based style magazine, *W*.[1] Enninful was following in the footsteps of Alexandra Shulman, who had successfully helmed *Vogue* for more than twenty-five years and whose departure came as something of a surprise to the fashion establishment despite her long tenure. Her career at *Vogue* had been marked by a notable expansion of the magazine's appeal to a wider demographic through the incorporation of popular culture and celebrity lifestyle content.[2] She also accelerated the magazine's promotion of star models such as Kate Moss, whose cockney-bohemian image seemed to capture the mood, first of 1990s 'Britpop' culture and even early Blairism, and later of the Cameronian 'demotic Toryism' that dominated British popular media in the years between 2010 and 2016.[3] Shulman successfully engineered *Vogue*'s modernisation during this period, retaining its commitment to elite fashion while also positioning the magazine within the hegemonic discourse of an expanded meritocracy that dominated popular media culture during the economically stable decade of 1997–2007, and did not fully exhaust itself until the impact of austerity in the years after 2012.

Enninful's appointment was in some ways unsurprising, coming in the wake of growing pressures on the globalised fashion industry and its media ancillaries to better reflect and celebrate diversity and social complexity. As a black Briton who had grown up in London, he came to fashion consciousness as a teenager having been 'discovered' on the London Tube by the modelling scout Simon Foxton, and had then insouciantly taken on the role of fashion director at the hipster magazine *i-D* at the tender age of eighteen before moving to New York and *W* – Enninful thus seemed made for the role. His credentials encompassed both a degree of 'street credibility' conferred by his background, and an appropriately US-focused cosmopolitanism suited to *Vogue*'s profile as a grand-but-still-hip Anglo-American fashion bible.

Indeed, as Joanne Entwistle and Agnes Rocamora make clear in their study of London Fashion Week, 'perform[ing] effectively within any field one needs to have accumulated the appropriate capital and mastered the field's habitus' (2006: 739). Enninful successfully demonstrated his capacity to perform within the 'fashion field', to demonstrate his accumulation of cultural capital and familiarity with fashion's habitus and, importantly, he showed that he could contribute to the reconstruction of the field for new times. Enninful was already a well-known figure among the fashion elite before his *Vogue* appointment, having used his role at *W* magazine to build a public profile. His appointment as British *Vogue*'s first black, and indeed first male, editor served to herald a shift in the magazine's identity towards a more culturally inclusive profile while maintaining its alignment with the market exclusivity of high fashion.[4]

Enninful's appointment generated acres of media coverage, not only in the fashion press, but also across the mainstream print media. Profiles, interviews, articles and commentaries proliferated, all focusing largely on his racial background and the distinction that this conferred within the predominantly white world of high fashion. Enninful himself appeared keen to acknowledge and enjoy the publicity that his new job generated. In an interview with the BBC reported in the London *Evening Standard* in November 2017, he is quoted as saying:

> My *Vogue* is about being inclusive, it's about diversity. Showing different women, different body shapes, different races, class. To be tackling gender . . . You are going to see all different colours, shapes, ages, genders, religions. That I am very excited about. You are going to see less of models who don't look so healthy. (Davis 2017)

Indeed, there can be little doubt that the appointment was geared to a reinvention of *Vogue* at a point when the circulation of the 'glossies' – fashion and women's magazines with high production values and a strong emphasis on escapist forms of luxury consumerism – was in freefall, challenged by the rapid growth of free online content during the 2000s, including fashion and lifestyle blogs by 'influencers' whose power had begun to rival that of the traditional fashion editor. As *Vogue* saw its legitimacy start to wane, the need for a shake-up became clear.

The Grande Dame of Modernity

Vogue navigates the relations between femininity, taste, class and modernity with some aplomb. Originally established in the US in 1892 as a weekly paper, *Vogue* soon changed to a monthly magazine explicitly targeted at New York high society with an emphasis on fashion and social and leisure activities. Its British offshoot was first published in 1916 as a consequence of shipping restrictions during the First World War, and rapidly assumed a distinctive identity and readership of its own, with a blend of fashion, arts, travel and lifestyle journalism. Alongside other fashion magazines of the 1920s and 1930s, *Vogue* established itself as geared to a 'modern' woman who was financially and socially independent. Unlike more domestically focused magazines such as *Good Housekeeping*, which offered advice and helpful tips on running a home and rearing children, *Vogue* always positioned its imaginary reader as already possessing high levels of social and cultural capital – a woman for whom the importance of good taste and stylish living was axiomatic. *Vogue* has thus rarely acknowledged the work of femininity other than in its most culturally valorised form: as the beautification of the self and of the private sphere, and as the aestheticisation of the public realm through fashion as art. Its 'glossy' format – printed on high gloss paper with a focus on strong images rather than text – has always also aligned *Vogue* to a culture in which high end consumerism blends into style as a way of life.

As Margaret Beetham (1996: 90–1) points out in her history of women's magazines, from the outset, it 'produced a femininity which was both class- and status-specific *and* available to the aspirational reader, whoever she was . . . [*Vogue*'s] style of life was an aspiration or even a fantasy'. Sustaining the gauzy threads between these potentially contradictory elements has been essential. Crucially, the magazine has always been adept at responding to new inflections of power and at transforming itself for new audiences while retaining its readership base. *Vogue* epitomises what Alison Light (1991: *passim*) has called conservative modernity, a frame of consciousness or even a 'structure of feeling', in Raymond Williams's (1981) phrase, in which the gloss of newness is tempered by the desire for continuity.

The British edition of *Vogue* is both cutting edge and deeply conservative in its articulation of fashion discourse. As Angela McRobbie (1998) – drawing on the work of Pierre Bourdieu – has shown, British fashion is split between the idea of fashion as 'art' and the more prosaic model of fashion as a 'rag trade'. Designers aspire to the former and to the cultural status that it bestows. *Vogue* saw its role as the canonical text of fashion as art, successfully presenting itself as the arbiter of good taste and skilfully blending fashion with a more 'serious' focus on the arts, reportage and lifestyle material. It is renowned for using (and indeed establishing) leading photographers and writers, and runs an annual talent competition for the latter, from which a number of its own writers have been recruited, including British *Vogue*'s editor between 1988 and 1992, Liz Tilberis. The magazine's longevity, combined with this carefully cultivated reputation, have helped to ensure it has remained the Grande Dame of glossies. For this reason, *Vogue* editors and contributors have had an unusually high public profile, helping to sustain the magazine's status and power.

During the 1940s *Vogue* helped foster the career of the war photographer (and erstwhile fashion model) Lee Miller, and its editors have all been strong-minded, independent women, often claiming to have feminist principles. For example, Beatrix

Miller (only ever known as 'Miss Miller' to her staff), edited the magazine throughout the 1960s and up until 1984, and was a self-appointed ambassador for the British fashion industry, receiving a CBE for her efforts. Its most famous editor-in-chief is probably Anna Wintour, however, whose rigorous commitment to a glacial personal style and espousal of conservative modernity was reputedly given homage in David Frankel's feature film *The Devil Wears Prada* (2006). Alexandra Shulman has also been widely regarded as one of *Vogue*'s most important successors to Miller, sustaining the magazine's profile and, as noted above, building an extended readership. Perhaps Shulman's most interesting innovation was to create commemorative or collectible issues of the magazine, thus cementing its cultural significance, most notably the spectacular 'gold' and 'silver' millennium issues that appeared in December 1999 and 2000.[5] Shulman was also skilled at maintaining *Vogue*'s relationship with the ruling class, both in its traditional aristocratic form and in the newer, high bourgeois elements (lawyers, doctors, PR and advertising professionals) that now dominate Britain's somewhat fractured but still robust social hierarchy. The magazine's early role as a house journal for metropolitan high society was considerably extended and adjusted throughout the twentieth century as various social waves and transformations (from the Second World War through the 1960s 'youthquake' and beyond) rendered the British class system more porous. By the 1990s, however, the magazine had to calibrate its relationship with an expanded middle-class readership of economically independent working women due to the potential threat posed by rival 'glossies' such as *Elle* and, later, *Grazia* and the emergence of gossip and celebrity magazines.[6] Shulman steered a course in which *Vogue*'s tacit endorsement of consumer feminism (made easier by its disengagement from domestic topics) was balanced by its endorsement of upper-class privilege and an *ancien régime*.

The monarchy had always been a favoured subject, but Shulman enthusiastically continued the tradition of often fawning features on the female members of the Royal family, climaxing in the 'Royal Salute' issue in 2001, which featured Kate Moss with a tilted crown and brandishing a sceptre on *Vogue*'s glossy cover, together with a portfolio of royal photographs through the ages inside. In addition, Diana, Princess of Wales appeared twice on the cover during Shulman's tenure, and was followed by Lady Helen Taylor in August 2000 and by the Duchess of Cambridge in June 2016; the issue seen as Shulman's triumphant valediction.

Yet *Vogue* was always careful to balance its monarchism with politics. During Tony Blair's period as British prime minister between 1997 and 2007 he, and especially wife Cherie, a leading lawyer and controversial figure, were given equally flattering coverage, often of a kind not offered elsewhere in the popular media. This was never a matter of the magazine endorsing a specific political party or policy, but rather of *Vogue*'s discursive relationship with power itself. Later, the Blairs' successors David and Samantha Cameron were the subject of similarly gushing endorsements, particularly the latter due to her established connections with the fashion business as an employee of Smythson, the upmarket leather brand. In a queasily adulatory *Vogue* interview from January 2017, for example, Christa D'Souza (2017) quite shamelessly promoted Cameron's new fashion line, Cefinn, and then Cameron herself as the epitome of modern – working, driven, 'completely equal to her husband' – femininity, notwithstanding her profoundly privileged upbringing. In such features, the intersections of gender, class, race, taste and publicity in high fashion's relationship with power are completely naturalised. Indeed, the version of 'modern' femininity privileged by such articles is a powerful articulation of neoliberal ideology; its emphasis on 'empowerment', 'choice' and personal agency, and on self-management and self-discipline as a necessary component of female fulfilment is striking. Just as Cameron's husband promoted such values as public policy through his premiership, she is called on to embody them at a personal level. As Rosalind Gill and Christina Scharff point out, under neoliberalism and postfeminism, 'women are required to work on and transform the self, to regulate every aspect of their conduct, and to present all their actions as freely chosen' (2011: 7). We might add that it is the job of *Vogue* and other glossy women's magazines to present these imperatives rather than those of domesticity or motherhood as fundamental to the middle-class woman's economic and social success and her personal happiness and fulfilment.[7]

Savagery, 'Street', Exoticism: Visual Style and the Black *Vogue* Model

And yet high fashion glossy magazines are also a form of popular art. Often deploying a modernist aesthetic in which the fashion is partially subsumed within the wider artistic vision of photographer or stylist, the glossies do not present themselves as selling clothes so much as selling a cultural ideal. The interview with Samantha Cameron was both a puff piece for her clothes brand and an endorsement of her taste. Details of décor, food and music preferences are dropped into the article, ostensibly as 'local colour', but the relentless brand naming suggests that this is also part of the quasi-commercial promotion of a particular taste formation.

This creation of an idealised lifestyle extends to the fashion spreads themselves. Glossy fashion shoots always have a 'story', one in which the model is set against a series of backdrops which construct a narrative into which the reader may insert herself. *Vogue*'s stories invariably privilege upmarket (and aspirational) urban settings such as luxury hotels and architecturally striking buildings, or exotic adventures in India, Africa or South America, in which the model is a cultured and sophisticated traveller, never a dumb tourist, and various kinds of ironic slumming, in which the model implausibly scoffs greasy burgers in a seedy relic of 1930s Americana, or is posed against a bleakly picturesque urban landscape. These images invite an appreciation not simply of the clothes but of the composition and form of the image. In other words, they require a high level of traditional forms of cultural capital to be legible. Indeed, the human models who carry the meanings, aspirations and desires connoted by such images are themselves often anonymous, valued in this context for their chameleon qualities and ability to take on different and temporary personas. As Myra Macdonald observes, 'as a spectacular icon, carrying none of her own meaning, the supermodel [in these images] is supremely postmodern. As part of a transitory spectacle which momentarily seizes our restless attention and then disappears . . . the excess and extravagance of her presentation tell us she is a simulacrum' (1995: 112).

In fact, *Vogue* was one of the last of the glossies to name the models in its fashion shoots. Until 2001, the photographer and stylist received credits, the model did not; she was effectively treated as simply one beautiful object among many to be manipulated by the 'real' (usually male) creative artists involved. This was despite the fact that in other sections of the magazine *Vogue* had enthusiastically endorsed the growth of a celebrity culture around the supermodels of the 1990s, actively encouraging their claims to agency and the extension and monetisation of their individual 'brands'. Such contradictions perhaps capture the way that *Vogue* has always attempted to balance its supposedly high-minded commitment to fashion as art in one corner, while simultaneously vigorously supporting a culture of excessive consumption (and often vulgarity) in another.

Until the 2010s the presence of women of BAME heritage in *Vogue* and indeed other glossies was confined largely to these fashion spreads, which are, of course, in some ways the defining purpose of such magazines. Here, black models featured alongside their white counterparts, although they were also used much less frequently and the range of meanings associated with the manner and style in which they were presented was often highly charged in overtly racialised ways. Black lives, experiences, identities remained largely subordinated. Cosmetics and beauty features rarely included items on products geared to black or dark complexions, for example, except as a 'special focus', thus reaffirming white hegemony and black exceptionalism.

Historically, fashion's mobilisation of black culture and style has also been profoundly problematic. It has tended to foreground three discursive articulations: savagery, 'street' style, and exoticism. The first iteration can be traced back well beyond contemporary fashion to 1920s modernism and the 'discovery' of African art by Western aesthetes. This led to a mania for 'primitive' or 'tribal' cultural forms, from the genuine to the ersatz. Prompted in part by the postwar fashion for psychoanalysis and the impact of the first wave of jazz – a powerful synthesis of African and European music traditions – African art was embraced as both psychologically authentic in expression and as excitingly savage in style, in contrast to the restraint and romanticism of Western traditions. The connection between the aesthetic fetishisation of savagery and fashion was thus mediated by the fashion magazines and their preoccupation with modernity.

Artists, writers and, indeed, fashion designers, developed a fascination with the racist idea of Africa as both unknowable – the 'dark continent' – and as the repository for the Id, Sigmund Freud's term for the instinctual, basic drives for pleasure and gratification that dominate the unconscious. African clothing styles were raided and reframed for Western fashion: 'tribal' costumes of feathers, hair, beads, masks and headdresses were used to signify the freeing up of the inner self, the refusal of Western cultural norms, and the taking on of new and exotic identities. From the 1920s through the hippy styles of the late 1960s, which used the 'primitivism' of Native American dress to signify authenticity and the rejection of Western conformity, to the use of African animal prints in more recent fashion to suggest untameable sexuality, Western fashion has both appropriated the 'other' and shaped it to fit white cultural expectations.

Incredibly, the use of African or 'tribal' references to connote savagery remains a thematic trope in contemporary fashion. Anjali Vats (2014) points out that Alexander McQueen's oeuvre contained frequent uses of such elements, here presented as a commentary on white beauty and style traditions, but still deploying the same tropes of savagery to do so:

> [B]eneath the thin veneer of multicultural celebration and hip intellectualism, McQueen's designs are more concerned with appropriating oddities, stereotypes,

> and wild animals and placing them in a new and Western-appropriate context than any real and substantial engagement with race. (Vats 2014: 113)

The second key way in which black models appear in high fashion imagery is in material that claims to explore urban fashion or 'street style'. Such features draw on the resistant and iconoclastic genres of anti-fashion associated with youth subcultures and club cultures. The centrality of black subcultural forms to these became newly prominent in the 1980s, popularised initially by *The Face*, the ground-breaking style magazine launched by Neville Brody in 1980, and later by *i-D*, where Edward Enninful also learned his trade. These features are analogous to, and indeed often draw on the way that vernacular terms for black music – 'cool', 'hip', 'bad' – have been incorporated into mainstream, primarily white, culture as signifiers of a raw authenticity. Such references associate urban space with glamorised violence, gang rivalries and illicit entrepreneurship. These articulations form a striking contrast with more traditional high fashion references to the city as a site of civilised leisure and the flâneur.

Street style can, moreover, be an extension of the savagery discourse. It is grounded in genres of masculine dress that often exaggerate and parody conventional white good taste. Originating in the 1940s 'Zoot suits' associated with African-American communities in Harlem and Chicago, later iterations have included the 'Super Dude' styles seen in 1970s blaxploitation movies, featuring ultra-sharp tailoring, bright checks and strong colours which deliberately contrasted with the grey formality of middle-class white male dress. In the 1980s and 1990s, the rise of sports clothing alongside rap and hip-hop culture similarly dominated street fashion, again utilising exaggerated shapes in the form of baggy sports pants and oversized track tops. Since the early 2000s, street style has become an increasingly central strand in fashion's discourse, with the focus not on the distinction of specific outfits but rather on the distinction of specific brands – the new signifiers of authentic taste and insider knowledge. The use of street style in the glossy magazines has inevitably involved a feminisation and recuperation of its oppositional tropes and the forced association of streetwear with upmarket brands, however paradoxical this appears. It remains, nevertheless, overwhelmingly associated with black bodies and urban spaces, even when these are those of 'ordinary' people captured by photographers seeking inspiration from the pavements of central London.

The third trope is that of the 'exotic'. This too overlaps with 'savagery', but its use in high fashion is also linked to the way that black models are cast for shoots which foreground a highly aestheticised body as part of the *mise en scène* as opposed to shoots which use the body as a more neutral coat hanger for the clothing. In these spreads, the bodies of black models are heavily objectified, transformed into visually striking instruments of display which may be fragmented, distorted or dehumanised by the photographer's art. For example, a fashion spread from British *Vogue*'s July 2018 issue, 'Amazing Grace', shot in black and white to accentuate its stylisation of bodies, featured primarily black models posed against a stark white backdrop, heavily shadowed and with their faces obscured by giant sized hats and sunglasses (*Vogue* July 2018: 192–5). The images are arresting but clearly do not promote the clothes so much as an aesthetic in which models are little more than interesting and visually striking shapes.

Indeed, this exoticisation extends even to the way that established black models are represented more widely. Alek Wek, a Sudanese-British model has become famous for supposedly being the first model to be valued for her 'African' facial features. Wek's impact on the industry was even described by Louette Harding (2007) of the *Daily Mail* as being due to 'an uncompromising, sub-Saharan beauty . . . her industry saw her as new and exotic – *a savage beauty*' (my italics). The ideological loading of this description is extraordinary. Wek's round face and wide eyes do not remotely conform to anything savage unless we are to assume that blackness by definition equals savagery (which, presumably, Harding did). As with my earlier examples, fashion discourse's coding of blackness invariably returns it to the realm of the 'other', even when it believes that it is doing something more liberating.

'I haven't got a racist bone in my body': the Shulman Scandal

In August 2014, the British newspaper *The Guardian* ran an article by Tansy Hoskins (2014) pointing out that the UK edition of *Vogue* had not run a solo image of a black model on its cover since 2002 when Naomi Campbell was its star. Black models had been included in ensemble groups, but none had been featured in their own right. Hoskins went on to describe the interventions being made by models themselves into what they regarded as institutional racism in fashion more generally, including an open letter from three leading models, Naomi Campbell herself, Iman and Bethann Hardison, calling out the industry. They were, Hoskins reported, particularly angered by the attitude of *Vogue*'s editorial team led by Alexandra Shulman, who was asked why Jourdan Dunn, a black British model with a growing international reputation, had never appeared on the front cover of *Vogue*.

Shulman's response was that: 'We have put Beyoncé and Rihanna on the cover of *Vogue* and at least half our covers do not feature models. We love Jourdan Dunn and she was the cover star of the last *Miss Vogue* which previously had featured Cara Delevingne.' This suggested that somehow the celebrities were preventing Shulman from putting a leading black British model on the front cover of the leading British fashion magazine. Yet Kate Moss had featured on three *Vogue* covers in 2014 alone and continues to be the magazine's favourite. Campbell retorted by tweeting a group photograph of the *Vogue* editorial team under Shulman's stewardship in 2017 – an entirely white group. Not only that, the core team included a host of privileged 'Sloane-y' women (that is, female members of the upper classes and aristocracy whose base reputedly centres on Sloane Square in Chelsea), whose habitus was unlikely to encompass the kind of 'street' culture that *Vogue* finds fascinating. It featured Emily Sheffield, the sister of Samantha Cameron, who is also the daughter of a baronet.

Shortly after Enninful's appointment was announced, Shulman was interviewed for *The Guardian* by Decca Aitkenhead (2017) about her career at *Vogue*, and her attitudes towards racism and class privilege were made clear, albeit unwittingly to the woman herself, who claimed not to understand the basis of Campbell's criticisms. She defended veiled comments that she had made about the future of fashion journalism as not 'being photographed in a series of designer clothes with a roster of famous friends' – an observation widely believed to be a swipe at Enninful's glamorous lifestyle. When pressed on her apparent reluctance to put black models on the *Vogue* cover, she fell back on the 'some of my best friends are black' argument (actually, it was that 'my son's grandfather, Robert Spike, was one of the civil rights leaders. So it's very offensive to me and my family, the idea that I'm racist'), and went on to bluster that she 'didn't believe in quotas' so could not be expected to keep a tally of the number of black people that she employed or featured in the magazine. She also insisted that she 'hadn't got a racist bone in my body'.

This train wreck of an interview led to a scandal insofar as Shulman's words were widely reported and became the fulcrum for a spate of critical articles on the fashion industry. It was not simply revealing about Shulman's lack of self-awareness; it was important because it uncovered the extreme tensions around the way a culture of privilege at *Vogue* had been forced up against the economic imperative to change or perish. The decline of the glossy magazine among its traditional readership base, together with the increasing dominance of online content and changing demographics were forcing *Vogue* to modernise again. This time, it would have to work harder to reimagine and remediate the intersectional relations of gender, race and class.

The December issue(s): Enninful Takes Charge

Enninful's much awaited first issue came in December 2017. The cover featured a huge close-up image of the mixed-race model Adwoa Aboah, her head clad in an African-style turban, her face brightly made-up in jewel-like colours reminiscent of the 1970s – and presumably intended to deliberately invoke that decade's use of 'exotic' black models in an earlier iteration of glossy bohemianism. The main strapline beneath Aboah's face simultaneously celebrated and challenged patriotic sensibilities with its statement: 'Great Britain' (*Vogue* December 2017: front cover).

Alongside the main image, further strap-lines simply listed the (impressive) line-up of contributors and featured individuals, which was equally diverse, including Sadiq Khan, the Mayor of London; Salman Rushdie, the Indian-born novelist and leading postmodernist; the black British filmmaker Steve McQueen; the venerable actress and ex-Labour MP Glenda Jackson; and the ubiquitous (and it seems obligatory) Kate Moss. This multi-ethnic mix of people from the worlds of literature, film, politics and culture alongside the more expected fashion designers and models suggested that Enninful's vision for the magazine was an expanded and inclusive one. Shulman before him had modernised *Vogue* by incorporating elements of 1990s Britpop, Britart and lifestyle features, including a food column by the emergent star of modern conservative femininity, the 'domestic goddess' Nigella Lawson. But she had also carefully curated its status as the UK's leading 'fashion bible'. Enninful was signalling his determination to foreground multiculturalism and diversity in a revamped vision of a British meritocracy.

In addition to its deliberately iconoclastic front cover, Enninful's first issue contained a letter from the new editor that proclaimed his diversity manifesto:

> I hope you will be as gratified as I am to note how many of the amazing names featured on these pages didn't necessarily begin their lives here, or were perhaps born into families who emigrated here a generation or two ago (like my own). Regardless of where they were born or how they got here, however, they all share huge pride in their homeland, with an outlook that is pleasingly global. (*Vogue*, December 2017: 24)

These words, presumably intended as a shot across the bows, are in fact not particularly radical. Indeed, in some ways they simply rearticulate the ideology of inclusivity and diversity that has long been hegemonic in the largely (if frequently superficially) liberal domain of the arts and culture.[8] Fashion is nothing if not good at identifying what is 'in', after all, and deference to the principles of liberal values and inclusivity have been central to the fashion world's idea of itself for at least five decades, shaping the way it positioned itself at the centre of the twentieth century's youth and countercultures, for example. High fashion, and *Vogue* especially, deftly appropriated the style of such cultures and reworked them for an elite market, colluding with the designers and marketers whose brands sold a sanitised image of rebellion back to the public as exclusive style statements.[9] As Parmentier and Fischer point out:

> [T]he fashion system regularly appropriates style innovations resulting from consumer identity play, both producers and consumers have restrictions on their power in the face of fashion's incessant need for newness and its relentless production of obsolescence. To the extent that end-consumers have scope for agency over their practices and identity projects, it rests in their choice of rejecting dominant discourses. (2011: 9)

It has been the job of the fashion press to legitimate this process by removing the rough edges of working-class resistance and adding the gilt of class aspiration together with the gingerbread of patriotic cheerleading, all in the name of democratising style. Enninful added to this a much more overt assertion of a liberal-pluralist ideology.

What *was* radical here, then, was to see these tendencies presented as the blueprint for *Vogue*'s future. Yet Enninful was also careful to emphasise that inclusivity worked both ways; it was about bringing new people into the magazine but also ensuring that some of the 'old guard' would not be left out in the cold. His new team actually included quite a lot of the old team, or certainly those who had been around *Vogue* for a number of years. Grace Coddington, Venetia Scott and Juergen Teller had all been regular contributors during Shulman's tenure, and were here listed as important to the revamped magazine's modernisation, notwithstanding their relationship with its earlier iteration. As he pointed out, 'Our mission statement was to bring you an old friend with a fresh face' (*Vogue* December 2017: 24).

Enninful went on to garland his first choice of cover girl with high praise:

> I only ever had one woman in mind. I've known the soon-to-be supermodel and activist Adwoa Aboah since she was a child. Elite but accessible, uptown yet downtown, high fashion but street smart – with her digital forum Gurls Talk, Adwoa is also leading the fashion conversation for women into the modern era. (Ibid.: 25)

Yet a note of extreme caution should be added to these effusions. Despite her African name and Ghanaian heritage, Adwoa Aboah is by no means a straightforward outsider to the fashion industry or, indeed, to the British class system. Her mother is Camilla Lowther, a well-known fashion 'booker' (i.e. agent) and a member of the aristocratic Lowther family (Camilla's father is the Earl of Lonsdale). Aboah attended the notably prestigious and suitably liberal arts-orientated private Millfield School and studied drama at university, thus accruing the 'right' kind of cultural capital. Her mother's work as a booking agent has given her the kind of access to the fashion industry and further cultural capital that no 'ordinary' young woman could hope for. In this regard she is not very different from many of her peers and the generation of models that preceded them, a number of whom came from wealthy or aristocratic backgrounds (e.g. Scottish model Honor Fraser is a member of the land-owning Lovat clan), and who were therefore able to readily acquire the social networking skills that gave them an entry into the world of high fashion. Aboah's promotion to contemporary 'It Girl' by Enninful represents not a triumph for democratisation, but rather the successful recuperation of black British style culture by the establishment.

The unacknowledged nepotism of such privileged access is another important dimension to this practice. As well as giving employment to the upper classes, *Vogue* favours the scions of the already famous in its content, promoting the daughters (and sometimes sons) of established performers and celebrities, and especially those belonging to the new cultural elite of rock and media aristocracy; Georgia May Jagger, Romeo Beckham, Pixie Geldof and Lennon Gallagher have all been offered publicity in the form of fashion shoots, and even features lauding their talents. Again, the way that this recirculates and accrues cultural capital within a particular social group and its kinship networks is reminiscent of the privilege enjoyed by the *bon ton* of nineteenth-century high society. The inclusion of black or Asian members of this golden circle can be traced to the shifts that took place during the 1960s, in which pop music success gave an entry into high society for a handful of non-white performers. It is also at least partly predicated on their symbolic value as the apparent physical embodiment of liberal pluralist inclusivity.[10] It does not ultimately mean that the power structures have changed or that those from ordinary backgrounds can otherwise enter. While, since his tenure began, Enninful has featured no less than eight non-white cover models, including Zoe Kravitz, Naomi Campbell, Dua Lipa, Oprah Winfrey and Rihanna, it is notable that they are mainly from this new aristocracy.

Of course, in the wake of the resurgence of feminism and 'woke' culture, no cover girl can be content with a role as an image, as something only 'to be looked at', despite the fact that this is exactly what models must be – an idealised version of contemporary beauty. Such a role now provokes profound anxiety. Models must prove themselves to be more than an image: they have brains as well as beauty, talents as well as looks! Who knew? No profile of the modern model is complete without evidence of her education (preferably Oxbridge), her dedication to good causes and 'activism', her skills (preferably in a fashion-related occupation). And the current ideology of femininity as constant busyness, of women as multi-taskers, managers, carers and, most importantly, self-inventors, also imprints itself just as it did in the interview with Samantha Cameron. As Gill and Scharff point out, 'secure and stable self-identity no longer derives automatically from one's position in the social structure . . . individuals are left alone to establish and maintain values with which to live and make sense of their daily lives' (2011: 6), while women especially find themselves driven to continuous self-reinvention and improvement under a neoliberal economy and within post-feminist culture. In addition to being beautiful and well connected, then, Aboah is a busy career woman and blogger, 'leading the fashion conversation'.

Indeed, Enninful went even further in this December issue to promote the neoliberal ideology of the model as multitasker. He commissioned Naomi Campbell – the most globally successful black fashion model of our time and one from a genuinely working-class background – to interview Sadiq Khan, the British-born son of a Pakistani bus conductor who was at the time of writing the Labour Mayor of London. Here, the magazine's new focus on immigrant heritage and experience was brought to the fore. Khan and Campbell's 'shared experience' as the highly successful children of immigrants who had both grown up in London was emphasised as the reasoning behind this somewhat extraordinary encounter and its trumpeting of a new kind of British identity.[11]

Yet these interventions are, ultimately, a form of recuperation, operating to modernise and diversify *Vogue* just enough to extend its supposedly more democratic appeal while also shoring up the class system. The fact that the Duchess of Sussex was recruited as the 'guest editor' of the September 2019 issue crystallises the way in which these ideological tensions are held together wonderfully. Widely greeted as a 'modernising' influence on the Royal Family by virtue of her career, her espousal of vaguely feminist values and, of course, by her embodiment of non-whiteness, Meghan Markle is a suitably safe symbol of Enninful's redefinition of *Vogue* as the bible of an expanded pseudo-meritocracy. Markle's main achievement is to marry into royalty as a 'commoner' – without that, her opinions on women, ethnic identity and even fashion would not be seen as important. Her coronation as the most recent royal *Vogue* contributor is, therefore, an example of continuity masquerading as radicalism, and of conservative modernity presented as the shock of the new.

Brand Britain

Promoting British brands has been one of *Vogue*'s most frequently disseminated values. Yet *Vogue*'s world, like that of the social circles it celebrates, is ultimately one that is defined by a particular form of class-based consumerist cosmopolitanism. The magazine looks outwards, primarily towards the fashion capitals of New York, Los Angeles, Paris, Milan, Rome, perhaps Madrid, and increasingly Moscow, Delhi and Beijing (as oligarchs and billionaires dominate its purview), and it looks inwards towards the tightly bounded fashion quarters of London: Chelsea, Kensington, Belgravia, Soho, Camden Town, Bloomsbury, Marylebone, and now the newly hip parts of the East End, Hoxton and Bow. Its contributors and editorial staff are part of a continuous and globalised 'flow' between these locations, flying in from New York and on to Paris, stopping off at Borough Market or the latest hip boutique in Chelsea, yet never venturing further into London's suburbs – or indeed out of London.

Vogue's map of Britain not only frequently conflates 'Britishness' with Englishness, and Englishness with London, it also reiterates the global tourist gaze. Its non-metropolitan horizon extends only to the Cotswolds, Edinburgh (for its festival), the Scottish Highlands, the coastline of Cornwall (but definitely not its industrial heritage), the more picturesque seaside towns of the South coast and East Anglia, and Oxford and Cambridge. The modern exception is the obligatory pilgrimage to Glastonbury, whose festival is now included in the global cosmopolitan hipster's itinerary. Britain's other major cities, and the creativity of Manchester, Birmingham, Leeds and Liverpool, is rarely connected to these global power networks or to the 'Brand Britain' being promoted.

'British eccentricity' is a favourite theme, but is almost entirely imagined in relation to nostalgia for a narrow 'heritage' image of British identity and an upper-class way of life. For example, a spread on 'The Great British Summer' in the July 2018 issue starred various members of the celebrity aristocracy – Shirley Bassey, Lennon Gallagher, Lara Stone, the twin hurdlers Laviai and Lina Nielson – shot 'on location'. These backdrops included the extensive grounds of two country houses complete with neo-classical follies, a Belgravia pub and the terrace of the National Theatre. The patriotism that is frequently invoked in such material is one which privileges aristocracy (whether of the old money variety or the new) and cultural whiteness. As in the case of Meghan Markle, when black or Asian Britons are included, it is in order to refresh not overturn the class relations involved.

Conclusion

Of course, one hardly looks to high fashion for genuine iconoclasm, notwithstanding its solipsistic trumpeting of creativity and vision, and the undoubted cultural importance of a few figures such as Elsa Schiaparelli and Christian Dior, whose work really did transform our relationship with clothes. Notwithstanding *Vogue*'s partial reinvention, Enninful's magazine, like Shulman's, represents fashion in terms of international brands and auteur designers, and continues to circulate the discourses of exclusivity associated with a largely white elite. This limited paradigm is clearly connected to the magazine's dependence on advertising, which is itself dominated by the international conglomerates which control the major fashion and beauty brands such as LVMH, which owns the Dior, Givenchy and Marc Jacobs labels, among many others. Such brands constitute the majority of advertising revenue for glossy magazines and, especially in the context of online competition, cannot be gainsaid. But it means that *Vogue*'s claims to be extending and reinventing the world of high fashion so that it is genuinely inclusive and diverse is in many ways chimeric, a device to prolong the magazine's cultural role without abandoning its class allegiances or its networks. We should celebrate the appearance of more black models in the magazine and the belated recognition of Britain as a multi-ethnic society, but the power relations of fashion are complex, the field is self-policing, and the system is still a system. *Vogue* is always in with the in-crowd – and the in-crowd is rarely a democracy.

Notes

1. Originally established in 1972, *W* is an offshoot of the more staid and mainstream US fashion magazine, *Women's Wear Daily*. In recent years it has courted controversy in its use of highly sexualised content and 'edgy' fashion shoots.
2. Under Shulman's editorship the magazine achieved its highest circulation in December 1999, with sales of 241,001 copies.
3. Moss first came to public attention when Corinne Day shot her for a style spread for *The Face* in 1988. In 1993, in a controversial campaign for Levis jeans, her waiflike figure and the 'grunge-y' backdrop of a seedy flat provoked accusations that the feature promoted 'heroin chic'. Moss has nonetheless had an extremely successful career and has become one of the most famous and influential models of the past 50 years.

4. In fact, *Vogue*'s parent company, Condé Nast, has until recently always had male managing editors and chairmen. Indeed, the appointment of a male editor might be regarded as a regressive move redolent of an earlier history of women's magazines in the nineteenth century were it not for the fact that *Vogue* has always had high-profile female editors.
5. And which I have kept copies of!
6. The British edition of French fashion magazine *Elle* was launched in 1985; the Italian *Grazia* first appeared in the UK in 2005.
7. For more on fashion magazines and the 'modern woman' see Anna Gough-Yates (2007).
8. I say 'superficially' because there are also significant examples of fashion's racist heritage erupting into its complacent view of itself as a liberal space. Most importantly, in February 2001 John Galliano, the British-born head of the prestigious house of Dior was arrested in a Paris bar for making anti-Semitic comments and was subsequently put on trial for racism. He has since been partially rehabilitated but the fashion world was split over the case.
9. In the late 1970s, for example, the British designer Zandra Rhodes, hitherto associated with upmarket hippy styles, recast herself as one of the 'inventors' of punk, here represented as high fashion, turning a DIY countercultural style involving bin bags, ripped jeans and homemade garments into an expensive fashion statement.
10. A direct parallel can be seen in the marriage of Prince Harry to Meghan Markle. Markle's TV acting career, her beauty and her American nationality combined to make her a member of a cosmopolitan elite, but it is arguably her mixed-race heritage that makes her a particularly valued member of that group as a visual sign of liberal modernity's relaxed attitudes to race, and especially of the British monarchy's own modernisation in that context.
11. Campbell's public image has been significantly influenced by her race. Celebrated as the most successful black model of all time and famous for her romantic association with alpha-male celebrities such as Robert De Niro, it is also notable that she has since pointed out that she earned considerably less than her white peers in the 1990s 'Supermodel' generation. She was not awarded the lucrative cosmetics contracts with major brands that help to perpetuate a model's longevity and public name and has herself said this was because of racism in the industry. Since the peak of her career in the 1990s–2000s she also became a figure of fascination for the tabloid press and celebrity magazines when she was twice convicted of assault. The publicity surrounding these cases, together with the notorious 'blood diamonds' trial when she was subpoenaed to give evidence about a necklace linked to illegal diamond mining which had been a gift from the disgraced ex-President of Liberia, Charles Taylor, helped to perpetuate the stereotyped image of Campbell as an 'uppity' 'angry black woman' with an enlarged ego.

Works Cited

Aitkenhead, D. 2017. 'Former Vogue Editor Alexandra Shulman: "I Find the Idea that There Was a Posh Cabal Offensive"'. *The Guardian*, 10 November 2017 <www.theguardian.com/media/2017/nov/10/former-vogue-editor-alexandra-shulman-find-idea-that-there-was-a-posh-cabal-offensive> (last accessed 1 November 2019).

Beetham, M. 1996. *A Magazine of Her Own: Domesticity and Desire in the Woman's Magazine, 1800–1914*. London: Routledge.

Bourdieu, P. 1993a. *The Field of Cultural Production*. New York: Columbia University Press.

Bourdieu, P. 1993b. 'Haute Couture and Haute Culture'. *Sociology in Question*. Ed. P. Bourdieu. London: Sage. 132–9.

Davis, A. 2017. 'Edward Enninful: My Vogue is About Being Inclusive, It's About Diversity'. *London Evening Standard*, 8 November 2017 <www.standard.co.uk/fashion/news/edward-enninful-my-vogue-is-about-being-inclusive-it-s-about-diversity-a3685211.html> (last accessed 1 November 2019).

D'Souza, C. 2017. 'Samantha Cameron: Picking Up the Threads'. *Vogue*, 11 February 2017 <www.vogue.co.uk/article/samantha-cameron-fashion-label-cefinn-interview> (last accessed 14 November 2019).

Entwistle, J. and A. Rocamora. 2006. 'The Field of Fashion Materialized: A Study of London Fashion Week'. *Sociology* 40.4: 735–51.

Gill, R. and C. Scharff. 2011. 'Introduction'. *New Femininities: Postfeminism, Neoliberalism and Subjectivity*. Eds R. Gill and C. Scharff. Basingstoke and New York: Palgrave Macmillan. 1–17.

Gough-Yates, A. 2007. 'What do women want? Women, Social Change and the UK Magazine Market'. *Information, Society and Justice* 1.1: 17–32.

Harding, L. 2007. '"I Went Hungry, Not to Fit into a Dress but Because I Was a Refugee," Says Model Alex Wek'. *Daily Mail*, 9 November 2007 <www.dailymail.co.uk/home/you/article-489840/I-went-hungry-fit-dress-I-refugee-says-model-Alex-Wek.html> (last accessed 1 November 2019).

Hoskins, T. 2014. 'Does Lack of Black Models on Cover of British *Vogue* Amount to Racism?' *The Guardian* 12 August 2014 <www.theguardian.com/sustainable-business/black-model-british-vogue-naomi-campbell-racism> (last accessed 14 November 2019).

Light, A. 1991. *Forever England: Femininity, Literature and Conservatism Between the Wars*. London and New York: Routledge

Macdonald, M. 1995. *Representing Women: Myths of Femininity in the Popular Media*. London: Edward Arnold.

McRobbie, A. 1998. *British Fashion Design*. London: Routledge.

Parmentier, M-A. and E. Fischer. 2011. 'You Can't Always Get What You Want: Unsustainable Identity Projects in the Fashion System'. *Consumption, Markets and Culture* 14.1: 7–27.

Vats, A. 2014. 'Racechange is the New Black: Racial Accessorizing and Racial Tourism in High Fashion as Constraints on Rhetorical Agency'. *Communication, Culture & Critique* 7: 112–35.

Williams, R. 1981. *The Sociology of Culture*. Chicago: the University of Chicago Press.

12

'Leaps and Bounds': Feminist Interventions in Scottish Literary Magazine Culture

Eleanor Bell

While there have been relatively few feminist magazines in Scotland, a study of literary and cultural magazines more broadly over the past few decades has revealed a strong focus on asserting women's rights and re-writing masculine discourses. From the 1960s to the 1990s a variety of important magazines and journals in Scotland engaged with the intersections of Scottish literature, culture and politics. While *Chapman* (1970–) and *Cencrastus* (1979–2006) were primarily literary focused, magazines such as *Radical Scotland* (1982–91) and *Scottish International* (1968–74) were more politically minded. With a few significant exceptions, most of the editors and contributors to these magazines were men. In the 1980s, however, a shift began to take place in Scottish literary culture, leading to the need for a broader recognition of women's voices and the re-publishing of the work of many women who had been out of print for decades, including Willa Muir, Catherine Carswell, Nan Shepherd, Jessie Kesson, Lorna Moon and Dot Allan. As cultural critic Joyce McMillan noted in 1983, 'the part played by women writers in Scottish literary life is increasing, at the moment, by leaps and bounds, and with that development there must come a change in old psychological patterns and tensions . . . Most Scottish women writers seem relatively free from the little-brother complex, the chip on the shoulder, the need to assert and re-assert Scottishness.' (*Chapman* July 1983: 71). As will be shown, while the renaissance in Scottish women's writing of the 1990s and beyond has now been well documented, it will be suggested that much of the impetus for this development began at least ten years earlier in magazine culture.[1]

This chapter therefore explores the ways in which many Scottish literary and cultural magazines from the 1960s to the 1990s generated significant outlets for critical debate, the importance of which have still to be properly taken into account in wider histories of modern Scotland. In particular, the chapter focuses on key moments of feminist intervention in magazine culture, which have had a significant role in shaping debate in literary and political culture, but which, ironically, have still to be fully credited for doing so. While women's contributions to Scottish literary and cultural magazines remained marginal from the 1960s to the 1990s, this chapter will suggest that their legacy must still be taken fully into account in histories of the development of feminism in Scotland more widely.

Scottish International and the Early Women's Liberation Movement

Scottish International first appeared in in 1968. Discussing the cross-cultural objectives of the magazine, editor Bob Tait (1997: 63) comments:

> Its full name was *Scottish International Review*. Its masthead simply proclaimed *Scottish International*. It was meant as an announcement, a declaration that here was a magazine fit to present Scottish life and culture in any international forum and set it in international contexts. It claimed a rightful place for Scottish work, not least for Scottish poetry, in that wider world. It insisted that Scottish concerns and products should jostle for attention, right there in the pages of the magazine, with signs and products of social and cultural developments elsewhere, and so help nourish and sharpen in Scotland an appetite for seeing our own society and culture as part of an often disturbingly changing world.

Through its interdisciplinary approach, *Scottish International* therefore attempted to understand Scotland at a time of significant change. As editorial board member Edwin Morgan commented, 'the sociological aspect was felt to be important because so much of modern Scotland was encrusted with myth that it seemed high time some attempt at mapping out the reality was made' (*Scottish International* September 1973: 28). Tapping into late 1960s radicalism, the magazine often adopted an experimental aesthetic in its challenge to convention and promotion of critical thinking, containing, for example, work by Allen Ginsberg, Alan Jackson, concrete poetry by Ian Hamilton Finlay and Edwin Morgan. For some readers, though, *Scottish International* was too focused on the international, rather than the national. For others, the engagement with national culture in the magazine, its 'adventurousness in Scottish thinking and culture', was similarly viewed with scepticism (Tait 1997: 65).[2] As John Herdman (1999: 28) noted in his memoirs of the period: 'The principal bugbear of the nationalist writers at the close of the sixties was Bob Tait's *Scottish International* . . . Hugh MacDiarmid was convinced that the whole project had been set up to counter the literary national movement.'

Scottish International thus often excited and annoyed its readers in equal measures, yet despite the controversy it caused, it undoubtedly played a role in shaping and challenging public opinion. Nevertheless, despite the prominent role of the magazine, it is clear, though perhaps not entirely surprising for the times (1968–74), that the voices directing the sociological and political discussions were, in the majority, male. Over its lifespan, however, the magazine did publish short stories by Elspeth Davie, poetry by Jean Milton, Liz Lochhead, and Margaret Hamilton, poetry and short stories by Joan Ure, art reviews by Cordelia Oliver, and some critical articles by Joan Aitken and Rosalind Mitchison. While these voices were in the minority, the magazine nonetheless demonstrated an openness to women's writing and inclusivity that was pioneering for its time.

Bob Tait stepped down as editor of *Scottish International* in 1973 (succeeded by Tom Buchan). Yet in the same year, Tait organised the hugely influential 'What Kind of Scotland?' conference in Edinburgh and some of the final editions of the magazine both previewed and reported on the conference in detail.[3] This conference, in bringing together a diverse group, including 'ecologists, economists, journalists, planners, social workers, criminologists, writers, educationists, artists, businessmen, historians and trade unionists – among others' sought to examine the state of Scottish life and politics, to find radical ways of bringing voices from leftist and nationalist circles together into a space of dialogue and connection.[4] Interestingly, one of the open sessions of the conference was devoted to a discussion of women's liberation (a session led by Margo Galloway and Marion Blythman). While this was a minor aspect of the conference overall, and much in the shadow of other events – such as the first ever performance of 7:84 Theatre Group's *The Cheviot, The Stag and the Black, Black Oil* – it is significant nonetheless to see a specific space being created for the discussion of women's rights and wider place in Scottish society organised on behalf of the magazine. While the onset of the 1970s were early days for the growth feminist consciousness in Scotland, from tracing through these magazine editorials and articles of the time we can see glimpses of cultural change becoming manifest, new perspectives beginning to emerge.

While *Scottish International* came to an end in 1974, it is clear that the magazine was becoming attuned to developments in the Women's Liberation Movement in the UK, and Scotland in particular. As with the wider UK, the first women's liberation groups began to appear in Scotland in 1970 and, as Esther Breitenbach (1990: 210) points out, 'by 1972 the Scottish women's liberation movement was strong enough to organise its own national conference', with Edinburgh hosting the UK conference in 1974.[5] Alongside the Scottish Women's Liberation Movement, several feminist publications began to appear, the most well known being the *Scottish Women's Liberation Journal* (1977–8), which continued as *Msprint* (1978–81). *Msprint* was produced by an editorial collective and had two specific aims: 'to stimulate debate in the Women's Liberation Movement and to develop an analysis of the position of women in Scotland and the role of women in Scottish politics' (*Msprint* August 1978: 1). While both of these responded to UK-wide campaigns, there was also a growing sense that 'feminists in Scotland had marked out the necessity of women in Scotland understanding their own particular history and experience and of developing their own political practice' (Breitenbach 1990: 216). While both of these magazines warrant further analysis and discussion in terms of their contribution to the women's movement, the particular remit of this chapter is to focus on literary culture in Scotland in particular. However, before returning to discussion of literary and cultural magazines it is useful to focus in more detail on the Women's Liberation Movement as it developed in Scotland, as this will provide further context for the discussion of gender politics that follows.

As Esther Breitenbach (1990: 216) has pointed out, by the mid-1970s the Women's Liberation Movement in Scotland had become increasingly focused on the particularities of Scottish-based experience, not least because 'Women campaigning for legal changes, and for better provision for women, whether in childcare, refuges for battered women, or abortion facilities, also had to develop their own demands that related to specifically Scottish laws and institutions.' Yet alongside this focus on the Scottish dimension was also a growing awareness that 'the apparent unity of Britain is a false imposition that works to marginalize, among others, women in Scotland' (Breitenbach et al. 1998: 50). Breitenbach et al. go on to suggest:

> Concepts such as 'British' and 'Britishness' often completely ignore Scottish experience (that is leaving aside our frequent incorporation into the concept 'English'),

> and that when some acknowledgement of Scotland or Scottishness is made it rarely goes beyond a form of tokenism, with no attempt to examine in any detail what is distinctive about Scotland. (Ibid.)

For women in Scotland, they suggest, this has led to a double form of marginalisation, a paradoxical situation where 'the debate on nationalism in Scotland has ignored gender, and feminist debates on nationalism have ignored Scotland' (Ibid.: 61). As will be shown, this is a dilemma which runs through many of the literary and cultural magazines.

Chapman (1970–) and Resisting the 'Double Knot in the Peeny'

For a short period, *Scottish International* crossed over with *The Chapman* (later *Chapman*), founded in 1971 by George Hardie and edited by Hardie and Walter Perrie. The editorials in early editions of the magazine contained dismissive references to other Scottish magazines of the time, setting themselves apart by presenting 'a magazine which will take due account of the worthwhile work being produced by younger writers in particular, without kow-towing to the peristaltic urgings of the latest fashion – political, literary or otherwise' (*Chapman* Spring 1972: 2). Joy Perrie began co-editing with Walter Perrie in 1972, becoming sole editor (as Joy Hendry) in 1977. In taking on sole editorship, it is important to note that Hendry became the first female editor of a literary magazine in Scotland. One of Hendry's objectives was to give the magazine more of a particularly Scottish grounding, which naturally included representing the voices of Scottish women.

One of the most prominent editions of the magazine was 'Woven by Women' (issue 27/28) in Summer 1980. In her editorial of this edition, Hendry begins:

> A certain well-known Scottish poet said to me recently, when he heard that I was devoting a double issue of *Chapman* to the women's contribution to twentieth century Scottish culture: Do you mean to say there *has* been one? He was, of course, trying to deny that women had made a significant impression on Scottish artistic life. Perhaps he was being provocative, looking for an argument, but his response was typical of the Scottish brand of chauvinism to be found not only in the arts, but in all walks of life. In Scotland, a country with a strong tradition of patriarchalism which delights in disparaging the efforts of almost anyone who steps outside the common round, it is easier to make that kind of remark than in most western countries. The unspoken strategy seems to be, not to bother dismissing what women do, but to ignore it for as long as possible, hence the need for this issue of *Chapman* which gives testimony to the fact that this contribution exists and is substantial in all fields. Faced with chauvinist attitudes, it is tempting to respond by assuming an equal and opposite chauvinism, but this temptation is easy to resist. (*Chapman* Summer 1980: 1)

'Woven by Women' was pioneering in its focus on the work of, or articles by, Scottish women. This particular edition specially commissioned articles which sought to recuperate the work of women poets, novelists, composers and visual artists, many of whom had been out of print for some decades, largely written out of the literary

Figure 12.1 *Chapman* 27/28, 'Woven by Women'.
(Image with kind permission of Joy Hendry, Editor, *Chapman*)

and cultural canon, including, for example, essays on the work of Willa Muir, Helen Cruickshank, Joan Ure and Jessie Kesson. In this respect 'Woven by Women' undoubtedly established important groundwork for the renaissance of Scottish women's writing that was to follow over the following decade, with important volumes including: Moira Burgess's (1987) collection *The Other Voice: Scottish Women's Writing since 1808*; Douglas Gifford and Dorothy McMillan's (1997) collection *A History of Scottish Women's Writing*; Catherine Kerrigan's (1991) *An Anthology of Scottish Women Poets*; Carol Anderson and Aileen Christianson's (2000) collection *Scottish Women's Fiction: Journeys into Being*; and Aileen Christianson and Alison Lumsden's (2000) *Contemporary Scottish Women Writers*.

Between 1993 and 1994 Hendry returned to the representation of women in literature and the arts under the title 'The Women's Forum: Women in Scottish Literature'. In her editorial of double-issue 74/75, Hendry reflects back on the importance of 'Woven by Women', the catalytic impact that particular edition had on Scottish culture:

> 'Woven by Women' appeared in summer 1980. It was something of a milestone, a landmark, a watershed, as the first Scottish publication to focus on women's cultural achievement across the artistic spectrum in Scotland. In those days you still had to argue that in almost every field not only *could* women encourage good

> work, but that they *already had* . . . Those were the dying days of domination by man of the cultural scene in Scotland. Yes, the big boys then were all boys, but the women, by 1980, were very much there and waiting in the wings. (*Chapman* Autumn/Winter 1993: 3–4)

As Hendry also notes, between 1980 and 1994, a sea change was underway in Scottish literary studies, a recuperation and broader recognition of the work of many women writers who had been previously marginalised in literary history.[6] Of particular note in *Chapman* 74/75 are articles by Margaret Elphinstone ('Four Pioneering Novels', taking a retrospective look at the legacy of Catherine Carswell, Naomi Mitchison, Willa Muir and Nan Shepherd) and Alison (Ali) Smith's 'Four Success Stories' (looking at the emerging work of Janice Galloway, A. L. Kennedy, Jackie Kay and Katherine Jamie). It is significant to note that in these articles, Elphinstone and Smith introduced many readers to previously neglected and relatively new writers, all of whom would shortly go on to become widely recognised in literary culture.

While these acts of recuperation were taking place in the 1980s and 1990s, there was also an awareness that feminist criticism was arriving relatively late to Scottish literary studies, which, as Susanne Hagemann (2006: 214) has pointed out, was often explained in terms of 'small nation syndrome':

> Gender is a comparatively recent issue in Scottish literary criticism. It is obviously true of all western cultures that women's writing and the theme of gender in literature precede the advent of feminist criticism; but Scotland lags behind in another, more significant way. While gender rose to prominence in Anglo-American criticism in the late 1960s and early 1970s, in Scottish criticism this did not happen until the early 1990s. One of the main reasons, it has been argued, is the quest for Scottishness. The small-nation syndrome involved focusing on the quiddity of Scotland.

This double bind of Scottish women being held back by their gender in discussions of nationhood, and by the nation in discussions of their gender, is something that Joy Hendry (1987: 38) went on to term the 'double knot in the peeny', ('peeny' being the Scots word for pinafore or apron, thereby symbolising the constraints of the domestic sphere):

> Writing is a claim to power. Scottish women are at one further remove from the seats of power by being first female and secondly Scottish. You can't deal with one without the other. Scottish culture as a whole is a neglected area, lacking in status and prestige. A Scottish woman writer shares that neglect with her male colleagues, as well as being overlooked and underestimated because she is a woman. Thus, the woman writer, rare enough anywhere, is even rarer in Scotland. The Scottish woman writer must overcome the inferiority feelings stemming from her femininity, and those stemming from her Scottishness. It's the double knot in the peeny.

In a culture that was particularly focused on the national question at the time, the Scottish woman writer was therefore placed in a frustrating double-bind. As Hendry goes on:

> Looking at anthologies and literary histories, you would be forgiven for thinking that the Scottish women writer didn't exist. Women tend to be mentioned in these volumes not for their writing, but for being the mother, mistress, wife, sister, or daughter of a male poet. The coverage of the women (chiefly novelists) who do peak like a sunbeam through the male nimbus, is scanty and patronizing. (Ibid.)

Further engagement with this 'double knot' can be found in one of the best-selling editions of *Chapman*, issue 35/36 in 1983, entitled 'The State of Scotland: A Predicament for the Scottish Writer?' (see Plate 7). After the failed Devolution Referendum in 1979, Scottish literary culture in the 1980s was often characterised by an intense focus on nationhood, with Scotland and Scottishness perceived as being in a fragile state (e.g. Craig 1996). This particular edition therefore sought to explore this artistic tendency, inviting a wide variety of writers and critics to submit articles on the theme of the 'state' of Scotland, whether or not the individual writer was placed in a 'predicament'.[7] For many of the contributors, the 'predicament' of Scotland was clearly considerably intertwined with its political status, the implication being that Scottish writers, were similarly placed in an inevitable quandary. In this 'Open Letter on the Closed Mind', Alan Bold, for example, discusses the predicament of the Scot in particularly masculinist terms:

> Secretly the Scot longs to be impressive, is dying to be a winner. The result is almost obscene. He expects to be battered into submission and readies himself for the challenge he is sure will come. He acts hard because the worst thing you can call him is a softie. The term has precise sexual connotations in Scotland. Way back the loss of Scottish independence, was experienced like a castration. To Scotsmen it meant a loss of independence, therefore a loss of manhood. Since 1707 at least . . . the Scot has been trying to compensate for the agonising sense of loss by acting hard. (*Chapman* July 1983: 3)

Bold then goes on to discuss the further implications of this national stereotyping with respect to women, whom, he suggests, 'have been treated with a mixture of terror and contempt in their twin roles as matriarch and mistress' (Ibid.: 4).

It was in *Chapman* 35/36, in her article 'The Predicament of the Scottish Writer', that Joyce McMillan suggested that 'the part played by women writers in Scottish literary life is increasing . . . by leaps and bounds, and with that development there must come a change in old psychological patterns and tensions' (Ibid.: 71). For McMillan, however, the fact that women have, historically, often not been as focused on the national question in quite the same, obsessive way as their male counterparts, places them in an ideal position to challenge the 'special dilemma' of the Scottish writer:

> At any rate, most Scottish women writers seem relatively free from the little-brother complex, the chip on the shoulder, the need to assert and re-assert Scottishness. In writers like Liz Lochhead and Marcella Evaristi, Alma Cullen and Joan Lingard, the Scottishness of theme and manner and often of languages is indisputably there; the need to prove it – the mental team of Scotland supporters distorting and disturbing their personal vision – is not; and their increasing prominence in our literary life can only have a positive and liberating effect. (Ibid.)

Another important contributor (and one of the few women) to this edition was Tessa Ransford. In 'Workers in the Spirit', she discussed the sense of marginalisation, both geographical and psychological, felt by some Scottish writers at the time. 'Literature in Scotland has limitations because of its subservience to the dominant culture of England, in the face of which it feels less important, misunderstood and overlooked', she wrote (Ibid.: 36). She went on to describe the ways in which this lack of confidence was also a specifically feminist issue: 'Lack of confidence also forces writers to define themselves (or let themselves be defined) by categories and labels, especially when writing for the media . . . Women particularly suffer from this' (Ibid.: 36). Ransford then mapped out her plan to begin to personally remedy this cultural diffidence through establishing a national poetry library for Scotland:

> One way in which I have tried to ease the deadlock is to begin the process of establishing a poetry library for Scotland. This is envisaged as a centre of information, a meeting point, the focus for people interested in and involved in poetry, a means of generating events and tours and visits, and a place where small press publications may be found. (Ibid.: 37)

Ransford was true to her word and went on to found the Scottish Poetry Library the following year in 1984. For Ransford, the focus on small publishers and little magazines was a particular aspect of her vision for the library, one which remains central to its remit and area of specialism more than thirty-five years later.[8] After establishing the Scottish Poetry Library, Ransford went on to become the second female literary magazine editor in Scotland, editing *Lines Review* from 1989 to 1999.[9]

Cencrastus (1979–2006) and *Radical Scotland* (1983–91): Inferiorism versus Superiorism

This cultural struggle for women's voices to be heard was also apparent early on in *Cencrastus* magazine. *Cencrastus* was founded by a group of postgraduate students at Edinburgh University and its first edition was published in 1979. Commenting on the origins of the magazine, editor Raymond Ross (1997: 3) writes: '*Cencrastus* was born in the dark days of post-referendum Scotland, in the immediate aftermath of the devolution debacle. The magazine took its name from the Curly Snake, the Celtic serpent of wisdom, the symbol of energy and infinity as embraced by Hugh MacDiarmid's *To Circumjack Cencrastus*.' As Ross continues, the magazine was predicted by many not to last long: 'some literary pundits gave it short shrift and predicted its life span in accordance with that of the common Scottish midge'. However, it was to continue for more than twenty-five years, its final issue being published in 2006 (Ibid.).

In an early edition of *Cencrastus* on Scottish film in 1983, Gillian Skirrow provides an edited version of papers delivered at the now-famous 'Scotch Reels' debate at the 1982 Edinburgh International Film Festival. As Skirrow points out, the role of women was much discussed at this event, a growing sense that the gender imbalance had to be addressed as a matter of urgency:

> For just as Scottish culture is invariably defined in relation to the supposedly more sophisticated English one, so are women defined in relation to men. In fact, it is true to say that Scottish women have to find their identities both as Scots and as women, and, in doing so, will experience many of the features of inferiorism and marginalisation which characterises the Scot in 'his' identity crisis. (*Cencrastus* New Year 1983: 3)

This reference to cultural 'inferiorism' refers back to an earlier issue of the magazine, Craig Beveridge and Ronald Turnbull's 'Inferiorism' (*Cencrastus* Spring 1982: 4–5). In this article, Beveridge and Turnbull set out to establish links between Scottish culture and Frantz Fanon's work on cultural colonialism, suggesting that 'if Scots in general suffer from a crippling lack of self-belief, if there exists a national "inferiority complex", this is related to the intellectual world view we have tried to identify' (Ibid.: 5). 'Inferiorism', they suggest, 'makes for a defeatist climate throughout national life, and can provide no basis for a creative, challenging nationalism' (Ibid.). However, as Skirrow's response indicates, in the early 1980s there was a growing frustration that cultural and national issues were still nonetheless being discussed in particularly masculinist terms.

Published one year later, Carol Anderson and Glenda Norquay's 'Superiorism', presents another self-conscious challenge to the gendered use of inferiorist discourse:

> The cultural life of Scotland, if the pages of *Cencrastus* and other literary magazines are anything to go by, has been largely dominated by men. Even a cursory glance over past issues of this magazine, and most others with similar concerns, will reveal the male monopoly over Scottish culture. (*Cencrastus* New Year 1984: 8)

They go on to suggest that: 'What is needed is some co-operative spirit, a collective effort to uncover the social and cultural history of women in Scotland. In this way we can gain a perspective on our own experience and establish identity in our own terms' (Ibid.: 10). In the same edition of the magazine, Rosalind Brackenbury has an article on 'Women and Fiction: How we Present Ourselves and Others', in which she takes stock of what the women's movement has achieved up until that point: 'Now I would like to hear from other women of how they envisage the future of the feminist novel, and what it will imply to you, as writers, to accept no limits on your creative power' (Ibid.: 12). Notably these articles caused controversy at the time, with the next few issues containing several responses and lively debate in the correspondence pages.[10]

Reflecting on the cultural shift that began to take place within the *Cencrastus* editorial team at the time, Cairns Craig, in a personal interview, explains:

> [V]ery quickly, the main conflict was around feminism, because the main group which had established the magazine regarded nationalism as the prime issue. But a lot of the women who had joined the magazine felt that nationalism was just a mask for masculinism and that the problem in Scotland was the lack of representation of women, or lack of resources for women . . . So there was quite a lot of, not conflict, but debate around what nationalism actually meant in Scotland and whether it could only be a Scottish nationalism if it was also a Scottish feminism, or whether feminism was a cosmopolitan movement that had very little to do with

> Scottishness. And so there were quite a lot of underlying tensions around those issues at the time.

In bringing these editorial tensions into a public forum, polemical pieces such as 'Superiorism', therefore, helped to initiate a broader questioning of gender politics in Scottish literary culture, encouraging the inclusion of more representative voices.

In *Cencrastus* issue 21, Esther Breitenbach published an article on 'Scottish Feminism in Print' in which she surveyed the feminist grassroots work to date, which is worth quoting in full as it provides an insightful synopsis of feminist activity at the time:

> In the early days women's groups produced duplicated newsletters which functioned more or less as internal bulletins and discussion papers, and also provided a means of exchanging information with other groups. Around 1975 a trickle of publications began to appear, which were aimed at a wider audience, though still with a very limited circulation. For example, there was a handbook for battered women produced by Women's Aid, a guide to the Equal Pay and Sex Discrimination Acts in Scotland by Chris Aldred and Margaret Marshal, a pamphlet on *Women and Housing* produced by Glasgow Women's Legal and Financial Independence group . . . The first feminist book to appear in Scotland was Eveline Hunter's *Scottish Women's Place* in 1978, and this has been followed by Stramullion's publications, *Hens in the Hay* – collection of poetry; *The Rime of the Ancient Feminist* by Stephanie Markman; *Incest – Fact and Myth* by Sarah Nelson; and *Moll Cutpurse* – a novel by Ellen Galford. There are also the present author's *Women Workers in Scotland*, and *Uncharted Lives* by Glasgow Women's Studies Group. Worth mentioning also is *Violence Against Wives* by Rebecca and R. Emerson Dobash, which, though written from a feminist viewpoint, is not published by a Scottish publisher, and is the product of academic research carried out in Scotland by American researchers. This list is not meant to be exhaustive. (*Cencrastus* Summer 1985: 45)

Breitenbach goes on to question, 'why so little?'. At least part of the problem, she suggests, is that 'political debates in Scotland often take place without any regard for the ways in which these issues are relevant to women' (Ibid.: 46). One aspect of this that is particularly illuminating for the present argument, however, is that magazines such as *Cencrastus* were nonetheless providing the outlets for such reflections to reach a wider audience, creating a space for these crucial debates to take place.

Notably several other magazines during this period also begin to trace the emergence of feminist activism in Scotland from overtly political and social perspectives. *Radical Scotland* (which ran for 51 issues from 1983–91), for example, was another magazine, like *Cencrastus*, which largely stemmed from political frustrations after 1979 and which had a particular focus on Home Rule.[11] While contributors were mostly male, from the first edition of the magazine there was a strong focus on pragmatic issues surrounding women's political engagement, and the Women's Liberation Movement in Scotland and beyond. *Radical Scotland* contained articles on women and the peace movement, the history of the women's movement, socialism and feminism, feminism and independence, Scottish Woman's Aid, and the 'Women Live' Festival, among many other issues.

In studying the emergence of literary and cultural magazines during this time, what becomes increasingly apparent is that many contributors were writing for several Scottish literary and cultural publications simultaneously. In *Radical Scotland* October/November 1983 (20–1), for example, Christopher Whyte, writes up his response to the *Chapman* 'Predicament of the Scottish Writer' event. In issue 8 in the following year, Tessa Ransford (*Radical Scotland* April/May 1984: 27) has a piece on 'The Spirit of Poetry', which marks the opening of the Scottish Poetry Library. Cairns Craig was also a regular contributor too, and member of the editorial board of *Radical Scotland*, as well as *Cencrastus*. The shared objectives of many publications therefore ensured a crossover of contributors as well as themes.

For Cairns Craig, both *Cencrastus* and *Radical Scotland* tapped into the cultural struggle of the period, the changing literary landscape and renaissance of Scottish writing taking place:

> It was quite clear that we were involved in what *Radical Scotland* came to think of as a life and death struggle with Thatcherism, because if Thatcherism succeeded, people in *Radical Scotland* felt Scotland would cease to exist, it would just disappear as a cultural economic entity, which is how they dreamt up the idea of the doomsday scenario that eventually Thatcher would be elected so many times that Scotland would just be wiped off the map, effectively. So there was a sense of cultural struggle, which had an energising effect, I suppose. But also there was the sense that lots of interesting things were happening in Scottish writing that were making it seem not just a historical issue, but a creative issue . . . There were lots of things that seemed to be, as it were, opening doors to new kinds of creativity. And there was also the possibility of people getting published, which hadn't been the case very easily in the 1960s and 1970s. (personal interview)

Harpies & Quines (1992–4)

In 1992 a new, innovative feminist magazine, *Harpies & Quines*, was first published (see also Chapter 18). As explained in the opening editorial: 'Harpies comes from the Greek harpazeim, to seize . . . Quines, also spelt Queans, is a word of Indo-European origin referring to . . . a bold impudent woman, a hussy or harlot.' It described itself as 'a Scottish feminist magazine devised by women, written by women, for women' (*Harpies & Quines* May/June 1992: 1). The tone of *Harpies & Quines* was upbeat and feisty, it aimed to 'campaign for the rights of women, snap at the heels of chauvinists, encourage secret stories to be told and take a cool, hard look at the reality of our lives' (Ibid.). While the magazine had a broad focus (containing articles on health, women's history, sexuality, spirituality and politics), it often contained literary reviews, occasional poems and short stories, as well as interviews with writers including Janice Galloway, Dilys Rose, Ellen Galford and Val McDermid. Throughout its relatively short history, the magazine was keen to interrogate the cultural stereotypes associated with Scottish identity. This was also largely the approach that it took in its often-sceptical look at establishment (including literary) culture. In issue 5, for example, in her article 'Poets, Penises and Pints', Lesley Riddoch, with reference to Joy Hendry's 'double knot in the peeny', is critical of the inherent masculinity within contemporary literary criticism, frustrated by the corresponding lack of outlets for women's writing:

> The only feminist press here has been 'Stramullion', which has produced good books but nothing like the volume that come from all the feminist presses in London. Though Virago and Pandora have brought out 'Scottish Classics' written by women, they haven't fully twigged that women still write here in the late twentieth century. (*Harpies & Quines* February/March 1993: 37)

Riddoch goes on to provide a specific example of this oversight when she states that 'a recent exhibition at the Scottish Poetry Library in Edinburgh confounded the theory that they [Scottish women poets] don't exist when some sixty women were named' (Ibid.). 'Female writing exists', she continues, 'but takes a different form to most of the work emanating from the pens of our national bardic heroes' (Ibid.).

Conclusion

In the introduction to her *An Anthology of Scottish Women Poets*, first published in 1991, Catherine Kerrigan (1991: 1) writes:

> After many years of neglect, and sometimes outright derision, writing by women has begun to find its permanent place on the cultural map. There is now available more work by women writers – past and present-day – than ever before. Novels, poems, journals and diaries have not only given great reading pleasure, but have also opened to women a new consciousness of their place in the world. The recovery of the past has played a significant part in this process . . . These works contain the trials and triumphs of women's experience and lead us to understand that women's drive to control their lives is not some kind of modern cultural aberration, but a long and continuing desire for self-determination.

Kerrigan's anthology was regarded as groundbreaking when it was first published in 1991. This volume was an important part of the active recovery of Scottish women's writing that would continue throughout that decade and beyond. However, as has been shown throughout this chapter, the germination of this renaissance in Scottish women's writing can actually be traced back to literary and cultural magazines from the early 1980s onwards.

While the past few decades in Scottish cultural and political history have been often been especially fraught, especially around the 1979 and 2014 referendums, by tracing through the significant contributions of writers and critics such as Joy Hendry, Tessa Ransford and Joyce McMillan, as well as many of the other writers mentioned above, it becomes clear that Scottish literary magazine culture helped to generate important new platforms for discussion and reflection along the way. Indeed, the feminist interventions within Scottish literary and cultural magazines offer nuanced readings of Scottish cultural identity over the past few decades which have still to be properly integrated into the history of feminism in Scotland more broadly.

Notes

1. For a fuller discussion of the context of this renaissance in Scottish literature, see Gavin Wallace and Randall Stevenson (1993).
2. As Bob Tait (1997: 65) comments, 'There were those who denounced us early and late for that *international* aspiration, as a diversion from the pursuit of Scottishness. But I believe there are those who will agree that *Scottish International*, although its ambitions inevitably outreached its resources, helped to seed and encourage more adventurousness in Scottish thinking and culture than the circulation figures might suggest.'
3. See *Scottish International* 1973 vol. 6, Nos. 2–5.
4. In 'What Kind of Scotland?', Bob Tait argued that 'Political leaders have to be re-educated. Specifically, those on the left have to be forced to face up to the powerful public pressure over issues affecting Scotland as a whole, and to recognise that there is no necessary contradiction between fighting for democracy at home and their allegiance to international socialist principles. Since it is widely believed that, of all the leftward groups, the Labour Party in particular in Scotland is all but intellectually bankrupt, nothing but gains can come from having fresh thoughts on the matter. Equally, nationalist leaders must be made to see that although the class struggle has had to shed some of its "auld sang", it still has its theatre of war, both here and internationally, and that its reality is not unconnected with the problems of gaining self-determination for small counties' (*Scottish International* February 1973: 13).
5. On the development of Scottish Women's Liberation Movement in Scotland throughout the 1970s, see Breitenbach (1990: 210–11) who writes: 'It is not possible to pinpoint the moment of the first Scottish women's liberation group, but certainly by 1970 there were groups in existence, for example, in Edinburgh and St Andrews. Early groups were often made up of primarily of women students – young, single, childless, middle class and articulate. But this was not exclusively the case. For example, the majority of women in the Dundee group, formed in early 1972, were married and had children. By 1972 the Scottish women's liberation movement was strong enough to organise its own national conference, and the first of these took place in the spring of 1972 in Glasgow.'
6. 'After *Woven by Women* came a deluge of publishing by women and of women; after the Women's Forum, I hope, will come an unstoppable drive towards genuine cultural and social parity, so that Scottish women's voices ring out as strongly and as vibrantly as some of our male colleagues in the past.' (*Chapman* Autumn/Winter 1993: 4)
7. In her editorial Hendry writes: 'My intention here is to provide a platform for serious discussion about the Predicament of Scotland, which is that of its writers also. I have asked writers to reflect quite uninhibitedly on the State of Scotland in their own fields – poetry, prose, journalism, criticism, folklore studies, theatre, philosophy, politics, education and publishing.' (*Chapman* July 1983: 1)
8. For a brief history of the evolution of the Scottish Poetry Library (SPL), see <http://www.scottishpoetrylibrary.org.uk/wp-content/uploads/2018/09/HistoryoftheSPLbooklet.pdf>. As former SPL Librarian, Lizzie MacGregor has noted in a personal interview: 'I would say certainly that the poetry library always had a great interest in the magazines and had determined to support them right from the word go . . . When the library was started they subscribed to as many magazines as was financially feasible . . . kept them in good order on the shelves and made them easily available for people to browse. Obviously they weren't borrowable.'
9. *Lines Review* was founded in 1952, specifically as a poetry magazine. It was published by Callum MacDonald. The first editor was Alan Riddell, others included Sydney Goodsir Smith, Tom Scott, J. K. Annand, Albert Mackie, Robin Fulton, Robert Calder, William Montgomerie, Trevor Royle and Tessa Ransford. It ceased publication in 1998. For more on Ransford, see also Tom Nairn's 'A Profile of Tessa Ransford' (*Cencrastus* 1987: 52–6).

10. See *Cencrastus* 16 (Spring 1984: 46) and 17 (Summer 1984: 43–4). For further discussion, see also Christianson (2002).
11. In the editorial of issue 4, 'A Window in Time', for example, Kevin Dunion writes 'need there be such gloom and despondency? We do not believe so. Evidence suggests increasing support for Home Rule as the months pass – a trend likely to continue under this reactionary centrist regime. With the Tories apparently installed in power on a long-term basis, the desirability of constitutional change is being increasingly accepted by the Scottish Left – some on the grounds of principle, some on the grounds of expediency. The widening gap between Scotland's potential and her reality over the next decade is the factor which analysts like Nairn and Hechter predict to be the very rocket-fuel of nationalism, whilst the differential development between the core of Britain (SE England) and the peripheries (Scotland, Wales and the North of England) will undoubtedly become more pronounced under this government.' (*Radical Scotland* October/November 1983: 3)

Works Cited

Anderson, C. and A. Christianson, eds. 2000. *Scottish Women's Fiction: Journeys into Being*. Edinburgh: Tuckwell Press.

Breitenbach, E. 1990. 'Sisters are Doing it for Themselves: The Women's Movement in Scotland'. *Scottish Government Yearbook: 1990*. Eds A. Brown and R. Parry. Unit for the Study of Government in Scotland, University of Edinburgh. 209–25.

Breitenbach, E., A. Brown and F. Myers. 1998. 'Understanding Women in Scotland'. *Feminist Review* 58: 44–65.

Burgess, M., ed. 1987. *The Other Voice: Scottish Women's Writing Since 1808*. Edinburgh: Polygon.

Christianson, A. 2002. 'Gender and Nation: Debatable Lands and Passable Boundaries'. *Across the Margins: Cultural Identity and Change in the Atlantic Archipelago*. Eds G. Norquay and G. Smyth. Manchester: Manchester University Press. 67–82.

Christianson, A. and A. Lumsden, eds. 2000. *Contemporary Scottish Women Writers*. Edinburgh: Edinburgh University Press.

Craig, C. 1996. *Out of History: Narrative Paradigms in Scottish and English Culture*. Edinburgh: Edinburgh University Press.

Gifford, D. and D. McMillan, eds. 1997. *A History of Scottish Women's Writing*. Edinburgh: Edinburgh University Press.

Hagemann, S. 2006. 'From Carswell to Kay: Aspects of Gender, the Novel and the Drama'. *The Edinburgh History of Scottish Literature Volume Three: Modern Transformations and New Identities (from 1918)*. Eds T. O. Clancy, S. Manning and M. Pittock. Edinburgh: Edinburgh University Press. 214–25.

Hendry, J. 1987. 'A Double Knot in the Peeny'. *In Other Words: Writing as a Feminist*. Eds G. Chester and S. Nielson. London: Routledge. 36–46.

Herdman, J. 1999. *Poets, Pubs and Pillar Boxes: Memoirs of an Era in Scottish Politics and Letters*. Kirkcaldy: Akros Publications.

Kerrigan, C., ed. 1991. *An Anthology of Scottish Women Poets*. Edinburgh: Edinburgh University Press.

Ross, R. 1997. 'Introduction'. *Scottish Poetry Index* vol. 7: *Cencrastus 1979–1992*. Edinburgh: Scottish Poetry Library. 3.

Tait, R. 1997. 'Introduction'. *Scottish Poetry Index* vol. 6: *Scotia:* 1970–2; *Scotia Review*: 1972–8; *Scottish International*: 1968–74. Edinburgh: Scottish Poetry Library. 63–5.

Wallace, G. and R. Stevenson. Eds. 1993. *The Scottish Novel since the Seventies*. Edinburgh: Edinburgh University Press.

Plate 1 *Rolling Our Own: Women as Printers, Publishers and Distributors* by Eileen Cadman, Gail Chester and Agnes Pivot, Comedia 1981. This is the first book to have analysed print culture in the Women's Liberation Movement, raising thorny issues, such as where the money comes from and working with men, as well as the positive achievements of women who set up their own printing presses, bookshops and publishing companies.
(Image courtesy of Ultra Violet Enterprises)

Plate 2 *In Other Words: Writing as a Feminist* edited by Gail Chester and Sigrid Nielsen, Hutchinson Education 1987. Cover illustration by Kate Charlesworth. 'A book for all women writers, professional, amateur or aspiring, in which 40 women talk about writing and the part it plays in their lives.'
(Image with kind permission of Kate Charlesworth)

Plate 3 *Spare Rib* cover, July 1989.
(© Mike Goldwater)

Plate 4 *DIVA*, Issue 1, March 1994, front cover.
(Image courtesy of DIVA magazine/DIVA Media Group)

Plate 5 *Picturegoer and Film Weekly*, 27 April 1940, front cover. (Courtesy of The Bill Douglas Cinema Museum, University of Exeter)

Plate 6 *Just Seventeen*, 20 October 1983, front cover.
(Image with kind permission of TI Media Limited)

Plate 7 *Chapman* 35/36, 'The State of Scotland'.
(Image with kind permission of Joy Hendry, editor, *Chapman*)

Plate 8 *Scarlet Women* 14, January 1982.
(Image courtesy of Leeds University Library)

Plate 9 *Women's Voice*, second series, Issue 49, February 1981.
(Image source: Feminist Archive North)

Plate 10 Screenshot of *The Vagenda*.
(Image reproduced with kind permission from Rhiannon Lucy Cosslett)

Plate 11 Cover of *Harpies & Quines*, June/July 1993.
(Image courtesy of Lesley Riddoch and Glasgow Women's Library:
Harpies & Quines Collection)

Plate 12 Cake: *Vogue* USA, June 2018.
(© Will Cotton)

Plate 13 *Good Housekeeping* UK, June 2018. 5. Images from 'Editor's note'. (Image with kind permission from Hearst Magazines Limited)

Plate 14 *Modern Woman* front cover, artwork by Francis Mortimer, December 1946. (©The British Library Board (*Modern Woman*/LOU.LON 173)

"Just what I was Wanting"

CLOTHES coupons are at their lowest ebb—if not non-existent! Shop windows simply a tantalizing range of forbidden fruit. What to show you this month puzzled me a lot until a member of the staff stopped at my desk and exclaimed over a pattern designed for a remnant, "That's just what I was wanting!"

So I decided to sketch it for you here, together with several other useful patterns which will help you make good use of remnants on hand, act as inspiration for re-cutting old garments or bring a touch of holiday spirit into a not-too-new summer wardrobe.

ELIZABETH TROY.

Two remnants make pyjamas 11640 A and B. Alternatively, an old blouse will help out for top. I like the pyjama top so much I would use it for a blouse in an emergency! Bust sizes 32-40 ins. Price 1/3.

11640

Backviews and Pattern Shop address—page 96. 1d. postage is charged on all patterns.

An odd piece of lace; remnant of silk make trousseau panties! Pattern 11454, waist sizes 24-32 ins.; price 1/3.

11454

10780

New rompers for baby from pattern 10780 and an old summer dress. Sizes 3 months to 2 years. Price 1/-.

11633

No Slippers? No Coupons? Use easy-to-make pattern 11633 A and B and bright felt, a suede skin, or canvas. Sizes 4-7. Price 1/3.

Skirt 11626, excellent style can be cut from old slacks or one yard only of 54-inch fabric! Waist sizes 24-28 ins. Price 1/3.

11626

Make an enliver jockey blouse from or three odd scrap fabric. Pattern 11 A and B. Bust si 32-40 ins. Price

11622

Bride's blouse in lace, no coupons! Pattern 11459 A and B. Bust sizes 32-40 ins. Price 1/3.

11459

11501

One yard only of 36-in. fabric needed for small sizes in this blouse! No. 11501. Bust sizes 32-40 ins. Price 1/3.

Plate 15 "Just what I was Wanting", Elizabeth Troy fashion editorial in *Modern Woman*. August 1943. 48–9.
(©The British Library Board (*Modern Woman*/LOU.LON 371)

13

Promoting Involvement in Performance: Performing Arts Journals and Women Writers, 1945–69

Charlotte Purkis

PERIODICAL CULTURE WAS important to postwar British creative industries because it both documented and stimulated the role of culture in rebuilding society. In particular, it reflected the increase in entertainment and leisure, the development of national state-supported culture, and the growth of the amateur sector. Performing arts journals offered elucidation on the training and education of practitioners and audiences. The journals discussed careers in the performing arts, gave critical context for performances and offered glimpses behind the scenes in articles and features. They also contained reports on recreational cultural practices linked to groups, societies and companies, and sought to develop consumption of the arts by offering tools for appreciation which contributed to taste-making. They enhanced participation in the performing arts by supporting skills development and by offering careers advice through role models.

This chapter considers how women writers developed performing arts coverage within newspapers, magazines and journals, and how they shaped readers' experience of leisure by relating to performance cultures – this had an impact on both the professional industry and amateur activity. Examples are drawn from women as reporters, reviewers, critics and editors, as well as written contributions from readers, audience members and participants. In this way, a spotlight is shone upon the growing presence of the female voice within performance culture and questions are raised about its impact. In the postwar years there was a growing involvement of women as professionals, amateurs and audiences in the performing arts and in this chapter it is argued that much of the contribution that women made to performance arts journals can be understood in terms of encouraging 'involvement' in the performing arts. This is a concept not dissimilar to today's Arts Council (2016) concept of 'everyday creativity' – acts constructive of democratic, accessible and open culture. This includes participation by amateurs, reader responses, as well as the ways in which specialist journalism in this sphere fostered dialogue between professionals.

British women writers interpreted the performing arts for enthusiastic readers looking for guidance and support. In doing so, women writers did more than engage reflectively with their times: they also acted as agents in the expansion of public culture. However, women were rarely employed as critics, and had to find their freedom of expression in writing more generally about topics of interest to do with performance and activities surrounding public stages. Some of the contributions to monthly magazines and newspapers by women were informal in tone, and specific to a contemporary moment or event. This was especially the case where women were writing as freelancers without secure appointment, for example, as reviewers rather than the in-house critic or as specially commissioned writers due to their particular expertise. At other times, where women were in charge of editorial or called upon as an expert, they became household names to regular readers, expressing authoritative opinions which were agenda-setting.

This chapter suggests an element of gendered writing in female performance arts journalism. Cassandra Laity has suggested that all writing is readable 'through a feminist/gendered lens . . . to recover underexplored modern women' (2018: 3). Here it is argued that certain forms of writing, combined with female-specific references and highly lucid styles of journalism, had greater appeal to female readers than the fact-driven observational pieces and top-down criticism typical of male critics. While some articles may contain little explicit feminism, the articles by female writers may be interpreted as foregrounding and valorising gendered points of view. Some women were writing from feminist perspectives, while others wrote from the tenuous dual position of professional-amateur. Laity has further suggested that 'modernism has yet to witness an intensive, wide-ranging recovery of lost and underappreciated writers' (Ibid.: 2). This chapter starts to recover those lost and underappreciated women writing for performance arts journals.

Tradition, Renewal and Change Reflected in Performing Arts Print

Performing arts magazines were a significant dimension of the postwar British creative industries. They responded to socio-political desires for change and rebuilding after the war through the ideals of increasing metropolitan entertainment, developing national state-supported culture and growth in recreation. There are three important postwar changes reflected in women's writing in performing arts print media. First, there are changes in the performing arts industry and women's positions and roles in that industry. Second, there are ways in which women in performing arts – both professional and amateur – used the journals to bridge that professional-amateur divide. Third, there are modes of female interpretation and expression that contribute to the cultural work of these journals.

In the late 1940s, performing arts magazines reflected the major changes that the war had brought to opportunities for women. For instance, *New Theatre* ran a series entitled 'I work in the Theatre'. The first article in this series by Sylvia Peters – 'In the Chorus' – was an enthusiastic but slightly dissatisfied account by a twenty-year-old wanting to get out of the chorus and into parts. It assumed that the chorus takes only women. By the end of the article it is clear that the intention is to demonstrate what a career in theatre might involve, and that the author is speaking to women readers:

> Just before I stop, a word to those who are thinking of going on the stage. Unless you are determined to be a straight actress, or you have influence, the chorus is your only way in. And to be a successful chorine you must have: 1. appearance

> and personality, 2. dancing talent, and 3. good health, in that order. It may help to be able to sing and act, but they are not essential. I like it; you might. It's up to you. (*New Theatre* June 1946: 9)

Peters discusses touring and the forced breaks between jobs, how her parents had not wanted her to go on the stage and how being in the chorus is actually 'just another job'. Keen to dispel myths about chorus girls, Peters says:

> We're a mixed lot and very unlike what people think . . . There are a lot of wrong ideas about chorus girls. Take immorality for instance. About five per cent of the girls are less particular than most, but so are about five per cent of factory girls or shop assistants or any other class of girl. It's true that some powerful theatre people expect a girl to sleep with them if she's going to have a part, but it is possible to become a leading lady without going to bed with a producer. (*New Theatre* June 1946: 9)

The second article in this series, 'Running Repertory' by Sally Latimer, emphasises her training, but ends with the remark that, in the repertory company that she had founded in 1936, Latimer 'acts, produces, arranges and washes up' (*New Theatre* July 1946: 3). The photograph accompanying this article shows two other women alongside Latimer, the designer and producer respectively. The article explains how the ten-year journey of the company through the challenging war years have built the idealism of the group: 'We feel too a new spirit . . . rising in theatre workers of to-day' (Ibid.). Other accounts in this series also point to the unusual patterns of women's careers in the performing arts at this time. Helen Dibley's account of 'Stage Manager' in the third article of the series, acknowledges that her success is an accident of history: 'It is largely a war-time feature that women are now accepted generally as stage managers' (*New Theatre* August 1946: 2). Evelyn Brierley, wardrobe supervisor at the Lyric Theatre Hammersmith, recounts the journey of her career in theatre, starting by auditioning for a comedy while working as a shop assistant in the fashion trade: 'during my lunch hour I had a brandy to summon up my courage and presented myself at the rehearsal rooms' (*New Theatre* September 1946: 21).

Another change in performing arts in this postwar period was the call for greater co-operation between the amateur and professional spheres. Read has argued that the world of drama supported significant crossover between professional and amateur involvements (Read 1993). This professional-amateur crossover was a key theme of the 1948 British Theatre Conference, and was reported by several of the performing arts magazines. Newspapers, journals and magazines both connected and educated enthusiasts, and linked professionals to each other and their audiences. The production and consumption of periodical texts linked a collective community of people passionate about the performing arts, and provided a forum for sharing skills and experiences. The November 1955 edition of *Amateur Stage*, for instance, contained a brief report on 'Amateur Drama on the B.B.C.' (13). Some magazines, such as *The Musical Times*, maintained a section headed 'The Amateur's Exchange' where connections could be made through notices placed for free. It seems that women readers were particularly instrumental in this aspect of performance arts. An example of the enthusiasm for a performing arts journal is provided by Patricia

Hastings-Hardy from Croydon in the form of an acrostic poem published in the *Amateur Stage* 'Forum':

> Actors' and producers' interests studied.
> Music suggestions.
> Authors' notes on their own plays.
> Technical advice.
> Entertaining articles.
> Useful addresses.
> Reviews of new plays.
>
> Stimulating controversies.
> Theatre news.
> Advertisements by play publishers.
> Generally interesting reading.
> Eagerly awaited monthly treat!
> (*Amateur Stage* September 1956: 47).

Figure 13.1 The Stanhope Choir outside the Royal Albert Hall at the national music festival organised by the National Federation of Women's Institutes (NFWI) 1950 (Image courtesy of the NFWI Archives).

Female readers, identifiable by their full names, wrote to journals such as *Amateur Stage* and discussed this amateur-professional crossover. One contribution by Muriel Kellett, for example, responded to the prompt 'what the amateur stage means to me' by explaining how she had 'gained a far deeper appreciation of the professional theatre, and have had my life immeasurably enriched thereby' and had progressed from taking part in multiple functions to 'watching on the amateur stage plays I had myself written and produced' (*Amateur Stage* October 1956: 36). In addition, some advice columns used humour to bridge the divide between amateur and professional activity. Elizabeth Brooke's 1956 series 'I want to be an actress' in *Amateur Stage* joked about female thespians as new recruits in the first-person and with feigned naivety. One of these claims how words:

> poured out from all parts of the house wherever I happened to be; attitudes were taken up at odd moments of inspiration . . . all this in the middle of cooking, dusting, gardening (although I had to be careful here in case anyone was in view), and last but not least, in my bath. (*Amateur Stage* January 1956: 45)

Another of these columns recalls feedback from a male adjudicator who 'commended one, deplored something in another, praised, cajoled'. She reports how she 'stood up to take what was coming' and saw 'a look of pleasure': 'I suddenly saw myself in a different light. Confidence surged through me.' The column deals with praise too: '"She was absolutely marvellous . . . she really was knitting." It was then that I knew that, as an actress, I was a very good knitter!!' (*Amateur Stage* February 1956: 29). Brooke's articles were clearly intended to encourage others. Further encouragement was offered by women writers in performing arts magazines who deployed language in particular ways to reach readers quite directly. This was in an attempt to foster interaction between expert author and lay reader to construct a shared experience. In the early 1960s, *Dancing Times* targeted diary entries by young professional ballerina Nora Telford at students, with aspirational articles on topics such as 'Touring Overseas': 'What new and wonderful things shall we see? What places shall we visit? One thing alone is certain, in a touring ballet company there is just never a dull moment.' (*Dancing Times* March 1963: 361).

Some articles in performing arts magazines seemed to be seeking to educate readers about what they could view on stage and how to perceive new work. Alan Sinfield (1983: 173) has argued that cultural change represented in stage performance between 1945 and 1970 'must be considered in relation to audiences'. This is pertinent to the style in which some articles in performing arts journals were written. In *Drama*, poet and playwright Anne Ridler drew upon Queen Elizabeth II's recent coronation, as well as radio 'soap opera' to help readers understand how ritual could be seen as a means 'to express the feelings which would otherwise be inexpressible' (*Drama* Summer 1953). Ridler seemed to have adopted a writing style that spoke especially to women readers, with references to the emotions and to motherhood. For instance, in one article about medieval mystery plays, she used a contemporary cultural example of a parallel emotional identification by women: 'Whenever a character in *Mrs Dale's Diary* is supposed to be having a baby, women listeners are sure to send in woolly bootees and vests which they have knitted.' (*Drama* Summer 1953: 16).

In a similar way, Caryl Brahms' review of the conversationalist Joyce Grenfell is full of references to female content and the female audience: 'Miss Grenfell has an avid public of the nicest people taking out their aunts'; it is an 'autumn world of Women's Institute and hard-tried educationists, with here a duchess and there a counterhand, and the inevitable Mum smiling bravely through the inevitable tears' (*Plays and Players* November 1957: 7). Doris Caroline Abrahams (1901–82) started out as a pianist, then in the 1920s and 1930s, wrote verses and captions for cartoons (with S. J. Simon) at the *Evening Standard* and on ballet and opera for *Time and Tide*. She changed her name to Caryl Brahms. From 1934 she deputised for Arnold Haskell as dance critic of the *Daily Telegraph* and contributed to *Tempo*. She also published many novels with Simon in the 1940s. After his death she developed her theatre criticism with *Plays and Players*, published collected editions and books on Gilbert and Sullivan and Chekhov. She collaborated with Ned Sherrin from the mid-1950s on musicals and radio and TV scripts and wrote for the *Spectator*. She became a governor of the National Theatre in 1978. Marjorie Bennett praised Caryl Brahms in *Plays and Players* for her, 'broad, all-embracing view of the theatre, as opposed to the one-eyed slant affecting the daily boys' and their 'monotonously vitriolic and boring daily criticisms' that she and her friends had decided to 'read no longer' (*Plays and Players* November 1960: 3).

Recognising the significance of women's interventions in the development of performing arts culture and its institutions expands historical perception of the changes in this period. Writers on these activities of production and interpretation who discussed, for example, how directors and performers reinterpret and re-engage as revisers of traditions, were themselves forming attitudes underpinning changing notions of what culture was for and who it was for. The socialist critic Raymond Williams, who himself contributed on 'new wave' theatre to 'New Left' journals in the 1940s and 1950s, termed this connecting of 'lived' and 'period cultures' the 'selective tradition', whereby 'cultural tradition can be seen as a continual selection and re-selection of ancestors'. Williams saw this process as both selection and interpretation (1961: 74). Brahms herself wrestled with new ideas and the standard national works. For example, she defended the tradition of Shakespeare against Joan Littlewood's Theatre Workshop 'distasteful and dishonest' representation. Concerned to protect authenticity, Brahms' article was headed 'Taking the Mickey out of Macbeth', and called to readers to debate how and why Littlewood had 'cut and . . . rationalised' the play: 'Because Shakespeare in modern dress is not . . . my dish, I am clearly not the best conceivable taster. So, go, dear reader, and judge it for yourself.' (*Plays and Players*, October 1957: 13). Yet a month before, Brahms had been far more tolerant about another modern reworking: 'we knew from the beginning that it is about as useful to go to a Peter Brook production with a preconceived idea of the play as it would be to go to a sack-race with an octopus . . . we do not go to the Stratford *Tempest* in search of Shakespeare but to enjoy . . . visual annotations to the text.' (*Plays and Players* September 1957: 9). The women involved in editorial work and the reviewers, reporters and commentators were joining in this 'cultural work' upholding the importance of inherited texts and considering what was being done with, and to, performing traditions, as well as heralding new ideas.

Figure 13.2 Caryl Brahms (Image courtesy of the National Portrait Gallery).

Women as Emerging Critics

In general, few women were considered 'critics' of the performing arts, because few were employed directly in this role. Even some of those women that were sent out to particular performances tended not to be present as experts offering analysis of the aesthetics of particular works. Instead, they were regarded as reviewers and encouraged to discuss an opinion but not to pass judgement. Dan Rebellato's view on the theatre context of the mid-1950s is that professional critics offered perspectives drawing on audience response as well as their own; they were there 'unabashedly not merely to inform but to mediate' (Rebellato 1999: 117).

The association of the role of critic with men was deep-rooted. J. C. Trewin's introduction to Audrey Williamson's *Theatre of Two Decades* – which reprinted articles from *Theatre World*, *Tribune*, *Theatre*, *The Shakespeare Pictorial* and *The Gilbert and Sullivan Journal* – commented that 'her enthusiasms are wide, her expression is considered' (Williamson 1951: vii). But the book is 'like a long talk about the theatre with a friend' (Ibid.: viii). He explained his reluctance to term her a critic: 'I must always hold that the prime duty of a writer on the theatre is to appreciate. There is no need to harp upon the word "critic"' (Ibid.: vi). Is this a compliment or exclusionary? Trewin falls back into the more authoritative third-person, gendering the critic as male: 'Let us get it right. A critic looks first for what, within reason, he can praise . . . he knows it is possible to discriminate, to select, to keep faith with himself and to serve the reader' (Ibid.: vi–vii). Nonetheless, Williamson was acknowledged as a critic by her publishers, for example, her previous book *Old Vic Drama* (1948) was marketed as the work of 'one of the best of our younger critics' who was 'well-known'. Williamson's next book *Contemporary Theatre 1953–1956* was received in *Amateur Stage* as the work of 'an eminent drama critic' (December 1956: 48).

Furthermore, although Caryl Brahms was excluded from the list of critics recorded at the front of the compilation *The Best of Plays and Players 1953–1968*, her work featured because it was a strength of the journal and she had been their writer from the start. Three of her four articles selected for the anthology were reviews. In this period, all of the magazines' editors had been male, as were the editors of the co-owned *Dance and Dancers* (1950–) and *Music and Musicians* (1952–), and the editor noted how *Plays and Players* 'played a useful role in providing a shop window for young critics' (Roberts 1988: 9). Brahms' article 'The Young Actresses' opened the celebratory volume. Using the expression 'we, the playgoers', Brahms positions herself in the audience, and, writes not as an arbiter of taste but as an associate of the theatre, chatting as an insider, sharing impressions: 'she [Yvonne Mitchell] is the only actress who has made Cordelia credible to me, and oh, Call-boy, have I seen a clutter of Cordelias in my time!'(*Plays and Players* October 1953: 18). Brahms acts as go-between for the backstage world, the front-of-house and the reader at home, to whom she poses questions. In the companion piece, 'The Young Actors', Brahms moved the discourse from 'a great actor' to 'your great actor', debating with readers through phraseology such as 'I have said that' and then asking questions to leave discussion open (*Plays and Players* November 1953: 23). When reviewing *Serjeant Musgrave's Dance* at The Royal Court Theatre, also for *Plays and Players*, Brahms provoked readers to disassociate themselves from the critics concerning the 'outstandingly important' play which had had 'a mixed press':

> Playgoers, I'm here to say that I'm ashamed of you – and I don't care what you say to me in the correspondence column. Surely you, the men and women who have time to live and feel and put your toes up and reflect – surely you should show more sense than a lot of word-obsessed and clock-ridden critics.

She then associated herself with the use of 'us': 'You must not let us keep you from this or any play of passion and poetry in prodigious confusion' (*Plays and Players* December 1959: 11).

Brahms' secondary position as a critic is now ironic, as current critical scholarship on twentieth-century playwrights frequently cites Brahms' commentary on new writing and prominent male playwrights whose work is seen as historically significant in the canon of British theatre. Other women theatre critics occasionally cited from the 1950s and 1960s in connection with new writing by British men are Frances Stephens (*Theatre World*); Penelope Gilliatt (*The Observer*), whose work features in study on censorship; and Hilary Spurling whose relationship with the Royal Court as critic of the *Spectator* is written into its history. Beyond these examples, the deep-rooted association of criticism and patriarchy has tended to discourage investigations of critical engagement by women in other types of writing. This issue is made even more complex by feminist historians who recover women as composers, playwrights and directors and yet rely on the negative critical press or ignorance of the male critic to suit the agenda of uncovering female creativity within a context of struggle. The opposition to women music critics in the twentieth century outlined, for example, by Jill Halstead (1997) in her discussion of late twentieth-century musicology, has affected an ongoing lack of historical investigation. Grace Barnes in *Her Turn on Stage*, a book which sets out to ignite debate about musicals and gender, acknowledges that the fact that most prominent theatre critics are male contributes to a lack of debate in historical scholarship about gender issues (2015: 83).

Women Writers and Performance Arts Networks

Although women authors are absent from many pages of arts periodicals, women were, in fact, active in all branches of performance culture as professionals, amateurs and teachers, and many were writing about it. The use of full names in signed articles has made it possible to recover some of the women's writing in this field.[1] The publications themselves were not marketed in gender-specific ways and print culture offered opportunities for micro-level interventions by women within specific networks. Men continued to dominate performance arts reporting because they were institutionally enshrined as the leading critics, whereas women were usually only identifiable as contributors. This situation changed as women gained editorial roles. Eventually, women writers became influential in their sphere and were nationally known figures and household names who have been recalled as role models by journalists from subsequent generations. Many women had long careers in journalism and mentoring often played a part in them getting established. Joan Chissell, for instance, was invited by Frank Howes, chief music critic at *The Times*, to become his assistant in 1948. Similarly, Frances Stephens, who dominated up-to-date reporting on theatre by developing the influential *Theatre World* as editor between 1940 and 1966, had been assistant to her male predecessor for the preceding ten years. *The Stage* commented on how Stephens' *Theatre World Annual Pictorial Review* (8th issue June 1956–May 1957) was 'excellently written and compiled' and that she, 'has the knack of being able to blend a warm love for the theatre with a critical approach' (*The Stage* 16 January 1958: 9). At her retirement lunch, Stephens commented that her intention had been to make *Theatre World* a picture of the theatre of its time (*The Stage* 5 May 1966: 13). Doris Hutton was assistant editor of *Drama: The Quarterly Theatre Review* – official magazine of the British Drama League – from the 1940s to the end of the 1960s working alongside editors E. Martin Browne and then Ivor Brown.[2]

Other female editors, such as Mary Clarke, achieved influence and legacy. Clarke was self-educated from spending evenings in the theatre as a young typist in London in the 1940s. She was encouraged through the British balletomane network and initially supported by Phyllis Manchester, who had started *Ballet Today* after the war when supplies of paper improved. Phyllis Winifred Manchester (1907–98), known as Bill, signed as P. W. Manchester. She started out as an amateur, and became dance critic of *Theatre World* in 1941, leaving in 1944 to become Marie Rambert's secretary. Having started *Ballet Today*, from 1951 she continued her career as a dance critic in New York. Manchester also gave Clarke a London correspondent position on American *Dance News* when she transferred to the US and Arnold Haskell invited her onto *Ballet Annual*'s editorial board in 1952. Clarke edited *Dancing Times* for forty-five years (1963–2008), starting in 1943 as assistant editor to Philip Richardson and continued to work with him for twenty years. Dance, as a performing arts form, had previously tended to be reviewed by music critics and Clarke was part of a shift to specialist dance writers. She was a very successful editor who came to dominate the field of specialist journalism on ballet because *Dancing Times* was the leading organ for the art form and because of the clarity of her own writing. Clarke's style had been described as 'lucid writing' which 'made the arcane mysteries of technical vocabulary and historical sources easily intelligible to the general reader' and 'was respected by the profession, even when she made no bones about criticising what she felt was artistically below par' (*Daily Telegraph* 30 March 2015). Clarke's influence can be seen in the work of others, such as Ninette de Valois, who was not only the founder and director of the Royal Ballet, but also a regular lecturer, writer and diarist. A volume of her collected writings, *Step by Step* (de Valois 1977) thanked Clarke for her advice.

It appeared that women had more opportunities writing for the newer magazines. *New Theatre* included more women writers than other journals. A relatively large number of articles were authored by women, with something in nearly every issue: Pauline Grant, Phyllis Bentley, Margaret Leighton, Brenda Cross, Freda Jackson, Vivien Leigh and Caryl Brahms wrote for *New Theatre*. Caryl Jenner's name appears on the masthead of the February 1947 edition of *New Theatre* as a 'contributing editor' and inside there is a request for support in assisting her with their enquiry into the problems of repertory production (12–13). Peggie MacIver became executive editor of the same periodical from April 1949, in a new role managing the two male editors. However, *Encore* – subtitled *The Voice of Vital Theatre* and described by its editors as a 'dogmatic, partial, principled, feverish' magazine for discussion of radical new drama – had five times as many men as women writing for it (Marowitz et al. 1981: 9). This may have reflected its field of new drama, in which men were more active as practitioners.

The magazines linked to amateur organisations were more egalitarian about opportunities for women and actively showcased women's work. *Amateur Stage* contained many contributions from women working professionally who wrote as advisers on theatre practices, such as Norah Lambourne.[3] The secure position of women in The British Drama League – a support organisation for theatre established after the First World War which offered a lending library, a training department and a country-wide committee structure – is particularly apparent in its magazine *Drama*. The book reviews section was full of books authored by, and reviewed by, women; news recorded in members pages frequently featured women; the cover illustration in the 1950s was engraved by Joan Hassall; and articles authored by women were regularly included. Furthermore, *Amateur Stage* magazine had a female patron, Dame Sybil Thorndike, who quite often appeared in print in various magazines from the 1940s to the 1960s.

Women journalists were in a position to highlight the achievements of other working women active on public stages, choosing sometimes to act as advocates. For example, Joan Chissell highlighted the contributions of several women to the 1965 London 'Proms' season, in the October issue of *The Musical Times*.[4] She commented how Jaqueline du Pré played Elgar's 'cello concerto 'more ripely than ever in her

Figure 13.3 Cover of *Drama* by Joan Hassall (© The Fitzwilliam Museum, Cambridge).

life', and singers Hermione Gingold (in Edith Sitwell and William Walton's *Façade*) and Heather Harper (in Benjamin Britten's *Our Hunting Fathers*) were selected for 'special applause' (*Musical Times* October 1965: 782). Chissell wrote with authority, although 'overwhelmed' by the whole season she stated that she would 'pull out the plums', identifying composer Elizabeth Maconchy's *Variazioni Concertanti* as a new work in 'pride of place' (Ibid.: 781). A few years later, Pamela Dalton acknowledged the breakthrough of Ruth Baker (Dr Gipps) in being the 'First Woman to Conduct Her Own Symphony on the B.B.C.' in *Time and Tide* (February 1969) and quoted Gipps' observation that 'This B.B.C. engagement is one of the first signs of the door opening' (*Time and Tide* February 1969: 21).[5]

Women reviewing one another's books demonstrates how there appears to have been an informal network of women writers. One example is Brahms' favourable review of Audrey Williamson's *Theatre of Two Decades*. Brahms saw it as a source for future historians of 'unpretentious' careful observation and documentation of plays and players, and described its style as 'like a long natter at night, with the voice of the author going on and on into the small hours, now excited, now soporific' (*Tempo* Spring 1952: 36). A few years later in *Drama* Janet Leeper reviewed Williamson's *Contemporary Theatre 1953–1956* declaring that each book she publishes 'enhances her reputation' giving 'the same alert mind and balanced judgment'. Leeper also commented upon Williamson's 'reliability on matters theatrical' (*Drama* Spring 1957: 36). Stephens' ongoing editorial work in *Theatre World* was also praised by Leeper for what it set forth 'in orderly fashion' as 'a useful record' (Ibid.: 37). Clarke (1953: 211) commented on Brahms' *A Seat at The Ballet* saying that she 'has covered the post-war period from her own point of view' in a style that 'can be infuriating, but she is another critic who knows her job'.[6]

Conclusion: Beyond 'Aunt Edna'?

It is essential to recover women's voices on the performing arts in order to ensure that they are not excluded from the historical record. Women's place in public discourse must be evaluated. Without a clear record of the female experience from within stage worlds, playwright Terence Rattigan's 'Aunt Edna' might be the surviving representative: 'nice, respectable, middle-class, middle-aged, maiden lady, with time on her hands and the money to help her pass it. She enjoys pictures, books, music and the theatre and though to none of these arts . . . does she bring much knowledge or discernment, at least, as she is apt to tell her cronies, she "does know what she likes"' (Pattie 2012: 119). This fictional satirical character which powerfully deployed humour in the service of misogyny was also called on by influential modern playwrights John Osborne and Joe Orton, leading to the circulation of assumptions after 1953 that contemporary work was not suitable for Aunt Edna.[7] If we also take into account Michelene Wandor's (1982: 135) recollection that '"feminism" was a dirty word in most theatre criticism in 1970', then the women working in print might too easily be explained away. Such an assessment is no longer as clear-cut and Wandor also recognised the emerging dilemma for women critics after the 1970s as to whether their role was to support other women by avoiding being too critical.

This essay has retrieved a selection of women's performing arts journalism in a variety of forms and examined it through the themes of communication with audiences, women's writing styles and networks of female critics and writers. It has begun to show how women's evaluation of events and performances contributed to the formation of a collective knowledge base and agency in readers. This particular periodical culture sought to educate readers and enhance their experience by encouraging involvement. The importance of recognising women journalists' participation as work, even if they were women of independent means, writing about what some readers considered leisure, and the impact of those neglected histories, is supported by the perspective of *Stage Women* (Gale and Dorney 2019). The large quantity of print on the performance industries by women journalists after 1945 is ripe for deeper investigation. Opening up this neglected material will facilitate consideration of an 'alternate' performance history that will take into account 'those who do the observing, chronicling and critiquing rather than the object of their musings', and reveal the ways that creative women were challenging the status quo as librettists, musicians, actors, composers, playwrights and arts managers (Haworth and Colton 2015: 3). In the period from the end of the war through to the 1960s, periodical culture was a supportive context for women to express views on the performing arts and to build the participation of women readers in British performance culture. The articles and letters presented here demonstrate that women's views were being noticed, heard and valued.

Notes

1. There are exceptions and notably Joan Chissell's name is absent from *The Times* (at a time when all reviews were unsigned). John Warrack writes in *The Dictionary of National Biography* 'anonymity was no bar to her work being recognised for its critical discrimination and fairness' <https://doi.org/10.1093/ref:odnb/30846> (last accessed 18 December 2019).
2. Hutton was noted as also running the 'coupons committee' which supported amateur companies finding material for costumes and for which the British Drama League was delegated by the Board of Trade. She does not appear to have authored any articles on theatre.
3. Lambourne was a British Drama League 'staff instructor', active as a costume designer in productions of national importance, and one of several authors connected to the teacher training colleges (in her case, properties tutor from Bretton Hall Yorkshire).
4. Joan Chissell (1919–2007) gained a piano scholarship to The Royal College of Music in 1937 and then taught there and at the Universities of Oxford and London during the 1940s and early 1950s. She was the first female music critic of *The Times* and wrote for thirty years as a music critic, starting as assistant to Frank Howes then working under William Mann. Her contributions are not signed. She also reviewed as 'J.O.C' for *The Musical Times*, wrote for *Music and Letters* and *Gramophone* and broadcast on the BBC.
5. Ruth Baker (also a performer, composer and lecturer) began her career as a professional conductor in 1946. She was the first woman to conduct at the Royal Festival Hall in 1957 in a programme which twinned Beethoven's *Choral Symphony* with her own cantata *The Cat*.
6. The publisher of Brahms' collection *The Rest of the Evening's My Own* (1964) declared on the dust jacket that: 'If criticism has a life of its own, then Miss Brahms's criticism is high life, observed with a wit that is as original as her own novels and plays.' Later, in her obituary, *The Times* classified her as 'a literary craftsman of great skill' (Walker 2006: 69).
7. Rattigan tried to retrench on this position and used Aunt Edna again to comment more favourably on Samuel Beckett's *Waiting for Godot* and Shelagh Delaney's *A Taste of Honey*, but her persona was set <www.bl.uk/collection-items/terence-rattigan-invents-aunt-edna> (last accessed 18 December 2019).

Works Cited

Arts Council. 2016. 'Everyday Creativity' <www.artscouncil.org.uk/everyday-creativity> and <www.docdroid.net/9HEVtmk/everyday-creativity.pdf#page=3> (last accessed 17 December 2019).

Barnes, G. 2015. *Her Turn on Stage: The Role of Women in Musical Theatre*. Jefferson NC: McFarland and Co.

Brahms, C. 1951. *A Seat at The Ballet*. London: Evans Brothers Ltd.

Brahms, C. 1964. *The Rest of the Evening's My Own*. London: W. H. Allen.

Clarke, M. 1955. 'The Printed Word: Books'. *Ballet: A Decade of Endeavour*. Ed. A. H. Franks. London: Burke.

De Valois, N. 1977. *Step by Step: The Formation of An Establishment*. London: W. H. Allen.

Dorney, K. and M. Gale, eds. 2019. *Stage Women, 1900–1950: Female Theatre Workers and Professional Practice*. Manchester: Manchester University Press <https://www.manchesteropenhive.com/view/9781526147271/9781526147271.xml> (last accessed 14 December 2019).
Halstead, J. 1997. *The Woman Composer: Creativity and the Gendered Politics of Musical Composition*. Abingdon and New York: Ashgate.
Haworth, C. and L. Colton, eds. 2015. *Gender, Age and Musical Creativity*. London and New York: Routledge.
Laity, C. 2018. 'Editor's Introduction: Toward Feminist Modernisms'. *Feminist Modernist Studies* 1.1–2: 1–7.
Marowitz, C., T. Milne and O. Hale, eds. 1981. *New Theatre Voices of the Fifties and Sixties: Selections from Encore Magazine 1956–1963*. London: Eyre Methuen.
Milne, D. 2000. 'Drama in the Culture Industry: British Theatre after 1945'. *British Culture of the Post-war: An Introduction to Literature and Society*. Eds A. Davies and A. Sinfield. London and New York: Routledge. 169–91.
Pattie, D. 2012. *Modern British Playwriting: The 1950s: Voices, Documents, New Interpretations*. London: Methuen.
Read, A. 1993. *Theatre and Everyday Life: The Ethics of Performance*. London and New York: Routledge.
Rebellato, D. 1999. *1956 And All That*. London and New York: Routledge.
Roberts, P. 1988. *The Best of Plays and Players Volume 1: 1953–1968*. London: Methuen.
Sinfield, A. 1983. 'The Theatre and Its Audiences'. *Society and Literature 1945–1970*. Ed. A. Sinfield. London: Methuen.
Walker, K. S. 2006. 'A Whirl of Words: British Dance Criticism, 1930–1950'. *Dance Now* 15.1: 68–78.
Wandor, M. 1982. *Plays by Women* vol. 1. London: Methuen.
Wandor, M. 1986. *Carry On, Understudies: Theatre and Sexual Politics*. London and New York: Routledge and Kegan Paul.
Wandor, M. 1987. *Look Back in Gender: Sexuality and the Family in Post-war British Drama*. London: Methuen.
Wandor, M. 2000. 'Women Playwrights and the Challenge of Feminism in the 1970S'. *The Cambridge Companion to Modern British Women Playwrights*. Eds E. Aston and J. Reinelt. Cambridge: Cambridge University Press. 53–68.
Wandor, M. 2001. *Post-war British Drama: Looking Back in Anger*. London and New York: Routledge.
Williams, R. 1961/2011. *The Long Revolution*. Cardigan: Parthian Books.
Williamson, A. 1948. *Old Vic Drama*. London: Rockcliff.
Williamson, A. 1951. *Theatre of Two Decades*. London: Rockliff.
Williamson, A. 1956. *Contemporary Theatre 1953–1956*. London: Rockcliff.

Part IV

Feminisms and Activisms

14

'It's capitalism, not me sweetheart': Women's Activist Magazines on the Left

Victoria Bazin

In 1970, writing in *Shrew* magazine, Hilary Rawlings pointed to the Left's failure to engage with feminist politics. According to the non-aligned Left's Marxist analysis, it was the economic system rather than patriarchal power structures that oppressed women, that led to the sexual division of labour in the home, unequal pay outside the home, violence against women, sexual objectification and exploitation. This analysis exonerated activist men on the Left, allowing them to adopt revolutionary attitudes in the public sphere while often continuing to adhere to conservative, even 'bourgeois' values in the private sphere. Male comrades, argues Rawlings, all too often hiding behind theoretical dogma, miss the significance of Engels's analysis of what he referred to as 'the antagonism between the man and woman in the monogamous marriage' (*Shrew* February 1970: 5). Marxist analysis, in other words, has always contained within it a feminist critique that recognises women's oppression under capitalism. According to Rawlings, what unifies revolutionary men across racial and class divides is a form of toxic, misogynistic masculinity that requires women's subordination. Any seeming support from male comrades comes at a cost:

> [T]he support of the male radical is always conditional: as long as you dedicate yourself to his political ideals and accept his buckpassing analysis of your oppression (it's capitalism, not me sweetheart) you will be given some time off and occasionally – when politically expedient – patronising interest. But you're not allowed to be serious about it, in other words, to be really radical. It's an interesting fact that on no other issue than the unanimous dismissal of the Women's Movement as 'revisionist' does the male Left agree, and that includes black male radicals as well. I do not intend to justify my struggle for liberation, I am oppressed and that is sufficient. I do not intend to seek permission from Pekin[g] before proceeding. I do not intend to neurotically consult Marxengelslenin before baring my teeth or my teats. I do not intend to give ladylike (read suckass) reassurance to male radical chauvinists during the course of this struggle; even if it means losing their friendship (i.e. patronage). Let us see just how revolutionary and how intellectually and morally rigorous the New Left is. See if they can bring their political values to where their cocks are for the first time in history. (Ibid.)

Rawlings concludes her critique with a call for feminists to be 'concrete', to produce a distinctly feminist analysis of oppression and to develop a theory that can inform social change. Of course, Rawlings was by no means alone in her frustration with Left politics. As a founding member of the Tufnell Park Women's Liberation workshop and a contributor to the early issues of *Shrew*, she was one of many women who were involved in developing an autonomous women's movement separate from non-aligned Left groups.

Much valuable work has been written on the ways in which the Women's Liberation Movement emerged out of the various New Left, anti-colonial and civil rights groups of the late 1960s and there is ample evidence within these magazines of a cogent critique of capitalism from an explicitly feminist perspective.[1] This chapter contributes to the history of Left feminism by examining how collective activist identities were formed and framed in activist magazines. It will focus on three magazines: *Shrew* (1969–78), one of the earliest Women's Liberation Movement magazines, produced by workshops in London; *Red Rag* (1972–80), a collective of women also based in London; and *Scarlet Women* (1976–82), a magazine produced by a collective of Left activists based in North East England.[2] Discussion, particularly in the early years, revolved around one issue: how to theorise the relation between gender and social class and how that theory might be put into practice. The feminists producing these magazines were also active on the Left as members of the Trade Union Movement, the Labour Party, various other non-aligned groups such as the International Socialists, as well as being involved in a range of campaigns on specific issues: supporting the night cleaners in their struggle for a living wage; fighting the Corrie Bill which threatened to drastically limit women's access to abortion; the Campaign Against Cuts protesting the reduction of government spending on public housing; health and welfare; the establishment of women's refuges; and local activism for nursery provision. Towards the late 1970s and early 1980s, what would later become known as 'intersectionality' is viewed from a socialist-feminist perspective providing textual space for black women to articulate the experience of a form of triple oppression. Transnational perspectives became increasingly significant, as the magazines sought to represent the voices of non-Western women, particularly in the wake of two international conferences in Amsterdam and Paris in 1977.

What becomes apparent in reading these often detailed and nuanced accounts of the struggle for a voice on the Left, is that through these dialogues, the magazines were developing theoretical approaches that inserted a feminist perspective into the Marxist critique of capitalism. The intellectual rigour of the discussion, often informed by years of studying Marxist theory, emerged out of the particular concerns and practical problems faced by activist women in their everyday lives. The women who were contributing to these theoretical dialogues understood well the challenges that they were facing and the challenges of organising actions specifically around 'women's issues'. Acutely aware of the heterogeneity of women's experiences across a number of divides that included race, sexuality and social class, they were engaged in dialogue with each other with the aim of developing a theoretical approach that might function to underpin a mass movement capable of affecting social change.

These feminist magazines might seem relatively inconsequential given their small circulation figures, but there are some very good reasons for focusing on them. While all three magazines were engaged in recording and reflecting the different views of women on the Left, they did more than simply reflect those views. As Laurel Forster (2015: 208) has suggested, the production of the feminist magazine is itself a form of activism, 'allowing women to name themselves, and to advance the cause'. Referring to the role of women's suffrage periodicals, Barbara Green (2012: 462) argues that activist magazines played a crucial role in offering 'mechanisms of identification and dis-identification by which women connected themselves to the new feminist communities and identities'. If activist agency is produced through activist magazines, then these magazines might provide ways of thinking about feminist agency beyond the current and in some ways debilitating debates in circulation around feminist identity and in particular, the identification of 'woman' as the subject of feminism. Activist magazines such as *Shrew*, *Red Rag* and *Scarlet Women* reveal the extent to which political agency is produced through collective identifications constructed in response to particular historical pressures. The production of even the smallest magazine is a collective endeavour based on compromise, negotiation and shared feelings, as well as intersecting interests. These are, to paraphrase Terry Lovell, 'ensemble performances' capable of telling us something about how activist identities are formed and how they affect social change. According to Lovell (2003: 2), 'transformative political agency lies in the interstices of interaction, in collective social movements in formation in specific circumstances'. Feminist magazines reflect the histories of activism but also point us towards the 'interstices of interaction', the textures and cultures of that activism, the affective glue that binds activists together in spite of their differences.

Maria DiCenzo, Lucy Delap and Leila Ryan's discussion of new social movement theory in *Feminist Media History* provides another good reason for focusing on socialist-feminist magazines. New social movement theory examines why and how social movements emerge at particular historical moments. More specifically, it seeks to explain the formation of the 'new' movements of the 1960s, as well as to characterise and distinguish them from previous forms of activism. As DiCenzo et al. (2011: 32) argue, Jurgen Habermas was particularly influential in this theoretical field, describing new movements as decentralised, non-hierarchical, non-class based, amorphous and fluid by comparison to the social movements of the past that organised to secure basic rights for workers and their families. The Women's Liberation Movement is often included in accounts of the rise of new social movements; with its emphasis on the political nature of the personal, it represents a shift towards an emphasis on equal rights and individual freedoms. Yet as Craig Calhoun among others has pointed out, the split between 'old' and 'new' social movements in historical accounts has tended to privilege the labour movement and marginalise organisations and actions that seemed less goal oriented. The justification for this is often coded in class terms: feminism and feminists are 'bourgeois', their cause a distraction from the real political and economic struggle. The socialist-feminist magazines under discussion in this chapter, therefore, offer evidence of the ways in which the history of the Left in Britain cannot be separated from the history of the Women's Liberation Movement. More importantly, perhaps, this uneasy alliance suggests how problematic it is to characterise the Women's Liberation Movement as 'new' when many of its strategies for action and analysis are drawn from Marxist, socialist and Left debate. In other words, along with DiCenzo et al., I argue for an account of women's activism that resists this problematic split between 'new' and 'old' social movements. The histories of the Women's Liberation Movement should retain a sense of its rootedness in, and connection to, a tradition of women's activism on the Left that extends back into the nineteenth century. Just as the suffrage movement anticipated the strategies associated with new social movements, the Women's Liberation Movement adopted strategies associated with old social movements.

The following discussion draws on examples from *Shrew*, *Red Rag* and *Scarlet Women* to examine, at a micro-level, the histories of socialist feminism in the late 1960s and the 1970s, making visible the ways in which these two social movements were connected in terms of both grassroots organisation and theoretical analysis. This involves not only tracing the formation of the magazines and analysing the theoretical debates within them, but also paying attention to the magazines as material objects and as media, their periodical codes, differentiation patterns, price, periodicity and internal and external dialogics (see Cohen 2015; Hammill et al. 2015; Ardis 2012). Comparisons across magazines become instructive, providing a sense of the slightly different discursive roles played by each publication. The broad church of *Shrew*, for instance, devoted more textual space to individual perspectives and was radically reinvented by each collective that produced the journal to reflect their particular interests. *Red Rag*'s bold visual style, its relatively consistent periodical codes and its comparatively professional production values was the result of stability produced by restrictions placed on membership to the collective. The dearth of images in *Scarlet Women* tells its own story. Produced by a small collective of women, this magazine drew together what it refers to in its masthead as the 'socialist feminist current'. The imagery associated with the push and pull of the tides, with the ways in which water is capable of making waves, signals the importance of allowing all the various theoretical debates to flow into feminist theory and practice. By comparison to *Shrew* and *Red Rag*, this is a quiet magazine that eschewed the loud graphic noise of its more boisterous sisters, offering another kind of textual space to reflect on the forms and the feelings associated with feminist activism.

Shrew and the Production of an Autonomous Women's Movement

The affects drawing women together in the first issues of all three magazines are associated with an anger and frustration with Left masculinity. This coincided, however, with a renewed sense of women's collective and powerful political agency. As Audrey Wise points out, the Women's Liberation Movement was at least partly produced by the critical attention paid to feminism in the pivotal year of 1968 (Wandor 1990: 201). That year was the fiftieth anniversary of woman's suffrage in Britain, which produced a proliferation of articles in magazines and newspapers reflecting on feminism and women's activism. That was the year that a women's rights group formed in Hull around the campaign initiated by Lil Bilocca and other fishermen's wives to improve safety on trawlers. That year also saw the strike action of sewing machinists at Ford's Dagenham plant, an embarrassment to a Labour government that was supposed to be supportive of women's rights. Wise points out that the first mass meeting of the Women's Liberation Movement was not the conference at Ruskin college in 1970 but the demonstration in 1969 organised by the National Joint Action Campaign Committee for Women's Equal Rights. Both Sheila Rowbotham and Wise identify a strong socialist current among women activists that was distinct from the style of Women's

Liberation that was coming from the United States (Wandor 1990: 14–15). It was the heady fusion of American-style consciousness raising with New Left politics that led to the formation of the first Women's Liberation Workshops and the production of *Shrew* in 1969.

In her account of the histories of Left activists living and working in London, Celia Hughes (2015) traces the connections between the Women's Liberation Movement and the non-aligned Left. She describes how the Vietnam Solidarity Campaign's London branch, based in Camden, split off and formed its own group, the Camden Movement for People's Power. One of the women involved was Sheli Wortis who, towards the end of 1968, formed the Tufnell Park Women's Liberation group along with other activist women. As Hughes (2015: 194) notes, 'prior to joining, almost all female members had been involved in non-aligned Left activist circles', but also important is the fact that 'many American members had also been active in New Left movements in the U.S. and the beginnings of the women's movement there'. The women who began to meet in women-only groups to engage in what was to become known as 'consciousness raising' and who brought the discourse of the 'personal is the political' into their meetings had already been active campaigners for many years. The Tufnell Park group was soon joined by collectives based in Peckham Rye, Ladbroke Grove and Belsize Lane.

Shrew's willingness to get all the arguments out in the open might perhaps be explained by the fact that many of its contributors had felt silenced for so long by the Left. As *Shrew*'s articles and cartoons suggest, what mobilised activist women was a frustration with grassroots politics, with the ways in which, even at a local level, women were being relegated to supporting roles. A sense of allegiance and a connection to the Left is evident in many articles, but so too is a palpable anger with male comrades who dismiss feminism as 'bourgeois'. In the cartoon 'When Women's Lib. Came along', the juxtaposition of text and image articulates the reasons why women began to organise separately (*Shrew* June 1970). According to the cartoon, initially socialist feminists believed that men were largely supportive. As the Women's Liberation Movement continued, however, it became clear that men were only interested in feminism if it made women 'better assistants for THEIR politics'. Initially 'encouraging', male comrades on the Left came to realise that the Women's Liberation Movement was challenging the practice and some of the theory on the Left. Women's Liberation asserts that the 'personal is political' resisting the ways in which politics 'is something separate from our own lives'. When it became apparent that the women were not, in fact, coming back to help with the 'revolution', to support the old agenda of the Marxist dialectic, men declared that 'they have no time for Women's Liberation'. The cartoon articulated the realisation that Left masculinity demands the 'assistance' of women to reinforce its revolutionary potency and not women's equal participation in the movement.

The fusion and sometimes the spectacular clash of radical feminism with Left politics is evident throughout the early issues of *Shrew*. Even though the composition of the group in terms of class and race was fairly homogenous, there were many different, competing and conflicting perspectives. This radical heterogeneity is reflected in the look and feel of the magazine. Produced by different collectives, *Shrew*'s discursive identity shifted, its preoccupations changed depending on which group took over temporary ownership. For instance, the Tufnell Park group was

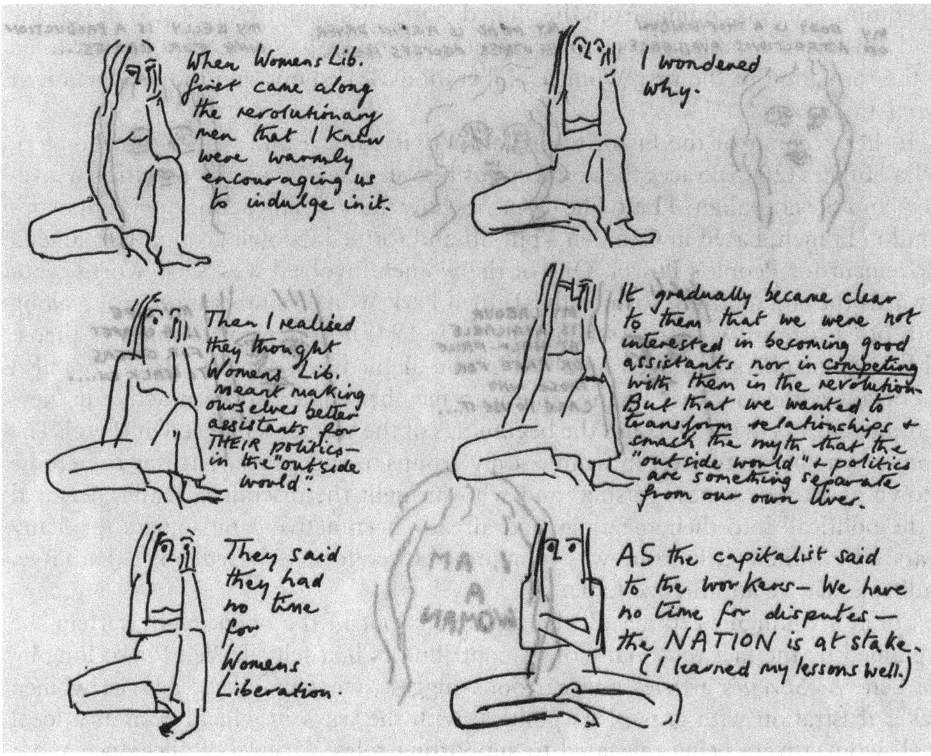

Figure 14.1 'When Women's Lib. Came along', *Shrew*, June 1970. (Image courtesy of Leeds University Library)

clearly preoccupied with issues relating to reproductive rights, childcare, motherhood and women's health, particularly after childbirth. Later issues moved away from concerns directly affecting members of the collective. The Spring 1977 issue, for instance, explored the role of religion in the patriarchal oppression of women and advocated matriarchal cultures that worshipped the 'Great Goddess'.[3] Underpinned by research into Minoan Crete, ancient Egypt, as well as studies of the Old and New Testaments, this issue is more radical feminist than socialist feminist (*Shrew* Spring 1977). While the 'Goddess' issue saw oppression in terms of 'male-based conditioning' (*Shrew* Spring 1977: 2), the Summer 1978 issue on 'Feminism and Non-Violence' provided a structural analysis of violence that linked colonial oppression, the nuclear arms race and the British occupation of Northern Ireland to the violence experienced by women in their everyday lives. The issue opened with a quotation from Andrea Dworkin exhorting women to consciously unlearn forms of 'masochistic submission' coupled with a statement by Sophie Laws that challenged 'patriarchal myths' reinforcing the essentialist fallacy that women are 'inherently nonviolent' (*Shrew* Summer 1978: 1). Articles in this issue pointed to gender-based violence as it operated within and across the institutions of the family, the state, the law and the media.

Red Rag and the Personal Politics of Socialism

By contrast, *Red Rag*, appearing in 1972, adopted a set of relatively stable periodical codes designed to signal a politically coherent collective identity. It was the consistently sexist and demeaning images in the *Morning Star*, the Communist Party's official publication, that spurred communist women to form their own collective and their own magazine. Val Charlton remembers composing, along with her communist sisters, a collage of women's naked body parts cut out from the *Morning Star* accompanied by a letter critiquing the objectification of women (Wandor 1990: 164–5). While the *Morning Star* never published the letter, it did curtail the reproduction of sexist images. Galvanised by this success, feminists in the Communist Party began to meet separately, an initiative that led to the formation of the *Red Rag* Collective. Persuading the Communist Party to support a feminist publication, however, involved intense negotiations, as Charlton recalls. The feminists resisted the party line and any interference from party officials concerning content. This was not to be a publication that used women's liberation as a way of luring women into the Communist Party. Charlton and her colleagues argued that 'to gain the confidence of the women's movement we had to be there as individuals in our own right, not as a front for the Communist Party' (Wandor 1990: 165). For Charlton and her feminist sisters, the women's movement had much more to offer the Communist Party than the other way around.

Communist officials, however, were appalled at the prospect of a journal that openly courted debate and that even invited non-party women to contribute. In this respect, the struggle for control of *Red Rag* reflects wider tensions between new social movements and the political parties from which such movements emerged. As Nicholas Owen (2013: 803) points out, the Women's Liberation Movement, like other new social movements, 'was highly participatory, open, and inclusive at the grassroots level. It placed great faith in free and non-judgemental explorations of personal experience' putting it at odds with formal party organisations. Feminists wanted to use *Red Rag* to reform the party from within, an ambitious project that recognised the revolutionary potential of fusing class-based politics with a critique of gender and that blurred the boundaries between traditional 'old'-style activism and the affectively charged personal politics of the Women's Liberation Movement.

Unlike *Shrew* and *Scarlet Women*, most of the original members of *Red Rag* had been attached to a political party resulting in its focus on developing a socialist-feminist critique that might gain political traction in the public sphere. Although Charlton remembers tensions between women within the collective, she also recalls the enormous pleasure that she derived from the production of the magazine, as well as the professional ethos that underpinned its style. Indeed, compared to *Shrew* and *Scarlet Women*, *Red Rag* looked much more like a mainstream periodical publication using a moderate differentiation pattern that deployed columns, boxed text and images to ensure that the layout was lively and visually engaging. *Red Rag* was, from its first issue, a magazine with a distinct identity signalled by its consistent use of its bold red logo. The colour red was deployed frequently to produce eye-catching front covers that linked the magazine's commitment to feminism with the iconography of Marxism. The cover of issue two, for instance, is a full-page black and white image of World War Two women workers in headscarves and overalls, wielding shovels and pickaxes, an image that reflects the collective labour of the women involved in the production of the magazine itself. To underline its commitment to the intersections of social class and gender, this issue featured a discussion on Selma James's 1972 pamphlet, *Women, the Unions and Work*. Other front covers are equally bold: for example, issue three featured a cartoon image of a top-hatted capitalist (similar in style to the 'fat controller' in the *Thomas the Tank Engine* TV series) who refuses to provide equal pay and threatens to replace his woman worker with a more efficient man. On the front cover of issue five, a bell-bottomed woman stands on the cowcatcher of a train that looks as if it has come straight out of a Western film. She embodies an image of sexual liberation as she rides the train, holding aloft a red flag, hair whipping behind her as she travels into the future.

This comparatively stable discursive identity was also reflected in the content and format of the magazine. *Red Rag* was by no means as conventional and commercial in terms of format as *Spare Rib* but compared to *Scarlet Women* and *Shrew* it adhered to a set of normative rules associated with commercial magazine production. There were some advertisements in the back of the magazine, although it is doubtful that they generated an income. *Spare Rib* itself appears in the back pages, as do other radical publications or book catalogues along with announcements of meetings and conferences. Text is arranged in two chunky columns punctuated by feminist logos, cartoons and photographs. Headlines to articles come in different fonts, subheadings break up what are often dense and complex arguments while hand-drawn sketches and cartoons sustain the homemade collective ethos of the magazine. These headlines often borrow from the punning, tongue-in-cheek style of the tabloids. For instance, in issue thirteen, published in 1978, Ellen Malos and Frankie Rickford discuss the 'nuclear couple' in 'Closed Encounters', referencing the recent Stephen Spielberg film, *Close Encounters of the Third Kind* (*Shrew* [c. Spring] 1978: 9–11). In the same issue, extending this political analysis of personal relationships, 'Falling in Love Again' by Daphne Davies featured an image of Marlene Dietrich, graphically reinforcing the author's interrogation of what she refers to as the 'mythical or fantasy construction' of love (Ibid.: 12). Fragments of the song that launched Dietrich as a *femme fatale* are boxed and interspersed throughout the article providing a critique of heteronormativity.

Scarlet Women and the Socialist Feminist Current

The formation of the collective that produced the slightly later magazine, *Scarlet Women*, was, according to Penny Remfry (one of its founding members), a response to 'men not taking us seriously'.[4] Remfry's personal history reflects the ways in which transatlantic feminist cross-currents intersected with anti-colonial forms of protest including the anti-Vietnam war protests, as well as the Black Power movement. Living in Montreal and studying at McGill University in the tumultuous years between 1968 and 1972, Remfry was exposed to a heady mix of radicalism. In 1968, the Montreal Congress of Black Writers 'temporarily transformed Canada and Montreal into the centre of the Black Power Movement' (Austin 2007: 525). Only a month later, a conference calling for an end to the Vietnam War brought together black activists, white radicals including French Quebecois, as well as anti-imperialist groups from across the world. It was in the context of this highly charged political atmosphere that students began to occupy the computer rooms at Sir George Williams University in protest against racial discrimination, an occupation that ended in the arrest of ninety-seven protestors and the fatal wounding of one black activist. That same autumn, as Remfry recalls, Quebecois students marched on McGill University to demand that it teach in French.[5] When Remfry returned to the UK in 1972, her consciousness was already raised and she was 'ready for feminist action'.[6] Working and living in North Shields in North East England, she met women in the Labour party, women in the International Marxist group, women involved in the Tyneside Abortion campaign, as well as the Campaign Against Cuts. They were all committed to social change but also frustrated with 'sterile cliché mongering' of the traditional Labour movement (*Scarlet Women* May 1976: 2).

The *Scarlet Women* Collective was smaller and therefore less prone to deep and damaging divisions. Having said that, the policy of the magazine from the beginning, as Remfry points out, was flexible and practical: 'We weren't about having a line. We were about exploring issues. What does our practice tell us?'[7] In the first issue of *Scarlet Women* in May 1976, the Tyneside Coast Women published a paper that had been prepared for the Women's Liberation Movement conference in Newcastle in April of that year assessing the position of the Women's Liberation Movement in the mid-1970s and reflecting on the collapse of the socialist-feminist conferences. These had been turbulent times for feminists. Articles refer to the Mile End conference of 1975 as a particularly divisive meeting that ended in acrimony. In the wake of that disastrous conference, this first issue outlined the three main challenges for socialist feminism:

(a) To cope with problems arising out of practice – to theorise practice itself.
(b) As a resolution to the contradiction felt by being a 'feminist' working in the socialist movement and a 'socialist' active in women's movement.
(c) To deal with the issues raised by the radical feminists – outside the scope of traditional socialist analysis; to theorise our 'gut reaction' – our own oppression. (*Scarlet Woman* May 1976: 2)

The most modest, in terms of its style and format, *Scarlet Women* was perhaps the most ambitious in terms of its intellectual reach. Formed slightly later than the other two magazines, *Scarlet Women* had the advantage of seeing its sister publications rehearse some of the important issues facing socialist feminists. It was clear that *Scarlet Women* was not aspiring to be a glossy, but it was also, in some ways, distinct from its feminist sisters. Comparatively quiet in terms of its visual aesthetic, with relatively few images, particularly in the very low-budget early issues, the magazine also offered a perspective from the margins, quite literally, from the edges of England. The North East coast location signalled an identity connected to but distinct from the feminisms emerging out of London. While the magazine articulated a strong grassroots, community-based politics, this located, rooted political identity sought to connect up with other activist communities to 'establish a communication network linking socialist feminists through the country' (*Scarlet Women* May 1976: 4). Perhaps partly because the women on the coast felt slightly cut off from their sisters in the South, *Scarlet Women* aimed first and foremost to keep the socialist-feminist current flowing in spite of the fractures evident in the Mile End conference. The rootedness of the magazine in local activism is evident not only in the articles produced by the *Scarlet*

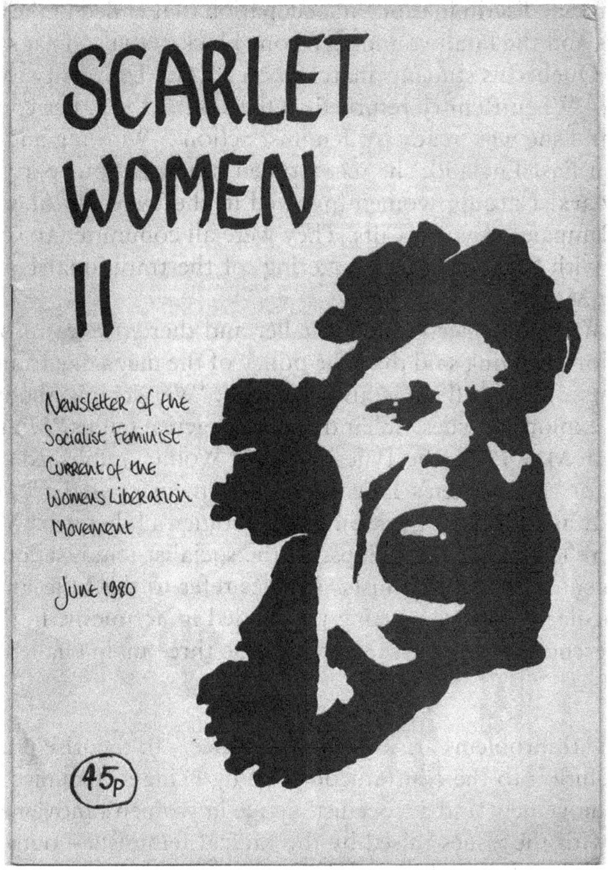

Figure 14.2 *Scarlet Woman* 11, June 1980.
(Image courtesy of Leeds University Library)

Women Collective but is also communicated through its discursive style. From the hand-written contents page that often served as the front cover, to the sentences that crossed the page from left to right, eschewing columns, the magazine resisted many of the normative rules of periodical publication. In doing so, it signalled its commitment to discursive debate, as well as its willingness to make a virtue of the small-scale, the locally produced and the modestly resourced. As the magazine moved from being the expression of the *Scarlet Women* Collective to being produced by a national editorial collective, its discursive identity shifted. Front covers become more expressive, deploying graphic art to convey key themes. For instance, the last issue on 'Women and New Technology' depicted on its front cover a woman caught in a web-like net (*Scarlet Women* January 1982) (see Plate 8), issue twelve on 'Women's Oppression Under Imperialism' (*Scarlet Women* [c. July] 1980) uses the feminist art work of Monica Sjöö on its front cover and the June 1980 issue on 'Women and Ireland' featured an inky black and white image of the face of an activist woman imposed on an outline of the island of Ireland.

Figure 14.3 *Scarlet Women* 12, 1980.
(Image courtesy of Leeds University Library)

By the late 1970s, socialist feminists were acutely aware that the decline of manufacturing and industry would have a profound effect on women and the women's movement. The *Scarlet Women* Collective continued to be active in the trade union movement and the Labour Party, as well as a number of other smaller issue-based groups. Yet they remained frustrated with the resistance on the Left to assimilating feminist concerns into discussion and political action. In an article reflecting on the three years of *Scarlet Women* – and three years where a socialist-feminist identity had been clearly articulated – Sally Alexander, Beatrix Campbell, Jean McCrindle, Lynne Segal, Sheila Rowbotham and Barbara Taylor summarised some of the key concerns for women on the Left. In 'Points for Discussion at Socialist Feminist Conference – 1979' there is recognition that women have mobilised and organised effectively but also a sense that feminist theory and practice has had relatively little impact on what might be described as a form of hegemonic masculinity on the Left:

> Lip service is paid to the women's movement while the male left continues to talk about the state, the class struggle, Eurocommunism, capital and the labour process without integrating socialist feminism's insights and revolutionary potential. Do they really read our literature or listen to our ideas – as applicable to the *whole* problem of socialist strategy? (*Scarlet Women* July 1979: 18)

While women had formed their own groups to analyse oppression from the perspective of gender as well as social class, these separate sites of analysis were not then informing debate in Left and socialist organisations. As the Tyneside Coast Women's Collective reminded its readers in 1979, it remained 'very difficult to develop a specifically feminist analysis and approach to traditional left areas of activity' (*Scarlet Women* July 1979: 4).

Most revealing, perhaps, is that Alexander et al.'s statement is published in *Scarlet Women* rather than *Red Rag*, given that some of the named authors, Beatrix Campbell and Sheila Rowbotham, for instance, were part of the *Red Rag* Collective. Many of the women attached to *Red Rag*, such as Val Charlton, had by 1979 become increasingly disillusioned with the Communist Party: 'I never felt that the Party changed very much in its attitudes towards women . . . I always felt the men made patronising token noises every now and again. They tolerated us, but I didn't really think they changed. That was why I ultimately left, out of total frustration and impatience with them.' (Wandor 1990: 166). The problem, according to Rob Henderson in 'Looking Over Our Shoulders', an article published in *Red Rag* in 1978, is not simply that the Left is unwilling to adopt some elements of feminist theory and practice, it is that some socialist feminists are themselves too wedded to the tactics of the 'patriarchal left' (*Red Rag* 13 [c. Spring] 1978: 7). These tactics sit uncomfortably with the anti-hierarchical, small-group, locally based activities of the Women's Liberation Movement and resulted in the damaging split at the Mile End conference in 1975, a split Henderson blames on the women in Trotskyist groups who took control.

These fractures, however, do not signal the demise of socialist feminism but rather its liberation. For instance, while in some ways the *Scarlet Women* editorial board saw little give on the traditional, hard-line Left to what was dismissed as 'bourgeois feminism', the magazine itself went on to produce several groundbreaking issues, remarkable for offering a feminist critique of oppression that extended beyond gender in order to think about what we would now describe in terms of intersectionality. This shift in perspective at least partly came out of the experience of attending conferences in 1977 in Amsterdam and Paris. The July 1979 issue of *Scarlet Woman* proposed a feminist conference in 1980 with an anti-imperialist focus. It also called for contributions to subsequent special issues of the magazine under the themes 'Women against Imperialism' (*Scarlet Women* July 1980) and 'Women and Ireland' (*Scarlet Women* June 1980). The 'Bolton bit of the *Scarlet Women* Collective' went on to produce the former, providing spaces for articles on 'Feminism and India', 'Women's Struggle for the Liberation of El Salvador', 'British Racism Institutionalised' and a particularly illuminating interview with Iranian women reflecting on the recent revolution and Iran's turn to Islamic fundamentalism. The Belfast Women's Collective produced the special issue on Ireland.[8]

From Transnational Periodical Networks to Grassroots Activism

The dialogic relations between these magazines throughout their publication histories point to the ways in which feminism flows across individual publications. *Scarlet Women* reproduced extracts from *Red Rag*, contributors from *Red Rag* wrote reports for *Scarlet Women* and particular issues are explored and then exchanged between publications. For instance, both *Shrew* and *Scarlet Women* produced issues, in 1978 and 1979 respectively, exploring the issue of violence, a subject capaciously defined in terms of the damage done to the environment by global capital, military conflict and forms of everyday violence experienced by women in the private and public spheres through sexual harassment and physical abuse. According to the editors of *Shrew*, this violence refers, for instance, to the Swiss cosmetic company that includes hexachlorophene (a poisonous substance) in its deodorants and baby soap. The same company has produced defoliants for use in Vietnam and was implicated in the Seveso disaster of 1976.[9] An anti-capitalist perspective is aligned to an anti-imperialist perspective that challenges Britain's occupation of Northern Ireland and the United States' recent involvement in Vietnam. Environmental concerns repeatedly intersect with the non-violent ethos in circulation in the magazine. The exploitation of natural resources, as the women contributing to *Shrew* recognise, is a form of what Rob Nixon (2011) has recently referred to as 'slow violence'. An emerging and powerful alliance between feminism and anti-nuclear activism is evident in the pages of *Shrew* (Summer 1978), rehearsing the arguments that would underpin the Greenham Common protest which began in 1981. The deployment of American cruise missiles at the RAF Greenham Common airbase becomes a specifically feminist issue when violence is reframed in a way that links acts of micro-aggression experienced by women in their everyday lives to forms of military and state aggression. This non-violent, 'peace' feminism flows into and consolidates the communication practices of the Greenham protest described by Hannah Feigenbaum (2013: 1–13) as effectively unifying feminists in their opposition to the government's policy on nuclear weapons.

In 1979, a year later, *Scarlet Women* addressed forms of institutional violence against women from a socialist-feminist perspective arguing in its editorial that 'the combination of the power of men and the power of wealth is a particularly lethal one for women' (*Scarlet Women* December 1979: 1). Parita Trivedy wrote from the front line about the sexual and racial forms of police brutality directed at the black women who were protesting about the killing of Blair Peach. Peach had been fatally wounded by a police officer, probably a member of the Special Patrol Group, at an anti-fascist rally in Southall in April 1979.[10] The Southall Action Committee, formed in the wake of Peach's death, demanded that charges against protestors should be dropped, that an independent public enquiry into Peach's death should be launched and the Special Patrol Group should be disbanded. The many and varied forms of violence experienced by women in the public and private spheres were signalled in the titles of other articles included in this issue: 'Reclaiming the Night', 'Pornography', 'Women, Violence and the Law' and 'Rape, Like Charity, Begins at Home'. One particularly powerful essay, 'Fighting Poverty Through Prostitution' by the English Collective of Prostitutes provided a searing critique of a legal system that forced women onto unsafe streets by criminalising soliciting and offering little to no protection against sexual violence. The treatment of sex workers in the media, the article pointed out, constructs them either in salacious terms or as downtrodden victims of sexual exploitation. The reality was more complex; there is no singular identity, no one 'truth' that describes the experience of women sex workers:

> We are like other women: mothers, students, full-time housewives, teenagers, black and white, lesbian or not. We come from different countries and different backgrounds. Some of us are young, some of us aren't. We are street walkers, callgirls, work for escort agencies or madams. Some of us are full time on the game but most of us are part-timers. The only difference between us and other women is the illegality which divides 'good' women from 'bad' women. It is a violence against women generally to force us to sell our bodies in order to survive but it's double violence when we're punished for it. (*Scarlet Women* December 1979: 20)

As the editors of this issue point out, 'it is important to look at the cultural and legal systems which reflect and support actual physical violence', as well as the everyday forms of violence undermining 'our integrity and autonomy'. This understanding of violence informed initiatives such as the Tyneside Rape Crisis Centre, established in the same year as this issue of *Scarlet Women*. In other words, here is a good example of the ways in which the theorising and debate within magazines provides the theoretical ground for feminist practice. As Penny Remfry, one of the founding members of the Tyneside Rape Crisis Centre points out, the trustees of the board still 'hold onto feminist ways of doing things' by listening to each other, discussing issues and reaching decisions through consensus.[11] The ethos of #WeBelieveYou underpins the centre's approach to gender-based violence, as does a specifically feminist and, one might argue, socialist understanding of the reasons for that violence. Shifting the emphasis away from the 'individual event' and the victim blaming that comes with that, the Tyneside Rape Crisis Centre's mission statement resonated with the socialist-feminist perspectives articulated in *Scarlet Women* by focusing on the structures of inequality that sustain forms of violence rather than individual agents or victims.[12]

Conclusion

According to the *Scarlet Women* Collective, 'We were not trying to reduce feminism to a set of Left phrases, nor yet trying to accommodate it to a workerist/economist framework. Our feminism broke that old framework apart.' (*Scarlet Women* May 1976: 2). That 'framework' referred to the patriarchal structures in Left organisations that marginalised women and the issues that most concerned them. Having found themselves silenced on the Left and by the Left, socialist feminists created textual spaces in magazines to articulate a critique of patriarchal capitalism but also to put that critique to work in their everyday activism. Through collaboration and contestation, a transformative political agency emerges in these magazines, a political agency capable of effective action at the grassroots, local as well as at the national and transnational levels.

While women's movement magazines return us to these discursive contexts and make visible women's contribution to debate in the public sphere, perhaps more importantly, they provide a way of understanding how activist agencies are formed and how they affect social change. As discussed at the beginning of this chapter,

Terry Lovell's theoretical engagement with a concept of transformative political agency in the work of Pierre Bourdieu and Judith Butler might be adapted in order to explain the role of the activist magazine in the formation of that agency. If, as Lovell (2003: 3) suggests, the ability of subordinate groups to act is a 'function of ensemble performances', such performances, I would suggest, are often constituted in and through activist magazines, in the intellectually rigorous and affectively charged debates within and between these publications. These magazines become sites of collective agency, not only in terms of the production of the magazine itself but in terms of the production of what Bourdieu refers to as a 'practical group' that acquires enough authority, in spite of its marginal position, to produce social change (Lovell 2003: 10). Crucially, this understanding of the role of magazines as ensemble performances shifts attention away from individual acts of resistance and instead compels us to focus on collective forms of activism, how social groups are formed and sustained and how they are mobilised. If, as Lovell argues, 'transformative political agency lies in the interstices of interaction, in collective social movements in formation in specific circumstances', I would suggest that the historical record of that interaction lies within the pages of activist magazines (Lovell 2003: 2).

Examining activist magazines points to the ways in which feminist agency might be understood as the function of 'ensemble performances' that emerge in response to contemporary contexts. These magazines return us to the debates as they were happening, reminding us of the historical circumstances that led to the emergence of particular campaigns and actions, providing us with an interpretive strategy that understands feminist agency as contingent, strategic and above all collective and making feminist activism visible within the wider context of social movement history.

Notes

1. See Browne (2014); Bruley and Forster (2016, 2018); Forster (2016); Hughes (2015); Jolly (2014); Rees (2010); and Setch (2002).
2. The first issue of *Scarlet Women* was called *Scarlet Woman*, but after the second issue the title of *Scarlet Women* was used consistently.
3. For a more detailed discussion of the 'Goddess' issue of *Shrew*, see Forster (2016).
4. Interview with Penny Remfry, former member of the *Scarlet Women* Collective, 26 July 2018. I would like to thank Penny for being so generous with her time and for assisting in the development of this chapter.
5. Penny Remfry's analysis of political activism in Montreal in 1968 provided a slightly different perspective to Austin's, highlighting the significance of the Quebecois separatist movement, as well as the division between the Catholic-French and Protestant-English in Quebec.
6. Interview with Penny Remfry.
7. Interview with Penny Remfry.
8. There were 3,500 copies of issue 13 on 'Women and Ireland' printed according to a letter sent from the *Scarlet Women* National Editorial Collective to the Belfast Women's Collective, 24 June 1980.
9. The Seveso disaster saw the accidental release of six tonnes of chemicals into the atmosphere above the small Italian town of Seveso, north of Milan.
10. Blair Peach was almost certainly killed by a member of the Special Patrol Group, an elite riot squad. As part of the investigation into the killing, Special Patrol Group lockers were raided, uncovering unauthorised weapons and a collection of Nazi regalia.

11. Interview with Penny Remfry.
12. See the Tyneside Rape Crisis Centre's website for its mission statement <https://rctn.org.uk>.

Works cited

Ardis, A. 2012. 'Editor's Introduction Mediamorphosis: Print Culture and Transatlantic/Transnational Public Sphere(s)'. *Modernism/Modernity* 19.3: v–vii.

Austin, D. 2007. 'All Roads Led to Montreal: Black Power, the Caribbean, and the Black Radical Tradition'. *Journal of African-American History* 92.4: 516–39.

Browne, S. 2014. *The Women's Liberation Movement in Scotland*. Manchester: Manchester University Press.

Bruley, S. and L. Forster. 2016. 'Historicising the Women's Liberation Movement'. *Women's History Review* 25.5: 697–700.

Bruley, S. and L. Forster. eds. 2018. *Historicising the Women's Liberation Movement in the Western World, 1960–1999*. London: Routledge.

Calhoun, C. 1995. *Critical Social Theory: Culture, History and the Challenge of Difference*. Oxford: Blackwell.

Cohen, D. R. 2015. '"Strange Collisions": Keywords Toward an Intermedial Periodical Studies'. *ESC: English Studies in Canada* 41.1: 93–104.

DiCenzo, M., L. Delap and L. Ryan. 2011. *Feminist Media History: Suffrage, Periodicals and the Public Sphere*. Basingstoke: Palgrave.

Feigenbaum, A. 2013. 'Written in the Mud: (Proto) Zine-Making and Autonomous Media at the Greenham Common Women's Peace Camp'. *Feminist Media Studies* 13.1, 2013: 1–13.

Forster, L. 2015. *Magazine Movements: Women's Culture, Feminisms and Media Form*. London: Bloomsbury.

Forster, L. 2016. 'Spreading the Word: Feminist Print Culture in the Women's Liberation Movement'. *Women's History Review* 12.5: 812–31.

Green, B. 2012. 'Complaints of Everyday Life: Feminist Periodical Culture and Correspondence Columns in *The Woman Worker*, *Women Folk* and *The Freewoman*'. *Modernism/Modernity* 19.3: 461–85.

Hammill, F., P. Hjartarson and H. McGregor. 2015. 'Introducing Magazines and/as Media: The Aesthetics and Politics of Serial Form'. *ESC: English Studies in Canada* 41.1: 1–18.

Hughes, C. 2015. *Young Lives on the Left: Sixties Activism and the Liberation of the Self*. Manchester: Manchester University Press.

Jolly, M. 2014. 'The Feeling Behind the Slogans: Abortion Campaigning and Feminist Mood-Work circa 1979'. *New Formations: A Journal of Culture/Theory/Politics* 82: 100–14.

Lovell, T. 2003. 'Resisting with Authority: Historical Specificity, Agency and the Performative Self'. *Theory, Culture and Society* 20.1: 1–17.

Nixon, R. 2011. *Slow Violence and the Environmentalism of the Poor*. Cambridge MA, Harvard University Press.

Owen, N. 2013. 'Men and the 1970s British Women's Liberation Movement'. *The Historical Journal* 56.3: 801–26.

Rees, J. 2010. '"Are You a Lesbian?" Challenges in Recording and Analysing the Women's Liberation Movement in England'. *History Workshop Journal* 69: 177–87.

Setch, E. 2002. 'The Face of Metropolitan Feminism: The London Women's Liberation Workshop, 1969–79'. *20th Century British History* 13.2: 171–90.

Wandor, M. 1990. *Once A Feminist: Stories of a Generation*. London: Virago.

15

Women's Voice, the Rise and Fall of a Socialist-Feminist Newspaper in Britain 1972–82

Sue Bruley

Introduction

The rise of the Women's Liberation Movement in the late 1960s led to an explosion of feminist activity in Britain throughout the 1970s and 1980s, sometimes referred to as 'second-wave feminism'. Unlike the US women's movement, the British Women's Liberation Movement had a distinctive socialist-feminist current, including both aligned (party members) and non-aligned women. Many left-inclined women had been involved in the 1960s Vietnam Solidarity Campaign and the Anti-Apartheid Movement. Organisation skills learnt in the new social movements of the late 1960s stood them in good stead when women decided to address the issue of gender inequality. An essential part of this activism was print media, particularly feminist periodicals. As Laurel Forster (2016: 812–31) has observed, engaging in print media was an inherent aspect of the feminist struggle. The new feminist print culture included a number of socialist-feminist journals. In many ways *Women's Voice* is the most interesting of these publications of this period, with the largest circulation and, at its height, there is evidence that it engaged working-class women more than any other socialist-feminist paper of the time. The intention of this chapter is to explore the rise of *Women's Voice* in the early 1970s and its troubled relationship to the International Socialists (IS), which was renamed the Socialist Workers Party (SWP) in 1976, and to account for its decline and controversial demise in 1982 (Bruley 2014). This research also aims to shed light on the Women's Liberation Movement of this period, and particularly the rise and decline of socialist-feminism. Given growing historiographical interest in the Women's Liberation Movement, it is hoped that this chapter will advance research in this important area of British postwar social history.

As Celia Hughes (2015: 248) has indicated, many women who joined IS found the experience transformative. However, IS also had an oppressive masculinist culture and attempts by IS women to explore the link between class and gender oppression were seen by the leadership as a deviation from the class struggle which, in their view, was the only route to women's liberation (Hughes 2015: 266; Birchall 2011: 463).[1] It is widely assumed that the centralised Leninist-style control of the membership prevented IS/SWP from engaging successfully with the socialist-feminist current within the autonomous women's movement. This chapter aims to demonstrate that, in attempting to account for the decline and demise of *Women's Voice*, it is crucial to focus more on the changing historical context, particularly the political impact of the economic downturn in the late 1970s and the changing nature of the late 1970s and early 1980s women's movement.

First, it is necessary to examine the background to IS/SWP. The USSR's invasion of Hungary in 1956 initiated a significant decline in the Soviet domination of Communist politics in Europe and a flowering of the movement which became known as the 'New Left'. Tony Cliff was a Trotskyist with considerable oratory powers who started an informal group around the theoretical journal *Socialist Review* in 1950. In the new political climate post-1956, Cliff's small group slowly gained momentum and political influence. By 1962 *Socialist Review* had about 100 members and relaunched itself as the 'International Socialists' (Birchall 2011: 201, 213, 463–4). Cliff's theory of the USSR as 'state capitalist' and the slogan 'neither Washington nor Moscow but International Socialism' appealed to anti-Stalinist Marxists, particularly in the growing student movement. IS was an influential force in both the Vietnam Solidarity Campaign and the student movement, leading to a membership upsurge to about 1,000 by the end of 1968 (Callaghan 1987: 95). Although IS was loosely based on Trotskyist ideas, it did not regard itself as *the* revolutionary party, but merely a group within the nebulous world of the Far Left in Britain (Callaghan 1987: 95). In contrast to more 'hard line' Trotskyist sects, IS members in the early years had a non-sectarian culture and, on some issues, engaged in collaborative work with other groups, principally the International Marxist Group. The gains made were not sustained and membership fell back, causing the leadership to turn increasingly to the syndicalist notion of political change through class struggle as manifested in industrial disputes. The IS leadership, and particularly Cliff, resorted to a simplistic form of 'workerism' with revolutionary activity seen as overwhelmingly male and organised at the workplace (Birchall 2011: 366–7). The industrial militancy surge of the early 1970s resulted in a membership rise to 3,310 and a print order for the IS paper *Socialist Worker* of 40,000 (Callaghan 1987: 98–9).

From 1975, industrial militancy declined, with fewer disputes and many strikes ending in failure. In late 1976, as the economy declined, unemployment rose and IS membership dwindled, the leadership decided to relaunch the group as *the* vanguard party and changed the name to the Socialist Workers Party (Callaghan 1984: 120). This move was accompanied by an increasingly sectarian stance with no pretence of collaboration with other Marxist sects. It did, however, attempt to exert influence through building broad left organisations around the issues of racism and unemployment. The Right to Work Campaign, aimed particularly at youth, had some success in attracting publicity through its Right to Work marches. The surge of racist activity at this time was a source of great concern among the Left. In an effort to staunch the rise of the blatantly racist National Front, the SWP launched the Anti-Nazi League in late 1977 and in April 1978 the league organised a Rock Against Racism carnival which attracted 80,000 people (Callaghan 1987: 102). By the early 1980s the postwar consensus was crumbling. The rise of the New Right led to an assault on the working class. The SWP's work with the unemployed and its opposition to Tory spending cuts led to a revival of interest in the Far Left, but very much in defensive mode, in contrast to the more assertive early 1970s.

The IS/SWP approach to the women's movement was typical in many ways of European Marxist parties since the late nineteenth century. Following the tradition of Engels, Lenin and Clara Zetkin, European Marxists saw the autonomous women's movement as a 'bourgeois diversion'. Using the slogan 'class war, not sex war' it was argued that the only road to women's emancipation was through socialist revolution (Bruley 1986). It was recognised, however, that as women were politically 'backward', special propaganda methods were necessary to recruit women to class consciousness and the revolutionary party. A women's paper was seen therefore as a useful propaganda tool. In early twentieth-century European Communist Parties, women constituted a very small percentage of the membership (Bruley 1986).[2] Both Russian Bolsheviks and the German Communists developed their own women's papers aimed specifically at recruiting working-class women (James 1980; Birchall 2011: 470).[3] The chief concern was that the wives of the male cadres would put a brake on the advanced male workers and therefore inhibit the working class as a whole.

The same view was held by the IS/SWP leadership in the period between 1968 and 1982. In addition, the group's culture was organised around the identity of the revolutionary as a masculine construct. Sexual harassment was normalised and most meetings were held in the evenings which prevented the involvement of many women. Although the more enlightened IS/SWP members were beginning to realise that their outlook was outmoded, the leadership, and Cliff particularly, failed to comprehend that the working class was undergoing significant changes. Steadily rising numbers of women in the postwar workforce meant that women workers aged 20–64 constituted 52% of the 1971 total labour force (Lewis 1992: 65). Starting with the strike by women sewing machinists at the massive Dagenham Ford plant in 1968, which held up production for three weeks, women were increasingly turning to industrial militancy, particularly over equal pay.

From late 1969 women in IS were beginning to engage with the Women's Liberation Movement, joining women's groups and taking on the ideas of second-wave feminism. About thirty IS women attended the first national Women's Liberation Movement Conference at Ruskin College Oxford in early 1970 (Paczuska 1990: 152–4).[4] Subsequently, an IS women's newsletter was launched and five issues were produced before it was officially adopted and transformed into *Women's Voice* in 1972. The newsletter was run by two volunteers, had no financial backing from IS and there was no official editorial policy. It was a very amateur effort with little attempt at visual display or design. Issue 3 reports that some IS comrades had made 'scornful and unhelpful remarks' about the newsletter (*IS Women's Newsletter* 3 April 1971: 1).[5] Sheila Rowbotham (1972: 99) also commented on the attitude of 'joking incredulity' when women tried to raise the issue of women's liberation with IS men. The newsletter also evidences that IS women held strong views that they had to fight for their socialist-feminism both inside IS and in the Women's Liberation Movement: 'For the revolutionary party, women's liberatison is not a luxury but a necessity if it is to perform its historic tasks.' (*IS Women's Newsletter* 3 April 1971: 6).

The First Phase, *Women's Voice* is Launched

Women's Voice was launched in Summer 1972 during the Conservative government led by Ted Heath, amid a period of industrial strife, raging inflation and Britain's entry into the European Economic Community (known then as the Common Market), covering a wide range of news and comment related to women. The paper attempted both to focus on and be accessible to working-class women. It was explicitly socialist, pro-union and openly used as a recruiting tool for IS. It supported activism, however small-scale, and encouraged women to be writers and organisers, promoting the idea that women should think of themselves as political actors capable of securing change. It minimised theory, instead aiming to provide practical support for activists and a 'good read'. It had an attractive layout, with plenty of humour, particularly relating to absurdly sexist behaviour. It was a sixteen-page bimonthly magazine, which IS members attempted to sell on housing estates, at shopping precincts, IS meetings and public demonstrations.

Women's Voice originated with very varied content, although by 1974 the coverage became much more slanted towards women in industry (see below). Equal pay was vigorously promoted and attention drawn to the deficiencies of the 1970 Equal Pay Act. Unequal opportunities which excluded women from large areas of employment and career progression through promotion were also exposed. Maggie Black wrote from Coventry about her work for a small engineering company. She refers to management's paternal attitude, whilst simultaneously paying women only half of the male workers' wages (*WV* 10, [c. March 1974]: 3).[6] In the 1970s, large numbers of women worked in offices, mostly restricted to menial work in the 'typing pool'. *Women's Voice* provided a more realistic view of secretarial work, attempting to undermine its romantic image. Mel Hartley wrote an amusing piece on the 'Lesser spotted secretary bird', describing a secretarial course which trained her to make coffee for the boss and arrange flowers. The course included two days of compulsory make-up, fashion and hairdressing which she found humiliating, 'I just had to call a halt when it came to being told that I was to sit down in front of a full length mirror and have make up smeared all over my face by the "instructor".' (*WV* 13, November 1974: 3). Considerable attention was given to union issues. *Women's Voice* admitted that there was a sexist and patriarchal culture in most trade unions, making life difficult for women, but argued that opting out was not the answer.

Women were at the forefront of industrial militancy during these years. The most important dispute involving women was the strike in GEC's massive Coventry plant, which began in July 1973 when 200 women walked out over a grading dispute. At the time, GEC was Britain's largest private employer. Sadly, the women had to fight both management and the union convenor, who refused to support the strike. After four weeks, with the strike still solid and spreading to other GEC factories, management capitulated (*WV* 8, September 1973: 8–9).[7] Women who had not previously been thought of as militant were becoming involved in industrial action. Health workers, including nurses, who were becoming unionised, featured regularly, making it clear that an angelic image was not enough, they wanted better pay and working conditions.[8]

Due to recent inward migration, British industry, particularly the clothing trade, employed many Asian women, often in conditions of sweated labour. An examination of *Women's Voice* in the early 1970s challenges the current view that the early Women's Liberation Movement was dominated by white middle-class women who failed to see oppression beyond their own personal lives (Thomlinson 2016: 1–2).[9] It consistently supported women of colour, both in the community and at work. The *Women's Voice* production team consisted mainly of white middle-class socialist-feminists who directed their energies towards developing working-class women writers, including

WOMENS VOICE

Number 12 5p PAPER OF INTERNATIONAL SOCIALISTS WOMEN

Fascist appeal to housewives

Hope

Racialist

Drudgery

EQUAL PAY

THIS YEAR NEXT YEAR SOME TIME NEVER!

£15,000 is being spent by the Labour Party on an advertising campaign to win women's votes for October's election. They're spending this money to convince us that Labour's done great things for women! Don't waste time trying to work out what they've done, because by the end of the year I'm sure we'll be saying that the only thing Labour did for women in 1974 was to dream up an expensive vote catching campaign! It's certainly let us down on the one most important single issue—Equal Pay for women by 1975.

Publicity

In June, Michael Foot told trade union leaders that the government would not be using its powers to compel employers to implement the Equal Pay Act. Instead the government are to embark on a publicity campaign telling employers about their obligations under the Act. They also plan to set up an Industrial Arbitration Board to which you can refer agreements that discriminate between men and women workers. BIG DEAL! That should really have Arnold Weinstock, head of the multi-million pound GEC combine shaking in his boots. He's the man who said, 'I'm all in favour of Equal Pay, so long as the men's pay is brought down to the level of the women's.'

A publicity campaign is not going to change his mind, and the Labour government knows it. The truth is that the government has effectively washed its hands of the Equal Pay Act, and is allowing employers to continue their discrimination unchecked. The government's decision means there will be no such thing as Equal Pay in 1975 [illegible] but they won't be telling us that in their advertising campaign for women's votes.

Hollow

It all makes Barbara Castle's statements about Equal Pay sound pretty hollow. 'My Act', she said in 197[illegible] 'represents the best possible formula for Equal Pay anywhere in the World. It combines statutory protection with the opportunity for strong collective bargaining.'

If what we have now is the best in the world—then God help the rest of the world.

And the trade unions aren't doing all they could to help women get a decent living wage either. One union, the UPW openly discriminates against women. It has a recruiting BAN on full-time female labour. At the other end of the scale, even unions who tack equal pay claims onto wage demands, like the AUEW make little attempt to win them.

Hopeful

However the most encouraging event on the equal pay front this year has in fact come from the unions—the battle by SOGAT, the print workers union, to abolish the lowest grade, Class 4, points the way for women workers to obtain meaningful equal pay. Abolition of low paid grades avoids all the pitfalls of job evaluation and the strings that employers attack to equal pay. Abolition of low grades ensures that *all* wages are living wages. In fact the strike that started the whole Equal Pay battle in 1968 was over the same issue. Women sewing machinists at Dagenham struck—not just for higher pay—but also in protest against low grading.

And now, in the autumn of 1975 the battle hots up again. Already we've seen women in various parts of the country taking up the fight—over threshold payments at Wingrove Rogers in Merseyside and for Equal Pay at GEC in Heywood, are two recent examples. Women workers everywhere must fight for Equal Pay now, if we are to get it at all.

FULL EQUAL PAY NOW WITH NO STRINGS!
ABOLISH ALL LOW GRADES!

Figure 15.1 Equal Pay, *Women's Voice* 12.
(Image source: Feminist Archive North)

articles which exposed racism and gave a voice to women of colour. They may not have had the terminology, but they were adopting an intersectional approach, seeing class, race and gender oppression as interlinked. In a 1974 article with the headline 'Sorry Mum, blacks are not invited', Martha Osamor described her life as a mother of three children and the persistent discrimination that her children experienced at school (*WV* 12 [c. September/October 1974]: 3). The paper was also concerned about police harassment of young black men. The disadvantaged position of Asian women at work was also raised by *Women's Voice*: in West London many women of Asian origin were employed in clothing sweatshops or catering and cleaning at Heathrow Airport. These women workers were increasingly making their voices heard: an article on the Wyuna factory in Southall in 1973 described their 'appalling conditions and incredibly low wages'. The article forcefully asserts that 'Verbally opposing racism and sex discrimination is **not** enough. Every conceivable pressure must be brought to bear to help better the conditions of women workers in these industries.' (*WV* 7, July 1973: 4).

Women's Voice supported women who were active on housing issues, most notably opposing the new 'Fair Rents' policy for council tenants which provoked rent strikes on some estates, plus articles on squatters and homelessness. The paper publicised the financial plight of low-income families created by 25 per cent inflation. *Women's Voice* supported women as consumers and attacked excessive profits in, for example, the dieting industry (*WV* 11, [c. July/August 1974]: 3). It exposed the practice of creating demand for unnecessary products such as 'Freshette', a vaginal deodorant containing harmful chemicals which destroyed the body's natural bacteria that fight off infections such as thrush (*WV* 5, March 1973: 6). The paper also provided coverage of the Northern Ireland 'Troubles', offering a woman's perspective on the occupation by British troops (*WV* 12, September 1974: 5). It also covered sex role stereotyping in schools, particularly the struggle for non-sexist reading resources.

One of the great strengths of *Women's Voice* was, unlike other contemporary socialist-feminist periodicals, its success in gaining working-class women writers who offered simple stories of women's working lives. Although frequently formulaic, such accounts gave prominence to readers and they did broadcast the message that these working-class women were noticed and valued. There were, however, some *Women's Voice* writers who were beginning, in more subjective ways, to reflect on the issues relating to women workers, particularly those with young children. Gillian Auciano from Ilford wrote that she was forced to find work which was near home and fitted in with her childcare responsibilities. She understood the limitations of such work: 'there's little chance of career prospects! Our priorities usually lie at home, our job is secondary.' (*WV* 8, September 1973: 7). *Women's Voice* gave housebound women opportunities to refashion an identity beyond the confines of home and family. This tendency was also reflected in the letters page where women responded, often in critical terms, to the magazine content. Sonia MacKay from Peterborough responded to an article on Northern Ireland saying that, although she found the article readable, it was 'too long and the print too small' which she thought would deter women readers. She added that she wanted 'more pointers to what can be done to change things' (*WV* 13, November 1974: 6). It is clear from the letters page that the views expressed did not necessarily toe the party line and offered room for discussion and engagement with non-IS political positions.

The way that *Women's Voice* developed genuine engagement with working-class women differentiated it from other contemporary socialist-feminist papers. International events, however, received poor coverage in the early years, with only the occasional article. *Women's Voice* did rather better on historical articles with regular features and reviews which were informative and inspirational, offering readers progressive women thinkers and activists as role models. Robyn Dasey from Portsmouth wrote about suffragette Sylvia Pankhurst, who broke from her mother Emmeline and sister Christabel to organise working women in London's East End (*WV* 7, July 1973: 10–11). The book reviews were also interesting and often challenging, sometimes publicising reprints of significant socialist-feminist works. The review of Bolshevik socialist-feminist Alexandra Kollontai's short tract *Communism and the Family* outlined her ideas for the family after the 1917 revolution. The reviewer then analysed the pamphlet's relevance to modern society, concluding that Kollontai placed too much emphasis on the role of the state in socialising children (*WV* 4, January 1973: 14).

Figure 15.2 The Perfect Mother, *Women's Voice* 7.
(Image source: Feminist Archive North)

IS blossomed during the years of student radicalism in the late 1960s – many IS branches were based around universities and many members were middle-class lecturers, students and teachers. The early 1970s upsurge in militancy led IS to the 'turn to industry' and particularly to the promotion of factory cells rather than geographically based branches. Women members of IS constituted 20 per cent of the membership, but very few of those were women in industry.[10] IS was faced with a dilemma: a significant aspect of the new wave of militancy was the number of disputes involving women, including women of colour. These workers had previously been considered 'backward' in terms of class consciousness, in contrast to male industrial workers who were considered 'advanced'. IS had to adjust to this new reality but was poorly equipped to do so. The leadership, accustomed to the idea of militants being white male workers in heavy industry and women (including their wives) full-time housewives, was becoming outmoded. The high demands on IS members for paper sales, attendance at meetings and so on, unsurprisingly meant that most IS members were young single men. IS culture, based around pubs, drinking, evening meetings and sexual permissiveness in student-dominated branches, aggravated matters, making it difficult for women with families to engage, especially Asian women. The 1974 IS National Conference launched a much more serious effort to recruit women in industry, part of which was pumping resources into *Women's Voice*.[11] In March 1975 the format switched from magazine to newspaper. Articles became heavily focused on work and editorial control was much tighter, with IS keen to promote the 'party line' and use the paper as an organiser rather than a magazine for socialist-feminist women. Much of the humour and visual appeal was lost, resulting in a narrow, strident work-focused publication.

The Middle Phase: *Women's Voice* Peaks

The 'workerist' strategy of shifting IS into workplace cells instead of geographic branches was a dismal failure and *Women's Voice* failed to take off as an industrial paper for women.[12] Despite this, the paper began to enjoy new success during 1975, due largely to the launch of the campaign to defend the 1967 Abortion Act. The Act, which sanctioned legal abortions in certain circumstances, provoked a counter movement. The Society for Protection of the Unborn Child was formed specifically to repeal the 1967 Act, with backing from a number of MPs and religious bodies. The threat posed by the James White Abortion Bill to the 1967 Act was serious, and consequently the Women's Liberation Movement responded with the formation of the National Abortion Campaign, cited as 'one of the most successful feminist campaigning organisations of second wave feminism' (Hoggart 2013). IS *and Women's Voice* were soon heavily involved in the National Abortion Campaign and urged members, including men, to support the campaign in every way possible, at branch, district and national levels, attracting many new readers to *Women's Voice*. In this way, *Women's Voice*, and therefore socialist-feminist perspectives, were at the centre of IS politics for the first time. On 21 June 1975 a demonstration in defence of the 1967 Act was attended by 40,000 people (*WV* 19, July 1975: 1).

On the strength of this, a *Women's Voice* rally attracting 600 attendees was held in Manchester in November 1975, focusing on the key themes of defence of abortion rights and equal pay (Anon. 2013). Although the James White Bill was defeated, it was clear that other attempts to undermine the 1967 Act, such as William Benyon's 1977 Abortion Bill, would follow, therefore momentum was maintained and *Women's Voice* continued to be a vociferous defender of the 1967 Act. Meanwhile *Women's Voice* was relaunched in January 1977 as a twenty-four-page socialist women's paper as part of the transition from IS to SWP. It had an impressive colourful format consciously emulating commercial women's papers *Woman* and *Woman's Own*, but also borrowing ideas for material and approaches from *Spare Rib*. In June 1977 the print order had increased to 8,500 with a paid sale of 63 per cent, almost double 1976 levels.[13] A staggering 800 copies of *Women's Voice* were sold at the abortion demonstration against the Benyon Bill.[14] In 1978 it was decided to launch *Women's Voice* as a national organisation and 'sister' to the SWP.[15] In fact, ad hoc *Women's Voice* groups had formed spontaneously on a local basis since 1974, many in London. Besides rallies and other public meetings, *Women's Voice* groups issued pamphlets, speakers' notes and publicity stickers. In June 1978 (the undoubted high point year of *Women's Voice*) a Sheffield *Women's Voice* rally was attended by 1,000 people (Birchall 2011: 465).

Although *Women's Voice* no longer aimed to be an industrial paper, it still devoted regular space to women's paid work, particularly the fight for equal pay. The Equal Pay Act – phased in during 1970–5 – raised women's expectations and *Women's Voice* covered many disputes on this issue. The Equal Pay Act was fraught with problems as, in many women's jobs, there were no men performing comparable work and, therefore, a case for equal pay was very difficult to make. Many employers responded to equal pay claims with job evaluation schemes which invariably failed to regrade women to anything approaching the lowest men's rate. In Spring 1977 the 400 women at the west Scotland Laird-Portch factory, manufacturing clothes for Jaeger and other premium clothing outlets, went on strike for equal pay. The union convenor Ellen Nicklin told *Women's Voice* that it was soon clear that the management 'had no intention of granting equal pay' (*WV* 6, June 1977: 16–17). As with many women's disputes, the union refused to make the strike official and often stated publicly that it would not support equal pay. In some cases, the union colluded with management to exclude the employment of women, as in the Rover plant at Solihull, Birmingham, where all new jobs had to be ratified by the Transport and General Workers Union. The only equal pay dispute which succeeded at this time was the strike at Trico windscreen-wiper factory in Brentford, West London, which started in May 1976 and continued for twenty-one weeks (Stephenson 2016). In September 1976, *Women's Voice* produced a special issue on Trico. The next issue reported the successful outcome of the strike and also that male workers in the factory had failed to fully support the women. *Women's Voice* groups actively supported striking women, supporting pickets and collecting for striking families. *Women's Voice* also spoke for part-time workers who were often highly exploited. In a period of rising unemployment, many unemployed married women did not bother to claim benefits: *Women's Voice* urged them to make themselves visible and campaign for the 'right to work'.

IS/SWP recognised that the National Abortion Campaign campaign attracted many middle-class women and also that a significant proportion of them were based at home, and the magazine content reflected this. In many ways the new *Women's Voice* of 1977 was an improved version of the early *Women's Voice* of 1972–3. There was more international coverage, including articles on the new Zimbabwe, and Turkish women – written in Turkish. Sexuality began to be discussed, with an article on 'Woman and Orgasm' based on the American Hite Report, which revealed that women were much more likely to reach orgasm from masturbation than penetrative vaginal sex with their husbands (*WV* 6, June 1977: 14). The article urged women to 'break out of the masculine model of normality' with regard to sex. Gay liberation had made an impact on the Left by this time and *Women's Voice* began to recognise gay pride and gave full support to the Women's Liberation Movement demand for an end to discrimination against lesbians.

The increased circulation of *Women's Voice* generated numerous letters, many critical. Maureen Tootoh, writing from 'one of the poorest parts of Manchester', urged the paper to 'drop the middle-class image' (*WV* 2, February 1977: 22). An article published on household budgets and the impact of inflation by Nikki Mellor, based on her own family, prompted Pat Harlow of Newcastle's response that many households had to manage on far less money than Mellor (Ibid.). Readers also complained about unexplained abbreviations that made new readers feel outsiders. Some of *Women's Voice*'s problems stemmed from being a socialist-feminist publication aimed at a range of audiences. It is very much to the paper's credit that it was responsive to readers and amenable to critical appraisal.

The Final Phase – *Women's Voice* Loses its Way

The rightward shift in British politics continued with Margaret Thatcher's Conservative government in May 1979. Unemployment remained stubbornly high as the manufacturing industry declined. *Women's Voice* continued with the familiar mix of material. In October 1980 the magazine exposed the Heinz Foundation scheme providing sports equipment for schools in return for Heinz product vouchers, revealing that £100 of baked beans would need to be purchased to obtain enough vouchers for a 'free' cricket ball. *Women's Voice* continued to fight racism, cuts to welfare services, homelessness, women's unemployment and women's health issues, and to attempt to provide inspirational coverage of working women – for example, in June 1978 it recorded the first woman to qualify as a train driver. In reality, there was little to be inspired by. Disputes involving women were recorded, but very rarely did these women workers win. The sad end of the Grunwick dispute after almost two years of struggle for union recognition in 1978 is just one example of this. The 1979 Corrie Abortion Bill reinvigorated the National Abortion Campaign, as forces were mustered to defeat the proposed legislation which would reduce legal abortions by 80 per cent (Hoggart 2013). On 28 October 1979, 60,000 marched against the Corrie Bill in the biggest demonstration on the abortion issue in British history (Hoggart 2013). Although *Women's Voice* and *Women's Voice* groups supported the campaign against Corrie, it does not appear to have resulted in *Women's Voice* readership gains, as it had done in 1975–7.

Despite its bright, colourful appearance and very amusing cartoons, (see Plate 9) worrying trends were developing in the paper. The lively sense of enquiry and debate of the early phase was now replaced by a much more dogmatic and polemical tone. Life stories of working-class women were still published, but the content was manipulated to read like recruiting propaganda for the SWP. *Women's Voice* attempted to engage with the new feminist campaign against sexual and domestic violence by supporting the 'Reclaim the Night' marches, including in the 'red light' districts of cities, but its approach was misguided. However, some articles were limited in their scope and reduced women's oppression to material circumstances only.[16] An article on the Corrie Abortion Bill linked the campaign to health service cuts (*WV* 35, November 1979: 5). *Women's Voice* supported lesbian rights, but the coverage was principally aimed at discrimination against lesbians at work.[17] The rise of different forms of feminism meant that *Women's Voice* was now struggling to relate to large sections of the Women's Liberation Movement. Another factor draining support for the magazine and its movement was the rise of the 'femocrats', engaged in political or official posts. In the late 1970s feminists were engaged with local councils in attempts to fund women's centres. This engagement with the local state led many feminists away from Far Left groups and unaligned socialist-feminism towards the Labour party, particularly in London where the Greater London Council was allocating large sums for childcare and projects involving disadvantaged women. An attempt by Sheila Rowbotham, Lynne Segal and Hilary Wainwright to unite non-aligned socialist-feminists, based around

Figure 15.3 *Women's Voice* October 1980, second series, back page. (Image source: Feminist Archive North)

the publication of *Beyond the Fragments*, created a lot of interest (Rowbotham et al. 1979). Unlike the non-sectarian stance of IS in the early 1970s, the SWP stood aside from this movement as it regarded itself as 'the revolutionary party' with no need of such movements. In any case, the attempt to build a movement around the idea of left socialist-feminist unity fizzled out very quickly in the harsh political and economic climate of the early 1980s.

The decision to launch a women's paper, and later a separate organisation for women, was always controversial inside the IS/SWP, with strong support on both sides. In 1975, after three years of *Women's Voice*, several branches sent resolutions to the 1975 National Conference proposing scrapping it.[18] Following the decision in early 1978 to encourage and support *Women's Voice* groups there was much internal discussion and disagreement over the nature of *Women's Voice* as a national organisation and its relationship to the SWP. Documents from the 1979 Conference indicate that there were fewer than 400 members in *Women's Voice* groups, with about half of those in the SWP.[19] There were also disciplinary problems, with expulsions from *Women's Voice* groups for breaches of party discipline. This is likely to relate, at least in part, to the Hackney branch of *Women's Voice* where members were expelled in the late 1970s. In an interview recorded in 2012, Celia Burgess-Macey described how her local SWP branch disowned her after her expulsion.[20] She was in fact purged, which for Celia, whose life revolved around Party activity, was a very traumatic experience (Bruley 2014: 165–6).

Although there were very real external factors leading to the decline of *Women's Voice*, it is also apparent that *Women's Voice* was undermined from within. In his memoir, Cliff (2000) argued that, instead of being a bridge to the Party from the Women's Liberation Movement, *Women's Voice* was leading women out of the SWP and into the women's movement.[21] As Ian Birchall (2011: 467) notes, Cliff's position on women's oppression was entirely class driven. He would not countenance the idea of gender division as it would undermine class solidarity. The only reason that he allowed *Women's Voice* to continue for as long as it did was that he did not want to alienate the women members. It is highly likely that other leading male comrades took the same position. By 1981 the issue had come to a head. Internal documents paint a very bleak picture of the situation indicating that there were only about 200 women in *Women's Voice* groups.[22] Of the sixty-two *Women's Voice* groups advertised in the paper, only twenty-two were said to be functioning, of which twelve were in London.[23] Many leading women comrades such as Sheila McGregor were no longer active in *Women's Voice* groups. The print run of *Women's Voice* was 9,000, but sales were given as 5,200.[24] Two full-time paid staff were funded by the SWP out of member's dues. The demoralised state of both the labour and socialist movements led to a decline in left wing activity at this time, resulting in a reduction in the SWP to fewer than 2,000 members in 1980 (Birchall 2011: 420). Although the situation was improving in 1981, it was argued that members were struggling to sustain local branches and that *Women's Voice* groups were a drain on finances and other resources. Against this view, *Women's Voice* had much vocal support: defenders argued that pressure had been mounted by central committee members to withdraw from *Women's Voice* activity in order to depict *Women's Voice* groups as demoralised.[25] Against this minority view, the 1981 Conference supported the recommendation from the centre to disband the *Women's Voice* groups but to maintain the magazine.[26]

Women's Voice struggled to survive. Orders from local SWP branches fell drastically. The paper was no longer connecting to working-class respondents in the same way, with very few writers submitting articles or letters for publication. The paper was largely written by two or three people at the SWP centre. Increasingly the paper was filled with book, theatre and film reviews, women's history, photographs and cartoons rather than real news. It had become a mere shell of its former self. *Women's Voice* staggered on until July 1982 when it ceased publication.[27] It was argued that its closure would mean that women's issues would no longer be in a 'ghetto' and that the issues previously associated with *Women's Voice* would be taken up by the whole Party. The decision to close *Women's Voice* proved to be very controversial as there was a minority of SWP branches who were loyal to the paper.[28] There were resignations, and it may be that the SWP lost several hundred members over this issue (Anon. 2013). Attempts to expand the coverage of women's issues in other SWP publications faded fairly quickly. The organisation no longer funded a women's officer, as all women's issues were officially 'Party issues'. It was only in the 1980s that the SWP admitted that this had been a mistake and changed its mind about the specific oppression of women, although, as David Isaacson pointed out in 2013, the SWP's policy on activity among women was never consistent and subject to 'countless zigs and zags' (Robinson 2007: 178; Isaacson 2013).

This chapter has demonstrated that the ideological incompatibility of Leninist vanguard politics with an autonomous women's movement was only one factor in the decline of *Women's Voice* as a socialist-feminist paper. What has previously been overlooked is that, to fully understand the rise and fall of *Women's Voice*, ideological difference needs to be placed in the context of changing economic and political circumstances. The period from 1968 to the mid-1970s was one of assertive working-class militancy which won some very important victories, putting the government on the back foot. The economic downturn of the mid-1970s and the subsequent rise of the New Right dismantled the postwar social contract and engendered a new political climate hostile to the working class and to the Left. Rising unemployment cowed the labour movement into a much more defensive stance. The women's movement also underwent important changes. In the early years, both IS and the Women's Liberation Movement were sufficiently fluid to allow for considerable overlap between the two. The socialist-feminist current within the Women's Liberation Movement was vibrant, strong and active and gave IS a position in the Women's Liberation Movement with which it could engage and thereby provide a market for *Women's Voice*. By the late 1970s the Women's Liberation Movement as a force of grassroots direct action and street protest was diversifying. Many socialist-feminists were joining the Labour Party and attempting to exert political power through more conventional routes. In addition, the rise of radical/revolutionary feminism exposed the failure of classic Marxism/Leninism to address the specific oppression of women, particularly the issues of sexual and domestic violence towards women. This trend was probably exacerbated by the tendency of many sections of the labour movement, both grassroots and in official structures, to collude with employers to prevent women from advancing the cause of equal pay. The success of *Women's Voice* was also linked to the campaign to defend the 1967 Abortion Act which did much to boost the circulation of the magazine. The early 1980 Parliamentary defeat of the Corrie Bill to drastically curtail legal abortions clarified that there would be no further attempts in the foreseeable future. There were also very few opportunities for successful industrial action for women. In addition, the SWP had failed to engage unemployed women in its 'Right to Work' campaign. These factors combined to set *Women's Voice* into terminal decline. Ultimately, *Women's Voice* died because the changing historical circumstances of the late 1970s and early 1980s meant that it no longer had an audience.

Notes

1. This also ties in with my own personal experience as a member of IS, 1969–71.
2. A report by Hertha Sturm for the Communist International gave the membership figures for European Communist parties as ranging from almost no women to about 20 per cent, *Inprecorr* (International Press Correspondence), held at the Marx Memorial Library, London.
3. The lost tradition of Clara Zetkin's *Die Gleichheit* and Kollontai's *Zhenodtel* is referred to in James (1980). Ian Birchall (2011: 470) also refers to the Bolshevik women's paper *Rabotnitsa*.

4. The initial demands of the Women's Liberation Movement as agreed at the Ruskin Conference of 1970 were equal pay, equal education and opportunity, 24-hour nurseries, free contraception and abortion on demand.
5. This newsletter is available in the Modern Records Centre, University of Warwick.
6. Two issues arose in referencing *Women's Voice* for this collection. First, there are only dates of publication given for some issues; some have only an issue number, while others have a date and an issue number. For clarity, the references refer to the issue number and either the actual date of publication or estimated date of publication. Where dates are estimated, this is noted in the reference. Second, following the relaunch of *Women's Voice* in 1977, issues were numbered starting again with number one. The use of date and issue number helps to distinguish between earlier and later issues.
7. A complete online archive of *Women's Voice* can be found in the Trotskyist History website 'Splits and Fusions' <https://splitsandfusions.wordpress.com/2017/03/08/womens-voice-isswp-womens-magazine/> (last accessed 29 January 2018).
8. See, for example, *Women's Voice* 5 March/April 1973: 3; *Women's Voice* 11 [c. March 1974]: 1; and *Women's Voice* 12 [c. September/October 1974]: 3.
9. The feminist critique of the Women's Liberation Movement from the 'race/ethnicity' perspective developed from the 1980s and has done much to challenge the dominance of white middle-class writers who were often taken to speak for the movement. The latest contribution to this historiography is Thomlinson (2016: 1–2), in which she refers to the 'white feminist project' as no longer valid.
10. Will Fancy Collection, Senate House Library, University of London (henceforth, WFSH), MS1171, Box 23–4 IS: Executive Committee Pre-Conference Discussion Document, April 1975, 23–4. These documents were distributed as internal bulletins and are not always easily identified.
11. WFSH MS1171, Box 23–4: IS Pre-Conference Papers 1974, Part X, Party Work with Women. 49–51.
12. WFSH MS1171, Box 23–4: IS Pre-Conference Documents, May 1975, David Widgery, The Women Question 1. 53.
13. WFSH MS1171, Box 13–1: SWP Pre-Conference Papers, June 1977. 10.
14. Ibid.
15. WFSH MS1171, Box 13–1: SWP Pre-Conference Papers, April 1978. 3.
16. For example, in an internal SWP bulletin article on the 'Yorkshire Ripper' by women's organiser Lindsay German, German links the issue to cuts in street lighting and public transport. (WFSH MS1171, Box 13–1: Pre-Conference, December 1980. 15).
17. For example, the sacking of Louise Boychuk for wearing a 'Lesbians Ignite' badge at work (*Women's Voice* 1, January 1977: 21. See also, Robinson 2007: 102).
18. WFSH MS1171, Box 23–24: IS Conference Agenda 1975. There were resolutions from Merseyside, Edinburgh and Bristol in favour of scrapping *Women's Voice*.
19. WFSH MS1171, Box 13–1: SWP Conference Papers, April 1978. 8–9.
20. Personal interview with Celia Burgess-Macey, 19 August 2012.
21. Cliff makes no concessions to the conventions of memoir writing and asked his colleague Lindsay German to write the section on *Women's Voice* for him, which is a clear indication of Cliff's lack of interest in this aspect of revolutionary politics.
22. Jeannie Robinson, 'Women's Voice Groups – SWP women have voted with their feet' (WFSH MS1171, Box 13–1: Internal Document 5, November 1981. 7).
23. Ibid.
24. Ibid.
25. Linda Quinn, 'The method of Duncan Hallas'. WFSH MS1171, Box 13–1: Internal Document 5, November 1981. 9.

26. 'Work amongst women', WFSH MS1171, Box 13–1: Internal Document 7, issued post-November 1981 Conference. n.p.
27. The issue was debated at the 1982 SWP Conference. See WFSH MS1171, Box 13–1: August 1982. 15–18.
28. This is evident in the SWP 1982 conference debate. For example, a piece headed 'Why we need specific women's propaganda' was signed by fourteen members of Brighton SWP (WFSH MS1171, Box 13–1: Internal Documents, August 1982. 16–170).

Works Cited

Anon [Renton, David]. 2013. '*Women's Voice*: In Retrospect'. *Lives; Running*, <https://livesrunning.wordpress.com/2013/09/26/womens-voice-a-retrospective/> (last accessed 29 January 2018).

Birchall, I. 2011. *Tony Cliff, A Marxist for His Time*. London: Bookmarks.

Bruley, S. 1986. *Leninism, Stalinism and the Women's Movement, 1920–1939*. New York: Garland.

Bruley, S. 2014. 'Jam Tomorrow? Socialist Women and Women's Liberation, 1968–82: An Oral History Approach'. *Against the Grain: The British Far Left From 1956*. Eds E. Smith and M. Worley. Manchester: Manchester University Press. 155–72.

Callaghan, J. 1984. *British Trotskyism: Theory and Practice*. Oxford: Blackwell.

Callaghan, J. 1987. *The Far Left in British Politics*. Oxford: Basil Blackwell.

Cliff, T. 2000. *A World to Win: The Life of a Revolutionary*. London: Bookmarks.

Forster, L. 2016. 'Spreading the Word: Feminist Print Cultures and the Women's Liberation Movement'. *Women's History Review* 25.5: 812–31.

Hoggart, L. 2013. 'Feminist Principles Meet Political Reality: The Case of the National Abortion Campaign'. Pro+choice Forum. <www.prochoiceforum.org.uk/al6.php> (last accessed 13 September 2017).

Hughes, C. 2015. *Young Lives on the Left: Sixties Activism and the Liberation of the Self*. Manchester: Manchester University Press.

Isaacson, D. 2013. 'SWP and Women: Countless Zigs and Zags over Women's Oppression'. *Weekly Worker*, 17 January 2013 <https://weeklyworker.co.uk/worker/945/swp-and-women-countless-zigs-and-zags-over-womens-/> (last accessed 23 January 2018).

James, L. 1980. 'Women and the Revolutionary Party: A Reply to Joan Smith'. *International Socialism* 2.7: 95–107.

Lewis, J. 1992. *Women in Britain since 1945*. Oxford: Blackwell.

Paczuska, A. 1990. 'Anna Paczuska'. *Once a Feminist, Stories of a Generation*. Ed. M. Wandor. London: Virago.

Robinson, L. 2007. *Gay Men and the Left in Post-war Britain: How the Personal Got Political*. Manchester: Manchester University Press.

Rowbotham, S. 1972. 'The Beginnings of Women's Liberation in Britain'. *The Body Politic: Writings from the Women's Liberation in Britain 1969–72*. Ed. M. Wandor. London: Stage 1. 91–102.

Rowbotham, S., L. Segal and H. Wainwright. 1979. *Beyond the Fragments, Feminism and the Making of Socialism*. London: Newcastle Socialist Centre and Islington Community Press.

Stephenson, G. 2016. 'The Forgotten Strike: Equality, Gender and Class in the Trico Equal Pay Strike'. *Labour History Review* 81.2: 141–68.

Thomlinson, N. 2016. *Race, Ethnicity and the Women's Movement in England, 1968–1993*. Basingstoke: Palgrave.

16

Spare Rib, *Ms.* and Reproductive Rights: A Comparative Analysis of Approaches

Claire Sedgwick

Introduction

Feminist media production had a particularly fertile year in 1972, with the founding of two key feminist magazines, *Spare Rib* in the UK and *Ms.* in the US. This chapter explores how reproductive rights – one of the most important issues for the feminist movement in the 1970s (Berkman 2011; Lovenduski and Randall 1992) – were represented in both magazines. Analysing primary data such as feminist magazines enables us to identify how feminist approaches to reproductive rights need to be understood in a historical context (Sedgwick 2016; Sedgwick 2017). I focus on how the differing geographical and political contexts in which the magazines operated shaped how they approached reproductive rights in different ways. The aim of this chapter is to analyse how these contexts affect the ability of feminist media to create narratives around reproductive rights.

Reproductive Rights and Second-Wave Feminism

Reproductive rights have been historicised as an important issue for second-wave feminists. Berkman argues that 'few issues in American history rival the fervour of the political confrontations between advocates and opponents over women's right to an abortion' (Berkman 2011: 43). Discussing the British context, Lovenduski and Randall (1992: 220) note that 'throughout the 1970s abortion was almost the definitive issue of the movement'. Similarly, the extent to which abortion was framed as a key issue is described by Bradley (2003: 185) as the '*Ms.* bottom line' suggesting that it was of specific importance.

The importance of reproductive rights can be seen by the amount of activism in the area from the late 1960s onwards. Dorothy McBride Stetson (2001:1) notes that 'expanding access to abortion was the only goal that could unify disparate wings' within the feminist movement. As a result, there was a huge amount of activism advocating for abortion access. In the US, the National Abortion Rights Action League (NARAL) was founded in 1969 (NARAL 2019). The Supreme Court's ruling in *Roe v Wade* legalised abortion in 1973 (Ginsburg 1985). In the UK, abortion was decriminalised by the Abortion Act 1967 that entered into effect in 1968 (Bristow 2012). However, as the analysis of *Spare Rib* and *Ms.* will demonstrate, this was not the end of campaigning for reproductive rights – there were many challenges from the

Right to a woman's right to choose. In both magazines, the importance of reproductive rights was reinforced by the combat imagery that was used to describe the issue. In Britain, this was seen when there were specific threats to abortion access, while in *Ms.* actual as well as metaphorical violence was described. One crucial difference between the two magazines is that, at times when threats to abortion were not imminent, *Spare Rib* was able to explore ambivalent emotions towards reproductive rights in a way that *Ms.* could not. In the US, abortion legislation was never secure enough that American feminists could do anything other than protect existing legislation, and could not therefore present the nuances of women's feelings about abortion as there was a higher risk that existing rights would be eroded.

To understand reproductive rights as an intersectional issue (Crenshaw 1989) it is important to go beyond discussions of abortion to include issues such as safe contraceptive drugs and the right not to be subjected to unwanted sterilisation and termination. Nelson (2003) argues that this was a particularly important issue for black women, poor women and disabled women. As the analysis will show, this understanding of reproductive rights as an intersectional and international issue differentiated *Spare Rib* from *Ms.* – *Spare Rib* was much more likely to present the issue as an intersectional one, whereas *Ms.* was much more likely to focus almost exclusively on abortion. I will now move on to provide a brief description of *Spare Rib* and *Ms.*

Spare Rib

Spare Rib was founded by journalists Rosie Boycott and Marsha Rowe in July 1972 and ran for more than twenty years before it finally folded at the beginning of 1993. Boycott and Rowe both had experience working within the alternative British press for magazines *Oz* and *Frendz* and it was this experience that led Rowe (1982: 13) to describe *Spare Rib* as the 'daughter of the underground press'. However, while the underground press was viewed as 'a more authentic voice for the concerns and mood of the youth movement than the mass media', the sexism that pervaded British culture existed even within so-called 'progressive spaces' (Rowe 1982:14). Rowe remembers how the 'women who worked on its magazines and newspapers served the men and did office and production work rather than editorial work' (Rowe 1982:15). *Spare Rib*, in contrast, provided a space where women could create their own media (Laing and Sutton 1999) outside the confines of patriarchy. Rowe (1982: 19) describes the magazine as 'an activity and consciousness-raising process combined'. Travis (2008) asserts that feminist media production provided space for feminists to practically apply the knowledge learnt through feminist theory. In addition, the magazine had a capacity building role and 'invited contributions from readers, including women not active in the women's movement' (Rowe 1982:19).

The explicit feminist aims of *Spare Rib* meant that the magazine differed radically from its mainstream counterparts in most of its content, with a much greater emphasis on political discussion and much less reliance on regular magazine content such as fashion and food. Winship (1987: 135) compares the 'fragile contentment with women's lot' that was seen in mainstream women's magazines with the 'critical discontent' of *Spare Rib*. Key to this was a largely DIY aesthetic. Advertising was generally for niche or feminist products in comparison to mainstream magazines (Sedgwick 2017). Although not as radical as some other British feminist magazines, as *Spare Rib* developed its anti-capitalist stance and broadened its scope and readership base, it became more likely to focus on issues facing the working class and women of colour. The magazine ran as a collective, and the decision was made in 1983 to actively make the collective more inclusive, leading to more women of colour working at the magazine (Sedgwick 2017). This had an important consequence for the discussion of issues such as reproductive rights, because the magazine was much more likely to focus on the way that reproductive rights affected women of colour and working-class women. In contrast, because of the different geographical and political context, *Ms.* was much more likely to assume a white reader and was therefore less likely to address the different oppressions that women of colour faced. (For a more detailed exploration of *Spare Rib*'s history, see Chapter 2.)

Ms.

Ms. was originally included in the December 1971 issue of *New York Magazine* as a sample insert (*Ms.* n.d.) and the first issue of the standalone magazine was released in July 1972. Founded by experienced journalist Gloria Steinem, *Ms.* staffers had extensive experience in mainstream women's magazines and news journalism (Steinem 2012: 4). Steinem (2012: 7) suggests that the aim of the magazine was to provide an alternative 'to all those magazines directed at men [that] were totally male owned and controlled'. *Ms.* widened the access for feminist journalists in the magazine publishing industry and allowed Steinem to 'control her own image' (Bradley 2003: 157). As with *Spare Rib* in the UK, *Ms.* became increasingly important for American feminists. Amy Erdman Farrell (1998: 1) describes the magazine as a 'popular icon of the women's movement, synonymous for many Americans with the women's movement itself'. Likewise, Thom (1997: 44) describes *Ms.* as 'a monthly advocate for the women's movement', suggesting that the magazine complemented the activities of the wider women's movement. *Ms.* aimed to appeal to a much more mainstream audience than *Spare Rib* and sought to achieve mainstream success (Erdman Farrell 2011). One consequence of this was that the assumed audience of the magazine remained relatively wealthy, white middle-class women (Erdman Farrell 2011; Sedgwick 2017), which inevitably affected the magazine's ability to engage with intersectionality.

Methods

This research is part of a wider project on the representation of second-wave feminism in *Spare Rib* and *Ms.* (Sedgwick 2017). The project used a directed content analysis (Hsieh and Shannon 2005) to identify the frequency with which specific feminist issues such as reproductive rights were discussed within the magazines. Five sample years were used: 1972, 1977, 1982, 1987 and 1992. Five-year intervals meant that the sample could consider changes within the magazines longitudinally. Seventy-three articles were coded as discussing reproductive rights across the total sample of 807 (387 for *Spare Rib* and 420 for *Ms.*). A textual analysis was then used to identify the key discourses that were evident in *Spare Rib* and *Ms.* Articles that were then selected based on how ideologically rich they were. For example, articles were chosen if they put forward a particularly interesting, typical or untypical opinion. Similarly, I identified whether the article was particularly timely and whether it engaged in key debates of the period. In the case of reproductive rights this is particularly important, as there are times when discussions regarding abortion become more prescient due to threats to abortion legislation. A textual analysis was then conducted out of these articles. In this chapter, I also analyse an additional article, by Eileen Fairweather, from outside of the main sample (*Spare Rib* October 1979: 26–30) because it has become particularly prominent in discussions of *Spare Rib*'s representation of reproductive rights

Abortion Campaigns and Parliamentary Bills in *Spare Rib*

Discussions regarding abortion intersected with political engagement in *Spare Rib*, especially when there were specific threats to existing legislation that created a heightened awareness of the issue. The Abortion Act 1967 was challenged by numerous parliamentary bills that threatened to restrict access to abortion, such as the Benyon Bill 1977, the Corrie Bill 1979 and the Alton Bill 1987, all of which were targets of *Spare Rib* campaigns. These 'threats to existing legislation' 'galvanise[d]' feminists to campaign (Lovenduski and Randall 1993: 244), evident in the increased coverage of abortion. For example, in 1977 there were seventeen articles that discussed abortion, in contrast to two in 1972 and seven in 1992 when there were fewer direct threats to abortion through legislation (Sedgwick 2017). *Spare Rib*, therefore, provides important evidence of how feminist periodicals are important documents for helping us to understand how feminists dealt with challenges to feminist gains.

Mandy Moore's article 'Anti-Abortion Bill Gains Ground' (*Spare Rib* April 1977: 17–18) is indicative of how *Spare Rib* responded to threats to abortion access. The article was written in response to the Benyon Bill – first introduced by MP James White in 1974 and then reintroduced in 1977 – that threatened to prevent private providers from conducting abortions because of perceived abuses in the system. The original amendment did not reach a parliamentary vote and was withdrawn by White after being 'defeated after a campaign by pro-choice groups' (Bindel 2011). This indicates the impact of pro-choice campaigns and provides an interesting context for the article, since previous legislation had already been defeated by campaigning.

Moore implicated both the medical establishment and the Church in restricting access to abortion. The picture illustrating the article features a priest and a doctor, standing in the street (see Figure 16.1). The priest gestures 'stop' with one arm and, with the other, points to a sign that reads 'back street'. Next to him, the doctor stands in front of a sign that states 'hospital closed' (*Spare Rib* April 1977: 17). The image suggests that the Church and patriarchal medical establishment pose a threat to women's access to abortion. The reference to 'back street' abortions reminds the reader that restrictions on abortion access in the past did not prevent women from seeking terminations, but instead forced them to visit unregulated and unsafe back-street providers.

The Benyon Bill was described as 'sneaky' and 'misogynistic, positioning anti-abortion opinions as anti-women. It was shown to represent a minority opinion as 'a massive campaign was launched against the bill' (Ibid.). One of Benyon's constituents described it as a 'provocation' that would cause the MP to lose his 'small majority', further presenting the bill as unpopular with the public and de-legitimising the bill (Ibid.). Alvarez and Brehm (1995) and Craig et al. (2002) argue that there is

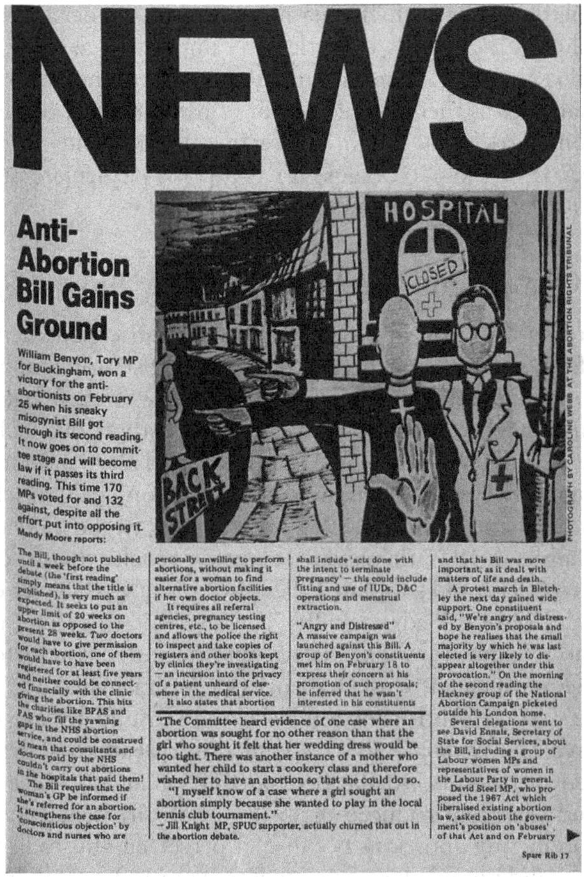

NEWS

Anti-Abortion Bill Gains Ground

William Benyon, Tory MP for Buckingham, won a victory for the anti-abortionists on February 25 when his sneaky misogynist Bill got through its second reading. It now goes on to committee stage and will become law if it passes its third reading. This time 170 MPs voted for and 132 against, despite all the effort put into opposing it. Mandy Moore reports:

The Bill, though not published until a week before the debate (the 'first reading' simply means that the title is published), is very much as expected. It seeks to put an upper limit of 20 weeks on abortion as opposed to the present 28 weeks. *Two* doctors would have to give permission for each abortion, one of them would have to have been registered for at least five years and neither could be connected financially with the clinic giving the abortion. This hits the charities like BPAS and PAS who fill the yawning gaps in the NHS abortion service, and could be construed to mean that consultants and doctors paid by the NHS couldn't carry out abortions in the hospitals that paid them!

The Bill requires that the woman's GP be informed if she's referred for an abortion. It strengthens the case for 'conscientious objection' by doctors and nurses who are personally unwilling to perform abortions, without making it easier for a woman to find alternative abortion facilities if her own doctor objects.

It requires all referral agencies, pregnancy testing centres, etc., to be licensed and allows the police the right to inspect and take copies of registers and other books kept by clinics they're investigating — an incursion into the privacy of a patient unheard of elsewhere in the medical service.

It also states that abortion shall include 'acts done with the intent to terminate pregnancy' — this could include fitting and use of IUDs, D&C operations and menstrual extraction.

"Angry and Distressed"
A massive campaign was launched against this Bill. A group of Benyon's constituents met him on February 18 to express their concern at his promotion of such proposals; he inferred that he wasn't interested in his constituents and that his Bill was more important, as it dealt with matters of life and death.

A protest march in Bletchley the next day gained wide support. One constituent said, "We're angry and distressed by Benyon's proposals and hope he realises that the small majority by which he was last elected is very likely to disappear altogether under this provocation." On the morning of the second reading the Hackney group of the National Abortion Campaign picketed outside his London home.

Several delegations went to see David Ennals, Secretary of State for Social Services, about the Bill, including a group of Labour women MPs and representatives of women in the Labour Party in general.

David Steel MP, who proposed the 1967 Act which liberalised existing abortion law, asked about the government's position on 'abuses' of that Act and on February ▶

"The Committee heard evidence of one case where an abortion was sought for no other reason than that the girl who sought it felt that her wedding dress would be too tight. There was another instance of a mother who wanted her child to start a cookery class and therefore wished her to have an abortion so that she could do so.

"I myself know of a case where a girl sought an abortion simply because she wanted to play in the local tennis club tournament."
— Jill Knight MP, SPUC supporter, actually churned that out in the abortion debate.

PHOTOGRAPH BY CAROLINE WEBB AT THE ABORTION RIGHTS TRIBUNAL

Spare Rib 17

Figure 16.1 'Anti-Abortion Bill Gains Ground', *Spare Rib*, April 1977.

ambivalence in how abortion is perceived; however, this is not present in *Spare Rib*'s discussion of threats to abortion. This was a necessary strategy, since acknowledging ambivalent feelings meant that the magazine ran the risk of being used by anti-abortion campaigners as evidence that abortion access was not welcomed by the general population.

Another common rhetorical technique used by *Spare Rib* when discussing abortion was to use combative language and metaphor. 'New Anti-Abortion Onslaught' (*Spare Rib* February 1977: 23) and 'Anti-Abortion Bill Gains Ground' (*Spare Rib* April 1977: 17–18) both framed parliamentary debates on abortion as attacks on women or attempts to gain territory over women's lives. The use of combat language emphasised the gravity of the debate and how it is constructed as a life or death issue. Other articles mirror this, such as 'Defending the Abortion Act' (*Spare Rib* July 1974: 25) and 'Glasgow: The Fight Against SPUC [the Society for the Protection of Unborn Children]' (*Spare Rib* July 1974: 20). Similarly, when the Corrie Bill was being debated in Parliament in 1980, articles such as 'Corrie Crushed?' (*Spare Rib* March 1980: 30–1) positioned abortion as a battle with distinct antagonists and protagonists.

War metaphors highlight the extent to which abortion was a polarising, emotive legal issue. Jolly (2014: 100) states that the tone of discussions was a 'measure of the mood' and had symbolic value since they also broached 'questions about gender, race, family, work, security and continuity'. The continued threat to existing rights defined by the 1967 Act meant that feminists were continually on the defensive, and this was reflected in the language used. It is also useful to consider whether these metaphors were unique to *Spare Rib* or whether they reflected imagery within the wider women's movement; although, without a detailed analysis of how reproductive rights were being represented outside of *Spare Rib*, this is hard to ascertain.

Ambivalence

Although *Spare Rib* was unequivocally pro-choice, Jolly (2014) argues that the public mood did not always reflect this. While the article on the Benyon Bill stated that a 'massive campaign' was organised against it, the public mood and the mass media were not as supportive (*Spare Rib* April 1977: 17–18). As Sandbrook states, 'there was a specific public anxiety about a "surge" of abortions since the 1967 act' (cited in Jolly 2014: 102). At times when there were fewer explicit threats to abortion, this was something that could be reflected in *Spare Rib*, and Eileen Fairweather's article 'The Feelings Behind the Slogans' identified the conflict between feminist rhetoric and the ambivalence that some women felt about abortion (*Spare Rib* October 1979: 26–30).

The article began with a reference to a letter from 1915 describing the 'suffering and courage' of a woman who had a failed abortion and was forced to continue an unwanted pregnancy (Ibid.: 26). Alongside this, Fairweather also referenced her own grandmother who 'died in childbirth' (26). The reference to real women grounded the discussion in the empirical, rather than the abstract. This is further demonstrated through the contrast between 'medical men and male legislators' and the 'working class women' who provided birth control but had been written out of histories of reproductive rights (Ibid.). Hoggart (2003) argues that the Abortion Act was not related to women's rights *per se*, but rather aimed to protect doctors from prosecution. Women's welfare was a secondary benefit, gained despite of, and not because of, male power. Even though abortion is inherently concerned with women's bodies, women's experiences have not been central to discussions about it. Through highlighting how women's experiences have been ignored in the abortion debate, Fairweather made the case for focusing on women's feelings.

Although Fairweather's article shares some similarities with 'Anti-Abortion Bill Gains Ground' (*Spare Rib* April 1977: 17–18) because it questioned male authority, it was critical of how pro-choice campaigns have assumed that women's experiences are universal and ignored the emotional complexity of abortion. Fairweather questioned whether pro-choice campaigns could be representative since 'the pro-choice movement cannot win the support of women overall because it does not actually reflect their experience' (*Spare Rib* October 1979: 27). While widening access to abortion is beneficial to women, this does not necessarily mean that all women are sympathetic to a feminist standpoint. Fairweather argued that as 'the women's movement was still very young when abortion became a political football', the response of the women's movement was to condense the issue into slogans, but this meant that 'the complexity of abortion and its emotional significance for women somehow got lost' since 'the trouble with all slogans, of course, is that they are shorthand for something more complex' (Ibid.). The use of combat metaphors, which were as likely to be perpetuated in feminist discourse as anywhere else, tended to flatten the emotional complexity of the issue by presenting polarised positions.

Jolly (2014: 105) describes how Fairweather's article became a catalyst for women to 'share abortion experiences' in a way that they had been previously unable to do. Women who have had abortions may experience ambivalent emotions that are neither positive nor negative, yet Fairweather argued that these were not discussed when feminists were fighting to defend existing rights because ambivalence could be used as an argument against abortion. For example, 'post-abortion trauma' was used by some anti-abortion activists to suggests that women's alleged regret can be pathologised as a form of mental illness (McNeil 1999: 158). However, a side effect of this was a 'legacy of shame, secrecy and often pain' (*Spare Rib* October 1979: 27).

'The Feelings Behind the Slogans' provided an alternative way of understanding debates around abortion, one that did not rely on polarising 'anti-abortion' and 'pro-choice' positions. Although *Spare Rib* did use conflict imagery as a rhetorical device, the magazine also critiqued this and provided space for contradictory arguments. Fairweather warned readers that 'it is a mistake to see all our opponents as women haters' (*Spare Rib* October 1979: 29). This contrasted with previous articles that positioned anti-abortion perspectives as inherently misogynistic. The link between anti-abortion sentiment and anti-feminism has been studied by Ginsburg (1989) who argues that anti-abortion activists are frequently presented as anti-feminist and associated with the political right. This is an understandable association given that, in both the UK and the US, anti-abortion legislation tended to be introduced by political conservatives, although David Alton (of the Alton Bill 1987) was a Liberal MP and an exception. Petchesky (1981) argues that the introduction of anti-abortion legislation was often linked to conservatives' concerns that women had gained more control over their sexuality.

Spare Rib did not discuss women who identified as feminists but were anti-abortion. Sheila Rowbotham (1989: 84–5) points to the existence of Christian feminists who do not know whether we can be 'sure that embryonic life does not "already possess a human individuality or soul"' suggesting that 'there was never – even at the height of the campaigning in the mid-1970s – a unified feminist position on abortion'. However, there is no discussion of this position on abortion in either *Spare Rib* or *Ms. Spare Rib* might have presented ambivalent discussions of abortion, but it would not go so far as to allow space for feminists who were anti-abortion and the feminist position is understood as pro-choice.

Feminist magazines such as *Spare Rib* are crucial for helping us to understand the nuances of an issue as sensitive as abortion and reproductive rights. I shall now move on to discuss how the issue was understood differently in *Ms.* The difference in approaches is useful for helping us to understand the ways in which geographical, political and economic contexts impact on how an issue is represented.

Abortion and American Politics

There are key differences between the way that abortion access has been campaigned and legislated for in the US and the UK. In the US, the most significant legislation is *Roe v Wade*, the 1973 Supreme Court decision that legalised abortion across the US (although, before the 1973 ruling, abortion laws had already been repealed and reformed across fourteen states) (Our Bodies, Ourselves 2016). However, whilst *Roe v Wade* overturned existing law, state legislation was often used to make abortions difficult to obtain. This is reflected in the way that abortion campaigns are discussed in *Ms*. Whereas *Spare Rib* often focused on national campaigns, *Ms.* was much more likely to focus on campaigning in specific states. There were more articles about abortion and reproductive rights in the 1980s in *Ms.* and therefore this chapter focuses on that period (Sedgwick 2017).

In Sgrignoli's 'Abortion: Winning at State Level' (*Ms.* April 1982: 26), the abortion debate was understood as adversarial; something that could be won or lost. The article referred to the 'Abortion Control Act' which had been debated in Pennsylvania and was described as 'one more attempt by anti-abortion groups to undermine the Supreme Court's 1973 ruling legalising abortion' (26). Staggenborg (1991: 58) argues that rather than settling the issue of abortion, *Roe v Wade* led to a new strategy where anti-abortionists tried to 'block implementation of the Court ruling' by making it harder to access abortions at state level, just as similar bills aimed to make it harder for women to access abortions in the UK.

The article described the Abortion Control Act as 'the most restrictive piece of abortion legislation in the United States' (*Ms.* April 1982: 26). The Republican Governor of Pennsylvania, Dick Thornburgh, vetoed the bill despite his opposition to abortion because of the amount of public opposition to it. In another article from 1982, Lisa Cronin Wahl described how the electorate may be influenced by the attitudes of candidates towards abortion, suggesting that '30 percent of pro-choice voters said they would vote against a candidate who advocated an anti-abortion amendment' (*Ms.* July 1982: 70). In both articles an anti-abortion stance was viewed as politically damaging. Abortion was seen as a strategic issue, since a politician's voting record could have an impact on their chances of re-election. Cronin Wahl quotes Nanette Falkenberg, the 'executive director of the National Abortion Rights Action League', who stated that there is a 'threat' in 'congress' that abortion rights would be undermined since 'frenetic legislative activity by anti-choice groups can be expected to continue' (Ibid.). *Ms.* presented abortion as a highly politicised issue where public opinion can influence the debate.

A politician's stance on abortion has a greater influence on the electorate in the US than in the UK (Durham 2005). In the US, the relationship between the Republican Party and evangelical Christianity has meant that attitudes towards abortion have been highly politicised. Evangelicals had influence on the Republican Party because they represented a sizeable portion of their supporters. In England, Scotland and Wales (although, notably, not in Northern Ireland) abortion legislation is an issue that affects all people equally in law (if not always in reality). In the US, state legislation can dramatically affect the access that women have to abortion services. As a consequence of this political context, *Ms.* was less likely to discuss feelings of ambiguity that women might feel about abortion and focused instead on how women were materially and emotionally damaged by anti-abortion campaigns. The magazine was also much less likely to include debate formats, or a variety of voices when discussing an issue, and therefore was more likely to present a singular argument.

Anti-Abortion Terrorism

Although *Spare Rib* used metaphorical combative language, terrorism against abortion providers in the US meant that descriptions of violence in *Ms.* were literal as well as metaphorical. Violence against abortion providers included bombing, blockades, arson and acid attacks (Bader and Baird-Windle 2015). As a result, *Ms.* was much less likely to discuss ambivalence for fear of conceding ideological ground to an increasingly hostile opponent.

This demonstrates why it is important to take context into account when attempting to understand how the magazines prioritised their focus on certain issues. *Ms.* featured articles about anti-abortion terrorism to help the reader to understand the extent to which anti-abortion activists were prepared to use violence. It also helped to personalise abortion providers and present them as sympathetic figures. The discussion of abortion in *Ms.* often focused on the extent to which abortion provision was about care, therefore framing it as a nurturing practice to counter negative stereotypes of abortion providers as emotionless.

Lisa Cronin Wahl's 1982 article 'Rise in Antiabortion Terrorism' fulfilled both of these aims. It discussed the emotional impact of anti-abortion terrorism and humanised abortion providers by giving an insight into who they were and the affect that terrorism had on them. The article describes the 'grave psychological toll on abortion clinics across America' because of the kidnapping of a doctor and his wife (*Ms.* November 1982: 19). Since anti-abortion terrorism aims to discourage abortion provision across the country, it cannot be an individual crime and must be seen within a wider context of intimidation and fear. The article implicated mainstream anti-abortion campaigns, suggesting that, although 'the leadership of major anti-choice organisations denies any involvement', the National Right to Life Committee (NRLC) would not give *Ms.* access to any of the organisation's picketing guidelines (Ibid.). This suggested that the NRLC had something to hide as they were not transparent about their conduct at protests. Doan (2009: 17) in her study of anti-abortion harassment states that: 'It is difficult to divorce the rhetorical absolutism as well as the individualised nature of protest activities endorsed by pro-life direct action organisations from the underlying context of violence that has occurred in the fight over abortion politics.' The culpability of right to life organisations was further suggested by 'Susan Hill, executive director of the 10-clinic National Women's Health Organization', who linked the rise in extremism to the rhetoric used by the anti-abortion movement. Anti-abortion leaders told activists that the clinics should be 'closed by now', leading extremists to 'start taking things in their own hands' (*Ms.* November 1982: 19). It suggested that anti-abortion activists reacted to the lack of progress made using non-violent processes, a suggestion further supported by reference to a 'lack of significant anti-choice victory' in the legislative arena.

Unsurprisingly, given *Ms.*'s pro-choice position and the criminality of anti-abortion terrorism, clinic workers were positioned as victims and anti-abortionists as illegitimate aggressors. One clinic worker was quoted as saying 'we've been nice people: the anti-abortionists think they can get away with anything' (*Ms.* November 1982: 19). Anti-abortion activists were portrayed as having no regard for the law or their victims, their acts represented as unprovoked with no justification for their violence (Luker 1984).

Anti-abortion terrorism was a recurring issue in *Ms.* In 1987, Michele Kort profiled an abortion clinic to humanise the workers there (*Ms.* May 1987: 48–53). The subtitle, 'On the Front Line at an Abortion Clinic', utilised combat imagery, mirroring the militaristic language that Doan (2009) argues is often used by anti-abortion activists. However, in contrast to *Spare Rib*, the combative language used was not metaphorical. Kort suggested that 'everything looks normal' at the clinic with the only 'visible reminder of the arson that nearly devastated the abortion clinic' being the 'once green and shiny shrubs [which] are now ashen gray, wilted' (*Ms.* May 1987: 49). Showing how the clinic was operating as usual set a defiant tone that indicated that violence had not worked as a deterrent. However, this is contrasted with the emotional legacy of the violence against them. Judith Widdicombe, the executive director of the Reproductive Health Services whose clinic was targeted, said '"it's like someone kicked you in the gut"' (Ibid.). The visceral language suggests an emotional legacy that lasts longer than physical damage.

The impact of terrorism on this clinic is presented as just one example: 'nationwide, abortion clinics are being invaded, vandalised, bombed and burned', whilst 'six' providers were 'damaged or completely destroyed' and a further 'six destructive attempts were made but failed' (*Ms.* May 1987: 49). Statistics from the National Abortion Foundation added further legitimacy to the claim that this was a serious issue. The emphasis on how abortion clinics are targeted reframes the combat metaphor since pro-choice activists and clinic workers are victims of persecution, rather than one side in an equal war.

The article was a personal profile of clinic workers, and the profile was a common feature in the magazine: for example, the same issue profiled Apple executive Debi Coleman. Erdman Farrell (2011) has argued that profiles were used to individualise feminism and de-politicise it. However, personal profiles were used to counter the stereotype perpetuated by the Right that the abortion provider was profit-driven and industrialised (Doan, 2009). Kort stated that 'one of the most frustrating aspects of front-line duty is the requirement to remain silent – to avoid starting a debate or escalating tension' (*Ms.* May 1987: 50). *Ms.* provided a rare opportunity for workers at the clinic to express their emotion publicly, something that they were prevented from doing because reasonable engagement with anti-abortion activists was impossible. Kort's article highlighted the emotions of clinic workers: as one worker stated, 'she hear[s] [herself] saying "I'm not looking forward to tomorrow" the evening before her shift, suggesting a sense of dread' (Ibid.). The suggestion that attacks on the clinic are 'like someone kicked you in the gut' further highlighted the emotional burden that workers in the clinic faced (Ibid.: 49). Preventing or deterring abortion workers from doing their jobs was considered a useful strategy by anti-abortion activists (Doan 2009). Another counsellor recounts a dream where the protesters 'wouldn't speak' to her and wondered if this demonstrated that 'there isn't room for dialogue', reinforcing how polarising the abortion debate was (*Ms.* May 1987: 50).

This polarisation created little space for discussing ambivalent feelings in *Ms.* Kort associated negative feelings with anti-abortion protestors who wanted to undermine the arguments of abortion activists. Statements by 'anti-choice wom[e]n who decided on an abortion but later expressed guilt and regret' are countered by a clinic worker who blamed 'increased patient anxiety' on 'the pressure being applied by the antis' (Ibid.). Emotional conflict was presented as something that is manufactured by a disapproving culture, rather than caused by so-called 'post-abortion trauma' (McNeil 1991: 158), a term that originated in America to explain negative emotions women had after their abortions, a term heavily criticised by feminists who argue that these negative emotions are as likely to be caused by the way abortion is framed as a source of regret and shame for women.

This brings to mind Ahmed's work on the role that 'emotions play in the constitution between subjects and communities' (Ahmed 2001: 10). Ahmed points to the way emotions 'are bound up with how we inhabit the world "with" others' and 'become attached to signs and bodies' (Ibid.: 12, 14). This can clearly be seen in the abortion debate where both women's bodies and emotions are highly politicised, while women's negative emotions are used against them by anti-abortionists. *Ms.* complicated this narrative by suggesting that these negative emotions were being produced by anti-abortion activists' intimidation tactics, not because of the way that women feel about abortion. The fact that *Ms.* featured a petition called 'We had abortions' (*Ms.* Spring 1972: 34–5), which featured high-profile women, suggests that the magazine aimed to provide an alternative to these feelings by normalising abortion as a decision that women should be entitled to take. In *Spare Rib*, ambivalent emotions were used to show the complexity of the abortion debate beyond slogans but, in *Ms.*, the polarisation of emotion meant that the emphasis on caring and nurturing was a more useful political strategy. This demonstrates how the magazines' rhetoric was partly influenced by different political contexts.

Competing Rights: Abortion and Disability

Spare Rib was much more likely than *Ms.* to view reproductive rights as an intersectional issue. A pair of articles from 1982 showed how the magazine viewed reproductive rights in relation to disability rights. In a discussion about the conflict between women's right to abortion and disability rights, Ruth Hubbard (2006: 101–2) acknowledged a woman's right to choose, but also argued that the termination of foetuses that carry defects or abnormalities involves 'a process of selection and a decision about what kinds of people should and should not inhabit the world' since 'decisions about what kind of baby to bear inevitably are bedevilled by overt and unspoken judgements about which lives are "worth living"'.

In the 1982 *Spare Rib* article 'Life: A Doctor's Right to Choose', Rose Shapiro described the case of Dr Leonard Arthur who was accused, but later acquitted, of killing a newborn with Down's syndrome. The article was not about the specifics of the case, or the legitimacy of the verdict, but focused on how the anti-abortion group Life campaigned for Arthur's conviction and how this could be linked to wider campaigns to restrict abortion access and pre-natal screening. Shapiro suggested that these restrictions meant that 'foetal abnormality (either physical or mental) would no longer be grounds for abortion' and this was a 'serious error of judgement' (*Spare Rib* January 1982: 26). For Shapiro, the medical establishment was a potential ally: while doctors' power had been negatively felt by 'women's health campaigners', she argued that 'the preservation of the power of doctors has been fundamental to the defeat of the moral right' (Ibid.). However, despite being potential allies, there was also the 'belief that doctors can play god' (Ibid.). In her study of abortion rights in the US, Staggenborg (1991) describes the importance of the US medical establishment in reforming abortion law. However, she also recognises the tension that could be felt between the medical establishment and abortion referral campaigns such as Jane, a US underground abortion service (Kaplan 1997), since the medical establishment was seen as patriarchal in contrast to the women-centred provision of Jane.

Shapiro questioned the sincerity of Life's campaigning, asking whether they 'actually care about the lack of facilities and support that exist for people with handicaps' and arguing that Life 'ignore[s] the contradictory feeling of a woman caring for a handicapped child 24 hours a day who finds this a terrible burden' (*Spare Rib* January 1982: 26). Although Shapiro focused on the lack of existing support for disabled people, the emphasis is on the mother. The use of the word 'burden' reproduces a discourse around disability that assumes that the disabled child is a liability. Although Shapiro did acknowledge how a lack of institutional or social support may be the cause of this, she reinforced the association of 'disability with unbearable suffering and stress, especially for the mothers' (Degener 1990: 87).

The following month's *Spare Rib* included a response to this characterisation of disabled people by Micheline Mason, a disabled woman (*Spare Rib* February 1982: 26). This is significant as it shows the magazine's willingness to provide a forum for different perspectives and to offer a form of deliberative democracy (Wahl-Jorgenson 2006) that presented multiple perspectives on an issue. Magazines are vitally important sites of discussion because they allow us to understand the wide range of perspectives that were being articulated by second-wave feminists. As contentious issues, abortion and reproductive rights are a good example of how feminist magazines can provide this space. The use of the debate format in *Spare Rib* made these kinds of debate visible while they remained invisible in *Ms*. This suggests that the form of the magazines, as well as the political contexts that the magazines were produced in, is important. However, while there was a diversity of arguments, *Spare Rib* was always broadly pro-choice. In contrast to Shapiro's article, Mason argued that 'the whole debate [around the Arthur case] shows up the horrendous prejudices that the able-bodied have towards people with disabilities' (*Spare Rib* February 1982: 26). As Garland Thomson (2002: 2) argues, 'feminist theories all too often do not recognise disability in their litany of identities that inflect the category of women'. Shapiro's original article demonstrated this lack of consideration; however, the inclusion of Mason's article suggests an attempt by *Spare Rib* to ensure that the debate included disabled feminists.

By using the pronouns 'you', 'I' and 'we', Mason used the personal to reject medical discourses that emphasise ideas such as quality of life, arguing that rather than wanting to protect the welfare of the mother or the foetus, abortion of disabled foetuses reflected a society that does 'not like "misfits" who may not be able to earn a living' (*Spare Rib* February 1982: 26). This corresponds with Degener's (1990: 1) suggestion that 'the eugenics movement has always relied on selective policies in its bid to reduce the number of disabled children in the population' and that pre-natal screening is one way that this is implemented. Mason lamented the lack of understanding of disabilities and suggested that able-bodied people were 'caught up in the stereotyped images of helpless vegetables needing 24 hours a day care' (*Spare Rib* February 1982: 26). Whilst Shapiro described caring for a disabled child as a burden, Mason's article highlighted how disabled people's experiences and rights are not properly accounted for in debates around abortion and disability as the focus is placed on the feelings of the pregnant woman and not on the experience of being disabled.

Mason rejected the idea that women who carry foetuses that will be born with disabilities have a 'choice' to 'keep alive a baby with a disability', given the societal pressure to abort (Ibid.). There has been much discussion regarding eugenics in the US and the UK (Nelson 2003; Saxton 2006) and Mason's statement points to the difficulty of ever being able to determine whether a woman's choice is truly free from societal influence, given that discrimination against disabled people is likely to affect how much a woman is encouraged to terminate her pregnancy. However, as Sharp and Earle (2002: 2) argue, 'the crux of the feminist position, as we see it, is that women have a fundamental right to bodily autonomy and this includes the right to terminate an unwanted pregnancy'. Nonetheless, there is a conflict between acknowledging that women have the absolute right to choose, and a potential eugenicist agenda where women are encouraged to abort disabled foetuses. In the final sentence, Mason argued that 'the right to choose to live or die' must lie with the disabled person, which contrasts with the dominant feminist approach to abortion that is predicated on the idea that a woman's right to terminate a pregnancy is fundamental and, as a result, the foetus will not become a person. The rights of a potential disabled person are presented as being in competition with the rights of the pregnant woman. Mason could not 'support the campaign' for abortion 'to be freely available', since this inevitably meant that disabled foetuses would be aborted (*Spare Rib* February 1982: 26). Shapiro's and Mason's articles highlight the contradictions within discussions of reproductive rights in *Spare Rib*, a contradiction less frequently reflected in *Ms.* because persistent and sometimes violent threats to existing legislation left no space for these discussions.

International Feminism and Discussions of Reproductive Choice

Spare Rib was also more likely than *Ms.* to see reproductive rights as an international issue. There were numerous articles about the safety of reproductive drugs such as Depo-Provera in lower-income countries. *Spare Rib* acknowledged that, for poor women and women of colour, the pressure to take contraceptives could be a form of population control (Nelson 2003). The inclusion of articles that question the ethics of contraceptive drugs demonstrates a concern both with access to those drugs and the ways that reproductive rights are curtailed because of coercion. This was not seen in *Ms.* – its focus on how lack of access to reproductive services affected American women shows that the magazine did not have the same intersectional approach.

The most common way that international understandings of reproductive rights were represented in *Spare Rib* was through articles about the perceived dangers of the drug Depo-Provera: contributors criticised how the drug was being prescribed in countries such as India and Bangladesh without being properly tested. In 1982, two articles about the use of the drug were included in the magazine, and due to space limitations, this chapter will analyse one of them, Carol Smith's 'Depo-Provera Control of Fertility: Two Feminist Views' (*Spare Rib* March 1982: 49–53). Smith spoke to one woman who opposed Depo-Provera and its use by Indian women and a second woman who supported its use. Smith introduced the article by suggesting that the discussion of Depo-Provera 'raises important questions about the imperialist framework within which western feminists carry out much of our political work' (Ibid.: 49). This demonstrated an awareness of how Western feminists benefit from imperialism even if they are not aware of it: women from lower income countries were used as 'guinea pigs' for Depo-Provera before the drug was made available to Western women. However, because the article is presented as a debate, the benefits of Depo-Provera are argued as well, demonstrating that *Spare Rib* understood the issue as one in which there was more than one perspective.

Smith interviewed Hari John, a doctor working in India, who saw Depo-Provera as positive because 'of the control it can give women over their fertility' (Ibid.: 49). However, although this gave an Indian woman space within the magazine, it was mediated through Smith. In contrast, the position of the campaign against Depo-Provera is discussed directly, without any editorialising. This might suggest implicit support for that perspective since Smith can express it in her own words.

The campaign against the drug argued that it 'removes the control more firmly from women' and towards a 'paternalistic medical profession' (Ibid.). The concept of control is utilised by both sides of the debate, as Depo-Provera is alternatively presented as something that both gives women control and takes it away. The emphasis on choice is central to feminist arguments about reproductive rights (Smyth 2002). However, as Nelson (2003) argues, the emphasis on choice ignores the fact that no choice is free from context and therefore this discourse ignores the limitations that affect the ability for women to make reproductive choices. The invocation of control by both sides of the debate points to the contradictions surrounding the issue.

Dr John is introduced by Smith as putting 'into practice what we too often only theorise about in the west' (*Spare Rib* March 1982: 49). This claim to authority suggests that John's opinion should be heard because she has first-hand experience working with women in India – she is asked to describe how her experience in India influenced her attitudes towards Depo-Provera – which Smith and *Spare Rib* readers lack. John was not wholly unsupportive of sterilisation, suggesting that 'there should be disincentives for not having lots of children *not* force' (Ibid.: 51). This contrasts with an understanding of sterilisation and population control as an abuse of women in lower-income countries. John described herself as 'an accepter of DP' who used the contraception herself. This contradicts the image of a Depo-Provera user as ignorant of possible side effects since John is a doctor. Furthermore, she suggested that the drug provided a safety net for women who are 'subject to constant sexual abuse' (Ibid.) and a range of health problems. Rather than being understood as an abusive tool, John presented Depo-Provera as something that helps women take back control in difficult circumstances. She argued that Western opposition to Depo-Provera showed that Western feminists were not listening to women from the developing world.

In contrast, Janet Hadley, a British feminist, saw the drug as a form of population control that did not benefit women. Hadley began her argument with an anecdote about Bangladeshi women who were 'refusing to accept injections of tetanus vaccine' because they were worried that they were being given the Depo-Provera injection instead (Ibid.). Depo-Provera was presented as something that Bangladeshi women were so afraid of that they were willing to risk contracting other diseases to avoid inadvertently being given the vaccine. As a British woman, Hadley had no direct experience of either using or prescribing Depo-Provera and the anecdote therefore served to ground the discussion in the experiences of Bangladeshi women. However, this appeal to real-life experiences was undermined by the fact that the Bangladeshi women's experiences were being mediated through the perspective of a Western woman. Hadley was cynical about the reasons that Depo-Provera was popular in South Asian countries, seen by her use of words like 'peddling' which suggests that the drug is not legitimate. Whereas John saw the drug as a way for women to gain control, Hadley saw Depo-Provera as a form of control, arguing that 'women's bodies are being assaulted' (Ibid.: 52). John saw the drug as a way for women who have been sexually abused to take back some control by not having an unwanted pregnancy whereas, for Hadley, the prescription of the drug itself was understood as a form of abuse.

The article demonstrates how *Spare Rib* discussed reproductive rights in a way that valued alternative viewpoints. The debate format was used when there was no clear consensus on an issue. It demonstrates an increased awareness of how reproductive justice is not only about access to contraception but may also be about women being able to resist being coerced into taking contraception against their will.

Conclusion

Both *Spare Rib* and *Ms.* represented reproductive rights as an important feminist issue. Both magazines also understood that abortion was a politicised issue. Whilst the Abortion Act was passed in 1967 and *Roe v Wade* was decided in 1973, the continued threats to access meant that neither *Spare Rib* nor *Ms.* took abortion rights for granted. *Spare Rib* used combat imagery when there was a specific threat to legislation.

The key differences between *Spare Rib* and *Ms.* were due to the different political contexts in which they operated, their assumed reader and the formats used to represent reproductive rights. The coverage of anti-abortion terrorism in *Ms.* shows how the different political contexts in the US and the UK meant that abortion, which is inevitably a polarising issue, was polarised even more. This made it difficult for *Ms.* to discuss the ambivalent feelings about abortion that could be discussed in *Spare Rib*. The British magazine also took a more intersectional approach, especially the relationships between reproductive rights and disability and race, reflecting the wider intersectional approach that the magazine took to several other issues (Sedgwick 2017). Because *Ms.* aimed to reach a wider audience and assumed a white reader, there is little discussion of the intersections of race and disability in discussions of reproductive rights. The comparative approach between *Spare Rib* and *Ms.* helps us to understand the impact that political context, format and audience have on the representation of feminism and highlight the importance of looking to feminist magazines to help us understand feminist history.

Works Cited

Ahmed, S. 2001. 'Communities that Feel: Intensity, Difference and Attachment'. *Affective Encounters. School of Arts, Literature and Music Publications*. Eds A. Kuoivunen and S. Paasonen. Turku: University of Turku. 10–25.

Alvarez, R. M. and J. Brehm. 1995. 'American Ambivalence Towards Abortion Policy: Development of a Heteroskedastic Probit Model of Competing Values'. *American Journal of Political Science* 39.4: 1055–82.

Bader, E. J. and P. Baird-Windle. 2015. *Targets of Hatred: Anti-Abortion Terrorism*. New York: St. Martin's Press.

Berkman, J. 2011 'The Fertility of Scholarship on the History of Reproductive Rights in the United States'. *History Compass* 9.5: 433–47.

Bindel, J. 2011. 'The Anti-abortion Lobby is Back on the Warpath'. *New Statesman* <www.newstatesman.com/uk-politics/2011/01/abortion-rights-women-life> (last accessed 17 March 2019).

Bradley, P. 2003. *Mass Media and the Shaping of American Feminism 1963–1975*. Jackson: The University Press of Mississippi.

Bristow, J. 2012. 'Britain's Abortion Law. What it Says, and Why'. *Reproductive Review* <www.reproductivereview.org/images/uploads/Britains_abortion_law.pdf> (last accessed 17 March 2019).

Craig, S. C, J. G. Kane and M. D. Martinez. 2002. 'Sometimes You Feel Like a Nut, Sometimes You Don't: Citizens' Ambivalence About Abortion'. *Political Psychology* 23.2: 285–301.

Crenshaw, K. 1989. 'Demarginalising the Intersection of Race and Sex: A Black Feminist Critique of Anti-discrimination Doctrine, Feminist Theory and Anti-Racist Politics'. *University of Chicago Legal Forum* 139: 139–67.

Deneger, T. 1990. 'Female Self-determination between Feminist Claims and "Voluntary" Eugenics, between "Rights" and Ethics'. *Issues in Reproductive and Genetic Engineering* 3.2: 87–99.

Doan, A. 2009. *Opposition and Intimidation: The Abortion Wars and Strategies of Political Harassment*. Ann Arbor: University of Michigan Press.

Durham, M. 2005. 'Abortion, Gay Rights and Politics in Britain and America: a Comparison'. *Parliamentary Affairs* 58: 89–103.

Erdman Farrell, A. 1998. *Yours in Sisterhood: Ms. Magazine and the Promise of Popular Feminism*. Chapel Hill: The University of North Carolina Press.

Erdman Farrell, A. 2011. 'From a Tarantula on a Banana Boat to a Canary in a Mine: *Ms.* Magazine as a Cautionary Tale in a Neoliberal Age'. *Tulsa Studies in Women's Literature* 30.2: 393–405.

Garland Thomson, R. 2002 'Integrating Disability, Transforming Feminist Theory'. *NWSA Journal* 14.3: 1–32.

Ginsburg, F. D. 1989. *Contested Lives: The Abortion Debate in an American Community*. Berkeley: University of California Press.

Ginsburg, R. B. 1985. 'Some Thoughts on Autonomy and Equality in Relation to Roe v. Wade'. *North Carolina Law Review* 63.2: 375–86.

Hoggart, L. 2003. *Feminist Campaigns for Birth Control and Abortion Rights in Britain*. Lewiston: Edwin Mellen Press.

Hsieh, H. F. and S. E. Shannon. 2005. 'Three Approaches to Qualitative Content Analysis'. *Qualitative Health Research* 15.9: 1,277–288.

Hubbard, R. 2006. 'Abortion and Disability: Who Should and Should Not Inhabit the Earth'. *The Disability Studies Reader*. Ed. L. J. Davis. London: Sage. 93–104.

Jolly, M. 2014. '"The Feelings Behind the Slogans": Abortion Campaigning and Feminist Mood-Work circa 1979'. *New Formations* 82: 100–13.

Kaplan, L. 1997. *The Story of Jane: The Legendary Underground Feminist Abortion Service*. Champaign IL: University of Chicago Press.

Laing, A. C. and L. A. Sutton eds. 1999. *Reinventing Identities: The Gendered Self in Discourse*. Oxford: Oxford University Press.

Lovenduski, J. and V. Randall. 1993. *Contemporary Feminist Politics: Women and Power in Britain*. Oxford: Oxford University Press.

Luker, K. 1984. *Abortion and the Politics of Motherhood*. Durham: Duke University Press.

McNeil, M. 1991. 'Putting the Alton Bill in Context'. *Off-Centre: Feminism and Cultural Studies*. Eds S. Franklin, C. Lury and J. Stacey. London: Routledge. 149–59.

Ms. n.d. 'About' <http://msmagazine.com/blog/about/> (last accessed 17 March 2019).

NARAL. n.d 'About US' <www.prochoiceamerica.org/about/> (last accessed 16 August 2019).

Nelson, J. 2003. *Women of Color and the Reproductive Rights Movement*. New York: New York University Press.

Our Bodies Ourselves. n.d. 'History of Abortion in the US' <www.ourbodiesourselves.org/health-info/u-s-abortion-history/> (last accessed 17 March 2019).

Petchesky, R. P. 1981. 'Antiabortion, Antifeminism, and the Rise of the New Right'. *Feminist Studies* 7.2: 206–46.

Rowbotham, S. 1989. *The Past is Before Us: Feminism in Action Since the 1960s*. London: Pandora.

Rowe, M. 1982. 'Introduction'. *Spare Rib Reader*. Ed. M. Rowe. London: Penguin. 13–22.

Saxton, M. 2006. 'Disability and Selective Abortion'. *The Disability Studies Reader*. Ed. L. J. Davis. London: Sage. 97–9.

Sedgwick, C. 2016. 'Feminist Magazines and Historicising the Second Wave: Whose Histories?' *The Past in Visual Culture*. Eds J. Kay, C. Mahoney and C. Shaw. Jefferson: McFarland. 84–100.

Sedgwick, C. 2017. *Spare Rib and Ms. and the Representation of Second Wave Feminism: 1972–1992*. PhD Thesis. De Montfort University, Leicester.

Sharp, K. and Earle S. 2002. 'Feminism, Abortion and Disability: Irreconcilable Differences?' *Disability and Society* 17.2: 137–45.

Smyth, L. 2002. 'Feminism and Abortion Politics: Choice, Rights, and Reproductive Freedom'. *Women's Studies International Forum* 25.3: 335–45.

Staggenborg, S. 1991. *The Pro-Choice Movement: Organisation and Activism in the Abortion Conflict*. Oxford: Oxford University Press.

Steinem, G. 2012. *Outrageous Acts of Everyday Rebellion*. Open Road Media: New York.

Stetson, D. McBride., ed. 2001. *Abortion Politics, Women's Movements, and the Democratic State: A Comparative Study of State Feminism*. Oxford: Oxford University Press.

Thom, M. 1997. *Inside Ms.: 25 Years of the Magazine and the Feminist Movement*. New York: Henry Holt.

Travis, T. 2008. 'The Women in Print Movement: History and Implications'. *Book History* 11.1: 275–300.

Wahl Jorgenson, K. 2006. 'Letters to the Editor in Local and Regional Newspapers: Giving Voice to the Reader'. *Local Journalism and Local Media: Making the News Local*. Ed. B. Franklin. London: Routledge. 231–41.

Winship, J. 1987. *Inside Women's Magazines*. London: Pandora.

17

Digital Feminist Cultures

Kaitlynn Mendes

WITHIN FEMINIST TRADITIONS across the globe, there is a long and rich history of women making their own media to spread feminist thoughts, ideas and goals, and to combat largely negative attention imposed upon them by the mainstream press (see DiCenzo et al. 2011; Piepmeir 2009; Zobl and Drueke 2012). In Britain, as in other nations, as new technologies emerged, feminists seized the opportunity to use these spaces for feminist thought, activism and writing. This chapter therefore provides both a background and new empirical evidence of the ways that British feminists have engaged in digital alternative media production to create and shape feminist discourse, engage in activism and engender a sense of feminist community through shared readings of these texts. The chapter will focus on three alternative British digital magazines: *The F-Word*, *The Vagenda* and *Feminist Times*. These sites were selected because of their importance within the history of contemporary British DIY feminism; their high level of visibility within mainstream media culture; and the surprising dearth of scholarship around them. Although there are many digital feminist initiatives which are worthy of scholarly attention, this chapter begins to map largely undocumented terrain and serves as an entry point for those interested in contemporary alternative, DIY feminist publications in Britain. Drawn from a combination of semi-structured interviews and textual analysis of primary and secondary sources, this chapter will provide some background and context on the rise (and in some cases, end) of these publications, highlight what they seek to 'do' and how they achieve this. Furthermore, the chapter adds important empirical evidence to document *why*, despite a long history of alternative feminist print cultures, contemporary feminists are turning to digital spaces to produce alternative media, while identifying key challenges encountered along the way.

The Emergence of Digital Feminist Magazines and Blogs in Britain

For many years, the focus on young women centred on their media *consumption*, rather than *production* (Kearney 2006) – a significant oversight given the ways that women in the UK and beyond have been engaged in media production practices for well over 250 years (Steiner 1992). In fact, there is ample evidence of the ways that feminists around the globe have long recognised the stakes in being able to control and produce their own media, as well as the way that they and their issues are represented (see Byerly 2013; Zobl and Drueke 2012). As such, the media has been an important site in wider struggles for equality. Looking back, scholars have documented the ways that newspapers, pamphlets, posters, scrapbooking, poetry and zines have been used to challenge and disrupt patriarchal ideologies and discourses (Piepmeier 2009; Zobl and Dreueke 2012). British suffragettes, for example, were prolific producers of their own newspapers, which they used in their campaign for women's suffrage (see DiCenzo et al. 2011). Similarly, second-wave feminists successfully ran the newspaper *Outwrite* (1982–8) and magazines/zines such as *Shocking Pink* (1980–2; 1987–92) and *Spare Rib* (1972–93), which provided feminist alternative perspectives and stories than those found in the mainstream media (see Chapter 2).

Around the start of the 1990s, just as feminism was routinely proclaimed to be 'dead', 'dying' or 'passé' (see Faludi 1992; McRobbie 2009), there was an explosion of alternative feminist cultural production, which embraced DIY aesthetics and principles. According to scholars, DIY cultural production is that which incorporates political resistance and blurs the boundaries between organiser, participants and audiences, often by inviting readers to collectively contribute in the production and distribution of media artefacts (Piano 2002; Piepmeier 2009; Zobl and Reitsamer 2012). Within the British context specifically, scholars such as Red Chidgey (2009) have argued that DIY feminist cultures were keen to embrace an anti-capitalist stance which favours self or collectively produced culture run on a not-for-profit or voluntary basis – principles which, for the most part, are seen within the three case studies profiled here. Initiated by what are now described as 'third-wave' feminists, or those informed by poststructuralist and postcolonial understandings of gender, race and identity, these young women used feminist lenses to engage with politics, popular culture, art and music as important sites through which they enacted political agency (Harris 2010; Henry 2004). While print-based artefacts such as zines were one of the most popular feminist media forms in the 1990s (see Chidgey 2012), by the early to mid-2000s, feminists, like many other DIY cultural producers, became more engaged with the opportunities afforded by digital technologies (Zobl and Reitsamer 2012). Leslie Regan Shade (2002), for example, has noted the ways that feminists around the globe began to use the Internet, and it is here that we begin to see discourses around the promise and potential of 'cyberfeminism' (see Braidotti 2003; Hawthorne and Klein 1999). In fact, since the turn of the century, the explosion of feminist blogs, e-zines, newsletters and social media accounts has been said to constitute a *fourth* wave of feminism (Baumgardner 2011; Munro 2013). 'Tech-savvy and gender-sophisticated' (Baumgardner 2011), fourth-wave feminists are engaged in projects such as digitally archiving experiences of sexism and hostility, fostering a collective call-out culture, amplifying marginalised communities and mobilising digital tools to highlight the continued need for (intersectional) feminism (see Mendes et al. 2019).

Because of the alternative, the DIY and sometimes underground nature of some feminist publications, combined with poor or scattered archives, one European study identifies fifty-one women-led feminist media projects in the UK since the 1960s, including thirty blogs and five e-zines (Zobl and Reitsamer 2012). To put this in a wider context, within Europe, Britain is one of the most prolific producers of feminist (digital) production. And while there has been much mainstream media attention paid to popular feminist campaigns and hashtags such as The Everyday Sexism Project (#EverydaySexism), Object!, or No More Page 3, there is surprisingly little academic attention, both empirically and theoretically, to digital feminist production in the UK and elsewhere (for an exception see Zobl and Drueke 2012). This is despite the popularity of feminist magazines such as *The Vagenda*, *The F-Word* and the *Feminist Times*. The rest of this chapter, therefore, begins to fill this gap.

The F-Word

Founded in 2001 by Catherine Redfern, *The F-Word* is one of Britain's earliest online feminist magazines which is 'dedicated to talking about and sharing ideas on contemporary UK feminism' (*The F-Word* 2013). After 'moaning for ages' to her partner about how great it would be to set up a feminist website, she returned home one night to find that he had bought her a URL (Chidgey 2010). Not long after discovering the rise of grrrl culture in the US – thanks to its explosion of feminist zines and websites – Redfern began to wonder if anything similar had been created in the UK. Frustrated at being unable to find any such equivalent publications, she decided to do something about it. *The F-Word* came about because 'it's the sort of thing that I would like to read, but didn't seem to exist anywhere else, so the only thing I could do was create it myself' (*The F-Word* 2011–13). Redfern chose the name after seeing it on a T-shirt Gloria Steinem wore for the cover of American feminist magazine *Bust*. As she recalled, 'I thought that was a really clever name for a website because it implied that it was unfashionable and uncool' (Chidgey 2010), but also because feminism was supposedly 'taboo' for young British women (*The F-Word* 2011–13). In this sense, like other DIY cultural producers, Redfern's choice of name is in and of itself an act of political resistance which brings attention to a movement (feminism) that is seen to be off-limits, challenging or even dangerous.

Well over a decade later, *The F-Word* has grown to be one of the UK's best-known feminist forums, producing a new issue each month by a wide range of contributors. The site is free to use, and members of the public can access content either by visiting the website or signing up to its mailing list to receive content directly to their inbox. Although the site has several categories that users can scroll through (e.g. sexual harassment, men, language, education and family), many of these are not heavily populated, nor have they been updated in several years. These digital remnants offer an insight into topics that site leaders perhaps envisioned would become popular – or at least were important enough to tag and organise using a header – but which never materialised. In this sense, in addition to functioning as a space where feminists can engage with contemporary feminist debates and ideas, the website doubles as a digital archive which documents development in feminist ideas and issues in the UK over a nearly twenty-year period. As it stands, at the time of writing, the main emphasis on the site is its 'features' section, which includes a combination of 'hard news stories', interviews, reviews and commentary about a wide range of topics (e.g. various feminist hashtags, sexist advertising, 'dress codes' at work and menstruation); and its blog, which includes a 'weekly round-up and open thread', providing short summaries and embedded hyperlinks to what they see as 'the most interesting and important articles from the previous seven days' (*The F-Word* 2017).

Although Redfern was the main site editor between 2001–7, it was never a solitary endeavour. After Redfern stepped down, *The F-Word* introduced a policy of rotating editors who have overall responsibility for the site, and section editors who are responsible for discreet sections such as music, film, comics and visual arts. While not quite a non-hierarchical *collective* – where work is shared-out equally among members who make decisions together – *The F-Word* certainly relies on collaboration and sharing out duties. Like many other contemporary alternative cultural products, *The F-Word* is an example of what Lieverouw (2011: 62) titles the 'new collectivism' which is based on 'community building, interactivity and participation in the design of the media as well as the organisation of the working and operation processes' (Zobl and Reitsamer 2012: 29).

When asked who her target market for the site was, Redfern emphasised that it was not aimed specifically at women, but was for people who were 'just interested in feminism, or wanted to say something [about feminism]' (Chidgey 2010). Although it accepts contributions from feminists of any age, like zines such as *Shocking Pink* before it, *The F-Word* is particularly aimed at showcasing the voices of younger feminists – 'those of us born during or after the feminism of the 60s and 70s' (*The F-Word* 2011–13). That this site continues the feminist tradition of opening up space for younger women's voices is a radical act in itself – as much research has shown the ways young people, girls in particular, are subject to increased scrutiny and regulation – factors which can lead to the silencing of their voices and their exclusion from the public sphere (see Harris 2004; Keller 2016). But here on the site, it is common to find articles from young women, some of whom are still in their teens. In addition, other articles specifically address challenges faced by teen feminists.

For example, in 2014, Chelsea Birkby wrote an article titled 'Teenage feminism – coming to a blog near you' which details the woeful underrepresentation of feminism as part of her formal curriculum in school, and the way that she sees this changing with the rise of popular sites such as the Everyday Sexism Project, No More Page 3, *The Vagenda* and popular authors such as Caitlin Moran and Hadley Freeman. Other 'agony aunt' sections deal specifically with sexism experienced by teens at school. For example, in 2010, Sarah wrote to *The F-Word* to ask: 'I get teased in school – what's the best way of shutting down boys who say girls can't follow football? What can I say to those that seem to think that girls and sports don't mix?' (McCabe 2010). In addition to functioning as a space for young women, which addresses their concerns and gives practical advice for dealing with sexism and other forms of oppression within institutionalised spaces such as school, the site also publishes articles about the relevance of feminism for men and gender non-conforming groups. Indeed, there are many articles which specifically address trans issues – such as the way that trans children are represented in the media (Violet 2016); reminders about annual International Transgender Day of Remembrance (Laura 2013); and reports about widespread discrimination against trans and intersex communities (G 2012). Many of these posts were written by trans or gender non-conforming authors. Indeed, the site, like many contemporary digital spaces, is committed to taking an intersectional view on issues. In its online guidance for potential contributors, while encouraging submissions from 'new voices' on a wide range of topics, even 'controversial' ones, they clearly state that they will not accept writing which is 'sexist, racist, homophobic, transphobic, classist or disablist' (*The F-Word* 2011–13).

In addition to providing a (safe) space for young (gender non-conforming) feminists to speak, Redfern articulated that a key goal of *The F-Word* was to challenge the idea that we live in a postfeminist moment where young women (and men) reject feminism (Redfern 2010). Indeed, in recent years, there has been a range of high-profile social media campaigns, such as *Who Needs Feminism?* or #INeedFeminismBecause, which invite the public to discursively challenge the notion that feminism is irrelevant (see Mendes et al. 2019). Similarly, within *The F-Word*, several articles focus explicitly on the challenges of identifying as a (teen) feminist. As sixteen-year-old Abigael Watson (2014) lamented in her article titled 'A generation that needs feminism', classmates at her all-girls school frequently misunderstand what it means to be a feminist ('does that mean you hate men?'), genuinely believe women are not equal to men, or 'regard sexism as an insignificant problem'. This is just one of many articles which explicitly and discursively reiterate the need for feminism and challenge postfeminist discourse. As scholars have argued, it is often at the *discursive* level that contemporary feminist activism seeks to intervene (see Shaw 2012).

The Vagenda

Founded in 2012 by Holly Baxter and Rhiannon Lucy Cosslett, these two 'impoverished graduates' decided to start a blog 'dedicated to humorously lambasting women's magazines' (Baxter and Cosslett 2014). After seeing the term 'The Vagenda' used in a broadsheet newspaper about women in the workplace with a hidden agenda, the two decided to use the name for their new blog. *The Vagenda* was an instant success. Overnight, the site attracted more than 30,000 hits and, as Cosslett recalled, she continued to watch the figures go up and up and up over the next few days (Cosslett 2017). Originally, *The Vagenda* was hosted on a simple, free-to-use Blogspot platform designed by Cosslett, who began building websites around the age of twelve or thirteen under her dad's supervision. As she recalled, by the time she initiated *The Vagenda* in her mid-20s, she was already 'quite experienced' with web design. Shortly after *The Vagenda* went viral, the pair initiated a Kickstarter campaign to fund a new, slicker website. In total, forty-three issues of *The Vagenda* were published between January 2012 and July 2015. Although *The Vagenda* is no longer updated, the website remains publicly accessible thanks to Cosslett's father, who pays the roughly £3 per month fee needed to keep the domain name and the site up and running (Cosslett 2017).

When asked why the pair chose a web-based site, rather than say a zine, newsletter or other printed format, Cosslett responded:

> I just think a blog allowed us to do the kind of writing we wanted to do – you know social media wouldn't have allowed that – Twitter was too short, Facebook felt too parochial I suppose. And you know, we wanted to write funny stuff, funny long form stuff, and you know, it was the way of reaching as many people as possible by doing that. I think a zine just wouldn't have crossed our mind. We didn't have money to do that – we couldn't be bothered to think of photocopy machines, you know, we didn't have the budget for it. A blog is free and theoretically, I mean I did quite a bit of photoshop design on it, but theoretically you can be up and running in five minutes. I think it was that that really appealed to us. (Cosslett 2017)

Although there is a materiality to zines which scholars argue matters deeply to publics (Piepmeier 2009), there are also capital (money) and resource (photocopier) implications which could make digital platforms more attractive for some contemporary young people. And while there is no doubt that the digital divide certainly exists – even among feminists who possess varying levels of media literacy, confidence and skills which restrict certain groups from engaging with digital platforms (see Fotopoulou 2016; Zobl 2009) – a new generation of young people are growing up with these skills, which in turn make them more likely to continue engaging with digital, rather than print-based forms of cultural production.

When asked what skills she thought were necessary to run a site like *The Vagenda*, Cosslett recognised that having web design skills, a clear vision of what the site would look like, as well as a good eye for design, all needed to come together to make the site a success. Unlike home-made DIY zines in the past, however, which were often produced via cut-and-paste and which lacked an overall professional look (Zobl 2009), Cosslett and a range of other contemporary feminists increasingly make use of media experts to give their platform a more professional look (see Mendes 2015, 2017; Mendes et al. 2019) (see Plate 10). In addition to having the right 'look', fundamentally, Cosslett argued that *The Vagenda*'s success was down to not only having a team of *good* but *funny* writers. Looking back, she reflected on how the writing was 'funny and cheeky and irreverent, and it spoke to readers in a tone that they knew intimately already because it was how they spoke with each other. And, that's why it took off while other feminist blogs didn't' (Cosslett 2017). Like many other alternative activist publications, humour and irony are key tools through which hegemonic ideologies about gender roles, and their representations in mainstream media and culture are critiqued (see Braidotti 2003; Lievrouw 2011; Zobl and Reitsamer 2012). Irony, as Rosi Braidotti (2003: 248) has argued, is simply a 'systematically applied dose of de-bunking'. Humour, on the other hand, has been identified as a particularly effective tool used to make online content 'sticky' – or to attract audience attention and engagement (Bore et al. 2018). Using both humour and irony, *The Vagenda* was able to tackle serious issues which are often considered taboo or excluded from mainstream content. For example, in June 2014, they ran an article titled 'Blushing and Bleeding: Why I'm sick of Period Apology Culture' which not only questioned why menstruation is seen as embarrassing, but highlighted issues around period poverty (*The Vagenda* 2014) – a term which, in the aftermath of a decade of austerity, has received mainstream media attention as the public initiates campaigns to make menstrual products tax-exempt, affordable and safe for our bodies and the planet (see Peck 2017; Period Equity 2017). Taking a humorous approach, other articles such as 'Dinner or Tampons?: The Modern Woman's Choice' (Rhodes 2015) critiqued the tax levied on tampons, while incontinence pads were tax exempt. As the author Anna Rhodes (2015) wrote, the tax on sanitary products:

> contributes to period shame: girls learn from a young age that they, and their bodily needs, are not valued by the government or the tax system. Girls' menstrual needs are valued lower than EXOTIC MEAT by the tax system, which is exempt. We are less important than a bloody Kangaroo burger, guys: it's a bit tragic.

By taxing sanitary products, Rhodes criticises the government for adding an additional burden to those living in poverty (including 13.5 million children) – many of whom are forced to choose between food and tampons each month. Finishing the article, Rhodes (2015) issues a call to readers to 'publicly voice our opposition to

Period Tax'. Although a small act, as Chandra Mohanty has argued, 'everyday feminist . . . practices are as important as larger, organised political movements' (2003: 4).

Indeed, it is these small, often humorous acts of identifying and calling out sexism, particularly within the mainstream media, that has led to real world change according to Cosslett. Although she was adamant that we are not yet at a point where we can say 'mission accomplished', as there is certainly more work to do, 'compared to what the landscape looked like five years ago, it's [*The Vagenda*] had a real influence', particularly on mainstream media who are beginning to adopt feminist views (Cosslett 2017).

The Feminist Times

In October 2013, seven months after founder Charlotte Raven announced that she would revive the historic feminist magazine *Spare Rib*, the online magazine launched as a member-led, not-for-profit, brand and sponsorship-free organisation which was funded by monthly subscriptions from the public (Raven 2014). The initial announcement received high levels of mainstream attention in left-leaning publications such as *The Guardian* – not least because of the history and esteem towards *Spare Rib* as Britain's most iconic feminist magazine, but also likely because Raven was a journalist herself with various media contacts. Although Raven initially hoped to name the magazine *Spare Rib*, because 'we love the 70s version of *Spare Rib* and didn't want to fall prey to the female compulsion to reinvent the wheel' (Dowell 2013), an alternative name was chosen after *Spare Rib*'s founding editors Marsha Rowe and Rosie Boycott threatened a legal challenge.[1] Aimed at providing more than 'one-dimensional' feminism, *The Feminist Times* was intended to be funny and satirical – a 'feminist Private Eye' which avoided traditional women's magazines' focus on lifestyle (Dowell 2013). Furthermore, although eschewing traditional funding models, Raven intended the magazine to be a 'mainstream' platform to 'represent the wonderful diversity of modern feminism' (*The Feminist Times* 2013). Unlike *The F-Word* and *The Vagenda* which targeted a youthful audience, *The Feminist Times* sought a broad audience, boasting that its members ranged from 'teenagers to grandmothers' (*The Feminist Times* 2013).

Despite a swell of enthusiasm from members of the public, the venture closed nine months later, in July 2014, after being unable to financially support itself as a 'not-for-profit, ad- and PR-free space' (Lusher 2014). According to the editorial team, this was because the magazine refused to accept commercial sponsors or engage in 'native' advertising – a 'form of paid media where the commercial content is delivered within the design and form of editorial content' (Conill 2016: 905). Instead, the magazine relied on membership, which began for as little as £5 per month (*The Feminist Times* 2014). In return, members received 'regular updates, offers & free entry to all our events while helping us give a platform to women and subjects often not heard in the mainstream' (*The Feminist Times* 2014). This membership model is not unique to *The Feminist Times* and has been used extensively in the past (see *Grassroots Feminism* n.d.).

Although the initiative ran for only nine months, it managed to produce nearly 500 articles. The site contained unusual categories such as 'angst,' 'speculum' and 'hard times', alongside more traditional sections such as editorials, politics, media, gender and culture. Indeed, before leaving, the editorial team composed a final segment titled,

Figure 17.1 *Feminist Times* logo.

'Utopia and End Times' (2014) which compiled 'some of your favourite moments, as well as some of our personal highlights'. This included an overview of eight 'theme weeks' including 'Man Week', '12 Days of Sexism', 'Sex Industry Week' and 'Mental Health Awareness Week'. Indeed, the variety of topics covered in the magazine are vast – from its 'War on Spanx' (Graham 2013) and 'Why Debt is a Feminist Issue' (O'Leary 2014), to highlighting lost histories of women who participated in the miners' strikes of the 1970s (Graham 2014a). Like the long history of feminist zines before it, *The Feminist Times* provided an outlet for personal expression, creative outlets, supportive spaces and forms of cultural resistance and political critique (Schilt and Zobl 2008).

Like *Spare Rib*, *The Feminist Times* faced many of the same challenges in trying to produce a mainstream feminist magazine using non-traditional business model or practices. In the wake of *The Feminist Times*' closure, the founding editors issued a statement to readers indicating that the main reason for the closure was lack of financial resources, noting that the magazine 'simply cannot survive any longer' (Moss 2014). As editor Deborah Coughlin elaborated, the only thing missing was money: 'It's the only thing that's been missing. It wasn't missing energy, it wasn't missing vision, it wasn't missing a gaping hole – it was very much filling a gap.' (Moss 2014). Perhaps the lesson to take from *The Feminist Times* is precisely how difficult it is to run a feminist publication which rejected both 'corporate advertising and slave labour' of unpaid interns (Raven 2014). Indeed, in modern times where people are often unwilling to pay for content – professionally generated or not – most grassroots, alternative feminist campaigns rely on free labour and public donations – the latter of which can be sporadic and is often viewed with suspicion. Although not a new issue, as I will outline below, the political economy of starting, running and maintaining media production – digital or not, historic or contemporary – remains one of the most challenging and pervasive problems in feminist cultural production.

Challenges of Running a Digital Feminist Publication

Although the three feminist publications discussed in this chapter are different in many ways, one challenge binding them together is financial sustainability. Previous research has noted the ways that feminists deliberately use (commercial) digital platforms or tools in their activism because they are free, affordable or relatively easy to use (see Mendes 2015; Mendes et al. 2019). For example, although the original site for *The Vagenda* was hosted on a free Blogspot platform, it is now hosted on a platform which costs around £3 per month. While the cost of actually *hosting* a site such as *The Vagenda* may not be too prohibitive (£30–40 per year), many feminists rely on *pro bono* developers, family or friends to design custom sites for them – sites which require upgrades every few years and which can become subjected to security threats as hackers seek to troll and disrupt these sites deliberately (see Mendes et al. 2019).

Accompanying the rise of digital culture in recent years, a healthy body of scholarship has emerged devoted to 'digital labour' – or that which takes place in online settings (see Andrejevic et al. 2014; Fuchs 2014; Terranova 2000). Like labour in offline settings, digital labour has been said to exploit the unpaid labour of those who use digital platforms and social media as sites of creativity, leisure and, increasingly, activism (see Duffy 2015a; Fuchs 2014). Although scholars have examined digital labour in relation to the ways that people produce free content for corporations (see Andrejevic 2009; Scholz 2013; Terranova 2000), little scholarship has focused on the *gendered nature* of digital labour (for exceptions, see Arcy 2016; Duffy 2015a, 2015b; Jarrett 2014), particularly within various digital feminist media production (see Gleeson 2016). Indeed, as I outline below and elsewhere in more depth (see Mendes et al. 2019), digital feminist labour is not only immaterial and affective, but precarious, highly exploitative and often invisible.

Although more often than not, such work is undertaken because of an individual's desire and passion for the subject, the fact remains that it is very difficult (and contentious) to earn money from these feminist initiatives. This sentiment was echoed by *Feminist Times* editor Sarah Graham who noted: 'So often women's work is unpaid, a labour of love, that women expect to work for free and, like many others in the digital age, expect online content to be free too. It's true of almost every feminist website online . . . but the fact is, beyond one-off donations, funding is so hard to come by for women's projects.' (Graham 2014b). Instead, feminist campaigns often rely on donations – a fact which Graham notes infuriates the public who ask, 'how dare we ask readers to contribute to the funding of the site' while being simultaneously quick to condemn them for 'selling out' if they accept funding from corporations (Graham 2014b). Anecdotally, from years of studying feminist platforms and campaigns, it is commonplace to see the presence of a 'donate' button. For example, with *The F-Word* and *The Feminist Times* the public can make a one-off or a standing-monthly donation. In both cases, funds received are reinvested back into the site. While the increased professionalisation of activism and solicitation of donations are controversial issues among feminists (see Mendes 2017), the fact remains that the labour put into these digital feminist platforms is real, and feminists often struggle to maintain this labour alongside (finding) paid employment and having a family or social life.

Indeed, in Britain's current climate of 'austerity', where a generation of 'precariat' workers are often expected to work for free, or for minimal pay, and where their lives are dominated by insecurity (Standing 2011), many engage in 'aspirational labour' (Duffy 2015b) where labourers are willing to contributing their time, creativity and efforts to these feminist platforms to raise their own public profile or gain valuable experience needed to secure future employment. As stated on *The F-Word*'s website, while it would make them 'very, very happy indeed if you wanted to contribute anything to the site', they are unable to 'pay for submissions. Everyone who contributes to the site is a volunteer' (*The F-Word* 2011–13). In a similar vein, under a tab titled 'Submissions', *The Vagenda* not only offers guidance on how to pitch a story, but a side note stating: 'Oh, and being as it is that we are two young women working out of our kitchens, we are unable to offer employment, work experience or internships – sorry.' (*The Vagenda* n.d.). Indeed, when asked what the biggest challenge of running *The Vagenda* was, Cosslett admitted that as a 'labour of love', neither Cosslett nor Baxter (nor any of the other contributors) were paid for their work. When the site took off, responding to emails, sourcing and editing stories became too much work, particularly when the pair began full-time employment elsewhere. As Cosslett acknowledged, the sheer amount of work is 'eventually why we had to stop doing it. It took so much time and energy' (Cosslett 2017).

Only *The Feminist Times* paid writers for their work and, while excellent in principle, it is also this fact which led to its closure. This presents a challenging double-bind – is it better to produce a feminist magazine that relies on exploitative labour practices, or to forego feminist intervention at all? Neither solution is ideal. Instead, as women's work continues to be undervalued and underpaid in various sectors (see Jarrett 2014), it is pertinent to recognise labour as a feminist issue and devote more time to studying the political economy of feminist initiatives – if only to make *visible* the largely *invisible* and un[der]paid labour needed to sustain them. And while I would personally like to live in a world where feminists get compensated accordingly for their work, it is unlikely to materialise in our current media environment or economic climate. On the other hand, I am also cautious that as feminism continues to enjoy a revival and unprecedented popularity, we must concurrently be wary about how it is co-opted and commercialised, where the profits are not evenly distributed, but become concentrated in the hands of the powerful few at the expense of the marginalised many (see Mendes 2017).

'Doing Feminism' in Digital Spaces

When looking across *The F-Word*, *The Vagenda* and *The Feminist Times*, it is clear that these three digital magazines have by no means re-invented the wheel for feminist cultural production. In fact, in many senses, they carry forward legacies of publications such as *Shocking Pink* and *Spare Rib* which sought to provide creative outlets for young women to speak, to provide an alternative to mainstream media content, and to critique a wide range of oppressive ideologies and practices. Like their forebears, these publications draw from a range of discursive strategies which include humour and irony as key tools of critique. Significantly, despite using digital technologies, the funding models have not changed dramatically over the years. Run by a core group of members, they accept submissions from members of the public who, more often than not, are not financially compensated for their work. Money is raised through crowdfunding, donations, subscription, and even out of their own pockets when necessary. These publications are also often discussed in highly affective terms – labours of love – work which they are happy to contribute but simultaneously can be exhausting, draining and ultimately too much at times.

When thinking more broadly then about what these and other alternative, self-published, digital feminist publications *do*, it is clear that, like printed publications before them, they provide at least the *potential* or *opportunity* to address 'taboo' subjects and perspectives – those which are often ignored in mainstream media. They also provide spaces for like-minded feminists to come together to create communities – even if only online ones. Although it can be difficult to tell what long-term impact these feminist publications have, Redfern reflected, 'I would like to think that it [*The F-Word*] has played a role in bringing more people to feminism, in fact I know it has, and has made more people feminists by reading it.' (Redfern 2010). As just one piece in a 'huge patchwork of feminism' (Redfern 2010) within the UK, *The F-Word* provides an important space for young women to better understand feminism and provide a feminist lens to the world around them. In a similar vein, Cosslett (2017) believes that *The Vagenda* has 'had a real influence' on the contemporary media landscape, noting the ways that publications such as *Elle* and *Vogue* are adopting feminist messages. Although *The Feminist Times* had a much shorter history, the fact that the magazine's closure received so much attention, and public statements of support indicates that it was valued and did matter. And although it is easy to take for granted that because these platforms are digital, they will be well-preserved and archived, this is far from the truth. So, while this chapter adds one layer to the preservation of knowledge about women's digital print cultures, how we archive this material has important implications for future scholarship and understanding of digital feminist cultural heritage – heritage which is certainly worth preserving for future generations of feminists to come (Withers 2015).

Note

1. This name was chosen after a vote by members. Alternative names included 'Hip Bone', 'FemText', 'Woman's Brigade' and 'The Purple Notebook' (see Blake 2013).

Works Cited

Andrejevic, M., J. Banks, J. E. Campbell, N. Couldry, A. Fish, A. Hearn and L. Ouellette. 2014. 'Participations: Dialogues on the Participatory Promise of Contemporary Culture and Politics'. *International Journal of Communication* 8: 1,089–106.

Arcy, J. 2016. 'Emotion Work: Considering Gender in Digital Labour'. *Feminist Media Studies* 16.2: 365–8.

Baumgardner, J. 2011. *F'em, Goo Goo, Gaga, and Some Thoughts on Balls*. Berkeley: Seal Press.

Baxter H. and R. L. Cosslett. 2014. The Vagenda*: A Zero-Tolerance Guide to the Media*. London: Square Peg.

Blake, I. 2013. 'Exclusive: Re-launched Feminist Magazine *Spare Rib* Changes Name to Hip Bone', *Ham & High* <www.hamhigh.co.uk/news/spare-rib-feminist-magazine-in-kentish-town-name-change-1-2266469> (last accessed 23 November 2017).

Bore, I. A. Graefer and A. Kilby. 2018. 'This Pussy Grabs Back: Humour, Digital Affects and Women's Protest'. *Open Cultural Studies* 1.1 <www.degruyter.com/view/j/

culture.2017.1.issue-1/culture-2017-0050/culture-2017-0050.xml> (last accessed 20 August 2019).

Braidotti, R. 2003. 'Cyberfeminism with a Difference'. *Futures of Critical Theory: Dreams of Difference*. Eds. M. A. Peters, M. Olssen, and C. Lankshear. Lanham MA: Rowman & Littlefield. 239–60.

Byerly, C. 2013. *The Palgrave International Handbook of Women and Journalism*. Basingstoke: Palgrave Macmillan.

Chidgey, R. 2009. 'DIY Feminist Networks in Europe. Personal and Collective Acts of Resistance'. *Transform! European Journal of Alternative Thinking and Political Dialogue* 5: 159–65.

Chidgey, R. 2010. '"No Rent-A-Feminist": An Interview with Catherine Redfern from *The F-Word* (UK)'. *Grassroots Feminism: Transnational Archives, Resources and Communities* <www.grassrootsfeminism.net/cms/node/668> (last accessed 17 November 2017).

Chidgey, R. 2012. 'Hand-Made Memories: Remediating Cultural Memory in DIY Feminist Networks'. *Feminist Media: Participatory Spaces, Networks and Cultural Citizenship*. Eds E. Zobl and R. Drueke. Germany: Transcript. 87–97.

Conill, R. F. 2016. 'Camouflaging Church as State'. *Journalism Studies* 17.7: 904–14.

Cosslett, R. L. 2017. Personal Interview, 17 November 2017.

DiCenzo, M., L. Delap and L. Ryan. 2011. *Feminist Media History: Suffrage, Periodicals and the Public Sphere*. Basingstoke: Palgrave Macmillan.

Dowell, B. 2013. '*Spare Rib* Magazine to be Relaunched by Charlotte Raven'. *The Guardian* 25 April 2013 <www.theguardian.com/media/2013/apr/25/sarah-raven-relaunch-spare-rib> (last accessed 23 November 2017).

Duffy, B. E. 2015a. 'Gendering The Labour Of Social Media Production'. *Feminist Media Studies* 15.4: 710–14.

Duffy, B. E. 2015b. 'The Romance of Work: Gender and Aspirational Labour in the Digital Culture Industries'. *International Journal of Cultural Studies* 19.4: 441–57.

Faludi, S. 1992. *Backlash: The Undeclared War Against Women*. New York: Anchor Books.

Fotopoulou, A. 2016. *Feminist Activism and Digital Networks: Between Empowerment and Vulnerability*. Basingstoke: Palgrave Macmillan.

Fuchs, C. 2014. *Digital Labour and Karl Marx*. New York and Oxford: Routledge.

G., H. 2012. 'New EC Report: "Discrimination Against Trans and Intersex People on the Grounds of Sex, Gender Identity and Gender Expression"'. *The F-Word* <www.thefword.org.uk/2012/06/new_ec_report/> (last accessed 21 November 2017).

Gleeson, J. 2016. '"(Not) Working 9–5": the Consequences of Contemporary Australian-based Online Feminist Campaigns as Digital Labour'. *Media International Australia* 16.1: 77–85.

Graham, S. 2013. 'War on Spanx'. *The Feminist Times* <http://archive.feministtimes.com/decommissioning-shapewear/> (last accessed 23 November 2017).

Graham, S. 2014a. 'Women Against Pit Closures: Memories from the Miners' Strike, 30 Years on'. *The Feminist Times* <http://archive.feministtimes.com/women-against-pit-closures-memories-from-the-miners-strike-30-years-on/> (last accessed 23 November 2017).

Graham, S. 2014b. 'On Leaving *The Feminist Times*'. *Huffington Post* 13 September 2014 <www.huffingtonpost.co.uk/sarah-graham/feminist-times_b_5586892.html> (last accessed 24 November 2017).

Grassroots Feminism. n.d. <www.grassrootsfeminism.net/cms/> (last accessed 27 November 2017).

Harris, A. 2004. *Future Girl: Young Women in the Twenty-first Century*. New York: Routledge.

Harris, A. 2010. 'Mind the Gap: Attitudes and Emergent Feminist Politics Since the Third Wave'. *Australian Feminist Studies* 25.66: 475–84.

Hawthorne, S. and R. Klein. 1999. *Cyberfeminism: Connectivity, Critique and Creativity*. Melbourne: Spinifex Press.

Henry, A. 2004. *Not My Mother's Sister: Generational Conflict and Third-Wave Feminism*. Bloomington IN: Indiana University Press.
Jarrett, K. 2014. 'The Relevance of "Women's Work": Social Reproduction and Immaterial Labour in Digital Media'. *Television & New Media* 15.1: 14–29.
Kearney, M. C. 2006. *Girls Make Media*. New York: Routledge.
Keller, J. 2016. *Girls' Feminist Blogging in a Postfeminist Age*. London and New York: Routledge.
Laura. 2013. 'International Transgender Day of Remembrance'. *The F-Word* <www.thefword.org.uk/2013/11/tdor_2013/> (last accessed 21 November 2017).
Lieverouw, L. 2011. *Digital Media and Society: Alternative and Activist New Media*. Cambridge and Malden MA: Polity Press.
Lusher, A. 2014. 'Editors of the *Feminist Times* Announce the Online Magazine's Final Week After Funding for a Print Version Falls Short'. *Independent* 14 July 2014 <www.independent.co.uk/news/media/editors-of-the-feminist-times-announce-the-online-magazines-final-week-after-funding-for-a-print-9606032.html> (last accessed 20 November 2017).
McCabe, J. 2010. 'Advice Needed: How Should Teenager Deal with Sexist Teasing from Boys at School?' *The F-Word* <www.thefword.org.uk/2010/07/advice_needed_h/> (last accessed 20 November 2010).
McRobbie, A. 2009. *The Aftermath of Feminism: Gender, Culture and Social Change*. Los Angeles, London, New Delhi, Singapore and Washington DC: Sage.
Mendes, K. 2011. *Feminism in the News: Representations of the Women's Movement Since the 1960s*. Basingstoke: Palgrave Macmillan.
Mendes, K. 2015. *SlutWalk: Feminism, Activism and Media*. Basingstoke: Palgrave Macmillan.
Mendes, K. 2017. 'Brand Feminism: Promotional Culture and Contemporary Feminist Activism'. *German Association of Communication Research*. Frankfurt/Main, 6 October 2017.
Mendes, K, J. Ringrose and J. Keller. 2019. *Digital Feminist Activism: Girls and Women Fight Back Against Rape Culture*. Oxford: Oxford University Press.
Mohanty, C. T. 2003. *Feminism without Borders: Decolonizing Theory, Practicing Solidarity*. Durham NC: Duke University Press.
Moss, R. 2014. '*The Feminist Times* to Close After Just 12 Months – Here's Why'. *HuffPost* 14 July 2014 <www.huffingtonpost.co.uk/2014/07/14/feminist-times-spare-rib-magazine-close_n_5584591.html> (last accessed 20 November 2017).
Munro, E. 2013. 'Feminism: A Fourth Wave?'. *Political Insight* 4(2): 22–5 <https://journals.sagepub.com/doi/10.1111/2041-9066.12021> (last accessed 23 November 2017).
O'Leary, F. 2014. '10 Reasons Why Debt is a Feminist Issue'. *The Feminist Times* <http://archive.feministtimes.com/10-reasons-worry-womens-debt/> (last accessed 23 November 2017).
Peck, T. 2017. 'Labour Promises £10m to End 'Period Poverty'. *Independent* 27 September 2017 <www.independent.co.uk/news/uk/politics/labour-conference-period-poverty-10m-angela-rayner-a7969326.html> (last accessed 21 November 2017).
Period Equity. 2017. <www.periodequity.org/> (last accessed 20 November 2017).
Piano, D. 2002. 'Congregating Women: Reading 3rd Wave Feminist Practices in Subcultural Production'. *Rhizomes* 4, Spring 2002 <www.rhizomes.net/issue4/piano.html> (last accessed 23 November 2017).
Piepmeier, A. 2009. *Girl Zines: Making Media, Doing Feminism*. New York: NYU Press.
Raven, C. 2014. 'Feminist Times: My Feminist Times' Journey'. *The Feminist Times* <http://archive.feministtimes.com/my-feminist-times-journey/> (last accessed 23 November 2017).
Redfern, C. 2010. Personal Interview, 24 May 2010.
Rhodes, A. 2015. 'Dinner or Tampons?: A Modern Woman's Choice'. *The Vagenda* 4 February 2015 <http://vagendamagazine.com/2015/02/dinner-or-tampons-the-modern-womans-choice/> (last accessed 21 November 2017).

Schilt, K, and E. Zobl. 2008. 'Connecting the Dots: Riot Grrrls, Ladyfests and the International Grrrl Zine Network'. *Next Wave Cultures: Feminism, Subcultures, Activism.* Ed. A. Harris. New York: Routledge. 171–92.

Scholz, T. 2013. *Digital Labor: The Internet as Playground and Factory*. London and New York: Routledge.

Shade, L. R. 2002. *Gender and Community in the Social Construction of the Internet*. New York NY: Peter Lang.

Shaw, F. 2012. '"Hottest 100 Women": Cross-Platform Discursive Activism in Feminist Blogging Networks'. Australia Feminist Studies 27.74: 373–87.

Standing, G. 2011. *The Precariat: The New Dangerous Class*. London and New York: Bloomsbury.

Steiner, L. 1992. 'The History and Structure of Women's Alternative Media'. *Women Making Meaning: New Feminist Directions in Communication*. Ed. L. Rakow. New York NY: Routledge. 121–43.

Terranova, T. 2000. 'Free Labour: Producing Culture for the Digital Economy'. *Social Text* 63, 18.2: 33–58.

The Feminist Times. 2013. FSWA Blog. <http://fwsablog.org.uk/2013/10/02/feminist-times/> (last accessed 24 November 2017).

The Feminist Times. 2014. 'Members Only.' <http://archive.feministtimes.com/members-only/> (last accessed 23 November 2017).

The F-Word. 2011–13. 'FAQ' <www.thefword.org.uk/about/faq/> (last accessed 20 November 2017).

The F-Word. 2013. 'About'. *The F-Word* <www.thefword.org.uk/about/> (last accessed 17 November 2017).

The F-Word. 2017. 'Weekly Round-up and Open Thread' <www.thefword.org.uk/2017/11/weekly-round-up-and-open-thread-120/> (last accessed 20 November 2017).

The Vagenda. n.d. 'Submissions' <http://vagendamagazine.com/submissions/> (last accessed 21 November 2017).

The Vagenda. 2014. 'Blushing and Bleeding: Why I'm Sick of Period Apology Culture'. *The Vagenda* 11 June 2014 <http://vagendamagazine.com/2014/06/blushing-and-bleeding-why-im-sick-of-period-apology-culture/> (last accessed 20 August 2019).

'Utopia and End Times'. 2014. *The Feminist Times* <http://archive.feministtimes.com/the-best-of-feminist-times/> (last accessed 23 November 2017).

Violet, M. 2016. 'Transgender Children Exist and They Need Our Help'. *The F-Word* <www.thefword.org.uk/2016/10/transgender-children-exist-and-they-need-our-help/> (last accessed 21 November 2017).

Watson, A. 2014. 'A Generation that Needs Feminism'. *The F-Word* <www.thefword.org.uk/2014/08/a_generation_th/> (last accessed 23 November 2017).

'What's on the Vagenda?' 2012. *Evening Standard* 22 February 2012 <www.standard.co.uk/lifestyle/london-life/whats-on-the-vagenda-7445736.html> (last accessed 17 November 2017).

Withers, D. 2015. *Feminism, Digital Culture and the Politics of Transmission*. London: Rowman & Littlefield.

Zobl, E. 2009. 'Cultural Production, Transnational Networking, and Critical Reflection in Feminist Zines'. *Signs* 39.1: 1–12.

Zobl, E. and R. Drueke. 2012. *Feminist Media: Participatory Spaces, Networks and Cultural Citizenship*. Germany: Transcript.

Zobl, E. and R. Reitsamer. 2012. 'Feminist Media Production in Europe: A Research Report'. *Feminist Media: Participatory Spaces, Networks and Cultural Citizenship*. Eds E. Zobl and R. Drueke. Verlag, Bielefeld: Transcript. 21–54.

18

'Alive, practical and different': *Harpies & Quines* and Scottish Feminist Print in the 1990s

Rachael Alexander

In 1993 Alexandra Howson claimed that 'There is scant opportunity for women in Scotland to exercise their cultural muscles, although some exceptional women do so' (1993: 47). Howson's article 'No Gods and Precious Few Women' – a play on the title of Christopher Harvie's history of twentieth-century Scotland (1981) – describes the cultural, social and political landscape of contemporary Scotland, arguing that 'women are marginalised and femininity is deployed as a symbolic category' (Ibid.: 48). Around the same time, Esther Breitenbach noted the 'spectacular growth of feminist historical studies' and argued that while contemporary feminism had existed for more than twenty years, 'this has only just begun in Scotland' (1993: 58). Libby Brooks, meanwhile, talked in *Trouble & Strife* of a women's lunch at the University of Strathclyde where she was speaking on the topic, 'Is feminism still relevant in Scotland?', to which the 'response was, not surprisingly, a resounding "yes"' (*Trouble & Strife* Winter 1992–3: 41). These comments indicate the cultural, academic and popular relevance of feminism(s) in Scotland, feminism(s) that had perhaps begun more vigorously elsewhere but were being actively used and adapted in Scotland in the 1990s. This was the landscape that *Harpies & Quines* functioned in. Styled as 'Scotland's New Feminist Magazine' it promised to 'campaign for the rights of women, snap at the heels of chauvinists, encourage secret stories to be told and take a cool, hard look at the reality of our lives' (*Harpies & Quines* May/June 1992: inside cover; hereafter *H&Q*). From its championing of Scottish women's writing and its humorous and controversial editorial tone, to its discussions of women's everyday experiences, the magazine aimed to offer something different to a specifically Scottish readership.

The magazine was not the first feminist periodical in Scotland. There were local and Scottish Women's Liberation newsletters; the earlier, but equally short-lived, *Scottish Women's Liberation Journal* (1977–8) and *MSprint* (1978–81); and the Scottish Women's Aid Newsletter (1983–97). What distinguished *Harpies & Quines* from these publications, as Breitenbach highlights, was that it 'represented the first attempt in Scotland to go for a more glossy popular feminist magazine, much more ambitious than the 1970s and early 1980s 'samizdat' productions, with a limited distribution, and all the work carried out voluntarily by 'a dedicated few' (1996: 6). This is not to say that *Harpies & Quines* did not rely on voluntary labour, but it was 'essentially set up on commercial footing' (Ibid.). While the publication did, of course, owe a debt in format and style to established feminist magazines like *Spare Rib* and *Trouble & Strife*, it attempted to address and give voice to a Scottish feminism seen as specific and different.

In an article in *The Herald*, journalist Lesley Riddoch wrote:

> In Scotland now it's clear that feminism is alive, practical and different. While London feminists have been tearing their hair out over slights delivered by power-dress American feminists, Scottish sisters have been doing it for ourselves, and doing it in the street. (*Herald* 1 February 1994: 9)

Riddoch constructs Scottish feminism as distinguishable from English (or British) and American feminisms, highlighting the practical campaigning and less-talk-more-action approach championed in *Harpies & Quines*. This fits with accounts of the Scottish feminist landscape at the time, including Joni Lovenduski and Vicky Randall's (1993: 359) comment: 'As we travelled to collect the material for this book, everywhere we went, except Scotland, we encountered a sense that numbers of activists were fewer, that old networks had broken down.' In contrast to the rest of the UK, the early 1990s saw a flurry of feminist activity in Scotland, much of which was covered in *Harpies & Quines*. The magazine itself was 'alive, practical and different', but not for long. By 1998, Breitenbach – along with Alice Brown and Fiona Myers – would cite the magazine while discussing Scottish literary and print culture: 'We have seen the birth and death of *Harpies and Quines*, a popular feminist magazine, which despite its popularity did not manage to survive' (Breitenbach et al. 1998: 47). The magazine folded in 1994, a month after its largest sale. In spite, or perhaps because of, its short life, the magazine offers an intriguing case study of feminist print, Scottish feminism and commercial publishing.

Lynn Abrams argues (2006: 3) that 'the right of women to exist historically in the Scottish narrative . . . is still a battle to be fought'. Breitenbach's commentary is one of the very few academic discussions of the magazine. She notes:

> From the point of view of a discussion of the women's movement in Scotland, its strengths and weaknesses, and organisation, it would be most helpful to have a good analysis of why *Harpies and Quines* failed, so that in future the same mistakes could be avoided. But it seems unlikely that this particular secret story will be told. (1996: 8)

Breitenbach's comments remain as true today as they were in 1996. *Harpies & Quines* is a crucial part of contemporary Scottish women's history, yet there currently exists no detailed academic discussion of the magazine.[1] The only recent reference to *Harpies & Quines* is in Angela Smith and Sheila Quaid's introduction to *Re-Reading Spare Rib*, where it is mentioned in a list of feminist magazines as '*Harpies and Queenies*' (2007: 12). This lack of attention is a fact that I seek to address – although by no means exhaustively – in this chapter. I hope to lay a foundation for future work by questioning the ways in which the magazine was, to borrow Riddoch's phrase, 'alive, practical and different' (*Herald* 1 February 1994: 9).

Beginning with a discussion of its birth, life and death, I will consider the magazine's aims and the challenges that led to its demise before moving on to how the magazine was 'practical'; how it appropriated and subverted established stylistic models and linked to broader Scottish feminist activity to position itself – and feminism – as relevant to its intended readership. Finally, I will look to how the magazine constructed itself as 'different', carving out a place in a broader, interconnected print culture through – among other methods – the construction of a relational periodical identity. Underpinning this interrogation is an understanding of the magazine as both collaborative text and commercial product, driven by editorial/ideological interests *and* commercial/market-dictated interests, two functions which did not always sit comfortably together. In this, I will examine how it functioned to construct and articulate a distinctly Scottish feminist identity and how it contributed to and interacted with broader print culture.

Alive

So what's in a name? Quite a lot!

(*H&Q* May/June 1992: inside cover)

Harpies & Quines – sometimes referred to as *Harpies and Quines* – was first published in 1992 by a collective of seven women: Lynne Bryan, Stella Coombe, Jackie Erdman, Fiona McGregor, Fiona Montgomery, Lesley Riddoch and Catriona Stewart. In the first issue they described themselves as 'community workers, students, journalists, film and TV technicians, some in paid employment, some with partners, some who have children, some who don't' (Ibid.). Of the collective, journalist and broadcaster Lesley Riddoch was certainly the most visible member and remains the individual most closely associated with the magazine. The collective changed over the course of the magazine, with journalist Libby Brooks – then still in her teens – one of the most notable additions. Yet the overarching editorial voice remained broadly the same. They emphasised that, while they did not represent all Scottish women, they hoped the publication could be a forum for women to represent themselves. The magazine took its name from two Scottish caricatures of women, explained in a characteristically upfront manner in the first issue. Readers are told, 'Harpies comes from the Greek *harpazein*, to seize. In ancient Aegean mythology living men were snatched to an early death by *harpuisi* . . . beautiful winged monsters with pale faces of women, bodies of vultures, the claws of eagles and the ears of bears!'. 'Quines' or 'Queans', meanwhile, survives 'only in Scots and chiefly in the north-east of Scotland where it retains its original unsullied meaning of an independent young woman' (Ibid.).

Scottish Women, another suggested name, was roundly rejected by the women who would become the collective. They wanted something that reflected the 'bold', 'sort of get-it-right-up-you kinda magazine' that they sought to create:

> It's like this almost describes the limits that women work within: they're either harpies, where they're like, you know, horrible, nasty kind of vicious creatures; or they're quines, innocent as the day is long sort of thing. And in the middle of that, actually, we have to live our lives. (Riddoch 2017)

While the magazine itself does not comment explicitly on the innocence associated with the word 'quine', the lasting Scots definition stresses that the word refers to: 'A woman, almost always a young, unmarried one, a lass, a girl, esp. one in young womanhood.' (*Dictionary of Scots Language*). The 'independence' mentioned by the magazine relates most closely to an unmarried status, which in turn is also linked to perceived innocence. The definition and examples of usage provided in the *Dictionary of Scots Language* are more complex than that provided by the magazine, although given that the *Dictionary of Scots Language* was not available until 2004, this is perhaps unsurprising. The readership of *Harpies & Quines*, in the main, would have been familiar with these words through colloquial usage. Combined with the definitions, an understanding of the title as representing two poles of feminine stereotypes is compounded by its illustrated style on the cover. 'Harpies' appears in a jagged, slanting font while 'Quines' follows in a rounded and neat one (see Plate 11). Similar stylistic and lexical choices were evident in feminist magazines like *Trouble & Strife* (1983–2002) and *Bad Attitude* (1992–5). From the first, then, *Harpies & Quines* takes aim at pervasive and limiting stereotypes of women while also rooting its feminist perspective in Scottish linguistic and cultural heritage. Etymological reasoning aside, the linguistic similarity to *Harpers & Queen* was not unintentional and did not go unnoticed.[2] Following the first issue, the National Magazine Company (the publishers of *Harpers & Queen*) claimed that the name infringed on their trademark, caused confusion and threatened the collective with legal action.

Stories abounded in the press about the plucky Scottish start-up that had dared to defy one of the largest magazine publishers in the UK. Articles like 'Feminist Magazine Upsets the *Beau Monde*' talked of the 'elegant ladies' of *Harpers & Queen* pitted against the 'wimmin' of *Harpies & Quines* (*The Times* 27 June 1992: n.p.), the latter threatening the 'cool sophistication and urbane tolerance' of the former's 'languid scribes' (*Evening Standard* 22 May 1992: 8). The furore even made it to the front page of the *Independent*, where *Harpers & Queen*'s 4,000-copies-per-month circulation was compared to *Harpies & Quines*' 'sold out . . . first edition of 5500 copies' (*Independent* 27 June 1992: 1). These articles simultaneously constructed *Harpies & Quines* as the scrappy underdog and commercially successful – a fact that no doubt had much to do with Riddoch's experience of working in the media. Riddoch was quoted as saying, 'There was no deliberate attempt to flatter *Harpers* by imitation', with Jonathan Foster commenting, 'Ms Riddoch has a fine sense of humour' (Ibid.). The similarity was a deliberate – if serendipitous – marketing ploy. And it paid off. The publication had no budget for publicity; supported as it was by subscriptions, donations, a Community Enterprise Strathclyde grant, and £3,000 from Lesley Riddoch's mother, Helen Riddoch (Riddoch 2017). As Riddoch (2013: 374) notes in her later book *Blossom*: 'thanks to the free publicity we had quietly been banking on in the absence of any cash for publicity or advertising, *Harpers* backed down.'

The victory against *Harpers & Queen*, while substantial, paled in significance to the long-running and finally ruinous battle with magazine distributor and retailer John Menzies. Early issues made consistent reference to the collective's distribution problems, telling readers in no uncertain terms who was to blame:

> The first issue of *Harpies & Quines* was a huge success – distribution by ourselves from Shetland to the Borders, the first print run was a virtual sell-out. But of course there were some problems – we know some of you found it hard to get your hands on the magazine. That's because we've been side-stepping John Menzies and

> their near monopoly on Scottish magazine distribution. (*H&Q* August/September 1992: inside cover)

According to Riddoch, in the magazine and elsewhere, John Menzies demanded over half of the cover price for distribution and had 'some very firm ideas of which titles should be sold where' (*H&Q* May/June 1992: inside cover). The collective's resistance to John Menzies' demands meant the creation of their own distribution networks, which included women's organisations, Oxfam stores and independent newsagents. The small collective physically distributed the magazines to sellers themselves. Even then, this was not without complication. As the October/November 1992 issue of *Harpies & Quines* notes:

> Newsagents have told us that if they stock our magazine, this distribution firm will stop sending supplies of *The Scotsman*, *Herald*, *Record* and other main daily papers and big circulation magazines. They say retailers can't afford to stand up to the big boys and other so-called radical papers have decided they can't afford to tackle the distribution stranglehold that limits freedom of the press in Scotland. (inside cover)

The fight was both practical and ideological – the magazine could not afford to give up half its cover price, but it also refused to contribute to a publishing system and distribution structure that it viewed as exploitative. Dilemmas such as these demonstrate the continuing difficulties presented by the magazine's status as both collaboratively produced text and commercial product, especially when editorial and commercial interests are in conflict.[3]

In the end, *Harpies & Quines* relented. In what *Scotland on Sunday* reported as 'a startling compromise' (20 January 1994: n.p.), they signed a deal with a distribution company Fleetfoot and made the shift from bimonthly to monthly publication. In 1994, Riddoch commented:

> After slagging off firms like the mighty John Menzies for less-than-satisfactory treatment of small publications like ours, we're using them. After whipping ourselves into righteous frenzies about the dreadful sexist and exploitative nature of tabloid journalism, we're doing a deal with the pinstriped, fast-talking brother of one-time Sun editor Steve Sampson. (*Herald* 1 February 1994: 9)

This unapologetic acknowledgement may have been uncomfortable, if not destructive, for other feminist magazines; likewise, the seeming confession that, 'after roundly condemning adverts that sell goods by depicting sexy semi-clad women, we've done it ourselves' (Ibid.). The shift to monthly publication was accompanied by a provocative advertising campaign claiming the magazine was 'not just for dungaree-clad dykes'.

The advertisement was controversial. Joan Burnie, in a short article in the Glasgow-based *Daily Record*, addressed 'the seriously sexist sisters' clique', commenting that 'the allegedly feminist magazine' was, 'relaunching itself with a deeply offensive advert which whines that it is, "Not just for dungareed dykes. . ." Oh really? Having read the wretched thing, you could have fooled me' (*Daily Record* 25 October 1994: 15). This

Figure 18.1 Billboard featuring monthly launch ad campaign for *Harpies & Quines*, January 1994.
(Image with kind permission from Lesley Riddoch and Glasgow Women's Library: *Harpies & Quines* Collection)

attitude was typical in more mainstream publications, contradictorily proclaiming there to be no need for feminism while simultaneously expressing derogatory, anti-lesbian attitudes. Despite feminism(s) and activism flourishing in Scotland in the period, it was not exempt from the sort of 'backlash' described by Susan Faludi (1991).

But the advertisement also attracted arguments among feminists, as Riddoch (2017) puts it, 'about the tit' but she also notes, 'I always think, if you got a good argument about something like that you're on to something, you know what I mean?' This sense of provoking debate was integral to *Harpies & Quines*, which never positioned itself as a monolithic, perfect authority on feminism. The magazine demonstrates how, as Laurel Forster notes (2015: 208): 'A single magazine can be a kaleidoscopic representation of feminism, with different elements appearing, merging, overlapping and contradicting, in relationship to the other activities of the movement beyond the magazine.' The feminism that it presented was multifaceted, problematic, complicated and, perhaps most importantly, controversial. As its 1994 change in tagline highlights, it sought the attention of 'Women with Attitude' (*H&Q* February 1994: cover). And it had their attention. The prospect of monthly publication and a controversial ad campaign appeared to work, and circulation jumped from 5,000 to 15,000. But the move to a distribution company meant an extended wait period before the income from each issue was received. In March 1994 the magazine folded after its twelfth, and most successful, issue.

For a magazine that started with minimal investment, faced a lawsuit, and for two years challenged established distribution networks, *Harpies & Quines* did well to survive – and thrive – for so long. As Breitenbach comments, 'The size of the readership of *Harpies and Quines* demonstrates the degree of interest in a Scottish perspective to feminism' (1996: 8). Yet, equally, its eventual downfall highlights the challenging nature of the publishing landscape, particularly for feminist publications. The lack of support for magazines which were beyond the mainstream – combined with the collective's inexperience in the mechanics of publishing, typified here in economic models and commercial distribution networks – ultimately led to the death of the magazine. But *Harpies & Quines* demonstrated that there was a real appetite for a specifically Scottish feminist magazine. From the first issue, the abbreviation '*H&Q*' was used throughout the magazine's pages. Returning to the importance of the name '*Harpies & Quines*', it's interesting to note the similarity of the abbreviation to 'HQ' (as in headquarters). While this was never rendered explicitly in its pages, in its short life the magazine did function as something of a headquarters of Scottish women's voices, a place that emphasised the relevance of practical, engaged, at times contradictory, feminist thought and action to the lives of its readers.

Practical

> Dear H&Q
> I have just read H&Q No 5. Along with making a few points, I wanted to say what a great read & and very *practical* mag H&Q is.
> M., Glasgow.
>
> (*H&Q* April/May 1993: 3, emphasis in original)

Like contemporary feminist magazines published before the 1990s, *Harpies & Quines* made use of formal and stylistic models established in women's magazines and refined throughout the twentieth century. *Harpies & Quines* appropriated and subverted the classic model of the women's magazine through explicitly feminist content. It replaced features on celebrities, beauty, fashion and 'women's health' with features like 'Women Worldwide', 'Wanker of the Month' and 'Clitoris Awareness'. These regular columns appeared alongside articles on politics; national and cultural identity; film, TV and book reviews; and interviews with feminist activists and authors. *Harpies & Quines* certainly owed a great debt to earlier commercial feminist magazines, a fact acknowledged in the pages of the magazine. Some of the aspects of the magazine that most notably distinguished it from clear influences like *Spare Rib* were its focus on humour and its distinctly Scottish vernacular. In the range of content, though, it was highly similar. That this combination of content is consistently perceived – as 'M.' highlights in the letters section of the April/May 1993 issue – as practical, is thoroughly interesting and deserves closer attention.

In surveying the full run of *Harpies & Quines*, the method adopted combines close reading techniques alongside surface reading. Surface reading, as Margaret Cohen (2009: 151) points out, allows for the tracing of patterns across groups of texts, repeated characteristics that require the reading of the text – as opposed to digital humanities 'distance' methods – but not in-depth analysis. As demonstrated by a number of scholars in the recent 'Reading the Modern Magazine in an Interdisciplinary Humanities Lab' cluster, edited by Katja Lee and Hannah McGregor (2019), this approach is exceptionally useful for magazines and other texts which operate according to recognisable formulaic patterns. Magazines rely on repetition, the regular presentation of a format and range of content that remains recognisable to their readership. Thus surface reading offers a mode of engagement that allows for the interrogation of the issue while maintaining a sense of the broader publication. Such is the case with *Harpies & Quines*, where regular interests and concerns are brought to the fore. Consistently across the disparate content, central characteristics emerge: a strong and self-conscious editorial voice that frames discussions; sustained acknowledgement of the variety and complexity of women's experience and perspective; and a focus on feminist activism and campaigning. The practicality of the magazine is broadly two-fold: first, it provides practical advice and commentary that centres on a wide range of women's lived experience; and second, it represents feminism in practice on the ground in Scotland.

Elizabeth Evans (2015: 10) notes a renewal of interest in feminist activism over the past twenty years and questions, 'Is the term "Anglo-American feminism" useful?'. Evans acknowledges the commonalities between Britain and the US, but is careful to point out some notable distinctions. She notes that the 'third wave' label 'has not travelled particularly well from the US to Britain' (Ibid.: 3), and that while in the US a 'renewal of feminist activism emerged in the 1990s, a similar return to a more visible and high-profile form of feminist resistance did not appear in Britain until the early 2000s' (Ibid.: 2). Understandably, in her consideration of feminism specifically in relation to neoliberalism and the nation state, Evans focuses her attention on Britain as opposed to constituent parts of the UK. In Scotland in the 1990s, however, the founding of Engender (Scotland's feminist organisation) in 1993, the sustained campaigning of Rape Crisis Scotland and Scottish Women's Aid, and the groundbreaking Zero Tolerance campaign of 1992 suggest that feminist activity and activism was highly visible in the Scottish context.

Much of this activity was evident in the pages of *Harpies & Quines*. In her essay, 'The Women's Movement in Scotland in the 1990s', Esther Breitenbach discusses the variety of feminist activity in Scotland in the early 1990s. She comments on the May 1991 conference 'Women in Scotland – Agenda for the 90s', sponsored by *Scotland on Sunday* newspaper and Edinburgh District Council Women's Committee, which was attended by 2,000 women and from which 'a clear demand emerged for an information network on feminist activities in Scotland, for more communication and debate' (Breitenbach 1996: 4). This was the beginnings of Engender, Scotland's feminist organisation which is still highly active today. Perhaps most interestingly, in the context of *Harpies & Quines*, was the fact that Engender 'recruited a large proportion of its membership in its first year, following its membership launch, through a leaflet circulated in *Harpies and Quines*' (Ibid.: 8).

The leaflet – found rather serendipitously in an issue held at the Glasgow Women's Library – is evidence of an interconnected ephemeral feminist print culture, too often overlooked. It outlines the new organisation's aims as 'a new research and campaigning organisation for women in Scotland' that seeks to change 'the political culture and social climate to make Scotland a better place for women – and men'. Readers of *Harpies & Quines* were invited to join, contributing the target annual membership of £25. Advertisements for Engender also appeared in the pages of the magazine itself. That the campaign in *Harpies & Quines* was so crucial for Engender's initial funding speaks to the trust placed in the magazine as a headquarters of Scottish feminism. Yet it also emphasises the constraints of commercial feminist publications. *Harpies & Quines* could attract enough funding to start Scotland's feminist organisation but could not generate enough income in the commercial marketplace to keep itself afloat.

The vibrancy of Scottish feminist activity in the 1990s was also especially perceptible in the representation of the Zero Tolerance campaign. Like Engender, Zero Tolerance remains a vital part of the Scottish feminist landscape today. The magazine dedicated its fifth issue to the theme of violence against women and children, framed by the Zero Tolerance campaign.

Figure 18.2 Cover for special issue of *Harpies & Quines* on violence against women, February/March 1993.
(Image with kind permission from Lesley Riddoch and Glasgow Women's Library: *Harpies & Quines* Collection)

The stark cover, featuring the monochrome 'Z' of Zero Tolerance, was a dramatic stylistic departure that reflected the content within. In the editorial, readers are told: 'For the past four issues you have not been reading a fair representation of our mail bag. The reality is that every second envelope contains poetry, fiction, articles and press-releases about the abuse of women and children.' (February/March 1993: 1). The themed issue marked a sustained relationship between the magazine and the campaign, but took an interview with controversial American feminist Andrea Dworkin 'as a powerful starting point' (Ibid.: 1). This may, initially, seem to be an uncomfortable fit, but it speaks to the way that the magazine frequently situated Scottish feminist activity in relation to feminist theory, which often came from elsewhere. *Harpies & Quines* functioned in a landscape where academic feminist activity was beginning in earnest – if a little belatedly when compared to the US or the rest of the UK. But rather than undermining the sense of Scottish identity, which was so crucial to the magazine, interviews such as this constructed Scottish feminism as outward looking, internationally engaged and discursive.[4] They provided relatively accessible theoretical context to the practical campaigning and personal accounts found elsewhere in the issues and, reciprocally, imbued the feminist theory contained in the interviews with a demonstrably practical purpose for their readership. This popularisation of feminism was not straightforward, as Amy Erdman Farrell (1998) details in relation to *Ms.* magazine. Yet the potential of magazines – as an accessible, recognisable and relatively unthreatening medium – to position feminist theory as practical and practicable should not be understated. This is particularly true in the pages of *Harpies & Quines*, where it was presented through a familiar and localised editorial voice.

Returning to the campaign in what would be the final issue of *Harpies & Quines*, Riddoch discussed the scope and reach of the Zero Tolerance campaign. She commented on the wide range of attention-grabbing techniques, from men at football matches 'eating their pies out of cartons and boxes overprinted with *Zero Tolerance* statistics' to signs on Edinburgh's Princes Street with 'the bold message, "There is never an excuse"' (*H&Q* March 1994: 8). She noted the success of the campaign in securing Scottish Office support for a 'million pound TV advertising campaign', gaining council funding for new staff at Rape Crisis Scotland and increasing the number of women reaching out to Scottish Women's Aid (Ibid.). But perhaps the most notable section of this article is when Riddoch criticises the 'London Association of London's Authorities' for changing the thrust of the campaign, ignoring the success of Scottish feminists and asking 'southern sisters precisely what Scots have to do to get noticed and taken seriously?' (Ibid.: 9). The complexity of the magazine's relationship with feminism that came from elsewhere is rendered apparent here, with a seeming inconsistency in the treatment of feminist thought and activity from outwith Scotland. That said, the multivalence of magazines allows for competing or contradictory attitudes and perspectives to sit side by side. Arguably, the distinction lies in the perception of agency and involvement. Articles from international feminists, like Andrea Dworkin, can be framed and related to the Scottish audience, implying engagement, discussion and a degree of reciprocity. The apparent ignoring of Scottish feminist activity by London-based institutions and feminists alike does not. What this example shows most clearly is the practical and tangible nature of the Scottish feminism presented in the pages of *Harpies & Quines*, and one of the ways in which the magazine constructed itself as different in comparison to a south-of-the-border, London-centric feminism.

Different

> What a brilliant idea! About time too! At long last! I've always thought it was needed!
>
> (*H&Q* May/June 1992: inside cover)

Harpies & Quines first words to its readership, printed on the inside cover of the first issue, are anecdotally related reactions of women to the new magazine. From the first, the magazine centres on the women who – it hoped – would make up its readership. Yet, almost as quickly, it begins to construct its identity in contrast to other periodicals. It is 'Not the men's world dished up daily in our newspapers . . . not the unreal existence described in some women's mags, and not the London-based perspective offered by the rest' (Ibid.). This emphasises how *Harpies & Quines* entered and contributed to a far broader, interconnected print culture. In *Feminist Media History*, Maria DiCenzo et al. (2011: 200) argue for the need to understand feminist publications 'in relational terms, in other words, as embedded in a dynamic and widespread movement and part of a complex web of media and interests in the period'. While their discussions focus on the early feminist press, their emphasis on the relationality of feminist print is equally relevant in this context. By establishing its aims and ethos through contrast with male-oriented newspapers, mainstream women's magazines and London-centric feminist periodicals, *Harpies & Quines* starts to construct a relational periodical identity that rests on a specificity and difference that is gendered, genre-based and national.

Harpies & Quines is certainly not unique in the periodical landscape in establishing novelty, at both the level of the title and the level of the issue. As Natalie Houston and Margaret Beetham note, this has been a characteristic of the magazine form since the Victorian period (2014: 535). Magazines are both collaboratively produced texts *and* commercial products, guided by editorial intention and market demands that both require a degree of novelty. The magazine sets itself against the daily and weekly Scottish newspapers in its emphasis on women's writing and frequent lampooning of (largely male) journalists in 'Wanker of the Month' and against mainstream women's magazines in tongue-in-cheek features like 'How to Read *Cosmopolitan* and Still be a Feminist' (*H&Q* December 1993/January 1994: 26). Yet its construction of novelty is particularly interesting because it does not set itself only against traditional, mainstream media but – as rendered apparent in its discussion of the Zero Tolerance campaign – also London-centric feminist activity and publications. The feminism that underpins *Harpies & Quines*, the magazine argues, is practical, campaigning and grounded in the lived experience of the women that it seeks to address:

> Let's face it, being a Scottish woman is often an uphill battle but it doesn't have to be a lonely, frightening, boring or humourless one. That's how we see 'feminism' – not the media hi-jacked stereotype or second runner to American ideas. (*H&Q* May/June 1992: inside cover)

This introduction sets the informal, accessible tone that became a crucial part of the magazine's identity. Being a Scottish woman need not be boring or humourless and, accordingly, a Scottish feminist magazine need not be so either. It also connects to

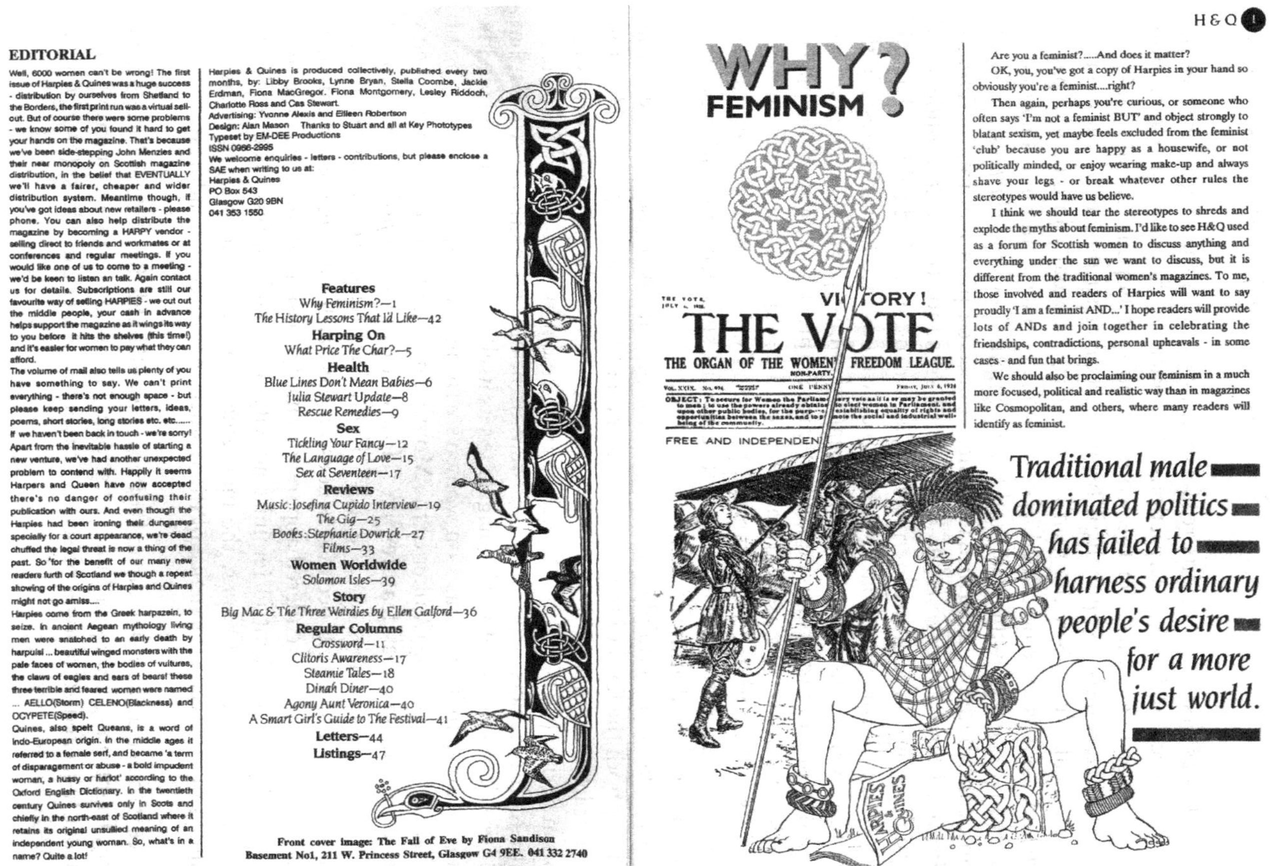

EDITORIAL

Well, 6000 women can't be wrong! The first issue of Harpies & Quines was a huge success - distribution by ourselves from Shetland to the Borders, the first print run was a virtual sell-out. But of course there were some problems - we know some of you found it hard to get your hands on the magazine. That's because we've been side-stepping John Menzies and their near monopoly on Scottish magazine distribution, in the belief that EVENTUALLY we'll have a fairer, cheaper and wider distribution system. Meantime though, if you've got ideas about new retailers - please phone. You can also help distribute the magazine by becoming a HARPY vendor - selling direct to friends and workmates or at conferences and regular meetings. If you would like one of us to come to a meeting - we'd be keen to listen an talk. Again contact us for details. Subscriptions are still our favourite way of selling HARPIES - we cut out the middle people, your cash in advance helps support the magazine as it wings its way to you before it hits the shelves (this time!) and it's easier for women to pay what they can afford.

The volume of mail also tells us plenty of you have something to say. We can't print everything - there's not enough space - but please keep sending your letters, ideas, poems, short stories, long stories etc. etc......

If we haven't been back in touch - we're sorry! Apart from the inevitable hassle of starting a new venture, we've had another unexpected problem to contend with. Happily it seems Harpers and Queen have now accepted there's no danger of confusing their publication with ours. And even though the Harpies had been ironing their dungarees specially for a court appearance, we're dead chuffed the legal threat is now a thing of the past. So 'for the benefit of our many new readers furth of Scotland we though a repeat showing of the origins of Harpies and Quines might not go amiss....

Harpies come from the Greek harpazein, to seize. In ancient Aegean mythology living men were snatched to an early death by harpuisi ... beautiful winged monsters with the pale faces of women, the bodies of vultures, the claws of eagles and ears of bears! these three terrible and feared women were named ... AELLO(Storm) CELENO(Blackness) and OCYPETE(Speed).

Quines, also spelt Queans, is a word of Indo-European origin. In the middle ages it referred to a female serf, and became 'a term of disparagement or abuse - a bold impudent woman, a hussy or harlot' according to the Oxford English Dictionary. In the twentieth century Quines survives only in Scots and chiefly in the north-east of Scotland where it retains its original unsullied meaning of an independent young woman. So, what's in a name? Quite a lot!

Harpies & Quines is produced collectively, published every two months, by: Libby Brooks, Lynne Bryan, Stella Coombe, Jackie Erdman, Fiona MacGregor. Fiona Montgomery, Lesley Riddoch, Charlotte Ross and Cas Stewart.
Advertising: Yvonne Alexis and Eilleen Robertson
Design: Alan Mason Thanks to Stuart and all at Key Phototypes
Typeset by EM-DEE Productions
ISSN 0966-2995
We welcome enquiries - letters - contributions, but please enclose a SAE when writing to us at:
Harpies & Quines
PO Box 543
Glasgow G20 9BN
041 353 1550

Features
Why Feminism?—1
The History Lessons That I'd Like—42
Harping On
What Price The Char?—5
Health
Blue Lines Don't Mean Babies—6
Julia Stewart Update—8
Rescue Remedies—9
Sex
Tickling Your Fancy—12
The Language of Love—15
Sex at Seventeen—17
Reviews
Music: Josefina Cupido Interview—19
The Gig—25
Books: Stephanie Dowrick—27
Films—33
Women Worldwide
Solomon Isles—39
Story
Big Mac & The Three Weirdies by Ellen Galford—36
Regular Columns
Crossword—11
Clitoris Awareness—17
Steamie Tales—18
Dinah Diner—40
Agony Aunt Veronica—40
A Smart Girl's Guide to The Festival—41
Letters—44
Listings—47

Front cover image: The Fall of Eve by Fiona Sandison Basement No1, 211 W. Princess Street, Glasgow G4 9EE. 041 332 2740

H&Q 1

WHY? FEMINISM

Are you a feminist?.....And does it matter?

OK, you, you've got a copy of Harpies in your hand so obviously you're a feminist....right?

Then again, perhaps you're curious, or someone who often says 'I'm not a feminist BUT' and object strongly to blatant sexism, yet maybe feels excluded from the feminist 'club' because you are happy as a housewife, or not politically minded, or enjoy wearing make-up and always shave your legs - or break whatever other rules the stereotypes would have us believe.

I think we should tear the stereotypes to shreds and explode the myths about feminism. I'd like to see H&Q used as a forum for Scottish women to discuss anything and everything under the sun we want to discuss, but it is different from the traditional women's magazines. To me, those involved and readers of Harpies will want to say proudly 'I am a feminist AND...' I hope readers will provide lots of ANDs and join together in celebrating the friendships, contradictions, personal upheavals - in some cases - and fun that brings.

We should also be proclaiming our feminism in a much more focused, political and realistic way than in magazines like Cosmopolitan, and others, where many readers will identify as feminist.

Traditional male dominated politics has failed to harness ordinary people's desire for a more just world.

Figure 18.3 Inside cover and first page of No. 2, August/September 1992.
(Image with kind permission from Lesley Riddoch and Glasgow Women's Library: *Harpies & Quines* Collection)

the magazine's complex relationship with feminism(s) that came from elsewhere, discussed earlier in relation to the featuring of international, often American, feminists. What this statement reveals most emphatically, though, is that this practical feminism with a sense of humour is positioned as nationally bounded, addressing the realities of Scottish women's lives and the relevance of feminism for those women in a manner – it is implied – that magazines like *Spare Rib* and *Ms.* do not.

This is compounded in the article 'New Mags and Old', where Fiona Montgomery reviews other feminist magazines circulating in the periodical landscape. The American *Ms.* – launched in the UK in 1992 – is 'informative and thought-provoking', but being ad-free and 'ideologically sound has its price – £2.95/issue in fact – pretty steep if you're on a low income' so it 'probably won't reach beyond the middle classes' (*H&Q* February/March 1993: 20). The review is favourable overall, concluding with the assertion, 'I enjoyed it and hope it hits on. (And hope I get a wage rise so I can afford it!)'. This is followed by a more critical assessment of *Spare Rib*, specifically described as 'London-based' and of minimal relevance 'for anyone living north of the Watford gap' (20). Riddoch asserts, 'I will continue to persevere with *SR* but I don't know many other Scottish women who still read it' (20). Yet through these assessments, *Harpies & Quines* distinguishes itself in relation to these more established, higher circulation publications on price (and accordingly class) and relevance, respectively.

The article follows this with attention to smaller publications. *EveryWoman* is described as a 'serious, news-based monthly mag that gives us good UK and international coverage,' despite 'its dull black and white layout and design and its worthiness' (Ibid.). *Bad Attitude*, 'Born from the ashes of *Shocking Pink*', is a feminist newspaper 'in the shocking, outspoken, anarcho-feminist vein'. A notable omission is *Trouble & Strife*, although this appears to be an oversight and apologies are issued in the following issue (*H&Q* April/May 1993: 3). *Harpies & Quines* was more closely connected to these smaller titles, in terms of the challenges they faced and their reciprocal advertising.[5] The only magazine that receives a scathing review is London-based *City Limits*:

> This is the only mag I've reviewed that's not collectively produced and in fact with a male editor, publisher and 50% male staff I wonder what it has to do with women at all. A look at the contents confirms this – reviews of quite unfemale productions – by men, men writing on women's issues (like Tampax and how we should get them free – do we really need to be told this???) a few hair-brained Cosmo-style pieces, the usual unisex listings and to top it all – blatant advertising-led articles – on cosmetic surgery! (*H&Q* February/March 1993: 20)

City Limits, here, is implicitly positioned by the magazine as a simulacrum for mainstream women's magazines, reiterating and emphasising the aspects of women's magazines seen as manipulative and toxic. Yet *City Limits*, was not a women's magazine but rather founded by former staff of *Time Out* with a similar scope and intended readership. Its inclusion points towards some of the limitations of volunteer-based feminist publishing, seen in inaccuracies and inconsistencies. Nevertheless, used here and in this way, it contributes to the two-fold construction of *Harpies & Quines*' novelty. *Harpies & Quines* vehemently and explicitly rejects the sexism of mainstream magazines and newspapers, ideologically aligning it with the feminist magazine genre. Simultaneously it distinguishes itself from other feminist titles along editorial and commercial lines, alternately on the basis of style, tone, geographical location, price and demographic. Through the magazine's construction of a relational periodical identity in this manner, it carved out a place in the broader publishing landscape.

Conclusion

> There are no copies of *Votes for Women* in any Scottish Museum – a fate we trust will not befall *Harpies.*
>
> (*H&Q* May/June 1992: inside cover)

Periodicals are shaped by their seriality and circularity. With that in mind, the above quote returns to where we started, with the first issue of *Harpies & Quines*. The editorial asserted that it was the first feminist magazine to be published in Scotland since the Scottish suffragette magazine, *Votes for Women*, which it states was first published in 1908. Indeed, I certainly cannot find the Scottish weekly penny paper in any library or museum. Yet this assertion is demonstrably inaccurate. As noted in the introduction, both the *Scottish Women's Liberation Journal* and *MSprint* preceded *Harpies & Quines*, although they did not have the same commercial aims. Both survive in the National Library of Scotland, as does *Harpies & Quines*, which is also held in the Glasgow Women's Library, among other gems. Yet all of these magazines have been overlooked since their collapse. *Harpies & Quines* assertion, then, is perhaps indicative of the lack of attention paid to the history of Scottish feminist publishing, a gap in scholarship that this chapter has attempted to begin filling. What has become most clear is just how much there is to say about *Harpies & Quines*. This chapter has touched on the magazine's representation of Scottish national and cultural identity, its treatment of race and racism in Scotland, its engagement with Scottish LGBTQ+ communities and publications through advertising of *Gay Scotland*, and Scottish women's writing in the magazine. Yet each of these topics – or simply the 'Wanker of the Month' column – would each provide ample material for interrogations of this length, making the fact that the magazine has been overlooked for so long all the more surprising.

This chapter has, perhaps, raised more questions than it has answered. What happened to the gap in the feminist landscape when *Harpies & Quines* folded? What more can the magazine tell us about the challenges of working as a feminist collective in Scotland, particularly in relation to competing ideological and commercial interests? And why, for twenty-five years, has the magazine been overlooked? In taking the opportunity now to dedicate much needed attention to the magazine, this chapter has opened up the space to ask these questions. Through an exploration of the magazine's history, the magazine as text and as commercial product, we have seen how in its short life it worked to construct itself as both practical and different. In its close links with on-the-ground feminist activity in Scotland as much as in its engagement with international feminists and other feminist magazines, it presented readers with a popular and plural form of Scottish feminism that was engaged, relevant and outward looking. It was this that underpinned its construction of the relational periodical identity that allowed the magazine to be, for a short time, 'alive, practical and different'.

Notes

1. This is notwithstanding a series of four short blog posts in 2017 by Charlotte Osalden as part of a student placement with the Glasgow Women's Library, <womenslibrary.org.uk/author/charlotte-osdalen/>.
2. *Harpers & Queen* (1970–2006), later *Harper's Bazaar* (2006–), was a popular glossy women's monthly that relied on an editorial and commercial formula often perceived as harmful and toxic by feminist critics and scholars.
3. *Spare Rib*'s careful, and often uneasy, relationship with advertising is another example of this; for more see Victoria Bazin's discussion on the 'politics and practices of consumption' which can result in conflict but also a 'productive paradox of feminist consumption' (2017: 199).
4. Interviews with other prominent international feminists – of varying perspectives – included Germaine Greer (May/June 1992), Suzie Orbach (December 1992/January 1993), Annie Sprinkle (February 1994) and Naomi Wolf, among others.
5. *Harpies & Quines* regularly featured advertisements for other smaller publications, including: *Bad Attitude* (1992–5), *Gay Scotland* (1978–97) and *Trouble & Strife* (1983–2002).

Works Cited

Abrams, L. 2006. 'Introduction: Gendering the Agenda'. *Gender in Scottish History since 1700*. Eds L. Abrams, E. Gordon, D. Simonton and E. Janes Yeo. Edinburgh: Edinburgh University Press. 1–17.

Bazin, V. 2017. '"A New Kind of Trade": Advertising Feminism in *Spare Rib*'. *Re-Reading* Spare Rib. Ed. A. Smith. Basingstoke: Palgrave Macmillan. 197–221.

Breitenbach, E. 1993. 'Out of Sight, Out of Mind? The History of Women in Scottish Politics'. *Scottish Affairs* 2 (Winter): 58–70.

Breitenbach, E. 1996. 'The Women's Movement in Scotland in the 1990s'. *New Waverley Papers*. Department of Politics, University of Edinburgh.

Breitenbach, E., A. Brown and F. Myers. 1988. 'Understanding Women in Scotland'. *Feminist Review* 58: 44–65.

Cohen, M. 2009. 'Narratology in the Archive of Literature'. *Representations* 108.1: 51–75.

DiCenzo, M., L. Delap and L. Ryan. 2011. *Feminist Media History: Suffrage, Periodicals and the Public Sphere*. Basingstoke: Palgrave Macmillan.

Evans, E. 2015. *The Politics of Third Wave Feminisms: Neoliberalism, Intersectionality, and the State in Britain and the US*. Basingstoke: Palgrave Macmillan.

Faludi, S. 1991. *Backlash: The Undeclared War Against Women*. London: Chatto & Windus.

Farrell, A. Erdman. 1998. *Yours in Sisterhood:* Ms. *Magazine and the Promise of Popular Feminism*. Chapel Hill: University of North Carolina Press.

Forster, L. 2015. *Magazine Movements: Women's Culture, Feminisms and Media Form*. London: Bloomsbury.

Houston, N. M. and M. Beetham. 2014. 'Introduction to the Special Issue: Tradition and the New'. *Victorian Periodicals Review* 47.4: 535–7.

Howson, A. 1993. 'No Gods and Precious Few Women: Gender and Cultural Identity in Scotland'. *Scottish Affairs* 2: 37–49.

Lee, K. and H. McGregor. 2019. 'A Provocation: Reading the Modern Magazine in an Interdisciplinary Humanities Lab'. *Modernism/modernity Print Plus* vol. 4, cycle 2, 3 July 2019 <https://modernismmodernity.org/forums/reading-modern-magazine> (last accessed 30 August 2019).

Lovenduski, J. and V. Randall. 1993. *Contemporary Feminist Politics: Women and Power in Britain*. Oxford: Oxford University Press.

'Quean'. *Dictionary of the Scots Language* <https://dsl.ac.uk/entry/snd/quean> (last accessed 20 August 2019).

Reynolds, S. 2006. 'Gender, the Arts and Culture'. *Gender in Scottish History since 1700*. Eds L. Abrams, E. Gordon, D. Simonton and E. Janes Yeo. Edinburgh: Edinburgh University Press. 170–98.

Riddoch, L. 2003. *Blossom: What Scotland Needs to Flourish*. Viewpoints.

Riddoch, L. 2007. Interview, *Glasgow Women's Library*, 6 April 2007.

Smith, A. and S. Quaid. 2017. 'Introduction'. *Re-reading* Spare Rib. Ed. A. Smith. Basingstoke: Palgrave Macmillan. 1–19.

Part V

Negotiating Femininities

19

'Doing Food' in *Vogue*

Janet Floyd

This chapter explores the realms of fear and uncertainty in writing on food and cooking in women's magazines. Of course, what we eat and how our food is cooked are always troubling matters. The preparing of meals has always and very obviously been charged ideologically: crackling with identity and gender politics, class and caste tension, ethnic difference. Cooking food for others, too, has always had profound significance in terms of how meals may situate but also vex the self, the guest and the stranger. To this trans-historical landscape of danger and dissatisfaction, modernity has added its particular experience of loss. Migration, urbanisation and the mass production of food have alienated modern subjects from the familiar food ways associated with routine and tradition, replacing them with shifting practices of consumption. The writing of cookery, meanwhile, deals unceasingly with potent questions of nationality and foreignness, safety and danger, prosperity and want, value and 'junk'.[1] This charged field forms my starting point in approaching food and cooking content in women's magazines, and at *Vogue* in particular, first in contemporary culture and then in the period after the Second World War. I want to propose that food's problematic life and the fraught management of cooking are vividly realised in these periodicals. This is not to claim that the anxiety I am describing here appears uniquely in women's magazines. Fiction from the nineteenth century, for example, is dotted with chapters describing – and moralising – rebellious food, disastrous cooking and agonising meals. Rather, my argument is that the magazine proves hospitable to such experiences and responses and presents them in particular and vivid ways.

Of course, important arguments have already been made about how the representation of food and cooking in magazines offers the precise opposite of the truth that magazines practice to deceive in these areas. Roland Barthes' essay on 'Ornamental Cookery' argues that the coverage of food and cooking (both textually and in the culinary sense of 'garnishings') in magazines such as *Elle* operates to prettify the 'primary nature of foodstuffs, the brutality of meat or the abruptness of seafood' while obscuring 'the real problems concerning food', namely its scarcity for the poor (1972: 79). Feminist critics and women's historians have problematised this content differently, situating it as embracing a reactionary agenda that sets domestic responsibility firmly at the centre of women's lives, seeks to pin white middle-class women in the home, and drives home the social and cultural capital to be earned – and hard-earned – by cooking and entertaining in particular ways. The issue in both cases, then, has to do with all that this material *denies* with respect to food and cooking. My conception of 'the problem' with food and cooking in women's magazines is a different one. Certainly, there is no question that food and cooking content avoids discussion of the mass-murder of fellow creatures and approaches questions about poverty and access to food very gingerly indeed. In women's magazines, buying, preparing and serving food in a domestic setting are undoubtedly constructed as women's work. But these points, pertinent as they are, seem not to acknowledge the ways in which food and dealing with food act as a locus for feelings that are profoundly difficult; difficult in the sense of being challenging, puzzling and even painful, but also difficult to articulate and difficult to resolve.

This chapter begins by using recent issues of two mainstream housekeeping magazines of long standing (the UK edition of *Good Housekeeping* and *Australian Women's Weekly*) and from very different Anglophone traditions to make my general argument, before going on to explore how problems with food and cooking are treated with peculiar intensity in *Vogue* in its US and British editions. From there I move to considering food and cooking in *Vogue* at the turn of the 1950s, at a moment in which food and cooking at home became a particularly preoccupying cultural issue, before turning finally to look at how two great food writers for the magazine of the period produce anecdotes about food at its most troubling. Using *Vogue* as my primary example will perhaps seem an odd choice. This is not, after all, a magazine concerned with domestic routines. As Taylor Antrim, in the huge and extravagantly produced anthology of the US *Vogue*'s food illustration and articles, *Food in Vogue*, points out, proudly quoting the remark of a fashion editor: '"You know that we don't *do* food the way other magazines do"' (2017: 13).[2] But the issues that interest me here – the trouble with food and cooking, its unpredictable behaviour, its location – are never more sharply defined than in a magazine that is studiedly insouciant, that turns decisively away from problems of exclusion, and that presses domestic routine into a peripheral position. It may be objected that *Vogue* is not directed to the same middle-class audience as housekeeping magazines, but rather to an audience of privileged subjects. But, as George Douglas (1991: 3) puts it, 'smart magazines' such as *Vogue* could not survive if their sales were limited to the people they represent. Rather, they 'pass stealthily as magazines for imagined elites'. *Vogue* could never have survived so exceptionally long without its attention to a middle-class audience described by Catherine Keyser as having always 'longed for luxury and élite social status' (2010: 5).

My interest here is not, in any case, in questions of class and consumption nor in the 'dream of smartness' that magazines may offer (Barthes 1972: 78). Rather, I observe that *Vogue*'s focus on the lives of people not much bothered with cooking gives a particular intensity of engagement to its treatment of the material that I am concerned with here. First, though, I want to begin by grounding my argument in a discussion of the emotional range within current writing about food and cooking in mainstream housekeeping magazines, drawing attention to the feelings of anxiety and uncertainty that they explore, before tracking the same repertoire of response in contemporaneous editions of *Vogue*.

The Trouble with Food and Cooking

My point of departure here is the modest observation that, for all that women's magazines directed towards the figure of the middle-class white housewife are so frequently and problematically linked with domesticity and domestic consumption, it is nevertheless the case that material concerning food and cooking is rarely accorded the prominence or space given to other forms of content: celebrity, fashion, life writing and so on. Evidently food and cooking content is an indispensable element, but in contrast to the elaboration of strategies for self-development or the shifts of lifestyle that fill those sections of housekeeping magazines with the highest profile, matter concerning food and cooking generally occupies a position close to the back of the magazine and regularly has a more cramped layout than other copy. It is also extremely predictable in its form: not only does it unvaryingly feature (as does other content, of course), but it is also dominated by instruction. The writers that produce these articles are characteristically anonymous or shadowy figures, their 'voice' muted, and their opportunities for expressive writing restricted to a few opening lines. The recipe with extra instructional material and photographic illustration dominates. At the same time, while fashion content, for example, asks the reader to imagine *herself* in relation to choices, to select 'a look' for herself, food and cooking content, by contrast, appeals not to dreams of self-realisation but instead refers relentlessly to imagined routines within the middle-class family. Thus, thinly narrativised, these articles cannot offer the rewarding sense of completion offered by magazine articles in other standard elements, such as, say, narratives of surviving unhappy events or setting off afresh on a new enterprise, or even the task of creating a coherent seasonal wardrobe. They cannot emulate the cookbook's movement either, as it progresses through sections as if through a meal or through seasons, with its bright lists of equipment and provisions, and its evocation of a life or style of life; the TV cookery programme's illustrative scenes of the fulfilment of home and family life are likewise not available.

And yet, for all that is contained and formally predictable, food and cooking content is forever ostentatiously presenting a model of 'fool-proof' certainty in tension with the threat of failure. It is, in an important sense, *about* the limits of containment and predictability. Even as the recipe promises a dish and presses the reader to repeat the instruction offered exactly – copying the photograph, the celebrity, the expert chef and so on – it is nonetheless always clear that this will indeed constitute something of a test and, as such, a locus of uncertainty in which the reader's undoing looms. Meticulous imitation should *but may not* control food's energy. Looking at two distinctly different housekeeping magazines published in the month of writing is, I think, suggestive of the problems that food and cooking broadly and inevitably open up. In the June 2018 edition of *Australian Women's Weekly*, for example, a magazine deeply invested in cookery and housekeeping as women's work, there is no ignoring the gap that yawns between food that the writers are keen to guarantee and the provisional behaviour of food itself; between the confidence of reliable perfection – the 'best-ever schnitzels' (*Australian Women's Weekly* June 2018: 138) – and the constant exhortations to 'get ahead,' 'check you have . . .', the calorific values and all the rest of the material that warns of lateness, lack, loss of control, burning and so on. Even the recipe for 'triple tested' 'best-ever schnitzels' must still be accompanied by an extra 'tip' that warns of burning pans, sticking food, hot oil and shattered bowls and elaborate instructions on how to ward off disaster: 'To avoid loose breadcrumbs burning and sticking to the schnitzels, you can strain out the hot oil into a heatproof bowl or jug and wipe out pan with paper towel between batches. Add oil back to the pan' (Ibid.: 140). This is a world short on triumph and pitted with the threat of mayhem. Certainly, life-writing elsewhere in the magazine may offer tears as well as smiles, and disasters to be faced, but these are experiences shaped and resolved by life-writing's capacious conventions.

The UK edition of *Good Housekeeping* of the same month (bearing on its spine the motto 'TRIED TESTED TRUSTED') elaborates the combination of assurance and danger with considerable convolution. The cover announces '31 summer recipes' for 'Feelgood food'. 'Feelgood' gathers together a cluster of feelings that apparently need no further articulation: food that you feel good about serving, that makes you feel good, that is 'good' food, that will be good for you. The editorial describes the food content as 'summer on a plate' and pictures the editor, smiling and seated squarely on top of the pristine workstation of a sleek kitchen, mixer and food processor in the background. The logo 'Good Housekeeping Institute' is positioned above her head. It is an image exuding confidence. There is no food in view (*Good Housekeeping* June 2018: 5). Beneath it is another photograph, differently decorative, of a woman's hand holding an ice-cream cone in which five flavours and seven scoops of ice-cream are (somehow) precariously arranged. It is emphatically a grasp and a food behaviour wholly unattainable without the interventions of a stylist (see Plate 13).

Remaining on the same page, we have intense emphasis on how the recipes in the magazine are 'Triple Tested': 'as you know, every recipe that is developed for *GH* has to be Triple Tested', a claim that draws at least as much attention to the trouble that food and cooking can cause as to the efficiency of the magazine's 'Institute' (Ibid.: 5). Indeed, once we reach the food content on page 127 (only the tourism content and small ads are closer to the back of the magazine), 'feeling good' is set aside and the reader is instead plunged into a thicket of instruction that scarcely 'feels' particularly 'good' (Ibid.: 127). Some of this instruction belongs to the domestic-scientific discourse of testing in which each food article is stamped with the 'Good Housekeeping Institute' logo, each recipe has calorific and food group information per serving added, and extra 'GH tips' appear in superimposed circles, along with a 'Get Ahead' instruction. Then there is the slightly different advisory strain represented by product placement: across most recipes, specific products are mentioned with the 'we used' recommendation, as in '35g sachet fajita spice mix, we used Old el Paso' (Ibid.: 129). In another vein similarly related to advertisement, we have descriptive material where hyperbole reigns as, for instance in 'All-Star Burgers' where 'ultimate' burgers become 'real crowd pleasers', spice mix gives 'maximum ease' and so on (Ibid.: 127–35). All this co-exists with illustration across the nine pages of the article (and this is a lavishly illustrated piece) of which six out of eight photographs show sauces of various kinds dripping or slipping off the burger, while four show food leaning to the point of falling over. These visual images convey a glossy, even slightly excessive wetness that seems intended to recall or predict the desire to eat – quickly – but also a precariousness even in the finished dish. There is always and obviously a gap between the stylist's image and the cook's production. This is a difference that is popularly acknowledged, sometimes ruefully, sometimes with pleasure at the messy authenticity of home cooking. What remains, however, structuring this content, is the strange and unresolved interplay between the certainty delivered by detailed instructions and the uncertainty opened up by the substance and handling of the food itself.

What makes the periodical so hospitable to this material? Of course, the magazine stands or falls on creating a predictable miscellany of content that enjoyably enfolds the surprising and shocking within its pages. Knowledge in multiple forms is central to the offer that the magazine makes to the reader, and this is combined with what we might term the folk knowledge of everyday experience. Its seriality lightens the burden of conclusiveness. It handles a hierarchy of content easily. The magazine may also offer peripheries in which the terrible or the frightening, the inevitable and the uncontrollable may reside in a form that is apparently lightly mediated. This last offer is suggested in the housekeeping magazines' treatment of food and cooking – its appearance on covers and in editorials and its position at the back of the magazine – but when we turn to *Vogue*, we find this practice of marginalisation becomes more vividly evident. The same sense that food and cooking are problematic categories is retained, but the tactics of discipline and containment are accentuated. This content is pressed right into the recesses of the magazine and now kept quite apart from material about fashion and celebrity. But, even as this 'smart magazine' suppresses discussion of food routines or responsibilities and is uninterested in cookery, the anxieties and confusions provoked by food and cooking elude concealment.

Turning first to the June 2018 edition of British *Vogue*, we find fruit and vegetables (both uncooked) very occasionally appearing in relation to advertisements for cosmetics, but dining tables (a common subject for illustration in women's magazines generally) pictured either as empty of food (again, this is common), or bearing fruit or arrangements of vegetables. A single page of food ads at the back of the issue draws our attention to food forms superfluous to nourishment and requiring no cookery (sauces and jams), along with such extravagantly superfluous gadgets as a brownie maker; a small, single recipe for a 'North End margarita' appears on page 117 of the edition. Cooking resides about as far from the danger zones of the kitchen as can be imagined, as nominees for the BFC/Vogue Fashion Fund are pictured in miniature undertaking the confounding task of 'ic[ing] their own gingerbread magazine covers' (*Vogue* [UK] June 2018: 48). As Barthes would have observed, the difficult and contentious activities of killing and eating non-human creatures with their associations with masculinity, aggression and death appear in the most obscure corners of the magazine. The 'wild dining experiences' to be enjoyed in rural Scotland are depicted in a tiny image of a lobster dish and associated with the lifestyle of the country estate (Ibid.: 95). Cooking as an activity appears only once (unillustrated) in the form of 'fried fish' that may be enjoyed in a Jamaican café. It is consumed in a style that '*Vogue* editors swear by' (Ibid.: 44). *Vogue* editors may vouch for it, but neither the method of producing this fried fish nor its qualities are divulged, and it is produced many thousands of miles away.

In the US *Vogue* of the same month, we find the same images of empty or decorated dining tables, the same arrangements of uncooked vegetables, and (as with the artwork made from gingerbread) the frosting of a cake categorised as 'more sculpture than baking' (*Vogue* [US] June 2018: 145). But this issue of *Vogue* deals more directly with cooking in 'A Cut Above', an article printed on the final pages of the magazine that explores the offer to make or provide a wedding cake for a friend, through a set of instructional encounters with expert cake confectioners The piece wrestles with the culinary social capital that the title suggests. It considers the production of a cake in the context of codified relationships that structure mainstream norms of social life: marriage, friendship, family. But, at the same time, we follow the writer, Tamar Adler (a regular and well-known food writer for US *Vogue*), in her uncertainty around this cooking task. We surmise from the start that the search for a model and the creation of the perfect cake will be hazardous, for a whole-page illustration depicting nine piled and toppling cakes, each iced and decorated, soft, slightly damaged, and balancing precariously, faces the first page of text (see Plate 12). And, sure enough, the presentiment that Adler will either not perform this duty or fail in doing so lies at the heart of the article. The reasons for such a derogation or failure remain indistinct. Perhaps she feels incapable of making such an important cake or finds these cakes unattractive in some way that is difficult to express, or rejects the expected gesture. Something, apparently, stops her from commissioning the cake from one of the confectioners encountered. In the end she doesn't make a cake and doesn't need to (her friend has made his own arrangements). But then Adler, we finally discover, didn't make her own wedding cake either; that was made by her mother and took a much homelier form that others described in the article.

Notwithstanding, then, the article's advertisement of fashionable (and doubtless expensive) cake confectioners, its nimble exploration of the kinds of cultural capital to be gained from various types of cake, and the knowledge of method that it provides, still the article shuttles anxiously between questions about what having or not having a wedding cake may mean ('romance or rebellion?'), what it means in relational terms to make a cake for someone, and indeed how it feels not to be able, or unable, to do so (Ibid.: 119). One wonders, indeed, what kind of 'cut' – unkind cut? – is really being referenced here: the complex act of cutting a wedding cake, the writer's friend's decision to cut her out of making his cake, the split between her mother's interpretation of the task and her own, or Adler's own sense that making the cake is 'a cut above' her. The piece is saturated with ambivalence.

Elsewhere in the issue, we find two other engagements with food and cooking. First, Lena Dunham, describing her experience of living singly after the break-up of a relationship in 'Table for One', mobilises food to organise her description of the intense pain and sense of failure she is suffering as a result. Scenes of consuming food are gathered up into scenes of discontent (though not into a narrative of the relationship). She disconsolately imagines 'sitting alone in an Indian restaurant, spooning paneer on to my plate unmolested' (for now, she says, no partner will torment her by helping themselves to her food) (*Vogue* [US] June 2018: 34). The relationship's most successful phase is recalled as involving piles of takeaway boxes – no cooking at all – while its nadir occurs in the kitchen: 'we sat in our shared kitchen of nearly four years and quietly faced one another' (Ibid.). Later in the issue the magazine's 'exclusive' projects its subject's self in two cooked dishes. The first is one that the subject has prepared (or had prepared) for the interviewer: 'a simple spread of veal Milanese and eggplant parmigiana'. The interviewer reads this dish as rendering the subject transparent and accessible. The second dish, the subject's cooking of 'chicken fingers and French fries' for her children on holiday, is offered as illustration of a friend's comment that 'she's one of the realest people I know' (Ibid.: 142). And yet, critically important as they apparently are to the writer as tools for prompting understanding, this is a language that resists explication. How, after all, is 'veal Milanese and eggplant parmigiana' an authentic expression of feeling? The humble food form of 'chicken fingers' may be evoked as a sign of selfhood, but this is a very contingent language mobilised by individuals, couples and small groups as they express themselves in response to circumstance.

Here, then, is the sense of food and cooking as needing to be contained and yet difficult to control that troubles women's magazines. What *Vogue* adds is a more explicit articulation of those complex and elusive feelings that spiral out of the encounter with food and cooking, the preparation of meals, the world of the kitchen, and so on. We still have the insistent presence of instruction, advice and expertise that serves only to accentuate a painful distance between what can be attained and what has or will be achieved. But in *Vogue*, we have food and cooking content developed *in order to* express states of feeling and situations. It may be objected to that these conclusions derive from articles that speak to the peculiar emotional health of the early twenty-first-century western middle-class subject: lost in a society increasingly understood as a market, abandoned by the state, unable, in these circumstances, to make decisions (much less frosting) hold; surrounded, furthermore, by a profusion of food, at the mercy of lightly regulated producers, exhausted by proliferating possibilities? Can it be any wonder, one might argue, that we see a discourse of food and cookery – wherever it appears – hemmed around with uncertainty, distress and even collapse. In moving now to look at food and cooking content in *Vogue* during the decade after the Second World War, I want to review my argument in the context of a historical moment in which food and cooking in the middle-class household represented a field for the expression of national pride and cultural achievement, and an arena for all kinds of conflict.

Food Resolutions

Insofar as the decade after the Second World War was, as Ken Ohi (2005: 158) so eloquently puts it, 'devoted to frenzied epithalamia to the wedding of virtue and good housekeeping', then this surely is a moment deserving of special attention with respect to *Vogue*'s attention to food and cooking. The kitchen and all its works have rarely enjoyed such attention, especially in the US, where the freshly technologised kitchen was the object of attention and advertisement nationally and of display internationally.[3] This was the moment in which new food technologies and popular cookbooks gave precedence to the project of minimising toilsome work in favour of push-button, can-opening, defrosted cooking. To see Nixon and Khrushchev bickering about kitchens in their staged 1959 encounter in Moscow is to appreciate how new domesticities could be used to express national superiority. But the 'frenzied epithalamia' produced a response characterised by cynicism and doubt. To catch John F. Kennedy's rejoinder to the 'Kitchen Debates' is to grasp a sense of how triumphant power, too, could be imagined using domestic space: 'Mr Nixon may be very experienced in kitchen debates. So are a great many other married men I know . . . [but] neither smiles or frowns, neither good intentions nor harsh words, are a substitute for strength.'[4] The rise in the US of the convenient and the mass-produced created a matching interest in gathering French *cuisine* into a triumphant national culinary practice.[5]

In a situation where national tensions and possibilities could be explored through a focus on the kitchen and what food and cooking might signify, the writer, journalist and activist Mary McCarthy made the feminist argument that we might expect now, drawing attention to the ways in which women's magazines – and *Vogue* in particular – were implicated in enforcing a conformity to values and practices that included culinary know-how. Here, in an essay published in 1950, she chose the following passage to delineate what it meant to be the object of the expression of hectoring authority:

> Will you wear a star in your hair tonight . . . or a little embroidered black veiling hat? . . . Will you wear a close little choker of pearls or a medal on a long narrow velvet ribbon? . . . Will you serve a lunch in the garden, of *prosciutto* and melon and a wonderful green salad . . . or sit in the St Regis's pale-pink roof and eat *truite bleu*? (2002: 277)

This passage, to McCarthy, exemplified *Vogue*'s 'unflinching' approach: it was a punishing instruction in which the woman and the salad *must* be 'wonderful', and it was, she argued, delivered with barely disguised contempt for the reader's likely ineptitude. McCarthy picks up the sharpness of the star here, the closeness of the choker and a sense of threat created by the suggestion of a woman almost dangling on the ribbon. And at the climax of this tight prescription (the list is extremely specific) is the challenge of lunch outside: the 'wonderful' salad and, above all, the forbiddingly iconic *truite bleu*. McCarthy's article, then, was offering a challenge to the conventions she perceived to be forced on women by magazines, but also a furious response to what she saw as *Vogue*'s increasingly sneering celebration of élite cultural capital. The example of *truite bleu* was a particularly apt one in this latter respect in that it typified the Francophilia of the US elite of the day and the distinction available to the cook who could get access to a trout suitable for *truite blue* – a fish only *just* killed and gutted – and then achieve the exacting task of giving it the briefest cooking, serving it with no more than the most austere decoration.

Food and cooking content in post-Second World War *Vogue* does indeed imagine the domestic cook as the object of stern and unforgiving judgement in the way that McCarthy describes. In the same 1950 edition of US *Vogue* as that critiqued by McCarthy (buried in later pages), Marian Maeve O'Brien, who, interestingly, produced cookery material for a range of periodicals from the *St. Louis Globe-Democrat* to *House and Garden*, dwelled on the same severe simplicity as that expressed in McCarthy's example: 'A salad, to give us the true enjoyment of its fragrance and texture must . . . remain simple'; 'there are far too many of us who use this as an excuse to call the "green leaves slightly lubricated with oil and flavoured with vinegar" "a salad"' (Vogue [US] April 1950: 127). The emphasis is on getting it right: 'Remember, first of all, that the prime requisite for a good salad is coldness. After coldness, freshness, crispness and appetizing flavor.' (Ibid.: 138). The cook must be skilled and watchful, but make the least possible intervention if the perfection required is to be achieved. Again, as with McCarthy's example, there is an emphasis on sharpness. The article is called 'Embroidery for a Salad,' evoking the daintiness, the delicacy, artistry, skill and separation from demeaning activity of the needlewoman, and yet the image of *embroidering* a salad – piercing it with needles to make a pattern – gives an estranging quality to the portrait of cooking practice.

In fact, McCarthy was playing a little fast and loose with her quotation. The article that she was using to exemplify a cruelly inflexible instruction was actually exploring the problem of achieving a sense of self that might be able confidently to choose and bear the consequences of that choice. As consumption practices proliferated dramatically (although before the social sciences and feminisms of the second wave identified middle-class white suburban domesticity as profoundly destabilising), *Vogue* was conjuring up confusion and a doubt close to dread on the part of the reader, as well as an inadequacy that went well beyond questions of cultural capital. Here is the complete quotation (the parentheses are the article's own):

> Will you wear a star in your hair tonight . . . or a little embroidered black veiling hat? A straight black linen sheath, to lunch . . . or an easy-skirted shantung shirt dress? Dance in pointed shoes of spinach-coloured satin . . . or a pointy-heeled toe tied on with black violin strings. Cut your hair the shape of your head (or the shape *you'd* like your hair to be) . . . or pin a chignon on the back . . . *or* wear it easily, semi-long and soft and ruffling in the wind? Will you choose a dress that is a Paris copy in grey and apricot . . . or a straight-from-America beige linen jacket dress? Will you wear a close little choker of pearls or a medal on a long narrow velvet ribbon? These are some of the little things you'll be making up your mind about this spring; all of them are part of the looks that add up to *your* look. (Some of the answers may be in the pages of this issue of *Vogue*.)
>
> Will your house be clear and cool and pearl-like in serenity . . . or warm and full of colour and pictures and books and sewing and plants and photographs and shells and things you like? And will you choose a table so 20th century that it is a theme without grace notes . . . or one that your Italian great-great-grandmother might have had in her red-tiled, wide-roomed palazzo? Will you serve a lunch, in the garden, of prosciutto and melon and a wonderful green salad . . . or sit in the St Regis's pale-pink roof and eat *truite bleu*? (*Vogue* [US] April 1950: 51)

This article (in fact it is the editorial) was called 'Vogue's Eye View of ??????????' and the piece was not so much concerned with dictating choices as with the simultaneously urgent and difficult task of making up your mind, a task on which the reader (contrary to McCarthy's claims) could expect no definitive guidance. Here, and later in the issue, the magazine warned that:

> In the intimate everyday realm of dress and decoration *where the self must be expressed at every turn, the woman who is unable to see herself clearly is up against it.* If she is even a little unsure, there is a kind of agony that comes over a woman faced with the potentially joyful prospect of buying some new clothes or doing over a room. (71: my italics)

The problem with *truite bleu*, then, was that, on the one hand, its expressive significance could not be fixed while, on the other, it stood as the epitome of a dish that a moment's uncertainty could ruin.

A couple of years earlier, the New Year editorial of British *Vogue* had given a similarly insistent direction to commit to choices that would confirm the self as having stability, while also raising the problem of *what* to choose. The British setting was not the same, of course. As the US limbered up for superpower rivalry, unleashed a second 'red scare' and claimed a commanding position in terms of modernity, Britain watched its empire fall away, began a radical programme to nationalise industries and still continued with some wartime rationing. Still, the Cold War generated shared organisations (e.g. NATO) and initiatives (e.g. the Korean War); Britain embraced supermarkets and washing machines similar to those celebrated in the US, was fascinated with the same 'New Look,' pursued the same interest in French traditions in cookery. Certainly, British *Vogue* imagined food within a strikingly similar landscape to the one evoked by the edition of US *Vogue* discussed above. '*Vogue*'s Eye View of the Coming Year' in January 1948 told readers that they must be 'first off the mark' and 'look ahead with curiosity, with the urge to know everything that goes on' (*Vogue* [UK] June 1948: 25). But the article immediately following this back-slapping exhortation to decisive action, 'Way of Life', dwelled on the apparently unsurmountable difficulty of interpreting 'everything that goes on': 'Something is in danger. But what is in danger? Our way of life? But what is our way of life?' Even reliance on self-definition – by any means – seems unrealistic when 'the person one knows least is oneself. One can live for years without forming more than a fragmentary concept of the person one is.' (Ibid.: 44). Again, the cooking and serving of meals is enlisted not as a refuge from choice but as the fulcrum in which choices have to be made. The 'home routine' of 'queer little ceremonials – the connection with the service of meals . . . the polishing of silver . . . evening dinner itself, irrespective of what there may be to eat': these 'queer little' practices are sustained in a way that would seem to be laudable; for whatever is 'let go' will surely be 'gone forever'. But adhering to convention and tradition is stultifying: 'I can but believe that in every home in Britain there is a woman battling not to let *something* go'; would it all be 'better gone?' (Ibid.: 92). The tone is different from 'Vogue's Eye View of ??????????', certainly, but in both cases the queasiness around knowing what to choose, the weight of uncertainty about what any decision would signify are expressed through food and cooking.

At a moment, then, when food and cooking were being mobilised in the service of national cultural triumph, *Vogue* examined questions of what and how to cook in the form of practices and choices to be braved against a background of continuous uncertainty where the wrong decision and the incorrect action were, in some unarticulated sense, profound and irrevocable in their impact. However, the fullest treatment during this period of the emotional and psychological cost of pursuing perfection, the exhausting pursuit of it, did not reside in brief references and short cookery articles, but in the new food writing that *Vogue* began, for the first time, to publish in the late 1940s.

'Desires difficult to explain'[6]

By the postwar period, *Vogue* had, on both sides of the Atlantic, long been publishing articles that described travels with conspicuous if not necessarily lengthy reference to food. Such reference had operated to authenticate knowledge and suggest familiarity or even immersion in a deliciously consumable foreign culture. This style of gastronomic travelogue in which (frequently though not exclusively) men offered narratives of their journeys to reposeful pre-modern spaces continued through the 1950s and into the 1960s. In this context, food and cooking content operated to give the most immediate sensation of categories of difference in 'race' and nationality, as when, for example, in the May 1954 edition of British *Vogue*, Beryl Gould-Marks described how, 'in hot countries, where Anglo-Saxons demand iced drinks and salad meals, the natives eat oily, highly spiced and sweet food,' producing 'strange flavours' with 'oil, hot peppers and even grated plain chocolate [going] into savoury dishes'. 'Strange flavours' were the journalistic currency here, offering a world of complete 'native' difference along with an imaginative escape from postwar Anglo-American culture. Gould-Marks assured her readers that: 'Most Iberian receipts can be toned down to suit our more sedate climate, but they are still colourful enough to conjure up bull fights and religious fiestas.' (*Vogue* [UK] May 1954: 160). It was in this setting, then, that M. F. K. Fisher and Elizabeth David, subsequently among the most distinguished postwar US and British writers of food and cooking respectively, fell into writing for the 'smart magazines'.[7] Published in issues of *Vogue* that continued to offer cramped little exhortations to make up your own mind while preparing a dish to a standard of perfection, these writers told gastronomic tales of enervating quests ending in disgust and self-denigration. The strains of pursuing and preparing perfection and achieving collapse are never more pointedly portrayed.

M. F. K. Fisher's 'Truffles for Weariness' of 1948 troubles the quest for the truffle, that most famously elusive and luxurious of foods, and yet one with a flavour difficult to express (*Vogue* [US] July 1948: 76, 101). The article takes the form of the anecdote typical of travelogue: the reader finds Fisher in 'a village high on a crag', a setting that seems at first to speak to the pastoral but which soon slips, with the appearance of her 'satyr' chef, into the faintly threatening. As readers, we never know, on any level, where we are. The article's conceit is that the treasured food is relentlessly pressed on Fisher in a nightmare of inescapable consumption in which categories of description dissolve. As successive dishes begin to sicken her, the chef offers her a dessert that will help her recover from her surfeit; but even that is somehow impregnated with truffles. This precious, expensive food quite fails in enabling her to identify as a gastronome or sophisticate. It does nothing to identify 'us'. On the contrary, this strange food engenders disgust and exhaustion.

Elizabeth David, in 'Dishes for Collectors', is also tracking down a singular 'oddity': *porc aux pruneaux*: in the perfect form of a 'row of little pork noisettes, the bronze and copper lights of the shining sauce, the orderly row of black, rich, wine-soaked prunes on the long white dish' (*Vogue* [UK] November 1958: 176). David's point that 'a dish of pork and prunes seems a strange one to chase 200 miles across France' is quite as much at odds with the gastronomic tradition (in which the long search for a food form is a favourite structuring device) as Fisher's ordeal by truffles, but like her, the experience David describes is of surfeit. By the time that David and her companion have reached Tours, the home of the dish, they have already eaten lunch – 'we settled down to some entirely entrancing white Vouvray while they cooked our *alose à l'oseille*' – and 'wrecked [their appetites]' with a 'hideously ill-advised cream cake at an Orléans patisserie' (Ibid.: 136). When they finally encounter 'the row of little pork noisettes,' the dish is pronounced 'worth the journey' but, as with Fisher, David is brought to 'near collapse,' as the *maître d'hôtel* and the *patronne* ply them with more and more of their specialities (Ibid.: 176). As with Fisher, this has been a quest for a dish for connoisseurs: 'food for collectors', the sophistication and unavailability of which would seem unquestionably to validate the quest. And yet it is the sheer 'weariness' of the experience that David and Fisher draw to our attention.

My argument about food and cooking in women's magazines rests on the way in which this material is positioned and the varying ways in which magazine articles may raise the stakes involved in cooking food, loading meaning on the task at hand. Writing about food is always about judgement – the *right* food – while writing about cooking food – as it spills and spits and spoils – is always about the need for control and management. But in these magazines, both food and cooking function to enable the representation of the difficulty of judgement and the failure to control. These are experiences that generate feelings that are difficult to summarise or even articulate. None of this lack and loss of resolution is given the same rein elsewhere in the magazine. Certainly both the directives of food and cooking discourse and the feelings that their instructions generate are inflected in ways that are distinctive to the historical moment. No one could read the issues of *Vogue* published on the cusp of the 1950s as opposed to the second decade of the twenty-first century without sensing that very different issues are at stake politically and personally and that there are different choices available. But what marks out the writing of food and cookery in these women's magazines is its apparent willingness to leave those choices and their significance hanging barely described and wholly unresolved.

Notes

1. I am drawing here on a range of commentary that shares roots in the work of Arjun Appadurai (1988); Roland Barthes (1972); Pierre Bourdieu (1984); Carole M. Counihan (1999); Deane W. Curtin and Lisa Heldke (1992); Luce Giard (1998); Mary Douglas (1975); and Claude Levi-Strauss (1966).
2. In the scholarship of magazines *Vogue* is almost universally described as exceptional: exceptionally successful financially; exceptionally long-lived; exceptional in the visibility and cultural capital enjoyed by its editors. There is not a huge scholarly discussion of *Vogue*, but I have drawn on the work of Diane Crane (2000: 210–16); Ane Linge-Jorlen (2009); Felice McDowell (2016); and Barbara Vinken (1999: especially 35–7).
3. See, in particular, Paul Betts and David Crowley (2005) in their excellent co-edited special edition of the *Journal of Contemporary History* 40.2 (2005). See also Caroline Hellman (2004). The technologisation of the postwar kitchen is variously dealt with in Sherrie A. Inness (2001).
4. John F. Kennedy's speech in Alexandria Virginia, 24 August 1960, is discussed in Hellman and can be accessed at John Woolley and Gerhard Parkes, *The American Presidency Project* <www.presidency.ucsb.edu/documents/partial-text-speech-delivered-senator-john-f-kennedy-alexandria-va> (last accessed 5 November 2019). The Kitchen Debates are discussed in Greg Castillo (2005) and Elaine Tyler May (1988: 16–19).
5. Christopher Endy (2004), especially Chapter 1, is a useful discussion of France's significance generally and its food ways. Some of the same issues are dealt with by Allison James (1996) and Janet Floyd (2003).
6. My reference here is to Joseph Litvak's (1997: 3) discussion where he explores a sophistication that has less to do with access or *savoir faire*, and everything to do with the 'embarrassment' of the desire to achieve it.
7. For a commentary on David's magazine journalism and her own comments on it, see David (1986); David (2000); and Chaney (1998: 237–42 and 338–40). M. F. K. Fisher's career is not as well served, although Joan Reardon (1994) is useful.

Works Cited

Antrim, T., ed. 2017. *Food in Vogue*. New York: Abrams.
Appadurai, A. 1988. 'How to Make a National Cuisine'. *Comparative Studies* 30: 3–24.

Barthes, R. 1972. 'Ornamental Cookery'. *Mythologies*. Trans. A. Lavers. New York and London: Vintage. 78–80.

Betts, P. and D. Crowley. 2005. Introduction. 'Domestic Dreamworlds: Notions of Home in Post-1945 Europe'. *Journal of Contemporary History* 40.2: 213–36.

Bourdieu, P. 1984. *Distinction: A Social Critique of the Judgement of Taste*. Trans. Richard Nice. London: Routledge and Kegan Paul.

Castillo, G. 2005. 'Domesticating the Cold War: Household Consumption as Propaganda in Marshall Plan Germany'. *Journal of Contemporary History* 40.2: 261–88.

Chaney, L. 1998. *Elizabeth David: A Mediterranean Passion*. London: MacMillan.

Counihan, C. 1999. *The Anthropology of Food and Body: Gender, Meanings and Power*. London and New York: Routledge.

Crane, D. 2000. *Fashion and its Social Agendas*. Chicago: Chicago University Press.

Curtin, D. W. and Heldke, L., eds. 1992. *Cooking, Eating, Thinking: Transformative Philosophies of Food*. Bloomington and Indianapolis: University of Minneapolis Press.

David. E. 1986. *An Omelette and a Glass of Wine*. Harmondsworth: Penguin Books.

David. E. 2000. *Is there a Nutmeg in the House?* London: Michael Joseph.

Douglas, G. H. 1991. *The Smart Magazines: 50 Years of Literary Revelry and High Jinks at Vanity Fair, The New Yorker, Esquire and The Smart Set*. Hamden CT: Archon Books.

Douglas, M. 1975. 'Deciphering a Meal'. *Implicit Meanings: Essays in Anthropology*. London: Routledge.

Endy, C. 2004. *Cold War Holidays: American Tourism in France*. Chapel Hill: University of North Carolina Press.

Floyd, J. 2003. 'Simple, Honest Food'. *The Recipe Reader: Narratives, Contexts, Traditions*. Eds J. Floyd and L. Forster. Aldershot and Burlington VT: Ashgate. 127–43.

Giard, L. 1998. 'Doing Cooking'. *The Practice of Everyday Life* vol. 2. Eds M. DeCerteau, L. Giard and P. Mayol. Trans. T. J. Tomasik. Bloomington and Indianapolis: University of Minneapolis Press. 149–223.

Hellman, C. 2004. 'The Other American Kitchen: Alternative Domesticity in 1950s Design, Politics and Fiction'. *Journal of American Popular Culture* 3.2.

Inness, S. 2001. *Kitchen Culture in American*. Philadelphia: University of Pennsylvania Press.

James, A. 1996. 'Cooking the Books: Global or Local Identities in Contemporary Food Cultures'. *Cross-Cultural Consumption*. Ed. D. Howes. London: Routledge. 77–92.

Keyser, C. 2010. *Playing Smart: New York Women Writers and Modern Magazine Culture*. New Brunswick NJ: Rutgers University Press.

Levi-Strauss, C. 1966. 'The Culinary Triangle'. *Partisan Review* 33: 586–95.

Linge-Jorlan, A. 2009. *Between Edge and Elite: Niche Fashion Magazines, Producers and Readers*. PhD thesis. London College of Fashion, University of the Arts.

Litvak, J. 1997. *Strange Gourmets*. Raleigh: Duke University Press.

McCarthy, M. 2002. 'Up the Ladder from *Charm* to *Vogue*'. *Reporter* 18 July 1950. Reprinted in *A Bolt from the Blue and Other Essays*. New York: New York Review of Books. 277–94.

McDowell, F. 2016. '"Old" Glossies and "New" Histories: Fashion, Dress and Historical Space'. *Fashion Theory* 20.3: 297–316.

May, E. Tyler 1988. *Homeward Bound: American Families in the Cold War Era*. New York: Basic Books.

Ohi, K. 2005. 'Of Red Queens and Garden Clubs: *The Manchurian Candidate*, Cold War Paranoia and the Historicity of the Home'. *Camera Obscura: A Journal of Feminism, Culture and Media* 20.1: 277–94.

Reardon, J. 1994. *M. F. K. Fisher, Julia Child and Alice Waters: Celebrating the Pleasures of the Table*. New York: Harmony Crown.

Vinken, B. 1999. 'Transvesty – Travesty: Fashion and Gender'. *Fashion Theory* 3.1: 33–50.

20

'*FRANK*' – FROCKS, POLITICS, LIPSTICK, HANDBAGS, HUMAN RIGHTS, BABIES, GARDENING, STILETTOS AND FRIDGE MAGNETS

Mary Irwin

'You asked for it!'[1]

What was *Frank*?

In October 1997 *Frank*, a new British monthly magazine for women, was launched by the publishers of style magazine *The Face* (1980–2004) and the men's lifestyle title *Arena* (1986–2009). Editor Tina Gaudoin wrote in her opening editorial that, while 'nobody ever needed a new magazine', *Frank* would provide 'a candid, no-bullshit take on the way we live in the 1990s' (*Frank* October 1997: 97). Describing the modern British woman as singular in 'her sense of humour, her eclectic sense of style and her intelligent, irreverent approach to life', Gaudoin continued, 'we have given that woman a voice' (Ibid.). Concurrently, in delineating the magazine's specific offer to readers she referenced *Frank*'s genesis in the men's magazine market, asserting that 'we admit we have borrowed from men's magazines in our assumption that you'll be interested in more than just fashion' (Ibid.). *Frank* sought to avoid the dependable staples of the women's magazine – 'horoscopes, letters and sensationalised sex stories' (Griffiths cited in Gough-Yates 2003: 146) – and aimed, above all, to do a better job of representing contemporary women and their lives.

Despite the combination of idealism and high expectations which produced *Frank*, it closed in June 1999. Gough-Yates (2003: 146–8) presents the business case for *Frank*'s failure, identifying a combination of inadequate financial backing, insufficient market research and reader profiling, and an unfamiliar product. In an article written in the weeks after the closure, former deputy editor Lisa Markwell (1999) reflected that: '*Frank* was expected to compete with *Vogue* and *Elle* from issue one. And frankly, on a minuscule budget and approximately two thirds the staff, with no promotion or marketing department, that was always going to be tough.' *Frank* and its history, aside from Gough-Yates' work and a handful of articles and interviews, is now effectively absent from any scholarly and popular explorations or any more general overviews of British women's magazines.

Why Revisit *Frank*?

Frank's bold, stylish and optimistic reimagining of the women's magazine for the late 1990s and on into a new millennium, makes it a very significant subject for reappraisal. Moving beyond the established feminine formula of fashion, beauty and romance, *Frank* engaged with politics, history, the arts, science and technology and assumed that its readership was conversant with, and had intellectual curiosity about, such material. Concurrently, while clothes, make up and relationships were still all covered, the approach was to seek out the new and original, or offer fresh and provocative reappraisals of the tried and trusted tropes of women's magazines such as the 'underwear special' explored later in this chapter.

Of note too are *Frank*'s writers, the range and quality of their output and their subsequent achievements. Many of them were women. Original editor Tina Gaudoin went on to have a highly successful career editing a number of fashion and lifestyle magazines, then branched out into management of yoga and perfume companies. Katherine Viner became the first female editor of *The Guardian*. Other now well-known *Frank* contributors have also gone on to write for major newspapers, as well as publishing books on the cultural landscape of their lives. Examples include Sylvia Patterson, Barbara Ellen and Miranda Sawyer who are now long-established newspaper columnists; Vanessa Friedman who wrote for the *Financial Times* and is currently fashion director of the *New York Times*; and Caitlin Moran who has gone on to become both a regular columnist for *The Times* and a bestselling author.

Frank's agenda, this chapter proposes, was to fill a gap in the existing commercial women's magazine market with a publication for the successful, ambitious, culturally curious 1990s woman (or those aspiring to such status), which provided her with what she could not get from other titles. With historical hindsight, *Frank* also articulates the conflicting cultural currents of the context from which it emerged, where celebratory postfeminist positivity was simultaneously shadowed by the imminent backlash of returning regressive masculinities, as exemplified by the 'lad' culture of the *Loaded* magazine phenomenon and its ilk. This chapter reinserts the story of *Frank* – its achievements, what it says of its times and its ultimate demise – into the broader narrative of the twentieth-century women's magazine.

Frank: Origins and Heritage

Frank, as mentioned earlier, drew directly on the template of the UK men's style and lifestyle magazine format established by Nick Logan, proprietor of the independent Wagadon publishing house which produced *The Face* and *Arena*. *The Face* (1980–2004) was the first British monthly magazine to synthesise coverage of new music, fashion and culture, while *Arena* (1986–2009) was a men's magazine which used *The Face*'s style and culture mix as a blueprint. Logan, seeing a gap in the women's magazine market, had hired Tina Gaudoin 'as editor of project Arena Woman' (Maxwell 1999).

While there is little direct commentary on *Frank*, the magazine can be usefully situated within the substantial critical scholarship on the UK male style magazines of the 1980s and early 1990s. This scholarship provides a lens through which to make sense of both the ideas that underpinned *Frank* and the physical form that it took. As

Rutherford (2003: 2) argues in the preface to the *Sociological Review* special edition 'Masculinity and Men's Lifestyle Magazines', male style magazines articulate what it means to be a man. Men, he suggests:

> are called upon to invent our own identities; to live in our own way and be true to ourselves. If we fail to achieve this, then our life might be considered wasted or ill-spent. But there is little to confirm what is an authentic experience or to say what it means to be self-fulfilled as a man.

For Rutherford, 'men's lifestyle magazines were a response to this predicament' and 'established a new hegemony of masculine thoughts, values and behaviours, incorporating the two contradictory forces of the consumer market and the ethic of self-realisation' (Ibid.).

In *Men in the Mirror*, Edwards (2016) interrogates men's style magazines in terms of how the discourses presented around men's fashion oscillate within broader discourses around masculinity, identity and the consumer society. Mort (1996: 85) suggests that the creators of the style press had an 'expansive vision of style as "socially transformative"' which 'gave these journalists an evangelical sense of mission; a yearning to educate and to exert cultural influence in a broad sense'. These magazines located their vision of a modern and contemporary masculinity within the context of a very particular urban experience and location: London. As Nixon (1996: 155) says of *Arena*, it: 'constructed for its readers . . . a particular way of experiencing the city [London] which was built around the familiarity with certain shops, bars, clubs, sought-after menswear outlets and significant street names', representing 'an avant-garde metropolitanism'.

Frank drew on some of the characteristics of these men's magazines to produce a fashionable female version of Nixon's 'Londoncentric' avant-garde metropolitanism. *Frank* recommended very specific London shops, restaurants, services and cultural experiences, selected to enhance and enrich the lives of readers who were assumed to live and work in or around the capital. If, as Mort observed, the masculine style press sought to expand its readers' cultural capital and credibility, then *Frank* also traced for its female audience an affluent and elite lifestyle which took for granted the financial resources and the intellectual confidence to pursue it. *Frank*'s milieu was that of the professional urban intellectual bourgeoise. The average provincial young woman earning a modest wage and looking for a bit of glossy-magazine escapism was simply not on *Frank*'s radar.

While *Frank* built on the male style magazine template, its relationship with the contemporary publishing phenomenon, the 'lad magazine' that was about to redefine the men's magazine world, was somewhat different. Former fanzine writer and music journalist James Brown's creation *Loaded* was first published in May 1994. Brown's mission statement for the magazine was that it should be 'dedicated to life, liberty and the pursuit of sex, drink, football and less serious matters' (cited in Deason 2004). Former *Loaded* writer Martin Deason (2004) reflects that it was for 'a generation of men who had grown up skint during the recession, stoned during the boom, slagged off by feminists but egalitarian by inclination, and horny as goats'. *Loaded*'s irreverent, retrosexual, booze, birds and male mischief mantra, combined with its evident disregard for any form of feminism, set it very much at odds with what *Frank* represented, and embodied the type of toxic masculinity that feminism's second wave had worked so hard to challenge.

Loaded spearheaded a wave of lad magazine imitations that lacked the ironic humour of the original. Their most recent incarnation – in titles such as *Nuts* (2004–14) and *Zoo* (2004–15) – have become synonymous with pneumatic, scantily-dressed glamour models and soft-porn sensibilities. *Loaded* appeared in the mid-1990s in a cultural climate which many feminist media scholars have classified as postfeminist. Gill (2014: 271) identifies how media culture in the period articulated 'a distinctive postfeminist sensibility organised around notions of choice, empowerment self-surveillance and sexual difference and articulated in an ironic and knowing register in which feminism is simultaneously taken for granted and repudiated'. McRobbie (2010: 12) highlights how postfeminism 'positively draws upon and invokes feminism as that which can be taken into account to suggest that equality is achieved in order to assert a whole repertoire of new meanings which emphasise that it is no longer needed'. She invokes Helen Fielding's incredibly successful 1990s fictional creation, the endearingly haphazard publishing PR Bridget Jones, who embodies the zeitgeist where 'an infectious girlishness produces a generational logic which is distinctly post-feminist' (Ibid.). Furthermore, 'post-feminism in this context seems to mean gently chiding the feminist past, while also retrieving and reinstating some palatable aspects in this case sexual freedom and the right to drink, smoke, have fun in the city and be economically independent' (Ibid.). While postfeminism is a complex and much contested notion, and while McRobbie evidences here her scepticism about the concept, much of what she and Gill identify exemplifies the type of women's culture by which *Frank* was shaped and which it helped to shape. *Frank* worked to bring into print its negotiation of postfeminist structures of feeling, while as part of this nexus of cultural sensibilities evidencing a tacit awareness of burgeoning lad culture, even featuring a scathing, if in hindsight sadly inaccurate, prediction of its dwindling power and appeal.

Frank: The First Edition

Frank put its money where its mouth was in terms of what it delivered in its first edition of October 1997. This stands as a physical and ideological statement of intent. Printed on thick, matt, high-quality paper, slightly squarer in shape and size than the standard industry magazine format, with a front cover in cool muted shades of olive and cream, *Frank* looks more like an arts or design journal than the typical glossy woman's monthly. *Frank*'s 'cover girl' dressed in a retro, off-the-shoulder ruched red velvet dress and with a green apple incongruously perched on top of her head looks with apprehension towards the camera. What does she see, who is she, what does it mean? This is an image designed to catch the eye and provoke discussion, disagreement, irritation and amusement rather than conventional consumerist desire. The main strapline in bold – 'You asked for it' – suggests that buying *Frank* either offers readers a challenge or fulfils desires not met by other magazines.

The breadth and range of articles offered, accompanied by well-shot, artful photography, demonstrates a magazine living up to its self-proclaimed brief. A 'Who, Where, When, Why and What' directory section directed readers to a selection of the newest and most interesting things to read, see, experience and consume. This included 'new voice of feminism' Natasha Walter's upcoming book *The New Feminism* – 'Has

Natasha Walter got something to say or is she just Britain's answer to Naomi Wolf?' (*Frank* 1997: 33); the coolest things to do in Manhattan – 'The Big Bagel is still the World's most directional destination' (*Frank* 1999: 97); and Chinese film star Gong Li's Hollywood breakthrough – 'Gong Li has broken through the bamboo curtain. But can she break into Hollywood?' (*Frank* 1997: 15).

Articles included *Guardian* correspondent Ed Vulliamy on the treatment that he received after testifying at The Hague against the Bosnian detention camps that he and his ITN film crew exposed (*Frank* 1997: 190–5). This was a dense, detailed, highly political piece of writing which rehearses the allegations made by the magazine *Living Marxism* that Vulliamy's reporting was a fabrication. Yvonne Roberts' 'In Bed with Labour' delivered forensic insights into the 150-day-old New Labour Government, writing that 'analysis shows patronage and elitism already staining the snowy sheets of Blair's "modern, strong and fair" government' (*Frank* 1997: 133–5). Music journalist Ian Penman offered a trenchant and damning criticism of the 'lad culture' magazines mentioned earlier which had become a prominent part of the late 1990s media landscape, writing about what he saw as its creeping influence on how women were treated as they turned from what:

> may have begun as an ironic giggle in a post pub *Loaded* editorial meeting into a photospread routine whose message to Everywoman is that she can only validate herself in the eyes of the *Loaded* generation by donning Agent Provocateur underwear and posing for sweaty Pentax alongside all the other Ladlore chicks and babes and dolly birds. (*Frank* 1997: 166–9)

The highly stylised, period fashion advertising from desirable and frequently coolly intellectual designer labels of the period such as Prada, Manolo Blahnik, Nicole Farhi and Issy Miyake which permeate *Frank* attest to a sophisticated and cerebral aesthetic in which clothes represented something other than simply dressing to look sexy or attract a man. Throughout its run *Frank* continued to cover a diverse and challenging range of topics, combining the work of both established writers and emerging talent who would go onto build careers beyond *Frank*. As will be demonstrated, its coverage of arts, culture, politics, society and fashion offered readers a thought-provoking and provocative read which consistently broke from the customary diet of the women's magazine.

Frank: Politics and Society

Frank consistently demonstrated a deep and sustained interest in domestic and international politics and current affairs. Most significantly, *Frank* offered substantial and significant coverage of women in politics and public life. Noteworthy is that this was political journalism which positioned women and women's stories centre stage, frequently presenting topics of particular concern to women's lives or exploring the achievements of women in public life, setting these within the broader context of how women negotiate the challenges posed by their gender. This sensibility sets *Frank* apart, both from the lack of interest in such issues demonstrated by the women's magazine market generally, and the marginalised perspective afforded to 'women's issues' in the quality press. One would have to look to the pioneering explicitly feminist journalism of the second-wave feminist title *Spare Rib* (1972–93) or feminist academic scholarship to find any kind of comparable content.

Frank explored the burgeoning career of twenty-nine-year-old Oona King, the new MP for Bethnal Green and Bow and only the second black woman to become an MP. The article was even-handed, if at times a little sceptical, weighing up King's obvious achievements with the advantages that her wealthy and well-connected background had provided. It also explored how appropriate her international career ambitions were in the light of the poverty and need that her constituency faced. The article made clear use of an intersectional approach, bringing to light the complexity of the judgement on her actions and career path to date that King's racial and gender identity provokes. Of note is that the article was written by author Frances Howell, daughter of Tory peer The Rt Hon The Lord [David] Howell of Guildford and wife of former Tory Chancellor of the Exchequer George Osborne. *Frank* had some very well-connected contributors (*Frank* November 1997: 16).

A lengthy and extremely comprehensive article on the rise of Labour MP Yvette Cooper – 'Little Red Yvette' – explored the notable achievements and triumphs of a young, middle-class southern woman in contesting and winning the northern seat of Pontefract and Castleford, whose previous incumbent Sir Geoffrey Lofthouse was a local boy, former coal miner and rugby league player. It also interrogated Cooper's relationships with the inner court of the New Labour Government, her proximity to figures such as former prime minister Gordon Brown and former chancellor Ed Balls, whom she married in 1998. As with the piece on King, the article highlighted intersectional issues, in Cooper's case, the challenges of being middle class, female and southern while challenging the bastions of a northern, male, working-class clique. It also encapsulated something of the particular quality of the best of *Frank*'s political journalism: detailed, well-informed commentary, with an interest in female subjects and careers and written by a well-informed and often well-connected specialist, in this case Sion Simon, associate editor of the *Spectator* and political columnist at the *Daily Telegraph*. At the same time, in letting the readers know that Cooper got married in an eye-catching bespoke Vivienne Westwood midnight-blue velvet suit, the article also acknowledges that readers' interests encompass clothes as well as current affairs (*Frank* March 1997: 155).

Moving onto a more international stage in 'Free Radical', *Guardian* journalist and former African National Congress (ANC) member Gavin Evans examined the life and career of his friend and fellow former colleague Cheryl Carolus in the light of her recent appointment as South African Ambassador to the UK. It charted her struggles growing up as one of a non-white or 'coloured' family banished from Cape Town's white group areas, uprooted and deposited in the townships, to being detained and tortured without trial while a law student at University of the Western Cape. It documented her life as an ANC activist and revolutionary leader, as well as her unexpected refusal to accept Nelson Mandela's offer to stand for Parliament and the consequences of this decision. Evans combined reflection on Carolus's life and achievements with his own memories of ANC politics of the period. Like the Ed Vulliamy piece on Bosnian detention camps in the first issue, Evans' work exemplifies *Frank*'s continued interest in the world beyond UK politics (*Frank* February 1998: 144–9). Like the piece on Oona King, the article offered a nuanced take on the circumstances of gender, ethnicity and class against which Carolus's ambassadorial appointment must be set.

Frank was also concerned with wider issues which were central to women's lives, such as health. Two such examples were the comparative levels of care offered for breast cancer patients in the UK and US (*Frank* October 1997: 236–9) and the then record number of caesarean births (*Frank* November 1997: 212–14). Well-researched and thoughtful investigations such as these worked actively in readers' interests, offering new and relevant research which they may have had to work hard to find elsewhere, buried for example in the depths of the quality press.

Frank's approach to politics made space for serious women's journalism within the context of the women's magazine format, treating women as fully rounded and intelligent beings who sought to be informed as well as entertained. It is praiseworthy indeed that it looked regularly in its coverage to stories about women and of particular interest to women.

Frank and The Arts

Frank offered a rich diet of arts coverage with, as in the case of its approach to politics, a strong inclination towards women, female excellence and achievement. Unlike the usual recommendations of contemporary TV and film, profiles of desirable actors and occasionally suggested reading, *Frank* considered the world of the arts in depth, ranging from the gallery collection scene to satirical media depictions of the archetypal 1990s woman.

In an article entitled 'Icon: Peggy Guggenheim', Sarah Hartley chronicled the life and legacy of the art patron. She detailed her remarkable achievements and her escape from her wealthy but unhappy upbringing, focusing on her significant impact on the interwar and postwar art scene and her discovery and patronage of twentieth-century geniuses such as Lucien Freud, Max Ernst and Jackson Pollock. Hartley's emphasis was the singularity of Guggenheim as a woman who directed and led the art world (*Frank* June 1998: 161–3). The remarkable professional life of Dame Jane Drew, first woman president of the Architectural Association, was also profiled, highlighting her outstanding and groundbreaking successes in a profession where women had had little or no opportunity. These included starting her own mainly female practice, being an active advocate of environmentally aware design and the social significance of town planning, and being much respected for her work overseas (*Frank* April 1998: 28). An extensive examination of celebrated multimedia artist Sam Taylor-Wood, which describes her work as 'beautiful, twisted and subversive', probed her working practices and her involvement with the Young British Artist movement of the 1990s (*Frank* November 1998: 156–9). This offered a detailed critical analysis of many facets of her art, such as how her choice to shoot on film rather than video gave her work a cinematic quality, her use of her experience of many layers of London cultural life to shape and reinvent her work, and her ambivalence about being shortlisted for the Turner prize. The article ended with her citing playwright Harold Pinter's quote that he is 'the weasel under the cocktail cabinet' which echoes her own complex ongoing dialogue with the English class system.

Frank covered not only high arts but also popular culture. 'Funny Girls' by Barbara Ellen looked at Channel 4's *Smack the Pony*, the first British female-led TV sketch show. The article offered candid revealing interviews with its three stars – Fiona Allen,

Doon Mackichan and Sally Phillips – which interrogated what it was like for women working in 1990s comedy. They reflected on how *Smack the Pony* differed from what Ellen called 'the Bridget Jones-style whimsy about the thirtysomething blues and wearisome hair-trigger ladette smuttiness' which, it was suggested, was the routine female comedy of the period. For Ellen, *Smack the Pony* was more of a mix of 'an apolitical Chris Morris, surrealist cartoonist Gary Larson and a less twee Victoria Wood' (*Frank* March 1999: 116–19). Significantly, two of the key fictional characters of the era, TV lawyer Ally McBeal and Bridget Jones, are invoked in an essay about one of the quintessential female cultural constructs of the 1990s: the thirtysomething professional singleton, the demographic of many of *Frank*'s readers (*Frank* September 1998: 93). The piece reflected the complexities and confusions, the challenges and uncertainties facing such women in the late 1990s. *Frank* chronicled contemporaneously the specificity of the female culture of the era which brought forth now-notorious incarnations of the conflicting and contradictory currents of postfeminism in Bridget Jones and Ally McBeal, and the female 'ladette' whose response to the return of lad culture was to beat them by joining them. The magazine captured simultaneous criticism of all such figures in *Smack the Pony* whose stars made clear their distaste for ill-thought-through media stereotyping.

Frank's specialist interest in chronicling women and the arts provides valuable details about women and their creativity augmenting and enriching or adding to extant records where women artists have been neglected. Critical and popular representations of 1990s culture have tended to concentrate on men from Britpop to lad culture. *Frank* inserted women into the historical record, looking at the cultural climate of 1990s Britain though a different lens.

Frank and Fashion

Fashion was, on the face of it, the most conventional aspect of *Frank* and one of the staples of many women's magazines. However, *Frank* did not define fashion in terms of making oneself as sexually attractive and dateable as possible. It was not fashion according to the male gaze: the coverage was witty, provocative, challenging and assumed an interest in fashion as an aesthetic, as history, and as cultural statement. *Frank* assumed that the reader had interests and purchasing power beyond the best buys on the high street or what shoes or handbags to buy. Typical was an in-depth interrogation of the life and work of designer Yohji Yamamoto 'Red Hot and Yohji' (*Frank* January 1998: 2–77) which examined Yamamoto's career and influence and his re-emergence as a force in fashion in the late 1990s. Yamamoto is a highly intellectual designer whose philosophy of fashion included the notion that 'clothing could be more than a trouser or a skirt, that is, a resolved garment' and who made the 1989 film *Notebook on Clothes and Cities* with celebrated film director Wim Wenders. The same issue had a tongue-in-cheek piece on the emergence of the 1990s trend, the micro-mini, 'Fashionable fun loving girls or an exercise in sexist futility' (*Frank* January 1998: 43).

The so-called 'Lingerie issue' of December 1997 represented *Frank*'s very particular fashion sensibility. The editorial set the tone: 'Only on the third issue and we've got a blonde babe on the cover wearing her knickers and a tiara. But about that lingerie – Damart's best.' (*Frank* December 1997). The model is wearing a long-sleeved white cotton vest and comfortable, roomy, white cotton knickers. As the introduction to a special section devoted to lingerie stated:

> For centuries women have been roasted on the spit of indecision about lingerie's place in their world order. Is it for him or is it for you is the kind of polemic women's magazines have employed since their inception. Why do we bloody bother is the question most realistically asked outside the rarefied world of the glossy page or the feminist debate. The answer we suspect lies somewhere in between. If you like it wear it. If you don't, don't put yourself through it no matter who or what it's for. (Ibid.: 99)

The special section deconstructed, and had fun with, the cultural connotations of women's underwear. There was Kirstie Alley's upcoming sitcom *Veronica's Closet* which satirised the Victoria's Secret franchise and played with men and women's relationships with sexy underwear. The series is presented from a female perspective and has much to say about men's obsession with the lingerie model (Ibid. 57–8). Lesley White discussed designer Miuccia Prada and the launch of her lingerie line: 'I don't see a contradiction between beauty and politics; politics is man trying to live better. Aesthetics is man trying to improve the quality of his life.' (Ibid.: 110–11). In 'Foundation Course' Harriet Quick ruminated on the sexual and cultural ramifications of the fashion for visible underwear (Ibid.: 118–19).

Frank's approach to fashion challenged the trivialisation of an interest in clothes and appearance as merely frivolous, a typical component of the shallowness of women's culture. At the same time its perspective on fashion was not constructed for the male gaze. Rather, the commentary offered could be compared to the type of discourses around sport to be found in men's lifestyle and more general quality press. As found there, all aspects of the topic – skill, artistry, history, virtuosity – are to be critiqued and celebrated. A passion for the pleasures of the works of an Yves Saint Laurent or a Chanel are afforded the same space and consideration as the skills and expertise of a Pelé or a Maradona.

The End of *Frank*

Things at *Frank*, however, moved away rapidly from the original game plan. In August 1998, less than a year after the magazine launched, Tina Gaudoin, pregnant with her second child and keen to return to freelance work, decided to step down from her editorial role. The editorial that she wrote in relation to this decision encapsulated the complexities and the realities that were life for a woman, even one working in the world of the media and women's magazines that one might assume would have been far more attuned to women's lives and aspirations. She cited the discourses that, as she put it, 'misconstrued my actions as those of "a born again earth mother who was giving feminism one in the eye by retreating from work and chaining herself to the kitchen sink"' (*Frank* August 1998). She restated the beliefs of her and her team that 'a magazine like *Frank* created for independent intelligent opinionated women in the 90s could find its niche in an overcrowded market'. She signed off, 'Whatever. The ethos of *Frank* has always been individuality of expression and freedom to choose' and rather poignantly in hindsight, '*Frank* is poised to evolve into the must-read glossy for the new millennium' (Ibid.). For a magazine that seemed implicitly to situate itself amidst postfeminist discourses where women had won many battles, Gaudoin's editorial seems now more in keeping with second-wave feminist struggles for equable treatment with men.

After a caretaking shift by managing editor Richard Benson, a new editor was appointed. This was Harriet Quick, already a regular columnist on the magazine who like many of the names associated with *Frank* went onto become a successful journalist and is currently a contributing editor to British *Vogue*. Quick's takeover seems simultaneously business as usual, yet with little clear sense of where this new editor would be leading the magazine in the coming months. The magazine still used the same recipe and there was, right until the end of the magazine's run, the continued combination of interesting, intriguing and frequently provocative articles and genuinely thoughtful and reflective journalism.

Perhaps most instructive is to compare the intriguing and genre-challenging first edition of the magazine with the final one (that this was the final edition was not known at the time). *Frank* had become literally smaller: from 242 pages in October 1997 to 162 in June 1999, the offer that *Frank* held out to its readership was literally shrinking. Of special note is the difference in covers. The intriguing, challenging first cover jostling with attention-grabbing straplines and its quizzical and anonymous red-velvet-clad cover star which told its readership 'You asked for it', was in marked contrast to the bikini-clad supermodel Shalom Harlow whose image dominates the final cover. *Frank*, although it did not last long enough for many summer editions, had not until then featured any cover where there was there was such a scantily clad model on the front. Although Harlow with her etiolated, fashionable and fashion-skinny frame and dark casually tousled hair is a far distant cry from the conventional glamour of the usual front-cover model, there is much in the cover that speaks to the codes and conventions of the commercial fashion magazine. The straplines, rather than promising to mix coverage of frocks and stilettos with politics and human rights, offered sun, sea, sand, sex and chilling out, as well as Hollywood supermodels and killer bikinis. This is a formula which offered very little to distinguish it from other women's magazines on the stand.

Likewise, the editorial eschewed the ideological stance of the first edition and concentrated on promoting articles on spas for the 'stressed-out urbanite', bikinis and beaches. There were still interesting articles and one in particular which grabbed the attention was about the trend for a 'new romanticism' and '"a softer style" – a modern form of femininity that means that girls can be girls'. It concluded of the trend that the most pleasing indication of it was that 'The new VW Beetle has a vase placed in its dashboard. Now that's girl heaven.' (*Frank* June 1999: 136–9). This article reflected ideas about postfeminism and femininity which had been central to the magazine. The whole product has a rather different look and feel to the trailblazing game changer that was *Frank* in issue one.

However, nothing about the magazine actually suggested that it was about to close down. One of the back pages was a full-sized advert offering subscriptions for another twelve editions. Closure was a matter of the plug being pulled abruptly. Markwell writes that *Frank* publisher Lou McLeod had said: 'He looked at how much it was costing and had to say "I can't do it anymore"' (Markwell 1999). The very thing that *Frank* had been set up to challenge was what undid it in the end: the market. As Markwell concludes in recalling a comment made by Gaudoin on *Frank*'s remit: 'If you think *Frank* is 'nice' then we're not doing our job properly'. Markwell reflected, 'But nice sells, as we discovered when *Red* was launched four months later.' (Ibid). This is in reference to the EMAP title which was launched in January 1998. *Red* targeted a similar niche to that in which *Frank* had situated itself or perhaps attempted to open up, albeit doing so with a far more commercial mindset. The editor of *Red* Kathryn Brown said of the title, 'There's going to be a lot of lifestyle stuff – interiors, gardens, food and travel – but done in a down-to-earth way,' and further, 'there isn't going to be pages of loft spaces that no-one can afford . . . This is real stuff for real people' (Brown in Gough-Yates 2003). *Red* was not going to follow the *Frank* line of trying to change and reshape the women's magazine market. There is perhaps an implicit dig at *Frank* and what might be seen as the over-ambitious and unrealistic nature of the claims that were being made about it, what it stood for and what it could achieve.

An interesting angle on the demise of *Frank* comes from another of the very few pieces written about the magazine. Written by Lou Stoppard, a fashion journalist born in 1992, it comes from the perspective of someone for whom *Frank* can only be seen as an historical artefact and a reader who approaches the magazine from a 2010s perspective (Stoppard 2015). Stoppard interviewed former editor Harriet Quick on Nick Knight's Showstudio fashion platform for a section called Print, which 'puts the spotlight on a range of titles and style mags from the past that continue to inspire today's image-makers and writers'. Its aim is 'to question how a title's impact can be measured by far more than its print run' (Ibid.). In the interview, the combination of Stoppard's interpretation of the magazine and Quick's memories of what they set out to achieve leads to a nuanced understanding of what *Frank* was about and what its import might now be. Quick reflects on *Frank*'s difference from the industry norm and the new territory that it wanted to attack:

> We wanted really strong fashion with a strong stylistic and cultural bent as well as punchy socio/political articles and humorous essays. It was about reflecting different facets of women's lives. There was a tech page called 'Charlotte's Web', Miranda Sawyer contributed car reviews and Martin Maloney, a regular 'new art' spread. (Quick, in Stoppard n.d.)

At the same time, she also highlighted the polarising nature of the magazine: 'People loved or hated it. Some considered it too out there, too outspoken and others really responded to the provocation' (Ibid.).

Quick also highlights that the times in which the magazine was produced gave it a freedom to try things that might not succeed:

> I don't remember there being an awful lot of pressure from advertisers. I think it was sensitive but it wasn't that, sort of, tick every box, you must shoot this or shoot that mentality. The late nineties was a very different era in publishing, and audience engagement could not be measured in the same way it is today through digital and big data. Fashion was wildly different too – there weren't so many players in the arena, the global picture had yet to emerge and there were certainly far fewer 'ropes and barriers' to access. (Ibid.)

Stoppard sees *Frank* as being ahead of its time. She writes of its contemporaneity: 'A lot of the content you can just imagine working really well on social media, or on Instagram.' (Stoppard 2015). Indeed, she wonders if the problem was that its approach was too much out of the norms of the period, asking Quick: 'Do you think that was a part of the problem?' (Ibid.). Quick hones in on how it did really try to say things about its times:

> It was also coming out of that late nineties – the ladette, girl power, riot grrrls, female empowerment – conversations about sex and sexuality, taste, entrepreneurship and ambition. It was there but it hadn't really found a voice in magazines, which were all vacuum-packed niceness – *Frank* had a gritty edge. (Quick in Stoppard 2015)

It is worth considering that Stoppard's age and different cultural expectations allow her to adjudge *Frank* beyond the rigid conventions by which women's magazines have historically been measured. Her focus on content and in particular its 'Instagramability' or social media friendliness suggests an openness to the range of content offered, rather than buying into a coherent package offering one unified point of view. *Frank*'s multiplicity of voices plays into a reader culture where, just as music is now consumed as a continuous stream from which consumers select, *Frank* offers a platform with a scrollable set of possibilities, where quality and appeal to the individual is the true indicator of value.

Frank and Legacy

What is *Frank*'s legacy? Its failure attests ultimately to its lack of commercial acuity and understanding of the market. What the creators of *Frank* thought would attract the smart, curious young professional woman of the late 1990s and create a magazine for the future that would disrupt the complacencies of the commercial woman's magazine market, simply could not sell enough copies. Clearly it had not done the type of robust quantitative and qualitative research into its target readership that might have made for a product that would survive. *Frank* tried to span a number of identities and in so doing failed to develop a recognisable and coherent one of its own. In its very incoherency what it does is reflect the complex, confusing cultural climate that women inhabited in the late 1990s. This is a climate where discourses around postfeminism suggest that the previous generations of feminists had created a level playing field for the sexes that meant that women could now go about enjoying all the freedoms and possibilities this represented. It meant too that women deserved a magazine that took them and their intelligence and abilities seriously – one which moved beyond the limits of traditional female culture on the one hand and acknowledged female sensibilities on the other. As this chapter also demonstrates, concurrently the arrival of a rebounding lad culture hungry to regain the territory and casual sexism it felt that feminism had taken from it, was rapidly infiltrating the mainstream. Being a liberated woman meant increasingly having to accommodate the excesses of laddism and even possibly become one of the lads or ladettes.[2] *Frank*'s real legacy in attempting to capture and chronicle all these contradictions is to hand down a rich complex historical archive of the postfeminisms of these times.

Notes

1. Strapline of first edition of *Frank*.
2. A boisterous female equivalent of 'the lad', this was a young woman who was determined to keep up with and even out do young-male bad behaviour.

Works Cited

Cook, R. 1998. 'The Fall of the House of Wagadon'. *The Independent* 11 August 1998 <www.independent.co.uk/arts-entertainment/media-fall-of-the-house-of-wagadon-1170999.html> (last accessed 3 December 2019).

Deason, M. 2004. 'How We All Loaded'. 9 March 2004 <www.independent.co.uk/news/media/how-we-all-got-loaded-63411.html> (last accessed 3 December 2019).

Edwards, T. 2016. *Men in the Mirror: Men's Fashion, Masculinity, and Consumer Society*. London: Bloomsbury.

Gill, R. 2014. *Gender and Media*. Cambridge: Polity.

Gough-Yates, A. 2003. *Understanding Women's Magazines*. Oxford: Routledge.

Knight, N. n.d. 'Show Stopper'. <www.showstudio.com/> (last accessed 3 December 2019).

McRobbie, A. 2008. *The Aftermath of Feminism: Gender, Culture and Social Change*. (Culture, Representation and Identity series).

Markwell, L. 1999. 'Media: Franks for the Memory'. *Independent* 11 May 1999 <www.independent.co.uk/arts-entertainment/media-franks-for-the-memory-1092907.html> (last accessed 3 December 2019).

Mort, F. 1996. *Cultures of Consumption*. London: Routledge.

Nixon, S. 1996. *Hard Looks: Masculinities, Spectatorship and Contemporary Consumption*. London: Routledge.

Rutherford, J. 2003. 'Preface. Masculinity and Men's Lifestyle Magazines'. *Sociological Review* special edition 51.1: 1–5.

Stoppard, L. 2015. Interview: Harriet Quick on *Frank* (1 December 2015) <https://showstudio.com/projects/print/interview-harriet-quick-frank> (last accessed 3 December 2019).

21

Writing about Mothering and Childcare in the British Women's Liberation Movement, 1970–85

Sarah Crook

By the close of the first conference of the British Women's Liberation Movement, held at Ruskin College, Oxford in early 1970, four demands had been formulated: equal pay; equal educational and job opportunities; free contraception and abortion on demand; and 24-hour nurseries. Women's relationship with reproduction and mothering was invoked in half of these demands. From its inception, the women's movement confronted the essential ways that parenting affected women's lives.[1] Mothering was situated in feminist writing as an activity that, more than any other, changed women's relationship to the social world, redefining mothers' ability to undertake paid labour and altering their role in the family and the home. Set against the early postwar optimism that the family could ameliorate social woes through the nurture of future citizens, as suggested by John Bowlby (1953), and the subsequent disavowal of the family as a potentially noxious private space, as argued by Laing and Esterton (1964), the Women's Liberation Movement's attentiveness to the politics of mothering stands apart. For the Women's Liberation Movement, it was not the effects of mothering on society or on children that was the locus of concern, rather the concern about mothering was focused on its consequences for women themselves.

Writing was a critical tool to the feminist project of deconstructing the family and to exploring the politics of mothering. Opening *The Past is Before Us*, Sheila Rowbotham (1989a: 3) wrote that 'The Women's Liberation Movement erupted in the late 1960s in a literature of complaint which focused on the experiences of the family.' This chapter argues that motherhood was an area of creative discontent for British feminism between 1970 and 1985 and that the print materials produced by the movement played a critical role in developing critiques of maternity and articulating new ways of imagining parenting. Using pamphlets, books and feminist magazines such as *Trouble & Strife* (1983–2002), *Shrew* (1969–74) and *Spare Rib* (1972–93), I highlight the ways that mothering was configured as a site both of oppression and opportunity in this 'literature of complaint' of the 1960s into the mid-1980s. As I have argued elsewhere, while by the end of the 1970s the Women's Liberation Movement had fragmented, the activism, relationships and institutions that it generated endured (Crook 2018); the feminist periodicals examined here provide further evidence that the Women's Liberation Movement did not diminish in importance at its final national conference in 1978. These materials demonstrate that the print culture of the Women's Liberation Movement served as a crucial site for forging a political critique of motherhood.

Marsha Rowe (192: 13), one of *Spare Rib*'s two founding editors, wrote about the magazine in a metaphor of the family: *Spare Rib* was a 'daughter of the underground press', a 'product of the counter-culture and a reaction against it'. From its establishment, the editors of *Spare Rib* magazine considered it a consciousness-raising activity as well as a means of communication (Rowe 1982: 19). The *Spare Rib* collective saw the magazine as 'part of the process of women working together for fundamental change' (1982: 607). 'Women were discovering how many ways there were of "speaking bitterness"', observed Allison Fell (1979: 3), a member of the *Spare Rib* collective who became involved in the women's movement when she was a housewife and mother. Writing was, as Laurel Forster has described, a 'potential portal to power' (2016: 812). Members of the Women's Liberation Movement were explicit about this, observing in *Trouble & Strife* that:

> When you think about it, feminists do a lot of writing. If we added together all the leaflets and handouts, every poem and novel, all the articles and reviews, it amounts to a great deal of work. Much of our feminism exists through the written word, and it is often the only link with women in the past . . . writing is a form of power, a tool which women do have access to. (*Trouble & Strife* Winter 1983: 42)

Periodicals such as *Spare Rib* and *Trouble & Strife* provided a means of the dissemination of these poems, articles, notices, reports and reviews.

The commitment to writing was also a process of archive construction. Members of the movement were keen to ensure that their activism was documented and were actively engaged with the making of their own archive. The first edition of *Trouble & Strife* magazine inaugurated a column on 'Writing Our Own History', declaring: 'We hope that this project, by accumulating a published record of some of our own views, will go some way towards countering the attempt to write us out of existence.' (*Trouble & Strife* Winter 1983: 51). This impetus, as Natalie Thomlinson (2016: 8) has recently noted, stimulated a large number of first-person narratives, although, as she shows, this has led to white, middle-class voices dominating the historiography of the movement. Attempts to address this dominance have been made through oral histories of the movement, perhaps most notably through the British Library's Sisterhood and After Project, generating insights into topics including the politics of race and class within the movement (e.g. Bruley 2014; Cohen 2012; Jolly 2012, 2019). Beyond these oral histories, historians have underlined the value of magazines, conference reports and newsletters to understanding the feminist activism of the 1970s (e.g. Rees 2010; Setch 2002). Sheila Rowbotham – both a participant in and a chronicler of the movement – has also advocated for the use of ephemeral materials, noting that it is:

> always tricky to assess the relationship between what is said or written by the visible figures in the movement, which may well be in books, and the turbulent dissemination of the ephemeral in which the concepts of people who are not nationally known but remembered locally are more likely to find an outlet. (Rowbotham 1989a: xiii)

Discussions about the politics and experience of reproduction, parenting and motherhood reverberated across all of these literatures. The print culture of the Women's Liberation Movement allowed ideas about mothering and motherhood to travel, evolve and disrupt. It facilitated conversations between women from different regions and different ideological standpoints. Magazines played a particularly important role in shaping conversations about mothering because of their invitation to correspond through readers' letters pages. The letters page in the Summer 1985 edition of *Trouble & Strife* exemplifies this, with the editorial collective writing that:

> *Trouble and Strife* is read by thousands of women throughout Britain and is getting a longer list of overseas subscribers. We'd like any suggestions you may have about raising more money and getting the magazine better known. We need your letters and comments, your criticisms and contributions. (*Trouble & Strife* Summer 1985: 4)

Readers took up the call to engage. In the same edition, readers' letters began by stating their imperative to respond to an article about parenting: 'I must comment on Lynne Harne's statement', while another began, 'After reading Lynne Harne's article . . . about fathering, I felt that I'd like to expand the discussion about forms of parenting and question what radical practice might be' (*Trouble & Strife* Summer 1985: 4–5). While letters pages were a feature shared with non-feminist women's magazines and other forms of press, in feminist magazines they represented, in part, a broader commitment to the visibility of multiple viewpoints and to the aspiration towards a non-hierarchical structure.

Here, it is worth highlighting that the relationship between speech and literature was fluid within the movement: ideas that were presented at conferences were also diffused through feminist publications, extending their reach. Tracing the journey of publication shows the ways that ideas were disseminated. For example, a paper entitled 'Women and the Family', written by Jan Williams, Hazel Twort and Ann Bachelli who were members of the 'London Peckham Rye group, Women's Liberation Workshop', was presented at the Ruskin Conference in 1970 and printed in *Shrew* magazine in February–March 1970. It was then published in *The Body Politic: Women's Liberation in Britain 1969–1972* by Stage 1 two years later, and subsequently republished as an appendix in Michelene Wandor's *Once a Feminist*, published by Virago in 1990 (Williams et al. 1990: 227–34; 1972: 31–5). The first edition of *Trouble & Strife* magazine admired the American feminist magazine *Off Our Backs* for its detailed coverage of feminist conferences, and explained that it too would cover conferences, noting that:

> exciting political debate develops at our conferences, and events may take place which change many of our minds. But unless something is written down, what has happened is passed only by word of mouth, and this tends to increase the distance between those who are 'in' and those who are not. (*Trouble & Strife* Winter 1983: 42)

While the magazine admitted that there were challenges with reporting on conferences – noting the potential to misrepresent viewpoints – the magazine explained that it aspired to 'develop a way of reporting on conferences . . . so that new questions raised and arguments put forward can be more widely discussed' (Ibid.). Therefore, feminist periodicals gave ideas voiced at conferences and meetings a life beyond that moment.

Drawing on printed materials, I first trace the origins of the Women's Liberation Movement and explore the cultural and political landscape from which it emerged, drawing out the ways in which motherhood appeared as a discursive refrain in its printed texts. I then discuss how the uneasy and shifting negotiation of activism and mothering was articulated in feminist magazines. Finally, I explore how the creation of feminist sites of childcare were articulated in pamphlets and in women's liberation magazines. Writing about childcare, I argue, formed a bridge between the Women's Liberation Movement's practical interventions and ideological commitments.

Motherhood and the Birth of the Women's Liberation Movement

The development of the British women's movement was part of an international burgeoning of feminist activism. In Britain, the women's movement of the 1970s emerged from the political climate and activism of the 1960s, including the student movement and the New Left. These countercultural movements disavowed consumerist, materialistic and capitalist solutions to social problems and drew attention to the power structures embedded in human relationships. Involved in these movements, and later disillusioned with their place in them, feminist women came to consider the family as a vital constituent part of how power acted in society (Antonis 1981: 56). The internal structures of the family, it was argued, were not fixed or immutable; there too, power could be critiqued, challenged and changed. Angela Weir and Elizabeth Wilson (1984: 95) wrote that the nascent women's movement was initially influenced by Marx and Engels in its interrogations of the family under capitalism, drawing feminists' intellectual energies towards untangling the relationship between the family and production. The women's movement developed accounts of the conditions of mothering that took account of gender inside capitalism. It was through reproduction that women were 'exploited at work, and relegated to the home: the two positions compound their oppression', Juliet Mitchell (1971: 99) argued in her influential study, *Woman's Estate.*

It is worth pausing to note the range of ideas and analysis encompassed by the Women's Liberation Movement: thought was rarely unilateral, with some significant differences between socialist and radical perspectives. As Setch (2002) has argued, however, the tendency for historians to represent this as constituting two unbridgeable sides, with radical feminists bearing responsibility for the movement's demise, obscures the more fluid reality in which multiple viewpoints were accommodated within the movement's structure. Feminist print culture provides further evidence of this: although *Spare Rib* and *Trouble & Strife* magazines adopted different tones and audiences – *Trouble & Strife* magazine, established in 1983, adopted an explicitly radical feminist stance, while *Spare Rib* was more mainstream – *Spare Rib* gave the editorial collective of the nascent *Trouble & Strife* help with production and design, and the first edition of *Trouble & Strife* thanks *Spare Rib* for the use of their offices (Cameron and Scanlon 2010: 4).[2] The production of feminist print culture, therefore, exposes the relationships within parts of the feminist community that adopted different stances and positions.

As well encompassing multiple ideological positions, the Women's Liberation Movement incorporated other points of difference. Sarah Browne (2014) has used an oral history approach to examine the Women's Liberation Movement in Scotland and has highlighted the rich feminist activity and engagement north of the border. As George Stevenson (2019) and Natalie Thomlinson (2016) have recently and powerfully demonstrated, class and race both shaped the politics of the movement as well as women's relationship with it. However, while class, race, geography and ideology shaped women's perspectives on the family, the family shared a significant – if disputed – place in feminist thought. While ideological critiques of the family never fell from view, they were buttressed by practical interventions into the conditions of mothering that emerged through local women's liberation groups and that were detailed in feminist publications.

The feminist disillusionment with the family was particularly important given the focus on 'domestic citizenship' that emerged in the wake of the Second World War; that is, that after the war, good citizenship came to be constituted by appropriate family life and demonstrated in the correct care of children (Shapira 2013: 112–13). This placed a distinct burden on mothers, as members of the Women's Liberation Movement pointed out.[3] Family relationships became a 'crucial foundation for peaceful democratic culture' (Chettiar 2012: 108). Psychoanalysts played a critical role in drawing forth new psychological understandings of childhood, and in so doing stressed the significance of mothers to children's future wellbeing (Shapira 2013). The hypothesis that the separation of mother (or mother substitute) and child could have long-term effects was most influentially articulated in Bowlby's bestselling *Child Care and the Growth of Love* (1953). In 1973 *Spare Rib* published an article titled 'Are children loved enough, too much or too little?' that set out Bowlby's ideas and explored Bowlby's influence on other psychologists, noting that these theories had been used to 'attack women who go to work while their children are still babies' (*Spare Rib* August 1973: 15). In the 1980s *Spare Rib* again explained Bowlby's emphasis on 'total mothering' to its readers and argued that this served economic ends: 'the rhetoric of motherhood masks a reality where the retreat of the welfare state demands increasingly more of women. She is expected to be responsible for the abandoned social priorities.' (*Spare Rib* September 1982: 52). *Shrew* argued that the cultural permeation of Bowlby's views was a mechanism through which blame could be attached to mothers, emphasising the way working mothers were held accountable for their children, for 'You know what they'll say – if any of them go off the rails, they'll blame you for going off each day and leaving them.' (*Shrew* October 1972: 2). The centring of mothers in this model of domestic citizenship would go on to be a cause of significant ire to members of the Women's Liberation Movement.

The experience of mothering in postwar Britain was an impetus for the development of the women's movement itself – it provoked women into political activism. As Sue O'Sullivan (1996: 2) recollected, in the:

> first years of women's liberation many of the women involved were mothers and our concerns were reflected in our emphases on the privatized and often lonely nature of the family, on childcare, on issues of radical child-rearing and in our dismissal of biological determinism.

Elizabeth Wilson (1989: 15) reflected that many of the women involved in the beginnings of the movement in the early 1970s:

> had had children in the isolating circumstances which prevailed in the 1960s: they came to the women's movement to find a way out of that isolation and inequality. They did not reject motherhood; they did demand that the conditions of motherhood should change.

In the early years of the movement, *Spare Rib* argued, motherhood was 'discussed endlessly', considered part of the 'impossible demands' made on women and on 'children as dependent "future citizens" of a sick society' (*Spare Rib* July 1980: 26). Certainly the movement saw itself as a result of the:

> sense of frustration . . . over the isolation, drudgery and boredom which some . . . found in the role of full-time wife and mother; a role which they had been brought up to believe was their natural destiny and only possible source of fulfilment.[4]

Indeed, involvement in the movement has been framed in the language of birth: 'I remembered my first feminist involvement in the early seventies as a time which felt like being reborn in slow stages', recalled Marsha Rowe (1982: 13).

Feminist print culture mobilised the image of the unhappy mother as a symptom of the profound inequalities that shaped women's lives. Members of the Women's Liberation Movement argued that discourses of housewifery perpetuated a 'pleasant myth' that housewifery was fulfilling, instinctive and comfortable (*Shrew* August 1971: 11). For some this was exacerbated by an awareness of the challenges faced by their own mothers. As Celia Hughes (2015: 39) has noted, women activists were marked by an 'alertness to and rejection of contradictions and hypocrisies their mothers' lives seemed to represent'. She argues that:

> For women who formed identities within these circles the process of redefining moral values away from their mothers was not simply part of an unconscious social and cultural shift . . . Rather, the process entailed a more extensive change in the way in which they came to inhabit their own class and left identities.

Feminist publications created new arenas in which the relationship between identity, class, mothering and writing could be explored. 'I have often said that I write for my mother', Pearlie McNeill, a working-class feminist writer claimed in *Trouble & Strife*, 'In saying this I mean, that if years ago, my mother could have read the sort of material that I strive to write, then maybe her life and my earlier years might have been less painful.' It was with the knowledge drawn from her working-class upbringing that McNeill wrote and composed her identity: 'I am a writer. I am a woman writer. I am a feminist writer. I am a working-class writer.' (*Trouble & Strife* Spring 1984: 9).

Feminist publications argued that the relationship between politics, work and mothering was intimate. 'Women's militancy at work is never simply economic', a 1972 article in *Shrew* argued, for it 'raises immediately other issues about the family, relations between the sexes, and democratic control at work and in the unions' (*Shrew*

October 1972: 1). This blurring of the boundaries between the domestic and the public was famously enshrined in the exhortation that the 'personal is political'. Against this background, the feminist press disseminated practical information about how women could navigate the strictures of legislation and affirmed its importance. *Spare Rib* labelled maternity leave, for example, a 'basic ingredient of women's working life' in an article that explained women's entitlements (*Spare Rib* September 1973: 14).

Reproduction and the family were ubiquitous in feminist literature. *Shrew* adopted the theme of 'the family' for the May 1971 edition, explaining that 'We're writing about the family because we are all in one. You can't spend much time in Women's Lib without realising that the institution of the family is responsible for many (all?) of our hang-ups.' (*Shrew* May 1971: 0). Rowbotham (1989b: 82) claimed that the Women's Liberation Movement 'created a political space in which women were able to consider the whys and wherefores of motherhood'. Feminist magazines were one of the ways that this 'political space' was created. Indeed, feminist periodicals offered ways for awareness to be raised and solidarities to be established: the author of a poem about lesbian custody battles – a critical issue for the women's movement – wrote in the accompanying letter published in *Spare Rib*, that 'There are a lot of lesbian mothers freaking out about custody around the country, they need support, they need recognition.' (*Spare Rib* June 1981: 32). In feminist writing motherhood could be articulated as simultaneously a political practice, an affective experience, and a signifier and enabler of women's oppression. Motherhood was both 'an experience and institution', American feminist Adrienne Rich (1976) influentially explained. Changing the institutions in which women experienced mothering was not easy, however.

The Women's Movement, Activism and Motherhood

The tension between political activism and maternal responsibilities was a fraught issue for the women's movement. Both demanded time, energy, dedication and emotional investment. At times, the tug of the political and the domestic are to be found literally back to back. One hand-drawn pamphlet advertising a women's liberation rally at Trafalgar Square on 18 May 1969 has a shopping list scribbled on the back: 'rice tomatoes lychees lentils? Peas? Chick peas? Marmalade cornflakes washing up liquid'.[5] The tension imposed by these commitments goes some way towards explaining the attitude observed by Elizabeth Wilson (1989: 5) among some feminists, entering the movement in the mid-1970s, that 'They seemed also often to assume that feminism was saying that to be childless was the *only* feminist position, the only way of being a feminist.' The feeling that feminist motherhood was not well represented in the movement's print media was shared. As a lesbian mother wrote to the letter pages of *Trouble & Strife* in Summer 1984:

> A lot of what I read in the feminist press would make it appear that women in the WLM either don't have children, or wish they hadn't, or are phasing children out. But many women I know either have children (and feel wild with the conflicts and dilemmas imposed on them because of it), or *want* children – even though this is meant to be a negative and soul-destroying experience – or have just lost custody of their children.

'I'd like to write something that counterbalances this impression – women do have children and do love them', she wrote, 'and it is harrowing, tiring, unrewarded, unacknowledged – a very large chunk of our lives' (*Trouble & Strife* Summer 1984: 5).

In the 1990s it was noted that, when the current feminist project was not yet complete, mothering obliged feminist parents to raise children in ways circumscribed by the services available and within the boundaries of social norms (*Trouble & Strife* Spring 1992: 24–9). Judith Barrington, who raised two children with her female partner, observed that that mothering changed the horizons of women's struggle against patriarchy. 'But what can we, as single mothers or groups of parents, hope to do while the children are raised in the same patriarchal system, with the same schools, the same teachers, the same textbooks, the same television programmes and the same fathers?' she asked. For Barrington, feminist childrearing posed an alternative to other forms of activism, as she 'became convinced of the political sense of child-raising just when I was beginning to realise that my passionate commitment to feminist politics was unlikely to have any serious effect on the patriarchy.' (Barrington 1980: 153–4). These compromises were brought to bear in discussions of the reconciliation of feminist ideology and domestic obligation. 'Trying to make ideal families in the real world is a much more confused business', Rowbotham (1989a: 19) has observed, for it was difficult to 'dwell on the emotional intensity of nuance and intimacy that we experience in our personal world and translate such "knowing" into the public sphere of politics'.

For some mothers, coming into a feminist consciousness was the cause of domestic strife. In 1971 an article in *Shrew* observed that awareness of women's oppression and an ostensibly sympathetic partner did not entail practical changes to the distribution of domestic labour. The article's author's engagement with the women's movement encouraged her to ask that her husband share responsibility for childcare and domestic tasks. He initially:

> refused to agree to this until I found something to do as productive, idealistic and useful to society as his work was – this response, of course, carried with it the assumption that my work was menial, meaningless, and totally useless to anyone.

Eventually her partner capitulated, for her feminist engagement 'gave me a greater sense of conviction about what was wrong, and also the courage to fight' (*Shrew* March 1971: 4). Here we can see that exposure to feminist ideas – in groups and through feminist print cultures – created new patterns of being in the home and in women's understandings of their lives.

The problem of mothering sons was an area of sometimes fraught debate in the literature of the women's movement. The politics of rearing boys bubbled to the surface of the movement in 1980, attracting correspondence to *Spare Rib* (*Spare Rib* September 1980: 31). In *Spare Rib* Sue O'Sullivan grappled with the problems of raising boys within a feminist movement, noting that excluding boys from women's liberation events would exclude their mothers. Moreover, it encumbered them in regressive ways: 'I didn't and don't want the burden or responsibility of proving I can bring up two non-sexist, anti-capitalist boys. The attempt could too easily become an intensification of a traditional mother's role.' (*Spare Rib* July 1980: 26–7). In a letter first published in *Birmingham Women's Liberation Newsletter* in May 1982, and later republished in an anthology of women's liberation writings, two women wondered how they should raise their sons, given their sons' status as both their children and as members of the 'oppressor class'. They noted that they limited their conversation about men in front of their sons, and asked 'should we take small boys to women's socials, etc.?' Moreover, 'when does a boy become a man?' they asked, reflecting that even pre-adolescent boy children could disrupt a female environment, but acknowledging that imposing a ban would affect the mothers of boys. The letter rued the quandaries of mothering sons and ended by noting the impossibility of ignoring these issues: as mothers, these members of the Women's Liberation Movement felt they could not 'withdraw attention from our boy children' (Goodenough and Dogsbody 1984: 299–302). Under the auspices of debates about mothering, other, intimate arguments about nurture, politics and change could emerge. In 1985, beginning a monthly series on parenting, 'Astra' wrote in *Spare Rib* about her struggle with her hatred for men as the oppressor class and the need to nurture her sons away from the misogynistic culture that surrounded them. 'How many of us have been made to feel guilty about "putting energy into men"?' she asked, suggesting that 'those of us who agree that the challenging and confronting of males of any age is legitimate political procedure must now speak out' (*Spare Rib* November 1985: 8). In 1996 O'Sullivan (1996: 4), part of the *Spare Rib* collective, looked back on the importance of the magazine in providing a space for the consideration of these issues:

> I still admire the way in which we tried to take an issue, such as the scary and wild assertion by a few women that boy children be banned from women's spaces or even that feminists refuse to rear boy children, and turn it into a serious exploration of some of the problems boy children present to feminists.

Some women felt that the presence of their children regardless of sex rendered them unwelcome in the movement. In 1992, in *Trouble & Strife*, Dena Attar remembered that her initially enthusiastic engagement with feminist campaigns and groups was curtailed after she had children. 'There was more and more to do', she recalled, 'but then I had children and started cracking up and stopped going to lots of meetings and being in several groups at once.' Thinking back to her involvement in women's groups, she recounted a time that mothers felt pressured into denying that they had actively chosen to have children, and another experience where, in a free pregnancy testing group, 'we just assumed that every positive result was a disaster'. In another meeting, a vote was passed to charge mothers for using the crèche at a new women's centre, a decision that at least in part facilitated by the lack of mothers in attendance (*Trouble & Strife* Spring 1992: 24–30).

The process of running crèches at conferences was frequently fractious: a letter first published in the *London Women's Liberation Newsletter* criticised the 1981 Lesbian Conference for not providing a woman-run crèche, noting that 'it's about time we gave our daughters the women-only rights we demand' (Kanter et al. 1984: 294). Men's involvement in running conference crèches also caused consternation for the National Feminist Conference Planning Group, who decided not to use the male-run Crèches Against Sexism for their conference in 1982 and published a letter in the *London Women's Liberation Newsletter* explaining their reasons. 'You are not indispensable' the planning group told Crèches Against Sexism, 'you are supposed to be a part of a political movement, and it is only on these terms that we will ask you to run crèches' (Kanter et al. 1984: 293). When mothers brought their children with them to meetings the atmosphere was sometimes hostile; Attar recalled one meeting at which no one spoke to her when she arrived with her twin toddlers, and no one spoke to her when she left. 'I didn't go back for a long time and I'm still angry', she later admitted (*Trouble & Strife* Spring 1992: 27). Members of the Women's Liberation Movement sought longer-term solutions to the lack of childcare provision, and discussions about how best to do this took place in magazines and pamphlets from the early years of the movement.

The Women's Liberation Movement, the Politics of Childcare, and Feminist Day-Care Centres

'Women's Liberation thinks that publicly-funded, community-controlled facilities should be available for the care of children: not because there is anything wrong with looking after children, but because child-care should be a community responsibility', declared a pamphlet issued by members of the women's movement in 1976.[6] The body of feminist writing around nursery provision importantly bridged the practical and the ideological, connecting the everyday and prosaic with the socio-political goals of the movement. As Davis (2015) has noted, preschool childcare provision was uneven across the postwar period. While nursery expansion was a topic of government interest in the late 1960s – when the Plowden Report (1967) on primary schools was published – and the early 1970s, discussions within the Women's Liberation Movement drew mothers' needs to the fore. Pamphlets created by the Women's Liberation Movement advised that a 'woman does not cease to be a person when she becomes a mother, or to have normal human needs for rest, recreation and other work'.[7]

It was against this background that in 1971 *Shrew* made the case that day care was unfairly contrasted with 'mother care'. Those who defended full-time motherhood as the optimal form of childcare, *Shrew* argued, assumed that the mother was 'always pleasant, relaxed, stimulating', juxtaposed with the 'cold atmosphere' of a nursery, overlooking mothers 'too unhappy, too poor, too tired, too neurotic or just too ignorant to give much to their children' (*Shrew* 3 1971: 1). If alternative care was provided, mothers would be allowed to make personal choices about the kinds of mothering that they wanted to undertake (*Shrew* 4 1972: 2). The particulars of this alternative care remained uncertain. As a teacher declared in *Shrew*, the aim of 24-hour nurseries – agreed at the first women's liberation conference – was not suitably detailed. Rather, she argued, 'it is vitally important to know just what kind of child care, nurseries and schools we really want' (*Shrew* 3 1971: 14). Activist groups explored and articulated what women's liberation childcare might 'really want' in the print materials they generated. Members of the women's movement wrote pamphlets and in magazines about the process of establishing the day-care centres, disseminating feminist ideas (*Shrew* 3 1971: 6).

Angela Davis (2015: 181) has noted that playgroups attained government approval as they were cheap and congruent with the idea that families should provide their own childcare. As she observes, however, this conservative ideology masked progressive possibilities. The Women's Liberation Movement explored this potential. For example, as an article in *Shrew* explained, in the early 1970s in Tufnell Park, North London, a women's liberation group attempted to establish its own playgroup. This playgroup, the article explained, would 'break down some of the isolation experienced by mothers and young children alike', relieving 'at least some mothers of some of the strain imposed by coping with young children on their own'. Run in a 'truly communal spirit', it aspired to provide opportunities for children to create equal bonds with a variety of adults. Encouraging women to understand that 'there are alternatives to the way in which we live', the playgroup was argued to be a means 'to reach women who would otherwise remain strangers', allowing them to nurture 'meaningful relationships among women in the community', and to 'communicate the ideas of Women's Liberation' (*Shrew* March 1971: 6–8). The readers of *Shrew* did not uncritically embrace this, however, and *Shrew* later published a letter of riposte that declared this proposal to be worrying, as children did not want 'watching-care, but loving-care' (*Shrew* May 1971: 13).

Pamphlets were also written as short guides to share experiences and to disseminate ideas. One such pamphlet, *Our Experiences of Collective Childcare*, was published in 1974 by the founders of an establishment founded in 1972. The Children's Community Centre was founded at 123 Dartmouth Park Hill in Highgate New Town, an area of North London that was in the midst of extensive redevelopment during this period.[8] The Centre, which in 1974 hosted a maximum of fifteen children at any one time, was established by members of the Women's Liberation Movement, some of whom had cut their teeth on the campaign for 24-hour nurseries, but had realised that it was necessary to expedite this by establishing their own sites of childcare. Camden Council gave the group use of the three-storey house rent-free, although the basement's vinyl-tiled floor developed swollen bumps and the walls crumbled from the damp. The rooms downstairs were used for art and play and had access to a small outside space. On the upper floors, a wooden-floored kitchen and adjoining front room were used for lunch and snacks, as well as table-based play; the relationship between the kitchen and this room, it was noted, made food production visible. One level up, a room served as a children's library and an office, and hosted the Sunday meetings held by the group, as well as being used to 'put up mothers and children who need refuge from their home scene for a few nights'.[9]

The Centre vowed that 'it *is* possible to rear different kinds of people' than those moulded by patriarchal capitalism: collectivism and independence amongst the children was encouraged, as was, albeit unevenly, the disintegration of sex roles. Not staffed exclusively by members of the Women's Liberation Movement, and inclusive of different political standpoints, there was some disagreement about this aim. Nonetheless, its 1974 pamphlet cited Lee Comer's *The Myth of Motherhood* (1972) approvingly. It was argued that that the Centre was successful in providing nurturing care to its child attendees, for even the children who struggled, 'are best coped with collectively, by people who love and respect the child rather than by an isolated and frustrated mother burdened by the feelings of guilt which she believes are unique'.[10]

More than a hundred miles away, in Calthorpe Park, Birmingham, a group of men and women involved in women's liberation were undertaking a similar project. This was set out in a pamphlet, *Out of the Pumpkin Shell: Running a Women's Liberation Playgroup*, published in 1975 (Playgroup Pamphlet Group 1975).[11] The authoring of the pamphlet demonstrates the importance of print culture in providing models of practice for others, as well as a means of resisting the erasure of women's activism from the record. The pamphlet connected the practical with the ideological aims of the movement, providing a bridge between theory and practice: 'How can we, through and around a pre-school playgroup, begin to transform the nuclear family?' the pamphlet asked, 'And at what point does our perpetuation of the family begin to compromise our political experiments?' (Ibid.: 6). These questions framed a project that began in 1970, as a group of parents who had been involved in women's liberation, disappointed by the disjuncture between the ideals of the movement and their daily lives, brought their three one-year-olds together twice a week between 10 a.m. and 2 p.m. Just eighteen months later it had expanded to include twelve children, running once a week from a member's house (Ibid.: 9). The parents involved were 'part of a generalised, middle-class redefinition of family life – moving from the traditionally domesticated family of the past, to a more open, progressive, "symmetrical" family of the future' (Ibid.: 6).

The parents sought to establish a more formal setting. Between September 1971 and July 1972, the parents sought premises for a playgroup, and – after overcoming some administrative hurdles and bureaucratic problems – secured the use of a purpose-built play centre in Calthorpe Park, within the Balsall Heath area of Birmingham (Ibid.: 9–10). It opened in September 1972 and was staffed by volunteers for the first two terms, but by Spring 1973 it was agreed that it should employ a paid supervisor and subsequently expanded its opening times to four mornings a week. This posed a quandary for the group, which struggled with finances as it sought to keep it accessible whilst not under-remunerating a role that was undervalued as part of 'women's work'. Attempts to avoid gender stereotypes were deemed more successful. Fathers and non-parents were involved in the group and the effects of gender socialisation on both male and female children were explicitly considered and confronted (Ibid.: 6). For example, boys were actively encouraged to play with dolls and to play homes and families; girls were actively encouraged to play with cars and trains (Ibid.: 24–5). The group also developed non-sexist rhymes: 'Father's washing, father's washing/rub, rub, rub/Picked up Johnny's little shirt/And threw it in the tub.' (Ibid.: 23). This was not straightforward, however, and members felt at time that the values of women's liberation were not sufficiently strongly expressed in the children's activities.

As in Tufnell Park, the parents in Birmingham were explicit in their writings that the playgroup could serve multiple purposes: to communicate the ideas of women's liberation; to change social attitudes; and to nourish women's confidence in themselves – and their confidence in the movement (Ibid.: 12–13). The desire for inclusivity sometimes contradicted the principles of the group, it was argued, since in 'developing a distinctively Women's Liberation approach to childcare, we inevitably make it more difficult for women not already in the Movement to be fully absorbed into the collective' (Ibid.: 13). More generally, it was sometimes difficult to engage local mothers with the playgroup. This was explained as owing to the transient local population and the large non-English speaking immigrant community, although the group produced a leaflet in Urdu in an effort to reach out (Ibid.: 15). Attempts to establish inclusive and politically aligned childcare services were therefore fraught with challenges for the Women's Liberation Movement, but were also held to be fundamental to ensuring that women did not shoulder the burden of unsupported childrearing. These challenges were reflected in the writing that was published in pamphlets and magazines across the 1970s and into the 1980s.

Conclusion

The Women's Liberation Movement placed the contradictions and compromises that were necessitated by women's maternal status at the heart of its challenge to British patriarchal culture. Once redistributing the domestic labour of childcare was positioned as fundamental to liberating women from the intellectual, temporal and emotional strictures of the home, the question of what this might entail was raised. Discussions in magazines and pamphlets indicated that while children posed practical difficulties for feminist mothers, they also pointed to new models of the future that could be brought into being through feminist care. As one author declared in *Spare Rib*, 'children don't have to weigh us down or close us in, nor we them. I want a society where all relationships have been transformed' (*Spare Rib* July 1980: 27). While childrearing revealed the profound challenges of living within a society whose strictures feminists were trying to change, motherhood opened up new intimacies and new points of contact with their communities. Feminist print culture played a critical role in forging new discussions about motherhood and facilitating new sites of dissemination. Magazines produced and edited by women's liberation members and groups charted new intellectual terrain and enabled the communication of ideas across geographic boundaries. The flow of ideas was particularly important as the Women's Liberation Movement attempted to bridge the practical and the ideological through the creation of new childcare models. Some members of the 'second wave' argued that although mid-century parenting ideologies had been forged by patriarchal norms, mothering might also constitute an opportunity to disrupt the transmission of patriarchal ideals across and through generations.

Notes

1. Three further demands were added in 1974 and 1978.
2. The second issue of *Trouble & Strife* thanked the feminist bookshop Sisterwrite for use of their space (*Trouble & Strife* Spring 1984: inside cover).
3. This is expanded on in my forthcoming monograph, *Postnatal Depression in Post-war Britain: Women, Motherhood and Social Change* (Manchester University Press).
4. Bodleian archive (hereafter Bod.) M91B638: 'Women's Liberation, an Introduction' (1976). 2.
5. Bod. 91B638, 2.5.4.: 'Women Demand Equal Rights' (1969).
6. Bod. M91B638: 'Women's Liberation'. 4.
7. Ibid.
8. Bod. 26234 c.9: Children's Community Centre, 'Our Experiences of Collective Childcare'. 1974. 4–5.
9. Ibid.: 5–11.
10. Ibid.: 11.
11. One of the women involved was historian Catherine Hall. Hall discusses the centre with her husband Stuart Hall in Jolly (2019: 197).

Works Cited

Antonis, B. 1981. 'Motherhood and Mothering'. *Women in Society: Interdisciplinary Essays.* Ed. Cambridge Women's Studies Group. London: Virago: 55–74.

Barrington, J. 1980. 'Why Children?' *Why Children?* Eds S. Dowrick and S. Grundberg. London: The Women's Press. 144–67.

Bowlby, J. 1953. *Child Care and the Growth of Love.* London: Penguin.

Browne, S. 2014. *The Women's Liberation Movement in Scotland.* Manchester: Manchester University Press.

Bruley, S. 2014. 'Jam Tomorrow? Socialist Women and Women's Liberation 1968–82: An Oral History Approach'. *Against the Grain: The British Far Left from 1956.* Ed. E. Smith. Manchester: Manchester University Press: 155–72.

Cameron, D. and J. Scanlon, eds. 2010. *The Trouble & Strife Reader.* London: Bloomsbury.

Chettiar, T. 2012. 'Democratizing Mental Health: Motherhood, Therapeutic Community and the Emergence of the Psychiatric Family at the Cassel Hospital in Post-Second World War Britain'. *History of the Human Sciences* 255: 107–22.

Cohen, R. 2012. 'Researching Difference and Diversity within Women's Movements: Sisterhood and After'. *Women's Studies International Forum* 35: 138–40.

Crook, S. 2018. 'The Women's Liberation Movement, Activism and Therapy at the Grassroots, 1968–1985'. *Women's History Review* 27.7: 1,152–68.

Davis, A. 2012. *Modern Motherhood: Women and Family in England, 1945–2000.* Manchester: Manchester University Press.

Fell, A. 1979. 'Introduction'. *Hard Feelings: Fiction and Poetry from Spare Rib.* Ed. A. Fell. London: The Women's Press. 1–6.

Forster, L. 2016. 'Spreading the Word: Feminist Print Cultures and the Women's Liberation Movement'. *Women's History Review* 25.5: 812–31.

Goodenough, G. and E. Dogsbody. 1984. 'On Bringing Up Boys'. *Sweeping Statements: Writings from the Women's Liberation Movement 1981–83.* Eds H. Kanter, S. Lefanu, S. Shah and C. Spedding. London: The Women's Press. 299–302.

Hughes, C. 2015. *Young Lives on the Left: Sixties Activism and the Liberation of the Self.* Manchester: Manchester University Press.

Jolly, M. 2012. 'Assessing the Impact of Women's Movements: Sisterhood and After'. *Women's Studies International Forum* 35.3: 150–2.

Jolly, M. 2019. *Sisterhood and After: An Oral History of the UK Women's Liberation Movement.* Oxford: Oxford University Press.

Kanter, H., S. Lefanu, S. Shah and C. Spedding, eds. 1984. *Sweeping Statements: Writings from the Women's Liberation Movement 1981–83.* London: The Women's Press.

Laing, R. D. and A. Esterton. 1964. *Sanity, Madness and the Family.* London: Penguin.

Mitchell, J. 1971. *Woman's Estate.* Harmondsworth: Penguin.

National Jewish Feminist Conference Planning Group. 1984. 'Crèches: Two Letters'. *Sweeping Statements: Writings from the Women's Liberation Movement 1981–83.* H. Kanter, S. Lefanu, S. Shah and C. Spedding, eds. London: The Women's Press. 291–3.

O'Sullivan, S. 1996. *I Used to Be Nice: Sexual Affairs.* London: Bloomsbury.

Playgroup Pamphlet Group. 1975. *Out of the Pumpkin Shell: Running a Women's Liberation Playgroup.* Birmingham Women's Liberation.

Rees, J. 2010. '"Are you a Lesbian?" Challenges in Recording and Analysing the Women's Liberation Movement in England'. *History Workshop Journal* 69.1: 177–87.

Rich, A. 1976. *Of Woman Born: Motherhood as an Experience and Institution.* London: Virago.

Rowbotham, S. 1989a. *The Past is Before Us: Feminism in Action since the 1960s.* Harmondsworth: Penguin.

Rowbotham, S. 1989b. 'To Be or Not To Be: The Dilemmas of Mothering'. *Feminist Review* 31.1: 82–93.

Rowe, M. 1982. 'Introduction'. *Spare Rib Reader*. Ed. M. Rowe. Middlesex: Penguin. 13–22.

Setch, E. 2002. 'The Face of Metropolitan Feminism: The London Women's Liberation Workshop, 1969–79'. *Twentieth Century British History* 13.2: 171–90.

Shapira, M. 2013. *The War Inside: Psychoanalysis, Total War, and the Making of the Democratic Self in Post-war Britain*. Cambridge: Cambridge University Press.

Spare Rib Collective. 1982. 'Afterword'. *Spare Rib Reader*. Ed. M. Rowe. Middlesex: Penguin. 607–8.

Stevenson, G. 2019. *The Women's Liberation Movement and the Politics of Class in Britain*. London: Bloomsbury.

Thomlinson, N. 2016. *Race, Ethnicity and the Women's Movement in England, 1968–1993*. Basingstoke: Palgrave Macmillan.

Weir, A. and E. Wilson. 1984. 'The British Women's Liberation Movement'. *New Left Review* 1/148: 74–103.

Williams, J., H. Twort and A. Bachelli. 1972. 'Women and the Family'. *The Body Politic: Women's Liberation in Britain 1969–1972*. Ed. M. Wandor. London: Stage 1. 31–5.

Williams, J., H. Twort and A. Bachelli. 1990. 'Women and the Family'. *Once a Feminist: Interviews by Michelene Wandor*. Ed. M. Wandor. London: Virago, 227–34.

Wilson, E. 1989. 'In a Different Key'. *Balancing Acts: On Being a Mother*. Ed. K. Gieve. London: Virago. 11–23.

22

Beyond Utility: Pushing the Frontiers in Women's Monthlies: *Modern Woman* 1943–51

Fiona Hackney

Introduction: Active Citizenship and Feminist Consciousness

THIS CHAPTER EXAMINES a 'new consciousness' that emerged, albeit unevenly, in the women's 'service' monthly *Modern Woman* in the 1940s. Published by George Newnes, *Modern Woman* was a mid-range consumer magazine targeted at a readership of professional women and the wives of professionals that first appeared in the mid-1920s. Subject to rationing, magazines reduced in size, yet the women's press took on new importance as a conduit for government and as a vital support for women dealing with wartime conditions. This chapter argues that the ethos of publications also changed as the home became central to public discourse. The new conditions opened a space to rethink women's social and political participation as 'active citizens' and discursive articles took on a new prominence in the magazine.

Looking back on the woman's magazine industry in the early 1940s, James Drawbell – then newly appointed managing editor of George Newnes' weekly *Woman's Own* – recalled those years as a unique time when editors could focus on meeting their readers' needs unhampered by commercial considerations:

> This was the great time, and it would last only a few years, when magazines would sell solely on their reader-value. It was a journalist's dream. We could plan our magazine as a magazine . . . It was the quality of the editorial, in fact, which in those early days caused the magazine revolution to happen. (Drawbell 1968: 125)

> [E]ditors had complete freedom to compile their magazines as they saw fit, reflecting their readers' lives fully and accurately, and balancing 'service' with 'general interest', not fearing to be controversial where they judged this to be appropriate. (White 1970: 132)

For Drawbell, this meant magazines transformed by colour in the postwar years, but also the quality of feature articles that debated a raft of pressing social and political issues in which women, in their expanded role of wartime citizens, had a voice. Women's magazine historian Cynthia White concurs, acknowledging the vital importance of the home-service provided by *Everywoman*, *Good Housekeeping* and *Housewife* in helping the war effort on the Home Front. Noting the large amounts of 'general interest' material, controversial discussions and informative, thought-provoking articles sparking lively conversation, she argues that in terms of some issues at least, they were 'in advance of the rest of society' as 'the frontiers of modern women's journalism were being pushed right back'(White 1970: 125, 130–1). White lists topics such as equal pay, married women's employment, child poverty, child psychology, housing, state-funded nurseries, parenthood, adoption, divorce, the social sciences, starvation in Europe and women MPs, all of which appeared in *Modern Woman* in these years. Laurel Forster (2015: 41), looking at *Housewife* in the 1940s, identified 1943 as the date from which the magazine began to think progressively about an expanded role for women beyond the war. Citing a new 'international element' alongside feature articles by well-known authors such as Monica Dickens and MPs discussing equality, equal pay and encouraging women to become involved in wider society, Forster argues that a discourse of housewifely competence transitioned into an a 'emergent feminist consciousness' in the magazine in these years (Ibid.: 47).

This chapter takes these observations as a starting point to examine the discourse of 'active citizenship' in *Modern Woman* during wartime and the postwar years, and how it offered readers new forms of agency in public and domestic life. Tensions emerged – war stimulated diverse elements of feminism including the 'equal rights' tradition and championing women's interests as housewives and mothers. Ambivalence between 'equality' and 'difference' shaped the discourse in *Modern Woman*, just as it shaped debates among women's professional and voluntary groups and women MPs (Oram 1996: 55). Magazines, moreover, performed a 'dual role' as '[h]andmaiden of government and handholders of the female population' (Ferguson 1983: 19). 'Service' magazines which, prewar, had mediated between women and commerce – selling readers to advertisers but also representing their needs (Hackney 2018) – had to rethink this in terms of their duty to government: recruiting women to industry, providing practical advice about shortages and boosting morale, while providing a 'voice' for women on the national stage. This chapter concentrates on the years around three 'moments' in the 1940s: the height of wartime mobilisation in 1943; the start of postwar reconstruction in 1946; and when Sybil Chaloner, *Modern Woman*'s editor, resigned and the ethos of the magazine changed in 1949. Focusing on discursive features, understandings of fashion (1943) and the home (1946) are contextualised within wider debates about active citizenship that were taking place in the magazine and elsewhere.

The *Modern Woman* Family

> [W]e magazine editors formed an Editor's Group early in the war. Object to keep in close touch with the Big Boys who were running the war and so be able to let you know what we all had to do. Introduced to the Group and with our names before them, most of the Ministries became positively matey in time, and much good work was done. (*MW* April 1946: 21)

Women's magazines underwent a profound transformation in wartime. Print rationing (1940) and controls restricting the space devoted to advertising (1942) contributed to the cessation or amalgamation of many titles. *Modern Woman* incorporated its sister paper *Modern Home*, increasing its cover price from 6d to 8d and then to 9d in

October 1941 when it moved to a 'pocket-size' format. Depending on imports that were difficult to sustain through the U-boat blockade, paper stocks to each company were limited. Publishers opted to cut page and edition size so that circulations could rise with demand, and this in turn contributed to the increased importance of the women's press as war progressed (Reed 1997: 210, 229). Copies were also passed between multiple households before 'the tattered remains were bundled off to a Service camp or hospital' (Grieve 1964: 134).

From 1941, after much prompting from the industry, editors met regularly with ministry representatives at the offices of the Periodical Publishers Association and the women's press, alongside the cinema and radio, became a vital channel of communication for government to issue instructions and broadcast announcements (Ferguson 1983; Andrews 2012). Government-sponsored advertisements from the Ministry of Food or the Ministry of Fuel and Power appeared regularly in *Modern Woman* as 'domesticity became a public issue' (Summerfield 2013/1984: 185). The magazine also ran a regular column 'Will You Lend A Hand?' calling for women's services as Auxiliary Territorial Service mechanics, wireless operators for the Women's Auxiliary Air Force (WAAF), and drivers for the Women's Royal Naval Service, for instance, as well as for 'Make Do and Mend' and salvage duties (*MW* January 1943: 91). In 1943 the *World's Press News*, noting the 'phenomenal growth' in influence of the women's press, attributed this to 'the advance of woman herself as a political, economic and moral force in the life of the nation' (Ferguson 1983: 20). Editors maintained that magazines were not simply a 'doormat press' (Winship 1996: 127). *Modern Woman*'s Sybil Chaloner claimed that they resisted ministry requests to 'soften the blow' for women asking, where possible, for the truth unvarnished by Home Front propaganda (April 1946: 21). Even at their most influential, this dilemma reveals a central tension at the heart of wartime women's magazines as editors struggled to fulfil two potentially contradictory roles as a conduit for government at a time of national emergency *and* as a mouthpiece for women, representing their concerns on a national stage.

The women's press continued to be a significant force in the years of postwar reconstruction as scarcity and rationing persisted in support of an all-out export drive to get industry back on its feet, and hardship and deprivation increased (Kynaston 2007: 22–59). Some things, however, did return to normal. In December 1946, at the end of a particularly punitive year (Garfield 2004), *Modern Woman* reintroduced coated-paper stock, meaning more colour and visual appeal. A humorous illustration in Chaloner's editorial shows her team literally flying high, distributing copies by aeroplane, helicopter and parachute in a celebratory reworking of wartime propaganda. Employing the metaphor of 'magazine as woman' to bind readers to the reinvigorated but more expensive publication, she declares:

> [A]t last [*Modern Woman*] has shed her drab frock; that horrid dun garment that old Poppa Paper Control has forced her to wear for years. She has put on the white full-skirted new gown she has dreamed of, and it brings out, as good clothes always do, her best qualities – her friendliness, aliveness, good looks, and humour . . . She was never an hysterical girl, but she can tell you now there have been times when, in her grey paper frock, she wanted to yell and tear her pages off. All that is over and she's all set for a new life of adventure in the brave new world. (*MW* December 1946: 29)

Quota restrictions prevented the free play of market forces, limiting advertising, and paper allocation was fixed in proportion to prewar circulations, inhibiting growth (White 1970: 124). The magazine's cover price had to rise to one shilling to support the added costs, and Chaloner had to woo readers with the promise of 'brilliant' new artists and writers: *Modern Woman*'s 'new clothes and more exclusive accessories will cost us a lot more' but 'she knows you won't mind paying a little more in future for the fun of taking her out' (*MW* December 1946: 29).

While the magazine was depicted as a 'woman' for readers, for the editor, however, the magazine was her child, and the team that produced it was a family (Hackney 2018: 298). Celebrating the magazine's twenty-first anniversary, Chaloner reflected on its original pioneering status, 'covering the main interests of women' when it was launched in the mid-1920s:

> I had a clear field. Oh, happy days-and nights! For in those early months I often worked till two in the morning sprucing up this only child . . . the women's magazine industry was in its infancy then. Staffs were minute and trained staff few . . . Within a few years there were a dozen sixpenny magazines for women. (*MW* July 1946: 21)

As men returned from war, the names of established male illustrators and authors started to appear in the magazine (*MW* December 1946: 30–1). The expert editors and core editorial staff, nevertheless, remained staunchly female offering, in Chaloner's words, the 'promise of continued service'. A feature in the anniversary issue pictured the 'specialists': Dr Elizabeth (health club); Elizabeth Troy (fashion); Jane Howe (beauty); Hilda M. Whitlow (housecraft); Noel Ward (furnishing and decoration); Edith A. Browne (cookery); Grace A. Rees (careers adviser); and Ray Allister (personal problems); and named the editorial team: Sybil Chaloner; Barbara Vise (assistant editor); Sheila Webb (chief sub-editor); Vivian Belmar (sub-editor); and Winifred Bottomley (editorial secretary) (*MW* July 1946: 71). Along with Chaloner, Vise, Allister, Troy and Howe had been with the magazine since prewar days. Author, poet and illustrator Stevie Smith was a newer addition. She wrote a monthly book review page for *Modern Woman* from the early 1940s, contributing to its literary status (Spalding 1988: 44–54). Noting that Smith's celebrated *Novel on Yellow Paper* (1936) had satirised women's magazines, Chaloner added that was 'as they then were. They changed' (*MW* December 1946: 30). At its core the *Modern Woman* family was distinctly female.

For Chaloner and Vise *Modern Woman* was literally a family affair, both having relatives who contributed to the magazine. Many women had family in the business, and Chaloner was from a prominent family of London publishers and journalists (Hackney 2012: 2,018). Lenore Maude Chaloner who wrote articles and books under the pseudonym Len Chaloner and edited many magazines (*Ideal Home*, *Woman's Magazine*, *Decoration*, *Parents*, and *Home and Schooling*) was Sybil's sister-in-law, being married to her brother. Lenore's husband Ernest J. Chaloner who had edited a daily newspaper and contributed gardening columns to *Modern Woman* and other Newnes' publications. Jennetta Vise whose signature appeared regularly on *Modern Woman* artwork, was Barbara's sister and a prolific illustrator who worked all her life on books, comics and magazines. Their father Reginald Toye Vise was also a journalist. Philip Burton (2019), who had shared an office with Jennetta in Newnes' technical book publishing department, recalled her method, working late into the evening – 'as freelancers typically do' – in her small study at 75 Carter Lane, near St Pauls, as well as the sisters' different personalities: 'She had an older sister, Barbara, a successful journalist, gregarious and more extrovert, unlike Jennetta who was a very private but equally-friendly person'. Chaloner, the Vise sisters and Ray Allister were members of The Women's Press Club of London which, having been founded 'amid the ruins and desolation of the London Blitz' on 1 April 1943, provided an important forum for women to meet, exchange views, discuss trends and share knowledge with colleagues 'from all parts of the world', connecting them to a larger international family of female journalists (Deakin 1984: 7, 80).

Original signed artwork was an important part of *Modern Woman*'s visual appeal and Chaloner cultivated a stable of artists whose style, while rarely abstract, was distinctly modern. The early 1940s provided space for women to establish themselves and most of those named and promoted were women, including: Jennetta Vise, Audrey Wynne Hatfield, Pearl Binder, Mariel Deans and Francis Mortimer who signed her work C-M. Following modern precepts, their work was never solely decorative but served as a means of visual communication. Better binding machines and new ideas from European and American magazines, meant that art directors increasingly looked for opportunities to create two facing pages as a 'coherent space' (Reed 1997: 206). Illustration was employed as a mode of 'picture reporting', whereby the artist tells a story through images. Binder, an artist and writer, would sometimes contribute an original article and illustrate it, Wynne Hatfield created embroidered 'art' pieces for readers to copy, while Vise specialised in humorous board games to communicate complex information in an interactive way. Stevie Smith illustrated her Book Review page. Deans, Mortimer and Smith appear in a photo-feature where their continental, American or generally 'bohemian' credentials were emphasised. Deans lived in a 'Mayfair back-alley' and had worked in London, Paris and New York in fashion drawing and journalism before contributing 'lighter love stories and girl-to-girl beauty talks in the blackout' to the magazine (*MW* December 1946: 31). Frances Mortimer is described as 'young, gay, an unusual beauty'. The accompanying photograph shows a slim, dark, striking woman posed with cigarette in hand. American born, she ran a design studio in Paris with her husband and worked as freelance artist in London and New York. Mortimer created the artwork for *Modern Woman*'s 'out-of-the-ordinary' covers in the postwar years, which sometimes displaying a surreal twist, were contemporary, delicate and daring. Over a period of months towards the end of 1946, for instance, she consciously played with magazine conventions, in particular the visual rhetoric of the 'female gaze'. The women on the covers, sometimes with a hand obscuring part of their face, eye the reader ever more directly, culminating in a final close-up on the cover of the Christmas issue where the eye alone is visible: a 'mind's eye' that seems to challenge the reader to see herself differently (see Plate 14).

Chaloner employed a collegial, even feminist tone with readers addressing them as 'sisters' and the magazine's 'ideal reader' was always represented as active and engaged, whether at home, work or in Parliament. In her 1946 New Year editorial she imagines her readers:

> sitting behind that desk; beside that mountain of mending; in that store; hurrying through the ward; teaching that out-size class; lecturing; washing-up; travelling

> uncomfortably; making your maiden speech in the House; taking all those antenatal patients in your clinic; feeding the hungry. (*MW* January 1946: 21)

Written after the 1945 general election that brought a Labour government with twenty-four women MPs to power, when hopes were high for women's participation in reconstruction, the editorial positions *Modern Woman* readers as hard-working, professional, capable, civically minded active citizens. A trope that emerged from wartime emergency, belief in women's active citizenship was to become a central tenet shaping the postwar magazine.

'Fiction, Features, Fashion, Knitting, All the Facts on Wartime Living': Feminism and Fashion Agency

Feature articles exploring women's active citizenship, during and after wartime, took on new prominence in *Modern Woman* from 1943, the year in which the Equal Compensation Campaign achieved a landmark victory for female equality (Beaumont 2013: 148). This section explores the tenor of that debate and how arguments about women's rights and duties framed in feature articles filtered into more conventional areas such as the magazine's fashion page, helping to transform ideas about female agency, appearance and identity. In a *Modern Woman* interview from early 1943, MP Ellen Wilkinson, then Parliamentary Secretary to the Ministry of Home Security, ratified a government order making fire-watching compulsory for women's Civil Defence work at a time when, in her words, 'Total war comes right into the home' (*MW* January 1943: 40). Such wartime rhetoric linked women's equal participation with the promise of full citizenship and was used by feminist groups and others to support 'equal rights' arguments, above all for equal pay. Hopes were raised when women's organisations working with the thirteen cross-party female MPs in the national government succeeded in their campaign for women's equal compensation for war injuries (*MW* February 1944: 46–7). War, at the same time, reinforced gender difference, albeit in new ways, as the maintenance of the Home Front meant that social issues typically gendered as feminine – housing, children's education, family and health – rose up the political agenda, fostering a new sense of 'complementary but different' female citizenship. Feminists, as historian Alison Oram (1996: 63–5) points out, struggled to reconcile these differing positions by fighting for women's improved political participation and a 'new form of citizenship for the housewife'.

These debates were articulated for *Modern Woman* readers in a series of six discursive articles, billed by the magazine as 'challenging', by future Labour MP Elaine Burton (*MW* November 1943: 42). Burton was eager to redress the lack of women's voices in national politics. Described as 'an ardent but not aggressive feminist', she combined 'equal rights' demands for equal pay with advocacy for women's active participation in areas of special interest to them; from 1950 she became the 'housewives' voice' in Parliament as an authority on consumer protection (Sutherland 2004: 16–17). Burton wrote a weekly column on women's wartime difficulties for *The Star* in the early 1940s – the articles were published as *What of the Women* (1941) and *And Your Verdict* (1942) – and her *Modern Woman* series, effectively a call to arms for women, provided a touchstone for progressive thinking in the magazine. Written at the height of wartime emergency – her first article was triggered by government's drive to involve more married women in the war effort (Summerfield 2013/1984) – Burton, like many others, was also looking forward to envisaging an active role for women in postwar reconstruction. Her articles focused on salient themes: married women's right to work outside the home; raising the status of domestic service; improved housing; and the expansion of women's postwar employment (*MW* June 1943: 46).

Drawing inspiration from the success of the women's equal compensation bill – sadly to be the 'only clear feminist victory of the Second World War years' (Oram 1996: 58) – Burton argued for the power of women's collective action as 'good citizenship': 'It is our business as women to *get* the things we know are necessary for the welfare of the community' (*MW* August 1943: 46–7). To achieve this, she proposed a network of 'Group Action Councils', following the model of Soroptimist 'Standing Conferences', which would bring women together to talk, clarify ideas, and work collectively to put them into effect (*MW* August 1943: 42–3). These were to be run in collaboration with existing organisations, from the Women's Voluntary Service and the National Council of Women, to the Women's Institutes and the Co-operative Guilds; women in the countryside were also encouraged to set up their own 'village Council' for weekly or monthly meetings (*MW* November 1943: 43). All points of view were to be heard, 'pooling brains and goodwill' across party political and class lines, and facilitated by the women's press: 'As a reader of MODERN WOMAN you can join our Council *now* as you read this article!' (*MW* August 1943: 47).

Her articles – written in a style somewhere between conversational and adversarial – combined provocation with empathy to stir women into action, as Burton presented both sides of the argument before pressing her point home. Titled 'Women are lazy thinkers', the first in the series was termed 'an attack that will start the talk going in any group of women'. A question and answer format at the start and finish reproduces the discursive qualities of 'talk':

> 'Should women take a fuller share in the life of the country?'
> 'But they do-everywhere in factories, nurseries, homes, the Forces, here and overseas, the women are doing a grand job!'
> 'Yes, I know, BUT . . .' (*MW* June 1943: 46)

> 'If you do this you will be taking your share.'
> 'In what?'
> 'In citizenship, of course. (*MW* June 1943: 47)

The pronoun 'we' is used throughout the series to foster a sense of collectivity while enabling Burton to share her own experience of work and unemployment to enhance reader-identification, a tried and tested journalistic strategy (Hackney 2016: 113–14). Humorous line drawings by Audrey Wynne Hatfield lightened the mood.

The second article, 'An Englishman's Home is his Castle', was in fact an argument for 'Married Women and outside-the-home careers' (*MW* July 1943: 42–3, 46). '[I]t is not necessarily "old-fashioned" to say that a woman's place is at home, or "modern" to say that she should go out to work', Burton intones, adding, but 'why on earth shouldn't a married woman go out to work?' (*MW* 1943 July: 42). Points in favour – the wife with no aptitude for housework, the trained woman whose expertise was wasted at home – recall prewar arguments, but wartime emergency gave them new weight. 'Are *you* going to forbid her to give that service to the community?', Burton declared, claiming that work made married women 'better citizens' and aligning the issue with reforms shaping reconstruction and the Welfare State (Hackney 2016; *MW* July 1943: 42):

> Every human being, whether man or woman, has a right and a duty to work; to use his or her brain and hands for self-support and the benefit of the community . . . In the future, you and I have to see that adequate wages are paid; that children's allowances become law, that full medical service is available to all, and that the new houses are planned to save all unnecessary work. (*MW* July: 46)

Housing, domestic work and new areas of employment for women came next. Advocating such progressive ideas as state subsidies for households below a certain income to employ domestic help – 'our plan must be for all, not only those who can afford it' – Burton proposed a 'domestic workers charter' devised by a committee of housewives, workers in domestic service agencies, and domestic science teachers to raise the status of domestic work (*MW* August: 42–3). William Beveridge's term 'the Giant Squalor' became a metaphor for the housing problem: the 'national disgrace' of homes in cities through which evacuation revealed 'the Giant Squalor in all his strength' (*MW* September: 42–3, 46). Whereas, anxieties about the feminisation of jobs for women had characterised prewar employment discourse in magazines, the rhetoric now changed (Hackney 2008: 114–20). In anticipation of a newly inclusive postwar society, a declaration of the egalitarian right and national responsibility for men and women, both married and single, to work, accompanies jobs as interviewers, nursery workers, camp organisers, cooks, restaurant managers, housing managers, and older saleswomen in shoe departments, shoes being particularly scarce (*MW* October: 46, 81). The series ends with the headline Elaine Burton 'sums up the active attitude that alone can give you the right to the proud title of CITIZEN OF GREAT BRITAIN', foregrounding its central message of 'Active Citizenship', co-operation, and women's postwar participation (*MW* November 1943: 42).

Civilian consumption of clothing was rationed from 1941 to 1949. Introduced to establish 'fair shares' across all classes, points were allocated to garments according to yardage, and the Board of Trade adjusted the number of coupons allocated according to fluctuating materials and labour (Howell 2012: 95–6). The Utility Clothing Scheme was introduced to control prices and ensure availability of good quality new clothing. In May 1942 the 'Couturier Scheme' was launched, whereby leading British designers created models for manufacturers to reproduce. A 'Dress Revolution' with 'Mayfair designs for the masses!' *Modern Woman* (May 1942: 52–3) enthusiastically proclaimed. Coats were a significant purchase out of the annual coupon allocation and advertisements for utility brands such as Harella and Heatons – the latter promoted through their 'Good Citizen Series' – appeared regularly in the magazine (*MW* January 1943: 54, March 1943: 20). Fashion editors helped readers to manage their ration. Chaloner claimed 'mine was one of the many small voices that urged Sir Stafford [Cripps, Chancellor of the Exchequer] to reduce the coupon value of suits, coats and frocks' (May 1946: 21). Shoes, stockings and underwear were a constant cause for concern and Troy gave detailed updates on their quality and availability (*MW* September 1943: 50–1).

Corsets – 'voted the black sheep of the whole Utility scheme' – were particularly controversial, yet she put duty before beauty when she instructed women asking for improved fit and style that corset makers had to focus on 'supplying necessary support for the women who are working to win the war – and this means no frills and prettiness!' (*MW* May 1943: 51).

By the start of 1943, Troy's fashion page was almost entirely dedicated to helping readers preserve, renovate and repair clothing. The Board of Trade had launched its central propaganda effort directed at housewives to encourage 'clothing salvage' and help meet shortages: the Make Do and Mend campaign in 1942. Women's magazines were a lynchpin in the scheme. Paper patterns were an established part of the merchandising offer of 'service magazines' and women could save coupons by making rather than buying readymade (Hackney 1999: 76–9). Publishers, in addition, owned their own pattern houses and the *Modern Woman* 'Pattern Service' meant that Troy could swiftly respond to the changing wartime conditions of scarcity and coupon reduction. Her editorials reveal a range of strategies. In January 1943, assuring readers that 'Two or three colours in a frock, suit or coat is the new fashion', she provided patterns for 'clever jester clothes' made from 'coupon cheap remnants', an example of the 'mildly eccentric edge' that wartime outfits began to adopt (*MW* January 1943: 52–3; Howell 2012: 145). The ingenious 'Master Pattern' (1s 6d) appeared the following month – a 'versatile design' that could not only be adapted to make multiple dresses, but was also a customisable template designed to help readers 'cut fresh garments from old clothes' (*MW* February 1943: 48–9). In April 1943, 'Shirt Tails' gave hand-cut patterns for multiple items that could be made from a man's shirt 'past mending', including slips, cami-knickers, boy's pants and vest sets with a yoke to eliminate elastic, and a 'Coif Snood' designed for the magazine by a 'Famous London milliner' (April 1943: 54–5, 93).

'Mending – make it an art!', an article written by F. Conyers, coincided with the launch of the Board of Trade's *Make Do and Mend* booklet, the centrepiece of the Campaign (Ministry of Information 1943/2007). Handicraft teachers were in short supply and magazines helped address the skills gap in their advertising pages and editorial. *Modern Woman* carried monthly Board of Trade advertisements urging readers to be always ready to administer '"first aid" treatment' with a needle and cotton and prompting them to join 'Sewing and household jobbery' classes and 'mending parties' (*MW* January 1943: 6; March 1943: 4). Cuts in ration levels and the inclusion of household linen in the scheme in Autumn 1942 resulted in widespread complaints about towel rationing, which was considered 'a really heavy blow' (Zweiniger-Bargielowska 2000: 89–90). The Board of Trade advertisements tried to plug the gap by showing housewives how to cut, turn and resew sheets to extend their life and make towels from bedspreads (*MW* April 1943: 2; July 1943: 6). Commercial advertisements employed similar appeals. Lintas – the publicity arm of Lever Brothers – which, along with the major women's organisations had advised the government on the 'Make Do and Mend' campaign, devised the 'Wartime Clothes Service' sponsored by the 'Lux Washability and Renovation Bureau' to sell Lux soap powder through a seemingly endless roster of transformational tips: 'A Practical Playsuit from Parental Pyjamas!' (*MW* January 1943: 2), 'Off-Duty Dressing-Gown from discarded frock' (*MW* March 1943: 2), 'FROM cast-off pyjamas TO couponless blouse' (*MW* July 1943: 2).

Even at the height of war, many women wanted to feel feminine (Kirkham 1999: 143) and with their lively colour illustrations Troy's fashion editorials combined feminine pleasure with wardrobe patriotism. Editors fostered 'new fashion narratives' and a 'whole new approach to the buying and wearing of clothes' (Howell 2012: 98, 117). While utility styles favoured a streamlining of design, Troy's editorial strove to conjure up a sense of joyful fashionability for 'war-strained wardrobes' while keeping shabbiness at bay (*MW* May 1943: 48, September 1943: 53–4). Articles such as 'Just what I was wanting', for instance, responded to conditions of scarcity and women's desire for a contemporary, fashionable yet feminine silhouette. Published in August 1943 when, as Troy put it, 'Clothes coupons are at their lowest ebb – if not non-existent! Shop windows simply a tantalizing range of forbidden fruit', the striking image of a dark-haired woman dressed in a red and yellow pyjama suit brings a sense of Hollywood glamour to remnant-made items as 'ingenuity was given its own drama' (see Plate 15) (*MW* August: 48–9, Howell 2012: 147). The take-up of trousers was more prevalent among younger, London-based and, above all, 'better-off' women (Howell 2012: 119–20). Suggesting the wider age-range and distribution of *Modern Woman* readers, trousers rarely appear apart from an occasional article on etiquette, which advised consistency in the form of a 'masculine topcoat' and shoes to go with 'he-man' corduroy 'slacks' (*MW* June 1943: 42).

Opinions differ as to the success of 'Make Do and Mend'. Historian Ina Zweiniger-Bargielowska (2012: 120–1), considering much of the advice 'bizarre and impracticable', argues that the response was 'predominantly negative'. She draws on interviews with working-class women from a 1942 government report which attributed this to lack of time, the fact that 'mending and making do is nothing new', and difficulties accessing women's magazines. Women also complained that patterns were not provided for remaking clothes, something that may have contributed to Troy's pattern strategy. Compiled five months after the Make Do and Mend campaign launch and before publication of their booklet, the report could not represent the full range of women's interests. The numbers attending the 12,000 Make Do and Mend and dressmaking classes that the Board of Trade was running in their evening and technical schools by 1943 – women's voluntary groups offered a similar quantity – suggest greater enthusiasm, even if for many this was mainly a means to access society 'beyond the house' (Reynolds 1999: 331). Author and journalist Mollie Panter-Downes' (1941/1999: 77–94) gently humorous short story 'Literary Scandal at the Sewing Party' shows how, united in a shared purpose, women met across the social classes. Burton's ideal of active citizenship was fuelled as much in craft groups as it was in political groups, as knitting and sewing skills took on new status. Mass observation diarist Nella Last, for example, was celebrated as 'the Salvage Queen' (Broad and Fleming 1981/2006: 80). The new fashion skills and narratives combined an 'evolving sense of aesthetic freedom' for women with a culture of 'patriotic thrift' that caught the public's imagination, and women's magazines played an important part in this (Howell 2012: 147, 98). The high public profile of Make Do and Mend helped consolidate a view of women 'as capable, imaginative and lateral thinking' (Howell 2012: 185). Together with the calls from MPs such as Burton, and women's organisations for women's participation as active citizens, this signalled a new consciousness of female agency that was manifest equally as powerfully in fashion editorials as it was in the discursive articles in magazines.

Reconstruction by Design: 'a Pocketbookful of Stimulating ideas'

'Is-you-is-or-is-you-ain't my peace-time baby?' – Sybil Chaloner's editorial welcomed peace with a jaunty Americanism and a drawing of a fairground carousel bedecked with streamers – a 'burst of hope' by Jennetta Vise who, Chaloner joyfully observed, 'put so much zing into the flags they almost ripped off the flagpoles' (*MW* June 1945: 21). The years of postwar reconstruction, however, would prove challenging. A policy of austerity was imposed to overcome the serious deficit in the balance of payments and rationing continued for another eight years, becoming even more stringent. Magazine editors continued to be in close contact with government, helping to keep spirits up as shortages continued, and prices and queues increased (*MW* February 1947: 37–8). 'Whatever we may feel about this Spring, sisters, it is surely a far better one than the Seven Sad Springs that went before', Chaloner intoned, urging readers to look to the future and start planning (April 1946: 21). 'Reconstruction' and 'Planning', which had been 'ideological imperatives of the wartime total society', from 5 July 1946 became central to the new Labour government's vision of a postwar society (Mellor 1974: 37). Chaloner, nevertheless, could also be ambivalent, suggesting some impatience with the ongoing job of assisting government:

> the word *planning* is one to make any editor to-day feel weak at the knees. The more so if she has just returned from a two-hour session with one of our Ministries where she has had to swallow a large quantity of statistics and sympathise with the Minister's latest headache: shortage of men, women and babies, skirts, shoes, homes, midwives and shorthand typists. (*MW* May 1946: 21)

Questions about how women could best contribute to the reconstruction of society and, in turn, how society might serve them underpinned debates in *Modern Woman*'s feature articles, but in ways that Burton's wartime articles did not entirely anticipate.

Fashion continued to be popular, particularly with the introduction of colour printing, which was ideally suited to showcasing the flamboyantly feminine New Look (1947), for instance, but it was the expansion of interest in all things home-based – housing, house-keeping, architecture, interior design, home-making, home-crafts and decoration – that took precedence, followed by articles about women's employment. The magazine's June 1945 issue, for example, included a feature on the Victory Bride furnishing her home, *and* one on the women's employment in aviation (*MW* June 1945: 54–5, 44–5). The magazine's newly appointed careers adviser, G. A. Rees, penned a column helping readers translate wartime skills and experience into 'careers', or at least some form of remunerative employment. Chaloner, like many in government and industry, put her faith in design: 'War has stimulated all "designing" minds. We have seen the last of old-dull-stodge and frightful trimmings in clothes and furniture.' (*MW* June 1946: 21). Renewed postwar interest in culture was reflected in features on modern art, craft and theatre (*MW* January 1946: 40–4; October 1946: 28–31; March 1949: 68–71). Design came to symbolise the brave new world of reconstruction and 'Britain Can Make It', an exhibition showcasing the latest industrial design, which opened in London in September 1946 to great public acclaim (Bilbey 2019). 'Design for Living', two articles by the designer and writer Marian Speyer, employed a distinctly modernist design aesthetic (see Figure 22.1) to

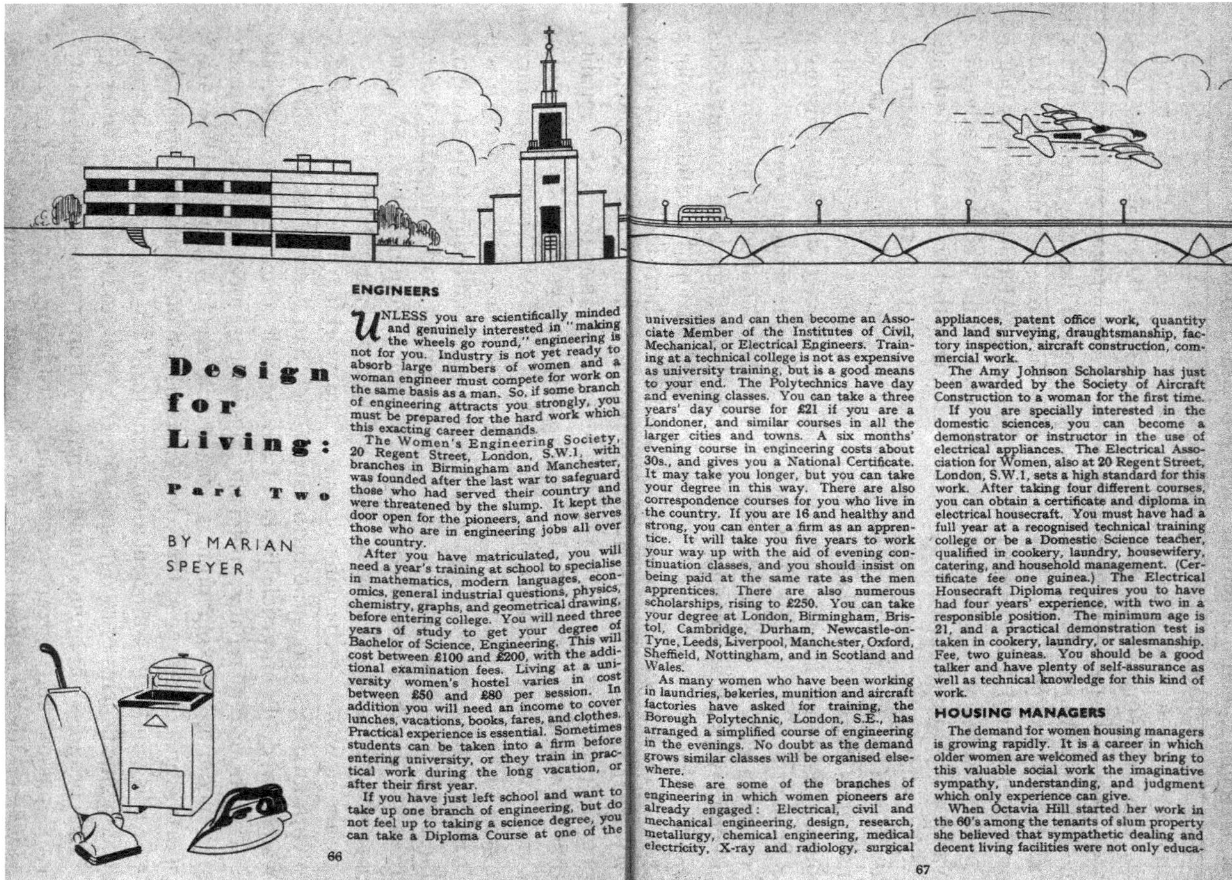

Design for Living: Part Two

BY MARIAN SPEYER

ENGINEERS

UNLESS you are scientifically minded and genuinely interested in "making the wheels go round," engineering is not for you. Industry is not yet ready to absorb large numbers of women and a woman engineer must compete for work on the same basis as a man. So, if some branch of engineering attracts you strongly, you must be prepared for the hard work which this exacting career demands.

The Women's Engineering Society, 20 Regent Street, London, S.W.1, with branches in Birmingham and Manchester, was founded after the last war to safeguard those who had served their country and were threatened by the slump. It kept the door open for the pioneers, and now serves those who are in engineering jobs all over the country.

After you have matriculated, you will need a year's training at school to specialise in mathematics, modern languages, economics, general industrial questions, physics, chemistry, graphs, and geometrical drawing, before entering college. You will need three years of study to get your degree of Bachelor of Science, Engineering. This will cost between £100 and £200, with the additional examination fees. Living at a university women's hostel varies in cost between £50 and £80 per session. In addition you will need an income to cover lunches, vacations, books, fares, and clothes. Practical experience is essential. Sometimes students can be taken into a firm before entering university, or they train in practical work during the long vacation, or after their first year.

If you have just left school and want to take up one branch of engineering, but do not feel up to taking a science degree, you can take a Diploma Course at one of the

66

universities and can then become an Associate Member of the Institutes of Civil, Mechanical, or Electrical Engineers. Training at a technical college is not as expensive as university training, but is a good means to your end. The Polytechnics have day and evening classes. You can take a three years' day course for £21 if you are a Londoner, and similar courses in all the larger cities and towns. A six months' evening course in engineering costs about 30s., and gives you a National Certificate. It may take you longer, but you can take your degree in this way. There are also correspondence courses for you who live in the country. If you are 16 and healthy and strong, you can enter a firm as an apprentice. It will take you five years to work your way up with the aid of evening continuation classes, and you should insist on being paid at the same rate as the men apprentices. There are also numerous scholarships, rising to £250. You can take your degree at London, Birmingham, Bristol, Cambridge, Durham, Newcastle-on-Tyne, Leeds, Liverpool, Manchester, Oxford, Sheffield, Nottingham, and in Scotland and Wales.

As many women who have been working in laundries, bakeries, munition and aircraft factories have asked for training, the Borough Polytechnic, London, S.E., has arranged a simplified course of engineering in the evenings. No doubt as the demand grows similar classes will be organised elsewhere.

These are some of the branches of engineering in which women pioneers are already engaged: Electrical, civil and mechanical engineering, design, research, metallurgy, chemical engineering, medical electricity, X-ray and radiology, surgical appliances, patent office work, quantity and land surveying, draughtsmanship, factory inspection, aircraft construction, commercial work.

The Amy Johnson Scholarship has just been awarded by the Society of Aircraft Construction to a woman for the first time.

If you are specially interested in the domestic sciences, you can become a demonstrator or instructor in the use of electrical appliances. The Electrical Association for Women, also at 20 Regent Street, London, S.W.1, sets a high standard for this work. After taking four different courses, you can obtain a certificate and diploma in electrical housecraft. You must have had a full year at a recognised technical training college or be a Domestic Science teacher, qualified in cookery, laundry, housewifery, catering, and household management. (Certificate fee one guinea.) The Electrical Housecraft Diploma requires you to have had four years' experience, with two in a responsible position. The minimum age is 21, and a practical demonstration test is taken in cookery, laundry, or salesmanship. Fee, two guineas. You should be a good talker and have plenty of self-assurance as well as technical knowledge for this kind of work.

HOUSING MANAGERS

The demand for women housing managers is growing rapidly. It is a career in which older women are welcomed as they bring to this valuable social work the imaginative sympathy, understanding, and judgment which only experience can give.

When Octavia Hill started her work in the 60's among the tenants of slum property she believed that sympathetic dealing and decent living facilities were not only educa-

67

Figure 22.1 'Design for Living', Marian Speyer. *Modern Woman*, December 1945. 66–7. © The British Library Board (*Modern Woman*/LOU.LON 486).

examine the potential of architecture, decoration, engineering and housing management – an area that Burton had anticipated – as careers for women (*MW* November 1945: 55–6; December 66–8). Arguing that 'Manufacturers are realising just how important good design is in raising exports' (*MW* November 1945: 55), Speyer gave full details of training, identifying those areas most open to women: interior design and decoration rather than engineering, for instance.

Chaloner, meanwhile, was deliberating the 'trials of the ex-service girl' facing a 'brave new Labour-saving world' (*MW* October 1945: 21). The majority perceived employment, especially in low-paid manual jobs, as a temporary wartime necessity. Domesticity was the predominant female aspiration in the early postwar years, which witnessed a decline in female employment, an increase in marriage, and a baby boom (Summerfield 2013/1984: 187–90). As one WAAF told a woman's magazine, she aspired to being 'a good cook and housewife, one who makes a house a *home*' (Waller and Vaughan-Rees 1987: 124). Hers, nevertheless, was a new model of housewifery that unlike her prewar predecessor took companionate marriage, labour-saving devices, and a part-time clerical job to fit around childcare and domestic responsibilities, for granted (Hackney 2018). Overall, these views were prevalent among younger, as yet unmarried, women. Many older married women, as historian Caitriona Beaumont (2013: 176) notes, hoped to continue working once the war ended, their experience of war work having 'given them confidence in their abilities as paid employees'. Rees's employment columns catered for both constituencies with suggestions for those caring for 'elderly relatives' 'invalid husbands or young children' who wished to work from home and others over thirty looking to start new careers (*MW* February 1947: 60–1; January 1946: 79). Scholars now acknowledge that 'employment did not necessarily result in female liberation or greater equality, and full-time housewifery was a locus of female power both within the family and in wider society' (Zweininger-Bargielowska 2000: 106; Giles 2004). Yet, as Zweininger-Bargielowska (2000: 105) points out, postwar official policy towards women was contradictory, 'combining pro-natalism and the desire to rebuild the family along traditional lines with female recruitment drives'. In a postwar world, magazine editors were increasingly caught between communicating the government line, no matter how inconsistent, and responding to readers' problems and aspirations.

Debates about women's changing domestic and working lives were inevitably bound up with anxieties about the birth rate, which had been in decline since the 1930s. 'Watch Sweden!', an article by Len Chaloner advocates the Swedish model of state intervention (rent rebates, maternity allowances, job security and nursery provision) to encourage working mothers to have children (*MW* January 1946: 46–7, 66–7). Reporting on a talk given at the Royal Commission on Population by Fru Alva Myrdal, a Swedish authority on population problems, Chaloner points to the wider social and economic benefits of recognising women's 'right to work *and* be wives and mothers'. 'Real progress' she argues could come only from realising the mutual interests of 'home-makers' and 'career women' and introducing legislation that valued 'women *as* women for the contribution they make to the community'. This vision, nevertheless, could not be realised without domestic support and Chaloner cites a Swedish campaign to establish 'Home Helps' and the Home Research Institute in Stockholm which, funded by government and run by housewives, explored the home as 'a centre of economic consumption and as a place of work'. The view that women had the right to marriage, motherhood and career seems radical for its time and to a large extent it was. Yet, as Beaumont (2013: 178) points out, in the 1940s, highly respected women's organisations such as the National Council of Women and the Mother's Union were 'foreseeing a future where mothers would take up employment and successfully combine paid work and motherhood'. Photographs of high-rise 'Dream towers' and 'idyllic' factory, tenement housing set in 'fresh-air' surroundings visualised the benefits of a system where, in Chaloner's words, 'the family makes the state' an argument developed by Jean Bird in an article in the same issue that reported on slum-clearance plans and the massive task of house building needed to give every family in Britain a 'dwelling of its own' (*MW* January 1946: 64–5).

The Utility Furniture Scheme which launched in 1943 offered new furnishings by permit only for those in need, chiefly newly-weds and bombees. Noel Ward, the furnishing and decoration editor, ran an early article on 'Utility Furniture for Wartime Brides' but restrictions meant that wartime articles were chiefly concerned with tips for economy, saving and making do with less (*MW* December 1942: 60–1). By 1946 the magazine's home section increased in size despite the desperate lack of available goods and furnishings. *Modern Woman* had a stand at the Ideal Homes Exhibition (1947) designed by Royal Designer for Industry James Gardner; Gardner along with Enid Marx, Gordon Russell and other proponents of 'good design' often featured in the magazine (*MW* March 1948: 117; February 1949: 72–5). Articles were full of longing for that 'new home' and plans for how to manage and furnish it. Ward made much of colour, providing newly married ex-WAAFs with ideas for light schemes 'after years of austerity' (*MW* May 1946: 64). Colour was important, symbolically and psychologically, for homes suffering 'colour starvation' *and* as a 'sign of freedom and fulfilment' for a nation escaping 'drabness' and 'mental or physical poverty'. We are returning 'pigment by pigment, shade by shade, to our lives', colour adviser Doris Langley Moore declared (*MW* December 1946: 28–9, 31). Plastics, as non-couponed materials, were attainable (*MW* June 1946: 60–1), while the Swedish home provided a future vision of 'comfort, colour, space-saving and cheerfulness' that could 'be applied to *our* homes – in time'. Ward showed photographs of modern Scandinavian interiors with fabrics based on homecraft methods and architect-designed 'blond' wood furniture which was 'mass-produced for flat package deliveries' and home assembly; a futuristic idea indeed (*MW* February 1947: 56–7).

Wartime publicity techniques that had been used to communicate information about saving and economy were now employed to foster consumer aspirations and educate readers about peacetime spending. A colourful two-page cut-out boardgame designed by Jennetta Vise – something between snakes and ladders and Monopoly – had players move from a dark tenement to their 'dream home', collecting information about a bewildering array of 'labour-saving' equipment along the way (*MW* April 1946: 68–9, 70). Dream 'labour savers' included an automatic washing machine, gas refrigerator, central heating, air-conditioning, even an automatic dust-collector installed all over the house, something that had featured prewar at the Ideal Homes Exhibition, an event that reopened the following year with a *Modern Woman* stand designed by James Gardner. This dream of future living, however, had its downside for the housewife whose responsibility it was to create a 'home' to the highest standards and, for the most part, manage it alone. A series of articles 'for inexperienced home-makers – married or single' by Hilda M. Whitlow, *Modern Woman*'s housecraft editor, set out the terms. Women were encouraged to build on their wartime experience but warned that, above all, the housework – which was extensive – must be done 'unobtrusively' by a homemaker who was not only 'well groomed' but also found time to keep up her interests in the 'outside world', ensuring that she would never become boring. Men did have a part to play, but one that seemed to add insult to injury; 'It is wise to let the men take a share in housework', Whitlow intoned, 'but as a pleasure, not a duty' (*MW* January 1946: 62–3). Advertisers, meanwhile, opportunistically used women's wartime expertise to transition them back into the home. An advertisement for mains-gas cookers pictures a woman welder next to copy declaring, 'She's been using the finest equipment in war – she'll want the best equipment in peace.' (*MW* February 1946: 2).

Features, however, countered this consumer-orientated domestic rhetoric with information about women's engagement in public life. The 1945 election returned twenty-four women MPs and *Modern Woman* celebrated with a double page photo-feature introducing them to readers (*MW* October 1945: 46–7). In early 1946 Elaine Burton returned to the magazine with a three-part series about women and politics. She contributed the first article about the situation in Britain, Labour MP Barbara Ayrton-Gould examined women in politics in France, and Christin Sandler in America (*MW* February 1946: 50–1; March 1946: 46–7; April 1946: 50–1, 52). 'Our 24: biographical jottings on the two dozen women in Westminster' hailed a new age of women's interest and involvement in politics. Claiming to base this on the large number of women she saw attending political meetings not only to ask about housing, social services and education, but also 'to see that something was done', the article was a postwar post-script to her 1943 series. Burton endorsed the 'different viewpoints' that women bring, reminding readers that much was still to be achieved, foremost the fight for equal pay. The article outlined women MPs' expertise in education, training, juvenile delinquency, international affairs and housing, so that readers could better envisage their future contribution to postwar society. Ending on a rousing 'this is a group of 24 who might be you or me . . . they are typical of us modern women and we wish them success in their big job', Burton's hopes were not entirely fulfilled.

Historian Helen Jones (2000: 217–20), while confirming that women 'joined political parties with alacrity and groups such as the WI [Women's Institute] and the TG [Townswomen's Guild] in their droves', has argued that it was in the 'symbolic meanings of active citizenship' rather than in policy making that they 'left their mark on the period'. Barbara Vise, in an article that expands Burton's ideas about constructive talk, develops similar ideas about the symbolic power of active citizenship when, declaring the postwar years 'the talking age', she examines the wider significance of discussion forums from 'brains trusts'–'a speaking part of our national life' – to the United Nations (1945). Ending with a story that could serve as a metaphor for the magazine itself, Vise describes a London Community Centre group as 'a "window onto the world"' that helps members 'share thought in talk' (*MW* November 1946: 22–3, 87; Hackney 2012). Utility furniture was popular in the period for its design, quality and fitness for purpose (Zweiniger-Bargielowska 2000: 95). Concomitant with interest in women's increased participation in public life, representations of the home as a modern, functional, easy-to-care-for space in *Modern Woman* suggested somewhere where the symbolic meanings of active citizenship, while not so evident in policy changes, were materialised in everyday life.

Conclusion: the Magazine that Keeps Your Spirits Up and Your Weight Down

The paper shortage was easing by 1947 and restrictions finally ended on 1 March 1950 when *Modern Woman* returned to its prewar size and format but without one key element: its long-time editor. Hidden away, among items on diets and corsets in at the back of the magazine's 'Notes and Letters' page the previous year, is Chaloner's magnanimous farewell to readers: 'Yes, sisters, I have resigned; and it hurts me much more than it will hurt you.'

> Well, let's get this business over! . . . I can honestly say that if the people of this island are as friendly, amusing, reasonable, generous with kind words as the many thousands who have written to us all in MODERN WOMAN'S offices through the years, then Great Britain, in spite of its dollar gaps and bomb gaps, is still a country fit to lead the world! Good-bye. SYBIL CHALONER. (*MW* May 1949: 118, 120)

C-M's cover depicting a woman's steady gaze as she seriously contemplates herself in a compact mirror, conveys a mood of editorial subjectivity, while the dark-toned still life – green purse, pink rose and acid yellow gloves – of her surrealistic final cover the following month – she left along with Chaloner – serves as a memorial device. 'Change,' Chaloner declared, 'is the essence of good magazine-making: something to highlight a new idea or give a fresh aspect to an old one, should be in every issue'. Her departure not only signalled significant change in *Modern Woman*'s ethos, content and appearance, but also coincided with wider changes in the women's press. Colour photography, which would increasingly 'rule the roost' in magazine publishing, replaced C-M's covers. The new editor Kay Smallshaw (2005/1949) came from *Good Housekeeping* – the most comprehensive purveyor of reliable housekeeping advice – and articles addressing the challenges of running a home alone replaced those challenging women to participate in politics. This was in tune with the nation's postwar fascination with the home, spurred on by the Festival of Britain where *Modern Woman* had a stand (*MW* February 1951: 18–19). Iris Ashely and *Woman's Hour* broadcaster Olive Shapley were part of new group of media-friendly journalists who wrote for the magazine as it reached out to wider readerships.

David Reed (1997: 203–6), in his history of popular illustrated magazines, takes issue with Drawbell's argument about the selling power of 'quality' features, pointing out that *Woman's Own* and *Woman* more than doubled their circulations during the last years of the 1940s, irrespective of their approach. Pointing out that whereas Drawbell enthusiastically employed American writers and illustrators that he met through the Goulds – editors of the phenomenally successful *Ladies' Home Journal* – he did not adopt the Goulds' tradition of 'civic responsibility'. 'Choices were made for which the staff were responsible', Reed darkly observes, resulting in the 'cult of femininity' that dominated British women's magazines for much of the twentieth century (Ferguson 1983). Arguably, however, editors were responding to readers' changing interests and needs. The surge in readership for mass-weeklies between 1947 and 1950 correlates with the growth in surplus disposable income for the mass of lower paid workers while the 'administrative class', who made up the majority monthlies' readership, did less well (Reed 1997: 209–10). Specificities of social class, culture and location also made it difficult for a middle-class, London-based, feminist such as Chaloner to understand wider popular taste. Nowhere was this more evident than in fashion. Dislike of clothes rationing and the exigencies of Make Do and Mend underpinned the widespread embrace of ready-made versions of Dior's New Look, particularly by working-class women (Partington 1995). Chaloner, in contrast, saw 'self-expression' as the antithesis of mass-production, declaring, 'British women have never tolerated mass-produced fashion and I hope they never will' (*MW* October 1946: 21). Her view that '[d]ress coupons have made us look twice and think three times before buying anything to wear . . . this is far better for general good looks than having too many and unsuitable clothes, as many of us did before 1941' speaks more to current concerns about fashion and ecology than to women facing their fifth year of rationing (*MW* July 1946: 21).[1] The discourse of 'active citizenship' so prevalent in the 1940s was absorbed by the burgeoning culture of consumption in the 1950s and *Modern Woman*, *Housewife* and *Everywoman*, all of which embraced challenging and controversial features in the 1940s, closed in the mid-1960s under pressure from TV and newspaper colour supplements (Cox and Mowatt 2016).

Note

1. As part of a research project examining how community groups using Make Do and Mend, upcycling and repurposing might instil more environmentally friendly clothing behaviour, Claire Dolman developed her own rationing system based on the Board of Trade coupon points system for 1942 to limit her consumption. See S4S: Designing a Sensibility for Sustainable Clothing <https://s4sproject-exeter.uk> and S4S Project <youtube.com>.

Works Cited

Andrews, M. 2012. *Domesticating the Airwaves; Broadcasting, Domesticity and Femininity*. London: Continuum.

Beaumont, C. 2013. *Housewives and Citizens: Domesticity and The Women's Movement in England, 1928–1964*. Manchester: Manchester University Press.

Bilbey, D., ed. 2019. *Britain Can Make It: The 1946 Exhibition of Modern Design*. London: V&A Publishing.

Burton, P. 2019. 'Jennetta Vise'. 7 March 2009. <https://bearalley.blogspot.com/2007/06/jenetta-vise.html> (last accessed 1 December 2019).

Broad, R. and S. Fleming, eds. 1981/2006. *Nella Last's War*. London: Profile Books.

Cox, H. and S. Mowatt, eds. 2014. *Revolutions from Grubb Street: A History of Magazine Publishing in Britain*. Oxford: Oxford University Press.

Deakin, P. 1984. *Press On*. London: Henry E. Walter Ltd.

Drawbell, J. 1968. *Time on My Hands*. London: Macdonald.

Ferguson, M. 1983. *Forever Feminine: Women's Magazines and the Cult of Femininity*. London: Heinemann.

Forster, L. 2015. *Magazine Movements: Women's Culture, Feminism and Media Form*. London: Bloomsbury.

Garfield, S. 2004. *Our Hidden Lives: The Remarkable Diaries of Post-war Britain*. London: Ebury Press.

Giles, J. 2004. *The Parlour and the Suburb: Domestic Identities, Class, Femininity and Modernity*. London: Bloomsbury.

Grieve, M. 1964. *Millions Made My Story*. London: Gollancz.
Hackney, F. 1999. 'Making Modern Woman, Stitch by Stitch: Dressmaking and Women's Magazines in Britain 1919–39'. *The Culture of Sewing: Gender, Consumption and Home Dressmaking*. Ed. B. Burman. Oxford: Berg. 73–96.
Hackney, F. 2008.'"Women are News": British Women's Magazines 1919–1939'. *Transatlantic Print Culture, 1880–1940: Emerging Media, Emerging Modernisms*. Eds A. Ardis and P. Collier. London: Palgrave. 114–33.
Hackney, F. 2012. *"They Opened Up a Whole New World": Feminine Modernity and the Feminine Imagination in Women's Magazines, 1919–1939*. Dissertation, University of London.
—. 2016. 'Getting a Living, Getting a Life: Leonora Eyles, Employment and Agony, 1925–1930'. *Women in Magazines: Research, Representation, Production and Consumption*. Eds. R. Ritchie, S. Hawkins, N. Phillips and S. J. Kleinberg. London: Routledge. 107–24.
Hackney, F. 2018. 'Woman Appeal. A New Rhetoric of Consumption: Women's Domestic Magazines in the 1920s and 1930s'. *Women's Periodicals and Print Culture in Britain, 1918–1939: The Interwar Period*. Ed. C. Clay, M. DiCenzo, B. Green and F. Hackney. Edinburgh: Edinburgh University Press. 294–315.
Howell, G. 2013. *Wartime Fashion: From Haute Couture to Homemade, 1939–1945*. London: Bloomsbury Academic.
Jones, H. 2000. *Women in British Public Life, 1914–50: Gender, Power and Social Policy*. Essex: Pearson Education.
Kirkham, P. 1999. 'Fashion, Femininity and 'Frivolous' Consumption in World-War-Two Britain'. *Utility Reassessed: The Role of Ethics in the Practice of Design*. Ed. J. Attfield. Manchester: Manchester University Press. 143–56.
Kynaston, D. 2007. *Austerity Britain 1945–48: A World to Build*. London: Bloomsbury.
Mellor, D. 1974. 'The Image of "Utility"'. *CC41: Utility Furniture and Fashion 1941–1951*. Exhibition Catalogue. Geffrye Museum. London: Inner London Education Authority.
Ministry of Information. 1943/2007. *Make Do And Mend*. London: Imperial War Museum.
Oram, A. 1996. '"Bombs Don't Discriminate!" Women's Political Activism in the Second World War'. *Nationalising Femininity: Culture, Sexuality and British Cinema in the Second World War*. Eds C. Gledhill and G. Swanson. Manchester: Manchester University Press. 53–69.
Panter-Downes, M. 1941/1999. *Good Evening, Mrs. Craven: The Wartime Stories of Mollie Panter-Downes*. London: Persephone Books.
Partington, A. 1995. 'The Days of the New Look: Working-Class Affluence and the Consumer Culture'. *Labour's Promised Land? Culture and Society in Labour Britain 1945–51*. Ed. J. Fyrth. London: Lawrence & Wishart. 247–63.
Reed, D. 1997. *The Popular Magazine in Britain and the United States 1880–1960*. London: The British Library.
Reynolds, H. 1999. '"Your Clothes Are Materials of War": The British Government Promotion of Home Sewing During the Second World War'. *The Culture of Sewing: Gender, Consumption and Home Dressmaking*. Ed. B. Burman. Oxford: Berg. 327–39.
Smallshaw, K. 2005/1949. *How to Run Your Home Without Help*. London: Persephone Books.
Summerfield, P. 2013/1984. *Women Workers in the Second World War. Production and Patriarchy in Conflict*. London: Routledge.
Sutherland, D. 2004. 'Burton, (Frances) Elaine, Baroness Burton of Coventry'. *Oxford Dictionary of National Biography* vol. 9. Eds H. C. G. Matthew and B. Harrison. Oxford: Oxford University Press. 16–17.
Waller J. and M. Vaughan-Rees. 1987. *Women in Wartime: The Role of Women's Magazines 1939–1945*. London: MacDonald and Co.

White, C. 1970. *Women's Magazines 1693–1968*. London: Michael Joseph.
Winship, J. 1996. 'Women's Magazines: Times of War and Management of the Self in *Woman's Own*'. *Nationalising Femininity: Culture, Sexuality and British Cinema in the Second World War*. Eds C. Gledhill and G. Swanson. Manchester: Manchester University Press. 127–39.
Zweiniger-Bargielowska, I. 2000. *Austerity in Britain: Rationing, Controls and Consumption 1939–1955*. Oxford: Oxford University Press.

Appendix

This appendix provides further details about the publications discussed in this collection. Compiling the appendix was very much a collective effort between editors and contributors and we are grateful for everyone's efforts in putting it together. The entries offer both a brief introduction to publications and provide a useful starting point for future research.

The entries also provide guidance on where to find print and/or online editions of the periodicals included. However, holdings in various archives are often incomplete. This is particularly the case with independently produced activist magazines where production was frequently short-lived and/or irregular. We have emphasised holdings in the UK and, where possible, tried to highlight holdings in a range of locations rather than to simply concentrate on those that are London-based.

It has proved challenging to give complete details for all entries. In particular, information about circulation has often been difficult to establish, especially for older and independently produced magazines. Where possible, we have included the names of editorial staff. However, in the case of many feminist periodicals, producing magazines was seen as a collective rather than a hierarchical endeavour and, therefore, individual names are deliberately obscure.

Locations

BL British Library, London
FAN Feminist Archive North, Special Collections, Brotherton Library, University of Leeds
FAS Feminist Archive South, University of Bristol Archives
GWL Glasgow Women's Library
HCA Hall-Carpenter Archive, London School of Economics
HSC Herstory Collection, 1956–74. Microfilm. Women's History Library, Berkeley/Bell & Howell Company, Ohio. A collection of newspapers, periodicals, magazines and newsletters relating to women (with many from the women's movement). Primarily US, but containing some UK feminist magazines.
NLS National Library of Scotland
NLW National Library of Wales (*Llyfrgell Genedlaethol Cymru*)
WL The Women's Library Archives, London School of Economics

Arena Three

The first lesbian magazine in Britain, published by the 'Minorities Research Group'.

Dates: 1964–71
Periodicity: monthly
Place of publication: London
Publisher: Minorities Research Group
Editors: Esmé Langley (managing editor) supported by a changing editorial team
Circulation: estimated 450–1,200 across lifespan
Location: BL; FAS; GWL; WL

Artemis

Subtitled 'The magazine for lesbians and all women who love women' and aiming to fill the gap left by the demise of *Sappho* magazine, *Artemis* was printed in black and white and stapled at A6 size. Later issues had a glossy cover, but the layout and design continued to be crowded and informal. Subscriptions were by an anonymous postbox service, and most issues were undated. It advertised the Artemis Club, a subscription letter-writing club that provided lists of members under *noms de plume* to other subscribers. Subscription to the club was around £6–10 including the magazine, which could also be bought independently. In addition, members could buy badges, hand-mirrors, pens and stickers to discreetly identify their membership to others. Advertisements were very occasional, and the magazine's revenue seems to have come mainly from the Artemis Club. It briefly changed its name to *Gay Girl and Artemis* in 1984 but reverted to *Artemis* after readers protested that *Gay Girl* was 'too brash, too modern, too loud'.

Dates: c. 1983–7
Periodicity: bimonthly in year one, then irregular
Price: approx. £1
Place of publication: London
Location: BL; FAN; FAS; HCA

Asiana

Glossy lifestyle magazine aimed at women of South Asian heritage published by Sarwar Ahmed with the tag line 'for the Asian woman who wants more'. Following the closure of the print edition, the magazine maintained an online presence. The magazine *Asiana Wedding* remains in print.

Dates: 2003–11
Periodicity: quarterly
Price: £4.50
Place of publication: London
Circulation: 30,160 (2004)
Location: BL

Bad Attitude

Not to be confused with the controversial American *Bad Attitude: A Lesbian Sex Magazine*, this *Bad Attitude* positioned itself as a 'radical women's newspaper'. Its editorial tone was similar to many other feminist periodicals of the time, explicit and combative.

Dates: 1992–5
Periodicity: bimonthly (until September 1993); biannual (from September 1993)
Place of publication: London
Editors: *Bad Attitude* collective
Location: BL

Bliss
Teenage girls' magazine launched by EMAP and a competitor to *Sugar* and *Just Seventeen*. The magazine's focus included pop, celebrity, fashion and beauty and, like *Sugar*, it had an upfront approach to sex.

Dates: 1995–2014
Periodicity: monthly
Price: £2 (in 2002); £4.99 (in 2014)
Place of publication: London/Tunbridge Wells
Publisher: EMAP; from 2007, Panini UK
Editors: included Helen Johnston and Lisa Smosarski
Circulation: 213,466 (2006); 50,043 (2012)
Location: BL

Blue Jeans
Aimed at young teenage girls, the magazine focused on pop and romance, alongside fashion and beauty.

Dates: 1977–90
Periodicity: weekly
Price: 12p (1977)
Place of publication: Dundee
Publisher: D. C. Thomson
Location: BL; NLS

Burnt Roti
Inclusive South Asian lifestyle magazine in digital and print formats that deals with questions about racism, gender and sexuality and campaigns on mental health issues.

Dates: 2016–present
Periodicity: annual (print)
Price: £10
Place of publication: London
Publisher: Peartree Productions
Editors: Editor-in-chief Sharan Dhaliwal (2016–present)
Location: BL; online, available at <www.burntroti.com>

Candida
Publisher enthusiasm for a new 1970s market in sophisticated women's magazines saw the ill-starred launch of *Candida*, billed in a prospectus as 'Modern, Serious,

Sophisticated, Stimulating', with a far exaggerated 750,000 copies printed for the first issue. Editorial confusion and disorganisation meant that the magazine folded after just seven issues, as it failed to compete with the racier, glossier *Cosmopolitan* on the one hand, and the more established traditional women's magazines *Women's Realm* and *Women's Weekly* on the other.

Dates: 1972
Periodicity: weekly
Price: 94p (first issue)
Place of publication: London
Publisher: IPC
Editor: Launch editor Jean Twiddy
Circulation: 750,000
Location: BL

Cosmopolitan
UK edition of the US young women's magazine published by Hearst. *Cosmopolitan* is distributed in more than 100 countries, which includes 64 international editions and publication in 35 languages. The British version is available in both print and digital editions.

Dates: 1972–present (print); 2006–present (digital)
Periodicity: monthly
Price: £2 (December 2019)
Place of publication: London
Publisher: Hearst
Editors: 2019 team includes Claire Hodgson (editor-in-chief), Jess Edwards (digital editor) and Amy Grier (deputy editor)
Circulation: 206,510 (2019 print circulation); 3.3 million unique visitors online
Location: BL; online, available at <www.cosmopolitan.com/uk>

The Debrief
UK-based digital-only lifestyle publication for young women by Bauer Media. After its closure, part of the team was incorporated into sister publication *Grazia*.

Dates: 2014–18
Place of publication: London
Publisher: Bauer Media
Editor: Rebecca Holman
Circulation: 852,522 unique visitors
Location: no longer available

DIVA
Magazine for LGBTQ+ women sold across the UK and Europe. Founded by Millivres Fowlers but owned by Twin Media Group since 2016, it celebrated its 250th issue in 2017.

Dates: 1994–present
Periodicity: monthly

Price: £3.50
Place of publication: London
Publisher: Twin Media Group
Editors: Frances Williams (1994–7), Gillian Rodgerson (1997–2004), Jane Czyzselska (2004–17) and Carrie Lyell (2017–present)
Circulation: 56,000
Location: BL; GWL; WL

Elle
British edition of the women's fashion magazine owned by the French Lagardère Group, whose Hachette Filipacchi magazine division was acquired by Hearst Corporation in 2011. There are 48 print editions and 44 websites worldwide.

Dates: 1985–present (print); 2007–present (digital)
Periodicity: monthly
Price: £4.50 (November 2019)
Place of publication: London
Publisher: Hearst
Editors: 2019 team includes Farrah Storr (editor-in-chief), Natasha Bird (executive director, digital) and Kenya Hunt (deputy editor)
Circulation: 152,756 (2019 print circulation); 739,000 unique visitors online
Location: BL; online, available at <www.elle.com/uk>

Feminist Times
This emerged with the hopes of being a re-boot of *Spare Rib*. After a dispute with *Spare Rib*'s founding editors Marsha Rowe and Rosie Boycott – who threatened a legal challenge – the name *Feminist Times* was selected after a public vote. It published more than 500 articles online.

Dates: October 2013–July 2014
Place of publication: London
Editor: Charlotte Raven
Location: The web link is no longer available. However, some links to articles hosted on issue.com/feministtimes can be found via Twitter (@Feminist_Times).

FOWAAD
Subtitled the 'Newsletter of the Organisation of Women of Asian and African Descent (OWAAD)', *FOWAAD* was a campaigning black feminist publication, combining news with more theoretical pieces that drew on Marxism to theorise the relationships between race, class and gender.

Dates: 1979–80
Periodicity: irregular
Price: 30p (July 1980)
Place of Publication: London
Publisher: OWAAD
Location: Black Cultural Archives, London; Institute of Race Relations, London

Fownes Street Journal
This journal was produced by a group describing itself simply as the Women's Liberation Movement, based in Fownes Street, Dublin. Five more issues followed, mostly giving very short summaries of themes relating to discrimination and violence faced by women, for example in relation to careers, reproductive choices and selling sex. The very cheap paper and poor-quality printing suggests a shoestring budget, although the group did begin to run hand-drawn advertisements in the September 1972 issue, including one for an important meeting point for the Irish women's movement, Gajs Restaurant on Lower Baggot Street.

Dates: 1972–c. 1974
Periodicity: irregular
Price: 4p
Place of publication: Dublin
Location: National Library of Ireland

Frank
Frank was created as a female counterpart to the UK men's style and lifestyle magazine format established by Nick Logan, proprietor of the independent Wagadon publishing house and was initially billed as *Arena Woman*. A commercial failure, it sought to offer an intelligent alternative to the style and content of the traditional commercial female magazine.

Dates: October 1997–June 1999
Periodicity: monthly
Price: £2.70 in 1997
Place of publication: London
Publisher: Wagadon
Editors: Tina Gaudoin and Harriet Quick
Location: BL

The F-Word
One of the UK's first feminist blogs. Founded by Catherine Redfern in 2001, it continues to be a key site for British feminism.

Dates: 2001–present
Place of publication: London
Editors: Catherine Redfern (2001–7), Jess McCabe (2007–13), Holly Combe (2016–17) and Lusana Taylor (current rotating editor – they change around once per year)
Location: available at <https://thefword.org.uk>

g3
Free magazine for lesbians and bisexual women. Distributed in bars and clubs.

Dates: 2001–13
Periodicity: monthly
Price: free
Place of publication: London

Publisher: Square Peg Media
Circulation: 40,000
Location: BL; WL

gal-dem

Founded by student Liv Little, *gal-dem* is a digital feminist magazine for women and non-binary people of colour that also produces an annual print edition.

Dates: 2015–present
Periodicity: annual (in print)
Price: £10 (print edition)
Place of publication: London
Publisher: gal-dem
Editors: Liv Little (CEO); Charlie Brinkhurst-Cuff (head of editorial)
Circulation: 4,000–20,000 unique visitors a day (2018)
Location: BL; online, available at <https://gal-dem.com/>

Glamour

UK edition of the American Condé Nast Publication, which pioneered the 'handbag size' format. In 2017 the magazine increased its focus on beauty content and went 'digital first', only appearing in print as a biannual 'beauty book'.

Dates: 2001–present
Periodicity: monthly until 2017
Price: £1 in 2017
Place of publication: London
Publisher: Condé Nast
Editors: Jo Elvin (editor, 2001–17); Deborah Joseph (editor-in-chief, 2018–present). The current team also includes Funmi Fetto (executive editor/beauty director) and Bianca London (website director).
Circulation: 3.1 million unique users (2019)
Location: BL; online, available at <www.glamourmagazine.co.uk>

Good Housekeeping

The US edition was founded in 1885 and acquired by the Hearst Corporation in 1911, which launched a British edition in 1922. With a primary focus on domestic life, the magazine is associated with a middle-class readership.

Dates: 1922–present
Periodicity: monthly
Price: £4.99
Place of publication: London
Publisher: Hearst UK
Editors: First managing editor, Alice Head; current editor-in-chief, Gaby Huddard (since September 2018)
Circulation: 464,000 (June 2019)
Location: BL; online, available at <www.goodhousekeeping.com/uk/>

Harpers & Queen

Harpers & Queen was a British women's magazine, established in 1970 after a merger of *Queen* and British *Harper's Bazaar*. It focused on fashion and 'high society' and had a general 'It-girl' image. In 2006 it was renamed *Harper's Bazaar* after its American counterpart, and positioned itself as more celebrity-focused.

Dates: 1970–2006
Periodicity: monthly
Price: £4.80 (2019)
Place of publication: London
Publisher: National Magazine Company; Hearst UK
Circulation: 103,000
Editors: included Vicki Woods (1990–3); Fiona Macpherson (1994–2001); and Lucy Yeomans (2001–6)
Location: BL; NLS

Harpies & Quines

The short-lived *Harpies & Quines* was established in Glasgow and positioned itself as 'Scotland's Feminist Magazine'. It was operated by a shifting collective of women in keeping with the non-hierarchical publishing practices of other feminist publications. Among the most long-standing members of the collective were Libby Brooks, Fiona Montgomery, Lesley Riddoch, Catriona Stewart and Charlotte Ross.

Dates: 1992–4
Periodicity: bimonthly
Price: £1.50 (1992)
Place of publication: Glasgow
Circulation: c. 5,000
Editors: *Harpies & Quines* collective; Charlotte Ross (June/July 1993 onwards)
Location: GWL; NLS

Housewife

A pocket-sized monthly with a focus on running a home, negotiating budget constraints and class-determination, and childcare. *Housewife* became subsumed into *Ideal Home* in 1968. It was targeted at both a lower middle-class and middle-class readership.

Dates: 1939–68
Periodicity: monthly
Price: 6d (1939)
Place of publication: London
Publisher: Hulton Press; Odhams Press
Editors: Bernard E. Jones and Margot Jones
Circulation: 238,600 (1957)
Location: BL

Jackie

Long-running teen magazine that included items on fashion, beauty, pop, boys and romance. It is frequently associated with the use of the romantic photo-story and the problem page, 'Cathy and Claire'. It found new life as the inspiration for the stage show *Jackie The Musical* in 2016.

Dates: 1964–93
Periodicity: weekly
Price: 6d (1967); 50p (1993)
Place of publication: Dundee
Publisher: D. C. Thomson
Editors: included Gordon Small and Nina Myskow
Circulation: c. 600,000 (mid-1970s)
Location: BL; NLS

Just Seventeen/J-17
The UK's leading teenage girls' magazine between 1983 and 1994 that capitalised on the success of the pop magazine *Smash Hits* and is credited with reviving and transforming the teen magazine market. Following declining sales and increased competition from new titles, EMAP rebranded it as a monthly magazine *J-17* in 1997.

Dates: 1983–2004
Periodicity: fortnightly (1983–5); weekly (1985–97); monthly as *J-17* (1997–2004)
Price: 45p in 1983 (as *Just Seventeen*); £2 in 2004 (as *J-17*)
Place of publication: London
Publisher: EMAP
Editors: launch editor David Hepworth
Circulation: up to approx. 500,000
Location: BL; NLS; NLW

Lesbian London
Newsletter produced without advertising revenue by a collective of lesbian feminist activists.

Dates: 1991–4
Periodicity: monthly/every two months
Place of publication: London
Location: BL; FL; WL

Lip
Lesbian magazine launched by Magda Devas in 1993.

Dates: c. 1993–4
Place of publication: London
Location: BL; FAN

London Women's Liberation Newsletter
The *London Women's Liberation Newsletter* was a title adopted in 1978, having been the *London Women's Liberation Workshop Newsletter* in its earlier incarnation. The newsletter was aimed at London-based women and contained opinion articles, illustrations and information about events and organisations. The newsletter was edited

by a collective and, in 1984, was published weekly and based at A Woman's Place, Hungerford House, London WC2.

Dates: 1978–85
Periodicity: weekly (from 1984)
Location: London
Editors: editorial collective
Location: WL; GWL

Marie Claire
British version of the French fashion-led women's magazine aimed at middle-class twenty- and thirty-something readers. With a focus on fashion and beauty, the magazine branded itself as a 'thinking woman's magazine' with a range of campaigning articles. In 2019, the magazine became digital only.

Dates: 1988–2019 (print); 2006–present (digital)
Periodicity: monthly
Price: £4.20 (2018)
Place of publication: London
Publisher: TI Media
Editors: included Glenda Bailey (1988–96); Liz Jones (1999–2001); and Marie O'Riordan (2001–9)
Circulation: 120,000 in 2018
Location: BL; NLS; NLW

Mizz
A magazine aimed at younger teenage girls that included topics such as relationships, sex, problems, pop, celebrity, fashion and beauty.

Dates: 1985–2012
Periodicity: fortnightly
Price: 45p (1985)
Place of publication: London/Tonbridge Wells
Publisher: IPC, purchased by Panini UK in 2005
Editors: included Lesley Johnston and Lucie Tobin
Circulation: 66,571 (in 2005)
Location: BL

Modern Woman
Modern Woman was one of the new 'service' magazines published by George Newnes Ltd. (Newnes and Pearson) in the 1920s to provide a reliable service for women with information about the home, housekeeping, fashion, beauty, features and fiction. Like most women's magazines, it reduced in size and rose in price during wartime (from 6d to 8/9d in 1941), merging with its sister publication *Modern Home*. It returned to full size in 1946 when its cover price rose to 1 shilling. While domestic concerns were important, it targeted at women with professional careers and the wives of professionals. Features debating contemporary issues relevant to women were also a big draw.

Dates: 1925–66
Periodicity: monthly
Place of Publication: London
Circulation: 97,000 in 1938; 190,600 in 1950
Editors: Sybil Chaloner (until 1949) then Kay Smallshaw (ex. of *Good Housekeeping*)
Location: BL

More!

Although initially launched as a magazine aimed at older teenage girls, it was relaunched as a lifestyle glossy aimed at young women in the early 2000s. With a focus on celebrities, fashion and beauty and relationships, it provoked considerable controversy for its explicit and forthright approach to sex.

Dates: 1998–2013
Periodicity: fortnightly; weekly from 2007
Price: £1.80 (in 2007)
Place of publication: London
Publisher: EMAP, later Bauer Media
Editors: included Lisa Smorsaski and Chantelle Horton
Circulation: 271,629 (2006)
Location: BL

Ms.

Ms. is an American feminist magazine aimed at a wide audience and featuring articles on key feminist issues such as reproductive rights, violence against women and American politics. *Ms.* was first published as an insert in *New York* magazine, and the debut stand-alone issue was published in 1972. It was bought by Fairfax in 1987, then by Lang, Inc. From 1998–2001 it was published by Liberty Media for Women, LLC., and is published today by the Feminist Majority Foundation. It has been distributed in the UK.

Dates: 1971–present
Periodicity: monthly, then quarterly
Price: $1 in 1972
Place of publication: New York
Publisher: Feminist Majority Foundation (current)
Editors: founding editors: Patricia Carbine, Joanne Edgar, Nina Finkelstein, Mary Peacock, Letty Cottin Pogrebin and Gloria Steinem. Current executive editor: Katherine Spillar
Circulation: 550,000 in 1989; 75,000–200,000 in 1993
Location: BL; FAN; WL

MSprint

MSPrint was created in May 1978 as successor to the *Scottish Women's Liberation Journal*. Like its predecessor, it was a collectively run publication that aimed to stimulate debate in the Women's Liberation Movement and to develop an analysis of the position of women in Scotland and the role of women in Scottish politics.

Dates: 1978–81
Periodicity: quarterly
Price: 25p (1979)
Place of publication: Edinburgh
Circulation: c. 1,000
Editors: *MSPrint* collective – Esther Breitenbach, Fiona Forsyth, Joanna Haynes, Sally Henry, Marian Keogh, Geri Smyth and Nina Woodcock
Location: NLS

Mukti

The magazine of the *Mukti* collective, the magazine sought to educate and politicise non-white women in the face of hardening forms of racism in Britain in the 1980s, and was available in English, Urdu, Hindi, Gujurati, Bengali and Punjabi. It was supported by Greater London Council and Camden Council funds; however, eventual budget cuts combined with lack of editorial focus meant that the magazine produced only seven issues in four years.

Dates: 1983–7
Periodicity: irregular
Price: 40p (1983); 70p (1987)
Place of publication: London
Editors: *Mukti* collective
Location: BL; FAS

My Guy

Magazine for teenage girls covering areas such as pop, fashion and beauty, and romance and relationships.

Dates: 1978–90
Periodicity: weekly
Price: 14p (1978)
Place of publication: London
Publisher: IPC
Location: BL; NLS

Nova

Magazine aimed at the 'New Woman' of the 1960s. Tackled 'taboo' topics such as abortion, racial equality and divorce.

Dates: 1965–75
Periodicity: monthly
Price: 3/6 (1970)
Place of publication: London
Publisher: IPC
Editors: included Harry Fieldhouse (issues 1–6) and Dennis Hackett
Location: BL; University of Cambridge; University of Oxford

Outwrite
A feminist newspaper run by a collective of second-wave feminists. It was dedicated to offering news for women, by women. Self-defined as an 'internationalist feminist' publication, the paper focused on 'the development of feminism worldwide' and an examination of women's oppressions 'in the context of imperialism, racism and class divisions'.

Dates: 1982–8
Periodicity: monthly
Price: 50p (1988)
Place of publication: London
Editors: A collective, The Feminist Newspaper Group
Location: BL; Birmingham Museum and Art Gallery; FAS; plus digitised samples available at <www.deedsnotwordstowardsliberation.com/herstory-publications-archive>

Picturegoer
Picturegoer contained a variety of material about film stars and new film releases in the UK and beyond, providing readers with a variety of photographic content, behind-the-scenes gossip, celebrity interviews, competitions and film news. The magazine began as *The Pictures* in 1911 and remained a prominent British film fan publication across the First and Second World Wars, undergoing the following name changes across its history: *Picturegoer: The Picture Theatre Magazine* (11 October 1913–14 February 1914); *Pictures and the Picturegoer* (21 February 1914–20 November 1920); *Pictures* (27 November 1920–August 1922); incorporated into *Picturegoer* (January 1921–July 1922); *Pictures and the Picturegoer* (August 1922–September 1925); *Picturegoer and Theatre Monthly* (October 1925); *Picturegoer* (November 1925–May 1931); *Picturegoer Weekly* (30 May 1931–16 September 1939); *Picturegoer and Film Weekly* (23 September–23 August 1941); *Picturegoer* (6 September 1941–23 April 1960).

Dates: October 1913–April 1960
Periodicity: fortnightly (although varies over lifespan)
Price: 3d (1945)
Place of publication: London
Circulation: 325,000 (mid-1940s)
Location: BL; Bill Douglas Cinema Museum (University of Exeter); Southampton University Hartley Library; online, available at the Media History Digital Library <www.mediahistoryproject.org>

Pride
The UK's first glossy women's lifestyle magazine aimed at women of Afro-Caribbean heritage.

Dates: 1991–present
Periodicity: monthly

Price: £3 (2019)
Place of publication: London
Publisher: Pride Media
Editors: included Joy Francis (2000) and Sherry Dixon (2004–7)
Circulation: readership of 146,000 in 2015
Location: BL; NLS; NLW

Psychologies
UK edition of the French glossy women's monthly lifestyle magazine focused on personal growth and wellbeing.

Dates: 2005–present
Periodicity: monthly
Price: £4.50 (2019)
Place of publication: London
Publishers: Hachette Filapacchi (until 2011); Hearst (2011–12); Kelsey Publishing (2012–present)
Editors: launch editor Maureen Rice (2005–9); Louise Chunn (2009–2012). Current editor Suzy Walker
Circulation: 150,000 (2008); 77,608 (2012)
Location: BL; NLS; NLW

Quim
A lesbian erotic magazine published with the strapline 'For dykes of all persuasions'.

Dates: 1989–95
Periodicity: irregular
Place of publication: London
Editors: co-edited by Sophie Moorcock (founder) and Lulu Belliveau
Location: HCA

Red
Red was launched to target the gap in the market for magazines for 'middle youth'. These were women with high disposable incomes who read *Cosmopolitan* and *Marie Claire* in their twenties but having reached their thirties struggled to find magazines that catered for their needs, interest and aspirations.

Dates: 1998–present
Periodicity: monthly
Price: £4.50 (2019)
Place of publication: London
Publisher: EMAP (at launch); Hearst (present)
Editors: Kath Brown (1998–2000), Trish Halpin (2000–6), Sam Baker (2006–13) and Sarah Bailey (2013–)
Location: BL; online, available at <www.redonline.co.uk>

Red Rag
An influential socialist-feminist magazine established by feminists who largely were already engaged in Left politics.

Dates: 1972–80
Periodicity: irregular
Price: 20p (1975)
Place of publication: London
Editors: *Red Rag* collective
Circulation: 4,000
Location: BL; FAN; FAS

Sappho
Lesbian magazine formed after the demise of *Arena Three* by several members of the *Arena Three* board. Its stated aim was to 'educate society about the true facts of lesbianism, support lesbians and women's causes'.

Dates: 1972–81
Periodicity: monthly
Price: 15p (first issue)
Place of publication: London
Publisher: Sappho Publications Ltd
Editor: Jackie Forster
Circulation: c. 900–1,000
Location: FAS; WL

Scarlet Women
A magazine for feminists working in the socialist movement and for socialists active in the women's movement.

Dates: 1976–82
Periodicity: irregular
Place of publication: North Shields
Editors: *Scarlet Women* collective
Circulation: 3,500
Location: FAN

Scottish Women's Liberation Journal
The *Scottish Women's Liberation Journal* lasted four issues, ending after a split in the collective as a result of ideological differences between socialist and radical feminism. It was based on an open editorial collective, cited as one of the reasons for division. The socialist-feminist members of the collection went on to create *MSPrint*.

Dates: 1977–8
Periodicity: irregular
Place of publication: Edinburgh
Editors: *Scottish Women's Liberation* collective
Location: NLS

Shebang
Lesbian magazine that began as a supplement to the *Pink Paper*. Circulated with no cover charge.

Dates: 1992–5
Price: free supplement
Place of publication: London
Editors: Linda Gibson (1992–3), Alison Gregory (1993), Lisa Sabbage (1994) and Vicky Powell (1995)
Circulation: 12,000
Location: FAN; HCA

Sheffield Women's Newsletter

First published in May 1971 as a two-page manifesto for women's liberation, it later morphed into a stapled booklet featuring hand-drawn illustrations. The content included accounts of personal experiences, women's health and reproductive rights, local events and campaigns, poetry and fiction. It was printed by the magazine collective itself. Learning to print was an important form of empowerment and revenue raising for feminist groups. The newsletter may later have morphed into the *Sheffield Women's Paper*, listed in Kanter et al.'s 1984 *Sweeping Statements* collection of women's liberation writings as an irregular, women-only production selling at 30p.

Dates: 1971–80
Periodicity: irregular
Price: 10p (in 1979)
Place of publication: Sheffield
Location: FAN; Sheffield Archives

Shrew

A Women's Liberation magazine produced by feminist collectives based in London.

Dates: 1969–78
Periodicity: monthly or less frequent
Price: 7 1/2p (1972)
Place of publication: London
Editors: Women's Liberation Workshop
Circulation: 5,000
Location: BL; FAN; HSC; FAS; WL

Shocking Pink

Low-budget magazine 'written by and for young women', *Shocking Pink* was a feminist challenge to the preoccupations of more mainstream magazines targeted at teenage girls. Its aesthetics were shaped by punk fanzines and its content was explicitly shaped by feminism. It was relaunched in 1987.

Dates: 1980–2; 1987–92
Periodicity: irregular
Price: 20p (issue 2); 60p (c. 1987)
Place of publication: London
Editors: changing editorial collectives

Location: BL; FAN; FAS; WL; PDFs available online at <www.grassrootsfeminism.net/cms/node/165>

Smash Hits

Launched by Nick Logan, *Smash Hits* was an irreverent and stylish pop magazine whose primary audience was teenage girls. It was a huge commercial success. The content and visual style of the magazine spawned imitators and had a significant impact on the teen magazine market. The *Smash Hits* brand was associated with a cable music channel in the 2000s.

Dates: 1978–2006
Periodicity: initially monthly, then fortnightly
Price: 25p (1978); £2 (2005)
Place of publication: Peterborough
Publisher: EMAP
Editors: included Nick Logan, David Hepworth, Mark Ellen, Mark Frith, Kate Thornton, Lisa Smosarski and Lara Palamoudian
Circulation: regularly exceeded 500,000 in the early 1980s, reached peak sales of 1 million in 1989 and dropped to 120,000 by 2005
Location: BL; NLS; NLW

Socialist Woman

This periodical appears to have had two lives. Initially produced by a group of socialist women from Nottingham, it later moved to London where it was published by the International Marxist Group, the British Section of the USFI (Trotskyist Fourth International). This later version billed itself as 'a new journal for an old battle' and classified itself as 'not anti-male' in its opposition to labour force exploitation and private property.

Dates: 1969–78
Periodicity: irregular
Price: £1.50 subscription for four issues (1978)
Place of publication: Nottingham, then London
Editors: editorial collective. Editorial board for first Nottingham-based issue: Jo O'Brien, Ann Torode and Antonia Gorton. Editors of October 1978 London-based issue: Sue Aspinall, Penny Duggan, Jo O'Brien and Celia Pugh.
Location: BL; FAS; HSC; digitised copies available at <www.marxists.org/history/etol/document/britain/socialist-women/index.htm>

SoFeminine

UK version of the women's portal by Aufeminin, a French digital media group present in more than 20 countries. In 2018 Axel Springer sold its majority stake of Aufeminin to Télévision Française 1 S.A.

Dates: 2004–present
Place of publication: London
Editors: included Anna-belle Woollcott, Ursula Dewey and Lareese Craig
Location: online, available at <www.sofeminine.co.uk>

Spare Rib

Launched in 1972, *Spare Rib* was Britain's only mainstream feminist magazine, available nationally at newsagents, including WH Smith's, until its closure in 1993. The magazine – which after 1974 was run as a collective – fused the politics, concerns and campaigns of the Women's Liberation Movement with a broad range of topics related to women's lives, from ethical fashion to psychology.

Dates: 1972–93
Periodicity: monthly or less
Price: 17 1/2p (first issue)
Place of publication: London
Editors: Marsha Rowe and Rosie Boycott, followed by a changing editorial collective
Circulation: 20,000–35,000
Location: BL (including extensive digitised holdings); FAS; HSC

Sugar

Drew on many aspects of the teen magazine *Just Seventeen*, such as pop and fashion, but combined these with an edgier style combined with a more upfront approach to, and preoccupation with, issues about sex and sexuality. The print edition was outlived online as the website Sugarscape which operated until 2016.

Dates: 1994–2011
Periodicity: monthly
Price: £1.30 (in 1994)
Place of publication: London
Publisher: Attic Futura followed by Hachette Filipacchi
Editors: numerous, but including founding editor Kathryn Brown and final editor Annabel Brog
Circulation: 422,179 (2000), 113,320 (2010)
Location: BL

Trouble & Strife

Trouble & Strife was a radical feminist magazine. The magazine emphasised the ways that men as a group benefitted from the exploitation of women as a group, as expressed in the magazine's first editorial in 1983.

Dates: 1983–2002
Periodicity: three times per year
Price: £1.50 (Winter 1983); £4.50 (Summer 2002)
Place of publication: London
Editors: original collective members were Lynn Alderson, Jalna Hanmer, Sophie Laws, Sheila Saunders, Diana Leonard and Ruth Wallsgrove. Membership of this collective changed over the period of publication.
Location: BL; the magazine's archive is available at <www.troubleandstrife.org/articles>

The Vagenda

A satirical feminist blog that was founded by two 'impoverished graduates' Rhiannon Lucy Cosslett and Holly Baxter. Cosslett and Baxter also authored a book of the same name.

Dates: January 2012–July 2015 (43 issues)
Place of publication: London
Editors: Rhiannon Lucy Cosslett and Holly Baxter
Location: <http://vagendamagazine.com>

Vogue
British edition of the US magazine launched in 1892, *Vogue* is a lifestyle and fashion magazine associated with an elite readership. It is usually seen as the UK's leading fashion magazine. *Vogue* currently has both print and digital editions and operates across a range of digital platforms.

Dates: 1916–present
Periodicity: monthly
Price: 2/6 (1960); £3.99 (2019)
Place of publication: London
Publisher: Condé Nast
Editors: included Audrey Withers (1940–60), Alisa Garland (1960–4), Beatrix Miller (1964–85), Anna Wintour (1985–7), Elizabeth Tilberis (1988–92), Alexandra Shulman (1992–2017) and Edward Enninful (2017–)
Circulation: 192,212 (2019)
Location: BL ; NLW ; NLS; Digital edition available at <www.vogue.co.uk>

We Are Here
Also sometimes referred to as *Black Feminists Newsletter*, this started life as a London-based newsletter focused on black women's experiences. It was later temporarily revived using a magazine format.

Dates: 1984–6; 1988
Place of publication: London (1984–6)
Location: FL

Woman
General interest magazine aimed at women in the home, providing guidance on cooking, dressmaking, shopping, relationships and health. Merged with *Woman's Illustrated* in 1961 and *Woman's Mirror* in 1967.

Dates: 1937–present
Periodicity: weekly
Price: 2d (1937)
Place of publication: London
Publisher: TI Media (current)
Editors: include Mary Grieve (1940–62)
Circulation: 1938 – 750,000; 1952 – 2,227,000; 1953 – 2,551,000; 1959 – 3,173,000
Location: BL; NLS; NLW; Northumbria University; University of Cambridge; University of Oxford

Woman's Mirror
General interest magazine aimed at women in the home. Underwent a revamp in 1965 with more radical content with the aim of appealing to 'modern' women. Merged with *Woman* in 1967.

Dates: 1960–7
Periodicity: weekly
Price: 6d (1964)
Place of publication: London
Publisher: IPC
Location: BL; WL

Woman's Own
General interest magazine aimed at women in the home, providing guidance on cooking, dressmaking, shopping, relationships and health.

Dates: 1932–present
Periodicity: weekly
Price: 4d (1949)
Place of publication: London
Publisher: TI Media (current)
Editors: included Elsa McAlanon, Catherine Westwood and Karen Livermore
Circulation: 1938 – 357,000; 1952 – 1,770,00; 1953 – 2,124,000; 1959 – 2,405,000
Location: BL; NLS; NLW; Northumbria University; University of Cambridge; University of Oxford

Woman's Realm
With a core audience of wives and mothers, *Women's Realm* offered knitting patterns and advice on decoration, cooking, health and children. In 2001, having failed to update its image for a more sexually liberal, self-indulgent readership, the magazine merged with *Woman's Weekly*.

Dates: 1958–2001
Periodicity: weekly
Price: 4d (1958); 29p (1987)
Place of publication: London
Publisher: IPC
Editor: Joyce Wards
Circulation: 1.2 million (down to 152, 000 in 2001)
Location: BL

Women's Struggle
Subtitled 'the newsletter of the women's liberation national co-ordinating committee', this journal was produced by different women's groups around Britain. It was typed and reproduced in a low-quality, black-and-white format. It listed women's groups and advertised upcoming marches and campaigns. The Women's National Co-ordinating Committee (WNCC) had established terms of reference in June 1970 which called for it to promote the aims of women's liberation and organise national and local conferences. The newsletter was a key component of this work. Women's groups were charged £1 to affiliate to the WNCC, but in a diverse and decentralised movement, payment was often sporadic or non-existent.

Dates: c. 1971–c. 1974
Periodicity: irregular
Price: 1 shilling
Place of publication: various in UK
Editor: various women's groups
Location: BL; FAN; HSC; WL

Women's Voice
Socialist-feminist magazine for women in the International Socialists (IS). From 1977 this Far Left Trotskyist-influenced group was called The Socialist Workers Party (SWP). The publication started as an occasional newsletter for IS women from 1970 to early 1972 and became *Women's Voice* in July 1972 as a bimonthly, becoming a monthly in January 1975. It was relaunched with a new series in January 1977 to tie in with the launch of the SWP.

Dates: 1972–82
Periodicity: initially bimonthly; then monthly
Price: 10p (c. 1977)
Place of publication: London
Editors: initially produced by IS volunteers including Anna Paczuska, Valerie Clark and Barbara Kerr. In January 1975, the editorial and production team included Margaret Renn, Anna Paczuska and Elana Dallas. From July 1975, there was a new editorial team of Sheila McGregor, Judith Condon, Lindsay German and J. Woodcock.
Circulation: estimated c. 10,000
Location: BL; FAN; FAS; WL; complete set in digital form available at <https://splitsandfusions.wordpress.com>

Woman's Weekly
General interest magazine aimed at women in the home, providing guidance on cooking, dressmaking, shopping, relationships and health.

Dates: 1911–present
Periodicity: weekly
Price: 3d (1954); £1.20 (2019)
Place of publication: London
Publisher: TI Media (current)
Circulation: 1938–498,000; 1952–1,746,000; 1953–1,816,000; 1959–1,512,000
Location: BL: NLS: NLW; University of Cambridge; University of Oxford

Notes on Contributors

Rachael Alexander is a research associate in journalism and a teaching assistant in English studies at the University of Strathclyde. Her work focuses on twentieth-century magazines, considering them as collaborative literary texts, cultural artefacts and commercial products. Her first monograph interrogates constructions of gender, consumerism and nation in American and Canadian women's magazines of the 1920s (Anthem Press, forthcoming 2020). Her current interdisciplinary project dedicates much-needed attention to Scottish feminist periodicals and print culture, 1970–2000.

Victoria Bazin is senior lecturer in American literature at Northumbria University. Her monograph, *Marianne Moore and the Cultures of Modernity*, was published by Ashgate in 2010, and her second monograph, *Modernism Edited: Marianne Moore and The Dial Magazine*, was published by Edinburgh University Press in 2019. She has also co-edited, with Mel Waters, a special issue of *Women: A Cultural Review* on 'Feminist Periodical Culture from Suffrage to Second Wave'.

Eleanor Bell is senior lecturer in English studies at the University of Strathclyde. She is the author of *Questioning Scotland: Literature, Nationalism, Postmodernism* (2004) and co-editor of *Scotland in Theory: Reflections on Culture and Literature* (2004). Her current research focuses on the literary culture of the Scottish 1960s, on which she has published two co-edited volumes: *The International Writers' Conference Revisited: Edinburgh, 1962* (2012); and *The Scottish Sixties: Reading, Rebellion, Revolution?* (2013).

Sue Bruley was formerly a reader in modern history at the University of Portsmouth and is now an independent scholar. Her research interests focus on women and gender relations in twentieth-century Britain, particularly in regard to oral testimony. She is currently working on women's movements in the UK from 1960 to 1990.

Gail Chester has worked in the radical book trade and been involved in feminist activism since the 1970s. She researches twentieth and twenty-first-century book history, and is widely published in academic, feminist and general publications. She co-authored *Rolling Our Own: Women as Printers, Publishers and Distributors* (Comedia 1981). Among her published articles are 'Producing Feminist History in

Electronic Form' in *Feminisms on Edge* (2000); 'The anthology as a medium for feminist debate in the UK' in *Women's Studies International Forum* (2002); and 'Sex, Race and Class: The radical, alternative and minority book trade in Britain' in *The Cambridge History of the Book in Britain* (vol. 7, Cambridge University Press 2019). She is a trustee of the Feminist Library and helped to set up the History of Women's Liberation (known as 'HOWL') to gather material from the Women's Liberation Movement, including records of local campaigns and small groups.

Sarah Crook is a lecturer in history at Swansea University. She has a particular interest in the histories of feminism, social movements and the history of medicine. Her research has been published in *Women's History Review*, *Medical Humanities* and *Contemporary British History*. Her monograph, which explores postnatal depression in Britain after 1945, is under contract with Manchester University Press. Her partner, Calum, looked after their baby daughter, Evelyn, while Sarah researched and wrote this chapter on mothering, writing and feminism.

Lucy Delap is a reader in modern British and gender history at the University of Cambridge, and fellow of Murray Edwards College. She has published widely on the history of feminism, gender, labour and religion, including the prize-winning *The Feminist Avant-Garde: Transatlantic Encounters of the Early-Twentieth Century* (2007); *Knowing Their Place: Domestic Service in Twentieth-Century Britain* (2011); and, with Sue Morgan, *Men, Masculinities and Religious Change in Twentieth-Century Britain* (2013). She is currently working on a history of modern feminism titled *Feminisms: a Global History* (Penguin Books, 2020), and is co-investigator on the Leverhulme-funded 'Business of Women's Words' project based at the University of Sussex and the British Library'.

Laura Favaro is a Postdoctoral Research Fellow at the Gender & Sexualities Research Centre, of City University of London. Her book project is an ethnography of the 'gender wars' in contemporary Britain, especially within feminism, and the arenas of activism, media and academia. With interests in feminist theory, contemporary media and cultural politics, she has published articles on topics spanning from pornography and evolutionary psychology (in *Australian Feminist Studies*) to male anti-feminism online (in *Feminist Media Studies*, with Rosalind Gill). Her doctoral thesis examined online young women's magazines from Spain and the UK.

Janet Floyd is professor of American literature and culture at King's College London. She has published on domestic work and its representation in Anglo-American settings. Her books include *Claims and Speculations: Mining and Writing in the Gilded Age* (University of New Mexico Press 2012) and *Writing the Pioneer Woman* (University of Missouri Press 2002). With Laurel Forster, she co-edited *The Recipe Reader: Narratives – Contexts – Traditions* (2003).

Laurel Forster is reader in cultural history at the University of Portsmouth. Her research interests are in women's twentieth-century history, women's magazines and women's modernist writing. She is author of *Magazine Movements: Women's Culture, Feminisms and Media Form* (Bloomsbury 2015) and numerous other articles on women's magazines and media cultures. She has co-edited a number of books, including *Historicising the Women's Liberation Movement in the Western World: 1960–1999* (Routledge 2018); *British Culture and Society in the 1970s: The Lost Decade* (Cambridge Scholars Publishing 2010); and *The Recipe Reader: Narratives, Contexts, Traditions* (Ashgate 2003).

Fiona Hackney is professor of fashion at Manchester Metropolitan University. She is a design historian who works principally on dress and fashion culture, interwar print media, crafting, co-creation and social design. Recent publications include *Women's Periodical and Print Culture in Britain, 1918–1939* (2018) and 'The Power of Quiet: Re-Making Amateur and Professional Textiles Agencies' in the *Journal of Textile Design, Research and Practice* (2016). Her monograph *Women's Magazines and the Feminine Imagination: Opening Up a New World for Women in Interwar Britain* will be published by Bloomsbury in 2021.

Joanne Hollows is a writer and independent researcher who previously had a long career teaching in British universities, most recently as a reader in media and cultural studies at Nottingham Trent University. She is the author of *Feminism, Femininity and Popular Culture* (Manchester University Press 2000); *Domestic Cultures* (Open University Press 2008); and *Media Studies: a Complete Introduction* (John Murray 2016). She is also co-author of *Food and Cultural Studies* (Routledge 2004). She has co-edited numerous academic collections including *Feminism, Domesticity and Popular Culture* (Routledge 2009) and *Feminism in Popular Culture* (Berg 2006).

Mary Irwin is an honorary research fellow at Queen Margaret University, Edinburgh. She is a specialist in television studies and has published widely on both historical and contemporary television. Most recently she published on the development of the television documentary in 'Civilisation and the Rise of the Television Blockbuster Documentary' in the *Journal of British Cinema and Television -Special Collection; BBC2 At 50: Historical Perspectives* (2017); and on television situation comedy in Scotland, 'Ah hink it's time for suttin blue n a BAILEYS!' – Subverting Scottish Male Identities in Gary: Tank Commander, the *International Journal of Scottish Theatre and Screen (Special Issue) TV in Scotland: Past, Present and Future* (2018). She is currently working on the monograph *Love Wars: Television Romantic Comedy.*

Tracey Loughran is professor of history, University of Essex. She is the author of *Shell-Shock and Medical Culture in First World War Britain* (Cambridge University Press 2017); co-editor with Gayle Davis of *The Palgrave Handbook of Infertility in History: Approaches, Contexts and Perspectives* (Palgrave 2017); and editor of *A Practical Guide to Studying History: Skills and Approaches* (Bloomsbury 2017). Her current research explores women's psychological, emotional and physical health in Britain between the 1960s and the 1990s.

Stevie Marsden holds a PhD and is a Lecturer in Publishing at the University of Derby. Their first monograph, *Prizing Scottish Literature: A Cultural History of the Saltire Society Literary Awards*, was published in 2020 by Anthem Press. Their research interests include literary award culture, celebrity book clubs, reader and writer identities, and inclusion and diversity in the publishing industry.

Kaitlynn Mendes is an associate professor in media and communications at the University of Leicester. She is an expert in feminist media studies and has written widely around representations of feminism in the media, and feminists' use of social media to challenge rape culture. She is author of five books including *Feminism in the News* (Palgrave 2011); *SlutWalk: Feminism, Activism and Media* (Palgrave 2015); and (with Jessica Ringrose and Jessalynn Keller) *Digital Feminist Activism: Girls and Women Fight Back Against Rape Culture* (Oxford University Press 2019).

Charlotte Purkis is principal lecturer in performing arts at the University of Winchester. A specialist in modernism and performance, she has written widely on topics across music, drama and dance, and has several publications on the career of Anglo-American thespian Velona Pilcher. Charlotte contributed to volume 3 of *Women, Periodicals and Print Culture in Britain, 1890s–1920s* on women and music criticism. She also writes on autoethnography in musicology as a creative practice.

Catherine Riley is a feminist historian and writer, and an expert on contemporary feminist publishing in the UK. She has taught English literature and gender studies courses at several institutions including Birkbeck College, University of London, where she completed her doctoral thesis on the feminist publisher Virago. Catherine now works as general manager of the literary festival Primadonna, while continuing to write about trends in gender theory and praxis, particularly as it applies to publishing and social change. Recent publications include *Feminism and Women's Writing: An Introduction* (Edinburgh University Press) and *The Virago Story: Assessing the Impact of a Publishing Phenomenon* (Berghahn Books).

Claire Sedgwick is a feminist lecturer and researcher. She completed her PhD in feminist media studies at De Montfort University, Leicester. Her thesis is titled "*Spare Rib* and *Ms.* and the Representation of Second Wave Feminism: 1972–1992". Her book, with the working title *Feminist Media: From the Second Wave to the Digital Age*, will be published by Rowman and Littlefield International in 2020.

Lisa Stead is a senior lecturer in film studies at the University of Exeter, specialising in women's writing and print cultures of cinema. She has published more broadly on adaptation, location filming histories, gender and fan magazines, and deaf community film histories. She is the author of *Off to the Pictures: Women's Writing, Cinemagoing and Movie Culture in Interwar Britain* (Edinburgh University Press 2016), and co-editor of *The Boundaries of the Literary Archive: Reclamation and Representation* (Routledge 2013). She is currently principal investigator on the AHRC Early Career Researchers Leadership Fellow Project 'Reframing Vivien Leigh: Stardom, Gender and the Archive'. Her monograph, of the same name, is due to be published by Oxford University Press in 2020.

Zoe Strimpel is a historian of gender, feminism, matchmaking and heterosexuality in late twentieth-century Britain. She was awarded her PhD from the University of Sussex in 2017. She is currently a research fellow on the Leverhulme-funded Business of Women's Words project based at the University of Sussex and the British Library, where she is researching *Spare Rib*'s business practices, relationship to profit, revenue and readership, and editorial and collective dynamics. Her monograph *Seeking Love* *in Modern Britain: Gender, Dating and the Rise of 'the Single'* was published by Bloomsbury in March 2020.

Estella Tincknell is associate professor in film and culture at the University of the West of England. She has published widely in the fields of media and film, and is concerned with representations of gender, aging, class and identity. Her books include *Jane Campion and Adaptation: Angels, Demons and Unsettling Voices* (Palgrave Macmillan 2013) and *Aging Femininities, Troubling Representations* (Cambridge Scholars 2012, with Dr J Dolan).

Amy Tooth Murphy is lecturer in oral history at Royal Holloway, University of London. Her research interests include lesbian history of postwar Britain, LGBTQ+ oral history, lesbian literature, queer narrativity and queer heritage. She is a trustee of the Oral History Society and a founder and managing editor of the peer-reviewed blog *Notches: (re)marks on the history of sexuality*. She is co-editor of an LGBTQ+ special issue of the *Oral History Journal* (Spring 2020) and her current research examines oral histories of butch identity and lived experience.

Georgina Turner is senior lecturer in media at the University of Liverpool. Her primary interest is in media representation, with a focus on gender and sexuality. She is particularly interested in magazines and print subcultures; her book looking at twentieth-century lesbian magazine discourse and the construction of subculture will be published by Bloomsbury in 2021.

Melanie Waters is senior lecturer in modern and contemporary literature at Northumbria University. She is co-author of *Feminism and Popular Culture: Investigating the Postfeminist Mystique* (2013); editor of *Women on Screen: Feminism and Femininity in Visual Culture* (2011); and co-editor of *Poetry and Autobiography* (2011). She has also published articles and essays on feminist periodical culture, twentieth-century women's writing and the contemporary Gothic.

Index

9781399546799